The Handbook of
INTERETHNIC
COEXISTENCE

The Handbook of

INTERETHNIC
COEXISTENCE

EDITED BY EUGENE WEINER

FOREWORD BY ALAN B. SLIFKA

An Abraham Fund Publication

CONTINUUM • NEW YORK

1998
The Continuum Publishing Company
370 Lexington Avenue
New York, NY 10017

Printed in the United States of America

Library of Congress Cataloging-in-Publication Data

The handbook of interethnic coexistence /
  edited by Eugene Weiner ; foreword by Alan B. Slifka.
      p.   cm.
  "An Abraham Fund publication."
  Includes bibliographical references and index.
  ISBN 0-8264-1056-1 (alk. paper)
    1. Ethnic relations.   2. International relations.
  3. Culture conflict.   4. Social conflict.   5. Conflict management.
  I. Weiner, Eugene.
  GN496.H363   1998
  305.8—dc21   97-31303
                                                            CIP

Contents

Coexistence Work: A New Profession

1 • Philosophy of Coexistence

2 • Applied Perspectives

4 • Tools for Coexistence Work

5 • Coexistence in Israel

Foreword

The Handbook of Interethnic Coexistence is designed to assemble and consolidate, from multiple perspectives, resources addressing the question of how interethnic coexistence might best be facilitated, and in the process make the case for the establishment of an interdisciplinary coexistence field. These articles make clear the interdisciplinary nature of coexistence knowledge and the need for its consolidation.

The Handbook is sponsored by The Abraham Fund, whose mission is to enhance coexistence, specifically through funding and promoting Jewish–Arab coexistence programs in Israel. Named for the revered patriarch of two great peoples, Jews and Arabs, through his offspring, Isaac and Ishmael, The Abraham Fund helps reconcile the children of Abraham while ensuring the integrity and continuity of both their identities and heritages.

Several articles in this *Handbook* focus on work done under the aegis of The Abraham Fund, and more broadly on the ethnic situation in Israel. However, The Abraham Fund's intention in creating this *Handbook* is to provide a central meeting place for a conversation that is presently occurring in diverse locations throughout the academy and around the globe.

It was almost a decade ago that I co-founded The Abraham Fund. The most important thing that I have learned over the years is that programs that augment coexistence, that help us to understand the "other" and touch the hearts of humanity, not only exist, but work. Although they may require special approaches and specialists to run them, they are gaining adherents and new importance all the time. What such programs promise makes them essential and makes it imperative to support them so that they have the opportunity to flourish and grow.

Active coexistence endeavors are inhibited in most places because they lack mainstream legitimization and understanding, and therefore do not receive appropriate support. Only by persistent and unremitting educational efforts will we one day see that mutual helpfulness and tolerance between differing peoples have become as important to our welfare as having clean air, clean water, and a healthy environment. Only with tenacious educational efforts will a field and profession of coexistence finally be recognized.

Coexistence can be made legitimate at all levels of society. At the micro-level, educational efforts can be fortified by programs that bring people together in projects to enable them to share common experiences to achieve common aims. In the process, they come to see their shared humanity, values, and concerns. Through direct understanding of the other, prejudice is diminished and replaced by a new sense of tolerance. Thus, each citizen can be taught that it is distance that depersonalizes the stranger, and that face-to-face contacts eventually bring home the similarities that exist between people of difference.

This *Handbook* is meant to help advance the field of coexistence in order that its ideas, techniques and methods can be utilized throughout the world before interethnic problems turn into interethnic conflict. As ethnic and nationalist passions rise all around with their destructive potential, it is crucial that everyone concerned with this issue come together to share their perspectives and the lessons that they have learned. It is not safe to leave the question of interethnic conflict and its resolution in myriad academic and social-activist niches, hoping that synchronicity will bring them together. I believe that *The Handbook of Interethnic Coexistence* can act as a focusing lens and a resource for all who work to promote a multicultural society, whether policy makers, educators, scholars, historians, or thoughtful citizens, in order that the field of coexistence be expanded and legitimized.

ALAN B. SLIFKA
Chairman of the Board
The Abraham Fund

Acknowledgments

Many people had a hand in creating this *Handbook*. Chief among them was Alan Slifka, who early in our joint efforts to create The Abraham Fund realized that a fundamental primer on coexistence was necessary. The first major publication of The Abraham Fund was *The Abraham Fund Directory of Institutions and Organizations Fostering Coexistence between Jews and Arabs*. This *Directory* demonstrated that there were, indeed, coexistence workers and activities in a society as deeply divided as Israel. Subsequently, we learned that coexistence activity is not limited to Israel alone. Our directory elicited an outpouring of interest in documenting similar kinds of activity all over the world.

Werner Mark Linz, the chairman of Continuum Publishing, accompanied us on one of our trips to Israel to meet coexistence workers in the Jewish and Arab community and was impressed with their dedication and practical wisdom. He was very encouraging in this project from the start. It was his suggestion that we employ Dr. Cynthia Eller as a consultant to help guide the work of putting this *Handbook* together. Without her ability and know-how this project would have bogged down several times. She has been indispensable. It was her unerring professionalism, good judgment, and practical sense of what was feasible that gave us the courage to persevere. In the initial research stage it was the conversations with her that helped give form and substance to our attempts to identify and organize the field. When we were ready to instruct the contributors about their essays and how they fit into the overall project she helped shape the instructions given. When the submissions were received and evaluated, it was her judgment that was relied upon in making final editorial decisions. Our lunches on West 116th Street and Amsterdam, when I came from the Columbia Library for nourishment, were memorable. I learned a great deal from her. It has been a great privilege working together.

The staff of The Abraham Fund has been particularly important in making this book happen. Vice president of The Abraham Fund and project manager, Joan Bronk, provided the administrative savvy required to prod the contributors to submit their work and then negotiated the hard process of redrafting, sometimes for three or four revisions. Considering the prominence of the scholars represented in this volume, this demanded both tact and persistence. The work was assisted by our Abraham Fund staff, particularly by Michelle Light, Randi Feinstein, and Carol Welker. Deborah Bing's contribution of the appendix is, we believe, a useful compilation of select bibliographic sources on coexistence, organizations that further coexistence work, and graduate programs in dispute resolution and coexistence. We hope it will prove useful to individuals who are interested in making their way into the profession of coexistence work.

Finally, I would like to thank Professor Hillel Levine, Dr. Reuven Gal, and Sharon Burde for their warm friendship and their many helpful discussions about this material, and Dr. Anita Weiner, who has accompanied this project from the start. Her thoughtful advice and critically creative editorial judgment helped to mold the Introduction, and is embodied in each of the sections of this work.

I hope that the case we have made for the professionalization of coexistence work and the foundation we have provided, will spark not only programmatic interest in educational institutions but will also motivate talented people to enter the field. We certainly need them.

EUGENE WEINER
Co-Founder
The Abraham Fund

Coexistence Work: A New Profession

EUGENE WEINER

This book is about the concept of peaceful coexistence—particularly as it impacts issues of contemporary ethnic conflict. The authors whose essays are included in this handbook are united in the conviction that coexistence work can play an important role in deescalating those dangerous ethnic conflicts now taking place throughout the world. Application of the coexistence concept takes place within the context of a civil society's institutions. We have chosen to call this application "coexistence work" and with this handbook we are both introducing its conceptualization and advocating its professionalization.

Three important assumptions form the basis of coexistence work: first is the assumption that irreconcilable differences and intractable conflicts must not be permitted to escalate into total conflict; second is our assumption that our human fate is ultimately indivisible; and third is the assumption that helping people see the human face of others is an indispensable prelude to humane action.

Although this book is neither about superpower interaction nor nuclear weapons, an experience recounted by Michael Gorbachev reveals most of the coexistence themes that will appear in its pages. Gorbachev wrote: "The ultimate absurdity of relying on nuclear weapons was dramatically revealed to me, and I am sure to President Bush as well, when we met in Washington in the summer of 1990. During that visit, we shared a helicopter ride together to Camp David. Near President Bush sat a military aide with the nuclear codes enabling him to destroy the Soviet Union. Near me sat my military aide with the codes required to destroy the United States. Yet President Bush and I sat together on that small helicopter talking about peace. Neither of us ever planned to use the awesome power we each possessed. Yet we possessed it. And we both knew how ordinary and fallible we both were."[1]

Coexistence work consists of getting people to participate in an intimate encounter with their ethnic enemies. Like the meeting between the two great enemies of the Cold War that took place in that helicopter, it is the absurdity that unfolds before their eyes that enhances conditions for ethnic peace. Although, as we shall see, the concept of coexistence had a controversial inception, it is a doctrine that enabled President Bush and Prime Minister Gorbachev to sit together in that helicopter. The commitment to coexistence at that moment may have saved the world from destruction in the twentieth century, and, if given a chance, it may succeed in doing so again in the twenty-first century as we deal with the horrors of ethnic conflict.

Questions about Coexistence

In this introduction, some of the questions that we will attempt to address will be the following: What is expressed by the term "coexistence"? What are the alternatives to coexistence and why do we reject them? Why is the term "coexistence" used to define the desire for peace, group identity, and international cooperation? Theoretically and pragmatically, who is doing coexistence work? How can different disciplines contribute to furthering our understanding of coexistence? Why is the Israeli–Arab conflict a particularly constructive and fruitful case study of coexistence work? What kind of interventions are likely to impact the potential for coexistence within a nation–state? The various essays in this book explore those ideas that support and reinforce the concept of coexistence.

Defining Coexistence

Coexistence implies not only that differences exist between individuals, groups, nation-states, and civilizations but that they are fundamental. Coexistence means "to exist together, in conjunction with, at the same time, in the same place with another."[2] According to the *Oxford English Dictionary,* the term was negatively expanded and applied during the course of the twentieth century to an essential *lack* of coexistence between the Soviet and capitalist ideological systems. The term "competitive coexistence" was sometimes used in this framework, but it was the term "peaceful coexistence" that was understood to be different in quality from "peace." Although "peaceful coexistence" began initially under Lenin's influence as an ideological cover for covert and overt aggression and deception, it has undergone development and finally transformation in the course of the past six decades. In its latest transformation, the concept has become a welcomed clarion call for a more enlightened and less antagonistic relationship between the Soviet Union and the West. In 1989, the Soviet policy of peaceful coexistence was redefined to include such principles as nonaggression, respect for sovereignty, national independence, and noninterference in internal affairs.

During the period of its most controversial usage, coexistence was deemed to be compatible with propaganda against, and isolation from, divergent groups as well as the encouragement of uprisings. There are, therefore, those who would say "good riddance" to a term so tainted by ambiguous usage. However, in our view such a move would be a serious mistake. The essays in this book will try to show that the ideas behind the term "coexistence" are indispensable when attempting to deal with contemporary ethnic conflicts.

First, the idea of coexistence has functioned as an important restraint on the self-fulfilling logic of many ideological movements. Ideologies with totalistic eschatological visions—and there have been many in the twentieth century—are dedicated to the destruction of their enemies. They require convincing reasons to justify anything less than a totally dedicated effort at such destruction. These totalistic, combative, confrontational visions—such as fascism, communism, and some nation-alistic, ethnic doctrines—sometimes need to be saved from themselves. This has been true as well for some missionary, zealous versions of the free-market economy. The concept of coexistence with the alien Other most fundamentally grants that alien Other the *right to exist*. It functions as a check and restraint on totalistic visions that seek the annihilation of an enemy viewed as the incarnation of evil. Once people are willing to agree to coexist, they begin to embrace a less toxic vision, one that may settle for something other than a complete victory over the enemy.

Second, the idea of coexistence also creates a useful and needed interregnum. Without the concept of coexistence there are only two orders of time for totalistic visions: the time of the totally dedicated struggle and the time of victory or defeat. The idea of peaceful coexistence creates a third order, an "in-between" time. It is a hiatus when one concedes that one will have to learn to live with the enemy "temporarily." In reality, it may turn into a hiatus without end: and that is precisely its social usefulness. The concept of coexistence provides a period during which other things can happen apart from the awful struggle itself. For example, when periods of peaceful coexistence begin, there are opportunities for noncombative personalities to emerge as leaders within the antagonistic groups. The onset of a coexistence era allows common interests (such as economic ones) to emerge among the antagonists, giving both parties a strong stake in making the temporary stage a permanent one.

It is this ongoing dynamic that, we believe, makes the concept of coexistence a particularly useful one in the resolution of intractable ethnic conflicts. Coexistence appeals to self-interest while affirming the right of the Other to life. The self-interested realization that one's own existence is dependent on the existence of the Other is an important stage in the humanization of conflict. It can be a prelude to a durable peace. We do not reject the ultimate desirability of such goals as reconciliation, amity, true peace, and cooperation. They are certainly desirable. However, it seems likely that the best means towards the achievement of these aims is to create a situation of minimalist coexistence, where antagonists "simply" allow others . . . to live. Although aiming low and succeeding may have the disadvantage of not resolving conflicts definitively, aiming high and failing can (and frequently does) lead to disenchantment, discouragement, cynicism, and helplessness, which can then contribute to the re-escalation of conflict.

Coexistence is at once a philosophical orientation toward reality, a goal to be achieved, and a method for achieving that goal. As a philosophical orientation, it is based on a tragic, pessimistic view of the human condition. The assumption is that many intended improvements are futile and achieve nothing, and some attempts to improve the human condition actually makes things worse. This is what Hirschhorn calls the "perversity of human interventions" and Merton calls the "unintended negative consequences of planned social action." "Improvements" frequently jeop-ardize achievements that are already in place.

Coexistence work thus tends to concentrate neither on the deep psychological level nor on the macro-societal, political, and economic levels. It does not pretend to resolve either deep-seated, long-lasting hatreds or fundamental, structural injustice. Coexistence work goes on where ethnic enemies actually interact: in the street, in neighborhoods, in institutions of higher learning, in hospitals, in sports clubs, in business enterprises, in community groups, in religious organizations. Its "live and let live" philosophy informs its work mainly within the institutions of civil society. Thus coexistence work, while taking a dim view of human nature, is nonetheless activist, pragmatic, incremental—and hopeful.

In Praise of Mere Existence

Coexistence as a concept has been controversial and appears to be regarded with suspicion and discomfort. It has yet to capture the popular imagination. Since the idea of coexistence contributed significantly to the prevention of world-destroying conflict, the question is—why has it been neglected or even vilified?

The first reason may well be the fact that coexistence is a concept and a policy that was not born in the West. It has no historical, cultural roots in the intellectual life of the West. As an announced policy of the West's former arch enemies, in the eyes of many, it can merit only oblivion. This is, I would submit, an error. It would be preferable to devote some attention to the policy that enabled the enemies of market economy and democracy to live with us in spite of their intentions to destroy us. Even though we, in the West, did not invent the concept, we have always been interested in what works.

The second reason that coexistence has not yet emerged as a desirable goal is because it seems to violate some deeply felt cultural value in the West. Although, in an imperfect world, we understand and value the necessity of choosing the lesser of two evils, we do not seem able to understand or value the option of choosing the lesser of two goods. In a world of happy endings and infinite possibilities, it is apparently difficult to willingly choose a lesser good that is realizable over a greater but less attainable good. Not attempting to achieve the greater good is somehow perceived as settling for too little. As a consequence, there is something tragic about living in a world in which people only "coexist" with one another.

Thirdly, accepting coexistence as the end state of human relations appears to deny a hopefulness that many feel is essential for the sustenance of people's morale. It seems to imply that we live lives in extremis, that there is no possibility of achieving "real peace and harmony." But must we clutch at the hope that the mythical lion and lamb will eventually embrace one another in order to continue working for peace? Is it not enough that the lion and the lamb drink from the same watering hole, although nervously aware of one another's presence, while drinking the life-preserving waters? Furthermore, those who advocate coexistence are not, of necessity, opposed to reconciliation, cooperation, and peace or other positive ways for groups to exist together. It is not a loss of hopefulness that impels one to embrace the benefits of coexistence, but a respect for the power of those forces that impel people toward deeds of tragic destructiveness.

Coexistence work involves an intimate collaboration between pessimism and optimism. As Roberto Toscano has written: "I have always believed one can be a realist when analyzing and an idealist when advocating (the pessimism of reason and optimism of the will) and also that mutual love is desirable, but coexistence is indispensable."

To let human beings live, no matter how hated or devalued, has attained a moral grandeur after Auschwitz. Talking of "mere existence," as though this were not a sufficiently noble value to pursue, overlooks an important truth: existence is the precondition for all else that we value. An obvious truth perhaps, but one frequently overlooked. In modern consciousness, it is the "image" and the mathematically logical formula that appear to be more indelibly stamped with truth—with existence—than human beings. Modern truth is supposed to reside in the slogans of the image maker ("if you define a thing as real it has real consequences") or of the behavioral scientist ("if you cannot count it, it does not count"). Try telling image-makers or behavioral scientists that when you say of a person or a thing that "they exist," you are saying that it is not an apparition, or the projection of an illusion or just a logical necessity; such a discussion is a difficult one. Lucy's insistent wail "I am a person that exists" in the comic strip *Peanuts* is not limited to her alone. It is a plaintive wail, because there seems to be so much around that is experienced as the denial of existence. It is more common to find "lifestyles" celebrated than life itself and public opinion is a matter of greater fascination than personal conviction. There is nothing "mere" about existence anymore. It is the last thing in the modern world that can be taken for granted.

Ethnic Conflict

Ethnic conflict has replaced the Cold War as the most explosive issue in the world. According to a recent report,[3] only 12 of the 111 armed conflicts in the 1980s involved the armies of two countries. The majority of armed conflicts involved warring ethnic groups. These conflicts are intimately related to the proliferation of ethnic groups who are demanding remedies for real and imagined grievances. In the former Soviet Union alone there are over 100 different ethnic groups each speaking their own language.

One complication of worldwide ethnic conflict is that state boundaries do not correspond to ethnic boundaries. As a result, ethnic conflicts frequently have an interstate dimension. It is the ferocity of ethnic conflict that has shocked a world already hardened by acts of atrocity. The genocidal acts against the Bosnians; the decades of strife generated by the "Irish troubles"; the ongoing conflict between Kurds, Shiites, and Sunnis in Iraq; the variety of atrocities committed against the Roma (Gypsies) in Eastern Europe; the war of the Hutus against the Tutsis in Rwanda: wherever one looks in the world today one sees ethnic strife—it appears to be universal.[4]

Although we are all witness to the dangerous potential of ethnic strife, there seems to be a general sense of futility with regard to engaging in any kind of constructive action about this issue. Such futility contributes to a widespread sense of malaise, and a general acceptance of the fact that ethnic conflict is inevitable.

There are several major points of view about the contemporary existence of ethnic strife that reinforce such inaction. The first point of view sees ethnic strife as the world's last gasp of tribalism before we all settle back to enjoy the modern benefits of a global village. According to this point of view, ethnic assertiveness is a temporary phenomenon, and the present painful fragmentation of groups is just a passing prelude to a greater, more inclusive unity. Those who hold this point of view generally feel that there is no point in doing anything about such conflict at present because, in any case, everything will turn out well in the end.

The second, opposite, point of view perceives the new ethnic assertiveness not as a passing phenomenon, but rather as an ever-present reaction to the homogenizing effects of globalization. As such, it is a central feature of our modern world. According to this view, the more the world unites the more it must fragment. With this perspective, there is no point in trying to do anything about ethnic conflict because it is the inevitable, inescapable price one has to pay for the globalization of a modern era.

There appears to be a silent pact between the optimism of those who think globalism is inevitable and the pessimism of those who think tribalism will persist. It is a pact that tacitly endorses inaction. Thus, when tribes kill each other in Africa the world is prepared to do nothing. Some say that the killing is an atavistic act that will disappear as soon as the warring groups get hooked up to CNN, multinational corporations, and regional markets. Others say that the killing is an inevitable concomitant of the "panic of modernity": precisely because the tribes are being exposed to modernity's unstoppable forces, they are reasserting their ethnic identity. In either case, containment is the only necessary action.

A third point of view attributes ethnic conflict primarily to a lack of democratic rights. It seems reasonable to assume that ethnic group rights are intrinsically linked to democratic values and the rule of law. Are not dignity and equality for all, individuals and groups, the principal components of democracy? However, the recent political changes in Central and Eastern Europe clearly demonstrate that granting equality cannot alone guarantee peace and stability in the region. As Helmut Tuerk, head of the European Union Commission on ethnic strife has indicated: "In the case of ethnic groups special measures are necessary for the purpose of ensuring that persons belonging to such groups have the right to freely express, preserve and develop their culture in all its aspects, free of any attempts at assimilation against their will. Only if members of such groups are genuinely convinced that the State in which they live is also their State, that they are not second-class citizens and have all the possibilities for their cultural, political and economic development, will they also be loyal citizens of the country concerned and committed to contributing to its well-being."[5]

Finally, there are those who believe that ethnic strife is not an issue of concern for them. Their approach is that the enmity between groups is "none of my business." It is frequently difficult to arouse the interest of these individuals in the significance of peaceful coexistence until the conflict reaches their doorstep.

In the face of this sense of futility regarding ethnic strife, there remains a pressing, unmet human need: the need for ethnic groups, many of which are poised to destroy each other and the social environments in which they live, to coexist in peace with one another. The social costs of not succeeding in this task are very great. It is overwhelming to contemplate the loss of life, mass dislocation, oppression, alienation, and protracted suffering through hunger, torture, and maiming that already exist, and that still await us if such a need is not met. Unfortunately, there are few guidelines for effective action in situations of ethnic conflict. This is true in spite of the fact that ethnic conflict constitutes a compelling social problem that has been studied historically and sociologically, and that is constantly in the news. The literature on effective interventions is very sparse despite the salience and visibility of the problem. For the most part, the body of knowledge that does exist about coexistence has not been adapted to practical use by professionals who could make a difference in the field. The strategies that deal with ethnic strife are often inchoate and untested. There are very few training programs to prepare people to take on the task of addressing ethnic conflict. Finally, in spite of the widespread conviction that it is imperative to enhance coexistence, most professionals in the behavioral sciences act as though nothing substantive is achievable. This is so in spite of the fact that many valuable insights about effective intervention are to be found in their very own disciplines.

The Nature of Coexistence Work

How could the creation of a new profession—the coexistence worker—contribute to the lessening of ethnic conflict, and what would the sphere of work specific to such a profession look like? As has been noted, the most ferocious conflicts in the world have tended to be between ethnic groups within the nation-state rather than between them. These have been some of the most devastating civil wars of the second half of the twentieth century—e.g., Sudan (the forty-year intermittent civil war between north and south), Nigeria (the Biafran Civil war, 1967–70), Pakistan (the 1971 secession of Bangladesh), and Lebanon (from 1975 through 1990).

Coexistence work between ethnic groups within a single nation-state encourages antagonistic groups to exist together in civil society by avoiding confrontation. It encourages measures of compromise that enable these groups to live together despite conflicting interests. It seeks to do this, no matter how hate-filled the environment has become, by persevering in its work of enabling groups to discover their common humanity. Coexistence work continuously attempts to blunt differences by making ad hoc arrangements to overcome crises and providing opportunities for face-to-face dialogue. It is based on the conviction that the cumulative effects stemming from a mindful awareness of common existence are far-reaching in their influence. Through the recognition of a common humanity and making compromise into a habit, a climate of hopefulness is created. In such a climate social and political arrangements can be designed to address long-standing grievances and to redistribute privileges equitably, which have been selfishly monopolized.

Coexistence work is predicated on the belief that all its efforts *will* eventually pave the way toward greater consensus, cooperation, reconciliation, and a generosity of spirit, and that if this is not achieved, at least excessive violent conflict will have been prevented. Coexistence work is a way to get through the day—alive. Coexistence practitioners work in the most difficult of times when coexistence is the only alternative to continuing all-out conflict. It is the last gasp of civilized hopefulness, the hope that human beings can be brought to their senses by not indulging in their fantasies of domination and the destruction of enemies, real and imagined.

Coexistence work attempts to call forth habits, skills, and qualities of character that form effective democratic citizens. It helps create civic virtues such as the capacity to listen and hear alternative views and interests, to attend to the common good, and to create a greater sense of belonging. It is the work of creating moral anchors that hold the overall societal framework intact and expose the absurdity of attempting to deny the human face of one's antagonist when it is actually seen.

Coexistence work can occur on many levels, but fundamentally it adopts a bottom-up perspective, in which one pays less attention to national politics (who is in power, how they use it, and how likely they are to keep it), or to the issues of war, peace, or territorial integrity. It is therefore frequently damned with faint praise, and is regarded as noncontroversial and somewhat innocuous. The really high-impact work of social amelioration is viewed as taking place on the level of legal rights, human rights, economic readjustment, etc. Increasing the civility in a society is seen as beneficial, but it is often viewed as a palliative to paper over deeper cleavages and inequalities. The truth is that there are, indeed, times of acute crisis, when this view is basically right. However, in the scheme of everyday life, coexistence work does make a difference. It matters more than a little whether one's ethnic food differences are taken into account when sick in a hospital, or if, because of ethnic origins, one is discriminated against in getting a job, an apartment, entering a university, getting a governmental entitlement, or simply being related to politely. These events are not the stuff of history but they are the stuff of everyday life for most people, most of their lives. Consequently, our answer to those who would neglect the less glamorous aspects of creating a civil society for the more dramatic, fundamental structural changes, is that the work of coexistence must continue until those more basic changes are in place. Indeed the work of coexistence must go forward or those structural changes may never happen. It is the example of coexistence work that may cause the structural changes to occur, precisely because people have not lost hope, and because they have seen that coexistence is possible.

For almost a century now in many parts of the world, this bottom-up perspective has been systematically undermined. Most notably in Eastern Europe and mainland

China, a major ingredient of democratic society has been missing. Among the first acts of totalitarian, ideologically based regimes has been the destruction of free, voluntary citizen associations. In those countries where civil society was destroyed, the state assumed complete responsibility for looking after the interests of the people. Voluntary associations of citizens in the pursuit of their economic, cultural, or religious interests were regarded as subversive competition to the state. It was the state's ideological agenda that determined what was good and bad, and therefore the state did not need to be prompted by the interests of citizens as they themselves defined these issues or sought to pursue them.

In the West, on the other hand, there has been a consistent appreciation of these voluntary associations. John Locke, the intellectual father of the American Revolution, saw government as the trustee of civil society (interests as defined and pursued by ordinary citizens). Insofar as it helped the ordinary people in the realization of their pursuit of life, liberty, and wealth, the government gained legitimacy or lost it. This is precisely the opposite perspective from the ideological world of totalitarianism. Under democracy, the government must prove that it is a faithful executor of the public will. Under totalitarianism, on the contrary, the people must demonstrate their embodiment of state aims or they are at the mercy of its coercive authority. However, while the democratic form of government has indeed given rise to a plethora of associations of like-minded citizens who pursue their interests, these associations have tended to be overshadowed by the sheer power and capacity of the state to achieve its goals. It is the President of the United States that we all know, rather than the president of the local neighborhood association, banking company, or tenant association. In comparison to the ultimate authority of the state, all these other forms of association may have seemed inconsequential.

This was true until 1989. It was in that year that some institutions of civil society succeeded in making the kind of major changes that everyone assumed no small association could accomplish. It was the Civic Forum in Czechoslovakia and the Solidarity movement in Poland organized years before that succeeded in creating a bloodless revolution that brought down one of the most despotic and coercive regimes in history. It was not the government bureaucracy, nor the military, nor political leaders that did this job. It was ordinary people who banded together to address the central questions in their lives. The movement had a moral force that was unstoppable. It was a revolution from the bottom rather than the top.

People in pursuit of their interests can, on occasion, achieve miracles. The voluntary organizations through which coexistence can be pursued are capable of doing things that central governments cannot easily do, and thus add further legitimacy to the coexistence project.

Coexistence Work in Israel, a Jewish Ethnocracy: A Case Study

The relationship between the Jews and Arabs of Israel is a case in point, which demonstrates the issues so far highlighted. Israel is both a Jewish and a democratic state. It is an ethnically Jewish state and must remain so in the eyes of the majority of its citizens. Although the Arab citizens of Israel have equal rights to vote and to governmental benefits, Jewish citizens are in many ways given preferential treatment. There is an inherent contradiction between Israel's democratic nature and this affirmative action on behalf of its already privileged Jewish citizens. This constitutes a moral and ethical problem for those who value civil society and its democratic expression. Theoretically, in a democratic society all citizens should be related to equally by the state regardless of race, creed, gender, or ethnic origin.

In a democracy it is believed that any ascriptive markers of identity will become increasingly unimportant as people pursue their own interests in the public sphere. In Israel, however, ethnic dominance has been justified on the basis of Jewish survival and security. For example, there are periodic needs to rescue Jews who are persecuted in various parts of the world. Although the Arab minority in Israel (17 percent) are full citizens, they are certainly second in the order of national priorities, and often feel themselves to be second-class citizens with first-class grievances. In spite of notable progress during the past fifty years since the establishment of the state, Israel's Arab citizens are disadvantaged in comparison to the Jews of Israel.

This presents a set of issues that need to be addressed. It is possible that the only way Israel may be able to maintain the distinctiveness of being a Jewish state will be to satisfy the ethnic needs of its minority Arab citizens. Throughout their thousands of years of exile, in which they have been a minority, Jews have fine-tuned the art of peaceful coexistence with diverse ethnic and religious groups. The need to continue to do this in the situation where they are the majority was pointed out by the well-known historian Salo Wittmayer Baron as early as 1947, on the eve of Israel's establishment. He wrote:

> Even after the establishment of a Jewish commonwealth . . . Palestinian Jewry would be confronted by a strong Arab minority and be surrounded by large Arab states. For generations to come, the majority of the Jewish people would still live outside of Palestine as a minority dependent on the goodwill of majorities. Such goodwill would certainly be affected, positively or negatively, by what Palestinian Jewry might do in regard to its own Arab minority. These Zionists trust, therefore, in the creative elan of their people to find some unprecedented answers. They believe that just as their prophetic ancestors, acting from necessity, discovered memorable new approaches vital to all Western Civilization, so will the Jews of a new Palestine, acting under the stress of new stupendous difficulties, help devise some new ways out of the present world crises.[6]

Israel, like all nation-states, has a particular stake in promoting the social mobility of minorities. Movement towards ethnic nationalism, with its nascent violence, invariably occurs when there is blocked social mobility, the prospect of humiliation, and the fear that the lives of children will be negatively impacted.[7] Paradoxically, it may well be that a majority can only live without fear of violence if those minorities living within its borders are also given the conditions necessary to maintain their separate identities. Or in terms already familiar to the reader, there may be no existence for majorities without coexistence with minorities.

Conclusion

Until now, coexistence work has been carried out by well-meaning amateurs, but its reliability and effectiveness can be increased by taking the necessary steps to professionalize the work. It is our conviction that the academy can make a significant contribution toward the generation of more effective strategies for dealing with ethnic and racial conflict. Such a contribution can be made:

(1) By helping to synthesize and critically evaluate the extant body of knowledge in the field of coexistence;
(2) By creating the training programs necessary to educate professionals, using the knowledge and skills necessary for dealing with these conflicts;
(3) By encouraging rigorous evaluational research to determine the effects of intervention on the moderation of conflict.

There are conceptual, empirical, and programmatic resources currently available to help inform the work of the coexistence professional. Some of these resources are illustrated in the essays of this book. They can be found most notably in the fields of conflict resolution, mediation, alternate dispute resolution, and ethnic relations. Fortunately for the development of coexistence work, virtually every academic discipline in the behavioral sciences, humanities, law, and business offers courses that are relevant to coexistence work. Some of these departmental offerings could be integrated into a graduate curriculum for the training of coexistence workers. Although the list is not comprehensive, the following are examples of such potentially relevant courses:

Anthropology	The Cross-Cultural Analysis of Conflict
Demography	The Migration of Populations and Their Impact on Ethnic Conflict Education
	Multicultural Education in a Pluralistic Society
History	Polyethnicity and National Unity as a Cause of Ethnic Conflict
Law	Law and Jurisprudence in Conflict Resolution
	The Many Applications of Alternate Dispute Resolution
	Theory and Practice of Negotiation
	Affirmative Action and Justice
	The Idea of Citizenship and the Mitigation of Ethnic Conflict
Linguistics	Multilingualism and the Education of Minority Children
Literature	The Difficulty of Imagining the Other: A Literary Perspective
Philosophy	Tribal Philosophies and Their Interaction

Political Science	War, Violence, and Conflict Resolution
	Strengthening Civil Society
	Coexistence Work with Minorities at Risk
Religious Studies	Religious Fundamentalism and Ethnic Conflict
Social Work	Moderating Racial and Ethnic Conflict
Social Psychology	Theories of Conflict and Conflict Resolution
	Laboratory and Simulation of Interpersonal and Group Conflict
	Community and Organizational Conflict
	International Conflict
	Attitudinal Change
Sociology	The Creation of More Inclusive Social Identities
	Social Conflict in Deeply Divided Societies

As can be seen from this disparate list of courses presently offered in universities, the academy is already engaged in areas of teaching and research that have great relevance to ethnic and racial conflict.

This *Handbook* brings together diverse perspectives. It gives the reader an opportunity to evaluate the promise of coexistence work in dealing with ethnic conflict. The selections are divided into five sections that span the gamut from theory to practice, and from analysis of the major issues to description of the concrete interventions that constitute the practice of coexistence. It is such integration of theory, empirical findings, and practice competencies that is required for the creation of professional education and training. We have designed this *Handbook* as a primer and first reader in the field. Our intention has been to provide a forum for the diverse disciplines now addressing issues of coexistence work and ethnic conflict to meet and converse, and, we hope, bring us all closer to an age of interethnic coexistence.

Notes

1. Gorbachev, M. (1995) *The Search for a New Beginning: Developing a New Civilization*. (San Francisco: Harper San Francisco, pp. 4–5)
2. *Oxford English Dictionary*
3. *World Directory of Minorities*, p. xiii
4. Ted Robert Gurr. *Minorities at Risk: A Global View of Ethnopolitical Conflicts*, (Washington, D.C.: United States Institute of Peace Press, 1993)
5. Tuerk, Helmut. "Ethnic Strife in Eastern Europe: An Austrian Perspective." From a speech delivered at Town Hall, Los Angeles, CA, April 15, 1994
6. Salo Wittmayer Baron. Modern Nationalism and Religion. (Meridian Books, 1947, pp. 246–47)
7. John A. Hall. Nationalisms: Classified and Explained, *Daedalus*, Summer 1993, p. 10

° 1 °

Philosophy of Coexistence

In this section, some fundamental orientations toward coexistence are explored. Based on their orientation, the authors present their interpretation as to the failure of coexistence, as well as some possible remedies to reverse this failure.

In the first article, David Hamburg considers the following issues and their contribution to the failure of coexistence: the lack of a worldwide human relatedness; the growing dominance of identity groups with mutually exclusive agendas; the dearth of common superordinate goals that can occupy all of humanity; an atavistic loyalty to national sovereignty; and the lack of institutionalized measures to prevent violence and activate "preventive diplomacy."

For Elaine Scarry, coexistence is problematic because of the difficulty we have in imaginatively identifying with the injuries we inflict on others.

Roberto Toscano notes that the failure to peacefully coexist has generally been attributed to a cluster of "narcissistic group identities" that justify killing the other and that turn concrete individuals into abstractions.

Ahmad Sadri attributes the breakdown in coexistence to humanity's tendency toward "tunnel vision." Using careful historical, ethnographical, and sociological texts, he points out how we all tend to start with an image of self based on a specific reading of the evolution of our own civilization. The image of the Other then presents us with a double vision that impedes peaceful coexistence.

For Saul Mendlovitz and Lester Ruiz, coexistence is impeded by territorially fixed identities and a lack of an inclusive myth and transformative practices that are oriented toward a notion of global citizenship.

James Will builds on the insights of historians, theologians, and the refined sensibilities of the humanities to argue that ethnonationalist loyalties are inevitable and are destined to continue to play an important role in conflict situations unless loyalties can be transformed to serve more universal purposes.

Wolf Emminghaus, Paul Kimmel, and Edward Stewart focus on the fact that recent conflicts, which they have termed *primal violence* have tended to be based on issues of cultural identity such as ethnicity, language, and race rather than on political differences and economic interests alone. They stress the need for a new paradigm, and indeed offer us one, which is penetrating and comprehensive, to understand the situation in which cultural variables and processes are primary.

Each of the authors has suggested different kinds of remedies to the causes of failure that they have presented. Hamburg stresses the strategic role of international institutions. He sees in the scientific community with its transnational, universal passion for truth, a model for the world community. For Hamburg, involvement in multiple associations that create greater heterogeneity and crosscutting loyalties is the key to a more peaceful world.

Scarry, who outlines our inability to imagine the Other, suggests that we cannot ultimately rely on what she terms "generous imaginings" and "unanchored goodwill" to guarantee that people will live well with those regarded as foreign. She believes that constitutional guarantees are required.

For Toscano the most efficacious remedies are those that prevent the erasure of the human face of the other. He believes that there is no idyllic interethnic community. Coexistence is a fragile—but possible—conscious mechanism of rapprochement, a sort of good neighbor policy finding its concretization in almost ritualized inclusion of the "different neighbor" who is loved or hated for concrete, not abstract reasons.

Sadri takes us past tunnel vision and double vision into the realm of depth perception through the merging of group stories into one and enabling the history of groups to merge and belong to one another. In order to progress toward a willingness to coexist, the two images must be overlapped in such a way that histories can be seen as belonging to one another.

Mendlovitz and Ruiz stress the centrality of transnational peace and social justice movements and a dedicated set of practices committed to nonviolent activism. Will presents a way for national loyalties to be transformed so they can serve more universal purposes.

In brief, what we are introduced to in this section is a broad overview of the philosophical grounded causes for the failure of coexistence and its possible remedies.

Preventing Contemporary Intergroup Violence

DAVID A. HAMBURG

The world of the next century will be different in profound respects from any that we have ever known before—deeply interdependent economically, closely linked technologically, and progressively more homogenized through the movement of information, ideas, people, and capital around the world at unprecedented speed. At the same time, it will be more multicentric in the devolution of economic, political, and military power to smaller adaptable units. Some nations will undergo a perilous fragmentation, as the centralizing forces that once held people together are pulled apart and traditional concepts of national sovereignty and nationhood are contested, sometimes violently. How these tendencies will be reconciled is far from clear.

One of the most striking facts of our time is the way technology has come to dominate and organize our lives, presenting unimaginable benefits, opportunities, and choices within a matter of decades, yet unleashing the destructive power of advanced weaponry that in an instant of history can do immense damage, even destroy humanity.

While the more complex and contradictory world that we have entered is of our own making, we often approach its problems with the biological orientations and emotional responses of our ancient ancestry, bringing attitudes, customs, and institutions that were formed largely in earlier times and that are perhaps no longer appropriate. Foremost is our tendency as a species toward prejudice, egocentrism, and ethnocentrism. In these times of rapid world transformation, as people have flowed like floodwaters across the earth, families, social support networks, old ways of forming group solidarity, and other traditional patterns of living have been strained or broken apart. Many individuals feel a heightened sense of uncertainty and insecurity. Some react with exaggerated intolerance of the outside world or with violence toward those who are seen as alien and threatening. Political demagogues can readily inflame these feelings in a context of severe vulnerability.

The historical record is full of every sort of slaughter based on the human capability to make invidious distinctions between in-groups and out-groups—often associated with the frustration of fundamental drives, deeply felt beliefs about identity, or a sense of jeopardy to group survival. In this century—a period of the most rapid industrialization and wrenching transition—human slaughter far exceeds any that has gone before. Just since the United Nations was formed in 1945, there have been upwards of 150 small-scale wars resulting in more than 20 million dead and easily four times that many disabled or displaced. Millions have perished at the hands of their own countrymen in Cambodia, Indonesia, Burundi, Rwanda, Nigeria, Paraguay, Tibet, Uganda, Angola, and the Sudan. Most recently the former Yugoslavia has generated at least 150,000 dead and more than two million refugees.

Today worldwide, fed by the powerful currents of aggressive ethnic nationalism, there is a virtual epidemic of armed civil or intranational conflict—the kind often thought of as "internal" but that can readily spill over the borders of nation-states. While international attention has been on the savage fighting in Bosnia, long-simmering antagonisms among deeply mingled ethnic groups have come to the surface in the successor states to the Soviet Union—exacerbated by the harsh economic conditions that prevail there as well as by the erosion of social norms. Hundreds of such nationality "hot spots" exist in these vast territories. Sixty-five million people in the former Soviet Union do not live in their primary areas of origin, and many are fearful about their treatment as minorities in the new nations. The international community is only just beginning to realize the potential gravity of these various conflicts. Russia herself, with her huge arsenal of nuclear weapons, has shown serious signs of instability.

New Wine in Old Bottles

Intergroup conflict is an ancient part of the human legacy, and tyrants have long understood how to exploit for their own ends the human tendency to attribute malevolence primarily or solely to other groups, deflecting anger onto the hated others, who are blamed for all their troubles. Many different political, social, economic, and pseudoscientific ideologies have been mobilized to support hostile positions toward those who are outside the primary community or who deviate from community norms.

All that is very old and once upon at time may have been adaptive, but these characteristics of our species have become exceedingly dangerous, primarily because of the enormous destructive power of the advanced weaponry we have created. Weapons themselves do not cause dangerous conflicts, but their availability in large quantities can easily intensify and prolong such conflicts. The use of sophisticated technology, moreover, enhances the risk that the consequences of local wars will become regional or global.

While nuclear warheads, which can be carried by missiles with tremendous accuracy over great distances, represent the ultimate in human violence, the increased killing power of enhanced conventional, chemical, and biological weapons also has the potential for making life everywhere miserable and disastrous. In the past, no matter how ferocious the conflict, humanity could not destroy itself even if it wanted to. Now it can. One of the most serious problems the world will face in the next decade is the proliferation throughout the world of these modern deadly weapons—or the knowledge and technical capability for making them—and the looming possibility that they will be used.

In this post–Cold War environment of many small wars and potentially large ones, a new approach to international problem solving may be needed. The system of international diplomacy that evolved over the past two centuries focused on power relations between nation-states. Yet the risks, costs, casualties, and tragedies of the twentieth century should tell us, if nothing else does, that this may be far from an optimal system for dealing with conflict between peoples of the same nation—or the problem of weapons proliferation.

Attachment and Aggression

The capacity for attachment and the capacity for violence are fundamentally connected in human beings. We fight with other people in the belief that we are protecting ourselves, our loved ones, and the group with which we identify most strongly. Altruism and aggression are intimately linked in war and other conflicts. My lifetime has witnessed terrible atrocities committed in the name of some putatively high cause. Yet there have also been vivid examples of the reconstruction of societies, major reconciliations, and real enlargement of opportunities for substantial segments of a population. What are the conditions under which the outcome can go one way or the other? If we could understand such questions better, maybe we could learn to tilt the balance in favor of a stable, enduring peace among human groups in the twenty-first century.

Even though in-group/out-group distinctions are ubiquitous in human societies, easy to learn and hard to forget, there is certainly the possibility that we humans can learn to minimize these tendencies. This may be one of the crucial roads we have to travel in order to cope with conflict in the transformed world of the future. Can we find a basis for common human identification across a diversity of cultures and national groups?

Below, I try to sketch some promising lines of inquiry and innovation that bear strongly on the two-sided coin of human cooperation and conflict and that suggest ways the world's institutions can cope with burgeoning threats to international peace. It is worth considering how the various approaches to the prevention of the deadliest conflicts and the promotion of international cooperation might be strengthened, particularly in light of superordinate goals essential for the future of humanity and our habitat.

The Search for Understanding

Given the myriad possibilities for world conflagration, the nature and sources of human conflict are deserving of the most careful and searching attention. Yet, until quite recently they have not been a major focus of systematic analysis and even today are rather marginalized in the world's great research and educational institutions. The scientists and scholars heavily engaged in such inquiry have been largely lacking in support. The field of ethnic conflict resolution, moreover, is relatively new and weakly institutionalized. The international community has nothing like an effective system for preventing the deadliest conflicts.

The powerful sectors of society everywhere, for their part, have tended to be complacent about such matters and to see them as someone else's problem, far away. Avoidance often substitutes for foresight, authority for evidence, and blaming for problem solving. The capacity for wishful thinking, as it is for self-justification, seems boundless in matters of human conflict.

All this may be beginning to change now, stimulated by deep concerns about the dangers of contemporary conflict and by the belated recognition of the ubiquity of killing and maiming in human experience. Conflicts have become everyone's business. The idea that states and peoples are free to conduct their quarrels, no matter how deadly, is outdated in the nuclear age and in a shrinking world where local hostilities can rapidly become international ones with devastating consequences. Similarly, the notion that tyrants are free to commit atrocities on their own people is rapidly becoming obsolete.

A substantial body of careful empirical research on conflict resolution and international peacemaking, detailing the historical experience with forms of negotiation, mediation, arbitration, recognition, and power sharing is at last beginning to emerge, and the results are providing new insights and guidelines useful to practitioners. It is apparent that there is no single approach to conflict resolution that offers overriding promise. Just as the sources and manifestations of human conflict are immensely varied, so too are the approaches to understanding, preventing, and resolving conflicts.

The field can benefit from more dynamic interplay between theory and practice. The great challenge is to move with a sense of urgency to organize a broader and deeper effort to understand these issues and, above all, to develop more effective ways in the real world of preventing and resolving conflicts short of disaster.

Additionally, there needs to be serious worldwide education about forms of nonviolent problem solving that can generate public support. The price of resolving international disputes by force of arms is becoming too high—even putative winners are beginning to recognize this unwelcome fact. But finding workable alternatives that are broadly acceptable, particularly in the realm of preventive systems, will challenge the international community beyond any prior experience. While it is certainly not beyond possibility to move this subject higher on the agenda of this nation and others, it will require a much deeper grasp of the dangers among leadership groups and the general public than now exists.

Sovereignty and Self-Determination

Most people everywhere live in multiethnic societies. Worldwide there are several thousand ethnic groups versus fewer than two hundred nation-states. In Europe, as in Africa, national borders were in large part imposed by external powers without regard to geography or shared ethnicity. Conditions were created in which members of the same identity group were split apart, leaving open the possibility that all groups could make territorial claims on each other. If now every ethnic, religious, racial, linguistic, or cultural group sought to establish its own nation, there would be no limit to fragmentation—precipitating violence, immense suffering, and a flow of refugees on an unimaginable scale.

Sometimes in the modern world it is possible to separate out ethnic groups that wish to have their own nation–state and create a situation in which borders essentially coincide with a living space of that particular group; but this is unusual. Although secession may be carried off democratically and peacefully, as in Czecho-slovakia, this is rare, and the quest to create a separate state or redraw borders will usually prove to be a chimera.

The attractive concept of self-determination was given an idealistic boost after both world wars, but the conflict in Bosnia shows how dangerous sudden secessions, rationalized on the basis of self-determination, can be. The creation of new states by sudden secession may trigger fierce fighting not only within a country but also across international borders. There is ample evidence of this in the states of the former Soviet Union, where the problem is complicated by an immense armory of highly destructive weapons. So the concept of self-determination will have to be reassessed in light of contemporary circumstances and the conflicting values involved clarified and dealt with peacefully.

Beyond this, there is an urgent need to create the conditions under which various identity groups can sort out their differences and learn to live in a state of harmonious interaction with their neighbors. Ways must be found to foster self-esteem, meaningful group membership, and internal cohesion without the necessity for harsh depreciation of out-groups and without resort to violence in the event of a clash of interests.

A fundamental requisite of mutual accommodation is development of a genu-inely free civil society within a democratic framework, where there is truly equal citizenship, respect for human rights, protection against the abuse of power, free-dom to express differences openly and constructively, and a fair distribution of opportunities. Many paths to mutual accommodation are possible: nonviolent agreed secession; peaceful, negotiated territorial border revision; federation or confederation; regional or functional autonomy; and respected cultural pluralism, within each nation and across national boundaries. Each case presents a particular set of opportunities and constraints, and each solution will inevitably be reached only after painful deliberation, taxing the patience and support of all. Whatever the outcome, it must eventually satisfy the reasonable claims of most citizens, though not necessarily the intolerant militants or extremists.

Shared Goals of a Single Worldwide Species

To an increasing extent, we will have to learn to broaden our social identifications in light of shared interests and superordinate goals across all of humanity. We must come to think of ourselves in a fundamental sense as a single interdependent, meaningfully attached, extended family. This is in fact what we are; but to state this is not to assimilate it as a psychological reality.

Superordinate goals have the potentially powerful effect of unifying disparate groups in the search for the vital benefit that can be obtained only by their cooperation. Such goals can override the differences that people bring to the situation.

What could constitute shared goals of this extraordinary significance? The avoidance of nuclear destruction is one. Protection of the environment is emerging as another, since it may well come to involve jeopardy to the human habitat. The creation of new forms of community, social cohesion, and solidarity in the face of the vast impersonal modern society we have wrought is another. The threat of worldwide economic deterioration might also become salient. At a regional level, the desire to improve economic prospects can impel two or more nations to cooperate in the development of agriculture, transportation, electricity, and water resources, increasing confidence and mutually beneficial interdependence.

These are mainly survival goals, updated to the modern era, where the reference for adaptation goes beyond the sense of belonging in the immediate valued group to identification with a much larger unit or ideal. The current, worldwide epidemic of severe ethnic conflict should help us realize that we are all in this huge leaking boat together in a gathering storm.

The ancient propensity toward narrow identity, harsh intolerance, and deadly intergroup conflict will confront us with new dangers in the next century and challenge us as never before. By the same token it will create a great opportunity to identify the fundamental properties of superordinate goals and their myriad possibilities in the world of small- and large-scale wars that have proven so contagious in recent years. How can all of humanity benefit—indeed survive—by adopting new attitudes, practices, and institutions?

Changing Principles of International Diplomacy

In the period following World War II, the international community put all too little emphasis on the protection of minority rights. Concepts of self-determination, sovereignty, and the sanctity of borders prevented outsiders from mediating ethnic tensions within or between states. International law on self-determination limited itself primarily to anticolonial movements.

When international intervention did occur, it was usually associated with partisan superpower support in the context of Cold War rivalry. In this environment and with its almost infinite respect for the nation-state, the United Nations was virtually helpless to intervene in most serious conflicts. Mediation by governments or nongovernmental organizations in intergroup conflicts also tended to occur only after fighting had erupted between opposing groups. This was the case in the Arab–Israeli disputes, in Ngorno-Karabakh, in Yugoslavia, and in the Sudan.

But with the ending of the Cold War, the growth of a dynamic and interdependent world economy, and the blurring of national boundaries by modern communication and transportation, nations have an opportunity to deal cooperatively with world problems unhampered by ideological rivalries. In particular they can now address seriously the paradoxically hostile separatism that is stirring up new conflicts around the world. They can begin to deal with the severe ecological damage and resource depletion, huge disparities between rich and poor, and denial of aspiration that are at the heart of much of intergroup violence.

Some experts, drawing on years of study and diplomatic experience in dealing with serious conflicts, envision a shift taking place in the nature of international relations—from the traditional power-oriented, authoritarian, and controlling model toward one that is more complex and multifaceted, in which mutually beneficial political and economic relations are of growing importance.

The older paradigm took it for granted that human beings were overwhelmingly selfish and therefore would respond mainly to coercion. Interests were defined narrowly in terms of power. This can now usefully be enlarged to a broader view that is more sympathetic to basic human needs for physical and economic security, social justice, and political freedom. Such a view relies less on coercive measures and more on the clarification of fundamental concerns and underlying common interests and on ways to change political environments toward democracy.

An indication of a shift in the paradigms of diplomacy is the recent willingness of states to yield some historically sensitive sovereign prerogatives in the interests of achieving larger political and economic benefits. But progress here is hard-won and subject to regression with little notice.

Still, the remarkably peaceful ending of the Cold War might in due course provide the basis for a new system of international, democratic, nonviolent problem solving aimed ultimately at prevention of the deadliest conflicts. This is an immense challenge to serious thinkers, penetrating analysts, and innovative practitioners.

A Post–Cold War International System

If aggrieved groups have recourse to a respected external authority—whether governments, multilateral institutions, nongovernmental organizations, or other bridge-building or mediating links—they might be less likely to engage in secessionist activities or appeal to their ethnic kin from outside to come to their rescue. Whatever can nurture a more cosmopolitan identity rather than a parochial, narrowly defined ethnic identity will be helpful in the long term.

To this end, the international community can formulate general standards for resolving disputes and for satisfying self-determination claims to a reasonable extent, in the context of an existing state if feasible. It can develop a preventive orientation, monitoring "hot spots," analyzing the potential sources of conflict, and becoming involved early as conflicts emerge. It can analyze ways in which economic access to and participation in the international economy can help ensure adherence to standards of decent behavior in intergroup relations. It can encourage ways of facilitating the growth of mutually beneficial loose associations or confederations.

A new international consensus toward conflict prevention and resolution could support the provision of visible, respected forums for the expression of grievances among the relevant parties and of organized settings that foster empathy and restraint, in which culturally accepted techniques for reconciliation are used to the maximum extent possible. It could instill a process of joint problem solving in which representatives of the different groups mutually explore their respective interests, basic needs, and fervent aspirations. It could have a means of identifying shared goals such as regional economic development and aid in the building of inclusive democratic institutions.

Such a consensus could lead to mechanisms for organizing an ongoing series of reciprocal goodwill gestures; for drafting possible agreements—even modest next steps—that show the possibility of finding common ground in a mode of civil discourse; for building institutions where parties can learn about negotiation and democratic ways of coping; and for utilizing multilateral, regional, and nongovernmental resources to create incentives and skills for negotiation, cooperation, and help with economic development.

These desiderata could apply to the resolution of a wide range of large, intergroup conflicts, spanning traditional international relations and contemporary ethnic tensions.

But what entities could implement such an international system for preventing the deadliest conflicts? The United Nations? The community of established democracies? Some interplay between the two? Other international mechanisms?

The United Nations

There is a growing interest by the international community in the possibility of broadening the role of the United Nations. With its legitimacy as the most significant global institution striving for democratic ideals oriented toward a peaceful world order, it might usefully intervene in some "internal affairs" to prevent deadly conflict, render humanitarian assistance, and aid transitions to more democratic systems of governance.

In January 1992, for the first time in the history of the institution, a special meeting of the Security Council of the United Nations was held at the level of heads of state. It was a summit meeting called to examine the functions of the U.N., particularly with respect to conflict resolution. Secretary-General Boutros Boutros-Ghali was asked to prepare a plan for strengthening the capacity of the U.N. to engage in preventive diplomacy, peacemaking, and peacekeeping. This was an unprecedented occasion and expressed a strong commitment to the original purposes and principles of the United Nations Charter drawn up a half century earlier.

The Secretary-General responded some months later with a remarkable document, "An Agenda for Peace," which drew upon many ideas and proposals from member states, regional and nongovernmental organizations, and individuals. Some aspects of the document are groundbreaking. In it Boutros-Ghali took note of changes in the concept of sovereignty: "The time of absolute and exclusive sovereignty . . . has passed; its theory was never matched by reality. It is the task of leaders of states today to understand this and to find a balance between the needs of good internal governance and the requirements of an ever more interdependent world."

The Secretary-General put emphasis on fact-finding and analysis—to identify at the earliest possible stage the circumstances that could produce serious conflict—and on the need for preventive diplomacy to resolve the most immediate problems, with attention to underlying causes of conflict. While placing a high priority on the U.N.'s having an early warning system and the means for early intervention, he did not ignore the necessity for it to deal effectively at later stages with its more familiar functions of peacemaking and peacekeeping. Improvement in the former could include strengthening the role of the International Court of Justice (the principal judicial organ of the U.N.) and introducing confidence-building measures, economic assistance, and, if necessary, sanctions and the use of military force. Boutros-Ghali considered the increased demands on the U.N. for peacekeeping and the complex organizational changes that will be necessary if the U.N. is to be more effective in these domains.

He also considered preventive deployment, which goes beyond earlier U.N. practice. There may be circumstances that justify deploying forces prior to the outbreak of fighting, if such help is requested by governments or parties to the fighting. The aim is to limit or control the violence, help ensure that security is maintained, assist in conciliation efforts, even establish a demilitarized zone before a conflict is well established, and provide humanitarian assistance.

To the functions he was asked to comment on, the Secretary–General added a fourth category—postconflict peacebuilding—having the aim of constructing a more durable foundation for peace. The creation of a new environment after a conflict is the counterpart of preventive diplomacy before conflict. While preventive diplomacy seeks to identify at the earliest stage the circumstances that could produce a serious conflict and remove the sources of danger, postconflict peacebuilding aims to prevent a crisis from recurring. It emphasizes, as does preventive diplomacy, cooperative efforts to cope with underlying economic, social, and humanitarian problems.

The Secretary–General's report underscored the importance of joint efforts to nurture democratic practices and, by implication, democratic institutions, since so many countries in a state of conflict have had little or no democratic experience. Similarly, in many arenas there is a need for the U.N. to provide technical assistance in the rebuilding phase and to place the conflicting parties on a sounder economic basis for their own internal development. As a practical matter, Boutros-Ghali cited the problem of how to get rid of the millions of mines that now litter the lands where conflicts have gone on. Doing so will restore not only agriculture and transportation but hope and confidence so that citizens can participate fully in the rebuilding. The Secretary–General recognized the importance of working with regional organizations and the nongovernmental sector in carrying out such functions.

Implementing this agenda will necessarily be difficult and the obstacles formidable. If the United Nations is to play these roles effectively, it will require much more substantial and dependable financial and political support than it has ever received before. For this to happen there will need to be a much higher level of public understanding about the U.N.'s current functions and its potential than now exists. And there will need to be some changes in structure and function.

The United Nations is not, and never will be, a world government. It is an intergovernmental organization of sovereign states that seek common ground for cooperation in their long-term self-interest. It is perforce large and multifaceted, disparate in its composition and in the outlook of its members, and emotionally charged from its past history and from current difficulties in the world. As such, it cannot be an optimal instrument for all efforts at preventive diplomacy or conflict resolution. Nevertheless, if it did not exist, something very much like it would have to be invented. There simply has to be a comprehensive, worldwide forum for global issues. Surely it is time to consider how some of its functions, and the components and mechanisms within it, could be extended, and new ones created if necessary, in order to strengthen the hand of the international community in preventing highly lethal conflicts.

The Established Democracies

The democracies of Europe, North America, Japan, and Australia have shown that they can live together peacefully even as they compete. On the other hand, they have failed badly in certain situations, such as Bosnia. Increasingly they are likely to take the lead in formulating international norms of conduct with respect to intergroup relations, the proliferation of highly lethal weaponry, economic development in poorer nations, human rights, and the growth of democratic institutions. They have the technological, economic, and political strength to establish such norms even if tyrannical governments are offended.

The established democracies may act on such issues with the approval of or on behalf of the U.N., or they may cooperate with it informally. Usually their actions will be political and economic in nature rather than military. In almost all cases they will need to consult widely with each other on a systematic basis.

The North Atlantic Treaty Organization is a prime example of the ability of established democracies to work together—initially to counteract an aggressive Soviet Union, provide for European security, and foster German recovery in a democratic mode. Could a similar alliance, involving a wider coalition of democracies, be organized to ensure security on a worldwide basis, fuel economic growth with fairness, protect cultural diversity, and foster democratic values?

Who Else Can Help?

As important as the United Nations is, there are other organizations of the international community that could be effective in preventing deadly conflicts. The involvement of the permanent members of the U.N. Security Council may be crucial for some regional conflicts, as in Cambodia, but other disputes may be handled at the regional level. The potential of regional mechanisms for dispute resolution in intergroup conflicts deserves serious attention in the next decade. The European Community, the Conference on Security and Cooperation in Europe, the Council of Europe and its European Court of Human Rights, the Association of Southeast Asian Nations, the Organization of American States, the Organization of African Unity, and the Arab League all need strengthening in this regard.

Various specialized international organizations, such as the General Agreement on Tariffs and Trade and the Law of the Sea Tribunal, can play a useful role in resolving disagreements surrounding a particular set of issues. Bilateral arrangements can also be created to adjudicate disputes between nations. The U.S.–Iran Claims Tribunal demonstrated that two hostile nations with different languages, laws, and goals were able to settle matters of considerable importance to both sides.

Nongovernmental organizations can also play an important part in resolving disputes, cooperating with the U.N. and with regional organizations. Former President Jimmy Carter, for example, has established through the Carter Center in Atlanta an international network for mediation and conflict resolution.

The Scientific Outlook

The scientific community is probably the closest approximation we now have to a truly international community, sharing certain basic interests, values, and standards as well as a fundamental curiosity about the nature of matter, life, behavior, and the universe. The shared quest for understanding is one that has no inherent boundaries. In any situation of potentially serious conflict, the scientific outlook can contribute to the construction of a framework for conflict resolution and for building a peaceful world. It takes a worldview that embodies multiple truths, not some simple ultimate truth; it seeks evidence, and it is prepared to learn from experience. This same empirical spirit is frequently helpful in defusing passions aroused by social conflict. It provides one of the pathways toward a broader-than-conventional perspective that can be learned by all peoples and that can build bridges across cultures.

In the realm of scientific research, the interactions of biological, psychological, and social processes in the development of human aggressiveness leading to violent conflict must constitute an important frontier in the decades ahead. A shared commitment to the humane uses of science and technology could offer a great vista of hope.

Bridge Building

This analysis suggests the importance of having crosscutting or overlapping group memberships in the modern world. Crosscutting relations are those that connect subgroups of society or connect nations in ways that overcome in-group/out-group distinctions and prejudicial stereotypes. They involve the opportunity for members of alien, suspicious, or hostile groups to spend time together, to work together, to play together, and even to live together for extended periods of time, gaining a sense of shared humanity.

On the international level, there must be concerted efforts to expand favorable contact between people from different groups and nations. Some measure of comprehension of a strange culture is vital. Educational, cultural, and scientific exchanges can be helpful. At a deeper level, joint projects involving sustained cooperation can provide, if only on a small scale, an experience of working together toward a superordinate goal. There are many ways to break down antagonisms between groups or, preferably, prevent them from arising in the first place. International organizations can do much to promote empathic personal contact and overlapping loyalties that cut across in-group/out-group antagonisms.

Those of us who have a deep sense of belonging in groups that cut across ethnic or national lines may serve to bridge different groups and help others move toward a wider sense of social identity. Building such bridges will need many people interacting across traditional barriers on a basis of mutual respect. Nothing in our history as a species would suggest there is a readiness for such a wider sense of personal identity; yet it must be possible to engender this in the next century and to do so on a broader scale than ever before.

Social Education

There are other ways to create positive connections between groups. Families, schools, community organizations, religious institutions, and the media throughout the years of human growth and development are pivotal institutions that can shape attitudes and interpersonal skills toward either decent relations or hatred and violence. In the twenty-first century it will be necessary in child raising to put deliberate, explicit emphasis on developing prosocial orientations and a sense of worth based not on depreciation of others but on the constructive attributes of oneself and others. Taking turns, sharing, and cooperating, especially in learning and problem solving—these norms, established on a simple basis in the first few years of life, can open the way to beneficial human relationships that can have significance throughout a person's life.

A secure attachment of infant to mother or other adult caregiver provides a crucial foundation for the development of prosocial behavior. It is important to focus on the nature of parental behavior that can promote or retard these tendencies. Not only schools but religious and community organizations should foster positive reciprocity, crosscutting relations, awareness of superordinate goals, and a mutual aid ethic in children and adolescents. The largely unfulfilled educational potential of the media can also be helpful in improving intergroup relations, as "Sesame Street" has shown. These same generic orientations and skills can be extended from childhood all the way up through adulthood to membership in larger units, possibly even including international relations in due course.

The painfully difficult effort to achieve decent, fair, peaceful relations among diverse human groups is an enterprise that must be renewed. While weapons of mass destruction pose the greatest danger, economic decline and environmental degradation will be a growing challenge to survival for many in the years ahead. People of humane and democratic inclination will need sustained cooperation throughout the world to build effective systems for dealing with these great problems. Ideas are emerging, analysis is proceeding, useful models exist. The current turmoil could provide a constructive stimulus for practical arrangements that help us learn to live together at last.

The Difficulty of
Imagining Other Persons

ELAINE SCARRY

The way we act toward "others" is shaped by the way we imagine others. This essay is centrally focused on the difficulty of imagining others.

Both philosophic and literary descriptions of imagining show the difficulty of picturing other persons in their full weight and solidity. This is true even when the person is a friend or acquaintance; the problem is further magnified when the person is a stranger or "foreigner." Cruelty to strangers and foreigners has prompted many people to seek ways of preventing such actions from recurring in the future. I will draw on a range of materials to suggest the difference between solutions that do and those that do not assume the "imaginability," or the "picturability," of other persons. Some solutions rely on the population to "imagine" other persons spontaneously and generously, and to do so on a day-by-day basis. Alternative solutions, in contrast, attempt to solve the problem of the Other through constitutional design: they seek to eliminate altogether the inherently aversive structural position of "foreignness."

We have the obligation to commit ourselves to both solutions, rather than to choose between them. But I weight my comments to the sphere of constitutional design because if this solution is in place, then the spontaneous acts of individuals have a chance of producing generous outcomes. But the reverse is not the case. If constitutional or legal solutions to foreignness are not in place, then the daily practice of spontaneous largesse will (in my judgment) have little effect, and all our conversations about "Otherness" will be idle.

The writing of this essay was directly occasioned by the cruelty to foreigners on the streets of Berlin and Mölln. My theoretical arguments are therefore anchored to those concrete instances of injuring, as well as to parallel acts of injuring on the streets of Los Angeles and on the streets of Paris. But my insistence on constitutional design is also strongly shaped by the fact that I have recently been at work on this same problem in another area: the nuclear weapons policy in the United States. Given the magnitude of potential injury, our current military policy may be seen as the Problem of the Foreigner Writ Large. In what follows I will try to show the alternative proposals of spontaneous imagining and constitutional design in the context of both local street cruelty and international arms. Neither spontaneous imagining nor constitutional design can alone guarantee the prevention of injury. Both solutions are needed: the second provides the frame in which the first can take place.

Are there large numbers of people who advocate the imaginative solution over the constitutional one? The answer is yes. Even many of those German intellectuals most passionately dedicated to stopping the injuries to Turkish residents often ignore altogether any discussion of altering citizenship laws and concentrate instead on practices that can be summarized under the heading of "generous imaginings." Meetings among international scholars dedicated to human rights often express an indifference to, or impatience with national protections on rights, and rely exclusively on foreign populations. Discussions about foreignness among American intellectuals display an increasingly shared animus against "nationalism" which is perceived to be an impediment to "internationalism." But on close inspection this attempt to replace nationalism by internationalism often turns out to entail a rejection (or bypassing) of constitutionalism in favor of unanchored good will that can be summarized under the heading of "generous imaginings." It is therefore important to come face to face with the limits on imagining other people, since in several different spheres it is used to legitimate the bypassing of legal provisions and procedures.

1. The Difficulty of Imagining Others: As Shown in the Treatment of "Enemies" or Persons That We Hurt

The difficulty of imagining others is shown by the fact that one can be in the presence of another person who is in pain and not know that the person is in pain. The ease of remaining ignorant of another person's pain even permits one to inflict it and amplify it in the body of the other person while remaining immune oneself. Sustained and repeated instances of this are visible in political regimes that torture. But the failure to see the reality of another person's pain has also been recently visible in each successive blow of the fifty-eight concussive strokes that fell in sequence on the body and back of Rodney King, as it has also been visible in the acts of burning alive ten-year-old Yaliz Arslan, fifty-one-year old Bahide Arslan, and fourteen-year-old Ayse Yilmac in their Mölln apartment house.

I focus on physical injury here because though the well-being of persons takes many forms—voting rights, access to education, the daily possibility of interesting work—all this is premised on bodily inviolability. It is precisely in order to minimize bodily injury that the social contract comes into being. The word "injury" is used repeatedly throughout Locke's *Second Treatise of Government*. Though the "injury" is not specified as, or limited to, "bodily injury," it takes its force from that original context. Locke, for example, uses the verb "injures" both where the object is the material reality of the body and where the object is freedom,[1] just as he speaks of "invading" another's body, invading another's property (the "annexed body"), or instead invading another's rights.[2] When Locke uses the idiom of "invasion" for a nonphysical object, he often immediately follows it by the word "rapine," in order to restore the physical referent. Persons enter the social contract for mutual security: the contract comes into being to "secure them from injury and violence," which is "a trespass against the whole species."[3]

The Social Contract prohibits us from trespassing across the boundaries of another person's body. Locke's concreteness, his sense of persons as embodied, reflects the fact that he was a physician: one of his biographers writes that until at least 1683 Locke "regarded himself as before everything else a doctor."[4] He collaborated extensively with Thomas Sydenham, then a controversial physician, now widely regarded as the "Father of English Medicine."[5] Locke accompanied Sydenham on visits to patients; he wrote a prefatory poem to Sydenham's treatise on epidemic and planned a preface for a second volume never completed; each sent his medical notes and manuscripts to the other for annotation.[6] The two also planned to coauthor a book reviewing "the whole state of clinical medicine."[7] Their correspondence reveals two key facts: Locke was extremely sensitive to his own pain;[8] more important, he was extremely sensitive to other people's pain and was able to describe it with unusual vividness and precision.[9] Locke's concern for the bodily integrity of others expressed itself not only in terms of individual patients but also in terms of the health of the public: he worked to create mortality tables in Ireland at a time when the concepts of state medicine and public health were just emerging.[10]

Locke's commitment to the practice of medicine is consistent with, and itself underscores, the emphasis in the *Second Treatise* on the Social Contract as the guarantor of bodily inviolability. The strong relation between the social contract and the diminution of injury is visible in social contracts that far antedate the Lockean social contract. In the eleventh and twelfth centuries, many of the five hundred major European cities came into existence. They did not accidentally emerge. They came about through explicit acts of oath taking and contract making: "a solemn collective oath, or series of oaths," writes Harold Berman, "[was] made by the entire citizenry to adhere to a charter that had been publicly read aloud to them."[11] Often called "sworn communes," "conjurationes," or "communes for peace," their very names memorialized the extraordinary verbal process by which they had come into being. In the language of these city compacts, as in the Lockean compact, we can hear the key association between self-governance and the diminution of injury. The founding of Freiberg, for example, emphasizes the guarantee of "peace and protection."[12] The Flemish charter of Aire promises, "Let each help the other like a brother."[13] The articles of the charter for Beauvais in Picardy begin:

> all men within the walls of the city and in the suburb shall swear the commune;
> each shall aid the other in the manner he thinks to be right;
> if any man who has sworn the commune suffers a violation of rights, . . . [the peers] shall do justice against . . . the offender.[14]

It is logical for clauses of the charter promising mutual defense to be followed by clauses arranging for jury trial because such compacts seek to diminish injury issuing from outside the city (war or armed attack) and from inside the city (crime).

One oath for mutual assistance from the Bologna region makes the coupling explicit: the members "should maintain and defend each other against all men, within the commune and outside it."[15] The "communes for peace" seek to secure their members from both sources of injury.[16]

The town's commitment to protecting its members from outside aggression by no means implied that outsiders were themselves subjected to aggressive treatment. On the contrary: Berman writes that "immigrants were to be granted the same rights as citizens [the right to vote, the right to bear arms, the right to a jury trial] after residence for a year and a day."[17] The relatively swift transformation from immigrant to citizen suggests that bearing the status of "foreigner" was itself seen to be an injurious condition and hence one that it was the obligation of the commune to remove. A 1303 guild statute from Verona, one of the oldest in existence, makes this thinking fairly explicit, in its specification of the recipients of special aid: one had the obligation to give "fraternal assistance in necessity of whatever kind," to give "hospitality toward strangers, when passing through the town," and to offer "comfort in the case of debility."[18] The listing of the three together indicates that "being a stranger" is perceived as parallel with being "in necessity" and with "debility." Being a stranger, in other words, is itself a form of injury. An immediate strategy for diminishing the debility is to extend hospitality to the stranger. A more long-lasting strategy (a more radical hospitality) is to eliminate the status of stranger altogether by granting the rights of citizenship.

Bodily injury is therefore of direct relevance to the social contract in both theory and practice, in both the Lockean contract and the earlier city contracts. The diminution of injury is the contract's raison d'être. At the same time, the ease of inflicting injury shows how easy it is not to know other persons. There exists a *circular relation* between the infliction of pain and the problem of "otherness." *The difficulty of imagining others is both the cause of, and the problem displayed by, the action of injuring.* The action of injuring occurs precisely because we have trouble believing in the reality of other persons. At the same time, the injury itself makes visible the fact that we cannot see the reality of other persons. It displays our perceptual disability.

The visibility or invisibility of injury in turn depends on its timing. Injury in the past is relatively easy to see. Injuring in the present is easier to see, but often still ambiguous. Injury in the future is most difficult of all. This is why our moral thinking is so different when the problem is *retrospective* than when it is *prospective.* For example, in the United States, nothing is easier for our population than to understand that there should not have been death camps in Germany in World War II. The subject arises frequently and is seldom controversial. Even when our own population has been the perpetrator of the injury, we often see it clearly: a great many people in the United States live every day with an awareness of the injury in Vietnam, just as many worry that the country will never recover from the grave injury of slavery. But nothing is more remote than the possibility that we ourselves may in the future injure another population with our weapons, on a scale as great or far greater than in the period of enslavement, or World War II, or Vietnam. I think it is accurate to say that despite my countrymen's and countrywomen's deeply genuine concern about the harms we have inflicted in the past, we are as a population almost empty of ethical worry about the future. This difference between the ease of thinking about the injuring of others *retrospectively,* and the difficulty of thinking about the injuring of others *prospectively* is especially ironic because we *cannot* intervene and change an injury that has occurred in the past. But we *can* intervene and prevent an injury in the future. Injuries that have not yet happened are the only ones that can be stopped.

Our injuring of others, therefore, results from our failure to know them; and conversely, our injuring of persons, even persons within arm's reach, itself demonstrates their unknowability. For if they stood visible to us, the infliction of that injury would be impossible. I have so far been describing the problem of imagining another human being as it is visible in one who is a stranger, a foreigner, an enemy, a person one is willing to hurt. But the problem of imagining people can be seen from an entirely different direction, the direction of imagining a friend.

2. The Difficulty of Imagining Others: As Shown in the Case of Friends

When we speak in everyday conversation about the imagination, we often attribute to it powers that are greater than ordinary sensation. But Sartre's study of the imagination shows more honestly and accurately that the opposite is the case. When we are asked to perform the concrete experiment of comparing an imagined object with a perceptual one—that is, of actually stopping, closing our eyes, concentrating on the imagined face or the imagined room, then opening our eyes and comparing its attributes to whatever greets us when we return to the sensory world—we at once reach the opposite conclusion: the imagined object lacks the vitality and vivacity of the perceived; it is in fact these very attributes of vitality and vivacity that enable us to differentiate the actual world present to our senses from the one that we introduce through the exercise of the imagination. Even if, as Sartre observes, the object we select to imagine in this experiment is the face of a beloved friend, one we know in intricate detail (as Sartre knew the faces of Annie and Pierre), it will be, by comparison with an actually present face, "thin," "dry," "two-dimensional" and "inert."

Sartre tries to imagine the face of his friend Peter while Peter is not present. The image, he complains, "is like the silhouettes drawn by children"; "It is something like a rough draft." It is "present but . . . out of reach."[19] "No development of the image can take me by surprise,"[20] he complains; and he summarizes how often consciousness consists of "a retinue of phantoms" all of which are "ambiguous, impoverished and dry, appearing and disappearing is a disjointed manner . . . a perpetual evasion."[21] So too "Annie as an image cannot be compared with the Annie of perception," and he goes on to specify how not only the image but the feelings toward his friend become "schematized" "rigid" and "banal."[22]

It seems that we tend to notice this phenomenon only when we are especially keen on seeing a face, only when we desperately care to have it present in the mind with clarity and force. We then notice the deficiency and like Proust's Marcel who berates himself for his inability to picture the face of Albertine or the face of his grandmother, we conclude that the vacancy or vacuity of our imagining is somehow peculiar to our feeling about this particular person, and that there must be a hidden defect in our affection. In fact the vacuity is general and all that is peculiar or particular to such cases is the intensity of "wishing to imagine" that makes us confront, with more than usual honesty, the fact that we cannot do so. It is when we are soaked with the longing to imagine that we notice, as Keats confessed, "the fancy cannot cheat so well as she is famed to do." By means of the vividness of perceptions, we remain at all moments capable of recovering, of "recognizing" the material world and distinguishing it from our imaginary world, even as we lapse into and out of our gray and ghostly daydreams. Aristotle refers to this grayness as "the feebleness" of images. Sartre calls it their "essential poverty."

This description of imagining a friend illuminates the problems that await us when we attempt to rely on the imagination as a guarantor of political generosity. Sartre in imagining Pierre on the Ku-dam or Annie while absent is only trying to imagine a single friend. The labor is unsuccessful even though the person is (1) an intimate acquaintance and therefore known in intricate detail; and (2) a solitary person. But now transport this to the imaginative labor of knowing "the other." Now we are talking about our ability to picture in the imagination not an intimate friend, but the face of someone who is merely a neighbor, or instead someone who lives five blocks away, or instead someone who has never entered your field of perception because she lives in a different section of town, or a different country, or perhaps works at night while you work during the day. So, too, now we are talking about our ability to picture in the imagination *not* one person, but instead five, or ten, or one hundred, or one hundred thousand; or x, the number of Turks in Germany; or y, the estimated number of Iraqi soldiers and citizens killed in our bombing raids; or 70 million, the scale of population that stands to suffer should the U.S. fire a nuclear missile, a conservative estimate. Or 30,000, the number of American eighteen-year-olds that were, without any Congressional deliberation or debate, not long ago sent to Somalia. Or 3.5 million, the number of illegal immigrants estimated to reside in the United States as we move through the final decade of the century. Most philosophic discussions of "the Other" are constrained by numbers: they contemplate the Other in the singular.[23] Even Max Scheler's extraordinary study of sympathy (which periodically speaks of a generalized "fellow feeling" for other human beings) primarily sets out to provide a map of possibilities for imagining solitary persons.[24]

The human capacity to injure other people has always been much greater than its ability to imagine other people. Or perhaps we should say, *the human capacity to injure other people is very great precisely because our capacity to imagine other people is very small.* In the section of the essay that follows, I want to go on to contemplate solutions that, rather than *requiring us to imagine Others,* instead require us *to dis-imagine ourselves* (a solution that is very bound up with constitutionalism). But before doing so, I want to remain for a few moments more with the strategy of picturing. I have so far been speaking about the poverty of mental imagining or daydreaming or contemplating. Here our ability to imagine is poor. But there is a place—namely, the place of great literature—where the ability to imagine others is very strong. What it therefore gives a population can be capacious, though even this solution, I will argue, has severe limits in terms of its ability to ensure the diminution of injury to live persons.

Great books, great poems, great films often achieve the vivacity of the perceptual world.[25] During the hours of reading Thomas Hardy's *Tess of the D'Urbervilles,* Tess comes before the mind with far more fullness, surprise, vivacity, and vividness than the two-dimensional images of Sartre's or our own daydreams. As so, too, does Tolstoi's Anna Karenina, Levin, Kitty. As so too does Franz Bieberkopf in Fassbinder's *Berlin Alexanderplatz.* We often in aesthetic discussions speak as though imagining-when-daydreaming and imagining-when-under-authorial-instruction are continuous. But it is crucial to notice that they are discontinuous. The flatness and two-dimensionality of the one gives way in the other case to a vividness that approximates the vivacity of perception.

The act of imagining oneself as another person is central to literature. How central it is can be seen by the position it occupies in the thinking of political philosophers. Whether political philosophers approve of or disapprove of the theater turns on whether they believe it is dangerous or instead advantageous for a population to place themselves imaginatively in the position of other persons.[26] For example, in his political treatise on reform, the Romantic poet Shelley argues that "a man, to be greatly good, must imagine intensely . . . himself in the place of others."[27] In contrast, Plato in the *Republic* or Rousseau in "Letter to M. D'Alembert on the Theater" disapproves of this imaginative emptying out of the self and replacement with others. What is at the moment relevant to my argument is not whether Plato or Rousseau or Shelley advocated or instead condemned this theatrical practice, but how consistently they associate theatrical practice with the practice of placing oneself in the space of mental "Otherness."

Because literary artists are dedicated to the labor of imagining others, they are appropriately called upon when the need to imagine others grows urgent. Throughout November of 1992, for example, Berlin's Schiller Theater, Distel Cabaret, Tribune Theater, Deutsche Theater, and Deutsche Oper all devoted programs to the difficulty of being a foreigner in Germany: there took place a poetry reading at the Schiller, for example, on the Constitution's Article I pledge to uphold as "inviolable" the "dignity of man," a cabaret performance at the Distel defending the Constitution's controversial "Asylum" clause, and a program of readings at the Deutsche Theater on the contributions of foreign philosophers, musicians, and writers to art in Berlin. So, too, in Frankfurt in December 1992 writers such as Saliha Scheinhardt, Darryl Pinckney, and Scott Momaday were called upon by Fischer Verlag to assist in sorting out the problem of Otherness in Germany.

Yet while a poem is far more able than a daydream to bring other persons to press on our minds, even here we must recognize severe limits on what the imagination can accomplish. One key limit is the number of characters. A novel or poem may have one major character. Or four major characters. It is impossible to hold rich multitudes of imaginary characters simultaneously in the mind. Presented with the huge number of characters one finds in Dickens or in Tolstoi, one must constantly strain to keep them sorted out; and of course their numbers are still tiny when compared with the number of persons to whom we are responsible in political life. Public life requires that we be capable of exercising not so much personal compassion as what, within medical writing, has been called "statistical compassion."[28] For this, literature prepares us inadequately, since even secondary characters (let alone second hundredth or second thousandth characters) lack the density of personhood that is attributed to the central character. Thomas Hardy's heroine Tess, in *Tess of the D'Urbervilles,* worries to her lover about the fact that her fellow milkmaids, themselves secondary and tertiary characters, are made to seem lesser persons than they are, merely by virtue of the fact that they are not themselves the heroine. Literature—even when it enlists us into the greatest imaginative acts and the most expansive compassion—always confesses the limits on the imagination by the structural necessity of major and minor persons, center stage and lateral figures.

There are other limits as well. The latent nationalism or tribalism of great literature may make it a seductive vehicle for an exercise in self-reflection and self-identification, rather than reflection upon and identification with people different from oneself. Despite, for example, the emphasis on artistic multiculturalism in the United States, it sometimes appears that Asian-American literature is being read by Asian-Americans, Afro-American literature by Afro-Americans, and Euro-American literature by Euro-Americans. But, of course, literature at least holds out to us the constant invitation to read about others, not only other ethnic groups within one's own country but the great Russian or German or Chinese writings; and universities are, in their departmental organizations, still structured to encourage this cross-country imagining. The potential of art to make an alien people knowable receives what is perhaps its most optimistic salute in French citizenship laws: a foreigner who enters France can become a citizen in *five* years; a foreigner who enters France with an undergraduate degree in French literature can become a citizen in *two* years.

A third limit is the lack of any anchor in historical reality. Sometimes fictional "others" do have actual referents in material reality. But more often they lack any reference to lived history. It has often been a criticism of literature that the very imaginative labor of picturing others that we ought to expend on real persons on our city streets, or on the other side of the border, instead comes to be lavished on King Lear or on Tess. Pushkin provided a stunning portrait of how we come out of the opera, weeping with compassion for those on stage, not seeing the cab driver and horses who are freezing from their long wait to carry us home.[29] William James was haunted by the same picture.[30]

Literature, it seems fair to conclude, is most helpful not insofar as it *takes away* the problem of the Other—for only with greatest rarity can it do this—but when it instead *takes as* its own subject the problem of Imagining Others. The British novelist Thomas Hardy is a brilliant explicator of this problem. He places before our eyes the dense interior of a man or a woman. He then juxtaposes this ontological robustness with the inevitable subtractions, the flattenings, the emptyings out that occur in other people's vision of the person. He shows the way a young woman like Tomasin in *Return of the Native* comes to be only "a piece of gossip" for the other people on the heath; how Tess in *Tess of the D'Urbervilles* is, even for her schoolhood friends, only "a [verbal] warning" to others of what can happen between men and women; how Michael Henchard in *Mayor of Casterbridge* can be reduced from his monumental proportions to a horrifying caricature of public shaming. In all these instances, Hardy maximizes the imaginary density of a person, then lets us watch the *painful subtraction* each undergoes as she or he comes to be perceived by others. He repeatedly contrasts the immediacy and weight of an embodied gesture—Tess standing on her toes reaching for a dish to take down from the family cupboard, or Tomasin in the attic plunging her heavy arms into a bag of ripening apples—with the weightless categories of "gossip," "warning," "moral example," by which even friends and genial acquaintances narrate their lives. The person in her full weight and solidity disappears.

"Otherness" can be, as it is in Thomas Hardy, depicted through an elaborate sequence of additions and subtractions. Two other essential methods of depicting the Other are underexposure and overexposure. Underexposure is illustrated by Ralph Ellison's *Invisible Man*. Overexposure is exemplified by the monster in Mary Shelley's *Frankenstein*. Monstrosity and invisibility are two subspecies of the Other, the one overly visible and repelling attention, the other unavailable for attention and hence absent from the outset. The two are common strategies for representing the Other in actual political life. Turkish persons in Germany can be underexposed, nameless,[31] while also being overexposed, as in the unclothed belly dancing by which they are known to German citizens and tourists.[32] Each representational strategy, far from contradicting the other, instead makes its counterpart possible: the dancing fills the field of vision and helps push complicated syllables like Yaliz Arslan, Bahide Arslan, Ayse Yilmac out of the way; in turn the absence of these names prevents the racial picture from becoming cluttered with psychological detail that might obscure the stark outlines of the dance. So, too, during the Gulf War, the Iraqi Other was underexposed, invisible, absent. No soldiers or civilians were pictured on United States television. If only one person was killed for each American sortie, then there must have been at least 10,000 people killed (and it is extremely unlikely that only one person was killed for each flight). Yet no injuries or deaths appeared before us. This underexposure had as its counterpart the magnified, overexposed, sexually caricatured image of Saddam Hussein.[33] As we watched missiles going into targets that appeared to have no people within, it was as though either no one would be killed or the Gruesome Tyrant alone would be killed.

The Saddam Hussein pictured may not have been a caricature of the actual Saddam Hussein, for the historical person seems to have many of the attributes that were credited to him. But certainly he was an unjust caricature—a magnified cartoon of swagger and cruelty—of the otherwise missing, hence featureless, Iraqi population. It is interesting that Sartre—who writes so eloquently about the dryness, thinness, and two-dimensionality of the daydreamed faces of our friends—is the same Sartre who shows in *Anti-Semite and Jew* how the racial caricature as a genre acquires the very vividness the imagined friend lacks. The "opinions" of the anti-Semite, argues Sartre, are as intractable as perceptions: "tastes, colors, and opinions are not open to discussion."[34] The stereotype is animated and energized by the anti-Semite's whole being: "Only a strong emotional bias can give a lightninglike certainty; it alone can hold reason in leash; it alone can remain impervious to experience."[35] "It is a faith."[36] It has the "permanence of rock."[37] William Hazlitt, the British essayist of the early nineteenth century, also talks in his essay "The Pleasure of Hating" about the way the energy of hate animates and vivifies: "We cannot bear a state of indifference and ennuie," he writes. "The white streak in our own fortunes is brightened (or just rendered visible) by making all round it as dark as possible, so the rainbow paints its form upon the cloud. Is it pride? Is it envy? Is it the force of contrast? Is it weakness or malice? But so it is."[38] These polarities of overexposure and underexposure, racial magnification and racial miniaturization, are richly excavated by the great literature about "the Other."

I have been calling attention to the limits on solving real-world Otherness through literary representation alone: the number of characters; the lack of a material referent; the seduction toward cultural egotism and self-identification. I have also been saying that literature ordinarily makes its contribution by critiquing the origins of (rather than by providing solutions to) the problem of otherness: it makes visible the perceptual disability that gives rise to otherness; it also makes visible representational strategies such as underexposure and overexposure whose operations we can then locate at work in the material world. Once these restrictions are acknowledged, it is appropriate to notice the one or two extraordinary instances in which literature has itself been part of the solution. Harriet Beecher Stowe's *Uncle Tom's Cabin* made blacks—the weight, solidity, injurability of their person-hood—imaginable to the white population in pre–Civil War United States. The scale of the book's immediate readership, its impact on actual political reality, is without an equivalent in Anglo-American Literature, though it also exemplifies, more generally, the politically radical work of sentimental literature.[39] E. M. Forster's *A Passage to India* has occasionally had parallel claims made about it: the book, overnight, according to Stephen Spender, enabled the British population to begin to reimagine India's population as independent.[40] But the Stowe and Forster examples are extremely rare, both because they required readers to imagine not just "a person" but "a people," and above all because they modified the well-being of actual persons, to bring about greater freedom and hence a diminution of the status of Otherness. More often we must say of literature what the poet Auden wrote in his elegy for Yeats: "Poetry makes nothing happen: it survives / In the valley of its saying."[41]

The section that follows turns from the literary to the legal, from daydreaming to constitution making. What makes Stowe and Forster remarkable is precisely that their writings were followed by legal and structural outcomes. If there had never been the Independence of India Act of 1947, or if the U.S. Constitution lacked the Reconstruction Amendments (prohibiting servitude; ensuring due process across race and religion; prohibiting racial restrictions on voting) no daily rereading of *Uncle Tom's Cabin* by the United States population, no daily rereading of *A Passage to India* by the English population, could in themselves have the smallest healing power. Some of the 1992 theater productions in Berlin described earlier also focused on constitutional solutions: rather than speaking in the voice of fictional characters, the artists spoke in the collective voice, the collective aspiration, encoded in the German Constitution's asylum and protection clauses. This essay concludes by turning to that sphere as well: it argues that the capacious vision implied by the "asylum" and "protection" clauses (Articles 16 and 1) as yet has no counterpart in the laws governing the process by which a foreigner may become a citizen. Solving the "problem of otherness" in Germany appears to require that these citizenship laws be changed.

The present arrangements allow foreign-born adults who have lived in the country legally for fifteen years to have the presumptive right of citizenship.[42] Again they permit sixteen to twenty-three-year-olds who have lived legally in Germany eight years, and who have attended German schools for six years, to have the presumptive right of citizenship.[43] These arrangements may be fine for people who are already in Germany and have fulfilled the temporal requirement. But, as Ulrich Preuss argues, for newly arriving immigrants, fifteen years or eight years are extremely long periods. Further, if the present 1995 deadline is held in place, then the statutes for adults will not even be open to present and future immigrants. The provisions are too slow for those already in Germany; and they are unmindful of those who have just arrived or who will come next year. Hence they are unmindful of the new century about to come forward. As Preuss observes, "They refer to the past, not to the future."[44]

Through its Asylum Clause, the country welcomes heterogeneity; but it does not at present protect the principle of heterogeneity through benign and rapid processes for citizenship.

3. Two Paths for Achieving Mental Equality: Giving to the Other the Same Weight as One's Own; or, Instead, Giving to Oneself the Same Weightlessness That Others Have

When we seek equality through generous imaginings, we start with our own weight, then attempt to acquire knowledge about the weight and complexity of others.

This is, as I have said, very difficult because of the constraints on imagining others. It is difficult to accomplish with the face of a friend, let alone the face of a neighbor, stranger, or enemy. It is difficult to do it with one person or five persons, let alone with the thousands and hundred thousands that deserve our labor of imagining. It is more possible when imagining under authorial instruction than under day-dreaming, but is limited in both instances.

The alternative strategy is to achieve equality between self and other not by trying to make one's knowledge of others *as weighty as* one's knowledge of oneself, but by making one ignorant about oneself, and therefore *as weightless as* all others. This strategy of imaginative recovery is exemplified by Bertrand Russell and, more elaborately and influentially, by John Rawls. It is also the strategy embedded in constitutional arrangements since they are independent of any one person's personal features.

Bertrand Russell argued that when reading the newspaper each day, we ought routinely to substitute the names of alternative countries to the reported actions in order to test whether our response to the event arises from a moral assessment of the action or instead from a set of prejudices about the country.[45] This ethical practice would obligate us *to decouple* a given action from country X and reattach it to country Y. An event occurring between the United States and Somalia, would be reversed and dispersed across imagined substitutes in Germany and France, Italy and Ethiopia, former Yugoslavia and Sweden and so forth. This ethical habit might be called "the rotation of nouns." It is equally valid for assessing the actions of ethnic groups toward one another inside a given country. The firebombing of a Turkish person's house by a German citizen would be mentally reversed so that a German household were burned by a Turkish noncitizen, or instead by an occupying British soldier, or instead by fellow citizen. The action of mentally detaching the action from one country or ethnic group and reattaching it to another helps ensure that moral claims about actions really are about those actions, and do not simply restate national prejudices or ethnic prejudices that are already in place. It protects against cultural narcissism by setting forth a sequence of locations that dislodges one from one's own geographical center.

A second example is John Rawls's "veil of ignorance" as a condition for achieving—at least in the imagination—just social relations. I say "at least in the imagination" because he requests us "to simulate the deliberations of this hypothetical situation, simply by reasoning in accordance with appropriate restrictions."[46] The "veil of ignorance" in Rawls's *A Theory of Justice* requires that one become temporarily ignorant about one's own physical, genetic, psychological, and even moral attributes. We enter into decisions about the best social arrangements without knowing what position within that social arrangement we occupy: "No one knows his place in society, his class position or social status; nor does he know his fortune in the distribution of natural assets and abilities, his intelligence and strength. . . . Nor, again, does anyone know his conception of the good, the particulars of his rational plan of life, or even the special features of his psychology such as his aversion to risk or liability to optimism or pessimism."[47] The act of making oneself featureless accomplishes the same outcome as making oneself a composite of all possible features: one makes decisions about legal structures as though one were saying, What if I were black, white, brown, yellow, red; What if my family lived in this town for thirty years, three years, three generations, three centuries, three days; What if I lived in the inland region, the eastern border, western border, north, south?

Like Russell's rotation of nouns, the veil of ignorance is a way of bringing about equality not by giving the millions of other people an imaginative weight equal to one's own—a staggering mental labor—but by the much more efficient opposite strategy, the strategy of simply erasing for one moment one's own dense array of attributes. By becoming featureless, by having a weightlessness, a two-dimensionality, a dryness every bit as "impoverished" as the imagined Other, the condition of equality is achieved. One subtraction therefore has the same effect as a hundred thousand additions. Through it we create what Rawls describes as "the symmetry of everyone's relations to each other."[48]

The stress here on temporarily dis-imagining oneself, on becoming featureless, on making oneself weightless, may mislead one into thinking that this strategy produces a featureless or homogeneous society. But precisely the reverse is the case: it is when a social contract privileges a certain set of features (for example, medium-length curly red hair) that the whole society drifts into acquiring those features. When a social contract is instead wholly independent of specific features, no political liability or credit is attached to any one of them, and hence the greatest possible diversity and heterogeneity are brought about. The only trait encouraged is psychological and moral "tolerance" of high levels of difference.

The problem with discussions of "the Other" is that they sometimes allow the fate of "the Other" to be contingent on the imaginer: now another person's fate will depend on whether we decide to be generous and wise, or instead narrow and intolerant. But solutions ought not to give one group the power to regulate the welfare of another group in this way. Picture, for example, a town in which third-generation light-skinned residents can vote but third-generation dark-skinned residents cannot vote. The light-skinned residents—through goodwill and large-mindedness—take into consideration, before they vote, the position of the dark-skinned residents. They ask themselves, for example, which candidate will best serve the needs of both themselves and the dark-skinned coresidents in their city. (This is a utopian assumption, of course, given the difficulty of imagining other people; but for the sake of argument, let us suppose they are able and willing to do it.) Thus they have acted to minimize the problem of foreignness or Otherness by holding in their minds a picture of those other people on the basis of which they go on to make their political decisions. Now contrast this to a second situation. The dark-skinned third-generation residents are citizens and vote for themselves. There is no longer the need for the light-skinned residents to act on behalf of the Others. Because a constitutional provision enables each group to act on its own behalf, no group any longer occupies the legal position of the Other. Even if we stipulate that in the first solution the light-skinned third-generation residents act with maximum generosity and largesse, the second solution is obviously much stronger. They would, even at best, be acting paternally, and hence operating outside the frame of social contract whose purpose, as Locke argued in the *Second Treatise of Government*, was precisely to decouple paternal power from political power.

What differentiates the first and second strategies of inclusion (let us call them Town One and Town Two) is the principle of self-representation, a principle perhaps too elementary and self-evident to require recitation. Yet I introduce the principle here because—at least to the ears of an outsider—discussions of the problem of Otherness in Germany sometimes seem not to take "self-representation" centrally into account. The words "protection" and "foreigner," for example, often seem to be used in ways compatible with Town One rather than Town Two. In its opening words, the German Constitution pledges to protect the inviolable dignity of persons, and this pledge of "protection" is often appropriately cited in lamentations over injuries to Turkish-German[49] residents. But since self-representation is the sturdiest form of "protection," it is not clear what any account of protection means that does not include the aspiration to change the current citizenship laws, voting rights, and other forms of procedural access (phenomena often omitted from the lament[50]). The "protection" clause in the United States Constitution has played a major role in shaping modern U.S. law: one legal scholar even makes the extraordinary claim that this sentence "has become the text on which most twentieth-century law is a gloss."[51] But this key phrase in the Fourteenth Amendment, "equal protection," is inseparable from a second phrase in the same sentence, "due process," and hence inseparable also from the equitable distribution of rights across different ethnic, religious, and gender groups. It would be inconceivable to propose that equal protection among adults in the United States could ever be secured by empowering an enfranchised group to look after a disenfranchised group by means of generous imaginings.

The use of the word "foreigner" illustrates the same problem. In her December 1992 reading in Frankfurt, Saliha Scheinhardt said that being called a "foreigner" was, for her, a painful insult. One respondent in the audience expressed genuine bewilderment about why this apparently neutral descriptive word, not intended to injure, should be perceived as negative. But to call Saliha Scheinhardt—or any other person who has lived in Germany five years, twenty years, two generations, three generations—a "foreigner" conforms to, and endorses, the Town One model.[52] If the light-skinned residents speak about the dark-skinned residents as "foreigners," the word cannot refer to a geographical location since both have resided in the same geography for substantial periods.[53] It seems instead to refer to, and to accept, the political geography of noncitizenship. The idiom soon comes to sound circular and self-justifying: the lack of voting rights is explained on the basis that the people are foreigners, but what makes them appear foreign is only the fact that they lack voting rights. The idiom places them outside the city gates, outside the political mechanism of self-representation that it is the very logic of the city to ensure. Even Chancellor Kohl's heartfelt response to the burnings in Mölln sounded like the words of a Town One imaginer, rather than one who desired to inhabit Town Two. He extended his sympathy to the families of those killed and "to the Turks *in our country,* who have lived here for many years, whom we asked to come here . . . and without whose assistance we would not have been able to achieve the level of prosperity attained *in our republic* over the decades."[54] Those pained to hear themselves called "foreigners" would probably also be pained to hear the phrases "our [not your] country," "our [not your] republic" at the very moment that their several-decade-long contribution to the formation of Germany was being acknowledged. The oddness of this language can be glimpsed by practicing Russell's rotation of nouns, and resituating the passage in another country. Picture, then, a U.S. President, after the beating of Rodney King extending his sympathy to the family, and "to the blacks [Vietnamese, Koreans, Irish, Germans] in our country, who have lived here for many years, whom we asked to come here . . . and without whose assistance we would not have been able to achieve the level of prosperity attained in our republic over the decades." To build a country, to form a prosperous republic, would seem to be the very meaning of "citizen." The opening passage in Locke's *A Letter Concerning Toleration* registers the difference between the magnanimous goodwill of Town One and the legal instantiation of Town Two. "But whatever have been the occasions [of our miseries and confusions] we have need of more generous remedies. . . . It is neither declarations of indulgence, nor acts of comprehension, such as have yet been practiced or projected among us. . . . *Absolute liberty, just and true liberty, equal and impartial liberty is the thing that we stand in need of.*"[55] Distributing the political mechanisms of liberty, however coldly procedural, is the more generous solution, precisely because it ensures that no group depends for its fate on the ability of another group to imagine it generously and accurately.

At present, most of us do not know the precise rules for acquiring citizenship in our own country, and are wholly ignorant of the rules governing citizenship in countries not our own. Given the constant pressure of migrating populations in the late twentieth century, it would probably be useful for us to become more widely knowledgeable about such procedures. Perhaps like poetry readings, we should have nightly coffee-house readings of the rules of citizenship, country by country. This has the disadvantage that it might begin to sound like a contest to determine the country most eligible to be regarded as the model of immigration. But an object over which people compete is also an object of emulation.[56] Competition designates a shared object of aspiration: if each population aspired to make its own country the outstanding instance, the benefit to the larger world would be great. More simply, a wider acquaintance with these procedures would make changing any one set of them "imaginable": legal arrangements that appear difficult to modify when one looks at one's own country's procedures in isolation suddenly come to seem remarkably malleable. The residency period—an almost universal precondition for application—is ten years in Germany,[57] ten years in Italy, ten years in Austria, twelve years in Switzerland, five years in Britain, five in France, five in the United States, five in Sweden.[58] The period is in some countries shortened, if certain other conditions are met. An undergraduate degree in French (as mentioned earlier) contracts the residency period to two years in that country. Marriage to a French person contracts the period to six months, and one need only live with the French spouse; one need not live on French soil. Marriage to a citizen contracts the residency requirement to three years in Sweden,[59] three years in Britain, three years in the United States, five years in Switzerland, five years in Germany (and three in Germany if one is both married to a citizen, and is oneself a person from a German-speaking country such as Romania or Transylvania). In Italy, marriage brings citizenship at once.

Our nightly recitations would have to include all the other preconditions for citizenship (such as the ability to support oneself, knowledge of the language), specify as well the amount of discretionary space reserved to the state after all preconditions are met, and list the impediments to citizenship. It would have to indicate the countries from which immigrants are accepted, and specify also whether those countries were once colonies or territories of the receiving country (both Britain and France have fewer preconditions in such cases[60]). It would tell us what happens to a foreign child adopted by citizen parents (in Germany, the child receives immediate citizenship; in the United States, some residency condition must still be met). It would include the country's willingness to tolerate dual citizenship (France permits dual citizenship with 105 other countries), and indicate whether the second passport can only be acquired passively or can be acquired actively without forfeiting the first. It would, finally, provide us with not only the theoretical rules of access but a concrete picture of the actual numbers entering a given country and the percentages of those eventually granted citizenship.[61]

I have for the sake of simplicity presented the acts of imagining others and unimagining oneself as two separate alternatives in order to stress the importance of creating laws that eliminate the structural position of the Other. Although when each is considered in isolation the second is stronger than the first, together the two are far stronger than either alone. Town Two only fully works when supplemented with Town One's magnanimous imaginings, especially when reciprocated across mutually enfranchised groups. Legal equality, as noticed earlier, encourages heterogeneity: the only trait it makes homogeneous is the capacity for toleration. To tolerate others is to make room for them in one's imagining; the act of toleration is the act of making imaginable the space in which other people's differences might be accommodated. In turn, a basic regard for a group leaves open the possibility of a heightened regard for—or more dedicated form of imagining—some *one* person within that group; thus toleration may become desire (as in turn desire for a single person may awaken one to a previously unfelt tolerance for an entire group).

Desire may even occur where, because of legal or cultural prohibitions on intermarriage, two different levels of reality have been assigned to the two groups, a kind of metaphysical disenfranchisement of the legally enfranchised Other. The prohibitions against intermarriage across class in nineteenth-century England, and across race in late[62] nineteenth-century America, meant that groups were perceived to be variable not only in their economic and social status but in their ontological status as well. Any sudden manifestation of desire was extremely threatening because it seemed (not simply to call into question but) to repudiate on the spot the separate levels of reality assigned the two groups. A brilliant apolitical model of this deeply political phenomenon is presented by Pirandello in *Six Characters in Search of an Author* where two supposedly ontologically distinct groups (literary characters and human actors) find their erotic desire straying across these boundaries.

Both the United States and Germany have in recent decades repealed all laws prohibiting intermarriage across race. Yet neither country is wholly free of a culturally sanctioned reluctance toward intermarriage that has gone relatively unscrutinized in recent years. A rule of thumb often invoked in the United States, for example, is that one out of four persons will marry outside his or her ethnic group. Yet the figures summarizing intermarriage between blacks and whites do not bear out this otherwise optimistic portrait. In 1970, the number of black and white married couples was 65,000 or .15 percent of all married couples in the United States. By 1980, the figure had risen to .3 percent of the total number of married couples (167,000 out of 49,700,000). It then remained at roughly that percent (.34 or 177,000 out of 52,286,000 couples) in the 1987 census figures.[63] Hannah Arendt's 1959 complaint about the country—that the adult population asks its children to solve black-white Otherness through school integration rather than themselves taking on the burden of otherness through intermarriage—has not wholly disappeared.[64]

Several intellectually glamorous vocabularies help to ensure separation while not openly announcing themselves as taboos on intermarriage. The first is the idiom of antiassimilation: it opposes racial mixing by equating it with racial erasure, thereby deflecting attention from its own fatal advocacy of racial purity and all that purity so unpleasantly entails. The second is the idiom of authenticity: by instilling in young people a dread of being "inauthentic" or "unreal," it proscribes for them the conservative obligation to reenact and perpetuate the racial, religious, or linguistic preferences of their parents or grandparents. It confines them to the coercive facts of natality and displaces their own volitional acts with the volition of those who define what counts as authentic. Both vocabularies urge sameness; both discourage shaping one's fate through allegiances with an Other.

The merits and liabilities of vocabularies advocating sameness need to be more openly debated in both countries. The champions of this language in the United States have not attempted to explain how this new separatism differs from the racial policy of "separate but equal" that so damaged the country in the past. Is it supposed that if blacks and whites *voluntarily* sit in different parts of the bus, an outcome substantially more benign will occur than when such spatial separation was regulated from outside? If blacks, rather than (as in the past) whites, are the architects of the separation, will a more benign outcome occur? In Germany, the concepts of "blood" or "race" that figure strongly in present arrangements about citizenship, also appear to themselves go largely uncritiqued. The concept tends to be acknowledged by rapid invocations of the opposition between *ius sanguinis* and *ius soli*,[65] as though its formalization into Latin eliminated the need to inquire into it more deeply. This lack of scrutiny is especially surprising because scores of constructs that were even obliquely or incidentally or accidentally entailed in the Third Reich are every day subjected to rigorous scrutiny in contemporary Germany. Yet the concepts of "race" and "blood" that were foundational to that era seem themselves to go unexamined and are permitted to play some part in citizenship policies of the present, in addition to their clear role in the infliction of injury to residents designated "foreigners." At the same time, intermarriage between Germans and "foreigners" occurs more frequently than one might suppose if one based one's conclusions about "Otherness" exclusively on the recent pattern of injuring or on present naturalization and citizenship provisions. In 1991, almost 10 percent of Germans married a foreigner (the category of "foreigner" includes both persons from other countries and residents of Germany who are not citizens). Figures compiled by the Statistisches Bundesamt in Weisbaden reveal a steady, year by year, increase from 3.6 percent in 1950 (18,216 intermarriages out of a total of 506,101) to 9.6 percent in 1991 (43,955 intermarriages out of 454,291). One percent of all 1991 marriages took place between German and Turkish residents. That 1 percent figure is much higher than the figure for interracial marriages between whites and Afro-Americans in the United States, despite equality of citizenship.

The importance of maintaining a Town One commitment to the practice of imagining (even after accepting Town Two constitutionalism) is, then, visible in the way both toleration and desire enable one to ally one's fate with the fate of other citizens. A second phenomenon that underscores the importance of maintaining Town One's commitment to the imagination is the existence of borders. While it is possible to eliminate the legal position of the Other within a country's borders, it is not possible to do so for people outside those borders. However odd, inappropriate, or cruel the word "foreigner" is when applied to a fellow resident, it is often denotatively exact when applied to those beyond the borders. Here the problem of Otherness, with its steady danger of injury, cannot be addressed through voting rights but might seem dependent on the largesse of the imagination alone. Even this practice of the imagination, however, can be constitutionally encouraged and safeguarded.

Right now, for example, the United States has a nuclear policy that permits a president, acting almost alone, to authorize the firing of nuclear weapons. How should people in the United States protect Other populations from the sudden use of this monarchic weapons systems? Should we hope that at the moment of firing, the president will suddenly have the imaginative powers to picture Other people in their full density of concerns, picture not one caricatured leader but the men and women of that country? But the United States Constitution was written to ensure that the fate of Other populations would never be left up to the accident of whether a U.S. president (or any other solitary person) happens to be resourceful at imagining other populations. It anticipates, and attempts to diminish, the problem of the other, by building in elaborate requirements for debate and deliberation, requirements that ensure that voices speaking on behalf of the About-to-be-Injured Population will be heard.[66] In other words, it distributes the responsibility to imagine other people to a large portion of the population. Since the invention of atomic weapons, these constitutional safeguards have disappeared. One day my country may annihilate another population: yet within the United States Constitution at this very moment are the provisions—the legal tools—to stop this from happening.[67]

Legal provisions to distribute the rights of citizenship across a country's internal population do not guarantee that those citizens will abstain from injuring one another; so, too, legal provisions to ensure that foreigners—those outside the country's borders—will be carefully imagined before a willful infliction of injury takes place cannot necessarily guarantee that their own specifications will be followed. But such legal arrangements at least objectify an aspiration; they set the standard of action; and they provide the mechanism for holding the population to the promises they have made. Civil Society can only exist if it is produced by the constituents of that country. The major constitutive act is the making of a constitution. The *Federalist Papers,* written as essays in advocacy on behalf of the United States Constitution at the time of its ratification, continually asked the question: what kind of arrangement will produce a noble and generous people? It seems that this is the question we have been repeatedly asking about Mölln and Los Angeles and Paris. What kind of arrangements, whether in France or in the United States or in Germany or any other country, will produce a noble and generous people. Or put another way, why is it in the midst of apparently noble and generous arrangements—as exist in all three nations—are there nevertheless steady inflictions of harm to some people.

Perhaps every group of constitution makers has asked this same question. Nor is it restricted to the liberal democratic ethos. Marx in the *Grundrisse* contrasts the question asked by contemporary economic societies—what kind of arrangements will make the most money?—with the question asked by more ancient societies, what kind of city-state will produce the best citizens? But he concludes that our present interest in production and distribution is only a partially veiled manifestation of the ancient concern with the creation of good people. Audible in works as different as the *Federalist Papers* and the *Grundrisse* is the assumption—everywhere present in the social contract theorists—that the social contract re-creates us, that it is a lever across which we act on, and continually revise, ourselves. More self-revision is needed, as we continue to repair our laws and prepare for a more generous future. That self-revision will best proceed through our constitutional structures and aspirations, and not simply through a reliance on expanding our imaginings.

The work accomplished by a structure of laws cannot be accomplished by a structure of sentiment. Constitutions are needed to uphold transnational values.

Notes

1. John Locke, *Second Treatise of Government,* ed. and introd., C. B. Macpherson (Indianapolis: Hackett, 1980), p. 52.
2. Ibid., pp. 115, 116.
3. Ibid., p. 10, see also 15, 16.
4. Henry Richard Fox Bourne, *The Life of John Locke* (1876; rpt. Darmstadt: Scientia Verlag Aalen, 1969) vol. 1, 446. See also Maurice Cranston, "The Physician," in *John Locke: a Biography* (London: Longmans, Green and Co., 1957), pp. 88–105.
5. Ralph H. Major, *Classic Descriptions of Disease: With Biographical Sketches of the Authors* (3rd ed., Springfield, Illinois: Charles C. Thomas, 1945), p. 194.
6. Kenneth Dewhurst, "Sydenham on 'A Dysentry,'" in 29 *Bulletin of the History of Medicine* (1955), 393–95.
7. Cranston, *John Locke: A Biography,* p. 117.
8. See Sydenham's 1674 letter to Locke reprinted in Kenneth Dewhurst, "Sydenham's Letters to John Locke," *The Practitioner* [1955], p. 315.
9. See Locke's 1675 letter to Sydenham reprinted in Dewhurst, "Sydenham's Letters to John Locke," p. 316.
10. Kenneth Dewhurst, "The Genesis of State Medicine in Ireland," *The Irish Journal of Medical Science* (August 1956), pp. 365–67, 379–81.
11. Harold Berman, *Law and Revolution: The Formation of the Western Legal Tradition* (Cambridge: Harvard University Press, 1983), p. 393. Petr Kropotkin describes how in Iceland and Scandinavian lands the entire body of law would be recited aloud before an assembly (*Mutual Aid: A Factor of Evolution* [New York: McClure Phillips, 1903], p. 158.
12. Berman, *Law and Revolution,* p. 375.
13. Henri Pirenne, *Medieval Cities: their Origins and the Revival of Trade,* trans. Frank D. Halsey (Princeton: Princeton University, 1925), p. 218. For the full text of the remarkable 1188 charter at Aire—which begins, "All those who belong in friendship to the town . . ."—see Kropotkin, *Mutual Aid,* 177.

    Despite their aura of revolution and volatility, the first French communes were brought into being by the desire for self-help: "to protect the town and keep the peace in circumstances where self-help seemed the only hope" (Susan Reynolds, *An Introduction to the History of English Medieval Towns,* [Oxford; Clarendon Press, 1977], p. 104. Reynolds's French sources are A. Vermeesch "Essai sur les origines et la signification de la commune dans le nord de la France" (Heule, 1966); Petit-Dutaillis, *Les Communes francaises,* (Paris, 1947); P. Michaud-Quantin, *Universitas: expressions du mouvement communautaire dans le moyen age latin* (Paris, 1970). 129–66.
14. Berman, *Law and Revolution,* 366.
15. Statute of the *Spade compagnia,* cited in Robert D. Putnam with Robert Leonardi and Raffaella Y. Nanetti, *Making Democracy Work: Civic Traditions in Modern Italy* (Princeton: Princeton University, 1993), p. 126. Putnam's recent book shows the startling contemporary relevance of the medieval contracts. Judging the "widening gulf between North and South [to be] the central issue of modern Italien history" (158), he argues that the differences in civic virtue in the two areas corresponds precisely with the differences in city contracts in 1300 (chapter 5) and with mutual aid societies in the 1800s.
16. According to Pirenne, the word "peace" referred not just to freedom from war but freedom from crime: "The peace of the city *(pax villae)* was at the same time the law of the city *(lex villae)*"; "peace" in the twelfth century "designate[d] the criminal law of the city" (207, 208).
17. Berman, *Law and Revolution,* 396.
18. Putnam, *Civic Traditions in Modern Italy,* p. cited from Kropotkin, *Mutual Aid,* p. 174. Though themselves in need of help, strangers are themselves helpful: "information may be obtained [from them] about matters which one may like to learn."
19. Jean-Paul Sartre, "The Imaginary Life," from *Psychology of Imagination* (Citadel, 1991). pp. 177, 178.
20. Ibid., 187.
21. Ibid., 193.
22. Ibid., 206, 207. Sartre goes on to say that "this unnatural, congealed, abated, formalized life, which is for most of us but a makeshift, is exactly what a schizophrenic desires." p. 211.

23. For two overviews of the philosophic literature on "the other," see Michael Theunissen, *The Other: Studies in the Social Ontology of Husserl, Heidegger, Sartre, and Buber,* trans. Christopher Macann, introd. Fred R. Dallmayr (Cambridge, Ma.: MIT Press, 1984); and Arleen B. Dallery and Charles E. Scott, ed. *The Question of the Other: Essays in Contemporary Continental Philosophy* (Albany, N.Y.: State University of New York, 1989).

24. Max Scheler, *The Nature of Sympathy,* trans. Peter Heath, introd. W. Stark (Hamden, Ct.: Archon, 1970).

25. I have attempted to give an account of how the verbal arts accomplish this in a separate essay entitled, "On Vivacity: the Difference between Daydreaming and Imagining-Under-Authorial-Instruction," in *Representations* (Fall, 1995).

26. My thanks to Athenaide Dallet (Conversation, November 1992) for this observation and for the supporting citations from Plato and Shelley.

27. P. B. Shelley, "A Philosophical View of Reform" (1820).

28. This term was invented by Walsh McDermott, a physician in the department of Public Health at Cornell Medical.

29. Aleksandr Pushkin, *Eugene Onegin,* rev. ed., trans. Vladimir Nabokov, Bolingen Series LXXII (Princeton: Princeton University Press, 1979), p. 44.

30. William James, *Habit* (New York: Holt, 1914), p. 63

31. Monika Schoeller called attention to the fact that throughout hundreds of media recitations of the deaths in Mölln, the names of those killed were almost never cited (Frankfurt, December 11, 1992). President von Weizsäcker expressed the same lament in his Christmas Eve address to his countrymen (December 24, 1992).

32. Saliha Scheinhardt, for example, critiqued the overemphasis on belly dancing (Frankfurt, December 12, 1992).

33. For a more extended account of these representational strategies, see E. Scarry, "Watching and Authorizing the Gulf War," *Dissident Spectators,* ed. Marjorie Garber (New York: Routledge, 1993).

34. Jean-Paul Sartre, *Anti-Semite and Jew,* trans. George J. Becker (New York: Schocken, 1948, 76), p. 7.

35. Ibid., p. 19.

36. Ibid., p. 19.

37. Ibid., p. 127.

38. William Hazlitt, "The Pleasure of Hating," in *Selected Writings,* ed. Ronald Blythe, Penguin, 1970.

39. Philip Fisher, *Hard Facts,* (New York: Oxford, 1985) chapter 2. Fisher describes the process by which a book like Stowe's may bring a whole new perceptual framework into place: having changed our perception, the book itself (the very agent of our change) now itself looks crude in retrospect and we repudiate it as politically unsophisticated.

40. Stephen Spender, in a course he gave at the University of Connecticut, described the specific impact of *Passage to India* on the British population, as well as Forster's ethical impact more generally: "When a British person woke up in the middle of the night, he might say, 'What would E. M. Forster think about this?'"

41. W. H. Auden, "In Memory of W. B. Yeats," *Collected Poetry* (New York: Random House, 1945), p. 48.

42. Section 86 of the *Ausländer Gesetz* came into force January 1, 1991. It is the rule most applicable to the circumstances of many Turkish residents. The ordinary guidelines governing citizenship, discussed at a later moment in this essay, specify a 10-year residency period ("Einbürgerungsrichtlinien," Section 3.2.1). But this 10-year period merely makes one eligible to apply; it does not, as in the case of Section 86, give one a presumptive right ("regeleinbürgerung").

43. Section 85, *Ausländer Gesetz.*

44. Ulrich Preuss, Conversation, December 5, 1992 and April 17, 1993.

45. Bertrand Russell, *Unpopular Essays* (New York: Simon and Schuster, 1950), p. 31.

46. John Rawls, *A Theory of Justice* (Cambridge, Ma.: Harvard, Belknap Press, 1971), p. 138.

47. Ibid., p. 137.

48. Ibid., p. 12.

49. I am avoiding the word "Turks" here because it does not differentiate between people residing in Turkey and people residing for many years in Germany: thus the word makes those residing in Germany sound as though they are "foreigners," a designation examined below.

50. There are, of course, times when procedural access is included. See for example Cornelia Schmalz-Jacobsen's article in *Die Zeit,* November 26, calling for naturalization, double citizenship, and other

forms of integration. But more often changes in citizenship are not stressed, even when the subject is the equal "legal protection" guaranteed by the opening of the Basic Law: see, for example, President von Weizsäcker's speech in Schwerin celebrating the second anniversary of the unification (October 3, 1993).

51. William E. Nelson, "Fourteenth Amendment (Framing)" in 2 *Encyclopedia of the American Constitution* 757 (L. Levy, K. Karst, & D. Mahoney eds. 1986).

52. Here I am referring not to negative statements about foreigners ("foreigners out," "foreigners are pigs") but to neutral or often even extremely positive expressions of comradeship with noncitizens spoken by statesmen, businessmen, and artists alike. For example, the word is used repeatedly throughout Von Weizsäcker's November 8 speech in Berlin; as it is again used in a parliamentary report showing the gigantic financial contributions that Turkish-owned businesses make to the German economy (Speech, Martin Frey, Leipzig, September 12, 1993).

53. Whether the light-skinned resident or instead the dark-skinned resident in any one instance has resided longer probably turns on age: for example, fifty-one year old Bahide Arslan had lived in Germany longer than the nineteen-year-old who brought about her death. Both the Bundeskriminalamt and the Verfassungsschuta reported (September 1992) that the average age of those making attacks in 1991 was eighteen, though the two offices differed in their count of the number of attacks, the first reporting 2,450 for the calendar year and the second reporting 1,483.

54. Chancellor Kohl, November 23, 1992. Italics added. Kohl here seems to be apologizing on behalf of the owners to the nonowners.

55. John Locke, *A Letter Concerning Toleration* (Buffalo: Prometheus Books, 1990), pp. 11, 12.

56. The relation between competition and emulation is made by Brooke Hindle in *Emulation and Invention*, a book about the invention of the steam engine and the telegraph.

In the gathering in Frankfurt where I originally gave this lecture, several speakers from France wished to argue the remarkable proposition that France, not the United States, was the model of immigration. The fact that different countries now aspire to be internationally recognized as the leading model of citizenship-by-immigration (rather than citizenship-by-descent) is a wholly benign outcome since the "competition" designates immigration a widely shared goal.

57. On the difference between the ten-year period and the fifteen-year waiting period described earlier, see note 42 above.

58. Rules governing citizenship in Britain, Switzerland, Sweden, Austria, and Italy were obtained from the respective embassies in Washington, D.C., and Boston, Massachusetts, in the winter of 1992–93 both by telephone and by written booklets issued by the offices. No written summaries were available from the German or French offices: information about these countries cited in the next two paragraphs was provided by Mr. Aberle in the German Embassy, and by Mr. Vasic and Ms. Philippart in the French Embassy (9 December 1992 and 22 March 1993).

59. The Swedish handbook on citizenship notes that, "As a rule, people cohabiting under conditions similar to that of marriage are treated as a married couple" (Elisabet Swartz, *Swedish Citizenship*, Bratts Trycheri AB, p. 4).

60. For a British subject, British Protected person, or person from British Dependent territories, the five year residency makes citizenship a right, rather than only a precondition for application that may or may not lead to citizenship. People from Algiers born before Independence, can ask for, and will be given, French citizenship the moment they begin residence. Persons from France's former colonies in Africa can ask for citizenship if they can show they have been living in France five years. If no negative answer arrives after a year, the person has citizenship (a much less rigorous restriction than the requirement for an explicit affirmative answer).

A country that never had colonies, or which separated from its colonies at a much earlier date than did France or Britain, would not, of course, have such provisions. Although the British and French procedures announce the recent connection of these countries to colonialism, they also underscore the fact that citizenship in these countries is independent of a concept of blood or race.

61. A study by M.I.T. and the London School of Economics places the overall yearly immigration figure in the United States at .3 percent of the total population. This would be the equivalent of Western Europe admitting 900,000 people each year as "primary immigrants or refugees" (Richard Layard, Olivier Blanchard, Rudiger Dornbush, and Paul Krugman, *East-West Migration: The Alternatives*, [Cambridge, Ma.: MIT Press, 1992], p. 49). The decades, 1870–80 and 1900–10, had the highest rate (the number of immigrants was over 1 percent of the total population): 8.8 million people

immigrated between 1900 and 1910. The decades of the thirties through the sixties were relatively low; the figure then rose to over .2 percent between 1970 and 1985 (p. 15).

Because newly arriving people often come to the cities, the immigration figures there are much higher than the overall national yearly rate of .3 percent. For example, in the city in which I live, Cambridge, Massachusetts, over 22 percent of the population if foreign-born. The cities adjacent to Cambridge have similar figures: in Boston, 20 percent of the population is foreign-born; in Somerville, 22 percent of the population; in Brookline, 21 percent. Consistently, then, between one-fifth and one-fourth of the city is first-generation foreign-born. A high proportion of these immigrants, close to 7 percent of each city's total population, arrived in the 1985–90 period. (Center for Labor Market Studies, Northeastern University. US Census. Reprinted in *Boston Sunday Globe,* October 11, 1992.)

For a summary of year-by-year immigration statistics in Britain, see *Immigration into Britain: Notes on the Regulation and Procedures* (London: Central Office of Information, 1990), pp. 15–17.

62. The prohibitions also, of course, existed earlier in the century; but I am drawing attention here to the laws against intermarriage that existed *after* the Reconstruction Amendments that distributed the right to vote across all races. The laws against intermarriage lasted in many states until the 1960s.

63. *Statistical Record of Black America,* compiled and ed. Carrell Peterson Horton and Jessie Carney Smith [Detroit: Gale Research Inc., 1990], p. 535).

64. Hannah Arendt, "Reflection on Little Rock" summarized in Elisabeth Young-Bruehl, *Hannah Arendt: For Love of the World* (New Haven: Yale U. Press, 1982), pp. 310, 311. According to Young-Bruehl, Arendt believed that the first target of integration should be the repeal of twenty-nine state laws against racial intermarriage still in force in 1959. Young-Bruehl also points out that Arendt's own marriage to a gentile in the United States would not have been possible under the Nuremburg Laws in Germany.

65. The first of the two terms is sometimes invoked as though it in itself explained the long residency period required of people wishing to become citizens in Germany. But other countries with relatively short residency periods, such as Sweden, also see their citizenship as following a descent model rather than a territorial model (see handbook by Elisabet Swartz, *Swedish Citizenship*, Bratts Trycheri AB, p. 1). In other words, a descent model does not obligate a country to adopt extremely encumbering rules for immigration.

66. Article I, section 8, clause 11 and the Second Amendment. For a fuller discussion of these two provisions, see Elaine Scarry, "War and the Social Contract: Nuclear Policy, Distribution, and the Right to Bear Arms," *University of Pennsylvania Law Review* 139 (1991), 1257–1316; and "The Declaration of War: Constitutional and Unconstitutional Violence," in *Law's Violence,* ed. A. Sarat and T. Kearns (Ann Arbor: University of Michigan Press, 1992), pp. 23–76. At the time of the writing of the constitution, the explanations given for these two provisions focused on safeguarding the United States rather than on making foreign populations imaginable. But the two are close: it is by enabling a country to think about the foreign population with whom it may wage war that the home country itself is made safe.

67. There is reason to hope that this constitutional deformation will be reshaped under President Clinton. Prior to the election Clinton quietly mentioned that he would never take his country to war without following the constitutional provisions. His comment went unnoticed by the press. Being true to this pledge would obligate him to make policies about both conventional and nuclear war compatible with the constitution. Should he do this, it would be a more important change for U.S. democracy than almost any other change in the second half of this century.

The Face of the Other:
Ethics and Intergroup Conflict

ROBERTO TOSCANO

Je dis seulement qu'il y a sur cette terre des fléaux et des victimes et
qu'il faut, autant qu'il est possible, refuser d'être avec le fléau.
—Albert Camus, *La peste*[1]

Introduction

The present article derives from the need felt by a practitioner to pause and
reflect, after twenty-eight years of diplomatic work, on the ethical foundations of
international relations, taking conflict (the most ethically problematic, ethically
charged aspect of the discourse on international matters) as the object of analysis.

But why, if this is the case, does the term "international" not appear in the title
of the present article? Why is it replaced by "intergroup"? The reason is not
superficially semantic, but has conceptual and even political roots on which I feel
it necessary to linger briefly.

In the first place, it would be practically impossible, in the present world situation,
to include or exclude concrete instances of conflict on the basis of the recognition
or denial of the status of a nation-state to a specific group. This sort of scholastic
dogmatism is unfortunately widely practiced, and not only by international lawyers,
who at least have both practical and conventional justifications for applying such
an abstract and unrealistic taxonomy. Let us take an example from another ethically
charged area: human rights violations. Since "only states can violate human rights"
(thus goes the conventional wisdom of most experts in the area), rebels, insurgents,
(still) unsuccessful separatists are to be considered, when they commit outrages
against people, common criminals, and not violators of human rights. The theoretical absurdity and practical awkwardness of this approach seems evident, and yet
the rearguard battle for the maintenance of exclusive subjectivity for nation-states,
though with growing difficulties, will probably continue for a while longer.

The issue, on the other hand, is not only one of categorization. The fact is that
the definition of a collective entity as being or not being a nation-state has never
been considered ethically neutral in its consequences. In terms of conventional
morals state-sanctioned group violence has been traditionally not only exempted
from ethical stigma but has been morally exalted. The "my country, right or wrong"
of an American patriot is only the naive verbal expression of a principle that is
sheer blasphemy from the point of view of ethics (if one admits that "partial ethics"

is a contradiction in terms), but that is not considered wrong within the context of nationalist culture. In order to consider the devastating effects of such partial ethics on ethics as such, it is enough to apply the same claim of irrelevance, of nonapplicability of ethical judgment, to other collective levels to which the individual may belong: Hitler's *Mein Kampf* may carry as a subtitle "My race, right or wrong"; Banfield's Southern Italian peasants[2] may have waved a banner with the inscription "My family, right or wrong"; Communists from Lenin to Pol Pot (but also from Bukharin to Neruda) believed, wrote, and stated "My party, right or wrong"—and behaved accordingly.

This is indeed the root of all violent conflict of a group nature. This is how the deafness to the rights of others is sanctified, made mandatory. How the human individual's tendency to refrain from shedding the blood of others is overcome by group solidarity and its concomitant rationalizations. The cause need not be noble—and besides, who is to judge among competing and mutually contradictory claims to nobility? It can even be the identity and the aggressive "honor" of a soccer team.[3] More significant still, the arbitrariness of ethically discriminating (alternatively legitimating and delegitimating according to personal, political, ideological preference) not only between causes—some of which are said to justify violence—but also between "moral" group violence and morally stigmatized individual violence does not withstand critical scrutiny.

In international relations, the followers of the realist school (by and large the dominating school, especially among professionals in the field) have traditionally been allergic to ethical issues, postulating instead the functioning of a system composed of intrinsically amoral subjects (nation-states) engaged in the disembodied pursuit of rational goals. What is singular is that this apparently Machiavellian approach eludes the explicitly ethical focus of Machiavelli's entire theoretical construction, a focus that has been analyzed with definitive clarity by Isaiah Berlin.[4] Realists in international relations, in other words, have the tendency to hide their own ethical preference in favor of the nation-state (their own brand of partial ethics) under a supposedly neutral, "extraethical" cover.

Since violent group conflict takes place at the frontier of different spheres of partial ethics, the object of a reflection on conflict should be the sphere of applicability of moral codes rather than their specific, culturally, and historically determined contents.

The premise on which this article is founded is that beyond all territorial issues, economic rivalries, mutual fears (necessary, but not sufficient conditions), violent conflicts are made possible only by the existence of partial ethics. The corollary is that only on the basis of nonpartial ethical approaches can differences and tensions be managed without recourse to group violence.

In the search for such nonpartial ethics we have found as the main point of conceptual reference the works of Emmanuel Levinas, who has rightly been defined as "the thinker of otherness *par excellence.*"[5] When trying to understand organized group violence we are necessarily led to focus on ethical attitudes, and in particular on the exclusion of the nonmember of the group—the Other—from the scope of applicability of ethical principles. Levinas places instead the face of the Other at the very center of all ethics, and even goes beyond this with a bold shift from ethics to ontology that makes the Other the necessary condition for the identity of the Self (for Levinas, identity without the Other is a contradiction in terms).

The appearance (the "epiphany," to use his term) of the face of the Other is for Levinas the starting point for ethics insofar as it functions as an inescapable call to responsibility. We reach here the total antithesis of the partial ethics that is so functional—so indispensable, one may say—to extragroup violence: reversing Cain's sinister disclaimer of responsibility, Levinas states that we are all our brother's keepers, and that our brother is the Other.

2. Identity and Narcissism

In this post–Cold War, end-of-the-Millennium disorienting and disoriented historical phase, it is fashionable to talk about the irrepressible urge of groups—having not only to cope with the destructuring of the previous international system, but also with the disturbing prospects of globalization—to find solace and reassurance in a strengthened identity as a prerequisite not only of psychic health but also of survival itself and of effective common action. At the same time, we are witnessing the horrors perpetrated by the violent pursuers of identity, from ethnic cleansing in former Yugoslavia to genocide in Rwanda. What are we then to think, in both political and ethical terms, about identity? Is it "bad" or "good"? Or perhaps—as many nationalists will tell you—are we just facing excesses, exaggerations (practiced by people who are for one reason or the other "savage") in something that is essentially good?[6]

Actually the problem is not a quantitative, but a qualitative one. Not all identity is conflict generating. On the contrary, identity is the prerequisite even of altruism and love and, in group terms, of all kinds of positive interaction in terms of exchange and solidarity. What is conflict generating is not identity per se, it is what can be called "narcissistic identity," the kind of identity whose affirmation, pursuit, and defense form an integral part of the essence of nationalism (and of its lesser but not less murderous counterparts ethnicism and tribalism).[7]

Why is this so? In the first place, because at the root of group identity lies . . . a lie, or—put in less blunt terms—a cultural artifact, an intellectual construct produced by elites that have been very aptly defined by Pierre Bourdieu as "professional producers of subjective visions of the social world."[8] It is commonly believed (especially by nondemocratic political leaders) that in order to maintain the cohesion of a group it is not enough to define its identity in objective terms: all those born on the same territory, all those sharing the same religion, all those speaking the same language.

To be fair, finding objective criteria for group identity is indeed problematic. If we go hunting for what have been defined as "crucial markers of identity"[9] and take for instance language, we see that on that basis no identity of post-Yugoslav entities would have been possible, since they all speak Serbo-Croatian; the same would happen in the case of Rwandan Tutsis and Hutus, all speaking the same language: in this case, not even the "crucial marker" of religion would work, since both Hutus and Tutsis are Catholic. More than hypothetical racial differences, or no longer intact social ones, often the deadly "crucial marker"—as in the case of the 1994 genocide of Tutsis—ends up being the most bureaucratic of all artifacts: a mention of ethnicity on identity cards.

For this reason, there must be what has been called "the invention of tradition,"[10] there must be the creation of "imagined communities"[11] there has to be a "founding myth."[12] The group must have in all cases noble, ancient origins (divine, if possible); it must bask in the past glories of invincible ancestors or it must brood over the historical injustice visited upon it by a military defeat or an alien invasion depriving it of previous power and well-being. The point is that such an artificial, ideological path to identity is inherently conflict generating: in the first place, because by abandoning factual, falsifiable criteria it opens the door to controversy that has no possible solution but force; in the second place, because myths are by definition not objects of possible compromise, especially when your neighbors hold about the same territory and the same history incompatible myths of their own[13]; in the third place, because the positive self-stereotyping that is an essential component of this narcissistic identity inevitably requires a negative stereotyping of the Other, of the neighbor. But, most of all, because narcissistic group identity, by making one's own group's value incomparably higher, qualitatively incommensurable with that of any other group, ends up denying the ethical relevance of the Other, i.e., expels the other from the scope of applicability of moral rules. Thus, when real or perceived conflicts of interests, real or perceived threats originate from another group, the human individual, who as a rule *abhorret a sanguine,* reacts together with the group in ways that are totally detached from the ethical standards that she or he would uphold as an individual without seeing, as a rule, any contradiction between being "a good person" and a ferocious soldier for the group (be it the nation state or the tribe).

We find in Nietzsche a description of this dichotomy of behavior—which Nietzsche finds totally natural, and not contradictory at all—that deserves to be quoted *in extenso:*

> The same men who are held so sternly in check *inter pares* by custom, respect, usage, gratitude, and even more by mutual suspicion and jealousy, and who on the other hand in their relations with one another show themselves so resourceful in consideration, self-control, delicacy, loyalty, pride, and friendship—once they go outside, where the strange, the *stranger* is found, they are not much better than uncaged beasts of prey. There they savor a freedom from all social constraints, they compensate themselves in the wilderness for the tension engendered by protracted confinement and enclosure within the peace of society, they go *back* to the innocent conscience of the beast of prey, as triumphant monsters who perhaps emerge

from a disgusting procession of murder, arson, rape, and torture, exhilarated and undisturbed of soul, as if it were no more than a students' prank, convinced that thay have provided the poets with a lot more material for song and praise.[14]

Moreover, the tragic destiny of narcissistic group identity (like the tragic destiny of narcissistic individual identity), is that by denying the Other it ends up not giving confidence but disorienting, not building but destroying identity, since in a vacuum there can be no identity.[15]

The result is inevitably violence. In the end, identity is no longer sought in the hypothetical common blood shared within the group but in the real alien blood that is spilled outside it.

3. Erasing the Face of the Other

Iver Neumann has written that foreign policy is about "making the Other," i.e., nourishing ontological enmity toward those who are external to the nation-state.[16] The effect of the presence of an external enemy on internal cohesion of any group—not necessarily with reference to a nation-state—is in fact part of politicological conventional wisdom. It is a point that would be hard to challenge, but one that is in need of some more refined definition.

If we want to try to explain from an ethical point of view the phenomenon of bellicose foreign policy or bellicose "group policy" it is not enough to stop at the "creation of the Other." Not all identity, not every self-definition is necessarily conflict generating and murderous. What we have to explain is *"la transformation—ou la non-transformation—du voisin en assassin."*[17] Besides, what is at stake here is not an attempt to explain individual violence that finds its roots in personal passions, desires, hate, greed. On the contrary, it is significant that the mechanisms of the two kinds of violent action (individual and group) are different and manifest themselves differently in the same individuals, who may have a radically different propensity to have recourse to group versus individual violence. To take one example, analysts of the Holocaust from Hannah Arendt to Susan Zuccotti have been impressed by the reluctance of individual Italians (even true believers in Fascism, even soldiers in war zones) to participate in the roundup of Jews, and their propensity, on the contrary, to give them assistance in escaping the Nazi machine of deportation and extermination.[18] Now, it would be a mistake to believe that those same individual Italians were less prone than individual Germans participating in the Holocaust to exercise violence, if we conceive it in individual and not group terms. On the contrary, very probably those same Italians would be much more likely than the individual "ordinary" Germans examined in studies on Nazi violence[19] to kill an unfaithful spouse or an obnoxious neighbor, but found it absolutely absurd and inhuman to participate in killing or even just harming unknown persons because of their belonging to an abstract category.

The point is that whereas individual violence is concrete, often intimate, group violence is by definition abstract. The Other—for the purpose of organized group violence—is not a real individual, whom you might in concrete terms and for specific reasons hate or love, but an abstraction. Xavier Bougarel's essay on Bosnian traditions of interethnic relations[20] supplies some very interesting elements. The analysis is not based upon an idyllic image of interethnic coexistence, but on the contrary reflects the awareness of the recurrent conflictuality that is historically inherent in the cohabitation of different groups on the same territory. What the article says is that in multiethnic communities coexistence is the fragile but possible fruit of conscious mechanisms of rapprochement, a sort of systematic "good-neighbor policy" finding its concretization in almost ritualized inclusion of the "different" neighbor, thus bringing about familiarization and appeasement, in intimate ceremonies like weddings or funerals. Again: real individual neighbors are not necessarily loved, but they are loved or hated for concrete, not abstract reasons. And especially they are not hated en masse. On the contrary, in order to apply group violence to the neighbor as belonging to a category, the concrete individual's face has to be erased[21]: the person must become an abstraction.

Here is where the role of violent, militaristic political leaders comes in. Here is where group violence loses its alleged "naturalness" to become a patent political creation. Differences as such are not sufficient to break through the resistance that average human beings feel when confronted with the use of group violence. One still needs what has been called "the reinforcement of differences"[22] and, even more important, the erasing of the face of the Other. The modalities and the degrees of sophistication of such processes can differ, but ethically and politically they are functionally the same.

Coexistence of different groups is indeed problematic and fragile, but at the root of violent group conflict (not simple tensions, not simple divergences, not simple controversies) we almost inevitably find the conscious, systematic, intellectually dishonest endeavor of political leaders aimed at convincing the group of: (a) its own uniqueness and nobility; (b) the despicable, treacherous nature of the rival group, stereotyped in abstract terms that leave no space for individual difference and exception; (c) the objective nature of certain group interests defined as "unavoidable goals" combined with the denial that—as Hoffmann writes—"there are . . . always choices"[23] and that they are also determined by subjective values and not only by objective interests; and (d) the absolutely "zero-sum" nature of the rivalry often to the point of mutually exclusive survival *(mors tua, vita mea)*. According to such terrorist technique, all issues (the use of a name or a flag, a few square miles of territory, the bank of a river or the top of a mountain) are presented as "vital" to the very survival of the group. To use Thomas Nagel's simile,[24] "the last eclair on the dessert tray" is always described, in nationalist propaganda, as "the last life jacket for your own child."

With this last point we reach a very crucial aspect of the ethical discourse, the incompatibility of ethics—any ethics—with the absolutization of a primordial striving for survival, what Spinoza calls *conatus essendi*.[25]

Here we are not just facing a variant of possible ethical options, but something much more radical. In fact, whereas ethics is by definition exclusively human, *conatus essendi* (i.e., the striving for the preservation of being) is, according to Spinoza, a property of "things" in general. In other words, if *conatus essendi*—a naturalistic law on a par with the laws of thermodynamics—is the only or the absolutely overwhelming guiding principle for action (both individual and group) we are in a dimension where only causality reigns. Actions may not be traced back to the subject accomplishing them by the process of "imputation," the necessary connection to responsibility. This evidently makes all ethics—and also legality[26]—inconceivable.

The tension between causality and imputation (i.e., between necessity and freedom) is another essential element for the definition of the field of ethics. One could say that, just as in premodern cultures even causation of natural events tends to be interpreted in terms of imputation and human responsibility (magic and witchcraft)[27] in the postmodern world human action tends to be "naturalized" and read in terms of causality. In the former instance the ethical discourse is distorted by hallucination, absurdity, and arbitrary assignation of guilt; in the latter, the universalization of causality to cover human action means the end of responsibility, in other words, of the very possibility of ethics. Only a never-resolved tension between causality (creating the framework, the limits, and the conditioning of human action) and imputation (allowing the attribution of responsibility) can leave space for a complex ethical discourse in which causality justifies compassion, but imputation legitimizes judgment.

Opting for an ethical approach means, in essence, opting for Humanity against mere Being. Emmanuel Levinas states this point with great clarity:

> Ontology—that is, the intelligibility of being—only becomes possible when ethics, the origin of all meaning, is taken as the starting point. Humanity must irrupt into Being: behind the perseverance, in being, of the beings or worlds—of men, too, insofar as they are themselves simple worlds—behind their *conatus essendi* or their identity, affirming its own ego or egoism, there must figure, somewhere, in some form or other, the responsibility of *the one for the others.*[28]

The primitive, vulgar brand of politics that puts the survival of the group as *suprema ratio* can boast noble politicological ancestors, and is often the vulgarized, cheap version of serious political works (just like the intellectual roots of Hitler's *Mein Kampf* can be found in much more respectable nineteenth- and early twentieth-century German theory). One could call such an intellectual tendency—cutting across epochs, countries, cultures—"reductionist political theory." Facing the complexity, the multicausality, the contradictory nature of the behavior of humans in groups, reductionist political theory finds a monocausal explanation in the friend/enemy dyad, to which all other aspects are subordinated. Thus violent conflict becomes "natural," and in a sort of perennial *jihad* of all versus all, peace is seen as a mere armistice of a temporary and somewhat artificial nature. Of course, this pseudorealistic approach is a way of smuggling in one's own ideological preference under the guise of an objective discourse, and yet if we want to refute it we will have to prove not that conflict is not possible (a patently absurd statement), but that it is not more "natural" than coexistence among different groups. And we will also have to linger on the conditions of coexistence, not only in terms of security, economics, territory, and politics, but also of ethics.

In other words, we will have to deal with the ethical premises of intergroup coexistence.

4. The Ethical Premises of Intergroup Coexistence

A. *Away from Dialectics*

The dialectical mode of thinking is shared far beyond the narrow circle of Hegelians (both "right-wing" and "left-wing," including Marxists). It is almost conventional wisdom—even for people with no philosophical training or concern—to believe that "stages" have to be "overcome," that historical reality proceeds through the spirallike ascension defined by the triad thesis/antithesis/synthesis.

The dialectical mode is, however, a conflictual mode, and it is conflictual in a very special way. Dialectical thinking tends to deny the right of existence of whatever—and, one could add, whoever—is "overcome." Actually, as the end point—the "final stage" in both Hegel's and Marx's philosophy reveals, dialectics originates from a nostalgia for Unity, a striving for fusion that eliminates alterity, and from the refusal of contradiction, seen as a temporary imperfection of reality (especially human reality), that has to be eventually eliminated in the framework of a Higher Reality (Fukuyama's overly famous "end of history" is but a younger and less brilliant offspring of the same family).[29]

Paradoxically, the rejection of group violence as an inevitable mode of human existence is not compatible with visions of a conflictless "Kingdom of Heaven" (or classless society), but only with a philosophical interpretation of difference and contrast as irreducible. Coexistence of different cultures, different groups, is compatible only with the abandonment of a dialectical mode of thinking and its replacement with a "dialogical" one.[30] Only if "thesis" and "antithesis" can never be subsumed and annulled into a higher "synthesis," but are instead destined to constitute the *permanent poles of a noneliminable tension,*[31] controversy and contrast between human beings (individuals and groups) do not need to be necessarily turned into zero-sum violence, into the denial and annihilation of the Other.

The goal cannot be, realistically, one of "perpetual peace"[32], an unrealistic and also dangerous goal. When facing the reality of conflict, however, we should instead proceed by degrees, first by distinguishing contrast and difference (inevitable) from violent conflict (not inevitable). But then, facing the possibility of violent conflict, we should distinguish between types of conflict that are different not only in magnitude and material consequences, but also from an ethical point of view. It can be said that contemporary intergroup conflict is a much more direct challenge to ethics than classical international conflict—which recognized the adversary's right to exist—ever was. The victim of organized violence, today, is often someone with a real and familiar face. Violence, in this case, is the result of the urge to get rid of an intolerable familiar but different face, a face that creates a permanent tension one is unable to withstand. It is, in short, the path to a narcissistic, if not autistic, synthesis where the Self (the collective self) is alone and unchallenged because the Other has been eliminated.

B. Away from Myths

Conflict requires bad philosophy, but it also requires bad history. More specifically, it requires what can be called a "pathology of memory." Conflict-prone groups (and especially political leaders who want to foster such proneness) manifest historical memory that is pathological, simultaneously, in excess and in default. The former for one's own glories (all princes)[33] or sufferings (all martyrs) and the latter for one's neighbor's dignity or rights. It would be enough to leaf through books used to teach history in our countries in not too distant times (and through history books presently used in countries that have not developed our more recent qualms and self-restraint) to gather an endless anthology of sometimes hilarious self-serving travesties of factual history.[34] The fact is that, being historical sufferings, injustices, horrors, and victimizations only too real, there is only an *embarras du choix* for anyone wanting to justify present injustice and violence practiced with past injustice and violence suffered. It is indeed a game anyone may play. The trouble is that just as abused individuals have a tendency to repeat as victimizers the same acts of violence of which they were the victims[35], there may be a tendency of "abused groups" (or—which is the same—those that convince themselves that they were historically abused) to exert violence on others whenever they gather sufficient power.[36]

In any case, the capacity of individuals to elaborate self-justificatory mechanisms that make collective violence not only admissible, but "sacred" is astonishingly boundless: in *War and Peace* Tolstoy quotes Napoleon's *Memoirs* in which the by then defeated and exiled Emperor, musing on his Russian adventure, claims (with Orwellian shamelessness) that his invasion was a *"guerre pacifique."*[37]

And yet historical distortion is not inevitable. It is enough to consider the post–World War II evolution of the reciprocal image of "traditional enemies" as the Germans and the French or the Italians and the Austrians to come to the conclusion that history (and the teaching of history) need not be pathological, but can be developed critically to include a healthy and honest (if not "objective") recount of rights and wrongs, glories, and miseries, violence practiced, and violence suffered.

C. Away from Narcissism

Ethics requires accepting that "one is for the other what the other is for oneself" and that "there is no exceptional place for the subject."[38] The same can be translated in group terms, leading to the recognition that there is no exceptional place, on moral grounds, for one's own: be it nation, ethnos, gender, race, class, party, or religion.

In other words, ethics requires impartiality.[39] There is no doubt, on the other hand, that in practice this is an extremely difficult endeavor. Suffice it to say that Levinas himself, when dealing with the State of Israel, has given ethically privileged status to "his own," i.e., Israel, that he refuses to consider it as "a state like any other."[40] It is the everyday experience of all human beings to be confronted with choices in which they are almost inevitably led to favor their own. And yet, the point about the essential ethical value of impartiality cannot, and should not be abandoned. In the first place, there is a substantial difference between favoring one's own by exercising the discretionary margin of choice that exists in most ethically relevant situations and favoring one's own by breaking ethically relevant rules and thereby harming others. If I give my only apple to my child instead of to another one I exercise my discretionary margin of choice. The same is true for the dramatic situation envisaged by Barry, in which an individual is confronted with the choice of saving either his own wife or another woman from a burning building.[41] But if I cut a line to a water fountain in order to let my child drink before the other children in line—or, on a more dramatic level, if I load my spouse onto a lifeboat reserved for children—I go beyond such margin and infringe upon someone else's right to see a rule respected. In the second place, what is especially dangerous in the partiality exercised in favor of one's own tribe, nation, or ethnos is not just its practice, but its theorization. No mother would theorize that her child, qua hers, has a preferential right to drink before the other children; and this works as a built-in limitation to possible claims and to the violence that, facing resistance, can be put to work in order to make them effective. But when one speaks of "morally sacred" rights of a community, such restraint is nowhere to be seen. The fact of partiality is transformed into the right, even the duty, of partiality: and from that the step to the use of violence is a very short one.

What does this have to do with narcissism? If narcissism is the denial not of the physical reality of others, but of their moral reality (i.e., of their relevance in terms of our ethical choices), then ethical partiality is tendentially narcissistic, insofar as it eliminates the Other as a moral subject, leaving the Self—and "one's own," actually an extension of the self—[42] as the only morally relevant reality. When—as Buber says—the Thou has been turned into an It, the Self is alone. Narcissistically so.[43] Contrary to what Levinas says, one can actually remove or cancel the face of the Other. Only thus, as a matter of fact, can the Other be killed as an abstraction, for collective reasons and in a collective, organized mode of violence.

But how can the face of the Other be brought back against all narcissistic blindness? In cultural-pedagogic terms, one could point at intercultural experiences and initiatives, be they student exchanges or other ways of familiarizing the individual (especially the young individual) with the Other. In political terms, we are talking, for example, about what is called "preventive diplomacy" or "postconflict peace building." One could say indeed that both instances should be aimed at such construction or reconstruction of the face of the Other. And yet, in order to avoid all overly optimistic, *illuministe* illusions, one should not think that knowing the Other is enough to prevent the erasing of his face and the narcissistic concentration on oneself and one's own. Tzvetan Todorov, in analyzing one of the historically more significant encounters with the Other, the discovery of America, has clearly and convincingly pointed out that knowledge ("the epistemic level") is only one component of the recognition of the Other (one could venture to say that cognition does not necessarily imply recognition), to which one should add the value judgment ("the axiological level") and the action of getting closer or distancing in relation to the other ("the praxeological level").[44] But if this is so, then, though we have clearly defined the problem, we cannot hope to find easy solutions. We will have to conclude that the ethical urge (and its devastating eclipses) remain largely mysterious, or alternatively say—which actually amounts to the same thing—that the production of ethical phenomena is subject to such a plurality of causal elements that it is practically impossible to decipher them in their origins, evolution, and possible reversal.

D. For an Ethics of Responsibility

Recognition of the Other is the essential, antinarcissistic "passage to ethics." Yet, it does not completely define the essence of ethics. Again, let us go back to the lesson of Emmanuel Levinas: *L'Autre me regarde,* in the double meaning of "looks at me" and "concerns me." The relationship that is thus established is not just one of acceptance, recognition, or tolerance, respect. It is one of responsibility.

Having said that the concept of responsibility is an essential component of the ethical discourse, we should also be aware of its possible distortions.[45] Responsibility, as a matter of fact, can be the last refuge of the political scoundrel, in the sense that it can supply a handy all-purpose justification for ethically horrendous action, especially in matters of peace and war. Levinas's responsibility for the Other is the exact opposite of that "responsibility" to the nation-state or to the group that is employed as a justification of injustice and violence.

E. Ethics and Legality

Having said that ethics (ethics that inhibits the recourse to group violence) requires cognizing and recognizing the face of the Other, making the Other concrete and not abstract—we should be very much aware of the fact that there are some faces we will never see. The problem of the use of group violence, in other words, is not only limited to the violence used literally against the neighbor (see the cases of Bosnia or Rwanda), but also the violence visited upon distant peoples by our own group (the case of America's Vietnam War).

How do we deal with the anonymous, distant Other? The ethical premise of our refraining from using or condoning violence can remain the same. Yet it will not take us far enough, and risks establishing a perverse proportionality between the geographical and cultural remoteness of a specific Other, the possibility to really *regarder son visage* and the degree of applicability of ethical standards. (Colonial violence was a clear example of this proportionality.)

For an orientation in the solution of this problem we can find interesting guidance in Levinas:

> Indeed, if there were only two of us in the world, I and one other, there would be no problem. The other would be completely my responsibility. But in the real world there are many others. When others enter, each of them external to myself, problems arise. Who is closest to me? Who is the Other? Perhaps something has already occurred between them. We must investigate carefully. Legal justice is required. There is need for a state.[46]

Thus the relevant pronouns are not only "I" and "Thou," but also "They." For a complete ethical cosmos, one needs to start from the freedom of the Self (an essential prerequisite of all moral action), but then move on to a respect of the "Thou" based on recognition and leading to solidarity. But there is a third component: for "Them," for those who are inevitably "third parties," since they do not concretely come into contact with us, we have to apply rules, we have to be guided by justice. All law, including international law, belongs to this level.[47]

What is important is that these three levels be constantly interconnected. Let us reflect, to prove this point, on the possible consequences of their disconnectedness. What is freedom of the Self without respect of the Other or justice? It is very significant, here, to see that the most radical defenders of extreme, nihilistic individualism—from Nietzsche[48] to Bataille—utilize a term that is characteristic of the discourse on international affairs: *sovereignty*.[49] Like the sovereign state, the sovereign individual is self-referential even in the realm of ethics. Like the sovereign state, the sovereign individual claims the right to kill in order to pursue specific ends.[50]

But what is the recognition of the Other without justice? Here we have to go back to the essential concept of impartiality. The Other that cannot be the object of a direct relationship, that cannot be "individualized," risks being relegated to the outskirts of moral responsibility. Risks being treated unfairly vis-à-vis the more immediate, more concrete Other. Only justice can be a sort of moral safety net allowing for the inevitable limitations of concrete experience, for the objective difficulties we encounter in the search for the face of the Other.

But, also: what is justice—what is the Rule—without the freedom of the "I," if not ethically precarious submission to rulers? And what is it without the concrete "Thou"? Justice without solidarity, and without compassion, turns into the opposite of ethics. Since the writing and the application of the rule require a system, specifically a nation-state, then abstract justice, the abstract rule, can be (has been, historically) the path leading to violence against those who are "outside the rule." If not checked, relativized by the "I" and the "Thou," the rule embodied in the state is indeed one of the mainsprings of group violence: violence that is abolished internally by the application of the rule and that is discharged externally, since the applicability of the rule (and of the justice that the rule is supposed to apply) is only coextensive to the legal system, that is, to the state. In this respect it would be of course absolutely absurd to maintain that German philosophy and political science (from Hegel to Schmitt, i.e., from the absolutization of the state to the centrality of the friend/enemy dichotomy) "produced" the Nazi phenomenon: but we can say that that philosophy and that political science were fully compatible with it.

I have said that group violence requires a narcissistic mindframe. One could also put it differently: violence requires *idolatry*,[51] meaning the absolutization of the group, its rights, its needs, its status, its glory. And in our historical times this absolutization is vested upon the nation-state, both in its defense and furthering when it exists and in its creation when it does not. Conversely, only a plurality of allegiances (therefore a plurality of identities) can be compatible with a nonidolatric view of the nation-state and of the group in general.[52]

To sum up, ethics and justice are distinct but interconnected: distinct because ethics needs a concrete Other, whereas justice is impersonal; because ethics is substantial, justice procedural; because ethics is independent from institutions, while justice can only be applied in their framework; because, as pointed out above, ethics and justice need each other as a limit.

On the one hand, we must avoid the paradox of "unjust ethics": not only the arbitrary privilege given, against justice, to a more proximate Other, but also the injustice of total self-sacrifice, forgetting that, as Jankelevitch says, justice must be even for oneself.[53] Without justice as an external limit, ethics can indeed go to the extreme of stating "The Other, right or wrong."

On the other hand, we must avoid the perversion of "unethical justice." It has to be noted, here, that this expression is not an oxymoron, since the term "justice" is used in this article as equivalent to "legality," and not with the moral connotation that is frequently attributed to it. Opposing justice to legality is just another way of shifting the former term into the field of ethics, and—I feel—of confusing the issue.

How does all this relate specifically to the problem of intergroup (and international) conflict? Both ethics and legality (justice) should be addressed in this context. In the first place, insofar as possible, the goal of those who want to prevent conflict should be one of the "ethicization" of relations, implying the attempt to shift from the abstract to the concrete, the effort to "give face" to the Other through political and cultural means. But if this is in part possible in the field of intergroup relations, once we shift to international relations ethicization runs the risk of becoming a well-meaning utopia. The main effort in this case can only be one of gradual "juridicization," not meaning of course the denial or ignorance of the realities of power, but the channeling and limitation of that power within rules, and necessarily also within institutions. The realistic goal cannot be that of "world government," and even less of "world democracy": power differentials will continue to weigh upon the different capacity of individual states in terms of rule setting; what is to be hoped is that gradually they will not affect the equal submission of all to rules. The latter, and not the former, is the real prerequisite of legality.

And yet not even in the case of international relations is ethics out of the picture. Even imagining the consolidation of legality beyond the borders of individual states—in other words, the strengthening of international law—ethics would remain as a necessary counterweight to pure legality. In terms of substantiality versus formality, individuality versus abstraction, or compassion versus intransigence. For example, sanctions imposed on a country by the Security Council on the basis of Chapter VII of the Charter are certainly "just"—but it remains to be seen case by case, in the light of actual consequences on concrete human beings and not just governments, whether they are ethically defensible. Or, again: no one could question the legitimacy, under international law, of the sinking of the Argentinian cruiser *Belgrano* by the British during the Falklands War, but it definitely was something that could (and was) questioned from an ethical standpoint.

Conclusions

Though, as we have seen, a complete ethical cosmos requires the three aspects I have mentioned (I for freedom; Thou for solidarity; They for the rule), one can say that the specific realm of ethics resides in the moving and contested territory lying between absolute freedom and absolute rule. Both absolute freedom and absolute justice (the absolutely sovereign individual and the absolutely sovereign state), in fact, are nonethical in their essence and violent in their potential.[54] Ethical individuals as well as ethical coexistence of groups require therefore a permanent, insoluble, nondialectic tension between the two polarities of freedom on one side and the rule on the other.

This theoretical approach has a practical corollary. If our agenda is strengthening the possibility of ethically inspired (or at least ethically compatible) life in a given society and/or intergroup relations, then our action should not inevitably and systematically orient itself on either one of the two poles (freedom/the rule). Instead, it should operate in a compensating mode in order to prevent either one from prevailing to the point of unduly invading and erasing the exposed and precarious territory of ethics.

Concretely, in situations of despotism and imperial domination (i.e., where an overwhelming absolute rule eliminates the possibility for ethical action) we should enlarge the territory of ethics by giving weight to freedom; where, on the contrary, anarchy destroys any possibility of ethical behavior by universalizing murderous sovereignty (both within a community or nation-state and in the international field) then ethics can be rescued only by working for the application of rules, i.e., for the strengthening of local, state, and international institutions.

But the ethical discourse can be developed following yet another bipolar approach. Vladimir Jankelevitch locates the territory of ethics in the space between absolute love—self-denial to the point of self-destruction—and absolute being, totally indifferent to ethics ("A being totally deprived of love is not even a being; a love without being is not even a love"). Only an unstable tension between these two poles can allow for an ethical dimension whose goal, according to Jankelevitch, is attaining the utmost level of love compatible with a minimal preservation of being *("le plus d'amour possible pour le moins d'être possible"),*[55] in other words, striving for "ontological minimum" and "ethical maximum."[56]

The implications of this approach for international (and intergroup) relations are quite evident: ethics does not necessarily imply absolute pacifism (which, in the presence of an aggressor, might mean the end of being itself); nationalism or tribalism are not "ethics-compatible" because they posit the existence and interest of the group in maximalistic, not minimalistic terms (so that being destroys the possibility of love, compassion, and humanity: in other words, destroys the ethical dimension). In concrete terms, ethically compatible group policies must steer a difficult and changing course—not lending itself to schematic formulas and prescriptions—between the need for survival (being) and the moral imperative of the recognition of the Other (love).

We can thus conclude by saying that, though admitting the mysterious complexities of ethical (or nonethical) behavior of humans both as individuals and as members of a group, we are not condemned, when facing intergroup violence, to fatalism and passivity (that some like to call realism).

In spite of all the intricacies of complex causation of human behavior, indeed the ethical premises of intergroup coexistence are far from obscure: certainly not obscure enough to relieve us of both political and moral responsibility.

Notes

1. "The only thing I want to say is that on this earth there are scourges and there are victims, and that one must, insofar as possible, refuse to be on the side of the scourge."
2. Edward C. Banfield, *The Moral Basis of a Backward Society* (Chicago: The Free Press, 1958).
3. "People fight because people like to fight. Soccer is the vehicle they use because they can justify violence as the defense of their team, town, or reputation." ("Hooliganism: An Ancient, and Still Lucrative, English Export?", *International Herald Tribune,* May 30, 1996.
4. Isaiah Berlin, "The Originality of Machiavelli," in: *Against the Current. Essays in the History of Ideas* (London: The Hogarth Press, 1980), pp. 25–79. Berlin argues very convincingly that Machiavelli's view of politics was not amoral, but was centered, instead, on a "higher morality" placing the supreme interest of the *res publica* above all other considerations.
5. Iver B. Neumann, *Collective Identity Formation: Self and Other in International Relations,* European University Institute, Florence, Working Paper RSC no. 95/36.
6. Nationalists have the amusing tendency to consider good only their own nationalism, which they often like to call "patriotism" to distinguish it from the nationalism of the Other, usually deplorable and threatening. On the dubious nature of the distinction between "good" nationalism and "bad" nationalism see Pierre Hassner, *La violence et la paix. De la bombe atomique au nettoyage ethnique* (Paris: Editions Esprit, 1995), pp. 297–98. One is tempted to suggest that the only possible distinction could be made, in clinical terms, between "mild" and "acute" nationalism.

7. Neumann, op. cit., p. 20; Gilles Lipovetsky, *L'ère du vide. Essais sur l'individualisme contemporain* (Paris: Gallimard, 1983). Lipovetsky, who explicitly mentions "collective narcissism" (p. 21), describes the "more and more narrow feeling of belonging to a group and the parallel increase of exclusion" (p. 93); he adds that "at the end of History we find Hobbes's state of nature," with "narcissism advancing in step with ever more barbaric and conflictive human relationships" (p. 99). Analyzing the roots of contemporary nationalism, Michael Ignatieff has spoken of "the narcissism of minor differences" (*The Needs of Strangers* [London: The Hogarth Press, 1984], pp. 130–31).

8. Quoted by Valery Tishkov, *Nationalities and Conflicting Ethnicity in Post-Communist Russia*, United Nations Research Institute for Social Development, Discussion Paper DP50, March 1994, p. 2. Tishkov (p. 6) speaks also of "illusions that see theoretically constructed classifications as objectively existing groups of people or as laws of social life."

9. Neumann, op. cit., pp. 4–6.

10. Eric Hobsbawm and Terence Ranger (eds.), *The Invention of Tradition* (Cambridge: Cambridge University Press, 1992).

11. Benedict Anderson, *Imagined Communities. Reflections on the Origins and Spread of Nationalism* (London: Verso Press, 1983).

12. Eric Hobsbawm, "The New Threat to History," *The New York Review of Books*, December 16, 1995, pp. 62–64. On the flimsiness of "objective" criteria to define ethnicity, Colin Renfrew has stated: "How precisely would one define a Serb living in Bosnia? And what if he were a Muslim by religion? How, precisely, would one define the ethnic identity of the Muslim population of Bosnia? Should the inhabitants of the former Yugoslav Republic of Macedonia call themselves Macedonians? It is my point that these, and others of this kind, are difficult questions, which cannot be answered satisfactorily in historical terms. Even when we understand properly the genetic, linguistic, cultural, and religious background, there is no good answer, because ethnicity is a matter of self-identity as much as a historical fact. It is to a large extent a matter of choice. To claim otherwise, and to place the responsibility for the decisions of today upon claims of historical truth is a fraudulent undertaking." ("The Roots of Ethnicity: Archeology, Genetics and the Origins of Europe," Conference at the Accademia dei Lincei (Rome), January 8, 1993, unpublished paper, p. 3.) Tishkov (op. cit., p. 4) expresses the same concept as follows: "Nationality or ethnic identity is not an innate human trait, although it is most often perceived as such. Nations are also created by people, by the efforts of intellectuals and by the state's political will. 'Nation' is an in-group definition: it is not possible to assign it strictly scientific or legal formulae. This also concerns the more mystical category of 'ethnos.'" Tishkov (p. 9) also quotes Karl Popper: "The attempt to uncover certain 'natural' state borders and, accordingly, to see the state as a 'natural' element leads to the principle of the nations state and to the romantic fictions of nationalism, racialism and tribalism. However, this principle is not 'natural,' and the very thought that natural elements such as nation, linguistic or racial groups do exist is simply fabrication." See also I. William Zartman, "Self and Space: Negotiating a Future from the Past." Paper presented to the International Studies Association, San Diego, CA., April 1996.

13. "The list of injustices committed against ethnic groups in the former Soviet Union is long and extremely painful. Therapy for past traumas may necessarily be lasting and costly, especially if resources and energy are directed to reconcile the past and to return the 'norm' of existence once lost. For some groups and leaders this might mean the moment before the collapse of the Soviet Union or before 1917 (groups of Russian national patriots), for others, before the start of massive deportations (the Ingush, Volga Germans, Crimean Tatars, and others), for a third group, before the prewar annexations (the Baltic peoples, Moldovans), for a fourth group before the Civil War and Red Terror (the Transcaucasian peoples), for a fifth group, before their inclusion in the Russian empire and colonization (the peoples of the Volga region), and for a seventh group, before the period of ancient state formations or even ancient cultures. In any case, the ideal is represented by that historical period from which the most arguments in favor of the currently desirable territorial borders, political status, and cultural conditions can be derived. The further one looks for the roots in the past, the more mythologized the concepts of 'historical territories,' 'nation state' and 'cultural traditions' become." (Tishkov, op. cit. p. 8) "In the same historicist rationale heard from Sarajevo to Tajikistan, the people defend their land-grab. 'It belonged to us once, whether 50 or 500 years ago, so we are taking it back now.'" (Alexandra Tuttle, "Europe's Other War: A View from Kelbajar," the *Wall Street Journal*, May 18, 1993).

14. Friedrich Nietzsche, *On the Genealogy of Morals,* in *Basic Writings of Nietzsche,* Walter Kaufmann (ed.), (New York: Modern Library, 1968), p. 476. Alain Finkielkraut, in his book on Levinas, writes something that could be considered a direct answer to Nietzsche: "Realism is not realist, it is simplistic: it eludes the problem of Evil by conferring upon it the status of a natural datum. Now, in man it is not nature that is homicidal or barbaric, but the aspiration to return to nature. Facing the Other, my life is indicted, the world is no longer my own home, there comes about an obligation that pushes back the sweet duty of preservation and flourishing of the self. Thus my existence is condemned not to find a justification in itself. Through Evil I appeal against this sentence. I express simultaneously both the resentment and nostalgia prompted by its severity. Nostalgia for a life that is no longer moral, but organic, that obeys only to its own internal dynamic. Nostalgia for *élan vital* and irresponsibility. Dream of a return to nature." (Alain Finkielkraut, *La sagesse de l'amour* [Paris: Gallimard, 1984], p. 146).

15. Lipovetsky, op. cit., p. 108. Or, as Neumann writes (op. cit., p. 10) quoting Mikhail Bakhtin's "dialogism": "'The Other' has the status of an epistemological as well as an ontological necessity, without which there can be no thinking self."

16. Neumann, op. cit., p. 18.

17. Xavier Bougarel, "Voisinage et crime intime," *Confluences Méditerranée* (Paris), n. 13, Hiver 1994–95, p. 75.

18. Hannah Arendt, *Eichmann in Jerusalem: A Report on the Banality of Evil* (New York: Viking, 1963); Susan Zuccotti, *The Italians and the Holocaust* (New York: Basic Books, 1987).

19. Daniel J. Goldhagen, *Hitler's Willing Executioners: Ordinary Germans and the Holocaust* (New York: Knopf, 1996); Christopher R. Browning, *Ordinary Men. Reserve Police Battalion 101 and the Final Solution in Poland* (New York: Harper Collins, 1992); Robert Jay Lifton, *The Nazi Doctors* (New York: Basic Books, 1986).

20. Bougarel, op. cit. *Komsiluk,* a Turkish-origin term meaning good neighborliness, is the term used in Bosnian culture to describe this mode of intergroup coexistence.

21. Finkielkraut, op. cit., pp. 164–65.

22. Stuart Hampshire, *Morality and Conflict* (Cambridge, Ma.: Harvard University Press, 1983), p. 175.

23. Hoffmann, op, cit., p. 10.

24. Thomas Nagel, *Equality and Partiality* (Oxford: Oxford University Press, 1991), p. 24.

25. Spinoza, *Ethics,* Part III (Of the Origin and Nature of Feelings), Propositions VI, VII, VIII and IX, French translation: *L'Ethique* (Paris: Gallimard, 1954), pp. 189–91.

26. On the essential replacement of causality by imputation for the very concept of law see Hans Kelsen, *Pure Theory of Law* (Berkeley, CA.: University of California Press, 1978).

27. Lipovetsky, op. cit., p. 262.

28. Emmanuel Levinas, "Prayer without Demand," in *The Levinas Reader,* Sean Hand (ed.) (Cambridge, MA.: Blackwell, 1989), p. 231.

29. "Beginning with Plato, the social ideal will be sought for in the ideal of fusion." (Levinas, "Time and the Other," in *The Levinas Reader,* cit., p. 53). Levinas also writes of "the gathering together of the world's diversity within the unity of a single order that left nothing out; an order produced or reproduced by the sovereign act of Synthesis." ("Revelation in the Jewish Tradition," ibid., p. 208).

30. Michael Holquist, *Dialogism. Bakhtin and His World* (London: Routledge, 1990); Tzvetan Todorov, *Mikhail Bakhtin: The Dialogical Principle* (Minneapolis, MN: University of Minnesota Press, 1981); Aileen Kelly, "Revealing Bakhtin," the *New York Review of Books,* September 24, 1992, pp. 44–48.

31. Levinas writes: "The idea that the Other is the enemy of the Same is an abuse of the notion; its alterity does not bring us to the play of the dialectic, but to an incessant questioning, without any ultimate instance." (Levinas, "Revelation in the Jewish Tradition," cit., p. 209).

32. Here we should head Hoffmann's warning: "Next to cynicism, the greatest threat to morality is disembodied idealism." (Hoffmann, op. cit., p. 18).

33. "The man of the people is almost invariably, in our land, a *déclassé* aristocrat." (Ernest Renan, quoted in Tzvetan Todorov, *Nous et les autres. La réflexion francaise sur la diversité humaine,* Paris: Editions du Seuil, 1989, p. 159).

34. "National histories, encyclopedias and cultural research often have little in common with the people's factual history and ethnography." (Tishkov, op. cit., p. 3).

35. "One study of a group of American rapists has established that as many as 80 percent were abused children. These men grew up with feelings of martyrdom, self-pity, and distrust, and characteristi-

cally lacked all compassion for other people." ("The Mind of the Rapist," *Newsweek*, July 23, 1990, p. 46.)

36. On the contrary, if violent conflict is to be avoided "identity must go beyond memory if it is not to be forever mired in the past, turning into a pathological view of the world which has no room for other people's sufferings." (Kanan Makiya, *Cruelty and Silence* (New York: Norton, 1993), p. 260.

37. L. N. Tolstoy, *Voina i mir* (Moscow: Sovremennik, 1979) Vol. II, p. 262.

38. Levinas, "Time and the Other," in *The Levinas Reader*, cit., p. 47.

39. Brian Barry, *Justice as Impartiality* (Oxford: Clarendon Press, 1995).

40. Emmanuel Levinas, "Zionisms," in *The Levinas Reader*, cit., pp. 267–88. For a harsh—but difficult to challenge—criticism of this philosophically inconsistent "exception," a clear case of partiality, see Neumann, op. cit., pp. 14–16: according to Neumann, "Levinas makes the political choice of being a nationalist first, and the philosopher of alterity who ostensibly has a responsibility to bear witness second." It is indeed remarkable that a thinker that can be considered as one of the most perceptive, most interesting of Levinas's disciples, Alain Finkielkraut, has shown the same kind of partiality when dealing with "his own," France. In an interview on self-determination and the end of Yugoslavia, the interviewer, puzzled at his blanket endorsement of separatist causes, asked him whether he was not afraid of sponsoring "less legitimate movements," such as that for the independence of Corsica from France. Finkielkraut's answer, indignantly rejecting any parallel between France and less glorious nations, deserves to be quoted: "France, do not forget it, is a republic that is one and indivisible . . . our country is an ancient nation." ("Le reveil des petites nations. Entretien avec Alain Finkielkraut," *Politique Internationale*, Printemps 1992, p. 56. In his French "patriotic exceptionalism," on the other hand, Finkielkraut is in good historical company: in Todorov's review of French thought on human diversity (*Nous et les autres*, cit.) we find Peguy upholding self-determination as an absolute principle but making an exception for *"la République une et indivisible"* (pp. 326–27); Michelet referring to "organic unity": *"Un seul peuple l'a—la France"* (p. 293); Tocqueville defending the right of Native Americans to be free while approving French colonization of Algerians (p. 279); and, finally, Chateaubriand, who "does not see any incompatibility between his criticism of the misdeeds of colonization, such as carried out in America, and the search for new colonies for the benefit of France." (p. 395).

41. Barry, op. cit., pp. 228–33.

42. Erich Fromm, *Man for Himself. An Inquiry into the Psychology of Ethics* (New York: Fawcett Premier, 1965).

43. Martin Buber, *Je et Tu* (Paris: Aubier, 1969), p. 98; Daniel Warner, "Levinas, Buber and the Concept of Otherness in International Relations: A Reply to David Campbell," *Millennium: Journal of International Studies*, Vol. 25, No. 1, 1996, p. 111.

44. Tzvetan Todorov, *The Conquest of America: The Question of the Other* (New York, NY: Harper, 1992, p. 185). Todorov remarks that Cortés knew much more about the Indians than de Las Casas, but definitely did not love or "recognize" them from an ethical point of view.

45. Roger Epp, "The Limits of Remorse: McNamara, Kissinger and the Ethics of Responsibility," paper presented to the Conference of the International Studies Association, San Diego, CA, April 16–20, 1996. Epp warns that Weber's "ethics of responsibility" can actually be turned into its opposite whenever the state, its monopoly of violence and the citizen's allegiance to the state are brought into the picture. Epp notes: "As Weber himself put it, 'Luther relieved the individual of the ethical responsibility for war and transferred it to the authorities.'"

46. Levinas, "Ideology and Idealism" in *The Levinas Reader*, cit., p. 247.

47. Paul Ricoeur, *Soi-même comme un autre* (Paris: Editions du Seuil, 1990); *Le Juste* (Paris: Editions Esprit, 1995).

48. Nietzsche speaks of "the sovereign individual, like only to himself, liberated again from morality of custom, autonomous and supramoral (for "autonomous" and "moral" are mutually exclusive)" (op. cit., p. 495).

49. Finkielkraut writes that violence aimed at the total annihilation of the Other is the product of the revanchism of an ego wanting to reconquer its "full powers," its sovereignty that has been made morally impossible by the presence of the face of the Other (op. cit., p. 155).

50. There is also a significant coincidence between arguments used by "realists" in international relations and defenders of the concept of the sovereign individual. The latter, smuggling their own ideological preference into an allegedly objective discourse (and ignoring all psychological and anthropological complexities) try to peddle "the phantasy that morality marks the spot where human beings discard

human nature." (Richard Wollheim quoted in Thomas Nagel, "Freud's Permanent Revolution," *The New York Review of Books,* May 12, 1994, p. 36).

51. According to Levinas, the state is also "the site of corruption par excellence and, perhaps, the last refuge of idolatry" (op. cit., p. 274). On the very important Jewish concept of idolatry, see Moshe Halbertal and Avishai Margalit, *Idolatry* (Cambridge, MA.: Harvard University Press, 1992).

52. Zartman, op. cit., p. 3. It is interesting to note, in the same context, that the ethics and the aesthetics of pluralism and coexistence versus group-centered intolerance tend to coincide, from Bakhtin's "poliphony" (aesthetics) and "dialogism" (ethics) to Salman Rushdie's both ethical and aesthetical concept of *métissage*. On the latter, see Annie Montaut, "Les mensonges de la purete ou l'Inde de Rushdie (a propos du *Dernier soupir du Maure)*" [The Lies of Purity or Rushdie's India (about *The Moor's Last Sigh*)], *Esprit,* April 1996, p. 108.

53. Jankelevitch, op. cit., p. 44.

54. "Absolute freedom is the right of the strongest to dominate. It therefore fosters conflicts that favor injustice. Absolute justice implies the suppression of all contradiction: it destroys freedom." (Albert Camus, *L'Homme revolté* [Paris: Gallimard, 1951], p. 345. A recent, extreme case of anomie proves this point: "Today Liberia more than ever is living up to its name: it is the freest place on earth—a place where anyone can give full vent to criminal instincts without suffering the least punishment." (Alfonso Armada, "Liberia, morir por nada" [Liberia, to die for nothing], *El Pais,* May 19, 1996.

55. Vladimir Jankelevitch, *Le paradoxe de la morale* (Paris: Seuil, 1981), pp. 88–90.

56. Ibid., p. 119. Also for Pierre Hassner (op. cit., p. 362) the essence of possible coexistence and avoidance of conflict is the maintenance of a never-resolved tension between the universal rule and particularistic needs.

Civilizational Imagination and Ethnic Coexistence

AHMAD SADRI*

1. Live and Learn

Every theoretical work is to some extent a biography. My insights on ethnic coexistence originate from my quest to understand what has happened during my lifetime in the country of my birth.

I, my twin brother, and fear were born triplets. The year was 1953 and our mother was terrified by the clatter of the CIA-induced machine guns that ushered in the second reign of the Shah of Iran. Twenty-five years later, when twenty-five hundred years of Persian empire came to an end and the old monarchy caved in under the pressure of a popular revolution, fears dimmed. New bright hopes for realizing perfection in government moved masses of enchanted Iranians overwhelmingly to ratify utopian blueprints for the first Islamic City of God. Now their massive disenchantment with that revolution is fomenting a different kind of rebellion expressed in revisionist thinking about Islam and its regulation of private, social, and public life.[1] It has been almost twenty years since that revolution and I am more convinced than ever that the horizons of those who have looked at it through the usual sociological methods in the context of Iranian society and Middle Eastern politics need to be expanded.

My current interests lie in placing the Iranian revolution and its aftermath in the broader canvas of cultural changes and civilizational exchanges within the Western world. This enterprise has had a few unanticipated dividends. The utilization of units of analysis larger than nation–states suggests a way to make sense of our world's fin de siècle dilemma: despite the realization of many of the promises of modernity in the second half of this century, we have also witnessed the rise of some of the most virulent varieties of religious fundamentalism and ethnic hatred. Reworking, adapting, and finally reviving such concepts as "civilization" provides a metalanguage for addressing, and even transcending, cultural and ethnic differences. In the meanwhile we have to acknowledge the apprehensions of current social sciences regarding such broad concepts, which is partly due to careless use or ideological misuse of them. For an illustration of these problems we need go

*I would like to express my thanks to the American Center for Oriental Research in Amman, Jordan, for their generous support of my research project on the Postrevivalist discourse in Islam (February to July 1997). The present paper provides the theoretical framing device for that study.

no further than Samuel Huntington's recent thesis on the clashing of civilizations.[2] In his controversial essay in *Foreign Affairs,* Huntington bases civilization on a vague set of commonalities of transnational populations; but, he ends up with a series of civilizations that have nothing in common. Two are world religions (Hinduism and Islam), one is a nation-state (Japan), one is based on a shared public morality (Confucianism), one is a continent (Africa), one is defined by a common language (Latin America), and, last but not least, one is defined by the direction of the movement of the sun (West). Indeed the only thing all of these entities have in common is the relative strategic interest they hold for the United States. This at once simplifies and reifies international tensions as signs of an impending civilizational armageddon.

2. "Civilization": A Conceptual Makeover

The world around us is being pulled in two opposite directions. There is no doubt that it is literally shrinking due to the technological enhancement of the means of transportation and the information revolution. Global news and computer networks, linked stock markets, and the formation of international bodies consisting not merely of national delegations but also of grassroots observers of environmental and political ills are all signs of the realization of the cozy modernist vision of a "global village." Despite the protestations of the "postmodernist" intellectuals, some of the most sanguine predictions of the much maligned midcentury modernists are coming to pass as well. There is no denying that the world is gravitating toward liberal democratic politics and capitalist economy.

Unfortunately for the modernists, however, the world is also gravitating toward new ethnic tensions that seem to lead with shocking spontaneity to mass brutalization and genocide. Besides, the existing ethnic and religious tensions are plumbing roots to new depths in the kind of tribalism that was supposed to have vanished from the modern world. The schizoid situation of the world calls for a descriptive as well as a prescriptive approach. Here I aim to combine the two without mixing them. But first, we have a lot of serious defining and redefining to do.

The term "civilization" has been used by philosophers of history, anthropologists, sociologists, and archaeologists. Instead of delineating the different stages and shades of meaning in the history of this term, I will simply offer my own definition in accordance with the needs of this project: *Civilization is the accumulation of organized and institutionalized rational responses of city-dwelling human societies to the challenges of their internal order (e.g., political legitimacy, social administration, economic system, religious cosmology, legal maxims, and libido economy[3]), environment (e.g., technologies of food production and architecture), and external enemies (technologies and organization of war and international relations). The practical and instrumental side of these rational responses comprise the "material culture" (e.g., art, architecture, and technology) of a civilization while their substantive and normative aspects amount to its "nonmaterial culture," which imparts meaning to the natural and social world and informs the patterns of social, political, and economic behavior. Thus, civilizations contain the sedimentation of two layers of collective rationality: a normative and substantive "core" and a practical and instrumental "crust."* Having defined civilization, I must hasten to add that civilizations must not be taken literally. They do not exist in the same way that planets, flowers, and cats do. They are not objective wholes nor do they enjoy an organic unity of their own. After the following four caveats regarding the ontological status of civilizations, we will return to the question of the state of the world as posed at the outset of this section.

A. The Inherent Instability of Civilizations

There is a level at which we can consider a civilization as an objective but rather tenuous and frail entity. The most basic characteristic of the substantive core of any civilization is *conflict*. I start with the assumption of an elemental incompatibility of axioms and values underlying every civilization. Further, practical problems are bound to flourish when applying principles to daily life. Value dissonance, inconsistencies, and contradictions between ethical, religious, and philosophical axioms, and between them and the practical demands of life, compel every civilization to work constantly at mending, patching up, dissembling, and even systematically deceiving to maintain the impression of an orderly and unified view of the world informing a clear set of guidelines for action. The fate of tragic heroes of fiction and drama such as Agamemnon, Hamlet, and Willy Loman provide opportunities to ponder the manifestations of deep cultural contradictions at the level of personal conduct.

Insofar as civilizations exist, they are weak and conflicted creatures who are too absorbed with their own maintenance to care much about "clashing" with other civilizations. In other words, the concept of civilization is useful only in the study of the internal complications of human societies and not terribly effective in explaining external conflicts.

B. The Question of Agency

In this sense civilization is an objective entity by proxy, that is, it owes its objectivity to a certain stratum of intellectuals who are its architects. The qualifying phrase *"insofar as they exist"* in the above paragraph signifies the fact that civilizations exist through the agency of the "intellectuals" who are their creators and carriers. The reason we date civilization back to the end of the fourth millennium B.C.E., when Sumerians first settled the first Mesopotamian cities, is that only at this time were human societies able to support a stratum of intellectuals (scribes, priests, schoolmasters, administrators, etc.) who focused on the elaboration of the instrumental and substantive collective responses to the challenges of their internal order and external adversaries. The invention of writing allowed the selection, preservation, and systematic development of collective rational responses and enabled successive generations of intellectuals to work on their elaboration and further rationalization. Of course the irrational cores of life (e.g., sexuality and aggression) and the sources of internal and external chaos (e.g., anomie, insurrection, and invasion) are never vanquished. These contribute to the inherent instability of civilizations. Therefore the recognition of the role of intellectuals in the definition of civilization is essential. To talk about civilizations in isolation from those who are its main creators and carriers is to hypostatize it.

C. The "Character" of Civilizations

Civilization could also be conceived of as a real, socially and historically specific, if pale, set of commonalities that have lost their moorings in particular historical circumstances. Our impression of the particular character of various civilizations is not precise, but it is not necessarily illusionary either. A lot of social scientists have opted not to pursue our vague impressions about the psychological and social characters of people from similar ethnic groups and national origins, let alone civilizations.[4] But it is possible to ground these differences and save them from the company of ethnocentric prejudices. National and civilizational characters exist because the lifestyle and worldview of a rather thin stratum is often used as the template for other classes, social groups, and strata.[5] In certain historical periods, a given status group or class takes a stance and adopts a way of looking at the world that distinguishes it. The cultural triumph of such a stylized pattern of life and worldview causes it to serve as the frame of reference for a society or a civilization as a whole.

D. Civilization as an Ideal Type

We may also use civilization as a heuristic device. In this sense it is mainly a "concept," an "ideal type" that allows a general view of the processes that might be otherwise too multifarious and rich in texture to be intelligible. Thus, civilizations also function as conceptual tools. To the extent that they do, they are creatures of mercury: they merge and divide according to the interests of the observer and the need to sum up the sociological or historical common denominators of similar societies. These commonalities may not be consciously present for the members of the societies in question. Here the scientist is given a license to lump and divide as long as the bases of his or her categorizations are accepted by the community of practitioners within the discipline. Of course this consensus itself represents a civilizational inclination but it is the aim of this article to argue that such civilizational distortions are not quite as pernicious as they might appear.

3. How and Why Civilizations Borrow

The current problem of the world to which we alluded at the outset consists of a split between the two forces of civilizational borrowing: centrifugal forces, such as modern communication, which bring civilizations together; and centripetal forces, such as ethnic tribalism, which thrust them apart. Social sciences have occasionally tried to come to grips with these two forces but never at the same time. They have tried to capture the meaning of worldwide unifying trends wearing such rose-tinted lenses as modernization theories and theories of global communication. Recently the postmodernists have spurned this approach as naive and have opted for less ambitious research projects that are best fitted to studying our world's discontinuities and divisions. Here we aim to provide a frame of reference that would make sense of both of these processes.

The most common form of intercivilizational contact occurs when civilizations borrow from each other.[6] The trade occurs at two levels. Exchange at the technological level is less problematic. To borrow at the level of ideas is much more complex. In particular, those ideas that relate to such spheres as religious worldview, political legitimacy, and libido economy are quite sensitive to sudden shocks of cultural borrowing. Another problem stems from the fact that in premodern times, civilizational borrowing occurred more gradually and through the agency of a few intellectuals who exercised control over the process of exchange. Continuous advances in the field of communications since the industrial revolution have both facilitated borrowing and expanded the base of contact between civilizations. Technological borrowing continues with such success that the cultural varieties of the world are threatened by the uniformities imposed by the adoption of Western technologies and their related patterns of life. But worldwide spread of culture is not the monopoly of the West; the internationalization of certain products of Eastern civilizations like acupuncture and martial arts proves this point.

In short, this is what has happened to the world: *the instrumental crust of all world civilizations has practically merged. Consequently, the distance between the inherently unstable substantive civilizational cores has been dangerously reduced.* This explains the simultaneous opposite pulls that we feel in our world. If this reading is correct, then the new forms of fundamentalism and ethnic hatred would represent a hurried withdrawal to the domain of ancient certainties in the face of encroaching ideas that provide a disconcerting variety of new options for organizing individual, social, and public life. The problem is that on the one hand borrowing and adoption at the level of core ideas has lagged behind technological borrowing. On the other hand, the adjustments necessary for accepting a global framework for the interaction of civilizations has not taken place.

4. Civilizational "Contacts"

The interaction of civilizations or indeed all culturally different groups goes through a certain number of stages which I will represent by means of an ocular metaphor. I do not mean to imply that these are evolutionary stages. Although there is a sense in which the dominance of the three patterns of looking at "the other" follows a historical order, the previous forms are not eliminated but often remain as alternatives on the list of options for intercultural understanding.

A. Tunnel Vision

At the most rudimentary stages of intercultural understanding, the vision of the other is obtained through a single opening into the exotic world. The resulting picture is not only vague, but also limited and one-sided.[7] But the one-sidedness and unfairness of this stage of relating to the other is the least of its problems. As an approach that exaggerates difference, it can hardly encourage the observer to find parallels in his or her own culture for the derogatory or laudatory characters attributed to the other. Nor is there any attempt to appreciate the self-understanding of the other. Worst of all, there is ample evidence to suggest that psychological projections play a significant role in this way of viewing the other.[8] Thus our tunnel-vision portrayals of the other reveal, more than anything else, our own neuroses.

B. Double Vision

The next stage in understanding the other comes with the realization that each civilization including our own is a complex and enclosed universe of meaning and signification, and that it is unfair to perceive—let alone judge—a foreign culture by only one of its parts. This recognition is the first requirement of the science of anthropology. The methods of living among the natives for long periods and suspending all judgments about them were adopted by early twentieth-century anthropologists. Armchair verdicts about the virtues and vices of"savagery" were thus shelved in favor of a value-neutral investigation and careful cataloguing of the varieties of cultural universes. Those Western moral philosophers who continued to enjoy the luxury of only reading about "primitive people" rather than facing a myriad of cultural varieties, have been scandalized by the inability of anthropologists to pass the most elementary moral judgments about the superiority of the West.[9] Thus, flames of philosophical debate have time and again been stoked around the straw man of "moral relativism."

Here I do not wish to enter into this debate. What I would like to emphasize is that this anthropological, relativistic stage represents a real advance over tunnel vision (of which the moral philosophers mentioned above often suffer) and a radical reversal of common ethnocentric prejudices. Yet I do not consider it the ideal cognitive springboard for ethnic coexistence, and this must be clear from the niche it has been assigned in our ocular metaphor. Like tunnel vision, double vision is a neurological disorder. It is caused by the inability of the brain to superimpose the two pictures relayed by the eyes to create a single perspective. The picture produced by one eye lacks depth, but seeing double causes confusion. Cultural relativism is a necessity at the beginning of ethnographic research. For those with an interest in ethnic coexistence, the creation of fairly objective portrayals of the other is an essential step.

C. Depth Perception

In the perception of a normal person the superimposing of the pictures provided by the eyes produces an integrated, three-dimensional view of the world. Now, by a grand leap of logic—compliments of our metaphor—we land in the field of ethnic relations. We start with a picture of the "self" by a specific reading of the evolution of our own civilization.[10] Then we produce a picture of the other, using the careful historical, ethnological, and sociological tools at our disposal. Ideally we must be able to overlay the two pictures and arrive at a unified view. Like games of optical illusion, this picture will allow us to look at it twice and see different things each time. It may even let the two stories merge into one, allowing us to read our own history as if it belonged to the other and vice versa.

Studying the history of any nation including our own would be a boring affair if we did not pause to ponder the question: "What would have happened if?"[11] Why not use this tool in the cause of interethnic relations? Why not read the different histories of the various ethnic entities, whether within a single civilization or across them, as if they were the same story with different endings? I think that we can utilize these methods in interethnic dialogue to gain a new perspective on, or probably "see through," our obdurate differences. If we look at our own history as a different version of the others' we will understand it in a new light. Reading the other's history as our own story with a twist leads to a more sympathetic reading. This method allows us to see many similarities between distinct identities and break down many differences into their common elements. We might be just a historical accident away from the fate of our neighbors. Sometimes intended or unintended consequences of a reform, an invasion, or even a natural disaster at a sensitive historical moment makes all the difference in the world.

It also could turn out that the only difference among civilizations is *time*. Since most conflicts occur within rather than between civilizations, we might even develop something akin to an evolutionary scheme. I am well aware of the tortured history of this concept in social sciences and will not belabor the point here. Suffice it to say that similar "objective possibilities" especially within civilizations could provide a finite number of possibilities. Comparing the destinies of nations within civilizational frameworks to determine whether and to what extent their inherent potentialities are actualized can be more than a clever way of understanding their course; it may be a good foundation for coexistence as well.

5. Islamic Revolution and the Rest of the West

Let me offer a synoptic example of the use of the comparative civilizational outlook suggested above. I start by viewing Western civilization as a whole, because its

Judaic, Christian, and Islamic subcivilizations are all steeped to their cores in the two rather incompatible sources of inspiration: Abrahamic religion and Greek philosophy. And they all seem to foster, among other things, a common temptation for ideal Republics (e.g., Plato), Utopias (e.g., More), and "Cities of Virtue" (e.g., Al Farabi). The Greek obsession with an ideal political community in combination with the Abrahamic belief in one omniscient personal God make a compelling case for theocracies.

Even the historical conditions that shaped the initial political positions and messages of these religions did not make much of a difference in the strength of this common desire. Christianity, based as it was on an apolitical gospel preached to the demilitarized Jews of Palestine, seemed to be the least likely candidate of the three to establish theocracies. Ironically, the apt political climate of Europe allowed it to get the most practice in crowning pontiffs, exalting "defenders of the faith" and "crusader kings," and founding occasional Christian republics (e.g., Calvin's Geneva). Such principles as religious tolerance, separation of church and state, and finally secularism were not the result of abstract insights, but the sweet fruits of bitter and protracted historical experimentation with centuries of papacy and long religious wars. "The Shining City on the Hill" of Western imagination cannot be wished away; it must be lived out, and, more importantly, it must be *outlived.* This is exactly what the Christian West has done. Once such a large-scale historical experiment has been performed, the way to the secular city will be wide open.

The wishes of fringe sects notwithstanding, it is safe to say that the Christian West is not likely to go back to theocracies. Secularism is ensconced in Western constitutions, but this is the effect of the civilizational changes, not their cause. Unless it represents a civilizationally grounded insight, no secular document can ever compete with the allure of a theocracy in the West. That is, the validity of secular constitutions depends on their historical experience, not vice versa. Theocracy is no longer within the range of "objective possibilities" of the Christian West because it has been outgrown; the temptation has been indulged. Few may contest this argument. But it will be difficult to account for it unless we assume a civilizational approach. Only within such a framework can we study huge social and intellectual processes that last for centuries and affect large cultural and transnational regions. Where are the results of such experiments stored? Certainly not in the quotidian consciousness of the masses. Rather they are preserved in the sphere of nonmaterial culture of a civilization whose carriers are the very-much-material, flesh-and-blood, intellectuals. They remember such experiments and maintain, reconsider, and advance them. They also help enshrine such lessons in constitutions and laws that perpetuate them, and in social institutions that reproduce them as laws, mores, and political culture.

Jews, partly due to their disembodied existence in the diaspora, seem to have jumped over the theocratic experiment to found a democratic, secular society. But it was exactly the conditions of the diaspora that galvanized the Jewish civilization as a whole from the effects of the Jewish enlightenment (Haskala) in a section of the Ashkanazim of the central and Western Europe. Enlightenment remained marginal to the Jewish civilization, as it did in the Islamic world, because it never pervaded the critical cultural areas where the temptation for theocracy resides. I am not about to argue that Jews *must* go through the theocratic stage as this would be the position of a dogmatic evolutionary theory. There are no paved roads, no ineluctable laws in history. Indeed, everything else being equal, Israel will probably continue its existence as a secular state. But if the increasing strength of messianic right-wing politics in Israel is anything to go by, the unindulged temptation is not quite extinguished. And, unlike the Christian West, everything may not remain equal in Israel. An economic or military disaster may revive the old longings for a "really" Jewish state. This is not an inevitability, but an objective possibility. Taking note of such possibilities and preparing for them would be prudent.

What we said about Israel also applies to the case of Turkey's jump to secularism. The case of modem Iran, however, is different. Here Moslems seem to have indulged for the first time their desire for a "City of God" free of all residues of traditional authority that accompanied previous Islamic Caliphates. Thus the present revisionist thinking of people like Abdolkarim Soroosh represents a real "civilizational leap." We cannot begin to estimate the importance of his revisionist Islam in isolation from the climate of postrevolutionary Iran. Soroosh is theorizing (with a great deal of intercivilizational borrowing, of course) the immense disappointment of Iranians after two decades of an actually existing theocracy. Most adult Iranians remember the revolution in which the overwhelming majority of them played a role at least by participating in demonstrations and referendums. The disillusionment especially after the anticlimax of the Iran-Iraq ceasefire, is expressed in an anecdote in which a man walks backward in the middle of the street repeating unintelligible syllables. When he is asked what he is doing the response is: "I am taking back my demonstrations!" The thought of Soroosh is original to Islam not because no one has thought of reforming Islam before, but because he represents a collective attempt to awake from a recurring nightmare of Western civilization. Civilizational borrowing will allow Iranian intellectuals like Soroosh to learn from the experiences of their civilizational neighbors, namely Christian theology and Western political philosophy. Civilizational depth perception will allow non-Iranian observers to go beyond apparent differences to gain a new empathy for what is going on in Iran.

This argument is pregnant and quite likely to raise more questions than it answers, especially in its present synoptic form. But I have posed it here as an example of the kind of flights of civilizational imagination that might ease existing ethnic tensions. We must try to see apparent conflicts less as arising from essential racial and cultural differences and more as a function of common civilizational, or intercivilizational problems. With the use of civilizational imagination we may see others at the same historic crossroads that we have faced and vice versa.

6. To Judge or Not to Judge

Rushing to judgment is almost inevitable in tunnel vision. If, out of consideration for the recent etiquette of political correctness, the judgment is not blurted out, there remains a suppressed inclination to "call a spade a spade."[12] Knowing the pitfalls of using one's own cultural system as a tribunal to judge others, social scientists have tended to renounce judgments altogether. The strong case for this attitude would posit the observer as an objective instrument that records but does not judge. Cultural relativism does not advance beyond registering the radical multiplicity and even incommensurability of human cultures. It does not aggravate ethnic tensions, the way prejudices and single-criterion judgments will do; but it is not much help either.[13]

In my view the process of engaging in ethnic dialogue cannot do without a good-faith attempt to understand the other by using all of the tools provided by the sciences of history, anthropology, and sociology. An attempt must be mounted to find common civilizational parallels, possibilities, and pitfalls. But we must not shy away from judgments either: our scientific protestations notwithstanding, we are all "human." I do not assume that excluding human judgments in the field of intercultural understanding is either possible or desirable.

Apprehensions of social sciences about judging others due to inevitable distortions that shape our views are misplaced. The problem arises from the assumption that the knowledge of the other is a one-way street. The gaze of knowing is assumed to be directed only from the Western to the non-Western world. But we are advancing to a point where we may not have to maintain this assumption any longer. If we agree that the task of knowing the other is not the solitary "burden of the white man," but a process in which different parties exchange glances, we might also assume that distortions, mistakes, misperceptions, and misjudgments will be corrected in time during the process of an intercivilizational dialogue. This is true because the economic and political hegemony of the powerful nations and their monopoly of the means of knowing is not nearly as total as it used to be a few decades ago.[14] In such a world we may finally be able to exchange the heavy burden of being saintly "objective" and antiseptically "nonjudgmental" for the lighter one of being fair.

7. Let Nations Speak

Finally, the colloquia of ethnic coexistence must avoid the discourse of cultural relativism and its questionable moral progeny: "sensitivity training." The worst thing that we can do is paper over our judgments. Even those judgments that are the result of blind prejudice or tunnel vision must be acknowledged and dealt with. The next necessary step for a useful dialogue involves a degree of cultural relativism. In order to gain a fairly "objective" view of the other we must consult, if not conduct, an objective historical, anthropological, and sociological search. This does not exclude engaging in moral judgments at a later stage of the game. Ethnic coexistence is itself a moral position and it cannot be accomplished by avoiding judgments, especially those that are rooted in civilizational positions. Of course, like charity, judgments must start at home: it is called self-criticism. Every meeting of the ethnic minds must begin with self-criticism. I prefer to start such a meeting with an

Alcoholics Anonymous-style washing of the proverbial dirty laundry in public. The next step would be holding a festival in which all confront their prejudicial and tunnel-vision pictures of each other. But any lasting attempt at conflict resolution must be extended beyond these stages to a nonemotional scientific plane where "objective" studies of one another are conducted and the results compared.

Civilizationally determined angles of reflection would only add character and interest to the perspectives that will be gained in "depth perception." Some of the inevitable distortions that are caused by mistaken interpretations will of course be corrected in the process of cultural exchange. But other distortions will remain as tokens of the civilizationally grounded differences of values and points of view. Such distortions are integral to our human condition: we are finite creatures whose interests are determined by the tiny slice of time and space allotted to us. Even the most scientifically minded among us cannot help but view our social world through the prism of a particular time and place. Acknowledging this rootedness will allow us to recognize our point of view as *a point of view* and use it as a tool for narrowing down the plethora of information in the subject of our study. To use yet another ocular metaphor, awareness of the blind spot will turn it into a discriminating lens.

Notes

1. Tehran's monthly, *Kian,* has for the last decade served as the most prominent venue for writings of such Moslem reformers as Mohammad Mojtahed Shabestari and Abdolkarim Soroosh. I have co-translated into English the first volume of collected essays by the latter at his request to be published by Oxford University Press. In Soroosh's thoughts one can recognize echoes of the last 100 years of Christian theology (e.g., hermeneutics) as well as a serious attempt to demarcate the domains of religion, society, and politics.
2. Samuel Huntington, "The Clash of Civilizations," *Foreign Affairs,* Summer 1993, pp. 22–49.
3. "Libido Economy" is used by Sigmund Freud in his *Civilization and its Discontents* to denote the various methods, and, the extent to which, "civilization" suppresses and transubstantiates our sexual drives in order to preserve order in society.
4. This is partly due to the sordid history of connecting such conceptions to theories ranging from geographical determinism to racism.
5. As Max Weber has shown in his *Religion of China,* the Confucian ethos of the state bureaucrats of the ancient Chinese empire spread not only throughout China but also through Southeast Asia. In a similar fashion Norbert Elias has shed light on the formation of the national characters of the Germans and the French in his famous book, *The Civilizing Process.*
6. Civilizational connections are seldom contentious. But, as the renowned historian Arnold J. Toynbee observed, such clashes—when they are not utterly deadly of course—tend to benefit civilizations as sources of external stimulation and crucial borrowing.
7. This is reminiscent of the Indian fable of *Pancatantra* where an elephant is kept in a dark room. A group of people who have not seen an elephant before enter the room. Later, each visitor describes the beast according to the part that he has happened to touch.
8. For instance in the study of the exotic world of the "orient" or that of the "savages."
9. In his otherwise brilliant book *Natural Right and History,* Leo Strauss taunts social scientists for playing a silly game of politeness by refusing to declare the superiority of Western religions and philosophies.

10. This reading is itself "specific" because it represents a narrowing down of the expanse of one's own history within the framework of specific "interests" that are probably already cued in to the needs of a comparative study.

11. Historians use these questions to build "counterfactual trends." Sociologists refer to it as determining the "objective possibilities" inherent in a historical moment. They also use this concept for engaging in futurology. They ask: What are the likely future scenarios given the existing possibilities in our society. Creating hypothetical historical trajectories allows social scientists to determine what was—or is—in the cards.

12. We owe this invaluable indication of the desire to make definitive judgments about others to Leo Strauss. See footnote 6.

13. The current "postmodem" anthropology has attacked the myth of the objective, nonjudgmental observer as yet another fantasy of modern social sciences. Yet the result has been merely to allow the expression of personal feelings and judgments. While, probably more honest, this attitude can hardly help the cause of ethnic coexistence.

14. Admittedly, inequalities and injustices (both past and present) are the bane of any dialogue. Thus rigorous safeguards must be devised (especially by those who represent the dominant side) to prevent the reproduction of the hegemonic conditions in the course of the exchange. Even among the well-intentioned, institutionalized and prolonged disparities in power and privilege can create complex pathologies: resentment, internalized oppression, and rage on one side, and, complacence, guilt, and patronizing sympathy on the other. The many difficulties of holding a dialogue in such an environment, however, must not lead us to choose the alternative and its ghastly consequence.

Myth, Identity, and the Politics of Conviction: Participation in the Struggle for a Just World Order*

SAUL H. MENDLOVITZ AND LESTER EDWIN J. RUIZ

The fact that one is a citizen of a particular state does not detract in any way from his membership in the human family as a whole, nor from his citizenship in the world community.
— Pope John XXIII, *Pacen in Terris*, April 10, 1963

A riot is the voice of the unheard.
— Martin Luther King, Jr.

My propositions serve as elucidations in the following way; anyone who understands me eventually recognizes them as nonsensical, when he has used them—as steps—to climb beyond them. (He must, so to speak, throw away the ladder after he has climbed up it.)
— Ludwig Wittgenstein, *Tractatus Logico-Philosophicus*, London 1981, p. 189

Introduction: Mythmaking as Political Practice

Myths and mythmaking are important to peoples' lives. Myths articulate a people's history, they bridge past, present, future; they bring together reason and desire, thought, feeling and action; they hold together time and space. All cultures and societies have mythmakers—storytellers—who spin their plots and narratives to capture the texture of their peoples' lives; their hopes, fears, and joys; their rituals, traditions, and institutions. Myths and mythmaking carry the spirituality and history of its peoples. In short, "myth . . . [is] a story usually of historical events that unfolds a worldview of a people; the origin, destiny, practices, and beliefs of a people."

---

*This is a revised and updated version of a paper which was published under the title "Algunas notas sobre mitos, politica e identidad: El sujeto, el constitucionalismo global y la identidad basada en la especie," in *Paz y prospectiva: Problemas globales y futuro de la humanidad*, eds. F. Munoz, et al (Granada, Spain: Servicio de Publicaciones de la Universidad, 1994).

As stories and worldviews of a people, that is, as historical constructions of identities and practices, myths and mythmaking have always been a significant, and indeed, difficult and complex—if not contested—part of the economic, political, and cultural terrain; and it has often been said that whoever masters the commanding myth of a society controls its politics.

Of the many constructed myths that are part of the human legacy, one is of particular interest to us. Part of this myth underscores the idea that since the neolithic period—when hunting and foraging human bands settled around the great river basins and created agriculture some 7,000 to 10,000 years ago—humans have lived with, and by, the myth of a territorially fixed identity. Not surprisingly, it was also during this period that war, slavery, patriarchy, and the state emerged. And while belief, religious systems, and blood lines have always transcended territory, and while human identities will continue to be shaped by gender, status, class, occupation, and the like, this myth of a territorially fixed identity has been the commanding myth of human polity.

However, according to other interpreters of this myth, our planet is at an "axial moment," a "great transition" comparable to the period noted above, when human societies moved from an essentially nomadic-hunting existence to this essentially territorial-agricultural way of life. In fact, this transition, precisely because it is a transition, is characterized both by the breaking down and resurgence of statist myths and values in the light of profound political, economic, and cultural transformations that shape human life, leading not only through a crisis of identity, but toward the emergence of a truly planetary civilization. Human history—and the many histories that comprise it—is undergoing a process of change that puts into question not only the structures and processes of the present world system, but also the underlying myths and values that inform these structures and processes.

Moreover, at the heart of this myth is the idea that in the context of the transformations in political, economic, and cultural life in this century, we are witnessing the creation, articulation, and the implementation of a new myth of human identity. It is a myth of "a planetary people," namely, the human race that is transcending the territorially fixed identity noted above. By this we mean the capacity in each of us to identify, empathize, and act—to imagine, to use the apt terminology of Benedict Anderson—with and on behalf of the human species, and in the end, for the planet we inhabit.

It is not our intention to suggest that this myth—the myth of specie identity (or global citizenship)—was the overarching political motif of the last twenty years let alone of the next two decades. Nor are we suggesting that this myth replace all other myths of identity that have been constructed and that continue to shape human life on this planet. Rather, we want to explore different dimensions of this myth; and see how such a myth can play an important role in the creation of political practices that are adequate to the emerging global polity of our time. And while myth and mythmaking are not the usual stuff for policy consideration, we want to suggest that participating in the transformation of the structures and processes of our time may require the articulation and construction of such a myth, not so much as a mawkish, sentimental, pietistic claim for the brotherhood or sisterhood of humanity, but rather as a challenge to develop cooperative solutions for a common political life for all the peoples of the planet. In short, we want to explore the ways in which myth and mythmaking (of the kind noted above)—as *historical and contingent constructions of human identity, interest, and practice*—can be dimensions of a transformative political practice for our time.

From Philosophies of the Subject to the Practices of the Subject

The connections between philosophy and politics have a long, not to mention contested, history. In fact, one could claim without much difficulty that many of the critical political issues of our day, including the meaning and significance of transformative political practice, are being worked out in the philosophical debates of our time. For example, the recent edited work entitled, *Who Comes after the Subject?* by Eduardo Cadava, Peter Connor, and Jean-Luc Nancy, asks rather provocatively the *philosophical* question that concerns us *politically* in this essay. Seeking to come to terms with the challenge posed by both structuralists and poststructuralists concerning the (philosophical and political) status of the Subject (including questions about subjectivity), contributors to this volume may be read as suggesting that despite—perhaps because of—the profound difficulties of identifying *who* the Subject is and *what* subjectivity is, it is nonetheless important both for philosophy and politics to come to some provisional understanding, if not resolution, of the problems arising around these issues.

To be sure, the philosophical question of the Subject—which has a long contested history—is of great significance, and will continue to haunt us in years to come. Without pretending to have overcome the philosophical *aporias* of the Subject identified by thinkers like Jacques Derrida, Michel Foucault, and Jean-François Lyotard and the poststructuralists, we want to pose the question of the Subject, less as a philosophical and more as a *political* problem, recognizing that in the end, philosophy and politics are inseparable, but believing that moving through these intractable philosophical problems may very well be achieved through the constructions of political practices. What is especially interesting to us, particularly in the context of our concern for myth and mythmaking, is the suggestion, underscored by much of the literature on "critical social movements," "civil society," and "democracy and democratization," that, perhaps, the impetus for social change, if not its bearers, will be those critical social movements, what the participants of the Global Civilization Project of the World Order Models Project (WOMP) have called "global civil society." And more important, that the practices of these critical social movements are articulations, however provisional, of this myth of specie identity, or of the global citizen.

In short, while we are sympathetic with the concerns raised by the poststructural-ists noted above, in this paper we want to explore a slightly divergent trajectory, namely, from questions of "Who and what the Subject and subjectivity are?" to the question of "What is entailed in being a Subject?" Put in its political/convictional and institutional form, the question is: "How is it possible to increase the number of human beings who realize that a just world order is possible?"

Different Narratives of the Current Situation

In order to answer the question, it seems sensible to review the ways in which our contemporary global society is presently operating. Consider, in this regard, the statement of former President George Bush at the UN Conference on Environment and Development (UNCED) after he declined to sign the Biodiversity Convention and watered down the Convention on Global Climate Change: "I am the President of the United States, not the President of the world, and I will do what is best to defend US interests." Even more instructive is the statement of James Woolsey, at one time the Clinton administration's nominee for Director of the Central Intelligence Agency, during his confirmation hearings:

> Yes we have slain a large dragon, but we live now in a jungle filled with a bewildering variety of poisonous snakes. And in many ways, the dragon was easier to keep track of.

Of course, as Richard Falk observed, the dragon referred to by Woolsey is the Soviet Union and the snakes referred to are all the myriad problems we confront today: Yugoslavia, Somalia, proliferation of weapons, terrorism, to name only a few. The fact is, having left the rhetoric of the new world order, as indeed Bush himself did, the Clinton administration still sees the world, if the statement by Woolsey is any indication, primarily as a jungle of competing and dangerous self-interests.

A second narrative, in contrast to the statements of Woolsey, is what is reflected in the work of UN Secretary General Boutros Boutros-Ghali, in particular, his 1992 "Report on the Work of the Organization" and the "Agenda for Peace"—two major documents that no doubt will shape the future of the normative order. In both instances not only is there a recognition that the "healthy globalization of contempo-rary life" is critical to the preservation of local or national identities, but, more significantly, that there is a sober acknowledgment that the "time of absolute and exclusive sovereignty has passed; its theory was never matched by reality."

To be sure (written) words do not always lead to appropriate action. At the same time anyone who has had to fight the battle of words in international organiza-tions and bureaucracies is very much aware that the words stem from embodiment in the real world. They arise from interest, values, and social forces, and they may be used to promote significant political change far beyond the original expectations of the authors. The "Declaration of Human Rights" and "Helsinki Accords" are two notable examples of documents that have had this impact. So, too, are the Boutros-Ghali documents noted above.

There is another point well worth mentioning. The statement of Boutros-Ghali, in contrast to those of Bush and Woolsey, affirms the promise rather than the threat that the present offers, and the sense that the old order of narrowly defined national interests could be passing away and a new, truly global order, is emerging. In fact, it may be argued that there are, at least, two narratives of the world that are today vying for dominance. And while they are not necessarily in contradiction with one another, they certainly provide very different emphases and perspectives and imply different trajectories, on our world. They embody, in a manner of speaking, contesting images—myths, if you will—of the global polity. One affirms the possibility of a truly global polity, the other retreats into a world of national polities.

A third narrative, even of greater contrast to the first two might be called a "popular internationalism," which is deeply critical of the present world system, while at the same time, cognizant not only of the limits of "enlightened self-interest" within a statist and capitalist-driven global polity, but also of the possibilities of creating an "effective front" built on the universalist values of the Enlightenment and of the socialist movement. And while this perspective places the emphasis on the role of what we call "global civil society" in creating a genuinely global polity, it accepts, as the other narratives do, the necessity of states, as we know them, for any future global polity. As Samir Amin writes:

> A humane and progressive response to the problems of the contemporary world implies the construction of a popular internationalism that can engender a genuinely universalist value system, completing the unfinished projects of the Enlightenment and the socialist movement. This is the only way to build an effective front against the internationalism of capital and the false universalism of its value system.

An Alternative Narrative of the Present Situation

It is possible to understand the first two narratives, as simply attempts by self-interested states or international institutions to gain better access to the world's political, economic, and cultural resources. It is even possible to read these events as the triumph of pragmatic realpolitik. We refuse this somewhat jaded view. For despite the differences in these readings, a number of profound underlying themes, best captured in the third narrative, seem to present themselves, not only as lessons of history, but as constructions of an alternative human identity, the articulation of transformative practices reflecting, if not an emerging global Subject, then surely, of a multiplicity of subjects (and subject positions) that are locally situated and globally oriented. These may be stated thus: the growth of an alternative normative order; the presence of a strong transnational peace and justice movement; and the preference for, and efficacy of, nonviolent activism.

First, the balance of power system based on national interest, national security states, shifting alliances, and ultimately, the willingness to use military systems, had its own normative framework. This century, however, has witnessed the growth of an alternative normative order in which the validity—in both a pragmatic and ethical sense—of the use of large-scale organized violence has been scrutinized and found wanting not only by policy officials, but by wide sectors of the world's population. The Hague Conference at the turn of the twentieth century with its regulations on the rules of warfare is followed by the Geneva Conventions, the League of Nations, the Pact of Paris, the United Nations Charter, Article 2(4), the codification of the Nuremberg Judgment, and the many declarations, resolutions and instruments, and, the special sessions on disarmament. Worthy of note, as well, are some twenty-five NGO fora—the global citizens' initiatives: Stockholm (1972), Nairobi (1975), Rio de Janeiro (1992), and, Beijing (1995), to name only four. These are all part of that normative movement. Again, as noted above, the practice does not always follow words; but words hammered out in negotiations, dialogue, and confrontations do have impact on behavior.

Second, there has been a strong transnational peace and justice movement in this century. It has drawn upon religious and traditional belief systems throughout the planet going back two or three millennia. While there are a number of movements that have focused on coherent alternatives, both short- and long-term, for resolving disputes and curtailing violence, for the most part, most movements have waxed and waned around particular wars. But their dialogue and practices have questioned the validity of large-scale organized violence and are attracting more adherents.

Third, nonviolent activism as a preferred method of achieving radical social change is another strand in this emergent myth of the Subject. Mahatma Gandhi, Martin Luther King, Jr., early Solidarity in Poland, and other formations of "civil society" in what used to be Eastern Europe, the Filipino peoples' deposing of Marcos, the Chinese students at Tiananmen Square, among many others, all attest to the growing realization of both the limits and possibilities of nonviolent activism. Not only are they another strand in the process of delegitimizing violence, but they also contribute to an ethos where the question of how to eliminate war and other forms of violence becomes a more credible political project for those concerned with the transformation of our planet in this "axial moment" of planetary history.

The Legacy and Promise of Historical Transformation: Democratic Global Constitutionalism, Global Civil Society, and Human Identity/Interest

Perhaps, most important of all, to read the current situation in this way is to suggest, at a minimum, that the war system, militarism, as well as other forms of violence need not be forever with us; they are not inevitable. Indeed, the historical achievements of the past—the delegitimization of the divine right of kings, of slavery and colonialism, and of apartheid—all attest to the fact that, as Margaret Mead once declared, war is a human invention and can be eliminated. The "Seville Declaration on Violence" puts it even more forcefully that while aggression is part of the human condition (or what might be called "human nature"), organized warfare (and, we might add, all forms of violence) is not. That the legacy of historical transformation includes the possibility of social change will need to be part of the story, the narrative, the making of myths, in order to convince others of the desirability and possibility of constructing a world that is peaceful and just.

Within the context of competing alternative interpretations of the contemporary scene, the various strands of delegitimatizing war, militarism, and violence, as well as the rich historical traditions of dismantling oppressive structures, we would like to suggest three additional propositions that could be part of the global transformative practices for our time. These propositions not only inform and motivate our practice, they are part of the historical construction of our identities. They are: (i) "a riot is the voice of the unheard"; (ii) *"Ubi Societas Ibi Lex"* (wherever there is society there is law); and, (iii) "to think, feel and act as a global citizen is essential for analyzing, prescribing, and implementing struggles for a just world order."

The first of these propositions has its origin in the lives and voices of the oppressed, and, in fact, is initiated by the voices of the unheard. It was Martin Luther King, Jr., who observed that "a riot is the voice of the unheard." We have the responsibility to identify where the unheard are located; what their grievances, needs, and claims are; what personal, political, and institutional opportunities they have to be heard, not to mention satisfying their aspirations; and yes, we also need to honor their sensibilities and feelings with our own evaluation of the validity of these aspirations. Surely one of the major matters we will need to attend to in all of this is the riot, and the use of violence. Since we are profoundly aware of structural violence, as well as direct violence that is visited upon the oppressed, our understanding and even empathy for self-defense or counterconflict is appreciable. At the same time we need to be aware that in legitimatizing this latter kind of violence, we may legitimatize violence itself. We need to weave these perplexing and vexing dilemmas into our narratives, practices, and identities.

Democratic Global Constitutionalism

It was Machiavelli who noted in *The Prince* that "there are two methods of fighting, the one by law, the other by force. The first method is that of men [sic], the second of beasts. But, as the first method is often insufficient, one must have recourse to the second." We take it that the task is to assist in the great effort to eliminate recourse to the second. And what we wish here to note is the roles that law, the constitutive order, and democratic global constitutionalism play in the construction of our narratives, practices, and identities.

The twentieth century has been the witness to two contradictory trends. On the one hand, it ranks as one of the bloodiest, war-ridden, and violent periods of human history. World War I, Manchuria, Ethiopia, Hitler's conquest of Europe, World War II, the Holocaust, the use of atomic weapons in Hiroshima and Nagasaki, the bloody partitioning of India and Pakistan, the Arab-Israeli wars, Korea, Vietnam, the Gulf War, Yugoslavia, Somalia, Rwanda, and more, are testimony enough to horrify any human being. Simultaneously, as we tried to suggest earlier, this century has produced a normative history unique in human society, including, among other things, the attempt to control and discourage by law large-scale organized violence. In short, the international community has embarked on a normative journey to outlaw war and crimes against humanity; to make recourse to aggressive war illegal and even criminal, and barbarous treatment of citizens by state officials; indeed, to outlaw and delegitimatize all forms of violence against both human beings and nature.

Under these conditions of divergence between practices of violence and the normative claims for peace and justice, the ideas of democratic constitutionalism as the formal and contextual political/legal foundation for global polity grows increasingly attractive. Here the developments around the League of Nations and the United Nations become more interesting. For as bilateral, regional, functional, and transnational treaties and organizational arrangements expand, such developments, almost of necessity, will refashion the state system, revealing its rigid tendencies and yet suggesting alternative political arrangements within and beyond the state. No doubt this is already happening as the activities around the Declaration of Human Rights, the two Covenants, and, the Rights of the Child have clearly illustrated.

Between 1930 and the year 2000 the world's population will have tripled from two billion to more than six billion. These six billion people will be more mutually aware of one another than every prior generation of earthly inhabitants. Furthermore, the process of interdependence, integration, and intermingling are producing transnational forms and structures of economic, social, cultural, and political relations that place great pressure on the old systems and suggest the urgent need for new forms of governance and polity. The year 1995 was the fiftieth anniversary of the United Nations. Citizen organizations throughout the world are beginning to focus on how to democratize the UN and how to make it more responsive and accountable to the citizens of the globe. It is becoming increasingly clear that a profound concern for new forms of democratic governance and polity at the global level is emergent.

And so let us be very clear that what is being called for here is *democratic* global constitutionalism. We noted above the maxim in Western jurisprudence, *Ubi Societas Ibi Lex*: where there is society there is law. We strongly believe, perhaps it is even demonstrable, that global society has emerged. We dare suggest, moreover, that some form of global law is emerging. Thus, the question that remains is: What kind of law? Administered by whom? And, for what purposes and values?

Global Civil Society

The emergence of a global civil society is also important to emphasize. Large-scale transformations always bring forth new political actors and new forms of political action. Social movements, as one of the important components of civil society, are particularly significant in this respect. Indeed, it is fair to argue that these movements that are transnational in scope are the critical mass from which global civil society is emerging and being molded. These transnational movements have, it should be pointed out, dealt with individual states, i.e., the antiapartheid movement against South Africa; clusters of states, i.e., the European peace movement against NATO, and the Warsaw Pact; multinational businesses, i.e., the campaign against Nestle's baby formula program; and international organizations, i.e., alternative conferences on environment, development, women, human rights, and the like. Greenpeace, Amnesty International, and other groupings have made themselves part of this transnational civil network; and it is fair to say that many states and organizations that are targeted by these groups recognize their influence.

At the same time, our efforts need to be directed toward exploring and explaining not only the emergence of global society and law, but of community; and how, in the final analysis, we should participate—and enable others to participate—in shaping it. We start with the idea, both empirically demonstrated and philosophically desired, that community is local in origin, but global in reach. We are concerned to know how many beings—whatever their differences and diversities that we, no doubt, are willing and sometimes eager to affirm—can and should be seen also as members of one "global" community. The lessons of human history do suggest that there is a "human condition," and that it is a valid, if not desirable, starting point especially if it is sundered from some of modernity's ontological or epistemological pretensions noted above. In this context, it will be necessary to modify our maxim *Ubi Societas Ibi Lex* to read *Ubi Communitas Ibi Justa Lex*: where there is community there is just law.

Human Identity/Interest

Finally, to think of society, community, and law, and especially at this moment of history with its emphasis on participation and democracy of people is to point directly to the notion of civil society and to the role of the citizen in it. This is where the third proposition finds its place, namely, to think, feel, and act as a global citizen is essential in the construction of human identity and interest.

It is extremely difficult to conceptualize, let alone construct, the idea and practice of human identity or interest. The historical, ideological, and epistemological weight of statist construals of identity and interest seem to inveigh against such a goal. One need only survey the literatures and practices under the sign of the realist consensus to realize that identity and interest are often tied to territorially, ethnically, and linguistically bounded communities. Often, these communities understand themselves as being in perpetual conflict and competition with other communities—a trace, to borrow a Derridean notion, of a Hobbesian "state of nature." Indeed, one might point to the present conflicts in the former Yugoslavia, the former Soviet Union—to name only the most prominent—as confirmation of the resilience, if not permanence, of conflicting and irreconcilable national identities and interests. Our third proposition, some may opine, is nothing more than utopian.

To be sure, not unlike the other two, this proposition that is essential to constructing the idea and practice of global citizenship calls for much broader, deeper, and wider discussion. The problems noted above have no easy solution; and it will not do to impose yet another identity, let alone an identity that aspires toward globally oriented norms and claims, on our multilayered, multistranded lives. Yet, it is precisely because such identities often tend to overlook some of the wider (some might argue, "ecological") dimensions of human experience that we make this almost nonsensical, if not arrogant, claim. Our politics is nourished by the conviction that the notion of citizenship will have to be extended beyond its present statist-, ethnic-, and gender-based limitations. We want to suggest further that any reconstruction of the idea and practice of citizenship must be accompanied by a corresponding deconstruction and reconstruction of the ideas of identity and interest, particularly as they are construed within the discourses of the so-called realist consensus.

Such a task is not to be taken lightly. But neither are we traveling the pathways of a *creatio ex nihilo*. Indeed, this idea of global citizenship that is sustained by the idea of a human identity (as opposed to ethnic, national identity) and interest, but especially of dignity, is being constructed by individuals and groups throughout the planet.

Political Practice as Mythmaking: From a Politics of Conviction to the Practices of Struggle for a Just World Order

Participants in WOMP and the Global Civilization Project have consistently maintained that convictions about political action proceed from moral imperatives as well as practical necessities. Such a perspective arises not only from profound reservations about the adequacy of the dominant myths and values under the sign of the realist consensus to interpret human history, and to provide both the moral ground and the political will for transformative practice in the present and the future; but, also from the deep realization of the limits of human reason and passion to comprehend what might be called the *Zeitgeist* and practices of our time.

If one reviews the literatures of "future studies," international relations, and political science, particularly in the last decade, it becomes fairly clear that scholars, public policy experts, and activists failed to comprehend what turned out to be profound and extraordinary transformations in human history that coalesced between 1989 and 1992. This is not simply the result of what is believed to be an imperfect, though perfectible, social-scientific method, but rather a reminder of the real limits of the human capacity to understand and interpret the world in which human beings find themselves. Rather than seeking refuge in the Cartesian pretensions of discovering that "Archimedean point," or modernity's illusion of the quest for certainty; and, indeed, rather than capitulating to the deception that lack of knowledge must be accompanied by lack of action, we prefer to argue for a "politics of conviction" that is rooted in *practices of struggle* for a just world order.

This politics of conviction is more than belief; and while it is always personal, it cannot be individual. It is a common practice that includes the articulation of preferred objectives for an *imagined community* that is global in reach, the identification of concrete social forces and agents of transformation, and, the creation and nurture of fundamentally new and better relationships, already in existence and still to be constructed, and the institutionalization of structures and processes that will bring about the transformation—without denying the major difficulties, hostile actors, and deep structures that need to be overcome. This politics of conviction is articulated as historical and contingent practice of transformation, which include, in the language of an earlier essay, articulating a "transition strategy," or better still, transition strategies, that takes seriously those struggles for a just world order as a "defining moment" within a larger quest for human identity and interest.

We noted above that the first proposition in our alternative narrative is "a riot is the voice of the unheard." This political idea has a methodological correlate within the context of a politics of conviction. Not only is political resistance critical, indeed, integral, to the process of transformation, but the sensibility of resistance (of what Hegel may have meant by the notion of "negativity"—or its embodiment in radical critique) dislocates these logics, particularly the logics of domination. It not only underscores the contingent and precarious character of what we seek to challenge, thereby opening it to transformation, but also reminds us of our own historicity, thus creating a climate where limits are affirmed as conditions of possibility rather than signs of failure; where empathy and shared vulnerabilities shape common aspirations even as they illumine the limits and possibilities of human action.

It is in this sense that our politics of conviction, which moves beyond an uncritical Weberian voluntarism, oriented around a structurally based "ethicotheoretical decision," is nourished by a commitment and call to individuals, groups, organizations, and leadership of progressive governments throughout the planet to join in a common effort and engage in practices of struggle for a just world order. It bears repeating that we are very much aware that war, imperialism, authoritarianism, poverty, social injustice, ecological instability, and alienation are problems faced by human beings throughout the planet; that the interaction of these problems produces and reproduces a global system in which militarism is deeply rooted and where the logics of the state system often go unchallenged. It is against this background that we commit ourselves to a set of interrelated aspirations: peace, social justice, economic well-being, ecological balance, and positive identity. These aspirations are not only normative, however. They form the basis of our analytical method in comprehending our world.

We also know and take heart in the fact that there are a growing number of people throughout the entire planet who are concerned and ready to act, even to resist, to change these structures and processes. Indeed, it is worth reiterating that we are at an "axial moment" in human history, a time when the old myths of identity are giving way to new ones. There are literally hundreds, indeed thousands, of struggles attempting to create local communities as well as a global society that are inspired by the imperative to provide acceptable conditions for material living, appropriate social and political participation, an ecologically sound environment, and a polity free from militarism. We recognize that the nation-state in the Third World has been a progressive institution and does provide some protection and some security against forms of domination by stronger states and institutions. Yet we also acknowledge that this very system of states as it is presently constituted is incapable of dealing with global crises.

Principles, Images, Norms

With a global system that is at once fragmenting and integrating, and a situation that is profoundly contested, conflictual, and uneven perceptually and empirically, we are the first to acknowledge the profound difficulties in offering principles, strategies, and tactics to overcome the problems we face. This is especially problematic where claims are being made, particularly by those perceived to be in positions of privilege, about the global applicability, not to mention desirability, of these recommendations. At the same time, not only does our politics of convictions refuse to yield to the luxury of inaction; more importantly, we are emboldened by the reality that our recommendations spring forth from the very practices of participants in an emerging global civil society—which we are here seeking to articulate. "The Iowa Declaration," the full text of which is included as an appendix is one such articulation that we offer as an example of these practices. One critical point also needs to be underscored. That is, the following principles, images, and norms are not in the first instance policy recommendations, but are articulations, indeed, constructions, of particular practices—and for this reason, are to be understood as part of the process of creating and nurturing a myth of global citizenship. They are, to return to Wittgenstein, "steps . . . to climb beyond them."

In this context, we emphasize three principles that are emerging in these practices, namely, accountability, participation, and transnationalization/globalization. These three mean, for example, that it is critical

(1) to the maximum extent possible, to form decentralized units of production, consumption, and community participation; units informed by globally oriented as well as locally constructed values and practices—with some right of appeal to some unit outside this formation;

(2) to develop unique and creative forms of transnational cooperation to pro-mote global values and practices; but to engage only in those political, social and cultural projects that benefit humanity. If that criterion proves to be too difficult, select only those projects that directly benefit the lowest 40 percent of humanity in terms of material well-being and meaningful participation in decision making, and, select projects that have the capacity to mobilize between 5 percent and 20 percent of the polity in which the project will take place;

(3) to increase accountability, wide participation in the creation and manage-ment of global institutions and global problems. Here, the use of violence should be avoided, if at all possible. If used, it should be used only against targets that are themselves the direct source of oppression. Further, the decision to use violence should be subjected not only to "local" people but wherever possible to a transnational group of like-minded individuals.

Conclusion: The Myth of the Global Citizen

We are "Citizens of the World." We demand that our borders be opened. We want commercial and cultural exchange, and the right to export our labor force abroad. We want freedom to leave China in order to study on a semistudy, semiwork basis. We demand to be able to travel freely, and to take care of our prerequisites.

The Alliance appeals for support from the Chinese masses, and from human rights organizations throughout the world.

—*Manifesto of the Alliance for Human Rights in China,* 1 January 1979
(Founding members: Ren Wanding, Zhao Xing, Xing Guang, Li Guangli, Quan Wei, Song Yi, Li Wei, and two other comrades)

This essay began with a statement by that good human being Pope John XXIII, introducing the notion of citizenship in the world community. That notion coming from Pope John XXIII—even given his extraordinary moral, intellectual, and politi-cal leadership—undoubtedly elicits the response that it is the statement of an idealist—it is at best, some would argue, aspirational, and at its worst, pietistic.

The quote above deploys similar language. However, it clearly comes from a much different context. Here we have a group in struggle, facing repression and oppression, and using the terminology of citizens of the world to express their grievances and claims. This is not a mawkish, sentimental declaration of "globalists" from Western society. Rather these are individuals who are confronting one of the most authoritarian governments in the world. Beyond that, what makes their statement so revealing in terms of the emergence of the myth of global citizenship is precisely the fact that it is occurring in China. According to traditional Chinese myth, China is the center of the universe; other cultures and civilizations are expected to live accordingly, as symbolized in the ceremony of the kowtow. In utilizing, therefore, universal terminologies, these dissidents may be interpreted as revealing the extent to which the idea of a global civilization of the kind we have been exploring resides even at the center of the universe in terms of the psychopolitical visions and feelings located precisely within the center.

The statement seems so arresting that we have attempted to discover who these individuals were. While we are unable to state definitively who they were, our research indicates that none of them were "cosmopolitan" in the sense of having traveled abroad. They seem to have been relatively well educated, so their internalization of the notion of citizen of the world is one that is quite significant and instructive.

There are other illustrations of the emergence of the myth of global citizenship that need recounting. Three, in particular, may be useful. First, Jimmy Carter, on the occasion of his inauguration as U.S. President, issued a one-page statement to the world with the following introductory paragraph:

> I have chosen the occasion of my inauguration as President to speak not only to my own countrymen—which is traditional—but also to you, citizens of the world who did not participate in our election, but who will nevertheless be affected by my decisions.

That this modest, very bright person, upon assuming what could very well be the most powerful office on the planet should feel the necessity of speaking to "citizens of the world" is still another indication of the emergence of the myth of global citizenship.

Second, we should also point to the statement made by Chancellor Helmut Kohl in November 1992 in eulogizing Willie Brandt. Chancellor Helmut Kohl described Mr. Brandt as a "citizen of the world," and saluted him for having built "bridges over walls and barbed wires, bridges to our eastern neighbors, bridges between North and South." That Chancellor Kohl, perhaps the most nationalist leader in Germany since Konrad Adenauer, would characterize Willie Brandt in his eulogy as a citizen of the world in affirming, positive terms is thus all the more significant.

And finally, as we noted earlier in this paper, the emergence of a global civil society, perhaps best exemplified by those citizens' initiatives that are often local in origin but global in vision, for example, the Nairobi world conference of women and the counterconference to UNCED at Rio, all attest to the existence of the myth of the global citizen.

It is our conviction, borne of our experience in an emerging global, indeed, planetary consciousness and practice, that the myth of the Subject, is today being articulated in the practices of an emerging global citizen: one who thinks, feels, and acts, as if he or she *belongs* to the planet earth, and who imagines that she or he is *responsible* for the planet earth. This is myth and mythmaking at its best: the creation of a narrative rooted in a practice that is already coming into being as both promise and fulfillment.

The Iowa Declaration

This Declaration, which is part of an ongoing process initiated by Saul Mendlovitz and formalized in 1992, has been discussed and revised in a number of workshops and conferences throughout the globe. The program outlined below for what we call here the Movement(s) for a Just World Order is based on the view that there are five major interactive problems facing human society. They are: militarism and war; poverty and maldevelopment; ecological imbalance; social injustice; and alienation. The Movement(s) attempts to address these problems by optimizing the values of peace, economic well-being, ecological balance, social justice, and positive identity through organized political, social, economic, and cultural activities. This value framework is used as an analytical frame for understanding the global social system and thus is seen as a supplement to or perhaps even substitute for a traditional power analysis.

In addition, the Movement(s) considers this period of history to be axial—that is to say, a fundamental change is taking place in the value system(s) of human society that has enormous impact on organization, norms, and concerns. Specifically, the nation-state system, state sovereignty, and practices and notions of governance as we have experienced and understood them for the past 300 to 500 years are undergoing profound transformation.

In selecting the particular program and projects, we have attempted to take into account the vast variety and disparity in income, power, and influence among the many groupings of human beings throughout the globe.

The Iowa Declaration

WE, PEOPLES OF THE UNITED NATIONS AND CITIZENS OF THE WORLD,

HAVING MET AT IOWA CITY, IOWA, FROM 12 TO 14 APRIL 1995 AND AT OTHER TIMES PRECEDING TO CELEBRATE THE FUTURE OF THE UNITED NATIONS ON THE OCCASION OF ITS FIFTIETH ANNIVERSARY.

DETERMINED

to save the world from the scourge of war, which often in our lifetimes has brought untold sorrow to humankind, and

to reaffirm faith in fundamental human rights, in the dignity and worth of the human person, in the equal rights of men and women and of nations large and small, and

to promote social progress and better standards of life in larger freedom, and

to protect and preserve the integrity and sustainability of our earth-space environment, and

to establish conditions under which justice and respect for the obligations arising from treaties and other sources of international law can be maintained,

DO HEREBY DECLARE OUR COMMITMENT TO PARTICIPATE IN MOVEMENTS FOR
HUMANE GOVERNANCE THROUGHOUT THE GLOBE AND, IN FURTHERANCE OF THIS
COMMITMENT, TO DEDICATE OURSELVES TO THE FOLLOWING CONCRETE GOALS
WHICH, SEPARATELY AND TOGETHER, CONSTITUTE OUR COVENANT WITH THE
WORLD BY THE YEARS 2010–2020:

1. a democratic constitutional framework for global institutions on global
matters, supported by a global tax regime and including a global court system
with compulsory jurisdiction (*democratic global governance*);

2. general and complete disarmament with a comprehensive global security
structure in place under civilian control (*demilitarization/peace*);

3. global and regional human rights regimes with compulsory law-making and
law-enforcing jurisdiction (*human rights/social justice*);

4. a basic-needs regime and the eradication of base poverty and maldevelopment for all humankind (*economic well-being/development*);

5. global and regional environmental regimes with compulsory decision-
making authority and control (*sustainable ecological balance*);

AND TO THESE ENDS, CONVINCED THAT WE ARE AT AN OPEN MOMENT IN HISTORY
WHEREIN REALITY — NEVER FIXED — CAN BE SIGNIFICANTLY TRANSFORMED, AND
RESOLVED TO COMBINE OUR LOCAL, NATIONAL, AND TRANSNATIONAL EFFORTS
TO ACCOMPLISH THESE AIMS, WE CALL UPON THE UNITED NATIONS, MEMBER
STATES, AND INDIVIDUALS AND GROUPS EVERYWHERE TO TAKE JOINT AND SEPA-
RATE ACTION IN RESPECT OF THE FOLLOWING SHORT-TERM (1995–2000) AND
INTERMEDIATE-TERM (2000–2010) TRANSITIONAL OBJECTIVES AND STRATEGIES:

A. *Short-Term Transitional Objectives/Strategies (1995–2000)*
Facilitating Political Processes

1. Establish and actively participate in coalitions, cadres, and cells of concerned
citizens resolved to fulfill globally oriented peace and justice agendas for local
and national governments, including: (a) active and informed citizen participation in political processes; (b) fair, equitable, and restorative criminal justice
systems; (c) the elimination of racism, sexism, and religious and other forms
of social intolerance; (d) enlarged provision for quality education, adequate
housing, expert health care, and income sufficient to ensure every person's
potential; and (e) effective laws and policies to ensure an ecologically sound
and healthy natural environment.

2. Support individuals for office, both electoral and appointive, who commit to
the values of a just world order within a globally oriented policy framework
for the governance of their local and national societies.

3. Initate a continuing summit of the world's religious leaders, moral philosophers, and other qualified persons who are committed to global governance to develop and recommend solutions to the principal problems dividing humanity, especially the problems of war, civil and political injustice, poverty and maldevelopment, ecological degradation, and sociopolitical alienation.

Democratic Global Governance

4. Work to ensure strong financial and political support of a reformed and revitalized United Nations system that takes seriously (a) an equitable sharing of power within the UN Security Council and General Assembly; (b) faithful adherence to principles of gender equality; and (c) increased participation by, and/or representation of, citizen action organizations (CAOs, also known as NGOs), indigenous peoples, and other underrepresented groups.

5. Publicize and promote the United Nations Decade of International Law, including submission to the compulsory jurisdiction of the International Court of Justice in respect of all treaties entered into after 1994, and otherwise work to expand and strengthen the world rule of law.

6. Support the movement for an international criminal code and court to deal with individuals and groups who engage in crimes against humanity, terrorism, torture, and other heinous behaviors that fall below standards of basic human decency.

Demilitarization/Peace

7. Campaign for a five-year, 50 percent reduction of national defense budgets (redesignated "national security budgets") that will (a) significantly reduce spending on offensive weapons systems; (b) provide for peacekeeping and peacemaking training and planning as part of the military mission; (c) encourage and adequately fund economic conversion programs for defense-related industries; and (d) allocate the resulting savings to meeting basic needs both domestically and globally and to United Nations peacekeeping and other multilateral peace operations.

8. Facilitate the successful resolution of an advisory opinion of the International Court of Justice on the illegality of the threat and use of nuclear weapons.

9. Work to establish a continuing United Nations Conference on World Security and Cooperation (analogous to the Conference on Security and Cooperation in Europe) and equivalent regional forums to define and develop mechanisms and institutions for the reduction of nuclear, "conventional," biological, and chemical arms, the clearing of land mines, the regulation of the arms trade, and the peaceful resolution of national and international disputes.

10. Promote the creation of a small but permanent and reliably financed United Nations peacekeeping force both for humanitarian intervention in civil wars

and instances of genocide and for monitoring and moderating violent conflicts between States.

11. Advocate and help to inculcate a culture of nonviolence at all levels of social organization and, to this end, develop popular and institutional support for both public and private conflict mitigation and dispute resolution initiatives, including an expanded right of individual and group petition to United Nations and regional bodies, peace teams, environmental negotiations, and reconciliation projects involving interpersonal and intergroup conciliation, mediation arbitration, and other means of peaceful settlement.

Human Rights/Social Justice

12. Assist in the investigation and exposure of human rights Violations everywhere, especially where egregious State behavior is involved, and, to these ends, help especially to enforce the 1948 Convention on the Prevention and Punishment of the Crime of Genocide and to secure worldwide ratification and enforcement of the 1966 International Covenant on Economic, Social and Cultural Rights, the 1966 International Covenant on Civil and Political Rights, the 1966 Convention on the Elimination of All Forms of Racial Discrimination, the 1979 Convention on the Elimination of All Forms of Discrimination against Women, and the 1989 Convention on the Rights of the Child.

13. Work to (a) promote the work of the UN High Commissioner for Human Rights; (b) ensure that the United Nations and regional organizations receive and act on early warning of interethnic conflicts; (c) establish regional human rights courts where they do not now exist; (d) further the World Decade for Human Rights Education launched by UNESCO in December 1994; and (e) encourage all nations to develop action plans stating how they will promote and protect internationally recognized human rights.

14. Help to implement "The Nairobi Forward-Looking Strategies for the Advancement of Women to the Year 2000" of the 1985 United Nations World Conference to Review and Approve the Achievements of the United Nations Decade for Women, participate in the 1995 Beijing Fourth World Conference on Women, and support its adopted "Platform of Action" promoting equality, development, and peace.

15. Promote the work of the United Nations High Commissioner for Refugees, and, to this end, (a) facilitate strong institutional and financial support to meet at least the basic needs of the more than 50 million refugees and other displaced persons presently existing; (b) expose and help to remove the conditions of militarism and maldevelopment, among others, that produce refugees and other displaced persons; and (c) otherwise help to cause refugee and displaced person status to be only a temporary evil of human existence.

16. Endeavor to inaugurate and strengthen economic and political democracy in all societies throughout the world.

Economic Well-Development

17. Help to bring about an effective worldwide basic needs regime, supported by an equitable global tax scheme capable of maintaining it and by an appropriate monitoring and regulation of transnational enterprises, each governed by principles of decentralization of production and consumption and by maximum community participation in decision making, involving especially representatives of labor in local and national communities.

18. Strive to eradicate economic misery and maldevelopment among the world's poor by (a) encouraging radical national and international debt-reduction programs, including the equivalent of bankruptcy proceedings, for heavily indebted developing countries; (b) supporting efforts to cause all wealthy countries to commit at least 0.7 percent of GDP for genuine and appropriate economic and technological assistance; (c) working to empower the Economic and Social Council (ECOSOC) or a substitute Economic Security Council to integrate issues of Socioeconomic development and security; and (d) helping to facilitate among all global and regional developmental agencies and institutions, especially the World Bank (IBRD), the International Monetary Fund (IMF), and the International Development Association (IDA), more democratic decision-making processes and enhanced communication, coordination, and accountability.

19. Promote economic security and equal opportunity for working men and women everywhere by (a) supporting the work of the International Labour Organisation to achieve full employment, the raising of living standards, and improvements in the conditions of work; and (b) encouraging greater access to labor-intensive services in the services regime of the newly formed GATT World Trade Organization (WTO).

Sustainable Ecological Balance

20. Prioritize and act upon Agenda 21 of the 1992 United Nations Conference on Environment and Development (UNCED) and, to these ends, work to secure universal ratification of, among other agreements, the 1982 United Nations Convention on the Law of the Sea and its progeny, the 1992 United Nations Framework Convention on Climate Change, and the 1992 Convention on Biological Diversity.

21. Initiate and promote a multilateral convention against ecocide that would make it a crime, in time of peace or war, intentionally to disrupt or destroy a human ecosystem in whole or in part.

B. Intermediate-Term Traditional Objectives/Strategies (2000–2010) Facilitating Political Processes

1. Continue to establish and actively participate in coalitions, cadres, and cells of concerned citizens resolved to fulfill globally oriented peace and justice

agendas for local and national governments (as recommended in Short-Term Transitional Objective/Strategy 1, above).

2. Continue to support individuals for office who commit to the values of a just world order within a globally-oriented policy framework for the governance of their local and national societies (as recommended in Short-Term Transitional Objective/Strategy 2, above).

3. Continue to sponsor and promote summits of the world's religious leaders, moral philosophers, and other qualified persons who are committed to global governance to develop and recommend solutions to the principal problems on the human agenda (as recommended in Short-Term Transitional Objective/Strategy 3, above).

DEMOCRATIC GLOBAL GOVERNANCE

4. Further ensure strong financial and political support to a reformed and revitalized United Nations system (as recommended in Short-Term Transitional Objective/Strategy 4, above) by, among other things, charging interest on unpaid United Nations dues and assessments and taxing international arms sales, international currency trading, and the transnational pollution of the "global commons."

5. Continue to promote the world rule of law and help to strengthen the international criminal code and court recommended in Short-Term Transitional Objective/Strategy 6 (above) and established in 1995–2000.

DEMILITARIZATION/PEACE

6. Continue to support the United Nations Conference on World Security and equivalent regional forums established in 1995–2000 to facilitate arms reduction, the clearing of land mines, the regulation of the arms trade, and the peaceful resolution of national and international disputes.

7. Work to provide effective United Nations and regional monitoring, inspection, evaluation, and reporting of the worldwide arms trade and all arms transfers.

8. Strive to eliminate all nuclear weapons and all nuclear power projects that could contribute to weapons production, and work to prohibit unconditionally the development, manufacture, and testing of all nuclear, biological, and chemical weapons on a worldwide basis.

9. Help to establish "nonprovocative defense" national security systems and continue to advocate a culture of nonviolence and peaceful settlement of disputes (as recommended in Short-Term Transitional Objective/Strategy 11, above).

HUMAN RIGHTS/SOCIAL JUSTICE

10. Continue to investigate and expose human rights violations, especially where egregious State behavior is involved and, to this end, continue to enforce the 1948 Convention on the Prevention and Punishment of the Crime of Genocide and all other fundamental human rights agreements and conventions.

11. Endeavor to require all nations to develop action plans stating how they win promote and protect internationally recognized human rights and redouble support for (a) the World Decade for Human Rights Education launched by the United Nations in December 1994, (b) the work of the UN High Commissioner for Human Rights, (c) United Nations and regional efforts to receive and act on early warning of interethnic conflicts, and (d) the use of established regional human rights courts whenever possible.

12. Help to ensure that women are guaranteed equity in all policy- and decision-making offices in the United Nations and in all legislative and executive offices in government, business, and professional organizations throughout the world.

13. Redouble support of the work of the United Nations High Commissioner for Refugees (as recommended in Short-Term Transitional Objective/Strategy 16, above).

ECONOMIC WELL-BEING/DEVELOPMENT

14. Strive to ensure adequate nutrition for all people through the world and, to this end, make adequate nutrition a first call on resources and secure the establishment of a global food agency to implement the right to food that would consolidate and give focus to the diverse food programs currently in existence.

15. Work to empower the World Health Organization (WHO) to provide basic health services for all human beings, including effective, medically safe, and noncoercive family planning on a universally available basis.

16. Further support and work for a serious and effective worldwide basic needs regime (as recommended in Transitional Objective/Strategy 17, above), and to this end promote the formal establishment of, among other things, a new System of National Accounts and broader Quality of Life indicators to provide a framework and criteria for development projects funded by United Nations agencies and other international institutions.

17. Continue to work toward the eradication of economic misery and maldevelopment among the world's poor (as recommended in Short-Term Transitional Objective/Strategy 18, above).

18. Further help to achieve economic security and equal opportunity for working men and women everywhere (as recommended in Short-Term Transitional Objective/Strategy 19, above).

19. Endeavor to secure the widespread adoption of a Global Code of Conduct for transnational corporations and State trading associations that would be accountable to the values of a just world order as well as the test of profitability.

SUSTAINABLE ECOLOGICAL BALANCE

20. Continue to act upon Agenda 21 of the 1992 United Nations Conference on Environment and Development (UNCED), paying particular attention to

safeguarding the genetic and biological diversity of flora and fauna throughout the world.

21. Work to secure the universal ratification and enforcement of a multilateral convention against ecocide that would make it a crime, in time of peace or war, intentionally to disrupt or destroy a human ecosystem in whole or in part.

FINALLY, WE BELIEVE THAT, ON THE OCCASION OF THE FIFTIETH ANNIVERSARY OF THE UNITED NATIONS, THE TIME IS LONG OVERDUE WHEN OUR ENTIRE PLANET MUST BE VIEWED AS THE BEGINNING AND END OF HUMAN IDENTITY AND LOYALTY. TO THIS END, WE COMMIT OURSELVES TO A NEW GEOPOLITICAL ETHOS OF PLANE-TARY STEWARDSHIP OR CITIZENSHIP. TO THINK AND FEEL AND ACT AS A GLOBAL CITIZEN IS, WE BELIEVE, ESSENTIAL TO THE REALIZATION OF A REVITALIZED UNITED NATIONS AND HUMANE GLOBAL GOVERNANCE GENERALLY. WE CALL UPON EVERYONE EVERYWHERE AND AT ALL LEVELS OF SOCIAL ORGANIZATION TO JOIN WITH US IN THIS STRUGGLE.

The Iowa Declaration was adopted at a symposium of 240 concerned citizens held 12–14 April 1995 at The University of Iowa in Iowa City, Iowa, USA to commemorate the fiftieth anniversary of the founding of the United Nations. The symposium, entitled "UN50: Preferred Futures for the United Nations," was cosponsored by the Iowa Division of the United Nations Association–USA, the International and Comparative Legal Studies Program of The University of Iowa, the World Order Models Project (New York City), and The Stanley Foundation (Muscatine, Iowa) in cooperation with the American Society of International Law (Washington, DC), the Center for Global and Regional Environment Research of the University of Iowa, The United Nations Association–USA (New York City), and the United States Institute of Peace (Washington, DC). The Declaration originated among the organizers of the symposium and in six preparatory community forums held in Iowa and in Illinois, Jamaica, and Nigeria during 1994–95, cosponsored by the Iowa Division of the United Nations Association–USA, the Iowa Humanities Board (a State Program of the National Endowment for the Humanities), The Stanley Foundation, and the World Federation of United Nations Associations (WFUNA). For additional copies of the Declaration, contact: Iowa Division of the United Nations Association–USA, 20 East Market Street, Iowa City, IA, 52245-1728 (Phone/Fax: 319-337-7290; E-Mail: unaiowa@igc.apc.org).

A Christian Theological Perspective on Ethnoreligious Conflict

JAMES E. WILL

Introduction

This essay addresses fundamental issues in what Paul Mojzes has properly named "ethnoreligious conflicts" in his recent book, *Yugoslavian Inferno*. Responding to the terrible violence in his homeland, he first notes, "There is currently no ideology in the Balkans which matches nationalism's profound effect upon individuals and groups"; and then laments, "those who have reignited the ethnoreligious hatreds have hurled entire nations into the inferno." But it is his more sober reflection in a corresponding footnote that gives most impetus to my thought: "The challenge of grappling with nationalism's negative effects as well as *strengthening its positive effects* deserves the utmost attention of politicians, diplomats, scholars, intellectuals, and citizens in the countries of the southern Slavs and elsewhere."[1] I intend to extend his "elsewhere" toward everywhere, and to make a basic thesis of what he relegated to a footnote. My hypothesis is that we must strengthen the positive effects of the ethnoreligious factor in our common life, and in so doing turn what I call "religionationalism" toward the relational universal found at its very heart, if we are to move toward the universal peace our global village now requires.

This thesis stands in some tension with the frequently articulated view that when religion regresses toward tribalism, it provokes and rationalizes war, but when it progresses toward universalism, it creates and sustains peace. The tension, however, is very dialectical. If I did not agree that religion should help create universal forms of human community, I would not have devoted four years of my life recently to writing *The Universal God* with its subtitle of "Justice, Love and Peace in the Global Village." But I also contended for some time with the publisher to keep my preferred title of "The Universal *Relationality* of God," before accepting their commercial expertise that *The Universal God* (without relationality) is a more marketable title (which perhaps only reflects the nonrelationality of a concept so abstract as a market). I remain convinced, however, that the religious and social ethos of any of us was not created by and cannot be understood in abstract universals. The universal God has created all of us in and through *concrete* universals, i.e., finite families and communities with particular ethnicities and cultures. Thus we cannot evaluate all forms of tribalism or religionationalism as regressive, nor all moves toward universalism as progressive. Some kinds of too abstract universalism may reductively miss or too easily dismiss the concrete relational reality that takes the form of a community of communities. Nevertheless, there are terrible forms of. . . .

Xenophobic Communalism and Conflicts of Identities

There is a "heritage of horror" in the ethnoreligious conflicts in many of our histories. We know it here in the U.S.A. in the Cherokee trail of tears that typifies for us the genocide practiced on Native Americans, and in the massive cruelty of the slave trade that took millions of Africans to their deaths or to slave labor for generations. Mojzes remembers it in Europe by the village of Očevad, which literally translates "Dig-out Eyes," located where the Greek Byzantine Emperor Basil II a thousand years ago blinded 15,000 captured soldiers in Macedonia, leaving every hundredth man blinded in only one eye to lead the others home. He also reminds us that the Carnegie Commission of Inquiry in 1913 published 400 pages of documentation of the mass murder of entire villages, rapes, arson, flogging, and pillage in the Balkan wars. During World War II at least 60,000 Serb, Jewish, Gypsy, and Muslim victims in the death camp at Jasenovač in Croatia were killed, often by the primitive means of knives and mallets. And typifying the horror of the current conflict was the gang rape of a twelve-year-old Muslim girl by a tank unit of Serbian soldiers, who then tied her battered body to their tank and drove around with it for months until only the skeleton remained.[2] Just one such awful story may bring home to us the meaning of a more abstract fact like the 16,000 children who have been killed and wounded during just the siege of Sarajevo in the last several years.

What are we to make of such vicious forms of human conflict? I am struck by the insight of Vukašin Pavlovič, a political science professor in Belgrade University, that so singular a degree of intolerance and cruelty cannot be explained by any conventional notion of "conflict of interests," but arises from far more intractable "conflicts of identities," where the decisive factors are not economic or material, but derive from culture, morality, religion, values, and associated emotions.[3]

Experiences in India support Pavlovič's insight. While at conferences in Kottayam in 1974 and Bangalore in 1975, one of the gravest concerns of our Indian hosts was what they called "communalism." Given the ethnoreligious strife in India since—punctuated by the assassinations of prime ministers Indira Gandhi and Rajiv Gandhi—the urgency of their concern was more realistic than we then realized. John Ferguson has characterized Hinduism as "a vastly extended and developed form of tribal religion."[4] Though now embracing a wide variety of spiritualities and beliefs, it nevertheless demands a broad acceptance of the Hindu way of life. Mahatma Gandhi, though a faithful Hindu revered by many for his leadership that restored Indian political autonomy, nevertheless paid with his life at the hands of a fellow Hindu for advocating a political role for a Muslim minority in the new Indian Republic he did most to establish.

Motilal Nehru, more secular than his mentor Gandhi, attempted unsuccessfully to transcend Hindu "communalism" with a nonreligious rationality where religion would be respected in a secular India while restricting its political and reducing its cultural power. The religious and cultural differences that inevitably would remain in India, Nehru hoped, would be subsumed in, and moderated by, a growing and enlightened national consciousness of simply being "Indian." Communal differences were to be resolved in the interest of the common good of the whole nation. It was the failure of this policy that cost the lives of his daughter and grandson, as they followed him in the office of prime minister. For many of their fellow Indian citizens, both for good and for ill, their national identity is strongly joined with their Hindu (or Muslim or Sikh) identity, and purely rational influences pale in contrast to the spiritual power of these traditional religions.

Who of us can miss the parallels with the tragic ethnoreligious conflicts between Israeli Jews and Muslim Arabs and Egyptians that has cost tens of thousands of lives in the Middle East and caused the assassinations of Anwar Sadat and Yitzhak Rabin by fellow citizens who judged any peace process to be ethnoreligious treachery? Parallels also abound in contemporary Africa, best known in Liberia, Rwanda, Somalia, and the Sudan, compounded by the remnants of colonialism and racism best known in South Africa. But even lesser-known conflicts, like that in northern Ghana where 1.4 million people still speak sixty tribal languages, reveal the same dynamics. Here the Nanumba and Dogomba tribes have dominated the Konkombas who "sharecropped" their land. A Konkomba leader affirms his people's tribalism: "Your tribe gives you a sense of belonging, a pride in who you are and what you are." But then laments the conflict, "It only becomes a problem when one tribe tries to dominate another."[5] We must recognize both the value and danger as we discern beyond and through the vicious conflicts. . . .

The Positive Effects of Religio-Nationalism

My perspective has been profoundly affected by the peculiar privilege and burden I had during twenty-five years of the Cold War to experience and try to understand religio-nationalisms that gave identity and dignity to Eastern European peoples as they struggled with the imposed universal of international communism.

When the Georgian seminary student Dzhugashvili became Stalin in the largely Russian Communist Party, he defined that party's policy for dealing with the "nationality problem" (of Georgians and others like him) in his report to the Sixteenth Party Congress in 1930:

> We must let the national cultures develop and expand, revealing all their potential qualities, in order to create the necessary conditions for fusing them into one common culture with one common tongue. The flourishing of cultures, national in form and socialist in content, in the conditions of a proletarian dictatorship in one country, for the purpose of their fusion into one common socialist culture,

common both in form and content, with one common tongue, when the proletariat is victorious throughout the world and socialism becomes an everyday matter—in this lies the dialectical quality of the Leninist way of treating the question of national cultures.[6]

Stalin's dictatorship imposed sixty years of "peace" on the more than one hundred ethnic groups comprising the Soviet Union, but with so heavy and terrible a hand that almost nothing of the transformation or fusion he talked about in 1930 had occurred when the Soviet Union unraveled in 1990.

The Eastern Orthodox tradition of autocephalous patriarchates, where each national church has its own head, with the so-called Ecumenical Patriarch of Constantinople—unlike the Pope—being only first among equals, led to a closer "symphony" of Christianity with nationalisms in the East than in the European West. The Russian Orthodox Church, thus, is almost as Russian as it is Orthodox, and the same can be said for the Orthodox churches in Bulgaria, Greece, Romania, and Serbia. When Islam vanquished Byzantium in this whole area, their millet system augmented this religio-nationalistic tendency by assigning representative and administrative functions to the churches of the nations that comprised the Ottoman Empire. Thus for long centuries in the Byzantine and Muslim empires, the churches of Eastern Europe held their nations together, and gave them their unique identities. When Patriarch Maxim was finally able to visit Bulgarians in the U.S. in 1978 after three decades of communist rule, it is not surprising that he called on his Bulgarian faithful to "bow down with humility before the altar of Bulgarian sanctity, the heroes of spirit and self-sacrifice in the name of faith and church, of nationhood and Slavic brotherhood."[7]

The Polish people, of course, are predominantly Roman Catholic, not Orthodox. The Polish Church, however, is arguably the most national of all the Roman Catholic—presumably universal—churches in the world. They are the last, so far as I know, to have their own Primate. Though not an Orthodox patriarch, he has sometimes functioned with more "autocephaly" than the Vatican preferred. Cardinal Wyszinski, the revered Primate through most of the communist years, understood his church as the "Polish Church," not as the church in Poland. He wrote:

> Since in the temporal order the nation was the most perfect human community, it became a particularly appropriate subject for the embodiment of the universal church. Thus, with God's will, there came into existence a truly authentic "Church on the Vistula"—the "Polish Church" and not just the Church in Poland. The church formed a locus for the creative convergence of religious and secular life and, in the course of common history, developed great social awareness, close communication with the community, and a unique ability of adaptation to the changing environment.[8]

Though the national power of the Polish Church can be, and sometimes has been, misused, it played a very creative role in the events that transformed Poland during the last decades.

My sociological conclusion from such experiences is that religion has played and continues to play a dynamic and probably indispensable role in the creation of most national cultures. And my theological conclusion is that God's everlastingly repeated lure to loving and just relations, contextualized over a long history in the dynamics of a concrete society shaped by its particular history, inevitably creates tribes and nations. Christians often speak of this as the guidance of God's Holy Spirit, while Jews may point to similar guidance as the power of the Torah. To help create, recognize, and celebrate such concrete community belongs to the essential functions of religion. Thus some form of religio-nationalism constitutes the permanent memories and shall continue to help constitute the social identity of most people in our world. To miss or dismiss this reality is to imperil our concern for real peace. Yet this reality also continues terribly to endanger, if not destroy, real peace. Thus we must set it dialectically within. . . .

A Relational Understanding of Universal Peace

The paroxysm of renewed religio-nationalisms that Europe now suffers is occurring, as it were, above thousands of nuclear missiles still nestled like vipers in their underground silos and under growing ozone holes on our one and only sky. We must, therefore, find ways of mediating the concrete communal values of our religio-nationalisms to help create the religious dimensions of a universal ethos necessary for a planetary peace. Those of us who think we discern a gracious God patiently guiding our world toward a planetary culture and a universal human community—as I do—may not only deplore and resist the dynamic religio-nationalisms whose narrower loyalties breed conflict and violence at their margins, as we are often tempted to do, because they also have the spiritual power to create real community at their centers.

The power of religion to create ethnic and national communities must be appreciated if it is to be appropriated to help create a more universal planetary community. The only universal we may ever hope to help co-create is a relational universal that builds upon the creative and redemptive relations that God already, and perhaps everlastingly, has with the nations. An abstract universal is almost powerless as a substitute for the concrete universals of particular communities. Ideological universals—even those as noble as "The Universal Declaration of Human Rights"—may provide criteria for critiquing reality, but the relatively "superficial play of discursive ideas" (Whitehead) is not powerful enough to transform it. Any attempt to substitute abstract ideological universals for the concrete and contextual universals that God already has co-created with our actual brothers and sisters shall not succeed. Mahatma Gandhi put this in a more memorable way: Unless one becomes able to serve his or her family and village, there is little possibility of genuine service to a larger or more universal cause, such as a "global village."

We have suffered in this century the earlier failure of the League of Nations, and the more recent failure of the Communist Internationale, while the fate of the United Nations hangs in the balance between, as it were, the absolute sovereignties of nation states.[9] The horror of our earlier ethnoreligious wars spawned by the Reformation and Counter-Reformation led the European Enlightenment to attempt to remove God to a deist heaven, or agnostically banish "him" from any active involvement in human affairs. Euro-Americans were then left with absolutely sovereign nation-states, whose unlimited nationalisms might and did take even more idolatrous forms, and whose cultures could become demonic under the guise of being the leading edge of evolutionary progress. If we do not yet sufficiently realize the resultant horrors, we must listen even more closely to the liberation theologians from the societies who suffered their/our colonialist hegemony in Africa, the Americas, and Asia. One of the results was Europe's second "thirty years war" of 1915–45, more horrible than the first one. Its "Treaty of Westphalia" worked out at Dumbarton Oaks and San Francisco fifty years ago has thus far given us little more than the oxymoron of the United Nations, terribly understaffed and almost financially bankrupt today. It may become what humanity and history now requires, but only if we develop the religio-cultural process to help co-create the universally relational ethos necessary for its political concretion.

To put this more positively: Our contemporary spiritual task is to create a planetary ethos that responds to the *universal* relationality of God now, with as much and more insight and power as religious nationalisms have responded to the *contextual* relationality of God in their national histories for centuries past. The reality of God active in human histories cannot be banished to any transcendent deist heaven—or inward pietist heaven either, for that matter. But our cultural ideologies and demonic histories can terribly limit, and sometimes viciously distort, the scope and nature of the universal community that God would now lead us toward.

Paul Tillich, the mentor of many of us on such issues, thought he discerned a *kairos* (i.e., a time of new and great possibilities) emerging after World War I for a theonomous age that would heal the destructive gap between heteronomous religion and autonomous secular culture that had developed in Europe during the long struggle between the Enlightenment and the churches. The failure of the Weimar Republic, the rise of Nazism, the Shoah, and World War II disabused Tillich of any such hope. Indeed, his total experience of, and between, these two wars (or what I would see together as the second "thirty years war") so reversed his sense of a kairos, that when I studied with him he had concluded that we were living through a historical period he metaphorically described as "a void, an unfilled space, a vacuum":

> Little is left [he wrote] in our present civilization which does not indicate to a sensitive mind the presence of this vacuum, this lack of ultimacy and substantial power in language and education, in politics and philosophy, in the development of personalities, and in the life of communities.[10]

Part of his sense of void after World War II was his intuition that neither of the superpowers then emerging had the religious or cultural resources to meet the challenges of this new era—just as his own Germany had proven not to have after World War I. He feared a repetition in the U.S.A. and the U.S.S.R. of what had occurred in Germany, and with good reason—as our long Cold War revealed.

Ernest Koenker, studying the period Tillich lived through, concluded in his *Secular Salvations* that "the erection of the National Socialist (Nazi) spiritual center can only be understood in its relation to the breakdown of the spiritual center which Christianity provided for the heart of Europe."[11] Though that contextual Christian center had its own terrible limits, as every ghettoized Jew certainly knew, it did have a genuinely religious and moral core. The issue today, as we seek to create a genuinely spiritual center, is no longer just the peace of Europe but the universal peace of God's whole creation. There is no guarantee that any of our attempts to fill the spiritual void at the heart of our planetary culture, which thus far shares little more than the technocratic values of international commerce, will not result in some similar idolatry. We still have reason to fear that any of our attempts to make the universal relationality of God concrete through any of our particular communities and theologies could again become idolatrous extensions of one or another of our religio-nationalisms—perhaps in the form of American civil religion or a renewed Russian slavophilism. Thus I am convinced that we need to develop:

Dialogical Hermeneutics for a Universally Relational Peace

Any contextually powerful universal theology shall have to be hermeneutical (i.e., interpreting tradition in relation to contemporary culture), because it must retrieve and interpret the grace and truth that has created genuine identity in particular communities. The Jewish hermeneutic tradition is abundantly available in the rich literature of Midrash and rabbinic commentary. A Christian theology of universal peace must be grounded in Jesus' gracious power, mediated through our peculiar ecclesial and cultural communities. Though some of us may have had Harvey Cox's kind of experience when he reports, "I have often found it easier to converse with universally minded Buddhists or Hindus than with fellow Christians, who not only dismiss such people as pagans but also want to dismiss me for not recognizing it," we must also come to his further insight, that "without the radical particularity of the original revelation, we would have no faith to share."[12]

Hermeneutics, however, may either harden into polemics or open into dialogue. Increasing clarity about our own tradition more clearly defines the margins where we meet the religiously and culturally Other. And that Other, as we now have been sufficiently reminded, may be seen as a perilous threat. Hermeneutics must become dialogical, therefore, if we are to move traditional horizons toward the universal by encountering the Other at our margins with the grace and truth we have learned at the center of our religious communities.

We learn as finitely free social beings the love and justice essential to any just peace only in the kind of concrete communities that Christians find in their churches, Jews in their synagogues, and Muslims in their mosques, at their best. To that extent Stanley Hauerwas's otherwise outrageous claim is right that there is "no salvation outside the church." "Such salvation," he writes, "is not meant to confirm what we already know or experience. It is meant to make us part of a story that could not be known apart from exemplification in the lives of people in a concrete community."[13] But this should mean that love and justice may be found in many religio-cultural forms deriving from peculiar communities with particular histories. Christians may then experience the reality of genuine peace first *in* their churches, as others do in their synagogues, mosques, and temples. But we must also learn there to open ourselves to the others at our margins with the same spirit we have learned at the center of our congregations. This shall require our increasing ability to live dialogically at the margins to create justice and peace *between* our communities.

The ethos of our Christian churches then must be seen as contextually relative, given their historical bond with Euro-American culture, from the Roman and Byzantine empires down to modern colonialism. Only a hermeneutics of suspicion that reveals and helps transform whatever relationships of power and domination are hidden in even relatively good modes of thought and praxis will allow the grace and truth they also carry to become transformative in the universal ethos that must emerge at the many margins of our contemporary world. A dialogical hermeneutics must thus be informed by both a hermeneutics of retrieval and a hermeneutics of suspicion.

Conor Cruise O'Brien, who suffers the ravages of religio-nationalism in his native Ireland, traces in his *God-Land: Reflections on Religion and Nationalism* the emergence of nationalism in Euro-American cultures to the Bible, and bewails the consequences of what he calls "holy nationalism." "Nationalism," he writes, "as a collective emotional force in our culture, makes its first appearance, with explosive impact, in the Hebrew Bible."[14] And he traces how we have been trying ever since to understand its relative permanence in Israel and other societies, as well as its spasmodic virulence.

Perhaps it was nowhere more virulent in ideology and praxis in our century than in Nazi Germany. The Congress of German Christians formulated a profession of faith in April 1933 that affirmed Hitler's kind of "holy nationalism":

God has created me a German; Germanism is a gift of God. [So far, so good; but then . . .] God wills it that I fight for Germany. War service in no way injures the Christian conscience, but is obedience to God. For a German the church is a community of believers, which is under the obligation to fight for a Christian Germany.[15]

This quotation comes from the work of Salo Baron, probably the greatest contemporary scholar of the social and religious history of the Jews, in his study of *Modern Nationalism and Religion* published shortly after World War II. What first amazed and then instructed me in Baron's thought, after his people had suffered so terribly from German religio-nationalism, was his continued affirmation of its value for the faith of his own Jewish community.

Even more instructive, however, is the distinction Baron made between the *cultural* and *political* dimensions of religio-nationalism, which Conor Cruise O'Brien completely missed in his discussion. Commenting on the roots of what he calls "Jewish ethnicism," Baron wrote: "The Israelitic prophets and priests may thus be designated the first exponents of a religious and cultural nationalism, in which culture was equated with religion but in which all political aspirations were considered secondary." His interpretation goes on:

> Of course, they did not object to their people's self-determination. But they found harsh words to castigate the abuses of power politics and the monarchy, the social inequalities and the degradation of the poorer members of an essentially egalitarian community—all of which had appeared to advocates of the established order as but natural consequences of state rule and land ownership.[16]

Baron is hermeneutically instructive: The heart of biblical nationalism is the creation of religious forms of just and loving community through law (halacha as "the way"), narrative, symbols, and kerygma (proclamation of God's saving action). But such justice and peace is endangered by any undialectical affirmation of the power of Israel's or Christianity's religious or political centers. Such power, when it moves from prophetic vision to political reality, so seldom attains or maintains the servant form taught by Isaiah of the exile and embodied in Jesus that it must be critiqued by those it marginalizes, so that it will not distort or corrupt beyond recognition the grace and truth that creates the genuine community it has at its center.

Thus we must relearn or reaffirm the wisdom of the Hebrew prophets in distinguishing cultural from political forms of religio-nationalism. Only so may we use its dynamic power to create identity and community now to help create the multicultural and interreligious ethos necessary to build the more universal structures we need today. The original social matrix for all our religious symbols was tribal and national, while the contemporary matrix in which they must now be interpreted is transnational and universal. In Gadamer's hermeneutical terms, we must learn to fuse their national horizon with our moving universal horizon.

To be more specific about our own nation as we conclude, the religio-nationalism we experience in our American civil religion derives from the Puritan revolutions, which Hans Kohn cites as "the first example of modern nationalism" where a people was "roused and stirred to its innermost depths, feeling upon its shoulders the mission of history."[17] Puritan notions of God's election and providential guidance of his chosen people toward messianic fulfillment are still to be heard in the political rhetoric of our American society. It is time to be done with it in this form! Whether in Jonathan Edwards's earlier messianic view of America as "the renovator of the world" or the more recent affirmation of Ronald Reagan that the United States is the biblical "city set on a hill," let us be done with it in this religio-*political* form.

We must all learn rather to speak in the religio-*cultural* terms of our own context in a way that Patriarch Paul I of the Serbian Orthodox Church and Franjo Cardinal Kuharic of the Croatian Roman Catholic Church began to speak in the agony of their Serbo-Croatian context when they met in Geneva in September 1992. Their appeal to the faithful of their churches to meet the others at their margins was eloquent in the midst of tragedy:

> We ourselves call, individually and together, for repentance before the God of love, for conversion of service to him, that we can live anew as neighbors, friends and brothers. Peace to all!
>
> Only by practicing a dialogical hermeneutics that builds upon the grace and truth our concrete communities have experienced over centuries in the *contextual relationality* of God may we move toward the more universal ecumenical and interreligious ethos for our emerging global village that discerns and responds to the *universal relationality* of God so often distorted in all of our communities. Only then may "all the families of the earth be blessed (Genesis 12:3) through the concrete particularity of each of our communities.[18]

Notes

1. Paul Mojzes, *Yugoslavian Inferno: Ethnoreligious Warfare in the Balkans* (Continuum, 1994) p. 86.
2. Ibid., pp. 45–47.
3. Ibid., p. 61.
4. John Ferguson, *War and Peace in the World's Religions* (Oxford University Press, 1978) p. 17.
5. "The Roots of War," *The Chicago Tribune,* 26 July 1995, sec. 1, p. 8.
6. Cited in Salo Baron, *Modern Nationalism and Religion* (Harper and Bros., 1947) p. 202.
7. Spas T. Raikin, "Nationalism and the Bulgarian Orthodox Church," in *Religion and Nationalism in Soviet and Eastern European Politics,* ed. Pedro Ramet (Duke University Press, 1984) p. 187.
8. Vincent C. Chrypinski, "Church and Nationality in Postwar Poland," Ibid., p. 137.
9. See Erskine Childers and Brian Urquhart, *Renewing the United Nations System* (Dag Hammerskjold Foundation, 1994).
10. Paul Tillich, *The Protestant Era,* tr. James Luther Adams (University of Chicago Press, 1948) p. 60.
11. Ernest Koenker, *Secular Salvations* (Fortress Press, 1965) p. 157.
12. Harvey Cox, *Many Mansions: A Christian's Encounter with Other Faiths* (Beacon Press, 1988) p. 18.
13. Stanley Hauerwas, *After Christendom* (Abingdon Press, 1991) p. 37.
14. Conor Cruise O'Brien, *God-Land: Reflections on Religion and Nationalism* (Harvard University Press, 1988) pp. 2–3.
15. Cited in Salo Baron, op cit., p. 146.
16. Ibid., p. 214.
17. Cited in Winthrop Hudson, *Nationalism and Religion in America* (Harper and Row, 1970) p. xxviii.
18. I am grateful to Rabbi Robert J. Marx and Rabbi Herman E. Schaalman, longtime colleagues, for their help in shaping the final form of this paper.

Primal Violence: Illuminating Culture's Dark Side

WOLF B. EMMINGHAUS, PAUL R. KIMMEL,

AND EDWARD C. STEWART

Since 1989, international conflicts have shifted emphasis from political and economic issues to ethnic and cultural issues. The resurgence of cultural identities based on ethnicity, language, race, tradition, religion, and region has generated primal violence such as ethnic cleansing. Traditional political and economic theories have not been effective in explaining these destructive conflicts. We need new paradigms to understand the cultural variables and processes underlying primal violence. This article provides such a paradigm and uses it to examine current destructive conflicts. We show how primal violence, cultural identities, and primordial sentiments are related and suggest some new directions for research and education in this field.

Most of the theory and research on international conflict has been the province of scholars of diplomacy, international relations, and economics. Their inability to anticipate and explain today's wars raises serious concerns about their traditional, disciplinary approaches to conflict and violence. We need new paradigms to improve our understanding of destructive conflicts. Recent suggestions for approaches that emphasize cultural variables more than the traditional political and economic variables seem particularly promising (Kimmel, 1984; Soeters, 1996). In this article, we suggest a paradigm for the explication of primal violence, that is, destructive conflicts originating primarily from cultural differences. Using this paradigm, we relate theoretical analyses and historical experience through concrete cases to illuminate the relations between culture and violent conflict.

Current Destructive Conflicts

Since 1989, major political developments that began in Europe and Asia are restructuring the world from an organization of national states toward groupings of peoples, or what we call cultural states. This restructuring in part has been nonviolent (as in the formation of the newly independent states, the separation of Slovenia and Macedonia from Yugoslavia, the division of Czechoslovakia and the integration of East and West Germany). Often, however, the restructuring has been hostile and has led to violence (as in the separation of the Baltic states; the Chechnyan rebellion; and the conflicts in Bosnia, Rwanda and Burundi, Sri Lanka, and East Timor). To better understand these situations, we examine the topics of peace and war from a cultural rather than a political or economic viewpoint (Huntington, 1993). The political and economic approaches have focused on the use of force or threats to achieve diplomatic and national objectives or prevent other national states from infringing on one's national interests or security (Morgenthau, 1978). From this traditional, Hobbesian perspective, peace is the absence of active, violent conflict, usually achieved through alliances and treaties among national states that end or prevent wars (Kimmel, 1985).

We believe that the emergence of cultural states is related to a decline in the power of national states both internally, by the loss of patriotism, and externally, by the breakdown of international relations (Fukuyama, 1992; Gottleib, 1993). When national states lose the allegiance of those they govern (Kaplan, 1994), and are superseded by cultural movements of peoples whose identities are primarily grounded in existential feelings called primordial sentiments (Geertz, 1973), the individual's sense of being a state citizen (civic identity) loses prominence. Subgroups of peoples dedicated to more specific cultural identities surface with cultural imageries that idealize their group and demonize others. The current situation in Bosnia exemplifies the disintegration of identities based on the civic actualities of law and the norms of socialist ideology, and the resurgence of identities based on ethnicity, language, race, tradition, religion, and region.

The United States is one of the few national states whose populace had a civic identity before it had cultural identities. In fact, it has been argued that for the United States to prosper, "ethnic identity has to go out the window . . . The bonds of family and kinship, which have proved their savage power since before history started, have to be dissolved for this country to succeed" (Tonelli, 1994, p. 50). At the other extreme is Japan, where, until recently, the cultural state and the national state with its economic interests were identical for most citizens. The formation of any group involves the principle of inclusion that identifies the members of the group (insiders) and the principle of exclusion that identifies those who are not allowed to become group members (outsiders). The primordial bonds or cohesiveness of a people are influenced by the relative degree to which inclusion or exclusion is stressed. For example, in the United States, peoples typically emphasize inclusion of members with similar interests and expectations, while viewing outsiders more neutrally than do many other cultures. This emphasis makes these U.S. groups more open or easy to enter. By way of contrast, in Japan, the people stress exclusion. Outsiders are seen as presenting a threat to the in-group, thus impelling group members to strengthen in-group ties and dependencies. The Japanese people rely much more on myths of categorical enemies to maintain cohesiveness than do similar U.S. groups.[1] In Germany, there is a delicate balance between inclusion and exclusion because of the variety of surrounding cultures and the different subcultures within the nation.

To understand the value and authority questions that cultural identities pose for national states and their citizens requires a theoretical perspective different from the political, sociological, and economic analyses that failed to anticipate or explain the major destructive conflicts that have occurred in the last few years. The dynamics of the ascendence of cultural states based on the social actualities of ethnicity, language, race, tradition, religion, and region are not well understood, but they hold the keys to a better explanation of many current destructive conflicts. When such states cannot accommodate the demands and influences of their environment and other peoples, their negative images of the broader ecology and those other peoples become so threatening or incomprehensible that primal violence becomes an attractive option for some of their members. Primal violence occurs when peoples are mobilized in support of the survival and promotion of their primordial sentiments. Such destructive conflicts are typically more personal and inhumane than wars for economic or political advantage initiated by national states.

Peace in the political and economic sense is not desired by the initiators of primal violence. Their interest is in total domination of territory, resources, and peoples, in being able to control the future of the loser's world. Primal violence without outside intervention is waged until one adversary is eliminated or decides that it can no longer endure the suffering of its own people, and unconditionally surrenders.

A cultural analysis is needed to understand the dynamics of such destructive conflicts. Instead of considering cultural forces to be subsidiary to political and economic influences, useful only when embedded in standard historical and realpolitik analyses of war and peace, we consider culture the primary focus or the ground in our analysis, and political or economic factors, or both, as situational figures needing cultural context. To provide such a perspective and analysis, we will use a paradigm we call the *cultural trilogy* (Stewart, 1995a). This cultural analysis will enable us not only to understand the etiology of primal violence, but also to prevent or manage such destructive conflicts.

The Cultural Trilogy

Individuals acquire a personal culture through interactions with other human beings and their environments. In this process, what becomes reality and common sense for each individual is selected and internalized from their social and physical experiences. Their consciousness is constructed through their contacts with others who have already incorporated certain alternatives from those experiences. Language, customs and traditions, ethnicity, race, religion, and region all contribute to the construction of consciousness through social bonding in a process called *enculturation*. Enculturation is a synthesis of social and psychological processes that continuously change and develop to create the psychic content of the individual's personal culture. Although the locus of personal culture is the individual, the nature and quality of its cultural meanings are socially constructed.

We will use a three-part paradigm (see Figure 1) to explain the development and functioning of personal cultures. Each part of this cultural trilogy has three

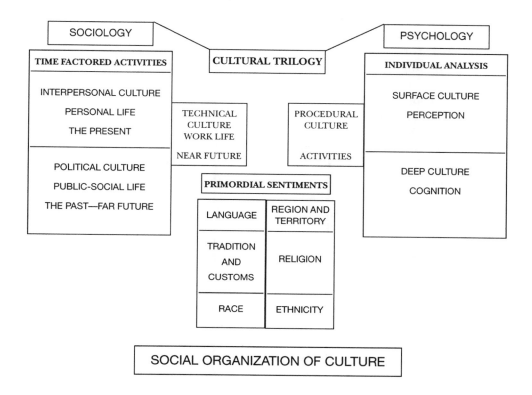

Figure 1. Social organization of culture.

synergistic aspects. The first triad provides a theory of situations, the second triad a theory of cognitive systems, and the third triad a theory of emotions and identification. The first part of this cultural trilogy deals with time-factored activities that exist in the present (one's interpersonal culture), the past and far future (one's political-social culture), and the near future (one's technical-economic culture).

Time-Factored Variations of Culture

Life as an ongoing stream of activities or cultural rhythms can be separated into the past, present, and future. The present consists of activities associated with physiological, security, and belonging necessities. These present needs and the structured activities associated with them make up the life-keeping activities of an individual or culture. Life keeping, or one's interpersonal culture, is the first synergistic aspect of the first triad of aspects of the paradigm: the time-factored variations of culture.

Interpersonal culture: Life keeping in the present. Life-keeping activities typically occur in the social context of the family and other intimate associates, and focus on routine endeavors that meet one's immediate needs. These personal activities include such things as eating, sleeping, sex, entertaining, and traveling. The experience of culture shock for travelers typically centers on experienced differences in these interpersonal relations and activities (Gudykunst & Ting-Toomey, 1988). Most people devote more time to and are much more interested in interpersonal life-keeping events than in life-making events at work, or in life-building issues concerning their state or nation. Primordial sentiments are very present and potentially arousable in the context of the individual's interpersonal activities. The cyclic rhythm of one's life-keeping activities is the bedrock for these existential feelings and their associated primordial bonding.

A society that adequately provides for the physiological, security, and belonging (life-keeping) necessities of all of its members has the potential for becoming or remaining a national state. One that does not is more likely to become or remain a cultural state, fragmented along culture's contours, especially in difficult times.

Political culture: Life building in the past and far future. Elections, national celebrations, and crises encourage the individual to identify with the political culture of the country as whole. The cultural rhythm of these life-building activities is the basis for political activities that are driven by power and status. The public environment of the political culture extends far beyond the circle of belonging characteristic of interpersonal culture. The individual enters the political culture with a dual identity: a civic identity based on nationality (American, German, Slovenian) and a cultural identity based on one or more of the primordial sentiments (an Afro-American, Prussian, Catholic). Historically, these two identities may be more (as in the United States, Japan, or Germany) or less (as in South Africa, Georgia, or Rwanda) concordant. The meanings of these different identities vary in different societies. Americans use the term to refer to idiosyncratic status as in one's personal identity or identity card. In contrast to this American stress on individuals, the Japanese have a social-centered identity structured upon the six primordial sentiments (see pp. 136–40) in unity with civil status. Japanese unity, in turn, contrasts with the complexity of traditional German identity and the diversity of identity types in contemporary Germany. For the German, identity reflects not only the dualities of the individual (as in American) and collective (as in Japanese) meanings of the concept, but also their own historical development of a civic and cultural duality. We will use the term *summit identity* to encompass the range of meanings of identity across societies.

The forms and meanings of summit identities come from a country's history as delineated by epochs. The use of this time form for reconstructing the past has the potential to arouse the primordial sentiments, especially when political leaders consciously bring these sentiments to the attention of their constituents (as happened in the former Yugoslavia). Under these circumstances, life-building activities focused on selective historic recollections arouse the power and identity interests of ethnic groups and lead to primal violence. For example, the civic identity of most Croats today has become secondary to their cultural identity in terms of Western Catholicism, region, and especially ethnicity, as these have been activated by the destructive conflict with the Serbs. The Serbs' summit identity in this conflict is also primarily ethnic, as well as traditional, regional, and Eastern Orthodox (Kaplan, 1994, p. 22). The focus of Croats and Serbs on cultural identities helps explain the primal violence in Bosnia (Kaplan, 1994, p. x).

Technical–economic cultures: Life making in the near future. Life-keeping activities are cyclic, with an emphasis on the present. Life-building activities are epochal, with an emphasis on the past and far future. In life-making activities, the time form is linear and the emphasis is on the near future. These activities typically occur in the workplace, require maximum effort, and focus on technical–economic endeavors that emphasize achievement and control by specialists and workers. There is little place for primordial sentiments in the technical–economic culture of life-making activities. By providing the cultural rhythm for problem solving, decision making, negotiation, and other processes of the procedural culture (see the second triad following), life-making activities can synthesize life-keeping and life-building activities of the individual. The more affective political and interpersonal cultures can be rationalized and integrated through the technical–economic culture. This integration is most likely when the cultural identities of different peoples in a national state are largely shared in both their daily lives (interpersonally) and their celebrations (politically), as in the United States. Otherwise, the procedural cultural activities may be too specialized and impersonal to integrate the richer life-keeping and life-building activities of an individual or nation.

The technical–economic culture has the potential to create violence, however. War has become work of a highly technical nature, employing sophisticated weapons for wounding and killing. When the cultural state coincides with the national state (as in the case of Japan or Germany in World War II), war assumes a moral quality that sanctions and rewards the military in the name of the national defense or aggrandizement. This type of integration of the interpersonal and political cultures through the technical–economic culture leads to maximum destruction.

The second part of the cultural paradigm deals with the psychological realm of analysis. Like the more sociological time-factored activities, this part of the cultural trilogy also has three synergistic aspects: the surface culture of perception, the deep culture of abstraction, and the procedural culture of action.

Psychological Analysis of Culture

Surface culture: The "what." The metaphor *surface* suggests the perceived features of all the items encompassed by the surface culture, such as the sounds of the language, nonverbal expressions, ways of dress, artifacts, art objects, and many other events and objects that qualify as the "what" of a culture. Perception brings these people, items, and events to the individual as images. To create these images, the brain first constructs a pattern registering the intensity of the sensory stimulation, called an impression, followed by a cartoonlike caricature of the object that is called a schema. The schema becomes an image with some depth called a prototype, which is compared with reconstructions of other images that have been perceived in similar contexts. This prototype becomes the constructed image, which has two features critical for the social perception of surface culture. First, the identity of the image emerges from a comparative judgment of past events and people in the perceiver's life, and second, the final image is colored by the needs, feelings, and beliefs that have entered into the perceiver's selection of the schema and the prototype. Thus, the individual's final perceptions are always embodied and contextualized; they have value.

Visual perception is an object-centered sensory modality used to construct objects. The vase I see sits firmly on the shelf as an object that is neither dispersed in space nor seen inside the perceiver's body. Whereas vision, hearing, and touch are all object-centered modalities, the sense of kinesthesis conveys an impression of movement and of the body. The most objectless sensory modality is that of pain. Pain also conveys an impression of bodily reality and of the body as a container of experience (Scarry, 1985). These distinctive features of pain and kinesthesis make them primary in the formation of body image and the combining of emotions and cognitions. It is in the nature of pain to find expression in negative emotions.

Pain is unique among the sensory modalities in that it lacks a center in the brain. A consequence of this pain physiology is that the primary qualities of the experience are those of aversion and desire for privacy. The greater the pain, the greater is the sufferer's sense of being alone. Intense pain destroys language, invades consciousness, and fills the brain with its own unbearable sentience.

Pain also warns the biological organism against dangers threatening its integrity. The objectless pain arouses anxiety that focuses on the agent threatening the organism. Through emotional and cognitive elaboration this pain and its associated anxiety readily acquire meaning in the surface culture.[2] The threat and meaning of pain are often elaborated by responses based on the emotion of fear (Stewart, 1995b), responses that convey emotional isolation and withdrawal. Fear creates a symbolic spatial structure that restricts movement into the social spheres of life, a narcissistic state of monism in which the world presses in against us.

Being objectless, pain exists in a frame with imagination and is available to leaders who want to transform pain into political meaning (Staub, 1990). The social management of pain through punishment instills discipline and can harden individuals to the use of violence and destruction. Pain and punishment are often used culturally in rites of passage and initiations or in preparation for battle. The pain associated with war can also be transformed by political leaders into the nationalistic serving of one's country.

Deep culture: The "why." The metaphor *deep* suggests concepts that underlie and interpret surface culture by providing an antithesis. The deep culture is made up of abstractions that are universal, unlike the surface culture that contains contextual features, accidental properties, and the emotions of perceptual experiences. Three transformations of perception form deep culture: (a) the particular identity of the percept is transformed into schemata that, in turn, are transformed by the refinement of their abstract features into systems of images and concepts; (b) the emotions and intuitions of perceptual experience are transformed into logic and reason based on cognitive forms; and (c) the logical ordering of refined images, concepts, and reason become systems of universal attributes. These transformations of perception into the universal abstractions of deep culture can best be character-ized in the individual's personal culture as styles of thinking, systems of knowledge (epistemologies), and constellations of values. These systems, styles, and constella-tions underlie and influence the everyday processes of perception that characterize the surface culture and activities in the interpersonal culture.

For example, social experiences of pain in one's interpersonal culture (e.g., in punishment) can convert the usual fear responses into anger in the deep culture, which associates pain with structures based on the emotion's physiology. Anger noticeably increases body heat and blood and muscular pressures. It also increases physical agitation, and interferes with perception. When we are angry, we narrow our conception of others into a dichotomy of the oppressed and the oppressors. The person who has become the target of another and has been angered takes the moral high ground—often in the role of a victim—while the perpetrator becomes an oppressor who deserves to be held responsible for the consequences of the anger unleashed. Thus, responsibility for deeds committed out of anger become the responsibility of the provoker of anger, not the victim.

The violent or dark side of culture is often first experienced when pain is used to redeem and discipline recalcitrant and nonconforming individuals. From the experience of pain and the associated emotions of fear and anger, individuals form moral imperatives that generalize to other events in their surface and procedural cultures. The scenarios for fear, anger, violence, and war are often related. Each can begin with a concrete offense that constitutes an injustice. Justice can best be restored by an act of retribution by the victim, who has a right to anger, with the oppressor serving as the target of the retribution. Because anger is insatiable, it is not unusual for retribution to escalate to violence and war. In the Western world, moral imperatives are often based on such an epistemology of right and wrong; but in Japan, the epistemology of moral imperatives usually oscillates between harmony and chaos. Because pain is not the only source of experience for forming moral imperatives, it is likely that other sensory impressions (besides pain) and emotions (besides fear and anger) explain differences among moral epistemologies from deep culture to deep culture.

The deep culture is distributed among all members of a people and is detached from any utility in real time or space, although it motivates both surface and procedural manifestations of culture. When individuals are made or become more conscious of their deep cultures, they become aware of the relativity of their styles of thinking, systems of knowledge, and constellations of values, and thus are better able to communicate with and understand individuals who have different cultural backgrounds and personal cultures.

The third aspect of the psychological triad of culture provides the abstract deep culture with more context, and furnishes a synthesis between the surface and deep cultures for the individual. This is the procedural culture.

Procedural culture: The "how." Procedural culture combines surface and deep culture in the individual and community by bringing context, intentions, purposes, objectives, and goals into experiences. Procedural culture involves activities and processes that occur in real time. This real time can be the present or, more often, the near future of the technical–economic culture. Some of the more important of these activities and processes are communication, problem solving, negotiation, and decision making. Procedural culture is the core of personal culture, the recipes for how to do things.

In relation to the dark side of culture, for example, there are in all societies bodies of learning and procedures on how to use pain in discipline and authority and how to commandeer the fear engendered by this pain in the service of political and social control. The organized use of terror and informing under Stalin and his subordinates aroused fear and anger in the people of central and eastern Europe in this century. These emotions became the impetus for joining Communist Party cells and work groups that provided a sense of security and comradeship in the midst of the people's fears of authority and punishment. Mass killings, genocide, and other forms of primal violence were incorporated into the patterns of interpersonal behavior performed by average citizens through the use of pain, fear, and anger in the procedural culture.

International negotiation styles illustrate different emphases on the three cognitive aspects of personal culture (Kimmel, 1994). Table 1 lists differences in German, Japanese, and American styles of negotiation as described in the research literature. In terms of this second triad in the cultural trilogy, it is apparent that in their face-to-face meetings the Japanese emphasize a procedural cultural style, the Germans a deep cultural style, and the Americans a surface cultural style. This is not to suggest that all three groups do not also understand and sometimes use other styles in their international meetings, but that there is a learned preference for different approaches to negotiation. All three different psychological levels of culture are always present in our cognitive systems. What differs are our cultural emphases in specific situations.

The Japanese, and to a lesser degree, the Chinese, often stress the actions of procedural culture. Germans stress deep culture and tend to theorize about how to get things done. Japanese attachments to methods and procedures contrasts with the German deep-cultural emphasis. Both in religion and in knowledge, the Japanese concern is more for what has to be done and for the style of doing it,

TABLE 1

Cultural Styles of Negotiation:
German, Japanese, and American Emphases in Negotiating

	German	Japanese	American
Primary purpose	To ascertain abstract truths	To establish and cement relations	To solve current problems
Target	Conversion	Consensus	Compromise
Before meeting	Logical examination of history of issues	Building support for feasibility	Brainstorming, finding options
During meeting	Arguing for ideas and positions	Showing ceremonial consensus	Evaluating by anticipating outcomes
After meeting	Assertion of authority	Rapid implementation of positions	Persuasion of decision makers
Valued information	Correct concepts and theories	Rules and precedents	Empirical data
Style of talking	Serious, critical, direct and certain	Formal, exclusive, indirect, cohesive	Informal, inclusive, frank and open
Valued traits	Knowledge and rhetoric	Graciousness and connection	Competence and creativity
Form of closure	Document with legal recourse	Oral agreement subject to change	Oral or written final agreement
Conflict tolerance	High	Low	Medium

less for beliefs or logic. The original Japanese religion is Shinto, and to be a Shintoist is to do Shinto things, not to hold Shinto beliefs (of which there are few).

Although the activities and emotions associated with procedural culture are more concrete and more available for analysis than are the abstractions of deep culture, they are still too general to assist us directly in our cultural analysis of primal violence. To reach the level of specificity that will allow such analysis, we must examine the primordial sentiments that provide a social organization for one's personal culture. Our social actualities and their psychological correlates, the primordial sentiments, comprise the third part of our cultural trilogy—the social organization of culture.

The Social Organization of Culture

The social actualities of language, ethnicity, customs and traditions, religion, race, and region evoke existential feelings or emotions called primordial sentiments (See Shils, 1957) during the individual's enculturation. These emotions are the basis for social connections called primordial affinities or bonds. Primordial bonds and sentiments are not in themselves good or bad, but they are the source of constructive (patriotic, humanitarian) and destructive (nativistic, xenophobic) behaviors with regard to others within and across cultures. Their specific development in a given people depends on ecological and social history.

Primordial sentiments exercise a pervasive influence on personal culture that is difficult for the individual to detect because they generate an internal sense of normality (e.g., in the use of one's native language). Only when these normative social actualities are distorted or contrasted with other social actualities does the arbitrary nature of one's own primordial sentiments and bonds become apparent. For example, in the United States, because of the influences of immigration, the frontier, and the slave trade, the primordial sentiments of race, region, and customs and traditions were predominant in the formation of the early American identity. After the Civil War and the closing of the frontier, the influences of region and customs and traditions gave way to a civic identity for most Americans, with race still an important primordial sentiment in contemporary America.

Given the strong civic influence in American identity, we shall look to Germany for examples of the potency of the six primordial sentiments to affect national life. Although the influence of these sentiments has lessened since 1946, they all have exercised a significant influence on German summit identity.

The Analysis of Social Actualities and Primordial Sentiments

Ethnicity

The members of a family are usually bound together by bloodline, physical resemblance, customs and traditions, and a common fate. When these relationships are examined in the context of a society, those individuals considered to belong to the same lineage (family name) become part of a community that may extend to ancestors, tribes, and clans. Thus, in some form, all socialized individuals (except perhaps the extremely marginalized) inherit the primordial sentiment of ethnicity.

For example, Germany has been the settlement area of different Germans who formed ethnic or tribal associations (Franconians, Saxonians, Alemans). Tribal characteristics often form the bridge for communication among ethnic groups who trace the heritage of a person by their name and start conversations by jokingly mentioning the respective stereotypes. In the current process of European unification, tribes are a resource for overcoming national borders (Alemans living in Germany and France; Frisians in Holland, Germany, and Denmark). Tribes are connected with regions, but they live together in one federal state. Huguenots have been assimilated from France, and workers from Poland are integrated into the Ruhr district. Minorities in Germany such as the Danes in Schleswig-Holstein and the Serbs in Brandenburg are entitled to a special parliamentary status. Although these ethnic groups are reminders of past wars and changing borders, they do not currently activate resentments.

Race

Personal belonging and identity also includes body image. Inherited physical characteristics such as facial features, head shapes, height, weight, skin color, color and texture of hair, and proportion of limbs are clustered among different groupings of humans, including families. Clusters of individuals with common physical features form the basis for the social actuality of race. Race may be introjected as a primordial sentiment in cultures that think of themselves in terms of this social actuality (e.g., the people or the race) or projected to others in cultures that think that race applies only to groups other than themselves. Anglo-Saxons with individualistic self-concepts (e.g., Americans, Australians, and English), project race onto others, especially Blacks. Arabs and Japanese, with self-concepts rooted in their interior life, introject race and stigmatize those not of their race for their inferior traditions, customs, and religion.

Although Germany was formed from different tribes, these were not seen as different races, but rather as different peoples (*Voelker*). The race question in Germany concentrated on the Jews inside Germany and the Pan-Slavistic movement outside Germany. Russia's policy of Pan-Slavism threatened the German tribes, whereas the Jews were seen as not wanting to participate in the integration of German tribes and states into one Germany. Hitler talked of a Jewish attitude of mind (*Geisteshaltung*) that he saw as wedded more to international affairs than to German development. Anti-Semitism was widespread in Europe. In the Third Reich, Jews were the categorical scapegoats being portrayed as capitalistic, communistic, nonpatriotic, and so forth.

Hitler's ideology was Darwinistic. Investigations were made of blood and body types to classify the races. The concept of race discriminated against the Jews for domestic purposes. In foreign policy, race included other nations such as Iran and Afghanistan. The idea of an Aryan race rather than a German race was developed to promote international relations among Aryans (including Scandinavians) and to recruit volunteers from other nations to the German side in World War II.

Language

The vocabulary and grammar of the family's native language, as well as their linguistic style of communication, become a key part of the family members' identities. The linguistic universe of the individual, which goes far beyond the family, is the social actuality most closely related to the individual's ways of thinking and reasoning in his or her deep culture. Individuals who speak the same native language and dialect share the social actuality of that language. Among many cultural groups (e.g., the Arabs), language serves as the primary marker of cultural identity and primordial sentiment.

During the time of the Holy Empire of the German nation, language became important to the feeling of belonging. The name German (*Deutsch*) literally means national (*Voelkisch*) in the sense of the colloquial language of the common people (as opposed to the educated Latin speakers). As the German national state formed, language gained importance for establishing cultural identity. The German language, which became the common language of educated people during the Reformation, was less related to the national state than to the German culture. For example, the German language ties together German literature in different states (Austria, Switzerland, Germany, the Czech Republic). The German dialects form an emotional tie for Germans living in different regions and outside Germany (Belgium, Poland, etc.). Language defines both regional and high culture for the German today.

Customs and Traditions

The customs and traditions of one's family, ethnic group, race, and language group extend into all areas of individual life and to all of the cultural rhythms. They include the rules and norms for living together that give content to the surface, deep, and procedural cultures of the individual. They are learned over a lifetime. Traditions provide precedents and antecedents for proper adaptive behavior and conformity with cultural styles and standards. They center on the interpersonal culture. Customs provide the collective habits and social manners for members of the group to interact with others. They center on the political culture.

Germany is rich in customs and traditions. These are related to the seasons (*Oktoberfest* in Bavaria), to the church and religion (*Karneval, Fasching*), and to national movements (riflemen tournaments). Some events are embedded in the tradition of the guilds (*Schaffermahlzeit* in Bremen, Winefests of winemakers). Besides these singular events, there is a tradition of regular meetings of associations, especially singing and sports associations.

German holidays are mostly religious and differ in number from state to state and region to region. They are in part Protestant and in part Catholic. Secular holidays also differ from time period to time period, such as the Emperor's Birthday during the time of Wilhelm II and the Führer's Birthday during the Third Reich.

Religion

Religion springs from the anguish of humans over the impermanence of their lives and the inequality among individuals, their commitment to the sanctity of life, and their fear of death. In some form, all human groups develop an idealized model of human relations and derive from it a moral imperative for regulating human affairs (e.g., Confucianism) and for coping with suffering, death, injustice, and destruction (e.g., Christianity, Islam and Judaism). Families pass on their religion by example and teaching. The primordial sentiment of religion is seen in ideal human relations, moral imperatives, and a view of life that extends beyond one's own life span.

The force of this primordial sentiment has both constructive and destructive potential. Its power comes from traditions. It is embodied in the faithful members of the culture and in artifacts and events. The emotional primordial sentiment of religion is transformed into a social ethic through scholars in organized religions such as Confucianism, Judaism, and Christianity. In today's world, the social ethic of organized religions has been embodied in secular social values.

Religion has been important throughout the history of Germany. The competing interests of the organized church and civic institutions in German identity raised social tensions at different points in German history. The power of the church has declined over time, yielding to state and civil institutions. In the First Reich there was a struggle between the Emperor and the Pope; in the Second Reich between the church and the civic legislature. In the Third Reich, Hitler managed the church by a Concordat with the Pope in 1935 and the establishment of a German Protestant Church.

In post-World War II Germany, the church was involved in public decisions. The West German *Ostpolitik,* for instance, began with a memorandum of the Protestant Church and was discussed in Protestant academies. In the German Democratic Republic, the churches were a refuge for opponents of the state and were the core of the 1982 peace movement. Church structures of administration remained officially in place. Even when the state structures of the German Democratic Republic and the Federal Republic of Germany divided, informal contacts and assistance never stopped.

The church is still strong in Germany and connected with the state (church taxes are collected by state authorities). Churches run kindergartens, hospitals, welfare organizations, and counseling offices. Religion defines region and tribe in part and is associated with different identities (Catholic vs. Protestant).

Region

Region is the broadest of the social actualities, as region may be characterized by geography, economy, or any of the other social actualities. The social actuality of region signifies primarily the means of survival provided by the nature of the region, its people, and economy. When a country is more a national state than a cultural state, the social actuality of land is often called territory rather than region. Regional contours refer to cultural areas, whereas territorial boundaries refer to political states when they become internalized as primordial sentiments.

Germany has a long tradition of a national identity within changing borders of territory. The First Reich covered an area from Sicily to the North Sea, divided into numerous states that had regional unities. After the Napoleonic Wars, territory became more important for the national state. Whereas France tried to establish natural boundaries (e.g., the Rhine river), the Germans included all the regions where German peoples lived.

The Second Reich did not include all German speakers (Austria was excluded) and contained other ethnicities (e.g., Poles). During the Weimar Republic, parts of the Rhineland were occupied by France and the Saar was annexed by France, activating the sentiments of belonging in the Germans in this region. Territorial questions, such as the identity of ethnic Germans living outside the borders of the German Reich in Czechoslovakia and Poland, also became an issue. The discontinuities between territorial and ethnic identity, provided Hitler the idea of a people without space (*Volk ohne Raum*). German territorial claims were accepted by other European national states that believed in territorial self-identification. Hitler regained the Rhineland without fighting.

The territorial questions of World War II were not settled until 1990, after a return of the Saar area from France to Germany in 1955, complete integration in 1959, and the abandoning of former territories in the East. Ties with ethnic Germans in Poland and the former Soviet Union developed in accordance with a minority policy in these countries. Today, German emigrés are returning at an annual rate of about 200,000.

Region determines primordial sentiments within Germany. There is a sense that Germans from the sea region differ from Germans in the hills and in the mountains. Differences in the geography call for differences in the surface culture, such as architecture. These regional differences were considered in creating the federal states that resulted from the division of Germany into occupational zones (e.g., Nordrhein-Westfalen). An article in the German constitution calling for an examination and reorganization of the federal states activates strong sentiments in those regions wishing their own administration and government. The framework of European unification (especially the Maastricht treaty) emphasizes the participation of German federal states as regions in the new Europe.

German regions can also be differentiated according to their traditional food and drink (wine, beer, potato, noodle areas). There are dishes that are typical for special areas and for special occasions in each area. Regional holidays are often an attraction for Germans living elsewhere who come to visit Germany.

Primordial Sentiments, Identification, and War

The power and relevance of the six social actualities (i.e., language, ethnicity, race, religion, territory, and customs and traditions) and their primordial sentiments for social organization and identification vary widely from place to place, time to time, and group to group. Constructively used, primordial sentiments provide anchors for a stable identity that is a precondition for creating respect, equality, and cooperation among individuals, as in modern Germany, where the former West is supporting and cooperating peacefully with the former East. Used destructively, primordial sentiments can lead to unstable identities requiring the kinds of confirmation that promote bigotry, arrogance, and violence among individuals. The formation of cultural identities about primordial sentiments without the parallel or subsequent development of civil identities has led to primordial violence in today's world. The potential of these emotions to demonize race, ethnicity, and religion, in particular, have transcended the life-keeping and life-making functions of culture for some individuals and led to suicide bombers, terrorists, and assassins as seen recently in the Middle East.

Cultural Identification

As individuals are socialized, they learn to center their judgments around values and procedures fundamental to their own culture. Other cultures and their assumptions serve to define the limits of one's own cultural group and its norms, especially in places such as Europe, where a number of different cultures are in proximity. In addition to learning that there are differences between one's own cultural group and other cultural groups, children also learn that the values, norms, and procedures of their people are natural and therefore better than other peoples' values, norms, and procedures; that they have the superior ways of handling the tasks of human existence. The cultural comparison of different groupings produces a judgment of in-group superiority and out-group inferiority. In some cultural states, the outgroups are seen as nonhuman (or having no culture), rather than having a different culture. These judgments are an outcome of the emotions of belonging (primordial bonding) and the formation of cultural meaning focused on the in-group (cultural identification).

A cultural identity is grounded in one's immediate community and kin connection, as well as in being born into a particular religion, speaking a particular language and dialect, and following certain customs and traditions. These congruities of blood, speech, land, and so on have an ineffable, and at times overpowering, coerciveness. This coerciveness involves personal affection, practical necessity, common interest, and incurred obligation, but is due primarily to the significance of the ties or bonds themselves. Primordial bonds flow from a sense of natural (or perhaps spiritual) affinity that transcends interpersonal culture (Geertz, 1973, pp. 259–60).

Thus, the roots of cultural identity in everyone are primordial (Stewart, 1987). The bridge between the social and personal culture is the identification process. It is this process that binds people together as cohesive groups and peoples. Associations based on primordial bonds create fellow feeling and a consciousness of kind that separates members from those who are different. There are other possibilities for individual identity formation beyond one's primordial roots, of course, but the primordial groupings of family and local community come first in the individual's enculturation (Volkan, 1992). Only later does the process of socialization provide other means of self-confirmation.

The effects of cultural identification also vary with the social and psychological situations of cultural groups. When a people is satisfied with its life-keeping activities and feels secure, there is less tendency to attack "outsiders" (beyond the aggressiveness sanctioned by the national state). In national states that have accommodated differences in primordial sentiments among their citizens, the peoples expect to continue their present situations into the future (through their children). Political activities in these countries include programs designed to improve and enhance the life conditions of the entire populace according to the dominant social norms and structures (e.g., the American dream). The hopes engendered by these life-building activities diminish life's inevitable personal discontent and pain, which otherwise accentuates primordial bonding and conflicts. Rather than being preoccupied with the dangers and uncertainties of the present and the ills and injustices of the past, peoples with a positive future (political culture) based on a satisfactory present (interpersonal culture) within their national state can work together toward political and economic goals and visions. They see themselves as belonging to countries having a public interest, striving for the common good. This optimistic point of view allows them to tolerate and even appreciate a range of cultural differences in their societies. Cultural identification takes on a positive social function in such hopeful civic states. It gives a positive summit identity to its citizens (patriotism) and encourages them to share their traditions and customs with others, including those from different cultural and national states.

However, when a people's physical or psychological security is severely threatened, their primordial sentiments heighten cultural differences so that cultural identification serves a negative social function: the promotion of their group values, norms, and patterns of thought at the expense of those of other groups. When a people are threatened or, more accurately, perceive themselves to be threatened, or when they have been humiliated (as in the case of Germany after World War I), there is a tendency for them to rigidly venerate themselves. Individuals with weak or negative civic attachments look to their primordial sentiments, which can be in opposition to their national states (as in the former Yugoslavia). Often an enemy is sought to serve as the focus of the fears and anger of the threatened or humiliated people. Peoples whose identity depends on the less flexible social actualities of subgroups with their feelings of kinship rather than on the more adaptable civic actualities of the national state with its emphasis on community, are less equipped to deal with today's rapidly changing economic and political conditions. They are rooted in the past. Lacking a vision of development and progress at the near edge of their future (their technical culture), these peoples fixate on past wrongs and retribution. In difficult political and economic times, other cultural states or peoples are readily seen as threats. Political leaders can encourage peoples to become defensive and intent on getting even. Pain, fear, humiliation, and frustration are followed by anger and a desire for revenge and inflicting pain that leads to primal violence in such cultural states. During such destructive conflicts, a people's feelings about other peoples become more negative, evaluative, and unchangeable. They develop stereotypes that denigrate and dehumanize outside groups and exalt themselves.

Yugoslavia Today

Until recently in Yugoslavia, the peoples' summit identity was orchestrated by Tito's government. Tito was responsive to the different peoples in his country. To restrain the political dominance of any group, he enacted a double constitution in 1948. One part of the constitution fixed the political boundaries within the country and the other concentrated on its cultural contours. There were sometimes contradictions between the political boundaries and cultural contours. For example, the political region known as Croatia included more peoples than just ethnic Croatians, and not all Croats lived in Croatia. So in addition to the state of Croatia, Tito also created a union or cultural nation of Croats. Likewise, all other ethnic groups (Serbs, Bosnians, Slovenians, etc.) had both a political region and a cultural union under the 1948 constitution. Consensus was to be reached by all members of a political region before an action (such as declaring independence) was taken. Only Slovenia, which was culturally homogeneous, ever reached such a consensus. Neither the political regions nor the cultural unions in Tito's Yugoslavia were very strong or stable, but until his death, the socialist ideology and procedural culture served to inhibit their differences. The national state was stronger than the potential cultural states.

Tito's ethnic policy restrained primordial sentiments in Yugoslavia, but he was unable to prevent the development of political parties that permitted ethnic groups to dominate after his death. The political situation was worsened by economic hard times when the bills came due for Yugoslavia's economic expansion in the 1960s and 70s. The richer republics, Slovenia and Croatia, carried much of the burden of paying off foreign indebtedness. Their economic resentment led to their declarations of independence from Yugoslavia in the early 1990s (Ignatieff, 1993).

After Tito died and his Communist government and economy eroded, many of the citizens of Yugoslavia took a renewed interest in their ethnicity (the cultural unions) and religion (Orthodox, Catholic, Muslim). As life-keeping resources became scarcer, former friends and citizens began to realign themselves culturally and to forsake their interethnic political and civic ties. As historical and territorial issues became more predominant (due to their association with ethnic and religious identities), regional and language differences were reactivated and added to ethnicity and religion as being central to people's changing allegiances and identities. Outsiders were no longer the non-Yugoslavians, but those with a different ethnicity, religion, or language. Insiders were not necessarily Yugoslavians, but those who could be identified in terms of a given ethnic, religious, regional, and linguistic background or history (Pecjak, 1994).

Encouraged by ethno-politicians, cultural identities and allegiances that had been controlled under the double constitution surfaced, replacing former civic identities such as Yugoslavian, Communist, and coworker. Ethnicity was defined in a divisive form by political leaders who benefited from exploiting differences among peoples. They objectified ethnicity and gave it negative meanings (Pecjak, 1994). The stereotypes held by different primordial groups in the Balkans today are often of this negative type: "Those destroying Bosnia are sick from history—from half-truths and ethnic prejudices passed from one generation to the next, through religion, political demagoguery, inflammatory tracts, and even, through abuse of folk song and tales" (Butler, 1992, p. C3).

In Yugoslavia distorted stereotypes and intolerant cultural identities led to primal violence, through pain, fear, and anger. Revenge and warfare are reshaping the physical and social landscape of this country, creating refugees and ghost towns. The peoples involved in primal violence see themselves as victims and their adversaries as oppressors. Primordial bonding in these cultural states provides peoples with antagonistic senses of identity and encourages them to separate themselves socially and physically from all those who are not culturally like themselves (become more exclusive). Even the more tolerant individuals lose their affinity for pluralism as destructive conflicts escalate and protract. Positive images and emotions give way to negative as relatives are killed or become refugees.

The Yugoslavian example is extreme, but the gradual erosion of national states based on political and social ties and the growth of cultural states based on ethnic, regional, religious, traditional, linguistic, and racial identities is occurring through-out the world. In Europe, only Iceland and Denmark are currently free from the tensions that come with the activation of primordial sentiments and the divisive negative identities and stereotypes associated with them. In Asia, only Japan is principally free of political fault lines caused by primordial sentiments. There are, of course, many nations whose political leaders work to channel their citizens' primordial sentiments away from destructive conflict. Perhaps the best example in Europe is Switzerland. Today, five different peoples live together in Switzerland in viable political integration. In Asia, Malaysia has developed a balance between Chinese business and professional groups and Malay farmers, politicians, and land-owners. In the Americas, the United States and Canada with their pluralistic tradi-tions have accommodated differences among many ethnic, religious, racial, and linguistic groups. These differences and the tensions associated with them are becoming accentuated as special interest groups based on primordial sentiments become more dominant, immigration becomes more controversial, and the na-tional economies and political systems in both countries weaken. American political integration is questioned, whereas Canada is somewhat unsettled by the French-speaking separatist movement in Quebec.

War

Ethno-politicians in cultural states are not the only force fomenting primal violence. National leaders and scholars who contend that war is an extension of national policy and diplomacy believe that there are winners and losers in international wars and that the losers will give up resources or beliefs when they are defeated. This view of domestic and international relations in today's world of cultural states fuels primordial sentiments on all sides and encourages revenge, dehumanization, and primal violence. Equally pernicious is the idea that war is an inevitable historical process inherent in the human condition. From our viewpoint, there are no "good wars," nor are wars inevitable.

Wars can begin as primal violence (Yugoslavia) or can become more cultural than political over time (World War II),[3] calling forth primordial sentiments in the participants. What begins as a tactical political policy (diplomacy by another means) and a plan to protect the groups in power, increasingly often becomes primal violence requiring total victory. In general, political-economic wars are becoming less frequent, whereas cultural-ethnic wars and primal violence are multiplying (Gottleib, 1993). The American-Iraqi War (known as Desert Storm) began as a political-economic war: Violent conflict was managed by the governments of powerful Western nations with minimal cultural ties to the Islamic state of Iraq. Political and economic peace (an absence of active conflict) was imposed when the war ended with the surrender of Iraq. However, many Islamic states saw this war in terms of primal violence: the godless Westerners against the true believers (Stewart, 1991). Security in this region today involves a precarious balance of power among religious cultural states and Western national states with civic ties based primarily on law. Recent attacks on Iraq by the United States were not supported by many of their allies from Desert Storm, suggesting that the potential for primal violence remains high.

In recent destructive conflicts among and within cultural states, the organized, technologically managed warfare of national states, exemplified in Desert Storm, has been replaced by primal violence. Hostilities that were formerly a part of political cultures of national states, controlled by public life, have shifted to the interpersonal cultures of cultural states and impact primarily on personal life (see Figure 1). Because of the pain inflicted on civilians in such hostilities, the enemy becomes inhuman and portentous. There are fewer rules and standards in such destructive conflicts than there are in national wars. Primal violence engenders fights to the finish with demands for unconditional surrender or total annihilation. There is little likelihood of a cease-fire, truce, or armistice, and no real interest in alliances, treaties, sovereignty, or the rules of war. The use of torture and massacre is frequent when ethnic cleansing and genocide become key objectives (Suedfeld, 1989). There are attacks on noncombatants, including murder, rape, starvation, and incarceration. These painful experiences strengthen the cultural identities of those who follow the demagogues that foment such primal violence.

A dilemma that arises for societies that legitimate the use of force to settle conflicts is the maintenance of internal law and order. They must deal with the aggression they create in socializing their members to fight and in training them for wars. Good participants in primordial violence come to prefer cultural identification over civic. They learn to regard those they are fighting as less worthy and less human than themselves. These stereotypes easily carry over into the denigration of other cultural groups within their own society. They often make bad citizens (as we see now in Afghanistan and El Salvador) while good citizens (who value cultural pluralism and civic identification) often refuse or fail to participate in primordial violence.

Without a greater understanding among peoples that neither ethnic cleansing nor winning wars are possible in today's world, and that everyone loses in the primal violence and cultural aftermaths generated by these seductive deceptions, the potential for primal violence within and among cultural states will increase.

The Cultural Trilogy and Primal Violence

Key questions that emerge from looking at primal violence from the perspectives of the cultural paradigm are: "how do individuals' primordial sentiments interact with the life-keeping, life-making, and life-building activities of their culture to produce cooperation and conflict; and are certain interactions involving different sentiments and situations more likely to produce primal violence than others?" Geertz (1973) suggests that whereas "economic or class or intellectual disaffection threatens revolution, . . . disaffection based on race, language or culture threatens partition, irredentism, or merger; a redrawing of the very limits of the state" (p. 261). The strong association anthropologists have noted between *Gemeinschaft* societies and life-keeping rhythms suggests that certain social structures and cultural processes promote cultural identities. *Gemeinschaft* societies, united primarily by primordial bonds of clan, religion, race, regionalism, tradition, and language, are likely to suffer more fracturing in times of trouble or political change than Gesellschaft societies, united primarily by civic ties of politics and economics (Soeters, 1996). The vision of the future and the radius of interdependence in the latter type of societies extend further, providing for more deliberate responses to life's difficulties (Fukuyama, 1995).[4]

All societies must meet the basic life-keeping expectations of their members to survive. The assessment of whether these expectations are met will vary from culture to culture. When enough resources are felt to be available, it is possible for peoples to develop and employ the more civilly oriented life-building and life-making rhythms of culture. But when these resources or the political and economic organizations needed to utilize them are lacking, destroyed, or unevenly distributed, civic discontent can lead to cultural identification and primordial bonding, as it has in Bosnia. At such times, aspiring political leaders can stir up primal violence by focusing on life-building activities at the state level and life-keeping activities locally. In East-Central Europe and much of Africa and Latin America, centralized economies have failed to meet the expectations of their citizens for a physical and social environment that provides primordial feelings of place, belonging, and security (Kaplan, 1994). Political failures, demagoguery, and primal violence in places like Georgia and Rwanda can be understood from this cultural perspective. In terms of our trilogy, such destructive conflicts are based on failures to meet the life-keeping expectations of peoples strongly united by primordial bonds.

Empirical work is needed to ascertain the point at which civic discontent is actually superseded by destructive conflict in these circumstances. Is it true, for example, that the more limited the life-keeping resources, the greater the danger of primal violence, as in Rwanda? Or is it a perceived decline in these resources that is more volatile, as in Georgia? Which of the six social actualities or combinations thereof is most likely to be associated with primal violence in times of scarcity, the religious and regional as in Bosnia, or the racial and linguistic as in South Africa? What role do leaders of cultural states play in forestalling or promoting primal violence in different situations?

What about societies based more on shared purposes and common ethical codes and values (moral imperatives) than on primordial bonds? How do these civic societies deal with shortfalls in the basic life-keeping expectations of their members? What will happen in the United States, for example, if a majority of the citizens find themselves unable to afford health care or housing? Will demagogues turn their civic discontent to primordial discontent and cultural identification (an "us against them" perception that some analysts see on the horizon), or will political and technical-economic organizations and leaders find ways to reframe or restructure such situations so that these voices are dismissed? Which social actualities will demagogic leaders emphasize to move peoples toward destructive conflict? How will civic leaders cope with any incipient tribalism? Even when life-keeping expectations are met in civic societies, it is possible to instigate some groups to fear outsiders who may threaten their standard of living or way of life, as can be seen in recent actions and policies involving immigrants in Europe and the United States. Which kinds of groups can be most easily affected by demagogues in a civic society?

In short, when and why do patriotism and sacrifice or bigotry and greed dominate difficult situations for different peoples? Do newer national states (e.g., Australia) or immigrant countries (e.g., the United States) have an advantage over those with longer histories and more entrenched primordial bonds in avoiding or controlling primal violence? The theoretical and research questions that flow from the cultural paradigm are intriguing.

In addition to analyzing and predicting primordial violence, we believe the cultural trilogy can be used to assist in peacemaking and peace-building efforts following destructive conflicts. It can help structure the dialogue among contending parties so that each can see where their activities, beliefs, and emotions fit in the paradigm and where the activities, beliefs, and emotions of their adversaries belong. Having such a framework for classifying the behaviors and ideas of protagonists can be of great benefit in overcoming cultural identification and facilitating discussion. Cultural differences can be better understood and analyzed within this common paradigm.

Conclusion

We recommend the use of the cultural trilogy as a geometry of critical cultural perspectives to understand and ameliorate destructive conflicts. This paradigm is a replacement for the more familiar disciplinary or single-issue approaches that have been used in the past to explain such conflicts. The trilogy helps us know where we are in the process of understanding and overcoming destructive conflicts.

We think that the primal violence taking place in many parts of the world today is best described as a result of the disturbance of the balance and integration of the time-factored activities—life keeping, life making and life building—within a society's procedural culture. Because procedural cultures are based on their society's primordial actualities, such disturbances can enable demagogues to use the primordial sentiments to instigate destructive conflicts. Just as our paradigm suggests that there is no single explanation of such conflicts, we also believe that there is no single solution to their management and resolution (Emminghaus, 1994). Peace-building efforts must restore symmetry to the time-factored activities through training, education, reconciliation, and economics (Emminghaus, 1995).

Notes

1. See Volkan (1992, pp. 6–8) for a more psychoanalytic interpretation of cohesiveness.
2. Anglo-Americans see pain as information about the individual's body, whereas Italians see pain as the disruption of interpersonal life. There is a Western metaphor that sees passions as uncontrollable beasts that are dangerous to awaken.
3. It was not until February 18, 1943 that Goebbels declared a state of total war.
4. The European Union is striving to become a *Gesellschaft* society that incorporates a number of more *Gemeinschaft* cultures.

References

Butler, T. (1992, August 30). The ends of history: Balkan culture and catastrophe. *The Washington Post, Outlook,* p. C3.

Emminghaus, W. B. (1994). Durch menschlichkeit zum frieden-konfliktlösung als alternative zu zerstörischer gewalt [By humanity to peace-conflict solution as an alternative to destructive violence]. In Deutsches Rotes Kreuz (Ed.), *Mit-menschlichkeitgegengewalt* (pp. 68–75). Bonn, Germany: Arbeitshilfe.

———. (1995). Kultur-kontakt und konfliktlösung: Psychologische aspekte in der interkulturellen beratung [Culture-contact and conflict-solution: Psychological aspects in intercultural counseling]. In A. J. Cropley, H. Ruddat, D. Dehn, & S. Lucassen (Eds.), *Probleme der Zuwanderung* (Vol. 2, pp. 114–145). Göttingen, Germany: Verlag für Angewandte Psychologie.

Fukuyama, F. (1992). *The end of history and the last man.* New York: Free Press.

———. (1995). *Trust: The social virtues and the creation of prosperity.* New York: Free Press.

Geertz, C. (1973). *The interpretation of cultures.* New York: Basic Books.

Gottleib, S. (1993). *Nation against state.* New York: Council on Foreign Relations Press.

Gudykunst, W. B., & Ting-Toomey, S. (Eds.). (1988, Autumn). Culture and interpersonal communication. *Sage Series in Interpersonal Communication,* 8.

Huntington, S. P. (1993). The clash of civilizations? *Foreign Affairs,* 72(3), 22–49.

Ignatieff, M. (1993). *Blood and belonging.* New York: Farrar, Straus and Giroux.

Kaplan, R. (1994). The coming anarchy. *The Atlantic Monthly,* 273(2), 44–76.

Kimmel, P. (1984). "Peace and Culture Shock: Can Intercultural Communication Specialists Help Save the World?" *Abstracts, Tenth Annual SIETAR Conference,* 1–4

Kimmel, P. R. (1985). "Learning about Peace: Choices and the U.S. Institute of Peace as Seen from Two Different Perspectives." *American Psychologist,* 40, 525–41

———. (1994). "Cultural Perspectives on International Negotiation." *Journal of Social Issues,* 50(1), 179–96

Morgenthau, H. J. (1978). *Politics among Nations: The Struggle for Power and Peace* (fifth ed.). New York: Knopf

Pecjak, V. (1994). "War Cruelty in the Former Yugoslavia and Its Psychological Correlates." *Politics and the Individual,* 4(1), 75–84

Scarry, E. (1985). *The Body in Pain.* London: Penguin

Shils, E. A. (1957). "Primordial, Personal, Sacred, and Civil Ties." *The British Journal of Sociology,* 8, 130–45

Soeters, J. L. (1996). "Culture and Conflict: An Application of Hofstede's Theory to the Conflict in the Former Yugoslavia." *Peace and Conflict: Journal of Peace Psychology,* 2, 233–44

Staub, E. (1990). *Roots of evil. The psychological and cultural origins of genocide.* New York: Cambridge University Press

Stewart, E. C. (1987). "The Primordial Roots of Being." *Zygon,* 22, 87–107

———. (1991). "An Intercultural Interpretation of the Persian Gulf Crisis." *International Communication Studies,* 4, 1–47

———. (1995a, March). "The Cultural Triology." *Newsletter of Intercultural Studies,* 21. Chiba, Japan: Kanda University of Cultural Studies

———. (1995b). "The Feeling Edge of Culture." *Journal of Social Distress and the Homeless,* 4, 163–202

Suedfeld, P. (Ed.). (1989). *Psychology and Torture.* Washington, DC: Hemisphere

Tonelli, B. (April 17, 1994). "The Amazing Story of the Tonelli Family in America." *Los Angeles Times* magazine. pp. 24–30, 46–50

Volkan, V. D., M.D. (1992). "Ethnonationalistic Rituals: An Introduction." *Mind and Human Interaction,* 4(1), 3–19

·2·

APPLIED
PERSPECTIVES

Each of the authors in this section attempts to increase the likelihood of coexistence between groups in situations of conflict by making important refinements to conventional methods used to decrease conflict.

Michael Walzer uses Israel as a case study in ethnic conflict. He describes the millet system, a holdover from the Ottoman Empire in Israel, which allows each religious community to run its own courts and system of education without creating a common culture, and which prevents Israel's national minority from finding its history mirrored in Israel's public life. Since the only thing these groups share is their common citizenship, Walzer looks to the democratic arena to provide the context for coexistence and advocates a common civic curriculum in the schools with a carefully elaborated philosophy.

Yehuda Amir explores the contact hypothesis in ethnic relations. He tests the assumption that intergroup contact reduces intergroup tension and prejudice. He refines this hypothesis by specifying the conditions under which contact between groups is likely to reduce tension and prejudice.

Louis Kriesberg's contribution to the refinement of conventional conflict-reduction methods is his clear and forthright definition of the nature of coexistence activity. Through clarifying the use of terms in the field, he makes the implementation of these concepts more accessible.

Building on empirical generalizations and on what has been called "theories of the middle ground" in the social sciences, Morton Deutsch advocates the development of a set of psychologically valid skills. These skills, when used by disinterested third parties, can help those directly involved arrive at constructive solutions to the conflict.

Jay Rothman, on the other hand, stresses the importance of the person engaged in intervention. His contribution to conflict resolution methods is to highlight the significance of true engagement to the process of intervention by those engaged in this work. Their role is central and Rothman argues that it should be engaged in self-consciously.

John Paul Lederach reinforces this position and points out that those engaged in coexistence work need to demonstrate a capacity for disaster management.

Lederach creates a series of heuristic devices constituting an inventory of factors to be considered to insure that the postconflict stage does not degenerate once again into active conflict.

The six articles included in this section utilize very different kinds of data to illustrate their points. However, whether the starting point is empirical, quantitative, or conceptual paradigms of analysis, all the authors are concerned with the application of available knowledge and insights gained from the past. These insights are then critically examined. The articles offer, in very differing ways, a refinement of coexistence methodologies.

Education, Democratic Citizenship, and Multiculturalism

MICHAEL WALZER

1

Arguments about democratic citizenship and education in a multicultural setting have to begin with a description of the setting. I don't mean only a list of the different cultural groups or a report on the last census (how many identified members of each group?) or a map of their residential concentrations or dispersions. We also need an account of the history that produced this specific assortment of "cultures" and of the institutional arrangements that have determined the character of their coexistence. Obviously, this account must be particularized, focused on *these* groups, coexisting in *this* time and place. But I want to begin with three ideal-typical accounts. For reasons that will soon become apparent, I shall turn to the particularities of Israeli multiculturalism only after presenting these three.

The first institutional history is that of the old empires and (some of) their successor states. Here the different cultural groups—nations and religious communities—were brought together through an ad hoc process of dynastic expansion: conquest, purchase, marriage, and so on. Sometimes the imperial elite tried to impose its own language and culture on all its subjects (czarist Russification is the most obvious example), but more often it was content to divide and rule—that is, to maintain the different groups in their differences, allowing them considerable autonomy in exchange for their acceptance of imperial hegemony. Thus there developed the millet system of the Ottomans, for which we could find many analogues in ancient Persia and Rome, in medieval Europe, in the various caliphates of the Islamic world, and in the European colonial empires.[1] Autonomy is by no means a singular arrangement: it takes very different forms. It can be regional or functional in character; it can encompass a wider or narrower range of communal activities; it can extend or not extend to the use of coercive power (including capital punishment). But it does have a singular effect: it gives legal standing to the various groups and so requires individuals to identify themselves with one or another of the groups and submit to its laws—most particularly in matters of family life, marriage, divorce, inheritance and so on; often also in matters of education.

The second institutional history is that of the modern nation-state, which virtually always incorporates a number of "national minorities." Nation–states have been variously formed, sometimes through long-term processes of consolidation (France, Italy, Germany), sometimes through partition (Pakistan), sometimes through liberationist or secessionist struggles against the old empires—all of these carried out under the aegis of a nationalist ideology, asserting the right of this group of people to govern themselves in accordance with their own history and culture, in their own "homeland." National minorities are simply smaller groups, usually associated with majorities elsewhere, whose members find themselves—so they are likely to think—on the wrong side of the border when the border is finally drawn. They now encounter a state that reflects and upholds the culture of the majority nation, making its language the language of public affairs, enforcing its calendar, celebrating its holidays, teaching its history in the public schools. Minorities sustain themselves as best they can in their families and voluntary associations. The state is sometimes tolerant and even supportive of these efforts, sometimes not. In either case, its aim is the cultural survival and well-being of the majority, while it makes no strong commitment to the survival of minority cultures.

The third institutional history is that of immigrant societies (the United States is only one among a number of cases, though I will draw upon its example in the account that follows). These societies take shape through the arrival of settlers, one by one or family by family, gradually displacing or subordinating an indigenous population. Perhaps one national group is dominant early on, the first settlers coming from the same "old country," but this dominance is unstable given a continuous flow of immigrants. Soon there are many "old countries," and many immigrant cultures in the new land. The state is forced into a kind of neutrality, which is first expressed in religious toleration and secularism and then in a slow disengagement from the national history and cultural style of the first immigrants. The disengagement is always partial and incomplete, which means that some newcomers find the public life of the country more familiar and congenial than others. Nonetheless, in principle, all the immigrants, including the first ones, must sustain their religious and cultural life, their national memories and customs, by themselves: the state is committed to none of them. It celebrates only its own history, creates its own holidays, and teaches in its public schools the general values of toleration, neutrality, mutual respect and so on—not the particular values of any of the groups its citizens form.[2]

To each of these three institutional histories there corresponds an (ideal-typical) set of educational arrangements. In the old empires, barring "Russification" programs, each of the autonomous communities organized its own schools and planned its own curriculum—sometimes with public support and one or another degree of public regulation. The successor states are likely to be wary of so radical a decentralization, taking education as one of their own prerogatives. But they, too, insofar as they are still nationally or religiously pluralist in character, must plan different curricula for the different communities or allow them some room for the teaching of their own history and culture. The language of instruction, at least for some part of the curriculum, will be the communal language, even if the language of the political center is required more generally.

Nation–states, by contrast, impose a national curriculum and a national language (France provides the best example of this: the Minister of Education is said to know at any moment in time what every schoolchild is reading). A unified school system presses a single history and culture upon its students—even if it rarely reaches to the radical curriculum proposed by Rousseau, who held that nothing but this single history and culture should be studied.[3] Minority cultures socialize their children at home or in private schools or after-school programs. In immigrant societies there is also likely to be a single public school system, which ignores all the constituent cultures or struggles, in the contemporary multicultural fashion, to give equal time and space to each of them. Many national and religious communities, the latter especially, run their own schools in competition with the public system or in addition to it, imposing extra hours of education upon their children.

2

These are ideal-typical accounts, as I have said, but Israel's specificity consists in the fact that it partakes in all of them. The pattern of its internal differences is highly complex because it is constituted by all three of these different institutional histories. Israel is triply divided. First of all, it is one of the successor states of the Ottoman Empire (the succession mediated by the British Empire), and it has retained the millet system for its various religious communities, allowing them to run their own courts and providing a (partially) differentiated set of educational programs in two languages. Secondly, Israel is a modern nation-state, established by a nationalist movement, and incorporating a substantial "national minority." Members of the minority are citizens of the state, but they do not find their culture or history mirrored in its public life. And, thirdly, Israel's Jewish majority is a society of immigrants, drawn from every part of a widely scattered diaspora, an "ingathering" of men and women who have in fact, despite their common Jewishness (itself sometimes subject to dispute), very different histories and cultures. Educational arrangements reflect this complexity, so that the schools have different and not entirely consistent aims: sustaining differences, both religious and national in origin; fostering a single national (Zionist or Israeli) consciousness; and incorporating and naturalizing immigrants, teaching mutual respect and self-respect.

No doubt, other countries enjoy or endure other sorts of complexity. But this combination of histories and institutions makes for an extraordinary intensification of difference among what is after all a fairly small population occupying a fairly small space: three religions (corporately organized, though each of them is in fact divided into subgroups); two nations; and many ethnicities. Since no one is likely to claim that these differences can be overcome or transcended, it is necessary to think of ways of living with them. In the United States, many people believe that all the immigrants will eventually become "Americans," forging a single identity through residential dispersion and social intermixing and intermarriage. Perhaps the same thing will happen to Jewish immigrants to Israel, Ashkenazim and Sephardim, Latin Americans, Moroccans, Russians, and Ethiopians emerging one day as Israeli Jews simply. But the long-established on-the-ground national and religious differences will not go away, not even over the long haul. How can they, then, be accommodated?

The only thing that all the different groups share is a common citizenship. They vote in the same elections; they obey the same laws (except for family law); they pay the same taxes; they participate in the same arguments about what the state should and should not do. Because Israel is a democratic society, the way is open for what might be called a "strong" citizenship, and indeed the rates of political participation and the levels of political understanding, among all the different communities, are quite high relative to other democracies.[4] The quarrels that difference generates have, so far at least, strengthened political commitment rather than producing alienation and withdrawal. So there is this commonality to work with—and the work is urgently necessary. Commonality has to be fostered and enhanced, because the same differences that make for political commitment also make for intolerance and zeal. No doubt, these latter qualities are intensified by Israel's international environment, but they have much to feed on at home. There are so many people toward whom one can be intolerant: ethnically, even racially, different Jews; secular and religious Jews; secular and religious Muslims; Christians, Muslims and Jews; Arabs, Druse, Circassians, Armenians . . . and Jews again. Can it be any help that all these people are also Israeli citizens?

Certainly, the democratic arena is very different from civil society with its multiple divisions. Even if political parties reflect social differences, they are at the same time driven by the logic of the arena to look for votes wherever they can find them—and then in the bargaining that follows the voting to make whatever deals are necessary in order to form a government. No one can govern without soliciting votes from the body of citizens, each of whom has only one to offer. If a narrowly ideological (religious or nationalist) partly focuses on a single group of voters, it cannot enter a government without negotiating with other parties differently focused. If it does not compromise its ideology in order to win votes, it must do so in the search for coalition partners. However difference is marked off in civil society, it must be bridged in the political arena.[5]

If we are interested in coexistence, then, the arena is a good place, despite all the shouting that goes on within it—and it could be a better place if the noise level were kept down. What that requires is simply (or not so simply) that the participants, all the activists and militants and their more passive, but no less opinionated, followers learn to think of one another as *fellow* citizens and to accord to one another the rights that democratic citizenship entails. They do not have to like their fellow citizens or attach any high value to their traditions, practices, and opinions. The fellowship of citizens does not have to be particularly warm. It is an alternative to, not an expression of, communal solidarity. We can hope that political participation will create over time a sense of mutual attachment, the recognition of common interests, even some degree of patriotic pride. But all this will come, if it comes, *over time,* the result of a process we might best think of as educational.

But the success of this process cannot depend only on adult education, which is notoriously chancy. Adults, I suppose, are at the lower end of the learning curve;

they have learned a lot already, and much of what they have learned does not help them to function within a fellowship of citizens. Democratic education must begin with children. That is chancy, too; we probably have less faith today than we once did in the effectiveness of schools. Children learn from their parents, and from their peers, and from the mass media, as much as, perhaps more than, they learn from their teachers. But they do learn something from their teachers, and so we have to pay attention to what the teachers teach. What should be required in an education for democratic citizenship?

3

I shall assume the existence of segregated schools on roughly the present Israeli model—that is, with national and religious groups largely separated and the various Jewish ethnicities integrated (except insofar as they are divided by religious and secular commitments). I leave aside class divisions, since the story I want to tell is complicated enough. Democratic education is probably best carried on in integrated schools, which anticipate the integration of the political arena. But a multiply divided society with a complex imperial/nationalist/immigrant history is unlikely to achieve anything like a full-scale integration, not now, when all the histories are, as it were, immediate and resonant, and not in the foreseeable future. Any effort in that direction would only outrage the constituent communities, each of which seeks to control, so far as it is able, the education of its own children. If it cannot shape the curriculum entirely to its wishes, it will still insist that whatever is taught be taught to *this* cohesive group of children—setting limits, that is, on personal if not mental associations. How else can communal survival be guaranteed?

So, every cluster of segregated schools will aspire to reach a particular set of students and teach them a particular history, culture, religion, and so on. Multiculturalism will then be a feature of the educational system as a whole, not necessarily of any particular school—though the world of secular liberals and leftists, committed in principle to pluralism, might generate a more local multiculturalism (in practice, Israeli secular liberals and leftists appear to learn very little about the life of religious Muslims or Jews). There are certainly good reasons to insist that all the students in all the schools should be taught something about the "Others," their fellow citizens, but it seems to me even more important that they be taught, first of all, something about citizenship itself.[6]

A common civic curriculum is necessary (and therefore ought to be legally required) for two reasons: because the state also has to do what it can to guarantee its survival, to produce and reproduce citizens, to ensure that the various particularist identities coexist with a more general identity; and because this more general identity provides the best possible motive for a sympathetic understanding of the various particularisms. Democratic citizenship in a divided society makes for a politics of difference, and people who come to value this kind of politics will, one can hope, want to know something about the differences that it encompasses.

The civic curriculum itself will not be multicultural—though when it is introduced into nationally or religiously focused schools, it may well represent the first suggestion of a different way of life. For democratic citizenship is not a neutral idea; it has its own particular history, and it points toward its own (political) culture. No doubt, its study will more easily be accommodated by some schools than by others. It is more likely to be resisted by some teachers than by others. A serious education in the commonalities of citizenship will require an uncommon political struggle; state officials will have to use their coercive powers—above all, but not only, the power of the purse. Now, what is it that they should insist on? Obviously, they must not be satisfied with some innocuous and soporific course in good government. Much more is necessary; I would suggest three critical requirements.

First, a *history* of democratic institutions and practices from ancient Greece forward—and, alongside this, an honest engagement with the Jewish (and Muslim) predilection for nondemocratic forms of government. It is, I suppose, difficult to determine just how honest this engagement ought to be. Consider, for example, the argument of a number of Zionist scholars, seeking to construct the best possible national history, that the government of ancient Israel, before the monarchy, was a "primitive democracy" of tribal elders.[7] This is not a claim, it seems to me, that can withstand critical scrutiny, but it is, as such things go, relatively harmless. If it makes possible what we might think of as the naturalization of democracy within a tradition that otherwise favors the rule of kings or priests or sages, why not include it in the curriculum? I am inclined to prefer the critical scrutiny: include the argument about the elders only if one also includes the counterargument denying their "democratic" character. After all, democracy is a culture of criticism and disagreement. There are different ways by which students can be made to feel at home in such a culture, and the claim that we have always lived there is not necessarily the best way. That said, I do not think it is wrong to tell the Jewish story (or the Muslim story) in a revised version, so to speak, that stresses points of access for a democratic understanding. But one must also tell the Greek story and insist on the genuinely formative moments in the history of democracy.

The second critical requirement of the course is a *philosophy* or political theory of democratic government, with all the standard arguments, critically reviewed. In a relatively new country like Israel, where crucially important constitutional questions are still undecided (what should the electoral system be like? should there be a bill of rights?), students should study not only the alternatives to democracy but also the different versions of democracy—and the arguments for and against each one. But the philosophy of democratic government does not stop at the analysis of constitutional arrangements. It extends to practices and attitudes: debate, compromise, tolerance of disagreement, skepticism about authority and so on. I do not know how one teaches such things, especially when it is not possible to count on reinforcement from outside the school. Certainly, a single course, however well-designed, will not do the job. A certain democratic consciousness—open, questioning, hostile to dogmatism—must be at work in every course. But this is not an easy requirement when schools are organized for the sake of religious or, for that matter, ideologically secular instruction. So there also has to be a specific place and time for students to discuss the texts in which a democratic consciousness was first exemplified and defended.

The third requirement is a *practical political science* of democracy: how-to-do-it for citizens, where the everyday working of government ministries, representative assemblies, courts, parties, social movements and so on are studied. This is probably the least controversial part of a democratic education, and also the easiest, since in this case, though not in the others, instruction in school is seconded by the daily news. But there is nonetheless important educational work to be done here: to teach students to think of themselves as future participants, not merely as more or less sophisticated spectators. The spectacle, no doubt, is often unedifying, so teachers must stress that it is in the nature of democracy that the system is never closed. There are always opportunities for people with new or different ideas about how things might be done. Students should be encouraged to experiment with political ideas and taught how to defend them in front of their peers.[8]

4

I have already suggested that a democratic education of this sort is likely to sit more easily with some of Israel's constituent communities than with others. Democracy has a substantive character; it is not a neutral procedure but a way of life. Now I need to address a more specific question: to what extent does this way of life, in its Israeli version, reflect the dominant cultures of Israeli society—Zionist, Jewish, Ashkenazi—so that all the other cultures must either reject democracy or transform themselves for its sake? Is the democratic education that I have just described (really) a program for cultural subordination?

It can hardly be denied that Israeli politics reflects the dominant cultures. Democracy as it is now organized has its beginnings in the Zionist Congress and in the *Yishuv*, where Arabs, obviously, had no place and Sephardic Jews were only minimally represented.[9] The state calendar is shaped by the Jewish, not the Christian or Muslim, calendar; state symbols and ceremonies derive from Jewish history. The political elite is still recruited largely from European immigrants and their children. Democracy was an early commitment of these people, even if they came from countries with little experience of democratic government, and the defense of democracy now looks very much like self-defense.

But democratic politics has a logic of its own, which is not subject to the control of its (temporarily) dominant groups. Even conceived as a way of life, which in some sense "belongs" to the people whose way of life it is, democracy can never be the exclusive possession of an ethnic group or a social class or any subset of the body of citizens. It is permanently open to what we might think of as friendly takeovers (insofar as the citizens are friends, at least in Aristotle's sense, which does not rule out the antagonism of political competition). Of course, it can only be taken over by people who learn the rules, and the takeover can only be called friendly if these same people have internalized the culture of democracy. And is not this a kind of assimilation—cultural loss as well as gain? Democratic schooling (practice too), if it works, will make for assimilation; I see no point in pretending that it will not entail significant changes especially in the various religious cultures of Israeli society. But once the give-and-take of democratic politics is opened up to everyone's giving and taking, even the dominant groups are unlikely to emerge unchanged. Their survival-as-they-are cannot be guaranteed. Political coexistence and interaction will erode the boundaries that divide them from the others; they will have to share power, and even surrender it. Democracy itself, assuming its survival, will appear in new versions, more plebeian, perhaps, or more populist, or more pious.

At the same time, it would be a mistake to overestimate the changes that democratic politics requires from (or imposes on) nondemocratic and predemocratic cultures. Modern societies are sufficiently compartmentalized, their individual members are sufficiently divided, to make it entirely possible, say, for orthodox Jews to elect their Knesset representatives without modifying in any way their loyalty to nonelected sages. Obviously, the potential will now exist for a rival orthodox leadership (though probably not for a rival orthodoxy), and a new, more public, more accessible argument will begin. But traditional authority structures have considerable staying power: rabbis, priests, mullahs, old families, local notables all continue to shape communal opinion long after modernity has called into being a host of eager successors. So there is no reason why democratic politics cannot coexist with a genuine and vital multiculturalism even if it is not equally in tune, as it were, with all the cultures. And we can help individuals from the different cultures to feel at home in the democratic arena without turning them into strangers in their own families or heretics in their religious communities.

But democracy is still, always, a politics of strain. One wins and loses, takes responsibility for governing without ever having power enough, lives for years in opposition, compromises one's deepest commitments, coexists with people one does not like or trust. I suppose that the strain must be especially great in multiply divided societies where some political leaders are struggling to build a consensus while others are firing up and mobilizing their own particularist constituencies. The politics of difference is both a product of democracy and a danger to it. That is why education is so important—school learning (also practical experience) aimed at producing the patience, stamina, tolerance, and receptiveness without which the strain will not be understood or accepted.

For it is always possible to escape the democratic arena, to hide in the closeness of one's own community, to surrender the responsibilities of citizenship and allow a small political elite to negotiate communal differences or a charismatic leader to override them. We know that multiculturalism can "work" in authoritarian regimes, as it worked in the old empires before the appearance of nationalist movements and successor states committed, at least in principle, to popular self-rule. Making it work democratically is a relatively new project, an experiment whose real subjects are our children and grandchildren. The point of a democratic education is to give them a fighting chance of success.

Notes and References

1. For a detailed account of how autonomy worked in medieval Islam, see S. D. Goitein, *A Mediterranean Society*, vol. II, *The Community* (Berkeley: University of California Press, 1971), especially pp. 311ff. On autonomy in the Ottoman Empire, see Bernard Lewis, *The Jews of Islam* (Princeton: Princeton University Press, 1984), pp. 125 ff. (on the millet system).
2. For the American experience, see Michael Walzer, *What It Means to Be an American* (New York: Marsilio, 1993).
3. Jean-Jacques Rousseau, *The Government of Poland*, trans. Willmoore Kendall (Indianapolis: Bobbs-Merrill, 1972), chapter IV (Education).
4. For example, in the pivotal election of 1977, the turnout among all Israeli citizens was 79.2% of eligible voters; in Arab cities, it was 77.4%. *Israel at the Polls*, ed. Howard R. Penniman (Washington, D.C.: American Enterprise Institute, 1979), pp. 63, 65.
5. No Arab party has yet been invited to join a government coalition, but the current government (1995) depends on Arab votes in the Knesset and bargains for them much as it does for the support of its actual partners.
6. For an account of Arab-Jewish division and mutual ignorance, see Michael Romann and Alex Weingrod, *Living Together Separately: Arabs and Jews in Contemporary Jerusalem* (Princeton: Princeton University Press, 1991). The situation of religious and secular Jews is similar to that described there. And the schools have little chance of changing what residence, daily life, and politics so consistently confirm.
7. Yehezkel Kaufmann, *The Religion of Israel*, trans. and abridged by Moshe Greenberg (Chicago: University of Chicago Press, 1960), p. 256.
8. For further arguments about and proposals for the education of citizens, see Amy Gutmann, *Democratic Education* (Princeton: Princeton University Press, 1987) and Benjamin Barber, *An Aristocracy for Everyone: The Politics of Education and the Future of America* (New York: Ballantine, 1992).
9. See Dan Horowitz and Moshe Lissak, *Origins of the Israeli Polity* (Chicago: University of Chicago Press, 1978).

Contact Hypothesis in Ethnic Relations

YEHUDA AMIR*

The impetus for writing the present article derived from a meeting between psychologists and some of the policy makers of the Israel Ministry of Education and Culture. Discussion concentrated on the possible contribution of psychologists to the newly planned changes in the structure of Israel's educational system. One of the problems raised concerned ethnic relations and the opportunity of intergroup contact among children and youth in Israel. Schools and classes in Israel are made up, to a large extent, of children from the same socioeconomic class and ethnic background. This situation is especially acute and calls for a change due to the high correlation between the social class and ethnic background of the different subgroups: the lower socioeconomic classes are composed mainly of immigrants from African and Asian countries, while the higher socioeconomic classes are composed of groups originating from Europe and America.

Residential areas in most parts of Israel are divided according to the socioeconomic and ethnic background of the population. Because of the policy that children should study at the school nearest to their homes, schools are also divided accordingly. The suggested plan for educational reorganization takes the divisions into consideration and aims at providing opportunities for interracial and intergroup contact within schools and classes. The assumption is that this contact will enable the children to know each other better and that this close contact will reduce ethnic prejudice and intergroup tension and improve relations between the various ethnic groups and classes in Israel. This problem is undoubtedly not limited to the Israeli scene. Similar problems and solutions can probably be found in many countries whose populations consist of a number of ethnic subgroups.

A major task for psychology is to evaluate the basis of the preceding assumption, that intergroup contact tends to produce better intergroup attitudes and relations. At present, there are conflicting views and evidence regarding this problem. Some goodwill programs are founded on the belief that contact between people—the mere fact of their interacting—is likely to change their beliefs and feelings toward

*Yehuda Amir was a professor in the psychology department at Bar-Ilan University, Israel. He founded and headed the Institute for the Advancement of Integration in the School System at Bar-Ilan. He initiated programs based on the principles of the contact hypothesis. He was awarded the prestigious Israel Prize in 1995 (Israel's Nobel Prize) for "Success in bridging social involvement and academic and scientific research. [Amir] has made a unique contribution to research on social integration, relations between groups, . . . and the manner of dealing with conflict resolution between these groups." He died in April 1996. The present article was written in 1969 and quickly became a classic of social psychology literature. This is an abridged version. The full article is found in *Psychological Bulletin* 71/5 (May 1969): 319–42.

each other. Such a view would maintain that people are basically good and seek understanding and mutual appreciation. If only one had the opportunity to communicate with the others and to appreciate their way of life, understanding and consequently a reduction of prejudice would follow.

This view, which seems to be held rather commonly, is exemplified in the explicit or tacit objectives of various international exchange programs: student exchanges or those of professional people, organized tours and visits to foreign countries, the sending of foreign students to visit or live with native families, etc. In the latter instance, the student from abroad gets in close touch with an American family and observes the American way of life firsthand. This contact gives the out-group member an opportunity to see and evaluate life from the in-group member's point of view and thus is held to enable him or her to appreciate, understand, and perhaps even adopt the latter's way of life. International seminars, international conferences and exhibitions, the Olympic games—all these—are often thought to be effective because of the opportunities for contact that they afford. The basic premise is typically that personal contact can overcome difficulties where tons of paperwork and memoranda have not succeeded.

On the other hand, there is much evidence indicating that intergroup contact does not necessarily reduce intergroup tension or prejudice and that it may even increase tension and cause violent outbreaks, racial riots, and slaughter. Historical documentation of anti-Semitism in Europe or the attitude toward African-Americans in the South of the United States are cases in point. In these instances, contact does not seem to have fostered friendly relations and mutual understanding.

This inconsistency in the effects of contact on attitude change observed in everyday life is also found in the results of more systematic social psychological research. There has been increasing research interest in the effects of contact between groups on changes in intergroup attitudes. Most of the relevant studies have been conducted in the United States, and almost all of these have dealt with contact between the white majority group and a minority group, and, in most cases, the minority group members were African-Americans. The question immediately arises whether relationships found with respect to intergroup relations in the United States can also be expected to be valid for other countries.

The purpose of the present paper is to summarize and evaluate studies of the effect of intergroup contact on the changing of attitudes and ethnic relations. Special emphasis is placed on the principles and generalizations emerging from these studies. As mentioned previously, it is questionable whether results from these studies can be uncritically applied to other countries. However, these findings could be used in Israel, and elsewhere, as a starting point for evaluation and research on the effect and importance of intergroup contact. Even without specific research on this problem in a specified country, principles emerging from research on this topic elsewhere may still be of use and may supply criteria for evaluating relevant opinions, concepts, and programs in that country. . . .

General Considerations

Although most studies have found the effect of contact to be positive, many investigators have remarked that indiscriminative generalizations may be misleading and warned against drawing hasty conclusions from the available evidence. Social psychologists generally agree that, in relation to attitude change, "contact" per se is an ambiguous and therefore an inadequate term. Sherif and Sherif (1953), for example, argued that "in any discussion on the effects of contact on intergroup attitudes, we must specify: What *kind* of contact? Contact in *what* capacity . . . [p. 221]?" Cook (1962) was of the opinion

> that "contact" has been used as the label for a multitude of different situations and experiences. In some studies, the "contact" whose results were investigated has been a very brief trip; in others, it had been a month's stay in camp; in still others, friendship of perhaps many years' duration. In some studies, the contact took place in a recreation group; in others, within a work situation; in still others, within the residential neighborhood. Some studies had children as subjects, others adults. Some dealt with college students, some with factory workers. And there have been almost as many different measures of "contact" as there have been studies [Cook & Selltiz, 1955, p. 52].

Summarizing this point, Cook (1962) stated that instead of asking: "Does intergroup contact reduce prejudice?" we should be dealing with the question of "In what types of contact situations, with what kinds of representatives of the disliked group, will interaction and attitude change of specified types occur—and how will this vary for subjects of differing characteristics? [p. 76]." Guided by this principle he analyzed carefully the relevant variables, namely, (a) the characteristics of the contact situation, (b) the characteristics of the individuals who are in contact, and (c) the attitudinal and behavioral results. Each of these categories can be subdivided into a number of components. The first category, for example, includes seven concepts descriptive of potentially significant variation in the contact situation itself. These concepts are degree of proximity between races, direction and strength of the norms of one's own group within the situation toward interracial association, expectations regarding interracial association believed to characterize authority figures in the situation, relative status within the situation, interdependence requirements (of the interacting individuals), acquaintance potential and implications for social acceptance. . . .

Allport (1954) thinks that "in order to predict the effect of contact upon attitudes we should ideally study the consequences of each of the . . . variables acting both separately and in combination [p. 262]." He then enumerates about thirty such variables, including categories of contact such as quantitative aspects, status aspects, role aspects, the social atmosphere surrounding the contact, the personality of the individuals experiencing the contact, and, finally, areas of contact. This large but still not exhaustive list of variables and categories serves only to emphasize the complexity of the problem. We should not, therefore, be surprised to find that research has not as yet satisfactorily covered all these variables. But, on the other hand, research has already advanced enough to indicate some of the relevant factors in this area.

In the following sections, the effect of contact on intergroup relations is discussed under several subheadings. This particular organization of the subject generally follows the suggestions advanced earlier (Allport, 1954; Cook, 1962). Topics related to the contact situation are discussed first, under the following subtitles: the principle of equal status, contact with high-status representative of a minority group, cooperative and competitive goals, casual versus intimate contact, institutional support. Following these sections is a discussion dealing with the characteristics of the interacting individual, namely, personality factors, and direction and intensity of initial attitude.

A preliminary section on the opportunities for contact opens the discussion because opportunities for contact may be regarded as prerequisite for intergroup contact. If no opportunities for contact exist, or if these opportunities are minimal, no contact occurs, and obviously no change of attitude as a result of contact can be expected.

Opportunities for Contact

Cook (1962) emphasized what he called the acquaintance potential, which "refers to the opportunity provided by the situation for the participants to get to know and understand one another. One may encounter another person every day for months in the reading lounge of a Manhattan men's club with no more than a whispered comment about the weather [p. 75]." Such a contact, undoubtedly, provides little opportunity for attitude change. On the other hand, contacts of the same proximity and frequency in a different social setting or with different individuals may produce more psychologically meaningful communications and thereby facilitate attitudinal or behavioral changes. . . .

Schild (1962) in a study conducted in Israel concluded that "In discussing 'contact' between hosts and strangers, it would seem necessary to take into account the differential opportunities for learning which the contact situation offers [p. 53]." Following his evaluations of different types of opportunities in foreign student exchange, it seems likely that differences will "be found in the changes produced where the study tour is based exclusively on sight-seeing and lectures and where they provide primarily opportunities for intensive participation [p. 54]." It seems that this differentiation between opportunities of contact can provide an explanation for the lack of change noted in a study evaluating the impact of an educational tour to Japan of California high school students (National Education Association, 1932).

Kelman (1962) in his evaluation of international Exchange-of-Persons programs also stressed the opportunity-of-contact variable. He stated: "In making opportunities available to the visitor, the emphasis should not be on group activities in which he engages along with other exchanges. There is no harm in arranging some activities of this sort, but these are not the important experiences [p. 76]." Kelman is also aware that when contact does occur it may produce negative results. On the other hand, contact may realize its full potential for producing favorable attitude change, especially if opportunities for involvement, including involvement with people in the host country, are provided. The importance of the opportunity for intergroup contact was also revealed in various housing projects (Deutsch & Collins, 1951; Wilner, Walkley, & Cook, 1952). In these studies, it was possible for white subjects who made contact with African-Americans to revise their initial attitudes and prejudices as a result of their contact. However, white subjects living in the segregated projects have little opportunity for contact and therefore no revision of attitude can be expected.

On the other hand, results from a study conducted in Israel indicated that people from different ethnic backgrounds, despite living in proximity to each other, tended to establish minimal social contact with each other. Weingrod (1965) observed:

> In general, an immigrant's primary bonds were to people like themselves. For example, when questioned regarding their social relations with neighboring villagers, Iraqi settlers responded that they rarely saw the Moroccans, Tunisians and Hungarians who lived near to them, but that they sometimes visited other Iraqi settlers who lived miles away! These informal ethnic-group ties were, of course, contrary to the official expectations for *mizug hagaluyot*—for group mixing. Government officials wished to diminish intra-group ties; for this reason entire villages, housing projects or even sections of larger communities were often purposely designed to include Poles, Yemenites, North Africans, Hungarians, and so forth. These "mixed" communities would, it was hoped, foster wider social contacts and new forms of behavior. These hopes were not often realized; alone, and feeling isolated, members of each group associated with their fellows. They might not necessarily be old friends, but at the very least, they spoke the same language [p. 33]. . . .

The Principle of Equal Status

Some of the conceptions advanced by Allport (1954) and by Allport and Kramer (1946) seem especially important and may serve as guiding principles in this whole area of contact in attitude research. Allport pointed out that for contact to serve as a factor in reducing prejudice it must be based on "equal status contact between majority and minority groups in the pursuit of common goals [Allport, 1954, p. 281]." If such contact is also supported by social institutions (such as the law, the community, etc.), its effect on attitude change should even increase.

Kramer (1950) suggested that the concept of "equal status" has to be refined in order to differentiate between equality of status *within* and outside the specific contact situation. He suggested that the relative status of group members within the contact situation may be an important factor in attitude change. A better understanding of the effect of relative status could be of great importance in our attempt to improve intergroup relations, since it is sometimes easier to assign members of minority and majority groups to equal status positions within a given situation than to bring together individuals who are of equal socioeconomic and educational status. . . . An experimental study in which equality of status within the contact situation seems to have prevailed was conducted by Mann (1959). He assigned seventy-eight graduate students at Teachers College, New York City, to six-person discussion groups. The groups, containing men and women, nonwhite and white, Southerners and Northerners, held four meetings a week for three weeks. At the beginning and at the end they were given sociometric tests and part of the Berkeley E scale for measuring prejudice. Contact in the group significantly reduced both the E scores and the use of race as a friendship criterion.

Occupational contact, too, may have a decisive effect on the attitude of white people toward a minority group, depending on the differential status in occupation of the members of the two ethnic groups. . . .

Watson (1950) was concerned with changes in attitudes toward Jews and African-Americans as reported in open-ended interviews by forty-five adult residents of New York City. Although the sample was not selected adequately enough to permit conclusive generalizations, it is interesting that most of the reported changes in attitude came as a result of contact experiences. From the obtained data it was concluded that "contact with minority group members having status equal to or higher than oneself usually leads to favorable attitudes toward that minority group. Contact with minority group members of lower socioeconomic status than oneself is conducive to the formation of negative attitudes toward that minority group [p. 36]." . . .

Equal status contact also served as the basis of a field experiment on intergroup integration in a summer camp. Yarrow, Campbell, and Yarrow (1958) found that the importance of racial origin in the establishment of friendship between white and African-American children decreased as a result of two weeks stay in an interracial camp. Although the children, at the end of the camp, still preferred their white cabin mates as friends, there was a significant drop in the extent that they were the favored group. At the end of the camp, white and African-American campers were almost equally desired as friends by the white group.

Similar results were obtained in an international setting. Bjerstedt (1962) summarized two studies conducted with eleven-year-old children in international summer camps in Scandinavia. He concluded that the most important observation with reference to social structure was that all differences between mean self-preference indices at the beginning and end of camp went in *one* direction only—toward lower segregation. The tendencies were toward less overpreference for the subject's own nationality and own language groups at the end of camp. . . .

In a study conducted in Israel, Sapir (1951) studied the adaptability of rural immigrant children who were placed with urban families owing to very difficult weather during the winter of 1950–51. This research is of interest because the ethnic contact was between groups highly differing in social status: Most of the children belonged to immigrant families of Near Eastern (low-status) origin, while almost all the host families came from Germany or East European countries (high-status). In her summary, Sapir pointed to an interesting negative factor that emerged in the way the children imitated people in their new environment.

> The behavior of the children in imitating the members of the host families, and the speed in which they rejected all their previous habits after just a few days shows that the children perceived the new environment as better in every way than their own home environment. . . . There is no doubt that very many of the children paid for the placement by developing feelings of inferiority and low self-esteem, as well as a low opinion of their families and their race. . . . It is interesting to note the large number of children (45.7%) who refused to return to their parents. . . There were also children, just how many cannot be determined from the existing data, who reacted negatively to the placement and revealed dissatisfaction, loss of self-control, a weakening of family values without any alternative values to take their place, and a formation of a serious emotional gap between themselves and their parents [p. 36].

In addition to these negative influences on the low-status group members, negative results were also found for the high-status group. This is elaborated later. The general impression from this research is that, in spite of the advantages of this project—that is, placement of immigrant children during a difficult winter—the results of the interracial contact between Near Eastern immigrant children and Western hosts are open to doubt. It is far from clear if the advantages outweigh the disadvantages. Perhaps even the opposite is true. The problem probably stems from the cultural gap and the large differences in social status between the groups in contact.

A somewhat indirect, theoretical analysis of the importance of status on the consequences of racial and ethnic contact was made by Lieberson (1961). He suggested two major factors that account for an orderly interpretation of differences in the nature of race and ethnic relations in contact situations. One of these factors is based on a distinction between migrant and indigenous groups. The other factor, superordination-subordination, refers primarily to the relative position of the interacting groups in terms of power, dominance, socioeconomic level, etc. Lieberson argued that the establishment of migrant groups of superordinate level is often accompanied by conflict. On the other hand, when the indigenous population dominates the political and the economic conditions, no great conflict occurs. It seems that Lieberson's distinction between superordination and subordination refers, to a large extent, to the social status of the groups or the group members taking part in the intergroup contact.

To summarize, from the foregoing studies, it seems evident that in cases where no hindering conditions are present, equal status contact is likely to produce positive attitude changes.

Contact with High-Status Representatives of a Minority Group

Several studies have indicated that friendly contact between members of a majority group and high-status individuals of a minority group tends to reduce prejudice toward the whole minority group.

. . . .One of the classic studies in this area was carried out by Smith (1943) on a group of students from Teachers College, Columbia University. These students visited on two weekends various places in Harlem, including homes of prominent African-American families, African-American leaders and artists. Attitudes toward the African-Americans for both the experimental group and a control group were tested at three occasions, first before the independent variable was introduced, then after it, and finally after eleven additional months. The results showed that members of the experimental group changed their attitude in a favorable direction as a result of the contact situation, while the control group remained practically constant. Moreover, after a lapse of eleven months from the visit to Harlem, the obtained change in attitude remained persistent. . . .

James (1955), in a study conducted in England, investigated the effect of contact between African women teachers and their white pupils. He found that as a result of their liking the teachers' personality, the pupils changed their attitudes favorably toward Africans in general. The writer noted, however, that the general atmosphere in the community was a positive one, including teacher-pupil and white-black relationships.

One study, however, reported negative results. Young (1932), in one of the earliest studies on the effects of contact on attitude change, used as subjects sixteen graduate students who had taken a course in American race relations, and "put [them] through a term's work consisting largely of unusual contacts with African-Americans who were in startling contrast with popular racial stereotypes [p. 16]." They visited an African-American hospital and watched a skillful operation performed by an African-American doctor, they were entertained by a wealthy and cultured African-American couple, and they visited the charming home of an excellent African-American pianist. The students were very cooperative and showed much interest in the whole subject of racial relations and racial attitudes. The results of their experience, however, were characterized by a lack of uniformity. Some students showed less prejudiced attitudes after the course than before it; others acquired more prejudice. Most of the variations were slight and no definite trend could be detected.

It is hard to discern the reason for such inconclusive results. It may lie in part in the fact that the visiting students may never have become a real "part" of the African-Americans group they visited. They observed African-Americans and evaluated their way of life as outsiders and not as fellow members of the same group. In relation to this, Sherif and Sherif (1953) observed that contact is likely to produce favorable attitude changes between members of socially distant groups only when the contact involves their "joint participation as members of an in-group whose norms favor such participation. . . . In situations in which in-group members meet with members of an out-group held at considerable distance on a very limited scale . . . there is little likelihood of change in attitudes of in-group members [pp. 221–22]."

Cooperative and Competitive Factors

Contact situations may differ in the degree to which they involve cooperative and competitive factors, such as questions of common or conflicting goals, shared concerns and activities, mutual interdependence or competition in the achievement of objectives and needs, etc. . . . Allport's principle of common goals was dealt with somewhat differently by Sherif. He was of the opinion that in many contact situations it is not sufficient to bring the antagonistic groups into contact and that these groups should have or should be given superordinate goals to make them cooperate across group lines. Only such superordinate goals can make the contact effective, thereby reducing prejudice and group tension.

> Only when erstwhile rivals come into contact in the pursuit of vital purpose that grips all participants can contact situations furnish opportunity for creative moves toward reducing intergroup hostility. The participants must feel a common steadfast pull in the same direction if not toward the same actions. . . . Without some interdependence among the parties in contact, face to face situations produce lowered thresholds for the verdict of "What else would you expect from such a ———?" . . . Contact is an effective medium for change when groups are directed toward superordinate goals overriding their separate concerns [Sherif, 1966, pp. 146–47]. [But] so long as the individuals belong to different in-groups with conflicting norms in relation to out-groups, such changes may be relatively specific to the area of contact or may be subject to fluctuations as the individual moves from one group setting to another, resulting in apparently inconsistent behavior [Sherif & Sherif, 1953, p. 222].

The concept of "superordinate" goals was also investigated empirically by Sherif (1966). He found that when previously antagonistic groups were brought into contact, the occasion was utilized only to further group conflicts even when the activities in the contact situations were satisfying in themselves for the group members. It was only in situations which provided superordinate goals of high appeal to both groups that they cooperated across group lines. This intergroup cooperation followed the realization that goals could not be attained through the energy and the resources of one group without the other one. . . .

Common and superordinate goals are generally absent where the contact situation itself is in contradiction to the objectives and the immediate needs of one or more of the interacting groups. When the contact between the groups is to the disadvantage of one of them (i.e., economic disadvantage, lowered prestige or status level, etc.), not only does the contact not reduce prejudice, but may even intensify intergroup hatred and violence. This point is illustrated in the studies reviewed next.

Sherif (1966) reported an experiment with groups of twelve-year-olds where the basis of common or superordinate goals was absent. He found that

> contact situations designed to bring together antagonistic groups as equals during sumptuous meals and entertainments did not reduce their antagonisms. On the contrary, the contact situations were utilized as occasions to exchange invectives, and degenerated beyond the point of reciprocal attribution of blame for existing tension [p. 144]. . . .

It seems that presence or absence of mutual concern or of common or superordinate goals can explain, in part at least, the negative results obtained in the two following studies. It should be noted that these two studies are based on several post hoc assumptions since we actually do not know the initial attitudes of the individuals or the groups, and we may only assume that they were similar for the different groups.

The first study by Dodd (1935) examined attitude changes between ethnic groups in the Middle East. He reported that

> social distances [there] are not determined by geographic proximity nor by abundance of contact, as by definite acts of a benevolent or malevolent sort between groups. . . . Groups that live side by side and have many commercial and other relations together are not nearly as close as groups who have fewer contacts, but are felt to be benefactors [p. 200].

The second study (Ram & Murphy, 1952) showed that the contact between hostile groups in India did not leave any substantial effect on the reduction of hatred or on the modification of attitudes between these groups. Also, the type of experience with other groups seems to have had no bearing on the attitude. "Hindu refugees who suffered directly at Moslem hands seem to harbor no more hostility to Moslems than those who made good their escape without suffering any such personal misfortune [p. 14]."

In addition to the explanations offered above for these negative results of intergroup contact, that is, the lack of common goals or mutual interdependence in the achievement of objectives, a cultural factor may also be involved. Murphy (1953) suggested that to be a good Hindu or Moslem implies accepting as true all the negative qualities and practices attributed by one's own group to the adversary.

Therefore, new information concerning the adversary, such as that obtained through intergroup contact, will not alter—for better or worse—the initial attitude.

Some research in this area has also been conducted in Israel, although, in most cases, the studies were not designed to explain the specific reasons for the positive or negative attitude changes stemming from ethnic contact. For example, the prevailing policy governing the settlement of immigrants for many years was to establish new settlements with mixed-ethnic populations. The assumption was that interethnic contact would further intergroup relations and create a united and homogeneous nation. The fact is that this policy often produced intergroup conflict and tension and was consequently abandoned. The reasons for this failure are not altogether clear and most likely are manifold. Unequal status seems to have been a major factor: In many cases each group considered the other as inferior because of different social and cultural norms. The differences in cultural norms also produced a threat situation thereby minimizing the possibility of establishing common or superordinate goals.

To sum up, it seems evident that cooperative and competitive factors may be significant and decisive in situations of intergroup contact: Cooperative factors seem to further intergroup relations; competitive factors generally hinder them.

Casual versus Intimate Contact

Social research has provided evidence that casual contact between ethnic groups in itself is not sufficient to change attitudes. Furthermore, high frequency of contact does not necessarily have to foster positive ethnic relations. It may even increase prejudice. Anti-Semitism flourished in those countries with large Jewish communities and where contact between Jews and non-Jews was relatively frequent. Pinkney (1963) concentrated on this very issue. He expressed doubts about the assumption that prejudice by members of the dominant group toward minorities is correlated with the ratio of a minority in the population of a community. He presented data from four American cities in an attempt to demonstrate that other factors aid in determining whether or not favorable attitudes will prevail. . . .

Another contact area in which intergroup relations were studied is work situations. Studies in this area have not reported any changes in the overall attitudes of majority group members toward members of the minority group. Some of the investigators did not report *any* changes in attitude. Others found some changes, but they were confined to work situations only (Gundlach, 1950; Alvin Rose, 1948).

Harding and Hogrefe (1952) state in a summary of the evidence on work contact that "equal status work contact between whites and African-Americans may produce large favorable changes in attitude among the white workers, small favorable changes, or no changes at all, depending primarily on the nature of the work situation and the type of attitude measured [p. 27].". . .

Why does intergroup contact in work situations tend to produce only limited attitude changes, if at all? One possible explanation leans for support on the hypothesis advanced in this section, that is, casual versus intimate contact. Perhaps, in general, work situations involve superficial interethnic contact, and even when the relationship becomes more personal, it is generally confined to the work situation only. This explanation may apply to such findings where no change in attitude was detected following interethnic contact, while whatever changes appeared were limited to work situations or issues.

In contrast to casual contact, better acquaintance and a more intimate relationship between members of different ethnic groups reduce prejudice. Evidence to support this hypothesis can be found in some of the studies already reviewed (Brophy, 1945; Irish, 1952; James, 1955; Mannheimer & Williams, 1949; Yarrow et al., 1958), in various other studies (Gray & Thompson, 1953; Segal, 1965; Stouffer, Lumsdaine, Lumsdaine, Williams, Smith, Janis, Star, & Cottrell, 1949), and especially in the following housing and residential studies. . . .

Studies on interracial housing in Israel demonstrated how specific circumstances, which may differ from group to group, are apt to influence the results of the contact. Shuval (1962) studied the relationships between neighbors in immigrant villages and new settlements and found that satisfaction with the neighborhood is related to the ethnic origin of the neighbors on both sides of one's house or apartment.

> Among European respondents it may be seen that satisfaction with neighbors drops markedly when they live in a completely heterogeneous micro-neighborhood, with North Africans or Near Easterners on both sides of their apartment. . . . The reverse picture is seen among the North Africans. [Their] satisfaction with neighbors rises markedly when North Africans live in a completely heterogeneous micro-neighborhood. Living "surrounded" by Europeans serves to increase satisfaction with neighbors. . . . The Near Easterners, on the other hand, react positively to any residential contact with Europeans [pp. 278–79].

Shuval elsewhere concluded that it would be advisable to have mixed-housing patterns, whereby a family has one neighbor with the same ethnic background and another one from a different ethnic background.

Soen (Soen & Tishler, 1968) arrived at different conclusions. He investigated one of the immigrant towns in Israel and reported two major findings on the relationship between intergroup contact and attitudes toward another ethnic group. First, most people in the community, of all ethnic groups, were indifferent to the ethnic background of their neighbors. Second, the more heterogeneous the neighborhood, the more receptive were its inhabitants toward members of other ethnic groups. In other words, people whose neighbors did not belong to their own ethnic group were more liberal toward other ethnic groups. This latter conclusion parallels findings from other housing studies, such as the Deutsch and Collins study. But here, too, it should be emphasized that a process of mutual selection might have taken place: Those who enjoyed living in the ethnically mixed area continued to live there, while those who disliked the intermixed housing pattern left their houses and therefore they were either not included in the mixed-ethnic group or else they appeared in the ethnically "isolated" groups. If such a process actually occurred, conclusions concerning the direct influence of intergroup contact on favorable attitude change may be an artifact and not necessarily valid. . . .

To summarize: The trend of evidence suggests that intergroup contact may produce different types of relationships. At one end are the casual and superficial relations; at the other end, the ego-involving and intimate relations. Proximity and frequency of contact as well as other factors may exert decisive influence in determining the amount of intergroup contact and also, indirectly, the nature of the contact. As to the actual outcome, casual intergroup contact has little or no effect on a basic attitude change. Intimate contact, on the other hand, tends to produce favorable changes. When intimate relations are established, the in-group member no longer perceives the member of the out-group in a stereotyped way but begins to consider him or her as an individual and thereby discovers many areas of similarity.

Institutional Support

The effectiveness of interracial contact is greatly increased if the contact is sanctioned by institutional support. The support may come from the law, a custom, a spokesperson for the community or any authority that is accepted by the interacting group. In many cases, institutional support comes simply from a social atmosphere or a general public agreement. . . .

Personality Factors

It can hardly be expected that contact will be so effective as to change the attitudes of all the members of the interacting groups. There are always hindering factors that resist the influence of the contact or may even counteract it. Certain personalities, too, will not be affected positively by interracial contact. Their inner insecurity and their personal disorder will not permit them to benefit from the contact with a group against whom they are prejudiced because they will always need a scapegoat. One study in this area concentrated on this problem.

Mussen (1950) studied the effect of contact on attitudes of white boys after a four-week stay of white and African-American boys in an unsegregated summer camp. The group as a whole did not change in its attitude toward African-Americans. However, about 25 percent of the white boys showed more prejudice after the camp experience, and just about the same percentage became less prejudiced. There was no question of unequal status because there was no racial discrimination in the camp and everyone enjoyed the same privileges and was treated equally, and yet the positive changes were practically equal to the negative ones. Further analysis of the data showed that the boys who became less prejudiced were those who enjoyed their stay at the camp more and who made better adjustment at the camp. The boys who became more prejudiced exhibited in their test-responses "greater needs to defy authority and strong aggressive feelings [p. 440]." This finding suggests that the determining factors in the attitude change were personality factors, or more specifically, the "aggression needs" of the boys. Mussen concluded

> that intimate contact with African-Americans per se does not insure a decrease in prejudice.... Whether or not a child will change his attitude toward African-Americans seems to be related to his personality structure and to certain factors in the social situation in which intimate contact occurs [p. 438]....

Direction and Intensity of Initial Attitude

The last study presented a different and new phenomenon. Apparently no relationship has been found between contact and attitude change: the percentage of prejudiced children was not affected by the contact situation. Contact, however, was clearly related to the intensity of the attitude. This phenomenon was also found in some other studies on the effects of contact on attitude change, which will be reviewed here briefly.

Hogrefe, Evans, and Chein (1947) found that white children who attended an interracial play center once a week for several months did not differ from a control group in attitudes toward African-Americans as measured by a social distance scale. However, a projective test showed a larger proportion of play-center children either favorable to racial segregation in play situations or strongly opposed to it....

Guttman and Foa (1951) demonstrated the importance of the intensity of an attitude. They investigated the attitude of the Israel population toward government employees. The respondents were also asked to indicate the extent to which they had contact with government officials. It was found that about half the sample expressed favorable attitudes, the other half unfavorable ones. The same fifty-fifty distribution held true for each level of contact. After further analysis, however, it was found that although there was no overall change in the direction of attitude, its intensity had increased with the amount of contact: The more contact with government officials, the more extreme, on the average, the attitude toward them.

Two possible explanations for this relationship were offered:

> Our explanation is that, before contact, a person has either a positive or negative attitude toward government officialdom based on various factors such as political affiliation, etc. Upon actual contact with officials, this attitude was sharpened, on the average, in its original direction. Some people may switch from positive to negative, and vice versa, but the average change is to reinforce the pre-existing attitude, or to increase the intensity. An alternative explanation is in terms of how the attitude is formed originally. Knowledge about government officials is accumulated primarily from two sources: Direct contact and way of mouth (or the press). Those who have little or no contact derive their attitudes from those with

more contact. Since the attitude is acquired more or less second-hand by the former it is less intense for these people [p. 52].

These explanations might very well be valid in understanding attitude changes in other contact situations, too. . . .

The importance of the initial attitude was also stressed by Sapir (1951) in her study on contact between low-status children and high-status hosts, which revealed, inter alia, that prejudice interfered with the children's adaptability.

> Prejudice either of the hosts towards the guests, or the guests towards the hosts prevents the creation of positive relations between them because it formed a background of reservations, suspicions, dissatisfaction and a lack of understanding. The prejudices of the guests (children) toward their hosts were mainly in a racial direction (negative attitudes towards Europeans). Interestingly enough, living together for a number of months was not sufficient, in most cases, to change these attitudes. The prejudices of the hosts had already been established, and, as with the children, these prejudices did not vanish as a result of the attempted absorption. Where the children were successfully absorbed in spite of the racial prejudices, and the family developed a positive attitude toward the child, the hosts would generally mention that "the child is nice in spite of his belonging to such an ethnic group." One of the hostesses expressed her opinion as follows: "It is a pity to leave such a nice and intelligent child in the hands of Yemenites." Not a single case was found where the hosts changed their general ethnic prejudice as a result of a positive attitude to a specific child [p. 28].

In the latter study, a somewhat different dimension was introduced. The studies reported earlier in this section considered the direction (i.e., positive or negative) of the initial attitude as a determinant and the intensity as an outcome. Specifically, it was found that initial positive attitudes tend to become more positive as a result of contact situations, and initial negative attitudes will tend to become more negative. However, in the last study, the intensity of the initial attitude emerged as a significant factor. Although attitude intensity was not controlled directly (i.e., no differentiation was made between subjects whose initial attitudes were more or less intense), it seems clear that the intensity of initial prejudice among the subjects in this study was quite high. . . .

In summary, two generalizations may be drawn: (a) Contact between ethnic groups may intensify the initial attitude of an individual; (b) the intensity of an individual's initial attitude may exert decisive influence on the outcome of the ethnic contact.

Summary of Findings from Research on Ethnic Intergroup Contact

By way of introduction, a few critical comments and words of caution regarding the drawing of generalizations from these studies are relevant. In spite of the very significant attitude changes reported earlier, it would be naïve to assume that *any* intergroup contact will produce the same results. When evaluating research on this topic we should keep in mind that investigators have generally sought and expected to prove something "positive," here a reduction of prejudice. In these experiments the social situation will thus have been selected with this aim in mind. Therefore, if most studies appear to prove that contact between ethnic groups reduces prejudice, it does not necessarily follow that these results are typical for real social situations. Intergroup contact under the circumstances studied is unfortunately quite rare in actual life, and even when it occurs, it generally produces only casual interactions rather than intimate acquaintances.

Furthermore, respondents in some of the studies may have been indirectly influenced by, and may have tended to comply with the expectations of, research teams or interviewers who generally intended to demonstrate positive attitude change. Similarly, studies in which prestigious persons such as teachers have led subjects through a series of experiences with African-Americans suffer from the danger that the research subjects simply cooperated by providing their leader with the changes they knew he was looking for. It should also be recalled that studies involving previous contact and current attitudes suffer from the obvious danger of contamination between the two; that is, current attitude may have influenced one's recall of earlier experience. More recent studies have been sensitive to these pitfalls and have striven to overcome them, hence they are more reliable. . . .

Following are the principles that seem to evolve from the studies on contact between ethnic groups:

(1) There is increasing evidence in the literature to support the view that contact between members of ethnic groups tends to produce changes in attitude between these groups.

(2) The direction of the change depends largely on the conditions under which contact has taken place; "favorable" conditions tend to reduce prejudice, "unfavorable" ones may increase prejudice and intergroup tension.

(3) If a change is produced, it does not necessarily follow that the change is in the *direction* of the attitude. Change may be found in the *intensity* of the attitude (or in other, not yet explored, dimensions).

(4) In many cases where an attitude change is produced as a result of the contact situation, change is limited to a certain specific area or aspect of the attitude (such as to work situations), but does not generalize to other aspects.

(5) Although most of the investigations on the effects of contact on the reduction of prejudice report "favorable" findings, this outcome might be attributed to the selection of favorable experimental situations. It is doubtful whether intergroup contact in real life takes place generally under favorable conditions and whether, therefore, in most cases contact actually reduces prejudice.

(6) Some of the favorable conditions that tend to reduce prejudice are (a) when there is equal status contact between the members of the various ethnic groups, (b) when the contact is between members of a majority group and *higher*

status members of a minority group, (c) when an "authority" and/or the social climate are in favor of and promote the intergroup contact, (d) when the contact is of an intimate rather than a casual nature, (e) when the ethnic intergroup contact is pleasant or rewarding, (f) when the members of *both* groups in the particular contact situation interact in functionally important activities or develop common goals or superordinate goals that are higher ranking in importance than the individual goals of *each* of the groups.

(7) Some of the unfavorable conditions that tend to strengthen prejudice are (a) when the contact situation produces competition between the groups; (b) when the contact is unpleasant, involuntary, tension-laden; (c) when the prestige or the status of one group is lowered as a result of the contact situation; (d) when members of a group or the group as a whole are in a state of frustration (i.e., inadequate personality structure, recent defeat or failure, economic depression, etc.)—here contact with another group may lead to the establishment of an ethnic "scapegoat"; (e) when the groups in contact have moral or ethnic standards that are objectionable to each other; (f) in the case of contact between a majority and a minority group, when the members of the minority group are of a lower status or are lower in any relevant characteristic than the members of the majority group.

Practical Considerations

Let us turn our attention now from scientific generalizations to the specific subject discussed at the beginning of the article. In view of the above studies, the assumption that contact always lessens conflicts and stresses between ethnic groups seems naïve. Ethnic contact may in certain circumstances lessen conflicts and strains, but in different circumstances, similar contact may intensify the existing prejudices, thus increasing the distance between the groups. The intention is not to dwell here upon the specific Israeli problem that was considered at the beginning of the paper, even though it probably exists in other countries as well. However, the situation that is likely to arise as a result of ethnic contact, due to the projected reorganization of Israel's educational system, is used as the basis for a short analysis.

The projected program is intended, inter alia, to create an educational structure in which children from different ethnic groups and diverse social classes study together, particularly from the seventh grade (age twelve) and onwards. What conditions will face these twelve-year-olds when they join the seventh grade, from the point of view of possible change in ethnic attitudes? Here, only the likelihood of a change in the relationship on the part of the children from the Western communities toward the Middle Eastern ones is considered. First, according to the principle of equal status, there is little chance that children from Western and Middle Eastern communities will be similar in socioeconomic level, intelligence, etc. Even if we do not consider the general factors of status, but, in accord with Kramer's theory, refer only to the status relevant in the contact situation, it is still doubtful whether we shall find the two groups equal in status. There is no clear indication from research which factors are likely to determine the status of twelve-year-olds at the time of contact in school. However, it is more than likely that some of the crucial factors will be scholastic achievement, social successes such as popularity or leadership, athletic abilities, external appearance, and perhaps clothing. It is also possible that elements related to the economic position of the child's family will also play a specific role in the status of the pupils at schools. Some of the above elements may be found equally in the different ethnic groups (for instance, athletic abilities), but we expect that on other status elements, most members of the Middle Eastern communities will find themselves inferior to the members of the Western communities. Moreover, in most cases where the Middle Easterners are superior, the Westerners may feel threatened, causing a rise in tension between ethnic groups. . . . On the other hand, in different circumstances the meeting between superior members of the "inferior" community may serve to increase the understanding between the ethnic groups, as was found in the study by Smith (1943).

It seems that the above considerations must raise doubts whether ethnic contact in school will necessarily improve the attitudes and the ethnic relations between the children. It is rather difficult to forecast whether this contact will cause a change in attitude, and if it does cause a change whether this change will be in a desirable or undesirable direction. At any rate, we should not be surprised if it turned out that no general or consistent change in the ethnic attitude of the children is detected as a result of the intergroup contact.

This latter expectation is based, to a certain extent, on findings from a different field of ethnic contact, namely, contact between ethnic groups among soldiers in the Israeli army. Here also the belief is prevalent that the army serves as an instrument for furthering understanding and closing the gap between ethnic groups. Despite the fact that soldiers differ, at least in age, from the children discussed above, there appear to be many parallels from the point of view of the conditions and status of the groups at the time of contact. For this reason, it is doubtful whether intergroup contact in the army situation really changes and improves ethnic relations. Findings from two unpublished studies seem to support this negative evaluation. One of these studies was concerned with sociometric choices, and the other, on a different population, was concerned with ethnic attitudes. Both of them point to a lack of change in the above aspects resulting from long and continued contact between ethnic groups in the army. These findings, together with those from studies discussed earlier, suggest the advisability of reconsidering and retesting the expectations held by administrators and policy makers that intergroup contact necessarily improves the understanding between groups.

In an area closely related to the present topic, Bronfenbrenner (1967) reached a similar conclusion. He stated:

> In many American communities the enlightened leadership, both African-American and white, and their supporters operate on the tacit assumption that once the African-American child finds himself in an integrated classroom with a qualified

teacher and adequate materials, learning will take place, and with it, the deficiencies of the African-American, and the judgments of inferiority which they in part encourage, will be erased. Regrettably, this is not the case. Neither the scars of slavery which the child still bears nor the skills and self-confidence of his white companion rub off merely through contact in the same classroom. This is not to imply that integration is impotent as an instrument of change. On the contrary, it is a desperately necessary condition, but not a sufficient one. Objective equality of opportunity is not enough [p. 910].

If one wants to achieve positive results in the area of intergroup relations, it would be wise to consider carefully if prevailing conditions are suitable to bring about such a change. Experimentation prior to policy making may eliminate illusions in this sensitive area and would enable the policy makers to choose those programs that have the best chances of producing the hoped for results.

References

Allport, G. W. *The nature of prejudice.* Cambridge, Mass.: Addison-Wesley, 1954

Allport, G. W., & Kramer, B. M. Some roots of prejudice. *Journal of Psychology,* 1946, 22, 9–39

Bjerstedt, A. Informational and non-informational determinants of nationality stereotypes. *Journal of Social Issues,* 1962, 18(1), 24–29

Bronfenbrenner, U. The psychological costs of quality and equality in education. *Child Development,* 1967, 38, 909–25

Brophy, I. N. The luxury of anti-Negro prejudice. *Public Opinion Quarterly,* 1945, 9, 456–66

Cook, S. W. The systematic analysis of socially significant events: A strategy for social research. *Journal of Social Issues,* 1962, 18(2), 66–84

Cook, S. W., & Sellitz, C. Some factors which influence the attitudinal outcomes of personal contacts. *International Sociological Bulletin,* 1955, 7, 51–58

Deutsch, M., & Collins, M. E. *Interracial housing: A psychological evaluation of a social experiment.* Minneapolis: University of Minnesota Press, 1951

Dodd, S. C. A social distance test in the Near East. *American Journal of Sociology,* 1935, 41, 194–204

Gray, J. S., & Thompson, A. H. The ethnic prejudices of white and Negro college students. *Journal of Abnormal and Social Psychology,* 1953, 48, 311–13

Gundlach, R. H. The effect of on-the-job experience with Negroes upon social attitudes of white workers in union shops. *American Psychologist,* 1950, 5, 300

Guttman, L., & Foa, U. G. Social attitude and an intergroup attitude. *Public Opinion Quarterly,* 1951, 15, 43–53

Harding, J., & Hogrefe, R. Attitudes of white department store employees toward Negro coworkers. *Journal of Social Issues,* 1952, 8(1), 18–28

Hogrefe, R., Evans, M. C., & Chein, I. The effects on intergroup attitudes of participation in an interracial play center. *American Psychologist,* 1947, 2, 324 (Abstract)

Irish, D. P. Reactions of Caucasian residents to Japanese-American neighbors. *Journal of Social Issues,* 1952, 8(1), 10–17

James, H. E. O. Personal contact in school and change in intergroup attitudes. *International Social Science Bulletin,* 1955, 7, 66–70

Kelman, H. C. Changing attitudes through international activities. *Journal of Social Issues,* 1962, 18(1), 68–87

Kramer, B. M. Residential contact as a determinant of attitudes towards Negroes. Unpublished doctoral dissertation, Harvard College Library, 1950

Lieberson, S. A societal theory of race and ethnic relations. *American Sociological Review,* 1961, 26, 902–10

Mann, J. H. The effects of interracial contact on sociometric choices and perceptions. *Journal of Social Psychology,* 1959, 50, 143–52

Mannheimer, D., & Williams, R. M., Jr. A note on Negro troops in combat. In S. A. Stouffer, E. A. Suchman, L. C. DeVinney, S. A. Star, & R. M. Williams, Jr. *The American Soldier.* Vol. 1. Princeton: Princeton University Press, 1949

Murphy, G. *In the minds of men.* New York: Basic Books, 1953

Mussen, P. H. Some personality and social factors related to changes in children's attitudes toward Negroes. *Journal of Abnormal and Social Psychology,* 1950, 45, 423–41

Pinkney, A. The quantitative factor in prejudice. *Sociology and Social Research,* 1963, 47, 161–68

Ram, P., & Murphy, G. Recent investigations of Hindu-Moslem relations in India. *Human Organization,* 1952, 11(2), 13–16

Rose, Alvin. Race relations in a Chicago industry (Unpublished study, University of Chicago, 1946) In Arnold Rose, *Studies in reduction of prejudice.* Chicago: American Council on Race Relations, 1948

Sapir, R. A shelter. *Megamot,* 1951, 3, 8–36

Schild, E. O. The foreign student, as stranger, learning the norms of the host culture. *Journal of Social Issues,* 1962, 18(1), 41–54

Segal, B. E. Contact, compliance and distance among Jewish and non-Jewish undergraduates. *Social Problems,* 1965, 13, 66–74

Sherif, M. *Group conflict and cooperation.* London: Routledge & Kegan Paul, 1966

Sherif, M., & Sherif, C. W. *Groups in harmony and tension: An integration of studies in intergroup relations.* New York: Harper, 1953

Shuval, J. T. The micro-neighborhood: An approach to ecological patterns of ethnic groups. *Social Problems,* 1962, 9, 272–80

Smith, F. T. An experiment in modifying attitudes toward the Negro. *Teachers College Contribution to Education,* 1943, No. 887

Soen, D. & Tishler, I. *Urban renewal: Social surveys.* Tel-Aviv: Institute for Planning and Development, 1968

Stouffer, S. A., Lumsdaine, A. A., Lumsdaine, M. H., Williams, R. M., Jr., Smith, M. B., Janis, I. L., Star, S. A., & Cottrell, L. S., Jr. *The American soldier.* Vol. 2. Princeton: Princeton University Press, 1949

Watson, J. Some social and psychological situations related to change in attitude. *Human Relations,* 1950, 3(1), 15–56

Weingrod, A. *Israel: Group relations in a new society.* New York: Praeger, 1965

Wilner, D. M., Walkley, R. P., & Cook, S. W. Residential proximity and intergroup relations in public housing projects. *Journal of Social Issues,* 1952, 8(1), 45–69

Yarrow, M. R., Campbell, J. P., & Yarrow, L. J. Acquisition of new norms: A study of racial desegregation. *Journal of Social Issues,* 1958, 14(1), 8–28

Young, D. *American minority peoples: A study in racial and cultural conflicts in the United States.* New York: Harper, 1932

Coexistence and the Reconciliation of Communal Conflicts

LOUIS KRIESBERG

Conflicts in which adversaries regard themselves significantly in terms of ethnicity, language, religion, or other communal identities are understandably matters of high concern at present. Such communal conflicts are often brutally violent and seemingly intractable. Even without the violence of civil wars or genocidal policies, peoples may suffer enduring oppression and exploitation. But most of the time, peoples live side by side and coexist with varying degrees of mutual accommodation. Furthermore, some peoples after bitter conflicts do find a kind of accommodation, forms of coexistence, and even reconciliation.

We need to understand how interethnic coexistence can be fostered and if destructive conflict erupts, not only how it can be overcome, but how it can be transformed and coexistence established or more likely, reestablished. In this contribution, we focus on the relationship of reconciliation to ethnic coexistence, particularly at the time when an interethnic struggle is brought to an end and intercommunal relations are transformed. After discussing the meanings of the terms coexistence and reconciliation, we examine the obstacles to achieving them out of the torments of protracted communal conflicts. We then examine bases for progress toward equitable coexistence and reconciliation, forms of reconciliation work, and strategies for conducting such work.

Meanings of Coexistence and Reconciliation

The terms "coexistence" and "reconciliation" are used in many senses; therefore any discussion of their interrelations in the context of ethnic and other communal conflicts first requires an examination of the terms.[1] They both refer to aspects of a relationship between antagonistic or formerly antagonistic persons or groups. Coexistence refers to a wide range of relationships, excluding ones characterized by overt struggle. Reconciliation generally refers to a relatively amicable and potentially stable relationship, generally established after a rupture in the relationship including one-sided or mutual infliction of extreme injury. Clarifying the several meanings of coexistence and reconciliation will not only reduce miscommunication, but suggest variations in the phenomena to which various senses of each word applies. Those variations are critical to understanding the relations between them and developing policies that foster achieving stable and equitable coexistence between formerly opposing ethnic groups.

Coexistence.

Although there are a great many understandings of the term "coexistence," it generally is understood to refer to relationships between persons or groups in which none of the parties is trying to destroy the other. But that still leaves a great deal of room for various forms of relations. Often, an adjective is added to clarify the meaning intended by the term coexistence. For example, in US–USSR relations during the period of détente, Soviet leaders used the term *peaceful coexistence* to characterize the relationship between the Soviet Union and the United States, and to convey a sense of mutual acceptance and equality.

Coexistence varies both in terms of structural and subjective aspects of the relationship between persons, groups, or other entities. First, considering the structure of relations among entities who may be adversaries, two dimensions should be noted. One is the degree to which the parties are integrated with each other or are separated from each other. Many entities whose members are not engaged with each other coexist in the world, but that is hardly worth mentioning; at least some nontrivial involvement is needed to make the coexistence meaningful. We are concerned here with entities that have significant interdependence and interaction, but that vary in the degree to which their relations are conflictual. Communal groups within the same country are generally highly integrated with each other, much more so than are two neighboring countries.

The other significant dimension of the structural aspects of the relations between coexisting entities is the degree of equality or inequality between them. In some cases, coexistence is stable with few overt signs of conflict, but the relationship is characterized by one group's dominating the other. The domination may be so severe that the subordinated party does not consider it feasible to raise any challenges and seems to accept the domination as if it were legitimate. Here we are most interested in the coexistence between groups in which no party greatly dominates the other and exploits its members.

In addition to the structure of the relationship, members of coexisting communities vary in their subjective state, in how their members regard each other and their relationship. Given the human tendencies toward ethnocentrism, members of each communal group are likely to regard themselves as superior and worthy of support and loyalty. In intense conflicts, each group may come to dehumanize the other, regarding its adherents as lower beings. But, there also may be considerable mutual respect, even for those who differ in language, religion, or other characteristics. At the other extreme, one communal group may regard the other as inferior and so dominate members of that group that its members internalize their own low ranking.

Whatever the rankings in group evaluations may be, they are often overlaid in varying degrees with sentiments of tolerance for differences in ways of life. The sentiments may be embodied in norms that constrain even a dominant group from acting in a highly discriminatory fashion against a subordinate group. Such sentiments and norms are enhanced by identities that are shared by members of the different groups, for example as coreligionists or as citizens of the same country.

Reconciliation

The term "reconciliation" generally refers to the process of developing a mutual conciliatory accommodation between antagonistic or formerly antagonistic persons or groups. It often refers to a relatively amicable relationship, typically established after a rupture in the relationship involving one-sided or mutual infliction of extreme injury. There are variations, however, in the meanings of the term reconciliation, and they should be explained. Clarifying the several meanings will not only reduce misunderstandings, but suggest variations in the phenomena to which different senses of the word applies. Those variations are critical to the development of policies that foster a stable and equitable relationship between formerly opposing groups.

Recognition of the importance of reconciliation between opponents in a struggle of recurrent cycles of humiliations, of revenge, and of violence, is growing. Reconciliation, however, has more than one meaning and includes contradictory elements. One meaning is to bring people back into concord with each other. But another meaning is to bring people into a state of acquiescence or submission to circumstances. The two meanings are not inconsistent in the present context. To bring people into accord often means that one or more parties accepts losses that cannot be avoided or changed. Furthermore, coming into concord does not mean equal gains and losses for the former adversaries. One side may have more to atone for and the other more to forgive. Reconciliation might refer to members of one side accepting the painful reality of their circumstances after a struggle in which they experienced devastating losses. Here I will use the term to refer to relationships with relatively shared views of who bore what losses and who bears what responsibility.

Reconciliation here refers to accommodative ways members of adversary entities have come to regard each other after having engaged in intense and often destructive struggle. They have somehow become able to put aside feelings of hate, fear, and loathing, to discard views of the other as dangerous and subhuman, and to abandon the desire for revenge and retribution. To set aside does not mean to have no such feelings, perceptions, and goals, but not to make them paramount nor to act on them against the former adversary.

Reconciliation varies in four noteworthy regards: units, dimensions, symmetry, and degrees. Each will be briefly discussed.

Units

Reconciliation may be attained between individuals, peoples, officials, families, or other groups or various combinations of them. Some individuals from antagonistic sides may become reconciled with each and yet most members of the enemy groups remain hostile. After intense struggles between large-scale adversaries, it is not likely that reconciliation will be universal among all members of the opposing sides. But official accommodation and reconciliation can still be achieved, even after something as horrible as the Holocaust by representatives of the German and Jewish peoples.

Dimensions

Reconciliation requires that members of the formerly antagonistic parties attain a minimal degree of four beliefs: they acknowledge with honesty the terrible aspects of what happened; they accept with compassion those who committed injurious conduct as well as acknowledge each other's suffering; they believe that injustices are being redressed; and they anticipate mutual security and well-being. This formulation is influenced by the use made of Psalm 85 by the conciliation team working in Nicaraguan villages to explain the agreement reached between the Yatama leaders and the Sandinistas.[2] The conciliators read the Psalm at the beginning of the meeting. It includes the verse, "Mercy and truth are met together; Righteousness and peace have kissed each other." The coming together of all those elements and the resolution of paradoxes arising from that encounter are crucial in the process of reconciliation.

A fundamental aspect of reconciliation is the open and shared recognition of the injuries suffered and the losses experienced. Official investigations, judicial proceedings, artistic productions, and mass-media reporting are all ways to face openly what many experienced covertly. Recognition ideally includes acknowledgments by those who inflicted the harm that they accept some responsibility for what happened. This may mean the offering of apologies and the expressing of regrets. All this is part of discovering and facing the truth.

In addition, many persons who have suffered from oppression and atrocities in the course of an intense struggle seek redress for the injustices they endured. Reconciliation often entails some degree of such redress. This may be in the form of tangible restitution or compensation for what was lost; it may take the form of punishment for those who committed injustices; or it may be exhibited in policies that offer protection against future discrimination or harm.

The third dimension element in reconciliation involves expressions by those who have suffered the harms that acknowledge the humanity of those who have committed the injuries. At the extreme, this may consist of expressions of mercy and forgiveness. But more likely this will only entail expressing the thoughts that many members of the adversary community did not personally and directly carry out harmful actions, and that the next generation is not responsible for what had been done by previous generations. Even less directly, persons who are from communities who have struggled against each other may engage cooperatively in projects relating to past harms, but not require any direct expressions of apology or forgiveness.[3]

Finally, the adversaries look forward to living together in peace without threatening each other, with mutual respect and security, perhaps even in harmony and unity. This may be in the context of high levels of integration or in the context of separation and little regular interaction. The nature of the anticipated peaceful relations vary, but the realization of the mutual preferences of the adversaries is critical.

Symmetry

The discussion so far suggests that one side in a relationship is the perpetrator of oppression and atrocities and members of the other are the victims. Frequently, however, antagonistic sides include individuals and groups who have inflicted great injuries upon each other. Several of the matters discussed are illustrated by the workings of the Truth and Reconciliation Commission established in South Africa after Nelson Mandela was elected president. For example, South Africa's former president, F. W. de Klerk, testifying before the Commission on August 21, 1996, said, "I have already publicly apologized for the pain and suffering caused by former policies of the National Party. I reiterate those apologies today."[4] He acknowledged that National Party Governments had approved "unconventional" actions that "created the environment within which abuses and gross violations of human rights could take place." The next day, Deputy President Thabo Mbeki, representing the African National Congress (A.N.C.), submitted a statement of the A.N.C. saying: "It would be morally wrong and legally incorrect to equate apartheid with the resistance against it. . . ."[5] But he added that some civilians had been caught "in the crossfire" and that "the leadership of the A.N.C. would want to express its regret and sorrow. . . . I'm sorry for the loss of life of those who might not have been members of the security forces."

Typically postconflict relationships entail only a few elements of reconciliation, often one-sided ones. For example, consider the relationship between a party that has suffered much in a struggle that it has lost and a party that has endured relatively small losses and is dominant. The overwhelmed party will likely reconcile itself to what has happened, sometimes enduring internal disorientation, while the dominating group denies or gives little attention to the injuries inflicted by its agents in its name. This can be illustrated by many of the struggles waged by conquering settlers in the United States and in many other parts of the world.[6]

Coexistence and reconciliation are most likely to be equitable when there is no clear victor and each side must attend to the concerns of their adversaries. This may occur if the relatively vulnerable side gains allies and supporters. Even if one side seems utterly defeated, the result may be regarded as mutually beneficial by the former adversaries. Thus a side that may seem to be defeated may become so transformed that only a small segment (perhaps the former leadership), loses and the other members believe that the new relationship with the former adversary is desirable. For example, this was generally true for the German people after the military defeat of Nazism.

Coexistence and reconciliation are also more likely to be equitable when the conflict has been settled using a problem-solving conflict resolution approach. This entails viewing the struggle as a problem that the parties face together and for which a solution is sought and jointly constructed. Often this approach is aided by the efforts of mediators. The likelihood of adopting this approach is also enhanced by the opposing sides sharing important identities, having high levels of integration, and not being greatly asymmetrical in resources.

Degrees

Clearly, all these dimensions of reconciliation are not fully realizable and in some ways are contradictory. For example, mercy and justice often cannot be satisfied at the same time, although they may be compatible if pursued sequentially or at the same time but by different members of the previously antagonistic sides. This discussion also indicates that there are various kinds of reconciliations, with different combinations of elements. For purposes of the present analysis, some degree of mutuality in the reconciliation is essential.

Recognizing that a widespread and comprehensive reconciliation is rare should not lead us to ignore the partial reconciliations which are achieved. Furthermore, there are other forms of accommodation that are stable but involve little reconciliation. For example, coexistence may be accepted as necessary. On the other hand, the failure to have achieved any degree of reconciliation or alternative form of accommodation leaves the door open to revenge-seeking.

The failure to carry out any measures of reconciliation endangers the stability in the relationship between former enemies. For example, the atrocities committed during World War II in Yugoslavia, particularly by the Croat Ustashi forces against Serbs were not explicitly and openly adjudicated or investigated by the Yugoslavian government headed by Tito. The government leaders, partly on ideological grounds and partly concerned about stirring up ethnic animosities, treated the internal struggles among Yugoslavs in terms of class and ideological differences. The unreconciled ethnic hostilities were available to be aroused later and contributed to the breakup of Yugoslavia in bloody wars.

Relations between Coexistence and Reconciliation in Different Conflict Stages

Coexistence and reconciliation come in many forms and are compatible in many ways, but some kinds of coexistence and reconciliation are not readily compatible. Much depends on the sequencing of coexistence and reconciliation and their social context, particularly the stage of the conflict in which adversarial groups are engaged.

Relations. In general, reconciliation is expected to emerge from interethnic coexistence and its realization helps stabilize and sustain coexistence. This is most likely to occur when the different communal groups are mutually interdependent and when the balance of resources in power, status, and economic conditions are not greatly asymmetric.

In many cases, however, such kinds of coexistence and reconciliation do not occur. Coexistence between groups whose relationship is characterized by gross inequality may result in submission and hidden opposition, hardly the soil for cultivating reconciliation. That is why the emphasis here is on equitable coexistence, the kind in which the coexisting groups accept to a significant degree the appropriateness of the terms of coexistence.

Sometimes adversarial parties separate themselves or are separated by outside parties. That can be the basis for a nonconflicting accommodation, but not one that is conducive to reconciliation. For example, the division of Cyprus into Greek and Turkish Cypriot communities—initially by Turkish military action—was institutionalized with United Nations peacekeeping forces maintaining the separation.

Conflict stages. Conflicts tend to exhibit a course of development: emerging, escalating, de-escalating, and ending. Actions that foster equitable coexistence and reconciliation are not restricted to the period when a conflict is ending. Even when a conflict is being waged and escalated, attention to future coexistence can affect the way the struggle is conducted. For example, if the adversary ethnic group is not treated as a single unit and all its members are not dehumanized and regarded as targets, reconciliation and equitable coexistence will be more readily achieved when the fighting ceases.

In de-escalating and ending a struggle, reassurances about seeking an equitable coexistence can hasten a settlement and even a resolution of the conflict. Ethnic and other communal conflicts are often protracted and seem intractable because one or sometimes both sides feel that their very existence is at stake if they are defeated. Convincing assurances that their existence as individuals and as people are not threatened becomes an important step toward settlement.

But requiring other kinds of reconciliation can act as barriers to ending a conflict and establishing equitable coexistence. For example, calls for justice by the aggrieved party may seem to pose unacceptable demands to the dominant party. Calls for justice in the form of judicial trials of the leaders of a collectivity charged with human rights violations are certainly likely to be rejected by those leaders. This obviously was a complicating factor in the efforts to end the war in Bosnia in 1996. But without some measure of justice, the resulting outcome may be the imposition of injustice and a coexistence that is far from equitable and ultimately unstable.

Once an ending has been achieved, establishing the conditions for an enduring and equitable coexistence becomes salient. Reconciliation that is balanced and mutual and not merely one-sided acceptance of an imposed settlement depends upon the establishment of an equitable coexistence.

Obstacles to Achieving Equitable Coexistence and Reconciliation

The obstacles and opportunities for coexistence and reconciliation vary greatly with several characteristics of the relationship between particular communal groups. Five characteristics are particularly noteworthy here: first, the degree and nature of the previous losses each has suffered at the hands of the other, recognizing that the hurts are likely to be asymmetrical; second, the extent to which one party is the winner and the other the loser in the outcome of the previous intercommunal struggles; third, the current relative political, economic, and military strength of the groups; fourth, the extent of continuity in the leadership (persons and structure) of each group; and fifth, the extent to which their current relationship is integrated or separated.

These characteristics are likely to vary depending on the particular set of groups chosen for consideration. The group members themselves are likely to disagree about the boundaries of their groups. For example, many Arab Palestinians consider the relevant parties to be on one side: all Arab Palestinians who live or whose parents or grandparents lived in what was British-mandated Palestine, and on the other side, Jews in Israel and elsewhere in the world along with people in Western countries supporting the Jews. For many Israeli Jews, the appropriate groups are the Jews of Israel on one side and all the peoples of the Arab world on the other. We will discuss the obstacles to reconciliation in general, but programs and policies must be suitable to particular relations to be effective.

Equitable forms of ethnic coexistence are not universally given the highest priority. Efforts to achieve them often face resistance and that needs to be understood in order to implement effective strategies to advance a relatively balanced coexistence. The same is true for the attainment of a mutually balanced reconciliation. Three general sets of obstacles will be briefly noted here: popular sentiments, ideologies, and vested interests.

Popular Sentiments

Relations shaped by ethnic and other communal identities have some bases in popular sentiments on each side of the relationship. Commonly, adherents of each side have feelings of pride and loyalty toward their own community and feelings of distrust and sometimes antagonism toward other communal groups. This is derived in part from general ethnocentric tendencies and social-psychological mechanisms of group identification. But the more serious manifestations of ethnic hostilities depend upon more particular manifestations of social processes. In many relationships, people on each side learn from parents, teachers, and religious and political leaders about the past in which they suffered losses by the actions of the members of the other side. Songs are sung, stories are told, and marches are held commemorating past victories over or defeats by the other side. In many cultures, these also give focus and direction to males' socialization to be warriors and to defend their people against dishonor.

Ideologies

In addition to the particular histories of relationships or the general cultural patterning of animosities, relatively well-articulated ideologies, varying in fashion, also guide intercommunal relations. Some ideologies attribute little significance to ethnic or other communal identities; they emphasize human characteristics that might be universally shared, such as supporting liberal democracy or advocating the cause of the working class.

Some ideologies, on the other hand, build on communal identities so that members of communal groups are readily pitted against each other. One such ideology is racism, claiming that some so-called races are biologically superior to others and that the superior race has the God-given or nature-given right to dominate lesser races. Another such ideology is nationalism, claiming that a nation should have its own land and government; a nation being a people who believe they share a common origin and many common qualities such as language, culture, and religion. The demand for a separate country for a nation, given the reality that many peoples live intermingled with each other, is often a source of strife.

Vested Interests

It is important to recognize that there are beneficiaries of struggles against other ethnic groups, of victories over them, and of their oppression. These beneficiaries tend to resist efforts to build peaceful and just relations between particular ethnic groups. Persons who believe they benefit from the continuing struggle or domination over another people are diverse. They may include intellectuals who believe their standing is enhanced by their privileged use of their language and the maintenance of a constituency for their cultural productions. They often include political leaders who believe that mobilizing ethnic or other communal bases for support is the road to attaining and keeping political power. They also may include those who wage the battle as armed fighters.

Bases for Progress toward Coexistence and Reconciliation

Despite the many obstacles to reconciliation, many people strive for it, and are often significantly successful. We will briefly note some of the motives and sources for such efforts, before discussing the methods of achieving reconciliation and the strategies for implementing them. Strategies to promote reconciliation are likely to be effective insofar as they are based on already available motives and sources of support for equitable coexistence and reconciliation.

Among the many kinds of motives and sources supporting reconciliation, three will be noted: personal, structural, and ideological. Individuals vary greatly in their readiness to seek and accept reconciliation with their erstwhile enemy. Some people are prone to feel sympathy and empathy for persons who have suffered, even if they belong to an enemy category. The sources of such variation has not been extensively examined, but the existence of the variation is clear. For some persons it is buttressed by their social role, religious sentiments, or personal experience with persons of the other side. This variability provides some people who can make the connections when steps toward reconciliation become feasible.

For example, in 1985 the South African Minister of Justice, Police, and Prisons, Hendrik Jacobus Coetsee, began effective secret meetings with the imprisoned leader of the A.N.C., Nelson Mandela.[7] Coetsee had some credibility for this task through his colleagueship with an Afrikaner lawyer who had legally defended Winnie Mandela, the wife of Nelson Mandela.

Many structural conditions provide the sources for reconciliation. They include the interests that members of different sides of a conflict share. An elementary shared interest is the avoidance of the great costs that ethnic strife can impose on all members of a society. In Malaysia, the eruption of riots by Malays against the Chinese worried both communities enough so that actions were taken to find a mutual political and economic accommodation that would ensure economic growth and allow members of both communities to prosper.

Another major source for reconciliation arises from pressure from the aggrieved community. The aggrieved persons may exercise passive resistance as unorganized individuals: for example, by withholding adequately performed services. Members of challenging communities may rely on more direct and organized forms of struggle, such as street demonstrations, written protests, and riots. More extended struggles include strategies such as nonviolent action and guerrilla warfare. All of these means impose costs on the challenged group, but also are often accompanied by persuasive arguments and the promise of improved relations if the goals sought are realized.

Another source for reconciliation that warrants emphasis is the way people view the world, including their ideologies, general thoughtways, and specific beliefs and values. For example, in many settings, norms of tolerance are widely held, often formed from the bitter experience of the costs inflicted by intolerance. Thus in Western countries, tolerance was a solution to the religious wars that caused so much destruction. More recently, increasingly shared views about the existence of universal human rights help provide minimum standards for relations between people who differ by religious beliefs, ethnicity, political ideology, or in many other ways that might be the basis for enmity. Finally, religious traditions generally stress moral injunctions such as the importance of demonstrating charity and mercy toward other humans.

Fostering Coexistence and Reconciliation

In this section, we focus on specific policies that often are seen to foster equitable coexistence and mutual reconciliation. They include structural, experiential, and interpersonal methods. They can make particular contributions to reconciliation by promoting the recognition of truths, the attainment of justice, the advancement of well being, and the expression of mercy.

Structural Methods

Structural methods include policies directed at reducing inequalities, developing crosscutting ties, fostering superordinate goals, and creating human rights safeguards. Each will be briefly noted.

Reduce inequalities. Methods to reduce inequalities that are the source of grievances may include compensatory policies such as affirmative action programs or the payment of reparations. They may take the form of creating more equal opportunities such as increasing the availability of schools and other educational facilities. Or they may take the form of combating discriminatory hiring and advancement practices in employment or actively seeking to recruit and promote persons from groups who had previously been discriminated against or otherwise disadvantaged. For example, the establishment of affirmative action policies, geared to economic growth, has contributed to accommodation between the relatively economically disadvantaged Malay majority and the relatively economically advantaged Chinese minority in Malaysia.[8]

Develop crosscutting ties. If many lines of cleavage coincide, conflicts are likely to erupt and be difficult to resolve, while crosscutting lines of cleavage and associations tend to mitigate the intensity and duration of struggles. Electoral procedures, for example, may foster broad and inclusive political parties or ones based on communal identities.

Foster superordinate goals and identities. Institutions may be established and practices and policies pursued that lead to a sense of common purpose.[9] These include educational practices within a country that emphasize a common history and identity among all the citizens, and forming institutions across ethnic or national lines for particular shared goals. For example, the establishment of the European Coal and Steel Community (ECSC) after World War II contributed to reconciliation between the Germans and the French.

Human rights safeguards. Much attention is now being given to shared understandings about human rights, including individual civil and political rights, and also collective rights of minority groups. Such rights are increasingly recognized and embodied in the laws of more and more countries. They may be reinforced by provisions that allow for some measure of power-sharing so that groups who are at risk have control of or access to at least a minimal degree of legitimate political power.

Experiential Methods

The subjective feelings and state of mind needed to bring about and sustain coexistence and reconciliation can be fostered by a great variety of experiences, both private and public. This is recognized in policies that channel and bring some degree of satisfaction to claims for justice, truth, retribution, and well-being.

Public trials of particular persons who are charged and proven guilty of crimes against specific persons, related to communal antagonisms and violence, can contribute to equitable coexistence and reconciliation in many ways. They provide information about the suffering that victims have experienced. They lay responsibility on particular persons, reducing the onus on the collectivity to which the perpetrators belong. They satisfy some of the desires people feel for retribution and punishment of the guilty. They serve as warnings against the recurrence of such crimes.

In recent years, variations on such kinds of trials have been undertaken. For example, in South Africa, a Truth and Reconciliation Commission was established in 1996, agreed to in the negotiations about the transition from white domination. It represents a kind of compromise providing a public accounting of killing and torturing under the previous government, but avoiding what might be thousands of criminal prosecutions. It consists of three committees: one collects and investigates victims' accounts, another considers amnesty, and a third makes recommendations about reparations for victims.

Education can be an important vehicle for developing beliefs and values that can support equitable coexistence and reconciliation; but they can also be the source of arousing and sustaining communal antagonisms. To advance the former and undermine the latter, the content of the curricular material and the day-to-day schooling experience must convey the reality of the shared humanness of members of antagonistic communities and the great diversities within each, as well as the validity of the cultural variations among them. For example, in the United States, education seems to have contributed to the decline in prejudice among whites regarding blacks. Portrayal and reporting about different communal groups in the mass media can also contribute to mutual understanding and acceptance or to fears and hostilities between ethnic and other communal groups, and thus must be done wisely.

Many social institutions can provide a setting in which interaction between members of different communal groups is the basis for exchanging information about each other and breaking down stereotypes. This is likely to occur in settings where interactions are between persons of relatively equal status.[10] Under such conditions, the experience of intercommunal encounters within integrated work settings can be conducive to prejudice reduction.

Many kinds of public events and products can generate experiences that support equitable coexistence and reconciliation. These include public ceremonies, parades, and monuments that celebrate historical and mythical origins. Their celebration helps form shared emotions, commitments, and identities. They may even provide opportunities for shared expressions of mourning and bereavement.

Expressions of forgiveness can be a powerful way to overcome suspicions and with the other side to acknowledge its mistakes and shameful actions. The offering of forgiveness is in many religious traditions.[11]

Another experiential method that contributes to equitable coexistence and reconciliation is the management of antagonistic incidents and disputes between members of different communal groups. Local agencies and centers, both private and public, can help in such management. For example, they can mediate a dispute, provide counsel to an aggrieved person, or offer training and consultations to prevent future disputes.

Finally, programs that provide private settings for people to work through the personal anguish produced by past intercommunal fighting can be helpful. Previous destructive struggles leave long-lasting traumas that reverberate intergenerationally. The treatment and management of such trauma, then, not only reduces the suffering caused by the past hurts, but helps reduce the chances that post trauma will be the source for renewed destructive struggles at some later time.

Interpersonal Methods

A great deal of reconciliation work is done on an individual basis, but more often it occurs within small groups in schools, workplaces, communities, or other settings. These small groups occur at a grass-roots level, but also at the level of high and middle ranking leaders. Some of this work is significantly facilitated by intermediaries who do not belong to any of the adversarial parties.

Individuals suffering posttraumatic problems may receive psychological therapy and so be better able to dissipate and control feelings of hostility that otherwise might be directed at members of other ethnic groups. Such emotions are especially relevant for survivors of intense communal conflicts.

Special workshops for small groups of students, employees, members of religious institutions, community leaders, and of many other groups provide a variety of training and experience directed at reducing intercommunal antagonisms. For example, many of these pertain to relations between Jews and Arabs within Israel, and between Israeli Jews and Arab Palestinians elsewhere.[12]

Finally, leading individuals from the antagonistic sides sometimes undertake personal meetings that greatly contribute to reconciliation. These meetings sometimes are the first face-to-face interaction leaders of enemy sides have had and signal mutual recognition of the sides they represent as well as a personal mutual acceptance. For persons and groups who have waged long and sometimes brutal fights, such meetings, often arranged by intermediaries, are a vital first step toward equitable coexistence and reconciliation.

Strategies for Coexistence and Reconciliation

In this section, strategies for achieving equitable coexistence and reconciliation of communal conflicts are discussed; they combine various methods, sequentially as well as simultaneously implemented. This discussion is organized by considering whether the agents who determine and execute the strategies are the top, middle, or grassroots leaders. For each source, we will also distinguish between persons who are based within one or more of the possibly antagonistic communal groups or based outside them.

Top Down

Strategies for coexistence and reconciliation are often initiated and encouraged by high-ranking leaders external to the contending sides, as well as internal to one or more of the adversarial groups.

From the inside. Within a country, high-ranking government officials often regard themselves as representing the collectivity of which the antagonistic communal groups are components. This favors recourse to structural and experiential methods to generate integration and shared identities. For example, leading officials of the U.S. government, particularly in the 1960s during the struggle for civil rights, implemented policies that were directed at reducing discrimination and deprivations suffered by black citizens. The policies were justified in terms of American values of fairness, equality of individual opportunity, and equality of rights.

Leaders of one of the adversary sides may pursue a step-by-step strategy to forge an accommodative relationship with an erstwhile adversary. This may include providing assurance of safety for the other side. It also may include an acknowledgment of some responsibility for the harm suffered by the other side in the past. It is likely to include fostering common overriding identities and establishing institutions that promise mutual benefits. Such policies offer a context for egalitarian social interactions and mutual interdependence. These strategies, it should be recognized, are pursued at the international level as well as within societies.[13]

From the outside. Powerful (and not so powerful) high-ranking intervenors sometimes pursue policies that contribute to adversaries' accommodation of and reconciliation with each other. In the post cold-war world, with the eruption and also the settlement of many large-scale internal struggles, such external intervention has become more frequent. This is evident in the steep rise of United Nations peacekeeping missions, and also in the increased cases of assistance in the implementation and monitoring of negotiated settlements between former enemies.

The range of policies external actors may pursue is large. They include, for example, the UN Security Council's creation of an international tribunal to prosecute perpetrators of war crimes in Bosnia. They include assistance in drafting laws and a constitution, in organizing and monitoring elections, and in demobilizing armed units.[14]

Lateral

Middle-range leaders are particularly likely to utilize experiential and interpersonal methods. They may be middle-range leaders within one or more of the antagonistic groups or based outside any of them.

From the inside. Leading figures in many local or even national institutions often play critical roles in fostering coexistence and reconciliation. They include religious, business, and political leaders, intellectuals and artists, news media personages, and many others. They help to forge interpersonal linkages between communities, to organize intercommunal dialogue groups and problem solving workshops, and to establish agencies to monitor and protect the rights of all citizens.

From the outside. External midlevel intermediaries and other kinds of intervenors include international nongovernmental organizations providing humanitarian and development assistance, fostering direct peace-building work, and advocating human rights protection. Such organizations are often associated with religious bodies, such as the Society of Friends or the Mennonites.[15]

Refugees and diaspora communities have always played significant roles in sustaining and also in resolving communal antagonisms. They can provide resources to sustain the struggle, but also resources to make accommodations more acceptable. In addition, they affect the policies of the countries in which they reside, influencing the government's possible intervention to aid one side in the struggle, to stop a conflict's destructive escalation, or to mediate a resolution of the struggle. For example, members of the Irish, Jewish, and Slavic diaspora communities in the United States have effectively played these various roles in conflicts not directly involving the United States. Dialogue groups with members drawn from opposing diaspora communities can contribute to peace building in their places of origin as well as in the new host societies.[16]

Bottom Up

Grassroots leaders can and do intervene from the outside to promote reconciliation work. They also exist within each of the adversarial sides and encourage, promote, and conduct policies that tend to help bring about equitable coexistence and reconciliation. They are likely to rely on interpersonal and experiential methods, and some of them exercise pressure to foster structural change.

From the inside. Local leaders for one of the aggrieved parties often engage in struggles to achieve greater justice for their constituents. This may include enacting legislation against discrimination, providing compensation for past damages, and permitting autonomy in culturally significant arenas. In many circumstances, such struggles are an essential component in the attainment of equitable coexistence and reconciliation.

Organizations with members drawn from antagonistic communities are often founded by grassroots leaders. As women, peasants, or residents of a particular locality, they see intercommunal strife as a danger to themselves and those they love. They encourage and promote policies of reconciliation to be pursued by high-ranking officials or nongovernmental leaders.

From the outside. External grassroots contributors in building equitable coexistence and reconciliation include a variety of transnational social movement organizations.[17] They also include citizens groups that engage in people-to-people diplomacy, such as instituting programs of social exchanges between "twin" cities in countries that are or have been antagonistic.

Combined Sources

The strategies pursued from any single level are not likely to suffice to bring about an enduring, equitable coexistence and reconciliation. Leaders at the top, middle, and grassroots levels are needed to reinforce each other. Resistance is likely, and some elements at each level may endeavor to thwart or undermine movement toward coexistence and reconciliation. Concerted efforts at each level are therefore needed to counter and overcome such resistance.

Whatever the strategies any particular group adopts, the context of changing social conditions provide unique limits and opportunities.[18] Changing economic, demographic, cultural, and many other relations between the antagonistic communities have profound effects on the likely effectiveness of whatever strategies are pursued. Changes in external conflicts, concerns and interests of external factors, and other such factors also provide settings for policies to work more effectively to bring about equitable coexistence and reconciliation. For example, the rise of the cold war provided a setting that encouraged policies of reconciliation between Germans and other peoples of Western Europe.

Conclusions

This review of the literature and practice regarding coexistence and reconciliation of communal conflicts indicates the significance of their relationships. To avoid either one-sided domination or recurrent destructive conflicts, a form of equitable coexistence leading toward reconciliation is crucial. A great many factors and policies may enhance one or another component of coexistence and reconciliation. No single factor or policy can be effective alone; rather various combinations are needed to achieve and sustain equitable coexistence and reconciliation.

The essence of having a long-term strategy is combining various policies in a coordinated manner. This often poses difficulties since some policies are not consistent with each other. One way to combine policies that might seem incompatible is to undertake them in a step-by-step sequence. Often, however, several policies are most effectively pursued simultaneously, yet the same parties cannot effectively pursue them all. One way of overcoming this difficulty is to recognize that a strategy may include the loosely coordinated efforts of various agents. There are significant roles to be played by many different actors to implement the many different kinds of policies that need to be pursued.

Developing and implementing policies to construct equitable coexistence and reconciliation always entails making moral choices. The priority given by some groups to one or another policy is affected by the values held by members of those groups. But the value preferences held are not simply expressions of taste or matters of faith; rather, they are influenced by and affect people's understandings about the empirical world.[19] Consequently, analyzing the way various methods affect the attainment of equitable coexistence and reconciliation helps us to make sound moral choices about policies.

Notes

1. Neil J. Kritz, ed., *Transitional Justice*, Vols. 1–3, Washington, D.C.: United States Institute of Peace, 1995.
2. John Paul Lederach, *Building Peace: Sustainable Reconciliation in Divided Societies*, Tokyo: United Nations University Press, 1995.
3. For example, a Southern plantation from the time before the American Civil War is being restored in the 1990s, and the work is being overseen by a group including a descendent of the family that owned the plantation and of one of the family of slaves from that plantation.
4. *New York Times*, August 22, 1996.
5. *New York Times*, August 23, 1996.
6. Robin M. Williams, Jr. *Mutual Accommodation: Ethnic Conflict and Cooperation*. Minneapolis: University of Minnesota Press, 1977.
7. Allister Sparks, *Tomorrow Is Another Country*, New York: Hill and Wang, 1995; also see: Hendrik W. van der Merwe, *Pursuing Justice and Peace in South Africa*. London and New York; Routledge, 1989.
8. McGarry, John, and Brendan O'Leary, eds., *The Politics of Ethnic Conflict* London and New York: Routledge, 1993.
9. Muzafer Sherif, *In Common Predicament*. Houghton Mifflin, Boston, 1966.

10. M. Hewstone and R. Brown, eds., *Control and Conflict in Intergroup Encounters,* Oxford: Basil Blackwell, 1986 and Y. Amir, "The Role of Intergroup Contact in Change of Prejudice and Ethnic Relations," in P. A. Katz, ed., *Towards the Elimination of Racism,* New York: Pergamon, 1976.

11. Michael Henderson, *The Forgiveness Factor.* London: Grosvenor Books, 1996.

12. For example, see; Herbert C. Kelman, "The Interactive Problem-Solving Approach," pp. 501–19 in Chester A. Crocker and Fen Osler Hampson and Pamela Aall, eds., *Managing Global Chaos,* Washington: United States Institute of Peace, 1996.

13. Louis Kriesberg, *International Conflict Resolution,* New Haven and London: Yale University Press, 1992.

14. Fen Osler Hampson, *Nurturing Peace: Why Peace Settlements Succeed or Fail.* Washington, D.C.: United States Institute of Peace, 1996.

15. Cynthia Sampson and John Paul Lederach, eds., *From the Ground Up: Mennonite Contributions to International Peacebuilding,* forthcoming.

16. Richard D. Schwartz, "Arab-Jewish Dialogue in the United States: Toward Track II Tractibility," pp. 180–209 in Louis Kriesberg, Terrell A. Northrup, and Stuart J. Thorson (eds.) *Intractable Conflicts and Their Transformation,* Syracuse: Syracuse University Press, 1989.

17. Charles Chatfield, Ronald Pagnucco, and Jackie Smith, eds., *Solidarity beyond the State: The Dynamics of Transnational Social Movements.* Forthcoming. Syracuse, NY: Syracuse University Press.

18. This can be seen, for example, in the varying degrees to which coexistence was achieved in central Europe during the decades after the end of World War II and in the Middle East in the decades after the establishment of the state of Israel. See discussion in Louis Kriesberg, "Transforming Conflicts in the Middle East and Central Europe," pp. 109–31 in Louis Kriesberg, Terrell A. Northrup, and Stuart J. Thorson, eds., *Intractable Conflicts and Their Transformation,* Syracuse: Syracuse University Press, 1989.

19. Louis Kriesberg, "On Advancing Truth and Morality in Conflict Resolution," in Richard E. Rubenstein and Frank Blechman, eds., *Conflict Resolution and Social Justice,* forthcoming as of this writing.

Constructive Conflict Resolution: Principles, Training, and Research

MORTON DEUTSCH

This article starts with a listing of several propositions to which most students of conflict, no matter what their discipline, would assent. Next, there is a discussion of such factors affecting the course of conflict as the orientation to the conflict of the parties involved, their personalities, the issues, and the conflict's social-cultural context. The following part discusses the skills involved in constructive solutions, an area that has been neglected by most scholars. The final part presents some suggestions for research.

The plethora of scholars writing about conflict from different disciplinary backgrounds and focusing on different types of disputes has given the study of conflict a fragmented appearance. Yet beneath this disorganized surface there appear to be some common themes that cut across the different disciplines and the different types of conflict. These themes can be summarized, in part, in the following propositions:

(1) Most conflicts are mixed-motive conflicts in which the parties involved in the conflict have both cooperative and competitive interests.

(2) Conflict can be constructive as well as destructive. Conflict has been given a bad reputation by its association with psychopathology, social disorder, and war. However, it is the root of personal and social change; it is the medium through which problems can be aired and solutions arrived at. There are many positive functions of conflict (Coser, 1967). The social and scientific issue is not how to eliminate or prevent conflict but rather to develop the knowledge that would enable us to answer the question, What are the conditions that give rise to lively controversy rather than deadly quarrel?

(3) The cooperative and competitive interests of the parties give rise to two distinctive processes of conflict resolution. Walton and McKersie (1965) have termed the processes "integrative bargaining" and "distributive bargaining," while I have termed them "cooperative" and "competitive" processes (Deutsch, 1973). Associated with the different processes are distinctive strategies and tactics of dealing with conflict, differing communication and influence processes, and different attitudes toward the Other.

(4) The relative strengths of the cooperative and competitive interests within the conflicting parties, and how they vary during the course of a conflict, will be major determinants of the nature of the conflict process and of whether the outcomes of the conflict are likely to be constructive or destructive for the conflicting parties.

This article has three parts: a consideration of factors affecting whether a conflict will take a constructive or destructive course, a discussion of the skills involved in constructive conflict resolution, and some suggestions for research.

Factors Affecting the Course of Conflict

The Orientation of the Parties to the Conflict

A "dual concern" model of motivational orientation has been articulated by many theorists (e.g., Blake & Mouton, 1984; Cosier & Ruble, 1981; Pruitt & Rubin, 1986, Thomas, 1976). The dual concerns are "concern for self" and "concern for the other," the two concerns are considered to be independent, each can range from "low" to "high." Cooperativeness is associated with high concern for self and other; accommodativeness with low concern for self and high for other; competitiveness with high concern for self and low for other; and conflict avoidance with low concern for both. Presumably there would be little conflict when there is little concern for self (as in "avoidance" or "accommodativeness") and, hence, the two major orientations to conflict in the dual concern model would be cooperativeness and competitiveness.

I have distinguished three basic types of motivational orientations to a conflict (Deutsch, 1973): *cooperative*—the party has a positive interest in the welfare of the other as well as its own; *individualistic*—the party has an interest in doing as well as it can for itself and is unconcerned about the welfare of the other; and *competitive*—the party has an interest in doing better than the other as well as doing as well as it can for itself. Since each of two parties can have any one of the three basic orientations, nine (3 x 3) combinations of orientations are theoretically possible. However, research (Deutsch, 1973; Kelley & Stahelski, 1970) as well as theory (Deutsch, 1982) suggest that only the reciprocal combinations are stable and that nonreciprocal combinations tend to move in the direction of mutual competition if either party has a competitive orientation Research results also suggest that an individualistically oriented dyad will move either toward mutual cooperation or mutual competition depending upon which is favored by external circumstances and situational facilities.

As a result of much research by my students and myself (Deutsch, 1973, 1985), I have developed a hypothesis about what gives rise to cooperation and competition. I have termed it, "Deutsch's crude law of social relations": *the characteristic processes and effects elicited by a given type of social relationship (e.g., cooperative or competitive) also tend to elicit that type of social relationship.* Thus, cooperation induces and is induced by a perceived similarity in beliefs and attitudes, a readiness to be helpful, openness in communication, trusting and friendly attitudes, sensitivity to common interests and deemphasis of opposed interests, an orientation toward enhancing mutual power rather than power differences, and so on. Similarly, competition induces and is induced by the use of tactics of coercion, threat, or deception; attempts to enhance the power differences between oneself and the other; poor communication; minimization of the awareness of similarities in value and increased sensitivity to opposed interests; suspicious and hostile attitudes; the importance, rigidity, and size of the issues in conflict; and so on.

In other words, if one has systematic knowledge of the effects of cooperative and competitive processes, one will have systematic knowledge of the conditions that typically give rise to such processes, and by extension, to the conditions that affect whether a conflict will take a constructive or destructive course. My early theory of cooperation and competition (Deutsch, 1949) is a theory of the *effects* of cooperative and competitive processes. Hence, from the crude law of social relations stated earlier, it follows that this theory provides insight into the conditions that give rise to cooperative and competitive processes.

Understanding the conditions that give rise to cooperative or competitive social processes, as well as their characteristics, is central to understanding the circumstances that give rise to constructive or destructive processes of conflict resolution. A constructive process of conflict resolution is, in its essence, similar to an effective cooperative process, while a destructive process is similar to a process of competitive interaction. Since much is known about the nature of cooperative and competitive processes, and the conditions that give rise to each from my work and the work of other scholars (Deutsch, 1973, 1985; Johnson & Johnson, 1989), much of this knowledge can be applied to understanding the factors that determine whether a conflict will take a constructive or destructive course.

The Personalities of the Conflicting Parties

Social scientists have written extensively about the factors within parties that determine their predispositions to be prejudiced or fair-minded and to engage in destructive or prosocial forms of social behavior. This literature is too extensive to summarize here. However, a brief perspective on it will be presented that represents a growing consensus among psychologists studying the relationship between personality and social behavior (Snyder & Ickes, 1985).

The once dominant dispositional approach that seeks to understand social behavior in terms of relatively stable traits, dispositions, and other propensities that reside within individuals is now considered to have a limited usefulness. Such an approach typically focuses on one or more enduring predispositions of the following types: motivational tendencies (e.g., aggression, power, pride, fear), character traits (e.g., authoritarianism, Machiavellianism, locus of control, dogmatism), cognitive tendencies (e.g., cognitive simplicity vs. complexity, the "open" vs. "closed" system), values and ideologies (e.g., egalitarianism—nonegalitarianism, cooperative—competitive, traditional—modern), self-conceptions and bases of self-esteem, and learned habits and skills of coping. Thus, some scholars have sought to explain destructive conflict in terms of an inborn or acquired need for aggression, others have emphasized the power motive or pride, still others have stressed "black" and "white" thinking, while others have employed ideologies and self-conceptions as the basis of their explanations.

The now dominant approach to explaining social behavior is one that seeks to understand its regularities in terms of the interacting, reciprocally influencing, contributions of both situational and dispositional determinants. There are several well-supported theses in this approach (see Snyder & Ickes, 1985), which I summarize as follows:

(1) Individuals vary from one another considerably in terms of whether they manifest consistencies of personality in their social behavior across situations—e.g., those who monitor and regulate their behavioral choices on the basis of situational information show relatively little consistency (see Snyder & Ickes, 1985) as do those who report a relatively low degree of private self-consciousness (Schier, Buss, & Buss, 1978).

(2) Some situations have "strong" characteristics and, in these, little individual variation in behavior occurs despite differences in individual traits (Ickes, 1982; Mischel, 1977) while other situations with weak characteristics permit the play of individual differences.

(3) Some situations evoke dispositions because they are seen to be relevant to it, make it salient as a guide to behavior, and permit modes of behaving that are differentially responsive to individual differences in it (Bem & Lenney, 1976); other situations lacking these characteristics will not encourage the manifestation of a disposition.

(4) Some situations evoke self-focusing tendencies that make predispositions salient to the self and, as a consequence, a more influential determinant of behavior than in situations where such a self-focus is not evoked (Duval & Wickland, 1972, 1973; Schier, Carver, & Gibbons, 1981).

(5) There appears to be a tendency for a congruence between personal dispositions and situational strategies (Deutsch, 1982) such that persons with given dispositions tend to seek out types of social situations that fit their dispositions and persons tend to mold their dispositions to fit the situation that they find difficult to leave or to alter (Snyder & Ickes, 1985). For a characterization of the nature of the cognitions, motivations, and orientations or dispositions that are congruent with the basic types of social relations (defined by their locations on the following four dimensions: cooperative vs. competitive; egalitarian vs. nonegalitarian; social-emotional vs. task oriented; formal vs. informal), see Deutsch (1982, 1985).

This more complex model of the reciprocally influencing, interacting contributions of situational and dispositional determinants of social behavior suggests a continuing reciprocal influence between the internal states and characteristics of the conflicting parties and their external conflict. That is, the causal arrow goes in both directions between internal characteristics and external conflict rather than simply from internal characteristics to the nature of the conflict process. This is also why parties in an extended conflict process, whether cooperative or competitive, often tend to become mirror images in some respects (Bronfenbrenner, 1961).

The internal needs of the conflicting parties may require a conflictful relationship and, in turn, a conflictful relationship may generate needs within the parties that further perpetuate the conflict. Thus, there are many kinds of internal needs for which a hostile external relationship can be an outlet:

- It may provide an acceptable excuse for internal problems; the problems can be held out as caused by the adversary or by the need to defend against the adversary.
- It may provide a distraction so internal problems appear less salient.
- It enables one to have a sense of excitement, purpose, coherence, and unity that is otherwise lacking in one's life. Conflict, especially if it has dangerous overtones, can counteract feelings of aimlessness, boredom, and weariness.
- It can provide an opportunity to express pent-up hostility arising from internal conflict through combat with the external adversary.
- It may enable one to project disapproved aspects of oneself (which are not consciously recognized) onto the adversary and to attack them through attack on the adversary.
- It may permit important parts of one's self—including attitudes, skills, and defenses developed during conflictual relations in one's formative stages—to be expressed and valued because the relations with the present adversary resemble earlier conflictual relations, and so on.

Parties to a conflict also frequently get committed to perpetuating the conflict by the investments they have made in conducting the conflict; also, those who have acquired special power, profit, prestige, jobs, knowledge, or skills during the course of conflict may feel threatened by the diminution or ending of conflict.

The Issues Involved in the Conflict

There are many different issues that can be the focus of conflict and a number of different typologies have been developed to categorize the content of issues—e.g., whether the conflict is over resources, preferences and nuisances, beliefs, values, or the nature of the relationship (Deutsch, 1973). Here, I shall focus on some formal characteristics of issues rather than their content since the likelihood that a conflict will take a constructive or destructive course is more determined by the former rather than the latter. Below, I shall consider such attributes of an issue as its type, size, and rigidity.

Type of issue. Certain types of issues are less conducive to constructive conflict resolutions than others; they lead the participants to define the conflict as a zero-sum or win-lose conflict. Such issues as "power or control over the other," having "higher status than the other," "victory of defeat," "exclusive possession of something for which there is no substitute or possible compensation" are the kind that are apt to lead to a win-lose definition of the conflict.

Size. One of the characteristics of destructive conflicts is they tend to grow in size or to escalate. The converse also seems true: small conflicts are easier to resolve constructively than large ones (Deutsch, 1973; Fisher, 1964). One enlarges a conflict by dealing with it as a conflict between large rather than small units (a racial conflict rather than a conflict between two individuals of different races), as a conflict over a large, substantive issue rather than over a small one (being treated fairly or being treated unfairly on a particular occasion), as a conflict over a principle rather than over the application of a principle, as a conflict whose solution establishes large rather than small substantive or procedural precedents. Many other determinants of conflict size could be listed. For example, an issue that bears upon self-esteem or a change in power or status is likely to be more important than an issue that does not affect these things. Illegitimate threats or attempts to coerce are likely to increase the size of the conflict and thus increase the likelihood of a destructive process.

Conflict size may be defined as being equal to the expected difference in the value of the outcomes that a party will receive if it wins compared with the value it will receive if the other wins a conflict. A party "wins" a conflict if it obtains outcomes that are satisfying to it; the more satisfying they are to it, the more it wins. This definition implies that conflict size will be small for a party who believes both parties can win and large if it thinks that one party will lose (have less than satisfactory outcomes) if the other wins. This definition also implies that the size of a given conflict may be larger for one party than for the other. One party may expect that its outcomes will be quite satisfactory even if the other wins, while the second may believe that its outcomes will be adversely affected if the other wins.

It is somewhat surprising that, in the literature dealing with the management of conflict, there has been relatively little focus on what Fisher (1964) calls *issue control*. Controlling the importance of what is perceived to be at stake in a conflict may prevent the conflict from taking a destructive course. Many conflicts may be defined in a way that either magnifies or minimizes the size of the disputed issues. In general, "here-now-this" conflicts, which are localized in terms of particular, delimited actions and their consequences, are much easier to resolve constructively than conflicts that are defined in terms of principles, precedents, or rights, where the issues transcend time and space and are generalized beyond the specific action to personalities, groups, races, or other large social units or categories.

Issue rigidity. The perceived lack of satisfactory alternatives or substitutes for fulfilling the interests at stake in the conflict makes for *issue rigidity*. Sometimes, motivational and intellectual limitations may lead the parties to perceive issues more rigidly than reality dictates so that they freeze themselves into "positions" (Fisher & Ury, 1981). However, it is also evident that a harsh reality may very much limit the possibility of finding acceptable substitutes and narrowly restrict the possibilities open to the conflicting parties. If there is insufficient food, shelter, clothing, medicine, or anything else required for physical and psychological survival, conflict over such necessities will often take on a desperate quality.

The Social-Cultural Context

Individuals, groups, or nations with different cultural backgrounds must often negotiate about their conflicting interests, beliefs, or values, and sometimes they must work closely together in organizations. Their cultural differences may give rise to barriers to interaction, misunderstandings, prejudices, and behaviors that are unwittingly offensive and these may reduce the chances that negotiations will be constructive.

In-group ethnocentrism reduces the likelihood that a productive problem-solving process will characterize the interaction among the members of different groups. In-group ethnocentrism may not be as universal as Sumner (1906) posited but it is ubiquitous (see Brewer, 1986, and LeVine & Campbell, 1972) and it clearly provides obstacles to constructive interaction among people from different cultural groups. Sumner characterized ethnocentrism as the

> view of things in which one's own group is the center of everything, and all others are scaled and rated with reference to it. Folkways correspond to it to cover both the inner and the outer relation. Each group nourishes its own pride and vanity, boasts itself superior, exalts its own divinities, and looks with contempt on outsiders. Each group thinks its own folkways the only right ones, and if it observes that other groups have other folkways, these excite its scorn. Opprobrious epithets are derived from these differences. (Sumner, 1906, pp. 12–13)

As Tajfel (1982a, b) has pointed out, the self-identity of individuals is very much linked to the characteristics of the groups with which they identify: these characteristics then help define their social identity. The expectations, beliefs, language, practices, rituals, norms, and values that members of an in-group have in common define their shared culture. The culture, in turn, establishes the symbolic meaning of actions, defining a type of action as appropriate or inappropriate, respectful or disrespectful, friendly or hostile, praiseworthy or blameworthy, etc. Cultural differences are established early and the cultural assumptions acquired in childhood often have heavily laden emotional connotations of good and bad. Hence, an ethnocentric orientation to cultural differences is apt to result in strong emotional reactions. Although the term *ethnocentrism* is usually employed in relation to ethnic and nationality groups, it is well to recognize that an analogous process can occur in the relation between various social categories—e.g., those based on gender, age, race, religion, class, occupation, physical disability, sexual orientation. Each social category has its own subculture and the differences between the subcultures (in expectations, practices, language, norms, values, etc.) may lead to misunderstandings, stereotypes, and prejudices that affect the ability of people in different categories to manage the conflicts between them successfully.

Ethnocentrism is conducive to the occurrence of conflict but not conducive to its constructive resolution. What are some of the factors affecting the occurrence and intensity of ethnocentrism? And what methods are effective in dealing with ethnocentrically based conflict? LeVine and Campbell (1972) have addressed the first question as have many other scholars concerned with the development of intergroup prejudice (e.g., Brewer, 1986; Brewer & Kramer. 1985; Stephan, 1985). Sherif (1966) has addressed the second question as have other scholars (e.g., Stephan, 1985; Wilder, 1986; Worchel & Austin, 1986) concerned with the reduction of destructive intergroup conflict.

There appear to be several reasonably well-established propositions relating to the occurrence and intensity of ethnocentrism that are supported by theoretical analysis (LeVine & Campbell, 1972) as well as by the existing research (Brewer, 1986).

(1) Ethnocentric in-group bias occurs most consistently with regard to such moral traits as "trustworthiness," "honesty," "peace-loving," "virtuous," and "obedient." As Brewer (1986) suggests, these are all traits that can be defined in terms of normative prescriptions that apply to intragroup, as opposed to intergroup, behavior—i.e., one is supposed to exhibit moral behavior toward the members of one's group but not necessarily to the members of other groups. When two interacting groups have each limited their "moral community" (Deutsch, 1985) to their own group, they are apt to have reciprocal stereotypes (Campbell, 1967) such as "We are loyal; they are clannish"; "We are honest and peaceful among ourselves; they are hostile and treacherous toward outsiders."

(2) The more intense the competition between groups, the greater the tendencies toward ethnocentrism in their relations; the more intense the cooperation between groups, the less the ethnocentrism (Blake, Shepard, & Mouton, 1964; Brewer, 1986; Deutsch, 1973; Sherif, 1966; Turner, 1975; Worchel, 1986).

(3) Reciprocal relations tend to occur between interacting groups—i.e., in-groups will return the perceived attitudes of out-groups toward themselves so that reciprocal attitudes (positive or negative) will tend to agree.

(4) Perceived differences between the in-group and out-group will generally be congruent with the maintenance of positive self-evaluation (Turner, 1975). Where the in-group's position is objectively less favorable than the out-group's (e.g., it has lost a competition), one could expect the perceived differences to be minimized rather than exaggerated or explained in a way which would reduce its implications for self-esteem. Otherwise, one would expect real differences to appear in exaggerated forms in the stereotyped images of the out-group.

(5) The pyramidal-segmentary, as compared to the crosscutting, type of societal organization is more conducive to in-group ethnocentrism and destructive

intergroup strife within a society (LeVine & Campbell, 1972). In the pyramidal-segmentary type, each smaller unit that an individual belongs to is included as a segment of each larger group that he is a member of. In the crosscutting type, the groups to which a member belongs cut across, rather than nest in, one another. His residence group is not necessarily included in his kinship groups, and his work group may be composed of people from different ethnic groups.

A number of different approaches to changing intergroup prejudices, stereotyping, and discriminatory behavior have been studied (Allport, 1954; Sherif, 1966; Stephan, 1985; Worchel & Austin, 1986): intergroup contact, information, and education, sensitivity training or problem-solving workshops, negotiations between group leaders, and the use of cooperative procedures. The research (see Stephan, 1985, for a summary) is much too extensive to permit more than several brief statements. First, it is evident that the most profound and enduring positive changes in intergroup relations occur when successful cooperation in the achievement of a joint or superordinate goal is promoted (Cook, 1984, 1985; Johnson & Johnson, 1989; Sherif, 1966). A social context of cooperation enhances the effectiveness of each of the other approaches, and without a cooperative context, the other approaches may have little lasting effects. A second factor enhancing the effectiveness of each of the different approaches is a favorable normative context in which accepted authority, or influential third parties, strongly favor positive relations between the groups.

Intergroup contact, per se, can either be positive or negative in its effects upon intergroup relations depending upon the context within which it occurs and the nature of the contact. Contacts are more likely to have positive effects if they are of equal status, extended over time, occur in diverse situations, permit individuation of group members, have high acquaintance potential, and have positive contexts and outcomes. In addition, contacts have more positive effects when the in-group and out-group members are similar in basic beliefs and values, they are of equal competence, and they are similar in numbers.

Studies of the effects of information, lectures, films, propaganda, etc., generally reveal positive effects (Stephan, 1985; Williams 1947), but most such studies do not have long-term follow-up and have not included behavioral data. Intergroup workshops, multiracial sensitivity training groups, and the like also appear to have short-run positive effects (Stephan, 1985), and such group techniques have shown some promise in dealing with intercommunal and international conflict (Burton, 1969; Doob, 1970; Kelman & Cohen, 1979).

Processes Involved in the Perpetuation and Escalation of Conflict

Some conflicts appear to take on a life of their own. They continue even though the issues that initially gave rise to them have long been forgotten or become irrelevant. Other conflicts are like malignant tumors; they grow out of control and enmesh the conflict participants in a web of hostile interactions and defensive maneuvers that continuously worsen their situations, making them feel less secure, more vulnerable, and more burdened. I have identified a number of the key elements that contribute to the development and perpetuation of a malignant process (Deutsch, 1983). They include (1) an anarchic social situation, (2) a win-lose or competitive orientation, (3) inner conflicts (within each of the parties) that express themselves through external conflict, (4) cognitive rigidity, (5) misjudgments and misperceptions, (6) unwitting commitments, (7) self-fulfilling prophecies, (8) vicious escalating spirals, and (9) a gamesmanship orientation that turns the conflict away from issues of what in real life is being won or lost to an abstract conflict over images of power.

In previous sections I have touched on some of these elements. Here, I wish to elaborate briefly on anarchic social situations and unwitting commitments.

The anarchic social situation. There is a kind of situation that does not allow the possibility of "rational" behavior so long as the conditions for social order or mutual trust do not exist. A characteristic symptom of such "nonrational situations" is that an attempt on the part of an individual or nation to increase it own welfare or security without regard to the security or welfare of others is self-defeating.

Such situations, which are captured by the Dilemma of the Commons and the Prisoner's Dilemma Game, have been extensively studied by myself (Deutsch, 1958, 1973) and other social scientists (see Alker & Hurwitz, 1981, for a comprehensive discussion). When confronted with such social dilemmas, the only way an individual or nation can avoid being trapped in mutually reinforcing, self-defeating cycles is to attempt to change the situation so a basis of social order or mutual trust can be developed or to leave it if possible.

Unwitting commitments. In a malignant social process, the parties not only become overcommitted to rigid positions, but also become committed, unwittingly, to the beliefs, defenses, and investments involved in carrying out their conflictual activities. The conflict, then, is maintained and perpetuated by the commitments and investments given rise to by the malignant conflict process itself. Within limits, the more costly the actions you take based on your beliefs, the greater the need to reduce any prior-to-action doubts that you may have had about your beliefs (Festinger, 1957).

One of the characteristics of a pathological defense mechanism is that it is perpetuated by its failures rather than by its successes in protecting security. An individual might, for example, attempt to defend him/herself from feeling like a failure by not really trying, attributing failure to lack of effort rather than lack of ability. The result is that the person does not succeed and does not quell anxieties and doubts about the ability to succeed. As a consequence, when again faced with a situation of being anxious about failing, the individual will resort to the same defense of "not trying"; it provides temporary relief of anxiety even as it perpetuates the need for the defense, since the individual has cut him/herself off from the possibility of success.

Although many individuals, groups, and nations appear to get enmeshed in malignant conflict processes, little is known about how to undo such processes. They are, undoubtedly, easier to prevent than to cure.

The Skills Involved in Constructive Solutions to Conflict

Third parties (mediators, conciliators, process consultants, therapists, counselors, etc.) who are called upon to provide assistance in a conflict in which the conflicting parties need help to resolve their conflict constructively require four kinds of skills. The first set of skills are those related to the third party's establishing an effective working relationship with each of the conflicting parties so that they will trust the third party, communicate freely with her, and be responsive to her suggestions regarding an orderly process for negotiations (see Folberg & Taylor, 1984; Kressel, 1985; Kressel & Pruitt, 1985; Rubin, 1980). The second are those related to establishing a cooperative problem-solving attitude among the conflicting parties toward their conflict. Much of the preceding discussion in this paper indirectly focuses on this area; this is elaborated more fully in Deutsch (1973). Third are the skills involved in developing a creative group process and group decision making. Such a process clarifies the nature of the problems that the conflicting parties are confronting, helps expand the range of alternatives that are perceived to be available, facilitates realistic assessment of their feasibility as well as desirability, and facilitates the implementation of agreed-upon solutions (see Blake & Mouton, 1984; Fisher & Ury, 1981; Janis & Mann, 1977; Zander, 1982). And fourth, it is often helpful for the third party to have considerable substantive knowledge about the issues around which the conflict centers. Substantive knowledge could enable the mediator to see possible solutions that might not occur to the conflicting parties, and it could permit him or her to help them assess proposed solutions more realistically.

Participants in a conflict need skills and orientations similar to those of a skilled mediator if they are to develop constructive solutions to their conflicts. They need the skills involved in establishing a cooperative, problem-solving relationship with the other, in developing a creative group process that expands the options available for resolving their conflict, and they need the ability to look at their conflict from an outside perspective so that they do not get ensnared in the many unproductive or destructive traps that abound in conflicts.

This factor of abilities and skills is not sufficiently emphasized in theoretical discussions. I suggest that many destructive conflicts between nations, groups, and individuals result from their lack of skills related to the procedures involved in constructive conflict resolution, and I further suggest that training in these skills should be more widespread (Deutsch, 1993). In recent years our International Center for Cooperation and Conflict Resolution at Teachers College has been doing a considerable amount of training of educators and students in conflict resolution and mediation under the direction of Ellen Raider. Several things have become apparent to us:

(1) *A significant change in behavior is unlikely to occur from the training unless there is emphasis on skills.* Knowledge, while important, is not enough to be skillful in engaging in constructive conflict resolution behavior. Thus, students in a course may come to know that "active listening," "taking the perspective of the other," distinguishing between "needs" and "positions," "controlling anger," "using 'I' rather than 'you' messages," "reframing the issues in conflict to find common ground," being alert to the possibility of misunderstandings due to cultural differences, etc., are good things to do when in a conflict. However, unless they are given guided and repeated practice in the use of the skills in various contexts, they may not be able to engage skillfully in the behaviors that exemplify them. This is not to deny that some people have relevant skills but are unaware of them or do not know that they can be usefully employed. For example, many parents can readily become successful mediators in disputes between children if they learn a few simple rules of mediation and employ them when a destructive conflict between children emerges (Deutsch & Brickman, 1994). Although knowledge by itself of the principles of constructive conflict resolution alone is usually insufficient to produce skilled behavior, it—along with skill practice in diverse contexts—can facilitate the generalization of these skills so that they are applied in a wide range of situations.

(2) *The social and cognitive skills involved in constructive conflict resolution are conceptually different than those involved in effective physical activities.* To understand the difference between the skills involved in physical and social activities, let us compare some of the skills required in tennis with those required for constructive conflict resolution. In tennis, if you serve poorly (e.g., into the net or outside the lines) the physical reality gives you immediate, relatively unambiguous feedback of your fault. In contrast, if you listen or communicate poorly during a conflict, the other (the social reality) may give you no, or ambiguous, feedback that you have been misunderstood or that you misunderstand. In tennis, internal feedback, the smooth coordination of your own movements and the movements of the tennis ball and racquet, often provides a reliable indication of whether your serve will be good or not. One can acquire many of the skills involved in serving well through solitary practice; this is not the case for conflict resolution. In conflict, people often do not question whether they have communicated well or not; they assume they have done so without checking with the other or examining their internal feelings. Direct and appropriate feedback from the environment or oneself is more common in relation to physical as compared with social skills.

In teaching a tennis novice how to serve, one must identify the component skills (e.g., how to place one's feet, how to hold the racquet, where to throw the ball, how to swing for different spins and different placements, etc.), provide practice in them, and also help the student to integrate them into a well-coordinated performance in which external and internal feedback during repeated practice develop an integrated skill. It is much the same for social skills. However, there are several differences in the two kinds of training:

(a) *No one is a novice when he/she starts training in conflict resolution skills; many are when they begin tennis lessons.* The fact that everyone has been a participant and observer in many conflicts from childhood results in preconceptions, attitudes, and modes of behavior toward conflict that may be deeply ingrained before any systematic training occurs. Much of a person's preexisting orientations to conflict will reflect those prevalent in his/her culture but some will reflect individual predispositions acquired from unique experiences in his/her family, school, watching TV, etc. Before a student can acquire competency in conflict resolution, he/she has to become aware of his/her preexisting orientations and the obstacles they may present and be motivated to change them. Awareness and motivation are developed by having a model of good performance that the student can compare with his/her preconscious preexisting one. Guided practice in that model that gradually shapes the student's behavior to be more consistent with it through modeling and feedback, and repeated practice, leads to its internalization. Once it has been internalized the reoccurrence of earlier incompetent orientations to conflict are experienced as awkward and out-of-place because there are internal cues to the deviations of one's behavior from the internalized model. Similarly in tennis, if one has internalized a good model of serving, internal cues will tell you if you are deviating from it (e.g., by throwing the ball too high). As with conflict resolution, if a self-taught tennis student has internalized a poor model of serving, training will be directed at making him/her aware of this and providing a good model.

(b) *How to obtain and use feedback is different in the two kinds of training.* In the acquisition and use of both social and physical skills, external feedback is important as is strong motivation. The tennis player need not exert any special effort to get clear and immediate feedback that his/her serve was effective or not. In contrast, without special effort and skill, the participant in a conflict may get no feedback or ambiguous or misleading information about the effectiveness of his behavior. Hence, training in conflict resolution involves training in the skills of eliciting and giving clear feedback to the others with whom one is in conflict. The skills that are required are considerably less complex in situations where one can be sure that the parties in conflict are not trying to mislead or deceive one another than when one cannot have this confidence. In the social science literature much has been written about giving and obtaining feedback in cooperative situations and various exercises have been developed to develop these skills (see, for example, Johnson & Johnson, 1987; Lewicki & Litterer, 1985), but little has been written about acquiring the skills in the art of lying or bluffing and knowing when the other is doing it to you (see Ekman, 1985, for an exception).

(c) *The implementation of social as compared with tennis skills requires considerably more knowledge and sensitivity to the social-cultural context in which they are to be employed.* A game of tennis remains much the same whether you are playing it in Japan,

Mexico, France, or the United States; little change is required in how you use your tennis skills. In contrast, conflict takes different forms in different cultures; to employ his/her skills effectively, a skillful conflict resolver will have to be knowledgeable about how the meanings of different forms of behavior may differ from those in his/her own culture. Knowledge of the rituals of politeness, of the social norms regarding behavior in conflict situations; of the steps involved in establishing mutual trust and a cooperative relation in the sociocultural context within which negotiations are to take place are essential to effectiveness. A scholarly literature about these matters is just beginning to emerge (see, for example, Binnendijk, 1987; Cohen, 1991; Fisher, 1980; Hall & Hall, 1990; Kimmel, 1989; Weiss & Stripp, 1985) but clearly much more research is needed.

(d) *The transfer of social skills from the training setting to real-life situations is more difficult.* It is easier to transfer tennis skills acquired during practice lessons because the rules of the game do not change with a change of players and both players have to play by the same rules. In conflict situations, this is not necessarily the case: a cooperative "game" of conflict has different rules than a "competitive" one; in a given conflict, one person may be following cooperative rules while the other is following competitive ones. Initially, it may be difficult to discern what kind of conflict rules the other is following, particularly if the other is trying to deceive you. Also, as previously indicated, the meaning of one's behavior varies in different sociocultural contexts much more in conflict situations than in tennis. Further, the difference in emotionality and ego involvement from the training situation to real-life situations is apt to be greater for conflict than for tennis; one could expect that this would make successful transfer of conflict skills less likely.

(3) *The use of these social skills is more likely if the social context is favorable to their use.* As I indicated earlier, the sociocultural context is an important determinant of whether a conflict will take a constructive or destructive course. It also may influence the readiness to use one's skills in constructive conflict resolution. In some social contexts, an individual who has such skills may expect to be belittled by friends or associates as being "weak," "unassertive," "afraid," etc. In other contexts, he or she may anticipate accusations of being "disloyal," a "traitor," an "enemy lover" if he or she tries to develop a cooperative problem-solving relationship with the other side. In still other contexts, the possibilities of developing a constructive conflict resolution process will seem to be so unlikely that one will not even try to do so. In other words, if the social context leads one to expect to be unsuccessful or devalued when one employs one's skills, they are not apt to be used; they are, if it leads one to expect approval and success.

The foregoing suggests that, in unfavorable social contexts, the skilled conflict resolver will often need two additional types of skills. One type relates to the ability to place one "outside' or "above" one's social context so that one can observe the influences emanating from it and then consciously decide whether to resist them personally or not. The other type involves the skills of a successful "change agent," of someone who is able to help an institution or group to change its culture so that it facilitates rather than hinders constructive conflict resolution.

I mention these additional skills because it is important to recognize that institutional and cultural changes are often necessary for an individual to feel free to express his constructive potential. This is analogous to what research has demonstrated in the area of prejudice: a favorable sociocultural context helps an individual to become less prejudiced in behavior as well as in attitude. When the context is unfavorable, the skills mentioned above are important to the maintenance and expression of one's skills in constructive conflict resolution. Sophisticated training in constructive conflict resolution will thus be directed at helping to bring about social as well as individual change.

Some Suggestions for Research

Like many other scholars working in this area, I have assumed that there are conflict processes and variables that affect the courses and outcomes of conflict that cut across the various behavior and social sciences. We have assumed that, although there are many different types of conflicts, it is possible to develop theories that can be applied to a wide range of disputes. But are such assumptions valid? Is it theoretically and empirically useful, for example, to discuss cooperative and competitive processes when considering intergroup and international as well as interpersonal relations? Do nations as well as individuals make misperceptions and misjudgments in the course of their conflicts? Even beginning to think clearly about whether such questions are answerable and, if so, how they could be answered, raises fundamental issues about the conceptual linkages as well as the empirical differences among the various behavioral and social science disciplines concerned with conflict. In terms of theoretically oriented research, I consider this topic to be of the highest priority.

In an earlier section of this paper and elsewhere (Deutsch, 1983), I have characterized the nature of malignant conflicts and have tried to identify some of the processes involved in them. Other scholars (e.g., Brockner & Rubin, 1985; Kriesberg, Northrup, & Thorson, 1989; Osgood, 1962; Patchen, 1987; Pruitt & Rubin, 1986; Smoke, 1977) have discussed insightfully the processes involved in the escalation of conflict. Yet it is evident that we are a long way from having the comprehensive understanding of the processes necessary to make constructive suggestions about how to prevent, abort, or deescalate such conflicts.

Mediation, conciliation, arbitration, problem-solving workshops, counseling, and other forms of intervention into conflict are widespread. However, as Kressel, Pruitt, and Associates (1989) indicated, there have been few good research studies comparing the outcome of mediation with other forms of third-party intervention such as court decisions or arbitration. There are even fewer that study the comparative effects of different approaches to mediation. It is evident that it would be of considerable social utility if research could help identify the conditions and methods of third-party intervention that are likely to be helpful in difficult conflict situations.

Despite the development of a growing industry of conflict resolution training, there has been little relevant systematic theorizing or research in this area. As the prior section has suggested, we know little about educating people in the skills, as distinct from the knowledge and attitudes involved in effective conflict resolution. Nor have we given much thought about how conflict effectiveness is to be defined and measured, nor whether conflict effectiveness is generalized or situation-specific.

The foregoing suggestions hardly exhaust the possibilities of significant areas of research. They indicate areas that must be systematically addressed if the theoretical and practical potential of this field are to be realized.

Let me conclude this article by stating that I believe there has been significant progress in the study of conflict since this area emerged as a field of scholarship. However, the progress does not yet begin to match the social need. In relation to this need, too few social scientists are working, and receiving support for work, on the scientific issues that are likely to provide the knowledge that may lead to more constructive conflict resolution of the many conflicts which await us all.

References

Alker, H. R., Jr., & R. Hurwitz. (1981). *Resolving Prisoners' Dilemmas*. Washington, DC: American Political Science Association.

Allport, G. W. (1954). *The Nature of Prejudice*. Reading, MA: Addison-Wesley.

Bem, S. L., & Lenney, E. (1976). Sex Typing and the Avoidance of Cross-Sex Behavior. *"Journal of Personality and Social Psychology."* 33, 48–54.

Binnendijk, H. (ed.). (1987). *National Negotiating Styles*. Washington, DC: U.S. Department of State.

Blake, D. R. S., & J. S. Mouton. (1984). *Solving Costly Organizational Conflicts*. San Francisco: Jossey-Bass.

Blake, R. R., H. A. Shepard, & J. S. Mouton (1964). *Managing Intergroup Conflict in Industry*. Houston: Gulf.

Brewer, M. B. (1986). The role of ethnocentrism in intergroup conflict. In S. Worchel & W. A. Austin (eds.), *Psychology of intergroup relations* (2nd ed., pp. 88–102). Chicago: Nelson-Hall.

———., & R. M. Kramer. (1985). The psychology of intergroup attitude and behavior. *Annual Review of Psychology*, 36, 219–43.

Brockner, J., & J. F. Rubin. (1985). *The social psychology of conflict escalation and entrapment*. New York: Springer-Verlag.

Bronfenbrenner, U. (1961). The mirror image in Soviet-American relations: A social psychologist's report. *Journal of Social Issues*, 17(3), 45–52.

Burton, J. (1969). *Conflict and communication*. New York: Macmillan.

Campbell, D. T. (1967). Stereotypes and perception of group differences. *American Psychologist*, 22, 812–29.

Cohen, R. (1991). *Negotiating across cultures*. Washington, DC: United States Institute of Peace Press.

Cook, S. W. (1984). Cooperative interaction in multiethnic contexts. In N. Miller & M. Brewer (Eds.), *Groups in contact; The psychology of desegregation* (pp. 155–85). New York: Academic Press.

———. (1985). Experimenting on social issues: The case of school desegregation. *American Psychologist*, 40, 452–60.

Coser, L. A. (1967). *Continuities in the study of social conflict*. New York: Free Press.

Cosier, R., & Ruble, T. (1981). Research on conflict handling behavior: An experimental approach. *Academy of Management Journal*, 24, 816–31.

Deutsch, M. (1949). A theory of co-operation and competition. *Human Relations*, 2, 129–52.

———. (1958). Trust and suspicion. *Journal of Conflict Resolution*, 2, 265–79.

———. (1965). A psychological approach to international conflict. In G. Sperrazzo (ed.), *Psychology and international relations*. Washington, DC: Georgetown University Press.

————. (1973). *The resolution of conflict.* New Haven: Yale University Press.

————. (1980). Fifty years of conflict. In L. Festinger (ed.), *Retrospections on social psychology* (pp. 46–77). New York: Oxford University Press.

————. (1982). Interdependence and psychological orientation. In V. J. Derlaga & J. Grzelak (eds.), *Cooperation and helping behavior: Theories and research* (pp. 16–43). New York: Academic Press.

————. (1983). Preventing World War III: A psychological perspective. *Political Psychology,* 3. 3–31.

————. (1985). *Distributive justice.* New Haven: Yale University Press.

————. (1993). Educating for a peaceful world. *American Psychologist,* 48, 510–17.

———— & Brickman, E. (1994). Conflict resolution. *Pediatrics in Review,* 15, 16–22.

Doob, L. W. (ed.). (1970). *Resolving conflict in Africa: The Fermeda workshop.* New Haven: Yale University Press.

Duval, S., & Wicklund, R. A. (1972). *A theory of objective self-awareness.* New York: Academic Press.

Duval, S., & Wicklund, R. A. (1973). Effects of objective self-awareness on attribution of causality. *Journal of Experimental Social Psychology,* 9, 17–31.

Ekman, P. (1985). *Telling lies.* New York: W. W. Norton.

Festinger, L. (1957). *A theory of cognitive dissonance.* Stanford, CA: Stanford University Press.

Fisher, G. (1980). *International negotiation: A cross-cultural perspective.* Yarmouth, ME: Intercultural Press.

Fisher, R. (ed.). (1964). *International conflict and behavioral science: The Craigville papers.* New York: Basic Books.

———— & Ury, W. (1981). *Getting to yes: Negotiating agreement without giving in.* Boston: Houghton-Mifflin.

Folberg, J., & Taylor, A. (1984). *Mediation: A comprehensive guide to resolving conflicts without litigation.* San Francisco: Jossey-Bass.

Hall, E. T., & Hall, M. R. (1990). *Understanding cultural differences.* Yarmouth, ME: Intercultural Press.

Ickes, W. (1982). A basic paradigm for the study of personality, roles and social behavior. In W. Ickes & E. S. Knowles (eds.), *Personality, roles and social behavior* (pp. 305–41). New York: Springer-Verlag.

Janis, I., & Mann, L. (1977). *Decision making.* New York: The Free Press.

Johnson, D. W., & Johnson, R. T. (1987). *Creative conflict.* Edina, MN: Interaction Book Company.

———— & Johnson, R. T. (1989). *Cooperation and competition: Theory and research.* Edina, MN: Interaction Book Company.

Kelley, M. M., & Stahelski, A. J. (1970). The social interactive basis of cooperators' and competitors' beliefs about others. *Journal of Personality and Social Psychology,* 16, 66–91.

Kelman, M. C., & Cohen, S. P. (1979). Reduction of international conflict. In W. A. Austin & S. Worchel (eds.), *The social psychology of intergroup relations* (pp. 288–303). Monterey, CA: Brooks/Cole.

Kimmel, P. (1989). *International negotiation and intercultural exploration: Toward cultural understanding.* Washington, DC: United States Institute of Peace.

Kressel, K. (1985). *The process of divorce.* New York: Basic Books.

———— & Pruitt, D. G. (1985). Themes in the mediation of social conflict. *Journal of Social Issues,* 41(2), 179–98.

———— & Pruitt, D. G., & Associates. (1989). *Mediation research: The process and effectiveness of third-party intervention.* San Francisco: Jossey-Bass.

Kriesberg, L. (1982). *Social conflicts* (2nd ed.). Englewood Cliffs, NJ: Prentice-Hall.

————, Northrup, T. A., & Thorson, S. J. (1989). *Intractable conflicts and their transformation.* Syracuse, NY: Syracuse University Press.

LeVine, R. A., & Campbell, D. T. (1972). *Ethnocentrism: Theories of conflict, ethnic attitudes and group behavior.* New York: Wiley.

Lewicki, R. J., & Litterer, J. A. (1985). *Negotiation.* Homewood, IL: Richard D. Irwin.

Mischel, W. (1977). The interaction of person and situation. In D. Magnusson & N. S. Endler (eds.), *Personality at the crossroads; Current issues in interactional psychology* (pp. 333–52). Hillsdale, NJ: Erlbaum.

Osgood, C. E. (1962). *Alternative to war or surrender.* Urbana: University of Illinois Press.

Patchen, M. (1987). The escalation of international conflicts. *Sociological Focus,* 2, 95–110.

Pruitt, D. G., & Kressel, K. (1985). The mediation of social conflict: An introduction. *Journal of Social Issues,* 41(2), 1–10.

Pruitt, D. G., & Rubin, J. Z. (1986). *Social conflict.* New York: Random House.

Rubin, J. Z. (ed.). (1980). *Dynamics of third party intervention: Interdisciplinary perspectives on international conflict.* New York: Praeger.

Scheier, M. F., Buss, A. H., & Buss, D. M. (1978). Self-consciousness, self-report of aggressiveness and aggression. *Journal of Research in Personality,* 12, 133–40.

———, Carver, C. W., & Gibbons, F. S. (1981). Self focused attention and reactions to fear. *Journal of Research in Personality,* 15, 1–15.

Sherif, M. (1966). *In common predicament: Social psychology of intergroup conflict and cooperation.* Boston: Houghton Mifflin.

Smoke, R. (1977). *War: Controlling escalation.* Cambridge: Harvard University Press.

Snyder, M., & Ickes, W. (1985). Personality and social behavior. In G. Lindzsey & E. Aronson (eds.), *The handbook of social psychology: Vol. 2 Special fields and applications* (3rd ed., pp. 883–948). New York: Random House.

Stephan, W. G. (1985). Intergroup relations. In G. Lindzsey & E. Aronson (eds.), *The handbook of social psychology: Vol. 2. Special fields and applications* (3rd ed., pp. 599–658). New York: Random House.

Sumner, W. G. (1906). *Folkways.* New York: Ginn.

Tajfel, H. (1970). Experiments in intergroup discrimination. *Scientific American,* 223, 96–102.

———. (1982a). Social psychology of intergroup relations. *Annual Review of Psychology,* 33, 1–39.

———. (ed.). (1982b). *Social identity and intergroup relations.* Cambridge: Cambridge University Press.

Thomas, K. W. (1976). Conflict and conflict management. In M. Dunnette (ed.), *Handbook in industrial and organizational psychology* (pp. 889–935). Chicago: Rand-McNally.

Turner, J. C. (1975). Social comparison and social identity: Some prospects for intergroup behavior. *European Journal of Social Psychology,* 5, 5–34.

Walton, R. E., & McKersie, R. B. (1965). *A behavioral theory of labor negotiations: An analysis of a social interaction system.* New York: McGraw-Hill.

Weiss, S. , & Stripp, W. (1985). *Negotiating with foreign business-persons: An introduction for Americans with propositions on six cultures, 85–86.* New York University Graduate School of Business Administration, New York.

Wilder, D. A. (1986). Social categorization: Implications for creation and reduction of intergroup bias. In L. Berkowitz (ed.). *Advances in experimental social psychology* (vol. 19, pp. 291–355). New York: Academic Press.

Williams, R. M., Jr. (1947). The reduction of intergroup tensions: a survey of research on problems of ethnic, racial, and religious group relations. *Social Science Research Council Bulletin,* 57, 1–153.

Worchel, S. (1986). The role of cooperation in reducing intergroup conflict. In S. Worchel & W. G. Austin (eds.). *Psychology of intergroup relations* (2nd ed., pp. 288–304). Chicago: Nelson-Hall.

——— & Austin, W. G. (eds.). (1986). *Psychology of intergroup relations* (2nd ed.). Chicago: Nelson-Hall.

Zander, A. (1982). *Making groups effective.* San Francisco: Jossey-Bass.

Dialogue in Conflict: Past and Future

JAY ROTHMAN

An Overview of Israeli-Palestinian Dialogue

The history of Jewish-Palestinian relations prior to the establishment of Israel is mainly a sad one, of each community looking beyond and in opposition to the other as it pursued its own supposedly separate future. When peace was sought between the two, it was primarily along the lines of efforts for an absence of war and violence. However, there were also significant efforts made to promote positive peace based upon national reconciliation and cooperation. Some visionaries struggled to create a positive relationship between the groups and find ways to reconcile and even coordinate their aspirations. While their efforts bore little fruit at the time, some of their ideas about creative interdependence, mutual understanding, and cooperation have provided a valiant legacy, providing inspiration and perhaps some practical blueprints for a more peaceful future between Israelis and Palestinians.

Despite the intense conflicts between the two communities prior to 1948 and the regularly violent confrontation between them since the establishment of the State of Israel, there has nonetheless also been continual dialogue between them since the founding of the first Jewish-Arab dialogue group called *Brith Shalom* ("The Covenant of Peace") in 1925. In surveying this history and piecing together a story that might contribute to new foundations for peace in the Middle East, one can identify at least four distinct (although also partially overlapping) types of Arab-Jewish dialogue efforts that have taken place over the years. These include: the *positional* approach, in which parties define the problem in adversarial "us versus them" terms; the *human relations* approach, where parties gather to break down fears and stereotypes and develop new trust and cooperation with individuals from the other community; the *activist* approach, in which parties from both communities who share a political platform organize joint activities in support of their platform; and the *problem-solving* approach, in which adversaries are brought together to articulate common definitions of their problem and generate joint solutions that may serve the separate self-interests of each side.

The Positional Dialogue Approach

The most common type of dialogue between adversaries may be labeled positional dialogue or, more pejoratively, "deaf dialogue." This is the time when Israelis and

Palestinians through the media, through proxies, or during shouting arguments in public settings, blame each other for the conflict. They loudly articulate mutually exclusive political platforms—i.e., autonomy or statehood—that contain both definition and solution. During the early years of conflict between Jews and Palestinians, positions were essentially articulations of mutual rejection. The Palestinians viewed the Jews as a continuation of colonial imperialism; the Jews viewed the Palestinians as linked to a broader body of Arab rejectionists who would not willingly allow Jews to live in peace among them. For many years following the establishing of the State of Israel, these positions of mutual rejection continued and hardened. They were articulated in statements by Israeli leaders like Golda Meir, who denied the existence of a separate Palestinian people, and by the Palestinian Liberation Organization, whose covenant vowed to destroy what it termed the illegal and imperialist Zionist entity.

Despite the perpetuation of the conflict, the final years of the 1980s witnessed major transformations in the way many Israelis and Palestinians began to define their conflict and consider solutions. For the first time in their history of mutual rejection, many Israelis, including powerful members of the Parliament and voices in the media, began to speak increasingly of the legitimate national and political rights of the Palestinian people. Simultaneously, many Palestinians, including prominent academics and powerful opinion makers in the PLO, began to speak increasingly about the legitimacy of the State of Israel. While few on either side spoke in ways fully acceptable to the other, all positions were new and notable in their basic acceptance of the existence and legitimacy of the other. Such new approaches were finally consolidated in the secret Oslo discussions leading to mutual recognition and a "declaration of principles" for peace signed at the White House in 1993 by then–Israeli Prime Minister Yitzhak Rabin and PLO–head Yasir Arafat.

The positional discussions prior to this signing, and many that followed them as well, were basically variations of UN resolution 242, summarized as "land for peace." They reflected the view of moderate Palestinians who wanted land but could not guarantee peace—only promise it to unbelieving ears. While admitting they had given up the dream of regaining the land, they also acknowledged that many among them were still not ready to accept a two-state settlement.

Many Israeli Jews claimed they sincerely wanted peace, but requested patience from a people tired of waiting and very wary of promises delayed. At best, these Israelis believed an incremental approach, with Palestinian self-determination growing as it was "earned" (through demonstrated and proven willingness to live side by side with Israel in peace), was the only way. On the other hand, even "incremental peace" was rejected by many Israelis, who feared that the land Palestinians wanted might be, at a minimum, the only insurance policy the Israelis still held against those who in fact wanted a great deal more.

In these largely dead-end discussions, even amongst moderates and especially among "rejectionists," parties walk ten paces back and turn facing position against position. They focus on scarce resources such as territory, and attempt to conduct a peace *process,* too long substituted for a rigorous peace *substance,* in which parties would find ways to narrow differences and build spheres of agreement. instead, they focus on compromises that are, at least at the outset, unacceptable to each—incrementalism versus immediate withdrawal—thus leading both to question the asserted "good faith" of the other.

It should be made clear, however, that such positional statements are no longer wholly in the realm of "deaf dialogue." While each side puts forward positions that are more or less at odds with those of the other side, the very putting forward of these types of positions and counterpositions illustrates that the conflict and discussion about its management has finally moved beyond the battlefields, where there is no room even for positions, as there is no recognition of a legitimate opponent.

Human Relations Approach

An illustrative survey conducted in 1988 of dialogue efforts between Jews and Arabs in Israel lists approximately forty-five contemporary *human relations* organizations designed largely to break down the barriers of mistrust, misunderstanding, and stereotyping between Arabs and Jews living in Israel (Rothman et al., 1988). In 1992 the Abraham Fund put together a comprehensive survey listing hundreds of organizations in Israel engaged in Arab-Jewish coexistence work (defined very broadly as fostering "a practical relationship of mutual respect" among Arabs and Jews): *The Abraham Fund Directory of Institutions and Organizations Fostering Coexistence between Jews and Arabs,* edited by Anita Weiner, Arnon Bar-On, and Eugene Weiner. The goal of such organizations is to help each side to see the human face of the other, and forge cooperative activity. Those working in this arena seek to influence interpersonal attitudes and relationships positively by fostering improved and understanding and interaction between Jews and Arabs. They endeavor to change certain institution norms (such as structural violence in the form of inequality and unequal access to goods and opportunities for the Arab minority in Israel). They attempt to influence legislation and the legal system to promote and ensure that the aspiration of democracy is achieved within the state of Israel.

One prominent example is the "Oasis of Peace" (in Hebrew: *Neve Shalom;* in Arabic: *Wahat al-Salaam*), a mixed village where since 1972 approximately 60 "Jews and Palestinian Citizens of Israel" have together built a community. Its statement of purpose puts forth a community that "gives tangibility to the ideas of understanding, partnership, and full equality between both peoples, [demonstrating that] true partnership between the two peoples is indeed possible on a permanent basis." The only such intentional Arab-Jewish community of its type in Israel, or anywhere else for that matter, it has also built upon its own experience in developing and operating, since 1980, a School for Peace.

At the School for Peace, a variety of different workshops are cofacilitated by some of the Jewish and Arab residents of the settlement for thousands of Jewish and Arab Israeli high school students each year. Most workshops last for a weekend and are designed to educate the students about each other, helping to foster new trust and respect between them. The idea is to help students break down the negative stereotypes born of lack of contact, and overcome enemy images built over the years. Other workshops are part of ongoing programs seeking to develop the leadership potential of participants so they can actively share their new knowledge and experience with others. Other activities include programs with university students and training sessions for teachers and others working in the human relations field, including group leaders of youth movements. Every spring, the community sponsors a fair dedicated to mutual understanding and coexistence. Many thousands of people come together from all over Israel for this an annual event.

Activist Approach

A third type of dialogue may be described as *activist* in orientation. In the Israeli-Palestinian context, pre-Oslo activism usually sprang out of groups of Israelis and Palestinians essentially sharing political convictions on the need to end the Israeli occupation of the West Bank and Gaza Strip. This mutual interest was often articulated for Israel's sake in order that it could cease being occupied and put an end to its damaging moral, political, and economic costs; and for the Palestinians' sake to cease being occupied and put an end to the attendant domination and indignities. These activists often undertook particular actions (frequently unilaterally but sometimes in cooperation with each other) to promote social and political changes necessary to achieve an end to occupation. Now with Israeli-Palestinian accords reached in 1993 on Israeli withdrawal from all of Gaza and much of the West Bank, the issues became those of when, how much, and in what ways such withdrawal would take place. In a sense the activists succeeded in achieving the principles behind their main goals of Israeli withdrawal, but continue their activism to foster their vision of depth and timing.

An early and most prominent example of this type of activism is the Israeli organization "Peace Now," founded in 1978 after President Anwar Sadat came to Jerusalem. Peace Now was founded to prod the Israeli government to seize this opportunity, and later forge new ones, for peace with the Arabs. It utilized educational activities, mass rallies, and articulation and publication of policy perspectives that are in contrast to those espoused by ruling Israeli leaders. "The goal of Peace Now is peace between Israel, the Arab states, and the Palestinians based on recognition of the State of Israel, recognition of the Palestinian people's right to national self-determination, and the principle of land for peace. Central to Peace Now's position is a commitment to negotiations among all parties to the conflict that are willing to participate, including the P.L.O." (from Peace Now Statement of Purpose, 1990).

Another example of this approach was the Beit Sahur-Yedidya group's "Guest Day," held in the spring of 1990. After a group of Israeli-Jews from Jerusalem and Palestinian-Arabs from neighboring Beit-Sahur had met for several months, predominantly operating on the human relations approach of building up understanding as barriers and mistrust were torn down, it decided to initiate a joint political action in protest of the Israeli occupation of the West Bank and Gaza Strip. In the town of Beit-Sahur, a "Guest Day" was announced. The Palestinian Intifada ("uprising") which had then been ongoing for more than two years, was locally put on halt for the day, and scores of Israeli-Jews came as "guests" (instead of "occupiers") of the local residents. Together the Israelis and Palestinians held a joint peace rally. While the Israeli military authorities tried to keep the event from taking place, they were circumvented and the event received much media attention.

Problem-Solving Approach

A fourth type of dialogue is the *problem–solving workshop* approach, in which influential Israelis and Palestinians meet with each other in workshop settings, guided by a panel of third party facilitators, to engage in carefully structured dialogue. The goal is to gain insight about their specific conflict and conflict processes in general, and to discover new means of creatively resolving the conflict.

Before describing its application in the Israeli-Palestinian context, an overview of the origin and nature of this approach will be useful. The first problem-solving workshops in the international arena were organized and run by a group of international relations scholars at the Centre for the Analysis and Resolution of Conflict at University College in London, England, in the late 1960s. Led by diplomat-turned-scholar John Burton, this group set out to demonstrate that conflicting parties in international settings could learn to employ concepts and methods of cooperative problem solving to most effectively resolve their conflicts. Through action-research, these scholars attempted to test their hypothesis that representatives of parties engaged in, or about to engage in, violent conflict, could interactively find more creative means of conflict management (Burton, 1969).

The earliest prototype of the international problem solving workshop was initiated at a series of meetings in which representatives from Indonesia, Malaysia, and Singapore were brought together in London for several weeks. After then—Prime Minister Harold Wilson had failed in his mediation attempts between these parties and war seemed inevitable, the group led by Burton, with their Prime Minister's knowledge and consent, succeeded in getting the three governments to send representatives to a series of private "controlled communication workshops." The participants met for ten days in meetings facilitated by a panel of five scholars from the London Centre.

A number of useful experiences and insights were generated from this groundbreaking effort. First of all, it demonstrated that it was indeed possible to bring high-level representatives from countries in deep conflict to engage in private, face-to-face discussions of a problem-solving nature. Second, out of such meetings, participants could gain many new insights about the nature of their adversaries' hopes, fears, perceptions, and motivations. And finally, new ideas for cooperatively handling shared problems could emerge from such exercises. The extent to which this meeting—private and therefore off-the-record—and scores of others like it that have followed in the decades since then, have actually been instrumental in averting or resolving conflict is hard to know. However, it clearly demonstrated that new insights could be generated and possibly new cooperative policy options drawn up.

The goals and purposes of problem-solving workshops may be summarized as twofold. One goal is to produce changes in participants' perceptions and analyses about the conflict and their opponents that may allow them to generate alternative solutions to the problem. The second goal is to influence policy directly by feeding insights derived during the workshop into the decision-making process. Kelman and Cohen write:

> The assumption is that the atmosphere created by the workshop has the potential for producing changes in perceptions and attitudes, and for generating new ideas and creative solutions that can then be fed back into the decision-making process. (1986: 325).

Building on this experience, a number of problem-solving workshops have been held with representatives of conflicting parties in several protracted communal disputes over the past twenty-five years. In particular, dozens of such workshops have been conducted between Israelis and Palestinians. In these workshops participants learn new insights about the conflict and each other. They have provided participants with new ideas for creative problem solving. Kelman (1991), who has been one of the major proponents of this approach in the Israeli-Palestinian conflict, suggests four key areas of learning that participants have derived from these workshops.

(1) Participants learn that there is someone to talk with on the other side and something to talk about—a discovery that may be limited, but is not insignificant in a conflict in which the abiding assumption has been that there is no one to talk to and nothing to talk about.

(2) Participants gain some insight into the perspective of the other party—their fundamental concerns, their priorities, their areas of flexibility, their psychological and structural constraints.

(3) Participants develop greater awareness of changes that have taken place in the adversary, of the possibilities for change under varying circumstances, and of ways of promoting such change in the other through their own actions—a kind of learning that is especially important because the dynamics of conflict create a strong tendency to dismiss the occurrence and the possibility of change

on the part of the adversary, which then make change less likely by way of self-fulfilling prophecy.

(4) Participants learn about the significance of gestures and symbolic acts, and become more aware of actions they can take that would be meaningful to the Other and yet entail relatively little cost to themselves. (p.152)

Since the early 1970s, many such workshops have been run between "influential" (e.g., advisors to policy makers, politicians, academic and business elite) and "preinfluential" (e.g., students, aspiring leaders, etc.) actors in the Israeli-Palestinian conflict. By no means designed to replace diplomatic or political negotiations, these workshops are instead designed to supplement them with a new emphasis on the human, social, and cultural dimensions of the conflict. It is hoped that insights generated from the workshops, both in terms of new analyses about the nature of the conflict and new means for creatively resolving it, will be communicated by participants to policy-making elites and negotiators as they set agendas, determine priorities, and build confidence that negotiation is desirable and successful outcomes probable. This author has himself conducted more than two dozen workshops with Israeli Jews, Israeli Arabs, and Palestinian Arabs and has developed a conflict-resolution methodology that shares common conceptual and practical roots with the problem-solving workshop approach (Rothman, 1989, 1992, 1997).

Strengths and Weaknesses of Past Approaches

The Israeli–Palestinian conflict, which sits within the broader context of the Arab–Israeli conflict and the overall Middle Eastern quagmire, requires new approaches to dialogue. Successful negotiation between the parties can emerge only when they gain the will, confidence, and fortitude to launch them. For the most part, all of these conditions had been lacking between the parties for decades. Effective dialogue helped foster them. Kelman argues persuasively that the many years of Israeli-Palestinian problem-solving workshops (or "track-two" efforts), helped build a constituency and conflict-resolution skillfulness that contributed to the successful outcomes of the secret Israeli-Palestinian talks held in Oslo—leading to mutual recognition and a greater degree of political cooperation between the two nations than ever before (Kelman, 1995).

In this regard, the fourth approach, problem solving, probably contributed the most to political accommodation. However, useful lessons may be learned from analyzing the strengths and weaknesses of the other three approaches as well. One of the problems with previous human relations, activist, and problem-solving dialogue efforts between Jews and Arabs is that they have largely been held amongst the already "converted." Thus, while participants may gain useful insights and generate creative suggestions for solutions, these dialogues are not fully representative of the mainstream perspectives of one or both sides.

Positional bargaining, for all its limitations does have one very important feature about it that may serve as a corrective in future dialogue efforts. Setting forth mutually exclusive positions where each side vents its anger and articulates its own truth can set broad parameters of the conflict and enable participants in dialogue to articulate the most common attitudes of their constituencies and/or get their own frustrations off their chests. In terms of searching for an adequate analysis and a full definition of a problem, positional statements help get the process started; the problem occurs when it ends there as well. The positional approach, in which both sides see each other as all wrong and their own side as fully just, leads to platforms that largely deny the legitimacy of the other side's claims. This inevitably leads to stalemate. After parties put their positions forward, a dialogue must then move parties to explore the underlying interests and needs beneath these positions; only then can overlapping concerns can be identified.

The human relations approach may well serve such a purpose. however, it is often viewed as soft and naive, and sometimes creates false expectations that all parties have to do is see the "human face" of the other side and the problem will disappear, or at least greatly diminish. In deep conflicts, dialogue between opponents should be only secondarily, or functionally, about trust building. Primarily it needs to be about hard-headed self-interest. "What we try to do," writes Kelman (1991), "is to create a working trust, based on the recognition of common interests despite profound differences, that allows participants to engage in the work of analysis and joint problem solving" (p. 154). As novelist and peace activist Amos Oz (1991) said in situations of such deep conflict as the Israeli–Palestinian case, sentimental motivations and foundations are not useful; instead parties must "make peace, not love."

In fact, as a facilitatory of dialogue, I am often concerned when parties develop too much emotional empathy with one another. I fear both for the quality of agreements and for the reentry and efficacy of the participants. A sure recipe for being disqualified as a representative of one's community in an intense conflict situation would be to return home after a meeting and say, "You know they're not so bad; in fact I kind of like and appreciate them now—we can make peace!" Instead, participants will retain and gain efficacy as representatives in peace-making efforts with adversaries if they can return to their constituencies and say, "Well, I still do not like them. I don't fully trust them, I don't like aspects of their culture, and some of their values seem negative, but I do now understand that they, like us, are motivated by deep needs and values and they will not stop until these needs and values are somewhat satisfied. While I wish they would go away or stop being so determined, they won't, just as we won't. But perhaps more importantly, I now know that we are motivated by many concerns that we can perhaps best, or maybe only, achieve through cooperating with them."

The difference in this approach from the human relations model, may be usefully distinguished in the terms *emotional empathy* and *analytic empathy*. In the first, as prescribed by the human relations approach, parties come to identify with each other and the other side's hurts and hopes and fears. In analytic or cognitive empathy, parties may instead come to understand the power and depth of their adversaries motivations, hurts, hopes, and fears, and the way their actions are conditioned by them, even if they do not necessarily believe that the other side's feelings and motivations are rational or correct.

Such analytic empathy could lead parties to accept that the other side, in ways quite similar to one's own side, is so deeply motivated to fulfill underlying needs and express their own values fully, to overcome past traumas and insure future safety and expression of identity, that coercion or suppression of those needs and values will probably be counter productive (e.g., lead to terrorism and other forms of extremism). Such analytic empathy could serve as a more solid foundation for joint problem solving based on hard-headed calculations of its necessity—for the sake of one's own side. "Since we can't avoid them, beat them, ultimately suppress them, or even eventually conquer them, and since they are as determined as we are to fulfill their needs and values, perhaps we had better find ways to cooperate."

Thus, somewhat differently conceived, the human relations approach may provide a vehicle for necessary transition from mutually exclusive positions to potentially inclusive analyses about the conflict. The human relations model certainly has much to offer, because breaking down monolithic enemy images and building empathy are certainly important in managing conflicts rooted in confrontations between living, human communities, and not only in the political institutions that represent them. Another positive contribution of the human-relations approach to dialogue is that it does indeed create a moral and universalistic foundation for peace. It is not unusual to hear such pleas as: "for the sake of the children, if not ourselves." But in the world of real politik, this plea often falls on deaf ears. Indeed, it is this kind of humanistic argument that many feel gives peaceseeking a simplistic taint. Peace, say politicians, comes from strength, not sympathy. For those espousing such a view, dialogue based most forcefully on discovery and articulation for overlapping self-interest, out of which moral benefits will derive, is quite probably the best way to make it appear to be a feasible, hard-headed option.

Perhaps the most useful aspect of activist dialogue in creating conditions and confidence for dialogue and peace is that it demonstrates the concrete possibility of cooperation between "adversaries." Thus, evidence is built against those who would say that Israelis and Palestinians cannot make peace because they cannot cooperate. Precisely this strength, however, is also a weakness of the activist approach; it is always launched against certain sectors (e.g., the government, the right wing, the pessimists, the realists). More to the point, activist dialogue is always a fringe effort conducted largely between "adversaries" who often share more in common with each other than they do with important constituencies on their "own" side.

While activist dialogue and concrete cooperative actions that ensure from it may foster greater moral conviction that peace is possible among those who already believe it is necessary, for those who think peace is a great risk, such fears will often be exacerbated by such activism. If seeking peace from the outset, even before negotiations begins, means that parties have to give up any of their own claims (e.g., Israeli control over the territories, Palestinian return to land inside Israel), political leaders and their constituencies will move farther away from a willingness to engage in negotiation and peacemaking with the other side. Nonetheless, if building upon the activist method of dialogue is not effective in showing the broader public that cooperation is useful and realistic, it may instead provide would-be peacemakers and negotiators, when they get to the table, with some concrete examples of agreements-in-hand, or pieces-of-peace, that they may build upon.

Identifying Identity-Based Conflict

One important effort in determining the best type of dialogue approach to use and when is to determine what kind of conflict is at stake. Some conflicts are fairly tangible and based primarily on competition over scarce resources. Other conflicts, while containing important resource elements like struggles over territory, are more complex and deeply rooted in the more abstract and interpretive dynamics of history, psychology, culture, values, and beliefs of identity groups. Israelis and Palestinians battle over issues of safety and control. These are identity-based conflicts because they derive from existential and underlying "psychocultural" concerns that are perceived as threatened or frustrated as a result of intransigent conflict (see Rothman, 1997). These disputes are usually, at their source, very complex, relatively intangible, and often hard to clearly define. However, they regularly become simplified and focused upon scarce resources that, while concrete, overshadow or even subvert the deeper elements at stake.

Rooted as they are in complex and multidimensional psychological, historical, and cultural factors, identity conflicts are marked by a difficulty in clear determination of their parameters and boundaries. They arise from the depths of the human heart rather than the material world. While theoretical distinctions between identity and interest conflicts may be valid, in practice the differences are not so neat or clear-cut. It is fair to say that all identity conflicts contain interest conflicts; not all interest conflicts, however, contain identity conflicts. Many do, however, particularly the longer they go on. What is most crucial at the outset of a conflict engagement process is analyzing the depth and type of a conflict at a given point in time, then ascertaining how to treat it appropriately. It can be difficult to discover the salience of the issues at stake—is the conflict based mostly in resources or identity issues? The challenge is to know which level should be addressed, and when. Conflicts that start primarily as resource-based, when ignored or poorly handled, may evolve into an identity conflict; the longer a conflict continues, the more people connect their dignity and prestige with the dispute. On the other hand, identity conflicts addressed as if they were primarily about resources may grow from bad to worse. Given the natural human disposition for the concrete and measurable, identity conflicts often are misidentified as resource-based disputes and approached inappropriately.

How, then, can intractable identity-driven conflicts be made tractable? How can cultural and identity issues be addressed in such a way as to allow more "rational" planning over resources and interests?

Prenegotiation

Existential or cultural conflicts are those conflicts fundamentally rooted in the identity and efficacy of the disputants, which have somehow been threatened or undermined in their encounter with each other. In such conflicts, stories and metaphors matter very much. They are ignored at the peril of any kind of constructive negotiation process. Storytelling can help transform identity-based disputes into interest-based disputes. Put another way, by having disputants tell each other what really matters to them and why, culturally based conflicts may be "ripened" or "softened" or "transformed," such that competing interests may be cooperatively negotiated.

The goal of cultural conflict discourse, or storytelling, must be first and foremost the *articulation* of disputants' organizing stories and metaphors, their core values, needs, and concerns in such a way that the other side can *recognize* them. In many cases, once such a discourse and mutual storytelling has occurred, it may well be that interest-based bargaining, including a partial separation of people from the issues, may be appropriate and useful.

Bryn Mawr College Professor Marc Ross, in his book *Culture and Conflict* (1993), suggests that deep conflicts contain a mix of psychological and cultural factors and tangible interest. The more a conflict is in its psychocultural phase and parties' interpretations and attributions of each other exacerbate tensions, the more prenegotiation is needed. Once the cultural elements have been adequately explored and new images constructed, including the possibility of inclusive metaphors (for example in addressing water conflicts: "We must learn to swim together if we are not to sink together"), interest-based bargaining is then appropriate and often necessary if concrete problem solving is needed to consolidate understandings and agreements (Lowi and Rothman, 1993). Once parties prenegotiate some common ground over the basic parameters and definitions of their conflict, they can much more easily begin to build common ground over technological solutions.

The Aria Method

Cultural factors may stimulate conflict and/or impede its resolution. Culture, like conflict, is highly reflexive. It is shaped and reshaped in its encounters with other cultures. While cultural encounters can and do have deleterious effects on negotiation, it is possible for a "cultural" approach to be employed consciously to assist adversaries in resolving their disputes.

In an effort to suggest concretely how culture may be used to promote cooperation—which may, in turn, encourage a consolidation of efforts for peace at the
political level—I will briefly summarize a conflict resolution methodology employed
and developed primarily in the Israeli-Palestinian context. Over the last decade,
through my personal interventions as a conflict-resolution trainer and facilitator
between Israelis and Palestinians, Greek and Turkish Cypriots, disputants in South
Africa, Northern Ireland, and Sri Lanka, I have evolved a four-phased dialogue
process which I call ARIA (1997). Based on a synthesis of the four approaches to
dialogue outlined above, the ARIA methodology is inspired by music and views
conflict as a potential source of great creativity. The ultimate goal is to foster
harmony and resonance from a full and honest expression between adversaries of
the respectively deeply felt human motivations that lie beneath their conflict.

In the first phase, *Antagonism,* parties focus on resources that they want and
blame each other for the conflict. Based on the positional dialogue approach, this
phase is a process of staged adversarial framing, whereby antagonism is surfaced
by focusing on the "What" of the conflict—what resources are at stake and what
solutions are being sought. This is the time for voicing the "Us" versus "Them"
sentiments, before moving into a phase of *Resonance.* In this second, reflexive phase,
the parties articulate why they want a given outcome. A period of reflexive reframing
fosters the articulation of core identity issues, as the focus is now on "Who?" and
"Why?" What is it in this conflict that means so much to the participants and why?
Resonance can emerge through the deep exploration and articulation of the needs
and values that are threatened or frustrated by the conflict. The human relations
approach to dialogue mentioned above shares a common analytical concern with
resonance in its emphasis on parties' own human hopes, fears, and needs.

A combination of the activist approach and the problem-solving workshop approach share a common focus with the next two phases of the ARIA methodology.
The third phase, *Invention,* focuses on the creation of joint solutions: the question
now becomes "How?" as participants search for integrative solutions as a means of
cooperatively resolving the conflict. Parties work cooperatively to solve common
problems that will address underlying motivations of both sides.

Finally, the cycle moves to *Action,* which addresses the tangible "What?" of
solutions, and consolidates the previous steps with an eye toward where to go next.
Parties cooperatively set an agenda for negotiation and/or problem solving.

What follows is a conceptual overview of this methodology:

(1) Antagonism: This type of outward antagonistic focus, in which disputants
see "the other" as the main problem, is the norm in intense conflicts, and culture
sets parties against one another by promoting ethnocentric and exclusionary perceptions. This adversarial pattern can be found wherever ethnic groups are engaged
in deep, identity-based conflict. The dispute is outwardly articulated and expressed
in terms of rivalry for control of tangible territorial, economic, and/or military
resources and for a monopoly over international support, to which the less tangible

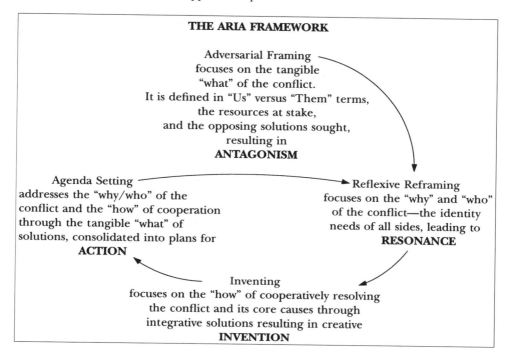

THE ARIA FRAMEWORK

Adversarial Framing focuses on the tangible "what" of the conflict. It is defined in "Us" versus "Them" terms, the resources at stake, and the opposing solutions sought, resulting in **ANTAGONISM**

Agenda Setting addresses the "why/who" of the conflict and the "how" of cooperation through the tangible "what" of solutions, consolidated into plans for **ACTION**

Reflexive Reframing focuses on the "why" and "who" of the conflict—the identity needs of all sides, leading to **RESONANCE**

Inventing focuses on the "how" of cooperatively resolving the conflict and its core causes through integrative solutions resulting in creative **INVENTION**

"cultural" issues of identity and recognition are intimately connected. Such an approach perpetuates fruitless negotiation, at best, and promotes repeated outbursts of violence, at worst. However, in the ARIA methodology, it is useful in bringing out the anger and putting it on the table for discussion. In effect, this phase provides a negative frame of reference for the phases that follow.

(2) Resonance: To break the cycle of antagonistic conflict framing and solution seeking, a reflexive telling of self can serve as a powerful vehicle for reframing and fostering resonance. In other words, changing the way parties define their conflict, from an outward view to an inward-looking analysis, can broaden significantly their analyses of the conflict. By describing reflexively their deepest motivations, traumas, hopes, and fears in the context of past and potential interactions, parties may begin to forge common ground and move beyond blaming.

Reflexivity is particularly effective in dialectical conflicts, since it is a process by which interrelationships between internal dynamics and external conditions are articulated. It leads disputants to inquire, interactively, into their respective values, needs, hopes, and hurts. In this way, the other side is provided with a window onto their opponents' reality from which mutual awareness can be engendered of the causality they share over such core concerns, past and future, and the way they are expressed and organized.

A reflexive approach would begin with an exposition of self: "Our experience at the hands of adversaries, including you, but surely not limited to you, has threatened our culture and our values, undermined our well-being, and led us to feel a profound sense of injury, insecurity, and mistrust." When parties in protracted conflict describe reflexively their motivations and the assumptions on which they act in the conflict and illuminate the cultural dimensions at play, constructive dialogue and intercultural encounter become possible.

For a tangible solution to be mutually acceptable, it must address disputants' underlying concerns including needs for identity, safety, recognition, justice, participation, and so forth. If solutions threaten or frustrate these deep concerns further, it is likely that they, as in the past, will be rejected.

The reflexive approach serves to unfreeze parties from total reliance on the adversarial "Us versus Them" mode and provides room for a more integrative mode. The underlying concerns for identity and cultural integrity have been underrepresented far too long in diplomatic efforts in the Middle East. Bringing such issues into focus within the context of concrete, practical issues may have a constructive effect on an overall peace process. If encouraged to articulate underlying concerns that are at stake in the conflict, parties would make more progress in spelling out what must be addressed for a mutually acceptable solution to be forged. In their book *The Practical Negotiator,* William Zartman and Maureen Berman (1982, p. 84) write, "Issues of recognition, of dignity, of acceptance, of rights and justice may be more important than the actual disposition of a material good, and taking them into account may facilitate a solution."

By shifting emphasis to common cultural concerns and relating them, where appropriate, to technical issues within the larger political conflict, the likelihood of successful joint problem solving is enhanced.

(3) Invention: After parties have described their reflexive analyses of the situation, they are asked to find the intersections of their underlying concerns. "Each of us seeks to sit under our own fig tree." This discovery then leads to an attempt at integrative inventing and bargaining, in which they are asked to propose cooperative solutions to their common problems (insecurity, poverty, threats to cultural identity, resource scarcity, and so forth).

Integrative solutions, where all sides gain mutually (if not symmetrically)—unlike compromise, where all sides sacrifice (often asymmetrically)—are those that all parties to a conflict are committed to internally. This internal commitment is due to the parties' sense that they gain from such solutions and, perhaps more importantly, because it can be demonstrated that such solutions are best suited to fulfilling their underlying needs. Disputing parties become motivated to "Help" the other side achieve certain goals because of the gains they can envision for themselves through such cooperation. For instance, insecurity or poverty of either side might be viewed as a concrete problem for both. In feeling insecure, each side will often act in ways that will lead the other side to feel insecure as well.

(4) Action: Having built confidence that peaceful cooperation is possible, and by seeing partial examples of how cooperative problem solving might benefit them, parties have now developed internal incentives to foster further cooperation. By

articulating common frustrations and perceived threats, an agenda for joint problem solving and action is set. This agenda can be both incremental and holistic at the same time. It can be designed to work on "pieces of peace" in ways that symbolically and practically are part of a total fabric of peace. Thus, as they set a substantive agenda for addressing concrete issues, they may now work together to set a procedural agenda for negotiation. That will engender a cooperative momentum to make the months and years ahead of necessarily difficult bargaining that much more promising and designed for mutual, instead of exclusive, gains.

Identity Conflicts and Reflexive Dialogue

One of the attributes of identity conflict is that it is intangible. Another way of putting this is to say that such conflict is deeply subjective; disputants locked in identity conflict often have a very hard time explaining the nature of their conflict to others who have not experienced it the way they have. When conflicting parties in identity conflict do describe its significance in historical terms, observers may believe different histories are being told. In many ways this is so. The subjective experience of disputants in conflict is shaped by and shapes their particular cultural reality and historical narrative. Moreover, disputants' experience of self and each other in conflict is subjective. One side's freedom fighter is very often another side's terrorist.

Seeking the "objective" truth about such a conflict, its history, and the merits of one side's interpretations and experiences against another's is futile; it leads only to deaf dialogue. However, it is possible and potentially transforming to discover the meeting points between the subjective experiences and interpretations—the "intersubjective" intersections between adversaries. This is what occurs in the resonance phase of ARIA, when a reflexive dialogue allows disputants to articulate to each other the impact of conflict upon their self-definition and experience, respectively and interactively.

One of the reasons identity disputes are so protracted and intransigent is that the stakes are very high: they have to do with disputants' needs for safety, dignity, control over destiny, and so forth (Maslow, 1943, Burton, 1990). Such needs usually resonate negatively between disputants locked in identity conflicts who share in common an experience of threat or frustration around such needs. At the core of such conflicts is the destructive relationship with the other side, viewed as the cause of threatened or frustrated needs.

The transformational potential that may be forged out of such negative conflict cycles occurs when the other side may become an ally in fostering or fulfilling each side's needs, instead of damaging them. This cannot occur, however, until both sides can become explicit and articulate about their motivations in the conflict.

Case Study: Jerusalem

My own work in reflexive dialogue began in Jerusalem, working with Israelis and Palestinians around their protracted conflict over this city. It continued in other deeply protracted ethnic conflicts and then took an interesting turn into the organizational arena. Describing my work in international conflict resolution at a workshop at a university, I was invited to apply this approach to transforming a decades-old labor-management conflict that had left the parties deeply divided and recycling the conflict annually. In the following pages I will summarize the reflexive approach in a stylized presentation of dialogues I have facilitated in Jerusalem (1992, 1997).

Reflexive Dialogue over Jerusalem

What follows is a summary of dozens of reflexive dialogues I have helped facilitate between Israelis and Palestinians since 1987 over the future of Jerusalem. First, the disputants articulate the "what' of the conflict, which is usually framed antagonistically. Then they begin to reframe their own concerns reflexively from an outward focus on what the "other side" did and how bad they are, to what they themselves care about and why.

FACILITATOR: In what way is Jerusalem core to your own people, their hopes and fears, in this conflict?

PALESTINIANS: *Al Quds* is our center. It is where our national, cultural, and religious life emanates. Walking to the golden dome of the Al Aksa Mosque, we gain a sense of elevation and calm simultaneously. While the whole Arab and indeed Moslem world claims this spot as its religious birthright, and with complete justification, to us our link with Jerusalem is equal to our own sense of national Palestinian selfhood. Moreover, Jerusalem has always been the main nerve of our intellectual and economic life as well. Without Jerusalem, we will remain what we have become, a fragmented, poorly led, somewhat unfocused collection of tribes. With Jerusalem, our national unity is assured.

IRAELIS: Jerusalem is the key to our continuity. For the past three thousand years, without break or exception, our ancestors either lived here or prayed here daily. We must pass it on to our next generations, as a birthright, for only then will we as a people, a culture, a religion, and a nation be ensured of a future. In other words, without Jerusalem, we are if we were not and thus will not be. Jerusalem and the Jewish people are really synonymous—past, present, and future. Moreover, politically, if we lose hold of Jerusalem, it is only a matter of time before we lose hold of the rest of the land of Israel, bit by bit.

FACILITATOR: The fears you each have expressed about Jerusalem are very powerful. Palestinians, you said that without Jerusalem you will remain fragmented and dispersed. Israelis, you said that without Jerusalem your past and future are wiped out. Say more about your hopes, values, and needs that are at stake in this conflict.

ISRAELIS: We need Jerusalem to be who we are and will become. Jerusalem is equivalent to our identity. We need it to be safe and recognized. This may sound a little grandiose, but we need Jerusalem to continue to be bigger than our size. We are small, but Jerusalem helps to make us larger. In short it gives us cultural, religious, national, and political meaning and purpose. Simply, without Jerusalem we shrivel.

PALESTINIANS: Our history has been marked by occupations by foreigners. The Turks, the French, the British, the Jews. We aspire to control our own destiny; this is only really or fully possible with Jerusalem as our religious and political core. With Jerusalem, we will gain the internal cohesion, politically and nationally, and the external recognition that we require.

FACILITATOR: Having heard such deep-felt articulations of self, please ask each other questions for clarification. Do not engage in the typical positional debate, as we already experienced at the beginning of this workshop, in which you try to prove the other side wrong. Instead, even if you doubt the efficacy of their perceptions, or that they really require the needs they assert they do, try to take them at their word that these are their perceptions and that they do believe they have these needs. Ask questions so that you may attempt to understand them and their values and needs as they perceive of them, even if you still do not necessarily agree with them. Only through deeply understanding what motivates the other side you will gain the tools needed to work with them, and not against them, to solve the conflict.

ISRAELI: You say Jerusalem is your unity, but this is only. . . .

FACILITATOR: Wait a minute, it sounds as if you are about to score a point. That's positional debate; here we want questions for clarification, for understanding, for analytic empathy. In a minute I will ask you to role play the other side and express their values and core concerns as you have heard them do. So you should now gather information and insight to help you do this.

ISRAELI: OK, then as a question. Why has Jerusalem become so important to you in terms of Palestinian peoplehood? This is a relatively new concern for you, less then a hundred years ago you cared about it only religiously, now you say it is your national core. Why?

PALESTINIAN: It is true that our national consciousness—at least in the Western sense of the word—is a relatively modern phenomenon; but it does exist and it is undeniable that it motivates everything we think and do. Jerusalem, for religious, historical, cultural, political, and so many other reasons, is the repository of us. While I cannot really explain it, I should think that you, of all people, should be able to understand this quintessentially spiritual connection we have with Jerusalem—even those of us who are secular!

PALESTINIAN: You speak of Jerusalem as your core, but why do you need to rule over us?

FACILITATOR: Can you make this question a little less provocative? We are engaged in listening for understanding, which requires both willingness to listen to what the other side has to say about themselves and also willingness to ask questions such that the other wants to answer honestly and nondefensively.

PALESTINIAN: OK, I'll try. If your safety and access to your holy sites as well as the Jewish areas were assured, wouldn't it be a relief not to rule over Palestinians in East Jerusalem who are hostile to you?

ISRAELI: Your question is just too hypothetical. Our security has never been assured and will only be secured by our own efforts. We can never again entrust our destiny to others, and certainly not to others who have at one time vowed to destroy us. When Jerusalem was divided we were not allowed access; now it is whole and everyone has access. Sure it would be fine if you could gain greater self-rule and control, but not at our expense, which our experience suggests is what would happen were Jerusalem ever again to be divided.

This type of reflexive dialogue may continue in this way for hours or for days over the course of an intervention, with many questions posed by me and increasingly by the parties themselves. It should eventually lead to a great deal of clarification and understanding about what is at stake and why it matters so much.

Finally the parties reach the point at which we test out whether they have developed the kind of "analytic empathy" sought (that is, the goal of such a dialogue is not persuasion, but rather deep insight). Each side in turn might, for example, reverse roles temporarily and describe "their" motivation, needs, and values as if they were the other side. It is always a powerful moment when, often for the first time, each side feels that their adversaries have truly heard them and at least recognized their deep concerns. When parties can indeed do this role reversal to the satisfaction of each other, a new foundation may be built on which the definition of the problem as "Us against Them" can begin to be replaced by a definition of a problem "we share," including a range of needs, goals, and values on both sides that are frustrated and threatened.

Conclusion

In reflexive dialogue, which operationalizes the ARIA framework, itself based upon a synthesis of the four types of dialogue discussed in the early part of this chapter, disputants reframe their perceptions and analyses of each other and their own identities; in short, they learn to articulate their own voice clearly and recognize each other's as valid. Where blame was, mutual responsibility enters. Where "us versus Them" dynamics prevailed, the way in which the disputants are locked into a relationship and in part defined by it becomes both clear and potentially constructive with a new use of "We." Where negative attributions clouded all differentiation of the other, a new analytical empathy may emerge in which they are viewed as "like self" in certain deeply motivated needs and values (for safety, dignity, recognition, and so forth). Finally, where pernicious projections where entrenched, a new awareness of disputants' own imperfections are acknowledged and accepted, promoting a less self-righteous or judgmental battle, and more tolerance for failings of the other side as well.

Kurt Lewin in his classic book, *Resolving Social Conflicts* (1948), suggested that when disputants are locked in bitter battles they must somehow "unfreeze" cognitions about each other and their situation that perpetuate the fight, in order to view them afresh and enable a new beginning. Folger and Bush give practitioners valuable new concepts for such unfreezing. Reflexive dialogue is one tool to produce the kind of transformational process they promote, whereby parties learn a great deal about their own needs and values through articulating them in guided dialogue, and come to reflexively recognize such deep motivations on the other side as well.

References

Burton, John W. (1969). *Conflict and Communication: The Use of Controlled Communication in International Relations*, New York: Free Press.

———, ed. (1990). *Conflict: Human Needs Theory*, New York: St. Martin's Press.

Kelman, Herbert (1995). "Contributions of an Unofficial Conflict Resolution Effort to the Israeli–Palestinian Breakthrough." *Negotiation Journal*, January 1995, pp. 19–27.

———. (1991). "Interactive Problem Solving: The Uses and Limits of a Therapeutic Model for the Resolution of International Conflicts." In V. D. Volkan, J. V. Montville, & D. A. Julius, eds. *The Psychodynamics of International Relationships* (Vol. 2). Lexington, MA: Lexington Books.

———, Cohen, Stephen P. (1986). "Resolution of International Conflict: An Interactional Approach. In S. Worchel & W. G. Austin, eds., *Psychology of Intergroup Relations* (2nd ed.). Chicago: Nelson-Hall.

———. (1993). "Coalitions across Conflict Lines: The Interplay of Conflicts within and between the Israeli and Palestinian Communities." In S. Worchel and J. Simpson. *Conflict between People and Groups*. Chicago: Nelson-Hall.

Lewin, Kurt (1948). *Resolving Social Conflicts*. New York: Harper.

Miriam Lowi and Jay Rothman. "Israelis and Arabs: The Jordan River." In Guy Olivier Faure and Jeffrey Z. Rubin, eds. (1993). *Culture and Negotiation*, Newbury Park, CA: Sage Publications.

Maslow, Abraham, "A Theory of Motivation," *Psychological Review*, 50 (1943): 370–96.

Ross, Marc (1993). *Culture and Conflict*, New Haven: Yale University Press.

Oz, Amos. (speaker). (March 10, 1991). National Public Radio.

Rothman, Jay (1997). *Resolving Identity-Based Conflict: in Nations, Organizations and Communities*. San Francisco: Jossey-Bass.

———. (1992). *From Confrontation to Cooperation: Resolving Ethnic and Regional Conflict*. Newbury Park, CA.: Sage Publications.

——— with Sharon Bray and Mark Neustadt (1988). *A Guide to Arab–Jewish Peacemaking Organizations in Israel*. New York: The New Israel Fund.

William Zartman and Maureen Berman (1982), *The Practical Negotiator*, New Haven: Yale University Press.

Beyond Violence: Building
Sustainable Peace

JOHN PAUL LEDERACH

I have been asked to reflect with you this morning on the challenges and dilemmas posed in building sustainable peace in the context of what has come to be known in international circles as the "postaccord" or what some of you here are calling the "postconflict phase." I am honored to be here with you, to be afforded such a privilege, and especially honored to have the opportunity to think with you, people for whom I have longstanding respect and admiration. I must say, however, that it is much easier to expound on these questions in the safety of the classroom back in America. In my experience, it seems that the further you get from a problem the easier the answers are. There are two things I have learned over the years in my line of work: (1) Never offer answers. Offer to think with people about ideas. (2) Learn to appreciate and to live with ambiguities. Ambiguity is good for your soul. It keeps you honest. It keeps you humble. It keeps you searching. So, I come this morning without pretensions, willing to wade with you in thick waters of wonderful Irish ambiguity, and hoping not to drown.

When I was first contacted about this conference by Dr. Fitzduff, she suggested I reflect on experiences and observations emerging from parallel postconflict situations. As I approached it, what seemed especially relevant was not the comparison of cases as much as the initial development of a set of lenses that might permit us to identify the broader patterns and dilemmas posed by a postconflict phase, which is a bit of a misnomer. Postconflict does not mean conflict has disappeared by some miraculous stroke of luck or genius; rather it simply indicates that the conflict has taken a new expression and is changing. And it is the changes of context, people, expectations, possibilities that is new, and as such creates a new phase. For this morning, I would like to make my observations based on two assumptions. *First,* we need a set of lenses to look at the peace-building process that can help us identify the problems and dilemmas posed by the particular moment in the process. *Second,* we must approach peace building like a system, a system with a design and architecture. The lenses, then, are used to look at this building. To draw a metaphor: we can approach peace building somewhat like a building inspector might approach a house. More specifically, I would suggest, we approach it like an inspector who has been tasked with discovering the heating patterns within the building. He is interested in knowing where the heat is going: is it sufficient? is it efficient? In our case, the lenses are focused on where energy in the peace-building system is expended. Is it spread evenly? Is it "overheating" some places and "underheating" others? With these energy-seeking lenses on, and looking not specifically at the Irish context but broadly across similar settings, I would offer three initial observations about postconflict peace building.

The system focuses enormous energy on immediate tasks too often decoupled from longer-ranging design of social change necessary for creating and sustaining a comprehensive approach. The system is driven by a hierarchical instead of an organic focus on political process. It moves with increasing narrowness, at times almost myopic, focus, on the technical tasks of political transition over the social, economic, psychological, and spiritual processes of transformation. I would like to look at each of these observations in more detail, providing some ideas and illustrations that I hope contribute to our discussions today.

Time Frames for Peace Building

Immediate and long-ranging peace building is a complex endeavor due to three phenomena: simultaneity of activities, gravity of issues, and the pressure for rapid response. Everything is happening at once. Everything is of critical importance. And everything is urgent. This is further exacerbated by the CNN effect. As described by Ernie Regehr: "Foreign problems not in the headlines should be ignored, but once they have the attention of CNN they should have been addressed yesterday." These characteristics point us toward the question of time, and more specifically how we think about time and our actions. I have found it useful to have a conceptual framework for thinking about time and action. My basic concern is to develop a mechanism that permits us to look at immediate needs as embedded in a longer-ranging design. In peace building I would propose a nested paradigm as illustrated in Figure 1.

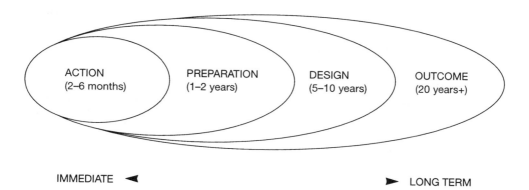

Figure 1. Time frame for peace-building © *John Paul Lederach*

The immediate, often crisis-driven, component is represented here by the word "action." It refers to the need we feel to respond to the evolving events. In the international NGO [non-governmental organization] community, recent crises like those of Bosnia, Somalia or Rwanda, have made popular the term "disaster management." In postconflict phases action is seen in terms of responding to emerging crises that put the peace process in jeopardy, often calling for crisis negotiation or mediation. The time frame of the "action" component is short-term, a matter of months. The driving question is "How do we respond to these immediate needs in order to keep the process alive?" Action is embedded, however, in the notion of "preparation." Here we refer to the need for equipping people to undertake better action. In a peace-building endeavor this is the component related to training and preparing the way. Preparation evolves into a more extended unit of time, often conceived in terms of projects that lay-out plans for one to three years.

At the far end of the paradigm is "outcome." I use outcome as a way of talking about vision and desired change. This refers both to structural as well as social change. What visions do people have for a given setting? For example, in a peaceful Ireland how would politics, economics and social systems be constructed and function? How would people relate? What would characterize their relationships? This "outcome" component of peace making is obligated to reflect in generational blocks of time, twenty to forty years. Between the two extreme ends of the paradigm we find the idea of "design." This component of peace building is characterized by its operational function of linking immediate action and long-term goals. Its primary task is to develop a conceptual plan, a peace-building architectural design for social change. It compels us to think in decades. Decade thinking is not easy, but in my mind, is absolutely critical for peace building. The design component pushes us to grapple with tough questions. How is our immediate action linked to desired social change? What are the steps we follow to move from where we are now to where we want to be?

Three keys are important for understanding this paradigm. *First,* it suggests that different activities related to peace building require distinct units of time within which we reflect and act. *Second,* the units of time are related to each other and must be seen as connected rather than isolated. *Third,* it is crucial that we develop the capacity to think operationally in decades in order to link immediate action, shorter term preparation with longer-ranging desired changes.

Taking this a step further, in Figure 2 I have devised a little scheme based on a set of questions that I find helpful as I think about specific pieces of work. The scheme is built as a matrix that cross-references time/relationship with purpose of the activity. There are four basic questions. What are we trying to accomplish? What is the nature of our relationship? What is the unit of time within which we can think and plan? How much do we know abut the context?

In response to the first question I suggest three categories that form one side of the matrix. *Purpose* refers to the bigger picture of what we are attempting to accomplish in the context or setting. *Goals* relate to narrower aspect of what a particular event is attempting to achieve. *Objectives* refer to the more specific activities within the event. These three categories can be cross-referenced with perspec-

	PURPOSE (within context)	GOALS (for events)	OBJECTIVES (within events)
EVENT (hours-days)			
PROJECT (1-2 years)			
PROGRAM (10 years)			

Figure 2. Matrix for peace-building activity © *John Paul Lederach 1994*

tives emerging from the nature of the relationship and the unit of time within which we plan. An event is a one-time activity that may be conducted for a few hours to a few days. A *project* refers to a series of events taking place across a year or two. A *program* connects the projects into a longer-term decade-length effort.

We can now return to our original point. If we overlay our two schemes we are situated to describe what typically happens in peace building and to suggest what should happen. Typically, the process of peace building is driven by a crisis orientation responding to immediate needs in the form of events with narrowly defined and short-term objectives. Projects and programs that relate to the longer-term agenda for social change are defined by what is necessary and possible emerging from the crisis. The suggestion of what should happen is the inverse. Peace building, I have argued, needs a social architectural design that thinks in decades and in which specific events and responses are defined by a measured understanding of the context, purpose, and program.

This seems especially true of the postconflict phase. The entire social, political, and economic system is changing. New realities and shared futures seem almost within reach. Yet the context is that of people who are emerging from years of stagnated cycles of violence, who by basic human nature find more security in hanging on to what is known and understood than by moving toward the unknown even if it promises to be qualitatively better. In this context, peace builders feel over-responsible to take care of every detail, lest the process fail. While vigilance is necessary, it is far more important to develop the capacity to think about immediate action as embedded in broader context and program developments.

Let me draw a brief analogy. I received a wonderful journal entry from my good friend Ron Kraybill written after election day in South Africa. Among other things he reported on this activity as a crisis mediator for the day. He and others were outfitted with cellular phones, connected to a central location. At a moment's notice they could be called on to respond to emerging conflicts, from any part of the city of Capetown and out into the Province. The effort was monumental, aimed at providing conciliation resources to deal with the potential sparks that could, if left unattended, rage into a fire. For election day it worked wonderfully, but is not recommended as an approach to the broader phase of postconflict peace building. It does suggest, however, an analogy. Too much of postconflict peace building is based on a cellular phone approach to social change. It can deal with sparks, but is incapable of generating and sustaining the broader context and design necessary to move fully toward desired goals.

In sum, let me make two points about time frame. First, peace building in postconflict phases must explicitly think about and develop the capacity of social change design as a discipline and responsibility. Second, we must learn to think in decades in order to contextualize our immediate actions. Notice that I am not suggesting what actions should be taken. I am suggesting that we need to develop the ability to think about social change as a *process needing a design* and that we need to think in longer units of time in order to locate the why, when and where of immediate action.

Levels of Peace-Building Activity

There are two main levels of peace-building activity, the hierarchical and organic. In the first section we made reference to the simultaneity of activity at various levels, and it is to this idea of levels that we now turn our attention. Figure 3 presents a conceptual framework that outlines three levels of peace-building activity: The top, middle, and grassroots. The top level of peace-building is what we could consider the official "table talks." My observation, stated earlier, suggests that during the postconflict phase the peace-building system is driven by a hierarchical instead of an organic focus on political process. In other words, the approach to peace building is top-down, where system energy centers on top-level leaders and activities. This is taking place at a time and in a context of significant and far-reaching change. Consider for a moment some of the dilemmas posed by this evolving contextual change.

(1) People experience a contradiction in terms of the pace of change. Simultaneously, the postconflict phase can be experienced as moving too slowly and too rapidly: too slowly because expectations have been raised by the possibility of peace; too rapidly because reformation of perspectives and concessions offered to create movement can feel like we have given away too much and received too little. We may feel like we are swept along by the rapid evolution of events.

(2) Everyone feels the identity dilemma, but it is especially critical for leaders who are caught in the public limelight. The identity dilemma struggles with the question

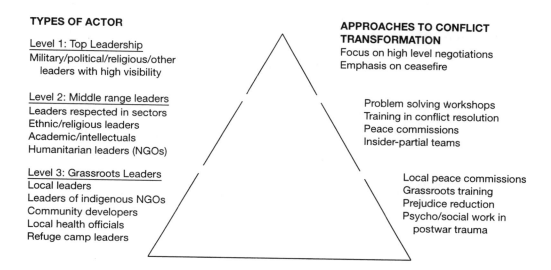

TYPES OF ACTOR

Level 1: Top Leadership
Military/political/religious/other
    leaders with high visibility

Level 2: Middle range leaders
Leaders respected in sectors
Ethnic/religious leaders
Academic/intellectuals
Humanitarian leaders (NGOs)

Level 3: Grassroots Leaders
Local leaders
Leaders of indigenous NGOs
Community developers
Local health officials
Refuge camp leaders

APPROACHES TO CONFLICT TRANSFORMATION
Focus on high level negotiations
Emphasis on ceasefire

Problem solving workshops
Training in conflict resolution
Peace commissions
Insider-partial teams

Local peace commissions
Grassroots training
Prejudice reduction
Psycho/social work in
    postwar trauma

Figure 3. Actors and peace-building foci across the affected population
© *John Paul Lederach*

of how to change and yet hold onto our core purpose. In settings of deep-rooted conflict identity is shaped in large part by defining ourselves against a clear sense of the enemy. "Clear" means that we have little room for ambiguity or gray areas. Postconflict processes change this clarity. Things become more ambiguous. Old answers no longer explain everything that is happening. Leaders, then are caught in this struggle: How may they create the space for remolding and shaping an identity not based exclusively on the enemy, yet clearly articulate the core purpose of who we are, and what we are about?

(3) People across the broader population, particularly at the grassroots level, not only feel the identity dilemma, but in addition are caught in a process paradox. They pay enormous attention to the official table as the measuring stick of personal and group validation, where their identity, sacrifice, and years of struggle are validated or invalidated by what happens at the "table," and simultaneously feel marginalized because they do not have direct access to the table.

All three cases can easily produce a sense of insecurity and disillusionment. It is in the postconflict phase that the past bumps up against the future. I have long carried with me the words that I once read on the walls of West Belfast. "While Ireland holds these graves, Ireland unfree shall never be at peace." I am not so interested here in the partisan view the phrase expresses as I am in the metaphor it weaves about conflict. Across our globe, across the thirty-five armed conflicts the graves are held present in people's minds because they represent the loss, the trauma, the deep pain, of years and generations of conflict. And here precisely is the dilemma that the image weaves: In the postconflict phase, the graves and great-grandchildren meet together. How can we change for the good of our children yet not forget the sacrifices of our parents?

As is the case with most dilemmas, we must not permit ourselves the luxury of choosing one over the other. We cannot afford to pursue a simplistic "forgive and forget" approach, nor be stagnated in a remember and refuse to change" cycle. The challenge of postconflict peace building lies in creating the individual and collective mechanism that provide us the space to remember and to step toward change.

I would suggest that enormous, nearly impossible, pressure be brought to bear on the official, top-level process to accomplish this task. The top level, "official" process is asked to bear fruit that it is incapable of delivering on its own. This is the weakness of the hierarchical approach to politics in the postconflict phase. As such we could suggest worst-case, postconflict scenarios emanating from two sources in other settings. The first are cases where the leadership is able to manipulate the context for personal gain because there is little or no accountability. In other words, power corrupts, and absolute power corrupts absolutely. The second is that people feel a lack of genuine access, participation, responsibility, and ownership in the process. In this case, on the other side of the coin, powerlessness is the seedbed of violence. Both are forerunners to the collapse of peace.

I believe the conceptualization and development of an organic rather than a hierarchical approach to politics is needed. An organic view of political process, or what Harold Saunders calls "whole body politic," envisions peace building as a web of interdependent activities and people. The web links and cuts across levels, types of activity, and time. It creates a binding effect, holding people and processes together. It is systemic in orientation, understanding that changes in one component of the system affect the whole system, but no one component controls the process of change in the whole.

In my view, the single most important aspect of encouraging an organic perspective of peace-building politics is creating a genuine sense of participation, responsibility, and ownership in the process across a broad spectrum of the population. People must move from sitting back and reacting toward a proactive engagement that helps shape and define the process. In other words, I would suggest that one of the key tasks of people in this room today is to seek the ways to engage and inspire others to a sense of their own responsibility and validation rather than turning it over to a process that is too often remote, rife with pitfalls, and incapable of meeting their needs. Peace building and politics in the postconflict phase must be seen as an open, accessible system that rests on a broad base of participation rather than the narrowness of official table.

Processes of Transformation

The final observation I suggested was the tendency of a postconflict peace building system to focus its energy on the technical tasks of transition over the broader processes of transformation. This is not easy to grasp purely at a cognitive level, and so I offer an attempt to visualize a postconflict paradigm in Figure 4. Again, this is best depicted as a web, made up here as a nested paradigm involving four related peace-building activities. Consider for a moment each of the four.

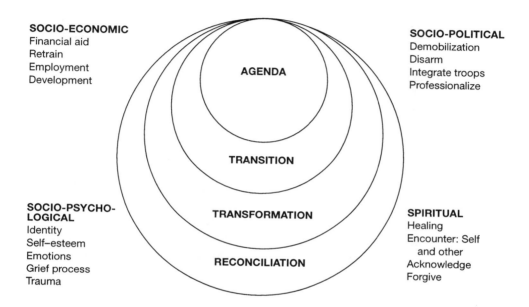

Figure 4. The web of reconciliation © *John Paul Lederach*

At its most immediate level, *defining the agenda* of the postconflict phase involves identifying the various tasks that need to be addressed. These include dealing with people, structures, and processes. Tasks may involve everything from demobilization and disarmament to governance and employment, as they relate to movement from destructive conflict toward redefinition of the relationships.

The second circle, *transition* suggests that each of the identified agenda tasks will move through a technical, logistical component of implementation. The technical aspect of repatriating refugees, for example, is the transport, location, and aid provided to them as they return to their country of origin.

This transition is embedded, however, in the third circle, the *transformative processes* that go beyond the technical aspect and reach toward the deeper questions. The technical side of disarmament, for example, is to remove the gun. The transformative side raises the question of the role and place of the military in a new context, under a newly formed structure of governance.

Finally, all of this takes place within the broadest circle involving the *search for relational reconciliation*. I say search because I believe that reconciliation represents a dialectic. It is both a place toward which we journey, and the journey once initiated opens a social space. In both instances, reconciliation is oriented toward restoring relationships, not merely resolving issues.

To this paradigm we can add four distinct and necessary dimensions in postconflict peace building: the *sociopolitical,* the *socioeconomic,* the *social-psychological,* and the *spiritual.* When I observed that many postconflict peace-building systems focus their energy too narrowly on political transition, I am referring to the top part of the paradigm. In this instance, the focus is reduced to the technical tasks of transition related to sociopolitical concerns, and times crosses over into socioeconomic issues. As such, the system rarely moves to encompass the transformative and relational concerns, or the social psychological and spiritual dimensions of human experience. This is perhaps best understood by tracking a specific task, such as the challenge of how to address the situation of former fighters in places such as Nicaragua or Mozambique.

From the sociopolitical perspective this is referred to as the process of demobilization, disarmament, and reintegration. The technical side involves the logistics of keeping troops encamped and separated, and simultaneously disarming them. The transformative aspect of the process is whether, how, when, and where the militias form part of a national defense or a policing force, and the nature and role of those institutions.

The socioeconomic perspective of the process is concerned with providing the demobilized soldiers with a fresh start, often in the form of financial aid or providing training for new vocations. The transformation aspect of the process is how a postconflict economy should be conceived, how to deal with unemployment, and how to pursue development and distribution of resources in ways that support the peace-building effort. For example, in some conflictive situations in the Horn of Africa the use of microenterprises development provided to small groups made up of people from different ethnic backgrounds, were strategically aimed at promoting interdependence, such that the success of one group is contingent on the success of the other.

The social-psychological dimension deals with a different set of concerns, aimed more at transformation and reconciliation. Here the demobilized soldier is seen as a person who is dealing with accumulated emotions and intense trauma. For this person, there are significant personal questions about identity and self-worth. The person may be resented by others for their actions, and likely carries deep feelings of anger, resentment, and loss attributed to others. There is a need to mourn and grieve loss of family, of friends, of youth and time. In other words, this phase represents more than the transition of social roles, it involves the transformation of the person.

This is coupled with what I have referred to as the spiritual dimension. Spiritual for me signifies moving beyond the issues and toward an encounter. It is a journey toward an encounter with self and the other. The purpose of the reconciliation journey is healing. Healing is in constant movement between self and the other, or in the case of postconflict peace building, between myself and my former enemy.

This involves a willingness to acknowledge the Truth and the pain of injustices experienced, and the openness to offer and accept forgiveness. The encounter with self raises the difficult question: What have I done? The encounter with the enemy raises the equally complicated question: What have they done to me? Both are necessary questions on the road to healing.

In our application here, the spiritual dimension suggests we see the demobilized individual, not merely as a soldier to be disarmed or retrained, nor as a person with psychological needs, but as a person on a journey to seek restoration and healing, embedded in a society that is seeking the same. The challenge posed by reconciliation is to open up the social space that permits and encourages individuals and societies as a collective, to acknowledge the past, mourn the losses, validate the pain experienced, confess the wrongs, and reach toward the next steps of restoring the broken relationship. This is not *forgive and forget*. This is not remember, justify, and repeat. True reconciliation is to remember and change. I see this as spiritual, because I have not found a better term to describe this search that goes beyond the political, economical, and psychological, and because, from a personal faith viewpoint, the journey toward reconciliation is necessarily a journey toward self, the enemy, and God.

In sum, I am suggesting we must extend our focus to include a broad set of dimensions that push us to operationalize the possibility of transformation.

This ultimately compels us to build a web of reconciliation aimed at sustaining the constructive initiation of change and builds toward the restoration of relationship.

The title of this conference is "Beyond Violence." I am suggesting that a sustainable approach to postconflict peace building requires moving beyond a number of frontiers. We must move beyond a short-term, crisis orientation and toward the development of our capacity to think about social change design in terms of decades. We must move beyond a hierarchical focus on politics and toward the construction of an organic, broad-based approach that creates space for genuine responsibility, ownership, and participation in peace building. We must move beyond a narrow view of postconflict peace building as a political transition and toward the formation of a web that envisions a whole body politic, whole persons seeking change in a radically changing environment.

Notes

1. Ernie Regehr, "War after the Cold War: Shaping a Canadian response," in *Ploughshares Working Paper* 1993, 3, Waterloo: Project Ploughshares.
2. This is articulated in *Building Peace: Sustainable Reconciliation in Divided Societies*, United Nations University in Japan, 1994.
3. Harold Saunders, *The Concept of Relationship*, Columbus, Ohio: Mershon Center, 1993.

·3·

The Role of
Governments and NGOs in
Coexistence Work

In this section we move from a variety of *perspectives* on coexistence (presented in chapters 1 and 2) to the search for *effective institutions* from which to launch coexistence interventions. The articles in this section consider six such institutions and evaluate their effectiveness.

Amitai Etzioni emphasizes the constructive role that can be played by the **nation–state**. He illustrates this role by pointing to numerous examples of successful mediation engaged in by the United States in recent years. U.S.-fostered reconciliations in such conflicts as Israel–PLO, Israel–Jordan, Israel–Syria, Russia–Ukraine, Northern Ireland, and Greece–Macedonia are analyzed. Etzioni advocates "embracing mediation as a major element of U.S. foreign policy" and believes that it "is particularly suitable for a period in which the United States is seeking to put its own house in order."

Roberto Toscano is partial to the use of **legal institutions**, particularly international legal institutions, to advance the cause of coexistence in the post–Cold War era. He argues for a radical redefinition of such legal concepts as sovereignty and self-determination. Such redefinition is needed to help mitigate the proliferation of demands by ethnic groups for their own states—a negative effect of some widely accepted legal rights that then become laws unto themselves.

Antonia Handler Chayes and Abram Chayes stress the relevance of good business practices for coexistence work. They emphasize the importance of **business institutions** and maintain that good business practices can provide the lessons needed to encourage coexistence. From their perspective, coexistence, like effective business, requires a culture that fosters flexibility and cooperation; a respect for autonomy; a vision that transcends selfish interests; and a strategic planning process to reach a common goal. While the authors maintain that these attributes of effective businesses are not directly transferable to the field of coexistence work, they spell out certain business themes that do make coexistence organizations more efficient and effective.

Herbert Kelman favors the **university setting** as an effective institutional base from which to engage in coexistence work. It is the university that can help create "a political environment conducive to conflict resolution" and such an environment can transform relationships between conflicting parties. In the university, it is possible to engage in a coexistence activity that he calls: "interactive problem solving." This is an academically based, unofficial third-party approach, bringing together representatives of parties in conflict for direct communication. He makes the case that the academy embodies norms favoring open discussion, attentive listening to opposing views, and an analytic approach that can facilitate coexistence. These norms tend to replace the polemical, accusatory, and legalistic approach more common in situations of conflict.

Louis Kriesberg examines the most deeply rooted and protracted conflicts, which he terms **intractable conflicts.** These are conflicts that are frequently ethnic, religious, or other intercommunal conflicts, which are waged destructively and persist despite efforts to settle or to transform them, and recur even after periods of dormancy. His major interest is the evaluation of a variety of institutional arrangements that move them toward "tractability."

Vamık Volkan advocates the use of **interdisciplinary facilitating teams** that include psychoanalysts, psychiatrists, (former) diplomats, historians, and other social and behavioral scientists. In his view, coexistence work essentially involves paying attention to unseen (unconscious) psychological factors that may blur real-world considerations. These factors lead to irrational actions and create resistance to change and to progress toward adaptive negotiations. Volkan's interventions utilize an array of sensitizing concepts derived from his own clinical experience. These include searching for "hot" locations (emotionally charged places like cemeteries and monuments); identifying mini-conflict displacement (the more immediate conflicts that emerge in the process of discussing the larger conflict); competition between chosen traumas and chosen glories; and attentiveness to the accordion effect (the way the groups come together and then pull apart in their understandings and willingness to compromise).

Raymond Shonholtz is partial to the creation of an institution he calls **Local Ethnic Conciliation Commissions** to handle ethnic conflict. He evaluates the use of such commissions in the context of the new democracies in Eastern Europe with particular stress on the need to change the cultural meanings of conflict, the perception of the opponent in a conflict situation, and the appreciation (or lack of it) for the positive functions of conflict.

All eight authors in this section search for the most effective institutional base from which to engage in coexistence work and present a wide variety of ways in which coexistence work can take place. For those who are interested in the implementation of coexistence work, it is clear that there are many alternatives available and that a wide variety of disciplines can contribute their perspectives and their skills.

Mediation as a World Role
for the United States

AMITAI ETZIONI

Gradually, and to some extent inadvertently, the United States has been developing a new role in the post–Cold War world. The new role is low-key and compatible with the need to focus on neglected domestic matters such as deficit reduction and welfare reform. Even in the foreign policy arena, the new diplomatic paradigm has been overshadowed by a grand theme left over from earlier years—the notion that the United States can and should foster democracy and human rights throughout the world.

The new U.S. role is that of the world mediator. Rather than acting as the world's police force, in several cases the United States has provided adversarial parties with its good offices and tried to broker resolutions to long-festering conflicts. As a rule the parties involved have found themselves at an impasse and believed that they might benefit from the assistance of a third party. The terms of the mediated resolutions and the compliance are not typically imposed by the United States or any other power, but are followed voluntarily by the reconciled parties. In some instances the United States offers economic inducements to encourage the parties to move forward in their reconciliation, to reward those who did move toward conflict resolution, or to ease the pain of transition for the parties whose dispute is being resolved, but that is about as far as it goes. The possibility of positioning forces between the previously conflicting parties has also been mentioned, for instance, for the Golan Heights, but basically the results of mediation—because they have been embraced voluntarily by the concerned parties—are self-enforcing.

To highlight the merits of mediation as a world role is not to suggest that this is the only role the United States plays or ought to play; clearly if Iraq were to invade Saudi Arabia, the United States ought to live up to its commitment as an ally and use its military might rather than offer mediation. And during the Cold War era there were occasions when the United States mediated. Still, as we shall see, there is a significant difference between mediation as one tool among many in one's diplomatic bag of tricks and mediation as a major U.S. tool in the post–Cold War world, in which numerous parties, released from their previous bloc commitments, are trying to sort out how to proceed in the new international environment.

U.S.-fostered reconciliations offer significant economic and social benefits in addition to helping to avoid the possibility that unresolved conflicts will lead to wars, say between Syria and Israel. As tensions abate over the longer term, more and more of the considerable resources countries have previously expended on troops, armaments, and intelligence gathering can be shifted to peaceful uses. New stability in the relations among neighbor countries can increase chances of trade with outsiders and enhance investment from abroad.[1] These developments, initially generated by reduced levels of internation tensions and conflict, in turn, undergird the evolving peace.

By and large, the U.S. role in fostering these developments has been appreciated, even celebrated. In this respect, local and international reactions compare very favorably to the reactions that have typically occurred in the wake of U.S. military interventions, economic boycotts, and pressures on countries to implement programs of economic "stabilization."

At the same time, if mediation efforts fail, the downside risk for the United States is minimal. The danger of military entanglement or of the type of difficult disengagement faced by U.S. troops in Somalia, not to mention Vietnam, is much reduced.

There is little need for major economic outlays because mediation, as a rule, entails little more than the use of skilled diplomats, shuttle diplomacy, state visits, and the like. As mentioned above, the United States has, on several occasions, provided some economic aid to help move the mediation process forward. This aid, however, is not an essential or even important part of the process because several mediation efforts, to be discussed below, have progressed successfully without economic sweeteners. And when given these were rather small in comparison to the aid used as a leading foreign policy tool.

A major reason mediation often bears at least some fruit is that the parties come to the table as a rule when they are tired of conflict and when their efforts to overcome differences on their own have failed. They come, in other words, when their conflict is "ripe" for mediation, and the opportunity provided by the United States is one they seek or at least welcome. In comparison, when the United States played a different international role, its help was not as obviously sought, nor as well received.

Even when a mediation effort is unsuccessful, it is often evident that the fault rests with an intransigent party (or parties), not with the mediator. And, because some dialogue has occurred, there is often the valid perception that additional mediation may still take place at some undetermined time in the future and may, ultimately, succeed. Thus, even under these circumstances, the U.S. basic role and intentions are appreciated, if not by all involved, then almost certainly by much of the rest of the world. The same cannot be said about the role the United States played when it acted more aggressively in places such as Nicaragua, Grenada, and Panama.

One reason why the United States has not further developed its role as a world mediator, and a large part of the reason why its contributions are not fully recognized, is that its leaders have allowed its successes in this role to be overshadowed by often futile efforts to pursue old-mode foreign policy. Old-style notions are at work in such hapless initiatives as the drives to make China respect human rights, to entice the former Soviet republics to embrace genuine democracy, and, most Sisyphean, to "restore" democracy to Haiti, where it never existed and is very unlikely to take root regardless of what the United States and its allies do. Even those who are much more optimistic than this author about the U.S. capacity to democratize the world should appreciate the benefits of allowing the role of world mediator to move to the center of the foreign policy stage, even as the United States continues to express its concern about the need to advance human rights and ideally democracy as well.

The United States as Mediator

Israel–PLO: Better Late. . . .

To depict the U.S. role in the mediation between Israel and the Palestine Liberation Organization (PLO), it is necessary to return to the period preceding the September 13, 1993, handshake between Yasser Arafat and Yitzhak Rabin at the White House. The basic political trade-off that led to the Declaration of Principles signed at that time was Israel's recognition of the PLO, and the PLO's acceptance of the Israeli model of autonomy. This was achieved through direct, secret negotiations between the Israelis and the Palestinians in which the United States was not involved. (The United States was, however, conducting an active shuttle diplomacy at the time between the Washington, D.C., hotels where Israeli and Palestinian delegations were at work. A State Department official explained that these rounds served to prepare "intellectual capital" for the rounds that followed the politically important but content-weak Oslo agreement).

After the historic handshake, the United States played a key role in overcoming major hurdles about which the two sides were deadlocked and that kept delaying the implementation of the accord. Among the issues the United States helped to deal with was the status of Jerusalem. The "solution" here was to table the issue until an indeterminate time. The parties agreed to discuss it during the final stage of negotiations. This allowed the Israelis to maintain that it was not on the active agenda and the Palestinians to feel that the subject was no longer taboo, but open to consideration, albeit in the indeterminate future.

Second, Palestinians living in East Jerusalem were granted the right to vote in elections for the Palestinian Authority, but so far their ability to hold political office has been left unresolved. For the Israelis this was a question again deferred, while the Palestinians saw it as a potential opportunity to expand their jurisdiction into Jerusalem.

Third, there was a question about the meaning of autonomy. Palestinians claimed autonomy over the land. Such autonomy, along with legislative power, would accord them a sense of sovereignty. The Israeli position was that the interim government was derivative of other authority and that, as that other authority, the Israeli government had the final determination of laws in Gaza and the West Bank.

The compromise mediators helped to work out granted the Palestinian Authority legislative powers, but the Israeli government retained review and rejection powers.

Fourth, the parties were helped to develop a compromise over border security. A complex Rube Goldberg rule, showing the ingenuity of those involved, was reached about the border crossing, which allowed Israel to control entry and the Palestinians to appear in charge. There are two terminals. At one, Israelis and tourists are checked by Israeli security. At the other, Palestinians are checked by Palestinian officers, with Israelis watching through a two-way mirror, accepting or rejecting certain persons.

To an outsider these issues may seem only somewhat more weighty than the shape of the table during the negotiations with Vietnam. For those in the area, however, only after these issues were resolved, compromised, or deferred by mutual agreement could the accords be implemented. The United States may have played at best an indirect role in getting the 1993 mediation going, but it played a growing role in keeping the process moving forward. Like many mediation endeavors, the work is far from done and one can never tell if, at some future time, last year's achievements will be undone.

Israel–Jordan: U.S. Role Rather Pivotal

The United States emerged as a significant factor in the Israel-Jordan give-and-take by putting aside its lingering ill will toward Jordan for its role in supporting Iraq during the Persian Gulf War. There were three main issues: refugees, borders, and water. With U.S. diplomatic help (and some economic sweeteners) these were resolved in the following manner: in July 1994, both parties agreed to postpone a resolution of the refugee issues until a later date, possibly because the Jordanians realized that Israel could not agree to allow the return of all or even most of the millions of Palestinians who had left Israel over the last decades.

Both sides agreed not to deal with the West Bank's Israel–Jordan border, which basically parallels frontiers drawn under a long-standing international agreement and is marked by the River Jordan. The disputes concerned short parts of the border north of the West Bank and south of the West Bank on the way to Aqaba. In both places it was resolved that some of the land was ceded to Jordan but leased back to Israeli settlers whose lives were not disturbed as a result, and some of the land was ceded to Jordan outright. (In the South, a really ingenious solution modeled on a section of the U.S.–Canada border has so far not been endorsed: turning the contested areas into transnational parks.)

The third major issue was water. Israel was mainly concerned about the water supply to the Negev from springs and wells. Jordan was most concerned about northern water from tributaries of the Jordan. The compromise? Jordan made concessions in the South and Israel in the North. Israel gets northern flow in the summer; Jordan in the winter. And Israel retains control over the southern aquifers.

These agreements were foreshadowed by a meeting on October 1, 1993, of Jordanian, Israeli, and U.S. leaders in Washington, D.C. At this meeting, the parties agreed to create a trilateral economic committee, ostensibly aimed at making plans for developing cooperative ventures and for development of territories in and between Jordan and Israel. A State Department source has indicated, however, that the underlying purpose was to enable the Israelis and the Jordanians to talk without being bound by the formal and rigid arrangements for Middle East negotiations set by the Madrid conference of 1991.

In July 1994, King Hussein and Prime Minister Rabin visited the White House to sign an agreement that ended the state of belligerency. In October, a treaty normalizing relations and resolving border and water disputes was signed in the Jordan Rift Valley. In both instances, President Bill Clinton presided over the festivities marking the successful completion of the trilateral mediation efforts. As these lines are written, in March 1995, this exercise in mediation seems particularly well rounded and its achievements solidly ensconced.

Israel–Syria: A Prolonged Beginning as the Cold War Ends

Syria became interested in joining the peace discussion when it lost the support of its patron superpower, the Soviet Union. It also felt that peace with Israel could serve as a foundation for better relations with the United States. Both goals could be advanced simultaneously if the United States served as the mediator. Israel recognized that the goal of peace with Syria could not be achieved without U.S. involvement.

From the outset, Syria wanted a prior commitment on full withdrawal from the Golan Heights by Israel. Israel had been reluctant to grant such assurances until Syria defined peace to show that it would not be merely nominal but encompassing, a peace that included full normalization of relations. Israel also wanted security guarantees in order to be able to prove to its citizens that their security would not be diminished by relinquishing the Golan Heights. Syria saw no reason to concede anything to get back what Syrians considered their land.

Since later 1993, U.S. diplomats, such as Secretary of State Warren Christopher, had been shuttling between Syria and Israel. In April 1994, to advance the talks, the U.S. officials suggested two new considerations; time and phases. Events could be stretched out over time using more phases, or completed more rapidly in fewer phases. This strategy opens up nearly limitless possibilities for schedules and types of relations. For instance, Israel initially wanted a seven-year withdrawal, all normalization in one year, and full security guarantees. Syria countered with a six-month withdrawal, five years for normalization, and no security assurances.

Gradually, differences in all these areas have somewhat narrowed, although the ground that is still to be covered is considerable. Israel is reported now to be willing to accept a four-year, nine-month withdrawal from the Golan Heights, while Syria is holding out for a sixteen-month withdrawal. On the issue of normalization of relations, the public veneer of relations has been improved, even if only slightly, by symbolic gestures such as the first-ever interview of a Syrian foreign minister on Israeli television and permission for one Israeli reporter (who is also a U.S. citizen) to attend a press conference with President Hafez al-Assad in Syria. Both sides agree on one point: there is a long row to hoe, and much for the mediators to achieve. This case has already proven to be a test of patience for those who offered to mediate.

Russia–Estonia: The Last Step

As early as January 1991, Russian officials were promising the withdrawal of troops from the three Baltic states of Lithuania, Latvia, and Estonia. But in October 1992, Russia reversed its course on troop withdrawals. It cited two reasons. First, there was insufficient housing in Russia to absorb the more than 100,000 Russian troops in the Baltics. Second, Russia felt a need to safeguard the rights of the ethnic Russian minority in the Baltics. For nearly two years thereafter, negotiations on this issue between Russia and the Baltic states can be characterized only as proceeding by fits and starts. No sooner would talks begin than they would be halted, unable to yield a resolution acceptable to all sides.

In October 1993, Secretary Christopher visited Latvia after his tour of the former Soviet Union. While in Russia, he pressed for a troop withdrawal. In Riga, Latvia, he suggested that the Baltics should extend citizenship to ethnic Russians. He feared that restricting citizenship might someday give Russia a plausible reason not only to keep troops in, but also to invade, the Baltics. While he was in Latvia, Secretary Christopher met with Aleksei Grigoriev, a journalist and spokesman for ethnic Russians. Grigoriev asked for U.S. mediation of the situation. Although his request was denied, Secretary Christopher suggested instead that an international committee review Latvia's restrictive citizenship law. Latvia promptly accepted the offer.

By 1994 Russian troops had completely withdrawn from Lithuania, where the situation was resolved without additional U.S. contributions. President Boris Yeltsin announced his intention to withdraw Russian troops from Latvia also, but stalled on a withdrawal from Estonia. Estonia turned to the United States for assistance.

The issue of a full withdrawal from Estonia was raised in communications between President Clinton and President Yeltsin. During the summit of the Group of Seven (G-7) in July 1994, President Clinton hand-delivered a letter from Estonian president Lennart Meri to Yeltsin. The letter requested a personal meeting between the Russian and the Estonian leaders. On July 15, the U.S. Senate voted to make all aid to Russia contingent on a full withdrawal from Estonia.

Shortly after the G-7 summit, Presidents Yeltsin and Meri met in Moscow. After a night of tumultuous negotiations a deal was truck. The last Russian troops were withdrawn from the Baltics on August 31, 1994, ending fifty-four years of military occupation. The U.S. mediation thus enabled completion of the process of Russian withdrawal from the Baltics. It helped remove the barriers especially in one remaining contested area—Estonia.

Russia–Ukraine: A Crowning Achievement

Following the fragmentation of the Soviet Union, the world faced the danger of instant nuclear proliferation because such weapons were positioned outside Russia in the now independent countries of Belarus, Kazakhstan, and Ukraine. Both the United States and Russia were interested, for a variety of motives, in eliminating these weapons or returning them to Russia. This matter was resolved relatively readily in negotiations between Russia and Belarus, and Russia and Kazakhstan but the negotiations with Ukraine ended in an impasse.

In May 1993, Leonid Kravchuk, then president of Ukraine, reported that talks between Ukraine and Russia were deadlocked and that Russia's ultimatums and pressuring were only making the situation worse. (The United States had shown decided favoritism toward the Russian position.) Ukraine declared that it had to hold onto its missiles. The situation seemed hopeless.

At the beginning of June 1993, the United States reevaluated its position in the dispute between Russia and Ukraine. In a visit to Ukraine, Strobe Talbott, special envoy of the secretary of state, listened to Ukraine's fears about Russia—its military superiority (conventional and nuclear) and its imperialist tone—and promised that the United States would mediate the dispute. As reported in *Arms Control Today,* Talbott stated, "we told our Ukranian hosts that the U.S. would like to try to find a way to serve as a facilitator in the complex relations between Ukraine and Russia, if that is acceptable to both sides."[2] The issues requiring mediation included security guarantees, assurances of territorial integrity, and compensation for denuclearizing. Out of the mediation was born a new proposal to disarm the nuclear weapons but store them in Ukraine. This proposal was unsatisfactory to the Russians. In July the Ukranians claimed full ownership of the weapons.

The Crimea Summit on September 3, 1993, produced a signed accord between Ukraine and Russia agreeing to the terms of withdrawal for all nuclear warheads in Ukraine. But less than three weeks later, Russia annulled the agreement, claiming that Ukraine had unilaterally altered the text. The word "all" had been crossed out and replaced with a handwritten phrase limiting the number and kind of nuclear missiles to be returned to Russia.

In November 1993, Secretary Christopher traveled to Ukraine to try to jump-start the negotiations between Russia and Ukraine. Ukraine sought $2.8 billion in aid for dismantling costs and firm security guarantees from the United States. Ukraine wanted a trilateral agreement closely linking the security of Ukraine to that of Russia and the United States. Secretary Christopher offered the Clinton administration's Partnership for Peace initiative—a plan that would offer alliances to former Eastern bloc countries that wanted membership in the North Atlantic Treaty Organization. Although this piqued interest in Ukraine, as of December 1993 Ukraine still feared Russia's nuclear and conventional military power and still worried about Russia's failure to acknowledge its borders. By mid-December, Russia was threatening Ukraine with economic sanctions that would have crushed their victim because Ukraine was dependent upon Russia for much of the fuel used to run its power plants.

The series of trilateral talks about nuclear disarmament among Ukraine, Russia, and the United States over issues such as how to split proceeds from uranium sales had, however, been in progress since mid-December. During this time President Clinton sent a letter to Ukraine's President Kravchuk urging a speedy solution to the standoff and Ukraine's deputy foreign minister visited the United States to push the negotiations. On January 14, a trilateral agreement between the United States, Russia, and Ukraine was signed in Moscow.

The jubilation that success brought was soured by Ukraine's noncompliance the following month.The Ukrainian government felt that the accord offered inadequate security guarantees. Further, the Ukrainian parliament failed to ratify the Nuclear Non-Proliferation Treaty, which had been a condition of the January 14 accord.

Following additional efforts by the United States, the light at the end of the tunnel reappeared as the Ukrainian parliament ratified the Strategic Arms Reduction Treaty, signed the Lisbon protocol, which declared Ukraine to be a nonnuclear country under the NPT, and resumed missile transfers to Russia.

This may well be one of the only cases in which the nuclear proliferation process was reversed: a country that had control of nuclear arms gave them up (as distinct from a superpower removing its nuclear forces)—all without a shot being fired. The interests of the parties, of the United States, and indeed of the world were directly served in this instance.

Northern Ireland: A Productive Tilt Away from an Ally

Both the United Kingdom and Ireland repeatedly offered to hold direct talks with the Irish Republican Army (IRA). Both countries demanded, however, that the IRA first renounce terrorism by announcing a permanent cease-fire and, second, acknowledge the right of unionists and republicans to self-determination of Northern Ireland. For most of 1994 Gerry Adams, head of Sinn Fein, the political wing of the IRA, refused to accept these conditions.

At the beginning of 1994, the National Committee on American Foreign Policy held a conference in New York on the prospects for peace in Northern Ireland after the Downing Street Declaration.[3] The New York conference marked a new foray into the mediator role by the United States. Gerry Adams sought to attend the conference, but was initially refused entry into the United States because of his links to terrorism. At the behest of Senators Edward Kennedy (D-Mass.) and Daniel Patrick Moynihan (D-N.Y.) and against the wishes of many key figures in his administration, President Clinton granted Adams a visa.

During the visit, Anthony Lake, President Clinton's national security adviser, pursued a secret exchange of views with Adams, urging the IRA's political leadership to accept the British conditions for attendance at the settlement table. U.S. willingness to vouch for the sincerity of the British offer provided the crucial weight that persuaded the IRA to adopt a unilateral cease-fire on September 1, 1994. During the same period, Lake maintained close contacts with Ulster Unionist Party leader James Molyneaux, a relationship that culminated in a meeting at the White House. Lake also spoke frequently with leaders of Northern Ireland's Social Democratic Labor Party. This proved useful in bringing that group to the table.

Aware of the influence of the Irish–American voting bloc, the IRA trusted the United States more than it did the United Kingdom, but in the past it had feared that the United States would stay out of the conflict to protect its "special relationship" with the United Kingdom. However, in a move not unlike the U.S. limited disengagement from its traditional close ties to Israel and its willingness to move, however slightly, closer to the PLO—thus facilitating its mediating role—the United States initiated a limited disengagement from the United Kingdom, opening space for the IRA to enter neutral negotiations. Note that in both cases the United States had built enough trust in its close allies to enable it to move toward a more neutral point without losing that trust, thereby enabling mediation. A further round of similar developments occurred in March 1995. Although the United Kingdom protested President Clinton's permission to Adams to raise funds for nonarms purposes. President Clinton encouraged him to "decommission" the arms of the IRA, as the United Kingdom has sought.

Since the cease-fire of September 1, 1994, the IRA has made overtures regarding the status of Northern Ireland's future. Some Sinn Fein officials openly admit that they are willing to accept that Northern Ireland might never be reunited with Ireland. Their opponents, the Ulster Freedom Fighters and the Ulster Volunteer Force which initially did not trust the cease-fire and were reluctant to join, came around to endorsing it.

The cease-fire, which was not permanent, gains more and more permanency as each day passes. As these lines were written, several months had passed in which there was next to no bloodshed in Northern Ireland and people were able to use public spaces freely. The U.S. role, while initially criticized by the British and by many U.S. journalists, politicians, and bureaucrats, now receives wide acclaim.

Greece and Macedonia: Maneuvering around Symbols

In 1992, after Macedonia declared its independence from a crumbling Yugoslavia, it took rapid steps to gain international recognition to ensure that it would not be invaded by Serbia. Among these actions were attempts to gain the recognition of the European Community (EC) and the United States. Although eleven of twelve EC countries ratified an agreement of recognition, Greece killed it by using its veto power. The United States declared that it would not act until the EC did.

Greece listed three reasons for its refusal to recognize Macedonia. First, the use of the name Macedonia, according to the Greeks, indicates that the former Yugoslav republic has designs on the region of Greece that is also called Macedonia. Second, the Macedonian flag borrows from very important Greek symbols, and is thus interpreted as another indicator both of Macedonia's plans to take part of Greece and its lack of respect for Greece. Third, Greece objects to amendments in Macedonia's constitution that guarantee protection for Macedonians everywhere. To show its overall displeasure, Greece has also established an export embargo on Macedonia.

Macedonia tried to assuage Greek fears by passing constitutional amendments that deny claims on Greek territory, by prohibiting interference in the internal affairs of other nations, and by reaffirming the inviolability of current borders. Macedonian efforts were fruitless until the United States took a more active role in the dispute.

The United States has attempted to broker agreements to end the Greek embargo and allow recognition of Macedonia by the EC, now the European Union. High-level State Department officials, Secretary Christopher included, have moderated meetings between both sides. According to Greek foreign minister Karolos Popoulias, "Differences have been narrowed." The United States has formally recognized Macedonia, but as of March 1995 had not sent an ambassador—a move aimed at appeasing Macedonia without angering Greece.

The United States, with very little directly at stake, skillfully dealt with a long list of largely symbolic issues, bringing the parties closer together. It also helped in the process to anchor the recognition of Macedonia as an independent state, which might prove helpful in preventing the war in Yugoslavia from spreading. In this sense, this is a case of preventive mediation: avoiding conflicts before they occur, often the best mediation.

North Korea: Mediation as a Limited Element

In the situations discussed so far mediation has played a key role. In other situations it has been but a part of a multifaceted approach to foreign policy; in these situations mediation has worked largely because it followed the application of other means. It nevertheless played a surprisingly significant role. A case in point is the developments in Korea in 1994.

The United States and its ally South Korea, backed by the world community, were at an impasse in efforts to make North Korea abide by the regulations of the International Atomic Energy Agency that required full inspection of all nuclear facilities. North Korea balked. The United States and its allies threatened economic sanctions and announced larger than usual military exercises. North Korea protested and in effect threatened war against South Korea, a threat taken seriously given the perception that North Koreans were irrational by Western standards.

Into the breach came former president Jimmy Carter, who in effect mediated between North Korea on the one hand and the United States and South Korea on the other. He brokered a nuclear monitoring agreement that all sides accepted. Moreover, after this agreement, the United States somewhat disengaged itself from its very close association with South Korea (as it did with Israel and the United Kingdom) and moved to deal with North Korea somewhat more as a mediator than as an ally of one of the parties. This led to a new, broader agreement and finally to South Korea's opening of economic relations with North Korea. Trade has been simplified and investment in the North by South Korean companies is no longer illegal, a sharp departure from earlier decades of very hostile relations.

An argument can be made that none of this would have happened if there had not been the initial threat of economic sanctions. Mediation, if this is true, served "only" to defuse the tensions and to build on the new openness, leading to peaceful results: it did not carry the full burden of conflict resolution. Even if mediation by the United States is seen in this limited manner, however, it still played a significant role and one that was much more welcome in the region (especially to China and Japan) and around the world than the previous U.S. role.

Haiti: A Noncase

At first blush, one of the most successful mediation efforts of the last years occurred when former president Carter, first single-handedly, and then in collaboration with Senator Sam Nunn (D-Ga.) and Gen. Colin Powell (ret.) persuaded the Haitian generals to yield power and allow a peaceful landing of U.S. troops rather than a military operation very likely to involve at least some bloodshed.

Actually the development in Haiti falls at the margin of this exposition for one reason and outside it for another. Mediation in Haiti was not the main mover; military threat was. As has been widely reported, the Haitian generals yielded only when reports were flashed that U.S. forces had actually taken off from military bases and were closing in on Haiti. More disqualifying is the fact that the United States did not mediate in this case between two other nations, helping them to resolve their differences without violence, but Carter and company mediated between Haiti and the United States. Although this is still a case in which mediation made a contribution, it is not a case in which the United States exercised its new post–Cold War mediator role.

Two Challenges

The thesis that the United States is wisely developing its role as the world peacemaker via mediation rather than on the nose cones of missiles called Peacemakers must address two questions. What is the relationship between mediation and other tools of foreign policy, because no one claims that it is the only tool? And what is the relationship between mediation and elementary justice, because mediation tends to the resolution of conflict even if this means appeasement of tyrants, an issue raised by President Carter's endeavors in this area?

Mediation is clearly part of a package of tools that all feed into one another. The mediation in Korea (and Carter's role in Haiti) might well not have been possible if it had not been preceded by the implicit threat of force and economic sanctions. And the same situation can be read the other way around: If mediation had not been successful, the United States would have had to apply force or sanctions when quite disinclined to do so for numerous reasons. But, the point is not that one can or should try to make mediation the only tool of foreign policy, or that there are no beneficial interaction effects among these tools; only that this particular tool should receive much more prominence given the new global situation and U.S. domestic needs.

The concern for justice is much more vexing. Studies of divorce suggest that when couples draw on mediators rather than on courts, their settlements are much less painful, much less costly, but often unfair to women. (Men often refuse to grant the mothers custody of the children, which mothers as a rule anxiously seek, until the men gain favorable economic terms.) Similarly it has been suggested that the mediation efforts with North Korea entailed too many concessions to a tyrant. Being aware of this trap, observers need to examine each case in its own right. By and large, however, the value of a peaceful resolution is very high, and if the costs are limited to matters of prestige (or "face") they seem, as a rule, well worth the price.

Mediation in Historical Context

Mediation is, of course, an age-old foreign policy tool and it played a role during the Cold War era as well. At that time, however, it was applied differently and typically had a much less central role. Mediation during the Cold War often took place among the superpowers on behalf of their clients. Thus, when differences between Syria and Israel were negotiated in this context, a good part of the dealing between the Soviet Union and the United States took the form of negotiation between two parties rather than mediation provided by a third party. Mediation among countries within the same bloc came closer to the mark, as illustrated by the Camp David accords. But even here there were superpower considerations in the background, such as how to prevent conflicts among nations in one bloc so that a unified front could be presented toward the other bloc, or how to prevent conflicts among the members of one's bloc and nonaligned nations so as not to push them toward the other bloc. And although mediation occurred, the main foundation of world "order" rested on relations between the superpowers.

True, in this earlier era, Henry Kissinger conducted shuttle diplomacy in the Middle East, and President Carter directly helped negotiate the treaty between Israel and Egypt. And indeed these early mediation efforts had a similarly attractive profile: little risk, limited economic costs, and significant humanitarian and political benefits. Yet they were considered at the time, as they have been since, sideshows, diplomatic efforts relevant chiefly for countries within the Western orbit. They were therefore peripheral to the main event: the worldwide confrontation between the superpowers, a confrontation in which the key policy tools were deterring arsenals of nuclear and conventional weapons, foreign military aid packages, U.S. Central Intelligence Agency and other covert operations, massive economic aid, and ideological warfare. Moreover, any mediation efforts were routinely structured so as not to undermine, however indirectly, the number one goal of "containing" communism and shoring up what was called the free world. In this context, simply dealing directly with, say, Syria, was not seriously considered because Syria was a Soviet client.

In short, the role of mediator was not viewed as a significant world role for the United States, and the architects of foreign policy did not suggest that it should be. The United States was a superpower confronting another superpower, not a globe-trotting broker of peaceful settlements. In the new post–Cold War order (or lack thereof), mediation—genuine mediation, largely free from extrinsic considerations—can play a much more pivotal role.

Embracing mediation as a major element of U.S. foreign policy is particularly suitable for a period in which the United States is seeking to put its own house in order. This focus benefits the United States because the costs of mediation are much lower than those associated with interventions such as those in Somalia and Haiti. Also, by being much less dramatic, mediation distracts the president and the country less from their domestic missions. Furthermore, it should be noted that no wide support exists in the country for a much more activist foreign policy. At the same time, there is strong sentiment in favor of some form of international engagement. Champions of pure realpolitik may want to act only when U.S. national interests are directly affected, but in the age of mass communications, public opinion plays a significant role in international relations and the idealistic side of public opinion—those facets of public psychology that found expression in the calls to help the people of Rwanda and to act in defense of beleaguered Bosnia—cannot be ignored. Mediation provides a constructive response for this compassionate side of the U.S. nature.

To be sure, it does not provide a complete one. The fulfillment of its foreign policy goals and ideals requires that the United States continue to contribute its leadership to the strengthening of international law through participation in the United Nations and various other international and regional alliances. It must continue to encourage the elimination of barriers among nations, remaining a major factor in the negotiation of international trade pacts. Where the well-being of its citizens or vital interest are threatened, it must be willing to project force outside its borders. And, where the preconditions for successful democratization exist, the United States may cautiously seek to assist in their development, although if it does, it must now do so with much more humility and sobriety than in the past. Success will be achieved more readily if mediation, in which the United States already engages with considerable success around the world, is given the recognition and attention that is its due.*

*The author is indebted to David E. Carney for research assistance and to Daniel Kurtzer, Michael McCurry, Michael Nacht, and Daniel Schorr for their helpful comments on previous drafts. He also benefited from a discussion following a presentation at the Council on Foreign Relations in Washington, D.C. The views expressed are his alone.

Notes

1. One example that highlights how peace brings business and prosperity is described in Amy Dockser Marcus and Caleb Solomon, "Growing Mideast Peace Is Opening New Worlds for Energy Industry," *Wall Street Journal,* January 16, 1995, p. A–1.
2. *Arms Control Today* 23 (June 1993), p. 25.
3. The Downing Street Declaration is a document produced at a meeting of the Irish and English political leaders in December 1993. The two main points were a recognition of the Irish right to self-determination in Northern Ireland and the acknowledgment that nothing would occur without the consent of the majority. The IRA/Sinn Fein rejected the Downing Street Declaration, as did various Unionist groups as well.

An Answer to War:
Conflicts and Intervention in
Contemporary International Relations

ROBERTO TOSCANO

> In moral terms, the problem we face is that of the rights of others
> beyond our borders: not merely the moral rights of other states, which
> have been enshrined in international law for a long time, but the
> rights of other human beings, either as members of other communities
> or simply as human beings.
>
> —Stanley Hoffman[1]

1. Conflict at the End of the Twentieth Century

One is almost embarrassed at having to stress once again the depth and radical nature of the changes brought about by the year 1989, the historical defeat of Communism, the end of the Cold War. And yet it is from this still recent turning point, unforseen and still far from being fully decanted, that a discourse on conflict must be begun.

In the first place, what has changed is the perception of a threat. We will not presume to interfere with historians as they debate up to which point the nuclear holocaust has ever constituted a real danger. What is certain, however, is that, both politically and psychologically, the counterposition of the two Superpowers in the field of nuclear armaments has contributed in a very fundamental way to determining the specific features of European (and in part, world) history throughout the second half of the twentieth century. It did so by determining alliances, marking borderlines, defining thresholds and activating "safety valves" not only for tensions between Moscow and Washington, but also for conflicts between others, even at times when such conflicts were played out in areas that were politically or geostrategically marginal.

If we want to ready ourselves for an understanding of the conflicts of our time, we will have to jettison the main bulk of the tools used for about half a century by the theory of conflict.

The risk that nuclear weapons may be used by someone somewhere has not disappeared, and may even be made more acute by proliferation. However, we should at last free ourselves from an obsessive fixation on the ghost of a World

War III. As we were anxiously waiting (ourselves in—nuclear—arms) for the dreaded coming of the nuclear barbarians, we did not lend sufficient attention to real wars, less apocalyptic but much more possible. For decades we expounded on "Megadead," and now that we are facing thousands, tens and hundreds of thousands of real dead, we find ourselves lacking a state-of-the-art, interdisciplinary culture of conflict capable of helping us understand and react.

One of the main reasons is that during the Cold War years the study of peace and war advanced mainly in the barren and disembodied terrains of technology, at times drifting into virtual reality. The discourse was disproportionately focused on the instruments of conflict: their number, their type, their possible uses and effects. Weapons held the center stage to the detriment of politics and history, the values and interests of men, both leaders and peoples. We will certainly not endorse the captious and disingenuous slogan of the NRA: *"Guns don't kill people. People kill people."* And yet even those who favor the control and limitation of the production and commerce of arms should have the intellectual honesty to admit that the slogan embodies a minimum of truth. How could we do otherwise when we have just witnessed the extermination in Rwanda, with machetes, of the equivalent in victims of at least seven Hiroshima-type nuclear bombs? Leaving aside games theory and the theology of deterrence we should at last focus our attention upon a real subject, on the mechanisms that bring about conflict and on those that can prevent it or stop it once it has started.

Another distortion typical of the study of conflict during the Cold War is the product of the systemic view that led inevitably, when considering any conflict, anywhere, to ask "who is behind it?" The planetwide confrontation of the two systems made such a question plausible, though not necessarily—and not invariably—well founded. What is true is that lingering on it today means losing precious time. It is banal and tautological, maintaining that those who have power exert it by the very fact of existing and moving (or even refraining from moving) on the international scene. It is quite a different thing, however, to interpret the clash among Somali clans or Rwandan ethnic groups in a mainly external key, be it neoimperial or neocolonial.

The fact is that inserting each individual conflict in the framework of the Great Confrontation was not only a handy key to understanding their causes, but also pointed at a path leading to their management and settlement. In the end, be it the Suez War in 1956 or the War in Vietnam, someone "was in charge," someone supplied military balance, diplomatic support, negotiated "ways out."

Today we live instead in a world that, when we speak of conflicts, is impressively polycentric and pluralistic. For decades many have hoped that someday we would overcome the division of the world in two opposed camps, the overbearing interference of the two Superpowers in the affairs of countries, peoples, ethnic groups, and political movements. Now, with a "regionalized" Russia and the U.S. as an evermore reluctant hegemonic power, one remembers what Saint Theresa had to say about answered prayers as being those apt to generate the bitterest of tears.

Irreconcilable claims of all sorts, nationalist obsessions, ethnic paranoias, demential fundamentalisms[2] reach the threshold of armed conflict without anyone (once the mobilizing effect of the Cold War is over) being willing to spend money or risk lives in order to prevent or stop the clash.

We will definitely not indulge in an obscene nostalgia for the good old days of the Cold War, and yet we are forced to live in a "postmodern" world that has been deprived of a handy interpretative tool and of an arbitrary but real international governance. We are all orphans of the Cold War, but instead of weeping the not-so-dear deceased we should try to grow up.

Focusing on the quantity of conflicts, on their pluralism, is important, but it cannot by itself supply the full measure of the problems we are facing in this disconcerting end of the twentieth century. As a matter of fact, the most disturbing feature is not the quantity, but the quality of present-day conflicts.

The term "war," indicating "organized violence carried on by political units against each other"[3] turns out not to be sophisticated enough to account for an important differentiation between two different types of conflict. The Greeks, for example—and especially Plato in *The Republic*—referred to organized violence using two different terms: *stasis,* i.e., a conflict between groups mutually recognizing a basic affinity, though seeking to solve by force a divergence of interests; and *polemos,* i.e., total war against the totally "Other," the barbarian, the threatening stranger, the alien.[4]

It is a fact that instruments created to prevent, limit for humanitarian purposes, or settle conflicts (from consuetudinary and treaty-based international law to the UN Charter) were developed by the international community with reference to war/*stasis,* and not to war/*polemos,* the latter not recognizing, by definition, either rules or limits. Thus it is false that, as critics often maintain, those instruments are invariably useless or ineffective.

Let us take a rather recent case: the war for the Falklands/Malvinas. It was a real war with many dead, and with the utilization of modern and lethal military hardware. Yet in carrying out this particular war, both the Argentinians and the British showed that their aim was neither the extermination nor the total crushing of the adversary. It was clearly a test of force with a very specific object performed by two subjects showing, even as they were fighting, that they were fully aware of the fact that after the war there would again be coexistence, relationship, mutual recognition. Hence the respect of certain self-limitations, rules of the game, internationally recognized norms (be it for the respect of noncombatants or the treatment of prisoners of war).

The problem is that such a kind of conflict is today the exception, not the rule. The rule is the proliferation of wars/*polemos*. And the real tragedy is that, contrary to what was true in ancient Greece, today the enemy is no longer the barbarian with an unusual appearance and an incomprehensible language, but literally (see former Yugoslavia or Rwanda) the next-door neighbor. It is indeed the neighbor that is to be identified as a threat to one's survival and identity. It is the neighbor that must be either forcibly removed or exterminated, with no space for compromise, coexistence, compassion, or respect for limits or rules in the clash.[5]

One may be tempted to maintain that, today as well as in the past, civil wars are invariably conducive to the concept of *polemos,* with its load of totality and ferociousness. But it is hardly so: the American Civil War—a wide, prolonged, bitter conflict—was basically fought as a war/*stasis.* Suffice it to say that it was during that very conflict that the foundations of what was later to be called international humanitarian law were laid.[6] Alternatively, one could suggest a differentiation between countries and cultures conceiving conflict in the former or in the latter variant: i.e., as a death struggle deprived of all rules or rather as a confrontation that is violent but limited both in its means and in its goals (the defeat, not the annihilation of the enemy). But history does not allow us to sustain this hypothesis either. The same country (Germany) in the same conflict (World War II) behaved vis-à-vis two enemies (allied between themselves) according to two different concepts of conflict: *stasis* on the Western front (as shown by the treatment of allied prisoners of war, as well as by the murky, but historically factual, attempts at a separated, negotiated peace) and *polemos* on the Eastern front (here too the treatment of Russian war prisoners, of which hundreds of thousands were starved to death in captivity, is revealing).

What is then the origin of this phenomenon, definitively not a new one as far as its roots are concerned, but ominously new for the breadth of its proliferation?

A methodological footnote is in order here. One would hope that the intellectual dominance of single-factor theories is at last waning. All the more so in a field such as the study of conflict (international and noninternational), one of the most complex due to the multiplicity and variety of factors at play, and where only a multidisciplinary approach and multicausal hypothesis can help us understand. We must at last rid ourselves of artificial dichotomies such as economics versus politics, ethics versus interests, diplomacy versus use of military means, internal versus international aspects: conflicts must be examined simultaneously under all these angles.

Turning now to the specific case of the kind of conflict characterizing our time, we see that the inevitable interaction between socioeconomic and politico-cultural factors unfolds in profoundly differentiated patterns according to different situations, geographical realities, levels of development, cultures.

For example, the conflict between Serbs and Moslems in Bosnia does not have the same causes (thus it does not demand the same "treatment") as the confrontation between Hutus and Tutsis in Rwanda and Burundi. But let us linger on these two so-called ethnic conflicts.

In the first place one has to reject the fatalistic pseudorealism of those who maintain that for certain peoples and certain ethnic groups—be it the Serbs or the Hutus—violence is more "normal" than coexistence. We must reject it not only because it is a more or less consciously racist statement, but also because it is a false one. History, even in the bloody Balkans, supplies evidence of alternating periods of coexistence and conflict, as matter of fact the former usually longer than the latter. Were it not so one could not account for the formation and the duration throughout several centuries of complex multiethnic communities. If today someone is trying to enforce ethnic cleansing it is indeed because groups coexisted for a long time, living together in the same territory. Who said, and on which grounds, that multiethnic coexistence is less "natural" than ethnic conflict? Can we not suspect the opposite to be true, so that only violence can separate what naturally tends to mix?[7]

And yet, we must make an effort to understand the roots of these conflicts.

In the first place, we must say that there are *also* material, socioeconomic causes. Let us take Rwanda. A Senagalese international civil servant, with extended experience in the country, wrote after the tragedy: "This small country, with the highest demographic density in Africa, is characterized by the most extreme proximity among its inhabitants. Yet individualism is sovereign, and fear of the other marks daily life."[8] African reality in general is often defined by a severe lack of resources and by a deep imbalance in person-to-land, person-to-environment ratio.[9] Such an imbalance creates situations that are "zero-sum," or can be presented as such by reckless and criminal political leaders. Given these premises, conflict becomes a paroxysmal and anomic clash described by the awful saying *mors tua, vita mea,* and that Hobbes rather than Clausewitz can help us understand.

And yet even in this instance what we are confronted with is neither "natural" nor automatic. Conflict between groups remains in the realm of politics, and not in that of nature, such as the mutual aggression among rats confined in ever more cramped spaces. What is needed to spark the conflict is a detonator: the "ethnic lie." If one wants the next-door neighbor to be considered as a threatening alien (to be exterminated before he exterminates you) the first step is describing him as such, exasperating the elements that make him different, or inventing them if they do not exist.[10] We detect here a task for intellectuals and propaganda workers, for the creators of positive myths about one's own group and of negative myths regarding the neighbor/rival. Such a process is very clear in the case of the Hutu–Tutsi confrontation.

Let us quote the General Secretary of "Medecins san frontieres," Alain Destexhe:

"When the colonizers arrived, there were groups, social entities distinguished from the others, but differences were not perceived in the guise of ethnic groups or races. Building stereotypes and supporting one group against the other, the colonizers contributed to the reinforcement, structuring and heightening of separate identities. After independence, such categories have been strengthened every time rulers have tried to overcome a politically difficult phase by exasperating the ethnic issue. What is true is that, though the Hutu–Tutsi confrontation does not coincide with a true ethnic differentiation, it has been assumed by the population as a whole, and has therefore become politically relevant."[11] Thus in Rwanda "human beings have destroyed each other in a conflict belonging to other times in the name of a fiction."[12] In other words, it is not enough, in order to account for genocide, to recur to history (Tutsi feudal power over which colonizers implanted their power and their administration), sociology (Tutsi herdsmen against Hutu peasants), economics (a country with dwindling resources subject to strong demographic pressures). These factors are only premises, and the same factors could have led to completely different outcomes if one had embarked on a different political path. What is still missing, in order to explain the tragedy, is the role of party and government leaders, of intellectuals, of media (in the first place the sinister *"Radio milles collines"*). Here too, when facing a specific case of conflict in which the degree of "material determination" is highest, naturalism and fatalism are absurd, if not suspect.

Even more blatantly absurd is a pseudo-realist interpretation on the inevitability of conflict in former Yugoslavia, and especially in Bosnia. Here the "material foundations" of conflict are even more flimsy than those applicable in the case of African conflicts. Here, on the contrary, we are in the realm of unabashedly creative politics. Bosnia: an ethnically homogeneous population (all Slavs), with the same language, and with religious-cultural differences that are not more marked than those existing between a Protestant of the Piedmontese valleys and a Palermo Catholic living together in the city of Turin. The only real difference, one which served as the starting point for a deliberate political project, is that between the city and the countryside: a sociocultural difference with political undertones on which was artificially superimposed a would-be ethnic mold. In a way, a sort of grotesque caricature of Lin Piao's vision of countryside-versus-cities: in this specific case, closed, sectarian, authoritarian countryside against open, multiethnic, cosmopolitan, democratic city.

2. An Answer to Conflict: The Issue of Intervention

We said that an analysis of conflict in our times can only be interdisciplinary. By the same token, the same interdisciplinary approach must preside over the search for a strategy aimed at preventing conflicts, at subjecting to rules and limitations those that break out, at stopping them.

But first we must make an effort at philosophical, and not merely terminological, exactitude. Conflict means, in this context, armed and organized violence. It does not refer to any divergence, radical opposition, dissent, dissonance. Paradoxically, the dream of eliminating not only war, but all conflict in the sense of contrast, rivalry, disharmony, has constituted, historically, one of the main roots of armed and organized violence. The utopia of ridding humanity of all conflict and contrast, of a "final solution of the political problem" has generated horrible wars-to-end-all-wars, sinister dictatorships meant to introduce the kingdom of freedom and harmony.

Every people, every group, has a precise and inescapable responsibility to embark on the path of coexistence instead of that of conflict. But having stated this self-evident principle, we cannot pretend we do not see its limits. In the first place, responsibility is directly linked to power (a commodity that, as is well known, is not equitably distributed among countries, peoples, groups). Secondly, washing our hands of alien responsibility does not seem to make much ethical or political sense.

On first sight, the "disconnection" between different crises brought about by the end of the unifying function of the Cold War may justify the belief that we are sheltered from the consequences of limited conflicts. Indeed, if we apply strictly geopolitical criteria, it is hard to see why we should consider ourselves threatened by genocide in Rwanda, conflict in Chechnya, or by war in Bosnia unless we happen to live in those unhappy places. Actually, wars are all near, thanks to CNN, but all equally distant insofar as the fact that they do not affect our daily lives. Today a citizen of Trieste may be morally and psychologically shaken by the war in Bosnia (distant only a few hundred miles), but does not feel more menaced than a resident of Washington's affluent Northwest section feels threatened by the piling up of murder statistics in the black areas of the city. And yet it is a mistake: that of believing that the negative effects of conflicts spread only by contiguous lines, as gangrene, whereas they spread the same way as blood poisoning. The very "blood" of the international community is being poisoned by the proliferation of "small wars." The defenses of the entire international organism are being weakened. Thus, in order to understand where our interest lies, in order to perceive the nature of the threat, to awaken our responsibility and prompt our action, we must not limit ourselves to measuring the repercussions of conflicts on international trade, lines of communications, refugee flows—but ask ourselves what will be the global effects of a creeping banalization/legitimization of the use of violence in the pursuit of the ends of more or less extended, more or less "historical" groups. In short, of the weakening of rules: both of those that tend to prevent conflict and of those that aim at regulating or limiting it for humanitarian ends. This is exactly what we are dealing with today.

A first level of action relates to the material conditions in which billions of people live. We should definitely refrain from drifting into the banal equation underdevelopment-conflict. We know of too many cases proving that conflict and violence can arise even without poverty and backwardness. We even know that the breach of previous solidarity, the fragmentation of previous political entities (the most frequent detonator of conflict) are often the work not of the most backward and poor, but of those who, from a position of relative advantage, feel they no longer want to share their destiny (especially in economic terms) with those who are more backward.

And yet how can one deny the linkage between poverty and reduction of the margins for compromise, struggle for scarce resources and temptation of *mors tua, vita mea,* social imbalance and readiness of entire social groups to identify an enemy, economic disorder and strength of demogogic and violent political leaders? Besides, it is hypocritical for Europeans to state that welfare does not eliminate conflict, when we know very well that a necessary, though not sufficient, condition for overcoming the century-old (and for some "realists," natural) enmities among the countries of the Continent—starting from those between France and Germany—has been the generalized rise of standards of living after World War II.

This is the reason that more advanced countries should "accompany" the diffusion of development and well-being as not only a moral duty, but also an objective interest that can be justified on the basis of realpolitik—i.e., of our clear interest in containing and reducing conflicts worldwide.

With all its possible economic roots, conflict remains a political phenomenon. Thus the international community must face it on political grounds.

We are confronted here with the very actual and very delicate issue of intervention. Definitions of intervention have changed in time, and they can also vary according to specific doctrine or approach (legal, political, moral).[13] What is essential is not to lose sight of the fact that the defining feature of intervention is its coercive nature. This is important in order to free the discourse on intervention, in any case an already complex and controversial one, from the ballast of an improper polemical usage that has led to claim intervention in all cases in which, in the real world of international relations, a stronger and a weaker subject come into contact. One should be very clear about it: it is no intervention when noncoercive political pressures are brought to bear; when conditionality or linkage are applied in trade; when classical peacekeeping is performed (which by definition is consensual, and not coercive).

As international lawyers well know, intervention is certainly not new, neither as a concept nor as a reality. And yet today it confronts us in new and pressing terms. Facing the proliferation of conflicts, and the fact they often escape from the "classical" boundaries of *jus in bello,* the problem arises of how the international community may establish certainly not a utopian "world government," but at least a measure of "world governance" supplying a framework for converting war/*polemos* into war/*stasis,* and replace military violence with political negotiation.

It is fully legitimate to maintain our aspiration to move toward a world freed from collective violence, just as within each country we want to ban individual violence. But the pursuit of this sacrosanct future goal should not prevent us from working today in order to impose rules on conflicts. In other words, we must realize that the pretense to deny in all cases the existence of a *jus ad bellum* would prevent us from dealing with *jus in bello:* outlawing war means also removing laws from war. It means transforming every conflict into *polemos,* i.e., doing exactly the opposite of what should be the common endeavor of the international community in developing, and if necessary imposing, a set of "minimum standards" applicable in every conflict (both internal or international) to both human rights and humanitarian law.[14]

Today armed conflicts are less frequently interstate wars and ever more frequently clashes, within states, between ethnic groups and tribes. At the same time, the issue of the nation-state remains at the center of conflict in the contemporary world, now that the aggregations (and the mystifications) brought about by the confrontation between the two ideologies, the two camps, have fallen.

The issue lies at the center of the discourse on conflict in the first place as far as the "right to be born" of states (self-determination) is concerned. Self-determination is of course far from being a novel concept, but the way we look at it today is profoundly different from what had been the case in the previous historical stage, when the principle had been universally conceived, and vindicated, in an exclusively positive light stressing its value in terms of freedom, justice, equality, and consequently also of peace.

Today, facing the harsh realities that surround us, we must have the courage to say that the principle of self-determination, far from being a guarantee of peace, a prerequisite for preventing and overcoming conflicts, is a problem rather than a solution. It is so for a series of reasons:

- Because it is a right that is proclaimed in the absence of clear criteria for the identification of the subjects entitled to it. What is a "people," and how can one distinguish it from an ethnic, cultural, linguistic group that is not a people? We will not delve into the disconcerting, absurd exercises carried out by the "organic intellectuals" belonging to each group, embarked in sustaining that one's own tribe is a people, while the next one is deprived of national characteristics, and speaks what is not a language, but a mere dialect, and claiming for one's own group on ethnic grounds what one simultaneously denies the other group by quoting history (or vice versa).
- Because self-determination is proclaimed without recognizing the existence of principles that are in contradiction with it (in particular, that of territorial integrity of states), and that should be simultaneously "cross-read."
- Because, in the new nationalist orthodoxy that in too many countries has replaced Marxist–Leninist orthodoxy, the national principle is affirmed regardless of consequences, costs, repercussions.
- Because, finally, the paradox is that the universalization of the pretense of building one's own nation-state threatens the end of the nation-state as a result of a sort of nationalistic overdose. This means that the principle of self-determination, if claimed in a generalized, absolute, and indiscriminate way, is inevitably a source of crisis and instability for the whole international system.

We are saying, in other words, that the revindication of the principle of self-determination is legitimate in the abstract, but, since it is applied without criteria and limitations, it ends up producing devastating results. We certainly do not lack concrete cases to prove this point, starting with those deriving from the collapse of two multinational entities: the Soviet Union and Yugoslavia.

The point is not denying self-determination, nor—of course—considering absolute and unconditional the opposite principle, that of the preservation of existing political-territorial realities, in short of the status quo. On the contrary, if we want to deprive conflict of one of its most fundamental legitimations, we must continue considering the principle of self-determination as one of the fundamental rules of international relations. But we must consider it as a relative, and not an absolute one.

We must stress in particular the following points:

- The international community lacks both instruments and legitimation to pass judgment on the foundations (historical, ethnic, political) of controversial and opposing claims in matters of self-determination, i.e., on whether in a specific instance we are or are not in the presence of "a people" having a right to its own nation-state. Instead, the international community is entitled to pass judgment, and to act consequently (to intervene, if it is necessary and possible on the basis of existing international rules), on the means to which groups of all sorts have recourse in order to pursue the goal of constituting—*or preserving*—their own nation-state. For example, we cannot plunge into the convoluted intricacies of Balkan history and ethnography, but we must react to aggression and ethnic cleansing, whatever the justifications that are advanced by those practicing them.
- The international community should mold its behavior, in matters relating to self-determination (and recognition of new state entities) to a sense of responsibility rather than to the adhesion to abstract principles whose application can bring about real tragedies. Such an ethic of responsibility implies a clear-headed calculation of the foreseeable consequences of actions that may be "just" in the abstract: we should beware of the terrifying logic embodied in the Roman saying *fiat justitia, pereat mundus* (let justice be done, though the world should perish).

The issue of the nation-state, however, lies at the center of the discourse on conflict mostly under another angle: that of sovereignty. This principle—politically substantial, historically sound, legally robust—seems to represent a major obstacle to initiatives forcefully (and sometimes forcibly) taken by the international community in order to prevent, regulate, stop conflicts.

Leaving historical and legal analyses aside, we will just state that from a political point of view (and not very differently from what we just said about self-determination) it would be absurd to relinquish this fundamental criterion of inter-state relations, which incidentally has the function of preventing the domination of the strong over the weak. But it would also be absurd and conceptually primitive to state that, since limited sovereignty imposed by one state on another is bad, unlimited sovereignty is good.

On the contrary, any hope for the prevention, limitation, and cessation of conflicts can only be founded upon the limitation of state sovereignty vis-à-vis principles and rules that are essential to coexistence. The Italian 1947 Constitution, in its Article 11, is extremely clear—and one could add very modern—in this respect: "Italy . . . accepts, in conditions of parity with other states, the limitations of sovereignty that are needed for an order assuring peace and justice among nations."

Nationalism threatens the end of the nation-state through mindless proliferation—and through the inevitable sequel of conflicts that such proliferation entails. Nonabsolute sovereignty, on the contrary, is the only way of ensuring that the nation-state may continue being—even in the imminent Third Millenium—the prevalent form of organized society. It is only a nonabsolute conception of sovereignty that makes the nation-state compatible (and European integration is there to show it) both with supranational linkages and with federal, regional, and local levels of government.

Only in such a way can the quest for identity that lies at the legitimate core of today's centrifugal drift avoid being turned into a pathological and conflictive denial of the other. Only thus can we defeat the urge to separate and lock oneself up with one's own tribe within the borders of an independent nation-state.

And perhaps we will also be able to dilute, mitigate, and balance through the introduction of rights tied to the person and to the community, wherever residing, the territorial obsession that lies at the very foundation of most armed conflicts.

We must in essence prove to groups that demand the recognition of their own identity that there exist other and more promising paths, besides self-determination, to acquire an institutional, political, economic, and cultural space of their own.

So far we have only mentioned the political and institutional elements favoring the prevention of armed conflicts. The most serious issue is, however, whether it is possible, in the contemporary international system, to intervene on conflicts from the outside in order to reestablish peace.

As we said before, one should be very clear about the fact that peacekeeping is *not* intervention[15]. The consensual nature that is one of its features represents one of its strengths, but also its gravest limitation, especially when one is trying (see today's Bosnia) to "keep the peace" where there is no peace to keep. And especially when the rule and the logic of peacekeeping must coexist, in a precarious and sometimes disastrous way, with instances and elements of intervention.

The limits of intervention do not derive only from classical international law (centered, as is known, on the principle of state sovereignty), but they are also embodied in the UN system. The UN Charter sets the principle of state sovereignty among its key foundations. The "interstate" nature of the system created in San Francisco half a century ago cannot be doubted: it is a system into which the founding states have injected many substantial guarantees against any hypothesis of loss of sovereignty or rise of "world government."

And yet in the Charter state sovereignty finds a limit on which it is worth lingering when discussing intervention. Let us read Article 2 (7), which indeed states that "nothing contained in the present Charter shall authorize the United Nations to intervene in matters which are essentially within the domestic jurisdiction of any state," but which continues: "but this principle shall not prejudice the application of enforcement measures under Chapter VII." In other words, domestic jurisdiction, the most tangible corollary of sovereignty, cannot render illegitimate an intervention decreed on the basis of Chapter VII of the Charter.

This limitation to sovereignty is so little theoretical and abstract that we find it included in every coercive action embarked upon by the UN or by individual states or groups of states with the legitimation supplied by a resolution of the Security Council. As a matter of fact, in its more recent praxis, the Security Council has had recourse to Chapter VII even in situations that one would have some trouble defining (as the heading of Chapter VII recites) "threats to the peace, breaches of the peace, and acts of aggression." The fact is that in the past few years the Security Council has utilized a reference to Chapter VII (thereby neutralizing the possibility of objecting national sovereignty) in a fashion that would be euphemistic to define "extensive" in cases such as: the protection of a minority (Iraqi Kurds and Shiites) against repression; peacekeeping bordering on peace enforcement (former Yugoslavia); instituting a tribunal to prosecute war crimes; protecting humanitarian activities (Somalia). It is true that on the basis of the Charter the Security Council has "the competence of defining its own competence." However, it remains difficult to accept that the repression against the Kurds in Northern Iraq or the pillaging of humanitarian supplies to Somali populations can really constitute a threat to world peace, the rationale for having recourse to Chapter VII of the Charter.

What is evident is that lately the instrument allowing the United Nations to overcome the limitation to international action represented by sovereignty (Chapter VII of the UN Charter) has been de facto extended from the field of international peace and security to other domains, i.e., to internal conflicts, to human rights violations, or to humanitarian concerns.

We should however ask ourselves whether the only way of legitimating intervention is pushing through this narrow door. The answer should be negative. Even before and outside the UN Charter, intervention can be legitimate. In the first place, the Charter itself, in Article 51, recognizes that "individual or collective self-defense" (which can imply acts of intervention) remains a right even in the new context and with the new rules of the game established by the Charter itself. Secondly, it is evident that the protection of one's own nationals in the territory of other states legitimates, in certain cases, forcible actions conducted even without the consent of the territorially sovereign states. The examples are numerous, even in recent times (it is enough to mention the operations repeatedly carried out in Africa by French and Belgian troops). What is interesting is to note that in certain cases such actions of armed intervention have been carried out also to rescue subjects other than the nationals of the intervening country. We are facing, here, a humanitarian action abstracting from the tie of a determinate individual to a determinate state, but that is legitimated by international law though it entails a violation of sovereignty.

The examples, however, are not only recent. It should be enough to mention radical, clear, and universally accepted instances of intervention in violation of the principle of sovereignty (evidently not considered absolute) such as those brought about in the framework of the long struggle of the international community against piracy or the slave trade. These are the historical and legal examples we should keep in mind when trying to extend the legitimation of intervention even without having recourse (in ways that are often dubious and that in any case presuppose the convergence of the permanent members of the Security Council) to the "umbrella" supplied by Chapter VII of the UN Charter.

Intervention is, therefore, possible. State sovereignty does not constitute an unsurmountable limit. The international community does possess the tools that are necessary to handle conflicts. We must not think, therefore, that the problem is one of legitimation, nor that it is created by the inadequacy of institutions or instruments. The real issue is one of political will.

In just three years, the optimism reflected in a cautiously courageous text, Boutros-Ghali's *Agenda for Peace,* has collided with some devastating confutations: Somalia, Bosnia, Rwanda. It was demonstrated that it is not enough to brandish Chapter VII, to define mandates, to dispatch military contingents. It was demonstrated that the option of intervention will remain a theoretical one or, even worse, will entail false starts, withdrawals, operational disasters, if, instead of dallying on the relatively easy issue of how intervention can be legitimated, we will not prove capable of tackling the much more problematic issue of how to proceed politically and operationally.

We think it is possible to identify some useful criteria:

(1) It is evident that there are differences in the power of individual states, and in their capacity to contribute to the definition and imposition of rules. Let us consider, for example, the differentiated status conferred by the quality of permanent member of the Security Council. More than that: no system of "world governance"—and in particular no system allowing the prevention, limitation, and cessation of conflicts—can abstract from what we could call real existing power. Whatever the process through which rules are defined (a process that, given present realities, cannot possibly be "democratic"), what is instead not acceptable are disparities in the respect of those rules, especially when vital issues such as state sovereignty are at stake. The fundamental principle of equality under the law does not mean that everyone contributes in the same way to the formation of law (and this is true both for the international system and for domestic legal systems: it would be absurd to deny the existence of legality except in cases where there is absolute egalitarian democracy). It must mean, however, that real existing power must be subject to those very laws to whose formation it has contributed more than proportionally.

Consistency is here of the utmost importance. No pattern of intervention that can be characterized by the formula "Strong with the weak, weak with the strong" can be, in the long run, neither credible nor functioning.

(2) Proportionality is another very important criterion. To act, through intervention, against the principle of state sovereignty remains a fact of the utmost gravity, which the international community should resort to only as

an *extrema ratio* and only against true transgressors of international norms, not mere *provocateurs* or mavericks. Moreover, intervention should go only so far as is indispensable to the attainment of specific ends: one should rule out the goal of *debellatio,* total crushing of the adversary. It would indeed be a paradox if the international community were to conceive conflict as *polemos* and not *stasis,* and were to drift into overkill.

(3) The option of intervention has to be matched by the will to support the costs it entails, including the possible cost in human lives for the military units that are employed in the operation. It is clear that, in highly conflictive situations and facing armed and bellicose groups, defining a "zero dead option" is the equivalent of espousing a doctrine of nonintervention. In Somalia the stern brandishing of Chapter VII, including the mandate of disarming the clans (definitely not a peacekeeping mission) did not last beyond the first casualties, with the consequences we all know. For example, the initial passivity vis-à-vis the crisis in Rwanda can be largely attributed to the devastating "lessons" from Somalia.

(4) Any hypothesis of intervention must be previously analyzed in trying to assess the chances for its success. One must prevent the rhetoric of intervention from going beyond the actual capacity to carry it out.

(5) One should think about the probable consequences of intervention even in case it "succeeds." It may well be, in fact, that intervention, though attaining its goals, ends up producing worse evils.

(6) The means at the disposal of individual countries and of international organizations (starting with the UN) are clearly limited, though perhaps limitations are political rather than financial or military. It is therefore necessary to carry out a certain triage among competing needs. One cannot do everything, but it would be absurd to maintain that, since you cannot do everything, you should do nothing.

(7) In situations of internal conflict, implosion of states, separatism, ethnic struggle, the possible goals of both coercive and noncoercive international action are necessarily manifold: from the respect of cease-fires to humanitarian assistance, from the prosecution of war criminals to the construction of a security framework allowing the search for political compromise.

We should not forget, on the other hand, that such objectives can turn out to be contradictory, sometimes downright incompatible:

- How is it possible to identify an aggressor, decree against him coercive measures under Chapter VII, and at the same time carry out peacekeeping and humanitarian activities that imply his consent?[16]
- How is it possible to maintain in war zones "peace soldiers" who cannot keep a peace that is not there, but cannot impose it either, in the absence not so much of a mandate but of adequate military capability, and especially of the necessary political will?

- How is it possible to handle a situation characterized by downright genocide (demanding the identification and punishment of the perpetrators) by operating almost exclusively in the humanitarian field, which by definition demands the indiscriminate protection of all human beings in need, without asking them (and without asking ourselves) whether they are victims or hangmen?[17]
- How is it possible, in the search for a political solution, to negotiate with interlocutors who are simultaneously defined and prosecuted (or should be prosecuted) as "ethnic cleansers" or genocides?[18]
- And most of all: how is it possible to increase the tasks mandated to the United Nations (from peacekeeping to humanitarian action) and at the same time insist for zero real growth in the UN budget or even, as the U.S. Congress is presently doing, for a significant reduction in assessed contributions?

These dilemmas are all very clear and real, but they do not lend themselves to easy answers. What is important, however, is not to hide them behind a veil of rhetoric. In the first place, not to find refuge in the great alibi of humanitarian action, a most important aspect of international reaction to armed conflicts, but something that possesses its own logic that cannot be arbitrarily extended outside its legitimate framework. We must not occult behind humanitarian flags the inescapable problem of the use of force by the international community. Not only of its legitimation (possible), but of its political, financial, human costs. Costs—especially the latter—that are very difficult to accept especially for all those whose moral and political urge to intervene derives from a rebellion against violence and death. And yet, inescapable costs, unless we decide to give up any attempt to contain, if not totally stop, the proliferation of conflicts that is today affecting the very texture of the coexistence among states and among human beings.

Notes

1. Stanley Hoffman, *The Political Ethics of International Relations* (Seventh Morgenthau Lecture on Ethics and Foreign Policy), Carnegie Council on Ethics and International Affairs, 1988, p. 19.
2. See Bernard-Henri Levy, *La pureté dangereuse* (Paris: Grasset, 1994). According to Levy (93) in order to understanding today's world we must set aside the concept of totalitarianism, indispensable to understand the century that is now ending, and replace it with the concept of fundamentalism (*integrisme*).
3. The definition belongs to Headley Bull, quoted in Geoffrey Best, *War and Law since 1945* (Oxford: Clarendon Press, 1994), 4.
4. The diffentiation between these two types of conflict is taken up by Massimo Cacciari, *Geo-filosofia dell'Europa* (Milano: Adelphi, 1994), who centers his whole reasoning about the peculiarities of the European essence on the possibility of pluralism, diversity, and the existence of the Other without having to accept the inevitability of violent conflict.
5. Van Creveld speaks of "non-Clausewitzian war," that he defines as war for existence (Martin van Creveld, *The Transformation of War* [New York: The Free Press, 1991], 142. It would be a serious mistake if we were to attribute the origins of this ruleless war to modern ideologies, to a nation-state that is organized and technologically equipped for the annihilation of the enemy. To quote

just one example, the Old Testament describes *milchemet mitzvah,* a true war of extermination against the enemies of the God of Israel. Ibid., 134–35.

6. At the start of the Civil War, the Union government assigned to an emigre German jurist, Franz Lieber, the task of codifying the basic principles applicable to war. The result was the so-called Lieber Code, which was to supply the basis for further work leading eventually to the Hague Conventions of 1899. Best, op. cit., 40–41.

7. Referring to class struggle, Simone Weil wrote: "Class struggle definitely has a meaning, but it is a struggle, not a war, and it is effective only insofar it is not a war. When, lured by the mirage of vacuous entities, we feel we have to turn it into war, when we aim at the annihilation of an adversary considered as an absolute evil, then class struggle, after bloody turmoils, can only attain illusory results. On the contrary, it is effective only if it is a permanent struggle pursuing exclusively the restoration of a balance that is continuously broken." Quoted in Simone Petrement, *La vita di Simone Weil* (Milano: Adelphi, 1994), 393.

8. Assane N'Diaye, "Rwanda-Burundi. Qu'est-ce qui me commande de parler?," *Africa International,* Sept.–Nov. 1994, 7. N'Diaye writes about "Hutu–Tutsi bilateral paranoia" (p. 9). The world is today generous with examples of the systematic ideological endeavor aimed at building up group identity on the basis of an exasperated (and usually artificial) differentiation vis-à-vis other groups, with which one has often co-existed on the same territory for centuries. It is the phenomenon that someone has called "the narcissism of minor differences." Michael Ignatieff, *Blood and Belonging* (London, 1993).

9. Robert D. Kaplan, "The Coming Anarchy," *Atlantic Monthly,* February 1994, 44. Kaplan paints an apocalyptic, but hardly questionable, picture of "disease, overpopulation, unprovoked crime, scarcity of resources, refugee migrations the increasing erosion of nation-states and international borders, and the empowerment of private armies, security firms, and international drug cartels."

10. See Eric Hobsbawm and Terence Ranger, *The Invention of Tradition* (Cambridge, 1983) and Benedict Anderson, *Imagined Communities* (London, 1983).

11. Destexhe speaks of "tribalism with no tribe," and "ethnicity without ethnic group." Alain Destexhe, Rwanda. *Essai sur le genocide* (Bruxelles: Editions Complexe, 1994), 58. "Hutus and Tutsis have always spoken the same language, called themselves by the same names, have shared the same religion (Catholic) and have often mixed through marriage. Many Rwandans maintain that divisions in their society are not ethnic, but rather those that differentiate cattle herdsmen from peasant serfs, a reality that one could also find in monarchical societies in Tanzania, Uganda, and Zaire. They also say that a rich Hutu can become a Tutsi after a special ceremony." Julian Bedford, "The Roots of Rwanda's Strife," *Reuters,* May 25, 1995.

12. N'Diaye, op. cit., 7.

13. Among the possible political definitions of intervention, the following seems to be one of the most adequate: "International intervention . . . connotes only those coercive actions (economic and military sanctions) taken by the community of States to alter the domestic affairs, behavior or policies of a targeted government or insurgency that flouts international norms and resists the expressed will of the international community." Thomas G. Weiss, "Intervention: Whither the United Nations?" *The Washington Quarterly,* Winter 1994, 110. It is a definition that coincides with the legal definition according to which intervention is "any authoritarian pressure exerted in order to bend the will of an international subject so as to obtain the performance or nonperformance of a specific art." G. Balladore Pallieri, *Diritto Internazionale Pubblico* (Milano: Giuffre, 1962), 257. For a very stimulating approach to the issue of intervention (examined in close relationship with the "relativization of sovereignty") see J. Bryan Hehir, "Intervention: From Theories to Cases," *Ethics & International Affairs* 9 (1995), 1–13.

14. See in particular the "Declaration on Minimum Humanitarian Standards," a document drafted by a group of experts in Turku, Finland, in December 1990 (published in *International Review of the Red Cross,* (May–June 1991). The text aims at overcoming a rigid distinction between human rights law and humanitarian law—a distinction to which, on the other hand, both states and practitioners in both fields remain very attached. On the relationship between human rights/humanitarian law and on minimum standards see also Best, op. cit., 67–79. As usual, practice tends to overcome the quandaries of theory: facing the conflict in Chechnya, international bodies (from the UN to the European Union) have taken positions through resolutions and declarations in which human rights and humanitarian law are jointly and simultaneously taken as a point of reference.

15. For a definition of peacekeeping, peace enforcement, peacemaking, preventive diplomacy, peace building, see the Report by the Secretary General of the United Nations: Boutros Boutros-Ghali, *An Agenda for Peace* (UN Document A/47/277. June 17, 1992).

16. In synthesis, the goal of peace and the goal of justice can turn out to be incompatible: "If peace should take precedence, intervention should support the mightiest of the rivals, irrespective of their legitimacy. If the United Nations had weighed in on the side of the Serbs, or had helped Aidid take control in Mogadishu rather than trying to jail him, there might well have been peace in Bosnia and Somalia long ago. If justice takes precedence, however, limited intervention may well lengthen a conflict. Perhaps putting an end to killing should not be the first priority in peacemaking, but interventionists should admit that any intervention involves such a choice." Richard K. Betts, "The Delusion of Impartial Intervention," *Foreign Affairs*, November–December 1994, 32. Betts lists the following "rules" in order to prevent intervention from giving rise to confused or counterproductive outcomes: recognize that making peace means determining who rules; avoid half measures; do not confuse peace with justice; do not confuse balance with peace or justice; be sure that humanitarian intervention makes sense from a military point of view. One must say that, as far as this last "rule" is concerned, we have recently reached a true dead end, and have produced contradictions such as the one embodied in the following statement: "The use of force is authorized on the basis of Chapter VII of the Charter, but the UN remains neutral and impartial between the parties, and does not have the mandate to stop the aggressor (in case he can be identified) nor to impose the cessation of hostilities." Report of the Secretary General to the 50th UN General Assembly: *Supplement to an Agenda for Peace* (A/50/60, January 3, 1995), Para. 19. Impartiality between the victim and the aggressor? But then, why bother with Chapter VII, the chapter of enforcement and intervention; why not stay within the boundaries of Chapter VI, the chapter of prevention, mediation, dialogue, consensus?

17. Facing this dilemma, "Medecins sans frontieres" has adopted, in Rwanda, a very firm stand, stating that "you do not stop genocide with doctors," and that therefore the situation could not be tackled in a humanitarian mode (Destexhe, op. cit., 79). The same author, though a "professional humanitarian," formulates a thought-provoking denunciation: "In a world in which it has acquired a quasi monopoly of international action, humanitarian assistance—unwilling and unable to draw a distinction among victims—has the shortcoming of reducing catastrophes to their minimum common denominator: compassion. All victims are the same and they all deserve our attentive care: the Tutsis that are the object of genocide as well as the murderer seeking shelter in a refugee camp and struck by cholera. Such is the servitude of humanitarian action: facing the victim, it does not want to choose sides, but only cure and nourish. Such noble gesture is however doomed to failure if, at the same time, there is no justice nor any political action. . . . The evil eating away at humanitarian action is called mindless apoliticism, with its corollary, neutrality. It has become an easy escape justifying the worst policies. The concept of neutrality does not make any sense facing a war of aggression or systematic genocide: neutrality means, in these cases, favoring the stronger party. The humanitarian system does not need more than one neutral organization: the International Committee of the Red Cross (ICRC) is at the same time indispensable and more than sufficient. The other organizations, hiding behind this now perverse concept, insofar as they refuse to draw a distinction between aggressors and aggressed, victims and perpetrators, partake in the general confusion and in a way are accomplices" (ibid., 85–87).

18. The problem is especially acute in the case of the Tribunal on crimes in former Yugoslavia, deciding, in July 1995, to indict Bosnian Serb leaders Karadzic and Mladic. In a previous interview, Justice Goldstone, Chief Prosecutor of the Tribunal, proved to be fully aware of this problem, but stated very clearly that justice cannot be derailed by political considerations: "I can give you the assurance that we won't respond to the political consequences either in what we do or in its timing." He added that even though a possible peace agreement for Bosnia were to include immunity for Karadzic and Mladic, the Tribunal should continue to pursue the case, since "immunity is a political decision (by which) we would not be bound." Roger Cohen, "Dilemma on Bosnia Puts UN in a Bind," *International Herald Tribune*, April 25, 1995. One cannot pretend that those who have the mandate to affirm justice accept the logic of political compromise. Likewise, we cannot ask those who pursue humanitarian ends to give priority to justice or to politics. But if this is true, who will define priorities among incompatible logics?

International Organizations
and Conflict Prevention
Lessons from Business

ANTONIA HANDLER CHAYES AND ABRAM CHAYES

1. Introduction

You cannot enforce peace when your own structure is an undisciplined
and often chaotic set of rival bureaucratic fiefdoms.[1]

Chester Crocker
Director, U.S. Institute of Peace

The international community has now accumulated wide experience within a short
period of time in its efforts to prevent and manage internal conflict and deal with
its aftermath. The proliferation of conflicts was an unexpected feature of the
post–Cold War landscape. Since the end of the Cold War, the UN has launched
eighteen major operations—more than in the previous forty-five years of its existence. Interventions into conflict situations have been made on every continent in
a wide range of political, social, and economic settings. In addition to the UN
and its agencies, many actors have responded—states, ad hoc coalitions, other
international organizations, regional and nongovernmental organizations. Some
responses come early, others not until the conflict has subsided. Many different
mechanisms have been used to stem conflict. These actors have performed all the
tasks set forth in Secretary General Boutros Boutros Ghali's 1992 *Agenda for Peace*
and its supplements, including conflict prevention by diplomacy and troop deployment, classical peacekeeping, so-called peace enforcement, the provision of humanitarian assistance at all stages of conflict, and physical and institutional
reconstruction of war-torn societies. The mere listing of organizations operating
in Croatia and Sarajevo in 1996 is two inches thick and includes organizations
ranging from the UN to "Clowns without Frontiers." These operations in the
aggregate have disposed of extensive resources—approximately $4 billion
annually.[2]

The results of international efforts have been disappointing, given the high
expectations for cooperation. On a case-by-case basis, many explanations are put
forward; some superficial, and others, quite penetrating. In some cases, it has been
nearly impossible to rouse international commitment equal to the magnitude of

the problem. This has been the case in the Great Lakes region of Africa, and in some of the states of the former Soviet Union. This same era bears witness to the frequent lack of consensus among even like-minded allies, as has been the case in Bosnia. Or there may be consensus that "something must be done" but deep disagreement about what that "something" is. This can lead to paralysis, or more likely, palliative measures.

This article examines one problem that seems to cut across interventions into most of these post–Cold War conflicts: the failure of the international community—international, regional, and nongovernmental organizations and states—to find ways to integrate their efforts into a coherent policy approach. Many of the organizations that intervene often do so with a strategy and presence that is ignorant of what has gone before them, and unaware how their efforts might be consistent and supportive of the efforts of others, rather than independent or in competition with them. Explanations for the failure of integration are also complex. They may be political on several levels at once—related to an international set of relationships, while simultaneously directed toward domestic constituencies. The reasons for independent, uncoordinated and even uncooperative behavior may be primarily institutional and bureaucratic. All result in inadequate resources to deal with the problems. Even when major powers can agree on a course of action, problems of effective implementation frustrate the goal of ending the conflict, and helping develop a peaceful society. The lack of cooperation has been marked in many cases by duplication, gaps in coverage, and waste of limited resources. As Jonathan Moore states in his trenchant monograph, *The UN and Complex Emergencies*, "The UN has not had significant experience until recently dealing with internal crises of multiple origins and parts, and its proudly autonomous operational agencies are not used to working in a coordinated way with one another and don't want to."[3] Since the UN agencies comprise only a portion of the complex mosaic of intervention, the problem is even worse.

We will argue that the best solution to this set of problems requires radical decentralization of operational responsibility to the field, with clear direction to cooperate fully there to develop an integrated approach—together with adequate delegation of authority to do so. The internal conflicts and complex emergencies of the post–Cold War era are too complex and fast-moving to permit central management. And the obstacles to cooperation at the top are too overwhelming for reform to begin there.

More than twenty years ago, U.S. business organizations began to question the way they were structured and operated, and began to make fundamental changes in their corporate culture to meet the challenges of rapid technological change, increasing competition in the world marketplace, and loss of market share. Business firms have developed innovative and flexible modes of responding to the complexities they face. Despite the very different contexts of business and international conflict, we believe that aspects of contemporary organizational theories and models derived from this experience may be relevant. In short, we believe that some change in the corporate culture of these international organizations is needed if they are to operate effectively in the complex post–Cold War context and be adequately supported. Business may offer some useful ideas.

2. Business Models for Improving Effectiveness

> The main dysfunctions in our institutions—fragmentation, competition, and reactiveness—are actually the by products of our success over thousands of years . . . so it should come as no surprise that these dysfunctions are deeply rooted.
>
> Fred Kaufman and Peter M. Senge[4]

The principal theme of the theory and practice of contemporary business organization is decentralization. The model of the fixed, pyramidal, hierarchial structure for business activity has been increasingly replaced by lateral organization. Business has found ways to move away from a rigid, centralized structure to decentralized, flexible structures that can adapt quickly to constantly changing business demands. In the 1970s, early attempts in this direction employed the model of a matrix in which a horizontal problem-oriented structure was created to foster communication and teamwork among separate corporate units. But "matrix management" represented only a partial shift in structure and operations.[5] It superimposed a new form of organization on top of the traditional centralized, bureaucratic organization. The delegation of authority was often unclear because either senior corporate management remained visibly involved, or the delegation of authority was so ambiguous that the results were anarchic.

New team-based organizational forms have been developed from those beginnings. They are functionally designed, project-oriented, and short-lived, with team composition that may change over the life of a project. The most successful are characterized by their nonhierarchical nature, flexibility, and interdependence. They are also problem-solving—designed to be responsive to situational demands, with free information flow made possible by advanced technology, and authority grounded in knowledge, not position. These lateral organizational forms include virtual corporations and other decentralized action groups called cross-functional, product development, and self-directed teams.[6]

Virtual corporations—This term denotes an arrangement in which the functions of a business entity are assembled without the permanence or structure of a corporation. In business, virtual corporations are, in effect, temporary joint ventures among companies for specific purposes. For example, the Italian clothing chain Benetton employs this concept to link 300 independent firms who supply material and manufacture clothing for the Benetton label. As one observer noted, the approach allows Benetton "to gain scale without gaining mass." Only entities needed for a given operation are part of the system.[7] At the same time, Benetton does not micromanage their activities. Its overall direction and quality control does not threaten the independence of members of the virtual corporation.

Cross-functional and product development teams—Teams consist of a core staff of functional experts from various corporate departments, and in many cases, many companies. A powerful example is the series of Boeing-Sikorsky product development teams for developing the RAH-66 Comanche helicopter—a complex, state-of-the-art stealth helicopter.[8] More than eleven companies worked on the first design team during the competition phase. Both Boeing and Sikorsky had more than 800 workers performing design and contractual negotiation functions at their respective sites in Pennsylvania and Connecticut. As described below, they were linked, as were other subcontracting companies such as Lockheed-Martin in Florida, by an advanced electronic digital design system and data base. In addition to frequent meetings and telephone and E-mail connections, team members were able to correct design problems as they arose, and to work concurrently on development and manufacture.

As with Boeing-Sikorsky, such teams may be supported by on-call specialists, often from other companies involved in design or supply aspects of the operation. Because teams include members from engineering, manufacturing, and quality assurance, as well as representatives from the customer, functions can be carried out concurrently, rather than sequentially. In the Comanche case, the customer—the U.S. Army—was part of the team from the beginning. Army mechanics presented problems they had encountered with other helicopters during the Gulf War so that designers could avoid them. The result was to speed up the entire process of producing a prototype that met demanding performance specifications while keeping costs and overhead low. In the end, Boeing and Sikorsky encountered far fewer than normal operational problems with the Comanche, despite the speed of its development.

Case studies of several different industries substantiate the Sikorsky experience. At Coors, for example, cross-functional teams cut the time it took to launch a new product (Winterfest Beer) by 50 percent. AT&T employed a similar technique with a team of twelve cross-functional experts that brought a new cordless phone from design to market within a year, instead of the normal two years. Not only were time and development costs reduced, but quality was improved as well.[9] Acting together at the operational level, team members were empowered to eliminate cumbersome vertical coordination mechanisms, and could reduce delays and inefficiencies because functional areas do not operate on separate tracks.

Self-directed teams—This is a slightly different business model in which the team is responsible not only for accomplishing tasks within its functional areas of expertise, but also for managing itself entirely. A self-directed team is responsible for an entire process such as manufacturing. The self-directed team is authorized to make key decisions concerning planning, implementing, and improving operations without consulting with senior management. Self-directed teams are found in some insurance companies where they are responsible for policy-holder services, including selling and record keeping. The self-directed team is the most autonomous of the models studied, and successful examples seem to be structured to take advantage of this attribute.[10]

What all these approaches have in common is that they are not merely a group of people working together to solve a problem or design a project. They have the characteristics of a high performance sports team, with broad authority and responsibility for results. A team, according to Glenn Parker, "is a group of people with a high degree of interdependence, geared toward the achievement of a goal or the completion of a task." "Interdependence," "commitment to a common purpose," "dedication" and "urgency" are the common descriptors. In high performance teams, individual success requires team success, and conversely, individual failure can sink the team. The key to creating a team from a group is creating a corporate culture that promotes team interdependence and permits a team autonomy from central management.

Because such teams evolved to enable business organizations to face complex, fast-moving, and highly threatening situations, it is worth taking a closer look at the key common characteristics of product development, cross-functional, and self-directed teams to explore the usefulness of such models for intergovernmental and nongovernmental organizations performing below optimal levels.

3. Attributes of Team Success

A review of recent writings on organizational theory yields some key attributes that analysts agree are necessary to the success of team operations. Though described differently by different theorists, these criteria are encompassed by the following concepts:

- A culture that fosters openness, flexibility, and cooperation
- Decentralization with autonomy
- Shared vision and common goals
- A strategic planning process to implement the common goals
- Clear allocation of responsibility to reach a common approach
- Transparency in planning and operations
- Authority based on knowledge, not position
- Mature leaders and members

In this section, we expand briefly on the content and significance of these attributes in the business settings. In the next, we discuss their potential relevance for international organizations operating in conflict. In the business setting, none of these factors ensures success, but neglecting any one seems almost to guarantee failure.

A culture that fosters openness, flexibility, and cooperation—The basic corporate culture of organizations that generate effective teams is one of openness to new ideas and willingness to make alliances with other business firms. The way an organization perceives itself—the core values that shape its mental model—will affect its operational practices in fundamental ways. Early efforts at matrix management often did not achieve their goals because a new corporate culture had not fully taken hold, and attempts at decentralization were undermined by an essentially centralized, hierarchical culture.

Business theorists praise "learning organizations"—those capable of responding to rapidly changing situations by altering their mental model, or "deeply ingrained assumptions, generalizations or even pictures or images that influence how we understand the world, and how we take action."[11] Unless an organization has the capability to learn and adapt, it may be left in the dust. Disseminating new approaches, and arriving at a new, widely shared mental model is, of course, part of the organizational learning process. Many cases have been analyzed in the literature in which firms have shed old mental models and set about creating a new corporate culture. The Xerox Corporation altered its basic corporate culture three times from 1961 to 1982, beginning with the entrepreneurial, risk-taking model of its founder, Joseph Wilson. It then moved into a period of consolidation, professional management and increasing bureaucratization, until the early 1980s, when it shifted to an emphasis on decentralization and innovation under David Kearns.[12]

Decentralization with autonomy—Each of the forms of business teams described exhibit a high degree of autonomy from their parent organizations. Long before team concepts had taken hold, aerospace had its "skunk works," the group of Lockheed designers established to make gigantic technological leaps in military aviation. This team was permitted to function in a sheltered, independent environment.[13] By contrast, other business organizations, such as airlines before deregulation, were highly centralized and hierarchical. When deregulation occurred, most airlines lacked the learning capacity to create new paradigms that might deal more effectively with vastly increased competition—to innovate, cut costs, and focus on customer satisfaction. Airlines were based on a rigid, bureaucratic model with numerous supervisory levels—each with a limited and well-defined span of control. Although this structure was successful in satisfying safety requirements, it limited individual initiative, punished risk taking, discouraged feedback, and demanded strict obedience to top-down authority. Efficiency suffered and, as might be expected, an adversarial relationship developed between management and workers.[14] The utility industry faces the same prospects, but has a longer lead time and the painful airline lessons to help it make the needed changes.

Not only is an organization constrained by a rigid, centralized, and bureaucratic structure from developing an internal capacity to respond to new demands and opportunities, it is unlikely to be able to respond rapidly to situations requiring joint ventures, alliances, and other forms of intensive cooperation with other organizations. Formal coordination processes or "treaties" at the highest levels of management do not achieve the objective, although they may be a necessary starting point. By contrast, the kind of teams described here create an environment in which experts and midlevel managers are motivated to function jointly across a single or several corporations; empowered to make the necessary alliances and decisions to bring results that cannot be easily achieved in the conventional structure. But it has taken business organizations a long time to permit autonomy. As discussed before, early matrix management constrained team potential because the culture of top-down management persisted. This is the situation that is also prevalent among international organizations. After experimenting with matrix management, it took business organizations a further cultural change to permit the decentralization and delegation that current teams enjoy.[15]

Shared vision and common goals—"Vision" is a term often used in American business and politics. It is not so often clearly defined, but it implies broad purpose and a clear sense of organizational goals. Vision is implied in the question "Where should this organization be three years from now?" Strategy is implicit in any answer to the query "By what means will you get there?" Vision describes a preferred end state that guides the development of strategy—broad in scope, possibly to communicate, easily grasped, ambitious, optimistic, and, if possible, somewhat inspirational. To be effective, it must be shared throughout the organization.

The responsibility for creating and communicating a corporate vision lies with senior management.[16] If a commitment to a clear mission is not adequately communicated, understood, and accepted, it will not be easy to develop a strategy to implement it. It has to be more than a public relations slogan to impress market analysts, shareholders, and customers. It implies a willingness to commit resources and change direction, if necessary, in the formulation of an implementing strategy. It must be sufficiently powerful and clear to empower employees and infuse them with clear direction in their daily work. Under new CEO George David, United Technologies Corporation completed its shift from a global corporation, though diversified, that still remained significantly dependent upon military contracts to one with an entrepreneurial world outlook whose motto became "Be there first."

Most important for this analysis, such a vision is necessary to permit corporate leadership to grant independence to teams especially if they cross organizational boundaries. It may not be too strong to say that it is a prerequisite for decentralization. The ultimate test is whether the vision mobilizes employees to pursue a common purpose without close central control of their activities.

A second level of vision, or common purpose, is also necessary to effective team operations. Even in situations in which the team is internal to one organization, it must develop its own vision and common purpose. "Most teams shape their purposes in response to a demand or opportunity put in their path, usually by management."[17] The "Zebra Team" at the Kodak Corporation was created to infuse life back into black and white film, eclipsed by the popularity of color film. Before plunging into specific production and marketing goals, it nurtured the common team vision and purpose.[18]

The problem of clarity of vision, and forging a common purpose, is more challenging and complex for teams comprised of several organizations. Not only must team members be imbued with their own organization's vision in order to operate independently, but must sustain a shared vision and common purpose for the project. These levels of vision and purpose must be in harmony with each other. If they are inconsistent, the team will fall apart. A joint enterprise requires agreement and support from senior management of participating companies in order to help the team overcome unanticipated obstacles and internal team differences. As Wheelwright and Clark point out, upper level management establishes the "framework of integration. How senior functional managers work together . . . the way they communicate . . . and the degree of respect and trust that develop . . . have an important shaping influence on the members of their organizations, and thus on the overall pattern of integration."[19] A consortium of companies competing for market share in the same product area and whose vision is dominated by increasing market share as against one another will have difficulty creating the environment to develop a shared team vision. The problem of lack of vision, or competing goals is one that besets international organizations operating in conflict areas, and is discussed in the next section.

It is crucial that the vision be sturdy and sustainable. The team project may persist over relatively extended time periods when many obstacles arise that threaten success. Team vision must not only be in harmony with the vision of its contributing members, it may have to be adjusted from time to time to take account of unanticipated issues.

A strategic planning process to achieve shared vision—A broad vision is made concrete by a detailed and well-communicated implementation strategy that engages corporate resources and the time and energy of people at all levels in the organization. The vision provides the framework for planning, but the implementing strategy translates the vision into concrete steps for achieving it. Corporate units develop elements of the strategic plan, with increasingly specific performance goals, milestones, and measures of success. The implementing strategy is not only cast in economic accomplishments over a given time period, but may detail the performance specifications of specific products, the capability of specific services, the markets in which they will be provided, and the profit margins they will yield.

As mentioned, United Technologies' vision was to "be there first." Its strategies involved making early investments in the Soviet Union, Eastern and Central Europe, and China. In the Soviet Union's waning days, Otis Elevator Company's partnerships with state elevator companies carried some risk, even though the opening of the society through glasnost meant a large market potential. The future of these partnerships were necessarily uncertain, since the entire political environment and transition to capitalism was itself uncertain. After dissolution of the USSR, UTC expanded further into Russia and Ukraine with new elevator partnerships for Otis, an aircraft engine partnership between Pratt and Whitney and Perm Engines in the Urals, and a partnership with Energomash Rocket Company, whose military technology made it a world leader. But the corporation's detailed strategies to reach its objectives developed in light of events on the ground. Originally, Pratt and Whitney planned to manufacture engines for Russian aircraft, but soon found that was not politically acceptable—it was necessary to form a partnership with indigenous industry, in order to penetrate the market, and to assist an ailing industry develop new technology.[20] These goals have been translated into increasingly specific and performance-oriented plans.

Where teams are accustomed to a broad corporate vision, a well-developed strategy with concrete performance goals helps to provide confidence that the delegation of authority that permits team autonomy is justifiable. Team members require concrete goals—a set of team products—to provide momentum for team efforts, and a yardstick for measuring success. "A team's purpose and specific performance goals have a symbiotic relationship; each depends on the other to stay relevant and vital. The specific performance goals help a team track progress and hold itself accountable; the broader, even nobler aspirations in a team's purpose supply both meaning and emotional energy."[21]

Even though problem-oriented teams develop cohesion and momentum through autonomy, it is necessary to assure that their goals remain in harmony with the overall corporate vision of participating members. Conversely, as team autonomy may impose awesome responsibility upon its members, a well-developed strategic planning process that allocates adequate financial and personnel resources for the magnitude of the task is crucial to assure the team that its objectives further the corporate vision. Motorola goes even further, and provides senior managers to act as team mentors to ensure that members are aware of front office interest.[22] Support from senior management for the team often involves clearing away bureaucratic obstacles that may impede the team's ability to achieve its goals.[23]

However, there is a fine line between a clear expression of interest and availability on the part of senior management, and the micromanagement that plagued matrix organizations. The value of a well-developed but flexible strategic plan goes far to deal with the need to reconcile an overall corporate vision with decentralization rather than central control. And more may be required in the way of support and goal adjustment, as unanticipated obstacles or significant change occur. For international organizations, not only is a culture change required to permit delegation of authority to teams in the first place, but many must develop far more expertise and experience in planning a detailed strategy to implement their vision before they can achieve the confidence to permit decentralization.

Clear allocation of responsibility to reach a common approach—Some organizational theorists believe that advance agreements about the allocation of responsibilities are a necessary corollary of the strategy development process and a key to high team performance.[24] Such up-front agreement signifies commitment and consent of those involved, and promotes a meeting of the minds among those who perform the work. Initial agreements can serve to limit confusion and potential "turf fights" by specifying what is required of team members. For example, Pacific Bell teams begin their projects by agreeing on the nature of the problem, the goals, and the time frame for achieving a solution. Initial allocation of roles and responsibilities not only binds team members closer to the project, but provides feedback to the functional departments that contribute the team members, thus informing the rest of the organization of priorities and resource requirements.[25] In a different context, the U.S. Corps of Engineers tries to achieve the same commitment and purposefulness through "partnering" with its major contractors on every project. This process begins with an initial meeting or set of meetings in which roles and responsibilities of each member of the project team are worked through, and mechanisms for dispute resolution developed. Allowing these agreements to fall into place by accident as work progresses may lead to overlapping, gaps, and disputes that may be difficult to resolve.

Other theorists emphasize the importance of forging a common approach that is broader than the allocation of roles and responsibilities. It involves agreement on how skills will be integrated, how weaknesses and strengths are assessed and planned for, how mutual trust is promoted and conflict dealt with, and how priorities are established and adjustments made.[26] A social contract is needed for effective team performance, but the working model may bear little resemblance to the initial charter. Flexibility is necessary in the fast-moving environment of contemporary global markets—nothing should be chiseled in stone. Agreements must be reviewed periodically and modified when it makes sense to do so. Securing initial agreement is a significant step to implementing a joint vision, but it is not the most critical element. Team integration and flexibility in dealing with problems as they arise seem to be more important. In the development of the IAE engine, Rolls Royce, Pratt and Whitney, MTU, Fiat, and Japanese Aero Engine divided ownership and responsibility for engine development. The "up-front" agreements were clear, but they turned out not to be very workable, since competition and politics plagued the project, with each partner withholding technology from the other. In the "up-front" agreement, Pratt held the presidency, and Rolls was responsible for the engineering. Despite the agreements, support from senior management was not uniformly strong, and capabilities did not match the division of work. The agreement was modified several times and after considerable delays, a solid product was finally developed.[27] As we discuss in the next section, international politics and the need to build consensus makes it very difficult to begin team operations with clear agreements in advance. But too often conflicts are addressed by many players with no or shifting-role allocation, and with insufficient attention to the importance of both clarity and flexibility.

Transparency in planning and operations—Given that decentralization and the delegation to field level is so difficult for many organizations, and given that each organizational unit tends to be jealous of its "turf," transparency in planning and operations is essential. The first and most important part of transparency is open and full communication among team members. It sounds simple and obvious that team members should share information, and communicate openly with each other about their activities. Nevertheless, this runs against the culture of many organizations and the tendency "to play the cards close to the vest" is hard to change.

Studies of business teams indicate that internal conflict among team members may be lessened significantly by clear communications and free information flow.[28] Much of the conflict that does arise occurs because of inaccurate or incomplete information, or unclear, misunderstood communication. Information flow must be clear and free from distortion. Methods of dissemination must be rapid and comprehensive; information must be readily available.[29] It is important that special attention be given to information sharing "up the stovepipe" to headquarters, especially at the beginning, when delegated authority is most in question.

What is called "boundary management"—maintaining good working relations with key external stakeholders and customers—is an important goal of transparency. In industry, key stakeholders include shareholders, suppliers, retailers, and lenders, among others. The business literature suggests that team failure is more often the result of inadequate attention to boundaries than of internal group friction. Successful teams develop processes that include the significant stakeholders whose support is essential.[30]

Authority based on knowledge, not position—The central principle of hierarchical organization is that authority goes with position on the organization chart. But for many aspects of business, this concept of authority is no longer adequate.[31] In effective cooperative ventures, authority depends on relevant knowledge and expertise, ability to balance power and priorities, ability to control resources, access to pertinent information, and the ability to reduce uncertainty for the organization.[32] Leadership may well rotate through the team with leaders designated or agreed under particular situations. Dow-Corning rotates leaders of product-design teams as products move from research and development, to production, to marketing. In the product development teams of the Boeing-Sikorsky venture designing and manufacturing the Comanche helicopter, authority shifted from engineering, to production, to marketing, to quality control, and back again, depending on the issue at hand.

This concept makes sense, but it is not without problems. Those in charge at any one phase may be reluctant to relinquish leadership. A British study of three high technology firms concludes that such new forms of leadership will cause a certain amount of tension among managers (who are traditionally generalists concerned with resources and bottom lines and whose authority is based on position) and experts (who were not generally in leadership positions in bureaucratic systems but who, because of their knowledge, now hold the keys to success in flatter, more organic organizations).[33] Functional experts may be loath to share "guild" secrets because by doing so, they give up a certain amount of power. Thus they may not be willing to help others gain relevant knowledge because they perceive it as a zero sum game. Moreover, such shifts can be difficult for members to accept because abrupt changes of style can be disruptive. Managers face a dilemma in that they must recruit and retain experts whom they may not be able to control in the way they are accustomed, given the breakdown of traditional authority paradigms and managers' lack of relevant knowledge in some areas.

Teams tend to assemble experts in a variety of fields. As a result, leadership is likely to be challenging. After all, as the British study demonstrates, it is difficult enough forging a team out of experts and leaders within one organization, much less trying to accomplish that goal in an ad hoc team comprised of experts and managers who owe their primary allegiance to other organizations. The ability to provide and accept leadership based on the relevance of knowledge, not position, will not only require an articulated and harmonious vision and a well-developed strategic plan, but also careful selection of team members.

Mature leaders and members—The strength of high performance teams also pose their greatest challenge to team members. Not only do teams require skills and expertise, but also individual maturity and confidence to cooperate fully with others and realize that team success requires success in a tightly choreographed whole. The willingness to take on responsibility, to assume and, when necessary, relinquish leadership, is a defining element of personal maturity, which is in turn one of the central requirements in constructing learning organizations.[34] Teams require members who can engage in collaborative planning, reach consensus on priorities, and work out adjustments as circumstances require. Members should be experienced, capable of formulating creative alternatives, possess good interpersonal skills, and have a high tolerance for risk, uncertainty, and change. Clearly, teams are not the place to send neophytes or those who do not fit in at corporate headquarters. Teams require members who work well with others and who understand that sharing authority can increase it.

Many industries take the selection of team members with great seriousness. The Matsushita Corporation uses a formalized approach for selection of personnel for overseas team positions that would seem to be useful for international organizations selecting field operating agents. Criteria include appropriate skills and knowledge level, as well as management ability (especially the ability to motivate others), willingness to learn, adaptability, language proficiency, and the willingness to persevere in the face of difficulty. NEC and Phillips use similar criteria.[35] International organizations—particularly NGOs—often lack the funds to send experienced personnel into conflict areas, or to provide adequate training to prepare them.[36]

4. Applying the Business Model to Organizations that Deal with Conflict

Do the foregoing precepts for business team success have any usefulness for the different context of conflict prevention? Among the many significant differences, two stand out. First, there is little opportunity for detailed advance planning. Despite often ample early warning, the attention of the international community is not directed at a potential conflict until a crisis erupts. Second, there is now no single international organization that is the natural conveyor of conflict teams. It may be the UN; it may be a nation seeking allies; it may be a regional organization. In business, even in the most complex alliance, the team is assembled by design, often under the leadership of one of the participating organizations, or by prior agreement of several. There is usually some time for strategic planning and goal setting, even though a crash effort may be required. The corporate initiators are able to establish the conditions under which others join in the common effort.

Before one turns away, thinking that conditions are so different that the analogy has no utility at all, it may be worthwhile to ask whether so many conflicts need to be "come as you are parties." It is a post–Cold War cliché that inadequate planning for dealing with internal conflict has been done, and that situations such as the Former Yugoslavia or Rwanda could have been anticipated and planned for. While the business precepts are not transferable on a 1:1 basis, they may in fact be very suggestive.

Teamwork and planning are needed even more in situations without a single organization with power to initiate action. Many organizations are needed to mount a complex multifaceted strategy. They are independent and not easy to coordinate. Even where the UN is involved, it cannot command the resources and skills needed to address a complex conflict. The World Bank and the International Monetary Fund (IMF) together dispose of the bulk of the financial resources available for reconstruction in the aftermath of conflict. The UN is not a superordinate body to which other international organizations are subordinate—other organizations have their own charters and constituencies. Regional organizations such as the Organization for Security and Cooperation in Europe (OSCE), the European Union (EU), and the North Atlantic Treaty Organization (NATO), consist of a roster of states very different from the UN, and different from each other. The same is true of the Organization of American States (OAS) and the Organization of African Unity (OAU). Even when they have substantially overlapping memberships, as some of them do in Europe, the state representatives on their governing councils come from and report to different agencies in their national bureaucracies, with different priorities and agendas. NGOs respond to an even more diverse set of managers and constituencies. Most important, the UN can only act by consensus of the nations that comprise the Security Council. We turn now to the business precepts to see how they may be used to help reduce the chaos and missed opportunities that have characterized conflict intervention. The need for greater organizational synergy is urgent, and the opportunities for improvement, vast.

An organizational culture that fosters openness, flexibility, and cooperation—An institutional landscape made up of a myriad of separate legal entities, with separate missions, governance, and resources, and characterized by strongly vertical structures is hardly a propitious setting for interorganizational cooperation. Moreover, these are not organizations with institutional cultures, cooperation, and teamwork. The functionalism that undergirded the architecture of the post–World War II system of international organizations seemed to imply that each organization could be matched to a single functional area—whether it was atomic energy, agriculture, telecommunications, health, or refugees—to be pursued in its own terms, without taking account of extraneous considerations. Each tub was to stand on its own bottom. Moreover, as Graham Allison showed in his classic *Essence of Decision*,[37] bureaucratic organizations develop standard operating procedures that resist adaptation and innovation. Thus, when the "complex emergencies" of the post–Cold War period began to generate new demands for cooperative and cross-functional action, the familiar international organizations were ill-equipped to respond.

Perhaps the most striking instance of this phenomenon is the international financial institutions, the IBRD (World Bank) family, the IMF, and the regional development banks. For four decades they maintained that their charters required them to make loans and advances on strictly "economic" grounds, without regard to "political" considerations. These provisions date back to Bretton Woods, where John Maynard Keynes insisted on them to prevent the new institutions from discriminating against Britain's postwar socialist polity. In practice this meant that the banks made loans to projects that met bankers' criteria of soundness, and the Fund required a country to which it advanced resources to adopt stringent monetary policies so as to be able to repay within a three to five year period. The Bank even continued to make loans to South Africa in the face of General Assembly resolutions calling for an economic embargo as a weapon against apartheid.

Although the Bank and Fund now say they take account of "enabling conditions" in their lending operations, in El Salvador, the IMF imposed monetarist requirements that prevented the government from fulfilling the nation-building undertakings it had made in the peace agreements designed to bring decades of civil conflict to a close. The UN, which had brokered the agreement, had not thought to consult the Fund before or during the process, and vice versa. The IMF-sponsored stabilization and structural reform program began in 1989, during the conflict. World Bank and IMF objectives were improved economic growth, reconstruction of the economy, and improvement in living standards for the poorest segment of the population. But at its heart were tight national budgets, austerity programs, and gradual reduction of the government's influence on the economy. As part of the 1992 peace accords, the government of El Salvador was required to undertake a number of costly social programs aimed at cementing the peace process and assuring demobilization and a stable transition.[38] One senior UN official observed "The UN and other bodies, including the International Monetary Fund (IMF) and the World Bank, are overseeing separate, simultaneous processes in El Salvador that could be on a collision course."[39] The UN Secretary General worked out an arrangement whereby the IFIs established a group of donors that raised $800 million, thereby preventing the collision.

In recent years, the World Bank has done extensive studies of requirements for reconstruction and rehabilitation in Cambodia, the West Bank and Gaza, Bosnia, and other conflict areas. They have provided the basis for UN appeals to donors, and, in some cases, a blueprint for action. But the Bank has not served as the coordinating agency for carrying out its recommendations. In fact, it provided scant resources of its own, and because of its cumbersome procedures, these have not often arrived in time to meet urgent postconflict needs. Indeed, because the Bank will only deal with a responsible sovereign government, Bank programs in Bosnia have been delayed for the first crucial nine months of the Dayton accords. Susan Woodward writes "The bureaucratic rules of the EU, IMF, and the IBRD require them to work with counterparts who can guarantee that they will eventually repay the loans. There cannot be aid without a country program specifying conditionality, and there cannot be a country program without a country."[40]

Calls for coordination, if not cooperation, between UN agencies are almost as old as the UN system itself. Indeed, much of the work of the Economic and Social Council (ECOSOC), as it was originally conceived, was the orchestration and coordination of the work of the specialized agencies.[41] When that proved an empty hope, the Administrative Coordinating Committee (ACC), made up of the major specialized agencies, was created, but it is now reduced to one or two meetings a year that deal with relatively routine matters. The complex emergencies of recent years have given birth to the Interagency Standing Committee (IASC),[42] and the creation of the UN Department of Humanitarian Affairs (UNDHA) in the Secretariat, headed by an Undersecretary General. It is too soon to tell how effective these new entities will be. Meanwhile, accounts of bureaucratic turf fights and struggles for preeminence even between agencies within the United Nations proper (like the UNDP, UNHCR, or UNDHA itself), remain drearily familiar in case studies of conflict operations.

Provision for cooperation with NGOs was likewise within the original purview of the UN. In what was, at the time, a startling innovation, ECOSOC was authorized to "make suitable arrangements for consultation with nongovernmental organizations which are concerned with matters within its competence."[43] ECOSOC discharged this responsibility by setting up a formal and rather cumbersome registration process, which has proved irrelevant to the actual needs of NGOs involved in UN activities, whether in peace operations or elsewhere. With a few exceptions, the necessary culture for cooperation has thus far not been much in evidence. Regrettably, despite the criticism of the UN and despite the shortage of funds—primarily a problem of U.S. domestic congressional politics—progress in making a major transformation in corporate culture has been agonizingly slow (there have been a few exceptions, such as UNHCR). The relationship between funding shortfalls and lack of coordination and cooperation has not been clear enough to provide the motivation for more rapid reform.

Decentralization with autonomy—It is no secret that intergovernmental organizations more often than not are textbook cases of hierarchical bureaucracies. They are excessively layered, with slow-moving reporting and decision processes. Secretariats or executive officials have little latitude for independent initiative. Organizational action is subject to elaborate requirements for approval, often by vote of the governing organs. Although the charters of most organizations provide for some sort of majority voting procedure, in practice action is taken by consensus, so that it can be blocked by a single determined member. Most major NGOs also seek to maintain control over field operations from headquarters to ensure conformity to organizational policy and responsiveness to constituency concerns.

International organizations, moreover, have deeply ingrained traditions of independence. The charter is taken as delineating an area of functional jurisdiction that is treated as an independent fiefdom where the organization acts on its own authority and without subordination to other entities. Again, NGOs also have a strong tradition of independent action.

Such bureaucratic organizations with vertical superstructures tend to view crisis response in a very narrow band, not as a system of interrelated actions. Instead of seeing other international organizations as potential partners, they concentrate on recapitulating standard operating procedures to address the facets of the situation within their traditional competence. Together these characteristic features of the culture of international organizations militate against cooperative effort and delegation of authority to operatives in the field.

Nevertheless, there are indications that the demands of post–Cold War international crises for flexible and innovative responses are forcing departures from these traditional attitudes. A prime example is the High Commissioner on National Minorities (HCNM) of the OSCE, who has had significant, and perhaps unexpected success in his efforts to forestall ethnic conflict in Eastern Europe and the former Soviet Union. Despite the traditional resistance to delegation, the HCNM's mandate authorizes him to intervene on his own initiative in a country with potential ethnic conflict.[44] He establishes contact not only with the government but with local and international NGOs as well as local ethnic representatives. His method is to try to set up round tables and other consultative processes whereby factions can cooperate in seeking agreed solutions to the problems of language, citizenship, education, and discrimination that are the substance of ethnic politics. Although he keeps the Chairman in Office (CIO) of the OSCE informed of his activities, and consults the Senior Council, as a practical matter the HCNM does not operate under their supervision and has broad flexibility in the tactics and methods he chooses to employ.[45]

What interorganizational cooperation there has been in peace operations and conflict prevention activities has occurred not in Geneva or New York, but has emerged ad hoc in the field, often in the form of regular informal consultative meetings among the public and private organizations on the scene. The paradigm is the Humanitarian Operations Council (HOC), established by Ambassador Oakley during the UNITAF phase of the Somalia operation. Attendance was voluntary but was open to all NGOs providing humanitarian assistance, the major international organizations in the theater, and representatives of the principal Somalian military factions. The parties exchanged information about the latest developments, NGOs outlined their plans and needs for military protection, and U.S. representatives often stated their intentions regarding action and policy and solicited reactions from the group. Current issues were often identified, discussed, and resolved on the spot.[46] The object is not to give instructions but to develop consensus on priorities and distribution of tasks in an immediate and volatile situation.

The working groups established in post–Dayton Bosnia by the High Representative display a similar format. They are organized along sectoral lines—electricity, housing, sewage, water supply, etc.—and comprise representatives from all groups interested in the particular question, including local government officials, NGOs, the EU, and IFOR. Again, the effort is to achieve consensus on the immediate problems in the particular sector and how to attack them. In the early days, these working groups were given impetus by American reserve officers trained and experienced in Civil-Military Operations Centers (CIMOCS). This pattern of coordination of military and civilian efforts has behind it long experience and recent successes in Haiti, as well as the UNITAF phase of Somalia, and make such efforts a valuable model for institutional coordination in conflict prevention.

Shared vision and common purpose—In the context of conflict prevention and mitigation, the "vision" is the definition of goals, objectives, and broad strategy. The "classical peacekeeping" operations of the Cold War period embodied a clear-cut and well-defined vision. It was first formulated by UN Secretary General Dag Hammarskjöld and his Undersecretary Ralph Bunche for the UN Emergency Force in the Middle East (UNEF), in the wake of the Suez crisis in 1956, and was authoritatively endorsed from the legal standpoint by the World Court in *Certain Expenses of the United Nations*.[47] Lightly armed forces contributed by member states were deployed after an agreement ending hostilities had been concluded between the parties, and their mission was to assist in implementing this agreement by interposing themselves between the armies of the parties and monitoring compliance. This concept dictated the three basic principles of peacekeeping operational strategy: (1) the UN force was deployed with the consent of the parties; (2) it was neutral as between them; and (3) it was authorized to use armed force only in self-defense. Since the agreements were signed by established governments, they were generally observed, and since the governments exercised control over their territories, the responsibility for supplying the necessities of their populations could be left to them, perhaps with modest international emergency assistance.

The "complex emergencies" that have engaged the international community in the post–Cold War period, however, have arisen from internal conflicts where the state was not in full control of its territory and people and, in the extreme cases, had collapsed entirely. Populations ravaged by war looked to international assistance for protection from violence and abuse and for food, shelter, and medical care—the bare necessities of life. And these demands, reinforced by scarifying images of suffering and brutality on Western television screens, would not wait for the conclusion of a cease-fire agreement. In this environment, international intervention could not be limited to the comparatively straightforward task of interposing forces between warring parties to implement a peace agreement between them. The objectives and scope of intervention had to be defined ad hoc by whatever combination of public and private organizations were prepared to assume its burdens.

In the Gulf War, the Operation Restore Hope phase of the Somalia operation, and in Haiti, the United States was willing to take charge and commit the major share of resources. Thus, like a corporate leader creating a product-development team, the U.S. was able to define the goals and objectives of the operation and ensure that the overall strategy and resources were well-matched to them. In the Gulf, it was the United States, for better or worse, that decided that the objective was to reverse the Iraqi invasion of Kuwait, but not to overthrow Sadam Hussein. In Somalia, despite constant and severe pressure from Secretary General Boutros Boutros Ghali, President Bush refused to undertake the disarmament of the contending military factions and clung to his vision of the mission as the provision of a secure environment for the distribution of humanitarian aid to starving Somalis. In Haiti, the objective was to oust the junta and install the government of Jean-Bertrand Aristide. Because of its dominant position in these three cases, the United States was able to impose its vision not only on other governmental members of the coalition, but also on NGO in the theater.

This clarity of vision and agreement on a common purpose is hard to achieve where the international action is truly multilateral. In the UNISOM II phase of the Somali operation, the Security Council, under pressure from the Secretary General and the new administration in the United States, changed the formal mission to one of disarming and neutralizing the military factions, in particular that of General Aideed. But the United States was no longer providing the bulk of the military resources. Countries that were major troop contributors (for example, Italy), did not share this vision and overall, the forces available were insufficient to sustain it. NGOs saw their objective quite differently, and worked to avert starvation and disease. Common purpose was lacking, both among headquarters of the major organizations, and at the field level.

Typically these differences of broad purpose or vision among the principal actors are buried in ambiguous language of the Security Council resolution or other instrument authorizing the operation. The need for political compromise results in the frequently remarked "vagueness" of the mandate given to the UN. Moreover, the original authorization is often followed by increasingly detailed and sometimes inconsistent resolutions in response to the evolving situation.

The prime example of this pattern was in Bosnia and Herzegovina where the thirty-three Security Council resolutions specifically dealing with that conflict (out of a total of ninety-two relating to the former Yugoslavia) reflected fundamental and unresolved policy disagreements among the Permanent Members of the Security Council. Britain and France, the chief suppliers of troops for UNPROFOR, were generally neutral among the parties to the conflict, and saw the main problem as the assurance of humanitarian assistance to the civil population. Meanwhile, EU and UN representatives sought to negotiate the cessation of hostilities. Thus the resolution authorizing the initial deployment of UNPROFOR to Bosnia defined its mission as implementing an agreement reopening the Sarajevo airport and ensuring a secure environment for the delivery of humanitarian aid. The United States, however, increasingly tended to side with the Bosnian Muslims and to see the Serbs not only as the aggressors in the conflict but as the chief perpetrators of brutal human-rights violations and outright genocide. Since Washington was not prepared to contribute the large ground forces that would have been necessary to defeat and punish the Serbs, however, it was unable to impose this vision on the Security Council. Nevertheless, in response to U.S. pressure, subsequent resolutions, without expressly adopting the U.S. view or formally taking sides, authorized the use of NATO sea and air power to enforce an arms embargo throughout the former Yugoslavia, to implement a no-fly zone over Bosnia, and to protect "safe havens" that the Security Council established in six Bosnian cities.

The incoherence of the fundamental vision of the operation led to questionable strategy and a severe mismatch between the resources available and the assigned tasks. The result was the continuation of the war and the growing loss of credibility and effectiveness of the UN operation as a whole. It has been argued that this same incoherence haunts the Dayton accords, which were unable to make a clear-cut choice between the vision of an ethnically mixed or ethnically partitioned Bosnia, and thus contain elements of both.[48]

Lack of clarity in the goals and objectives of an intervention stemming from political divisions among the principal participants in New York is a major—perhaps *the* major—problem in fashioning international responses to complex emergencies. Unfortunately, there is no easy solution. The countries that supply the resources for such interventions have different priorities, and face a variety of internal political pressures leading to very different views of the character of an international conflict and its impact on their interests. The requirements and practical possibilities of the crisis constitute only some of the factors shaping the response. Nothing will change these frictions of international politics.

As a practical matter, then, it will rarely be possible to develop a shared vision at the top, even in fairly broad terms. This is why UN Security Council resolutions have been both numerous and internally inconsistent, and not just with respect to the former Yugoslavia. One way to deal with this inevitable political situation would be to delegate more of the function of creating a shared vision and common purpose to the field. The arguments for decentralization are even stronger for international organizations than for corporations. In the field, it is more feasible to secure agreement on mission definition. In Cambodia, this seems to have taken place without prior design or plan. The Paris Agreements, which brought an end to the fighting in 1991, comprised a detailed wish list for the comprehensive reconstruction of the Cambodian economy and society after two decades of war and genocide. They mandated the disarmament and reintegration of the troops of the warring factions, the repatriation of 360,000 refugees and untold numbers of internally displaced persons, the enforcement of human rights, the conduct of free and fair elections leading to democracy, and the reestablishment of a functioning government and civil society. The UN Transitional Authority in Cambodia (UNTAC), with 15,900 military personnel, 3,600 civilian police, and 1,020 civilian personnel, with a total budget of $2.1 billion, was to oversee the process; and international donors pledged considerable funds for reconstruction and development.

Almost from the outset it became clear the Khmer Rouge was not going to carry out the demobilization and disarmament elements of the agreement, and the government troops followed suit. Much of the rest of the ambitious program laid out in the Paris Agreement, if it was not utopian from the beginning, became impractical under these circumstances. Nevertheless, UNTAC is widely regarded as a success. Why? Because Yasushi Akashi, the Special Representative of the Secretary General, and General Bernard Sanderson, the UN military commander, were able to define a narrower, more coherent, and practical vision for UNTAC, driven by the realities and limitations of the situation on the ground as they saw it.[49] In effect, they limited the mission to two basic elements: repatriation of refugees and the organization and conduct of the elections. The first was within the competence of UNHCR, one of the most experienced and effective UN agencies. And the UN force was adequate to provide sufficient protection to the election process, polling places, and voters on election day, permitting over ninety percent of the population to cast their ballots. The Security Council was content to join Ambassador Akashi in declaring victory.

Cambodia may have been an improvisation, or a practical redrawing of parameters on the ground, but it does suggest a more general approach. The team on the ground will inevitably be better acquainted with the needs and potential of the actual situation than diplomats in New York. Particularly if those with greatest responsibility in the field can be melded into a high-performance team, they may be able to generate more appropriate and workable goals than their central offices. Of course, the overall framework for the operation, including the legal basis for it and the resources allocated, will be established by high-level political negotiations. The Cambodian experience suggests that it may be productive to delegate substantial authority and responsibility to a well-constituted team in the field for something more than implementation of a predetermined vision of the operation, so long as adequate accountability can be assured.

A strategic planning process to implement shared goals—International organizations, whether intergovernmental or nongovernmental, have just begun to develop the skills to formulate detailed strategy to implement broad goals. Many are just beginning to see the necessity for strategic planning and recognize that they must look for help where the practice is well established, such as the military or corporate worlds. Few of the civil organizations involved in conflict have a strong tradition or experience in long-range or even midrange operational planning. Scarcity of funds have also been a barrier to adequate planning. For many of them, their involvement in conflict situations has been based upon ad hoc decisions at the top. The political and financial structure of the UN itself makes a systematic planning process difficult to develop. It must receive approval from the Security Council to mount an operation. Of course, the Secretary General may send a special representative to an area for developing facts and information in order to plan further action, and does so in most threatening situations. But the UN's capability to plan the operation that should follow has been rudimentary. In the last year or two, under prodding and with the assistance of the United States and other members of the Security Council, a concerted effort has been made to improve the military planning arm of the Secretariat: the Department of Peacekeeping Operations (DPKO). Even more recently, with the establishment of the Department of Humanitarian Assistance (DHA), a similar, if less intense effort has begun on the civil side.[50] UNHCR, through its increasingly demanding operational experience, has developed considerable capability in planning for the handling of refugees. Beyond that, planning at any level with other organizations is little more than perfunctory, and even interagency planning within the UN remains rudimentary. The European Commission is just beginning to develop its planning apparatus for Europe through its Directorate General for External Political Relations (DG1A), which has begun to explore the tools and methods that will permit it to anticipate crises and respond in a more deliberate manner.

Planning by the individual NGOs is even more rudimentary, with the possible exception of ICRC. As David Rieff points out, the decision to enter a country may be more a matter of internal politics and external pressures from funding sources or contributing membership, than as a result of a deliberate planning process.[51]

The contrast with the military is striking. In general, mature military departments contain robust planning staffs. They develop plans for a variety of contingencies and scenarios, dealing with all phases of the military operation: from weapons procurement and logistics to personnel training and exercises. NATO, for example, had nearly three years to plan for its role in Bosnia's postconflict peacekeeping phase. The United States announced well in advance that it was prepared to commit 20,000 troops to such an operation. Unlike the UN, NATO could draw on fifty years of alliance planning and interoperability to be fully prepared for the novel situation that ensued. Furthermore, it was able to include Partnership for Peace (PFP) countries of Eastern Europe in the first peacekeeping exercises, thus beginning to prepare them to participate in the International Force in Bosnia (IFOR). Because of the depth of NATO's history and its doctrine of broad delegation to field commanders, IFOR has been able to engage in collaborative planning at the field level, which is almost a necessity, given the division of the theater into country sectors and the inclusion of Russian troops in the force. How much more effective the post-Dayton situation might have been if civilian and military planning had been integrated.

It may be unfair to contrast the military and civilian sides of implementing the Dayton Accords. There was no advance designation of a team of civilian organizations to plan for the civil aspects of peace building. Partly at the insistence of the United States and partly out of its own desire, the UN was generally excluded from the picture, except for refugee repatriation and resettlement by UNHCR and, subsequently, the provision of civilian police. Although the UN had extensive experience with election monitoring on three continents, the task of preparing for and conducting elections nine months after the cease-fire was given to the OSCE. The Dayton agreements contemplated that a "High Representative" would supervise the nonmilitary parts of the settlement, but Carl Bildt was not appointed until late December 1995, therefore overall civilian planning could not begin until IFOR's sole year was already running. Nor were funds immediately available to jump start the reconstruction process. The World Bank made a study calling for a fund of $5.1 billion for reconstruction over a three to four year period; $2.1 billion for the first year.[52] Of this, the European Commission (EU) allocated 125 million ecus to be available on an immediate basis, but the first three months of the operation passed without substantial inflows of funds. Further, because of the fear of "mission creep," IFOR initially took an unusually rigid position about the scope of its operations and willingness to assist in essentially civil tasks.

Despite these impediments, it can be argued that some of the requirements could and should have been anticipated and planned for. It was clear, for example, that a strong police training and monitoring operation would be needed and that the responsibility for providing it would most likely fall on the UN's Civil Police unit (CIVPOL). Nevertheless, one of the most serious problems in the first six months of the Bosnian operation was the absence of this capability. Many of the most potentially explosive tasks under the Dayton accords, such as the transfer of territories and repatriation, were completed before an international police force was established. In March 1996, only 789 out of an authorized 1,800 members of the international police force were present for duty, and many of the police offered by nations failed to meet minimum criteria.[53]

Again, it was clear as the war wound down that a major problem would be the provision of housing and restoration of municipal services. But without early designation of the agency responsible for civilian reconstruction, little planning could be done. Thus, we heard anecdotes such as the delivery of window glass to Sarajevo, where it stood for months because there was no provision for installation.[54]

The fact that it is unclear at the outset whether or which organizations will be asked to intervene in conflict is not an excuse for the lack of a strategic planning process. First, generic planning against simulated scenarios developed from experience will prepare organizations to respond quickly and in concert. Since such contingency planning has been done for centuries by militaries throughout the world, there are ample models available. The U.S. Department of Defense has begun to help U.S. civilian governmental agencies exercise a joint planning capacity for conflict operations that may arise. Mechanisms for coordinating civilian and military planning must also be developed on an international basis.

Second, certain organizations or components have special skills and experience that make it likely that they will be called upon, since most conflicts will show need for those skills. For example, UNHCR does not wait to see if there are refugees, but monitors situations and prepares for response in advance, and while they may not be called upon in every case, the UN can plan for assembling and training a civil police element. Food and medicine are going to be universally needed. One lesson that can be learned from both business and the military is that the strategic planning process must be given high priority, regardless of the uncertainties of eventual participation, or the shortage of funds.

In many intergovernmental and nongovernmental organizations this process has begun internally for the organization itself. But it will be a large step for organizations to contemplate the joint planning that effective field teamwork requires, and such planning requires a major cultural change. Organizations have not fully recognized nor internalized the necessity to work together to develop a coordinated strategy to deal with conflict effectively. Internal, central strategic planning is a first step, but it will not be sufficient.

Planning almost necessarily implies training, and in practice almost all planning exercises include a training component. Both business and the military devote extensive resources to training. The U.S. Army conducts planning training exercises for peace operations exercises at Fort Polk, Louisiana, and at Hoenfels in Germany, where many of the troops now serving in IFOR were trained and where military personnel and civilians (including NGOs) can exercise their capacity to work together in a conflict situation. NATO's Partnership for Peace also includes a large training component—as noted above, some of the participating Eastern European troops participated in PFP exercises directed to peacekeeping functions.

The U.S. Department of Defense initiated training for a politicomilitary (POL-MIL) planning process some weeks in advance of the Haiti operation that included both military and civilian agencies represented by officials at the assistant secretary and deputy assistant secretary levels. The experience was so successful that the U.S. government has now instituted a program titled Interagency Training for Complex Contingency Operations in which officials from organizational units likely to play a role in actual peace operations participate in joint planning for a major U.S. intervention based on a scenario devised by the training managers. The plan is then exercised in a simulation of the operation, and ultimately debriefed and critiqued at a session attended by senior officials. Although NGOs and international organizations have not yet participated, the process takes account of their presence, and there is a possibility that they will be invited to participate in later training exercises.

It becomes clear that training is needed at a number of different levels to help develop effective strategic planning processes: (1) the internal planning effort now under way to assure that an agency can marshal its expertise and respond quickly—such as now done by UNHCR and the ICRC; (2) interorganizational training for joint planning at the highest levels, similar to training begun by DOD; and (3) training for cooperative planning for team action in the field. With respect to the third level, OSCE has conducted its first training for members of its missions of long duration. The U.S. Institute of Peace and the Army's Peacekeeping Institute conduct training sessions with staff members from a variety of agencies that are frequent participants in peace operations, and the World Bank is now organizing similar sessions.

Regardless of the training methodology used, participants become familiar with each others' organizations and agendas and discuss concepts and possible visions of crisis response. Over time, they are likely to understand the contribution that each organization can make, to feel more comfortable working with each other, and to work through various concepts and approaches together, thus enabling them to move more quickly to cooperative action in crisis situations. Such joint efforts and experience will not eliminate disagreements or tensions. However, disagreements that arise will perhaps be less disruptive and resolved more readily, so that joint energies can be turned to positive ends. It is much more difficult to arrive at a joint vision and strategy once conflict has erupted. Yet joint training is only beginning. To date, it remains a pitifully small effort reaching only a handful of the relevant organizational personnel.

Clear allocation of responsibility to reach a common approach—While advance agreements are clearly desirable for clarity in allocating roles and responsibilities of the major team participants in business, we have seen that flexibility and the need to adjust are necessary even there. In conflict situations there is little possibility that advance agreement can be made among the participating organizations that comprise a working team. But the need for clear allocation of roles and responsibilities remains strong, and some way must be found to achieve it, otherwise organizations will work at cross-purposes, wasting resources and energy fighting over their jurisdiction. Moreover, as important as it may be to "involve the customer," as Boeing-Sikorsky did in creating the Comanche helicopter, the parties to a conflict are essential parties to all agreements, and must play a major participatory role.

An axiom of classical peacekeeping was the requirement of a formal agreement signed by responsible governments ending hostilities between them, consenting to the presence of a UN force on their territory, with clearly understood rules of engagement, guarantees of freedom of movement, and other provisions regarding the status of the forces. But in contemporary complex emergencies, hostilities are often continuing, and in any case there is typically no effective government or other responsible authority that can guarantee the fulfillment of the terms of an agreement for the intervention of peacekeeping forces or the provision of humanitarian assistance. This is true even of such elaborate formal compacts as the Paris Agreements on Cambodia or Bosnia's Dayton Accords. They are consensual arrangements that depend on the continuing consent of the parties for their efficacy, a consent that may have to be renegotiated with each new implementation controversy. Moreover, the situation on the ground is ordinarily so complex and volatile that, as discussed above, only the most general advance agreement as to overall goals and strategy is possible.

Agreements among organizations participating in the process are often un-achievable in advance. In the first place, it is not clear which organizations will be involved. The UN itself was substantially excluded from the post-Dayton operation in Bosnia, as noted above, as well as from monitoring the 1996 ceasefire between Israel and Lebanon. Some organizations may have a monopoly of essential experience and expertise—for example, the UNHCR can generally count on being the lead organization in dealing with refugees. But, as noted, despite the UN's long experience with organizing and monitoring elections, Dayton assigned this task to the OSCE, which in turn, called upon the UN expertise for advice and assistance. Even with that uncertainty, generic scenario-based planning, as discussed above, allows the development of skill pools that then enable a rational allocation of resources.

Nongovernmental organizations in particular prize their independence. As a rule, each organization makes its own decision whether to enter a particular theater and how to conduct itself once there. At the same time, they are dependent upon funding sources for their participation, and few have the resources to make long-term commitments. Increasingly, though, NGOs are given contracts to perform tasks in a conflict situation—particularly in the postconflict reconstruction phase—by international organizations such as the European Commission, or governmental donors, such as U.S. Agency for International Development (USAID).

NGO participation is only loosely subject to control by any international political authority in the field. The NGOs regard independence from the political agenda of states and international organizations as essential if they are to be able to perform their own functions—the provision of food relief or medical care, aid to refugees, monitoring of human rights, etc. Few are likely to agree in advance to limit their activities or subordinate them to the direction of another organization.

In these circumstances, what may be more important than an elaborate formal agreement is a process to generate a kind of rolling consensus among the public and private organizations at the field level on a rough, but shifting allocation of responsibilities and a division of effort and resources. This is what seems to have been achieved by the mechanisms for coordination described above. One of the most successful features of the HOC process established in the Restore Hope phase of Somalia was its ability to establish a high degree of cooperation and open communication among the Somalian factions themselves, and between the factions and the military and civilian organizations operating in the theater.

Transparency in planning and operations—In such a process, information flow seems to be particularly important in order to reduce the misunderstandings and uncertainty that breed tensions and to provide data on which to base decisions and actions quickly. What seems to be needed is not a simple exchange of information about isolated events, but rather an ongoing mechanism that provides a venue to explore and evaluate ideas within the system that the team represents. There are cases where information sharing has dispelled mistrust and been a strong force in helping to develop teamwork. As noted above, information exchange was a principal purpose of the Humanitarian Operations Center (HOC) in the UNITAF phase of Somalia, and after earlier chaotic conditions in Rwanda, there were continuing attempts to provide information and coordination for the more than

200 NGOs on the ground, through UNREO, an On-Site Operation Coordination Center (OSOCC), and a NGO Liaison Unit.[55] In Burundi, UN Special Representative Ahmedou Ould Abdallah made sure that information was shared, and NGOs helped to maximize their effectiveness. The Burundi Forum continues Abdallah's efforts.

Processes for sharing information provide critical knowledge to all team members, and to their parent organization as well. Although, as noted above, transparency entails open and full communication among team members, information sharing is not the characteristic pattern among international organizations. In Tajikistan and Georgia, for example, there has been little interchange between the UN and the OSCE. In Tajikistan, the head of the OSCE mission had important contacts with opposition leaders and saw them frequently in meetings outside Tajikistan. The UN Special Representative considered himself unauthorized to participate in meetings outside of the country, and would not invite the OSCE Representative to meetings inside. Only after considerable effort on both sides was information shared between the two. Moreover, although the OSCE mission, in accordance with its instructions, had worked on the development of a new constitution, it was not permitted to participate in the drafting process chaired by the UN, and was able to review the drafts only in the very final stages.[56] More fundamentally, the various organizations in Tajikistan did not operate as a team at all. UNHCR cooperated with the representatives of both the UN and the OSCE, but no real synergy has developed. Similarly, in Georgia, the UN and OSCE have divided up the major conflicts—the UN is in charge of Abkhazia, and OSCE handles South Ossetia. Attempts to create a common center for dealing with human rights abuses in Abkhazia have been slow to materialize. Each operates independently for the most part, and even common problems are dealt with separately. There is limited communication.[57] On the NGO side, the ICRC is notorious for refusing to share information for fear of jeopardizing its traditional neutrality.

When it occurs, transparency in information and operations seems to be a matter of the determination and commitment of individual leaders. Conversely, certain players permit organizational rivalries to erect barriers to transparency, the importance of which is not fully recognized in interorganizational relationships, as it has come to be with business teams. Transparency is an element of developing effective teamwork that goes hand-in-hand with training for joint strategic planning, and is necessary to affect overall change in corporate cultures, moving them toward greater openness, flexibility, and cooperation.

Mature leaders and members with authority based on knowledge, not position—At first blush, members of the professions commonly engaged in peace operations would seem poor candidates for positions in an open and nonhierarchical structure. Military personnel are trained to give—or take—orders. Diplomats set more than ordinary store by the perquisites of rank. UN Bureaucrats are thought to be the most hidebound of their tribe. On the private side, NGOs, like political campaigns, are often staffed by committed but freewheeling younger people who possess little experience, strong convictions, and the ability to work around the clock under hardship conditions, sustained only by coffee.

As with most stereotypes, however, these are belied by practice. Military commanders of peacekeeping forces, in particular, have shown a remarkable ability to adapt to the unfamiliar requirements of operations based primarily on consent rather than coercion. It has been argued that in pre–Dayton Bosnia, there was little friction between UNPROFOR military and civilian officials. The difficulty came when headquarters called for more muscular use of force than military and civilian leaders in theater thought was appropriate. The Secretary General has assembled a corps of senior ambassadors and ex-ambassadors to act as his Special Representatives in a variety of trouble spots, and the OSCE has used similar people to head its missions of long duration. There have certainly been differences of quality among these, and not all have been successes. Nevertheless, many have been able to operate effectively in remote and difficult situations with little of the authority and few of the appurtenances of rank that are usual for ambassadors. In the UN, from Ralph Bunche and Brian Urquart in the 1950s to Kofi Annan, Yasushi Akashi, and Derek Boothby in the 1990s, the peacekeeping enterprise has drawn the most dedicated, imaginative, and effective officers of the Secretariat. And many NGOs have developed professional staffs able to pursue their organizational goals with audacity while cooperating with others engaged in the common effort.

What is needed, it turns out, is not the "follow-me" brand of leadership. People who perform well in these operations are comfortable with uncertainty and ambiguity, open to new ideas, imaginative and innovative in their own thinking, pragmatic and problem-solving in their approach, and able to help build and maintain the kind of rolling consensus described in the last section.

5. Conclusion

We began by examining the theory and practice of contemporary business organization for its relevance to the persistent problems of coordination and cooperation among organizations—public and private, national and international—involved in peace operations. We saw that the emphasis in the business arena is on decentralization and particularly the delegation of broad authority and responsibility to cross-functional teams at the project level. From the literature, we culled a series of successful operational attributes of such teams. We make no strong claims for this list. Different readers might generate a somewhat different formulation. Moreover, as we anticipated, not all of these attributes are transferable directly to the field of international operations to prevent conflict or its recurrence. Nevertheless, we think the study of business teams provides valuable approaches that may be adapted to the problems developing a coordinated strategy for such organizations. Three overarching themes have emerged that we think have powerful application to the coordination of international organizations engaged in conflict operations to develop synergies and make them both more efficient and more effective.

- There must be a major redistribution of tasks and responsibilities between the center and field, with the principal objective of empowering the field.
- The functions of mission and goal definition, strategy development, and planning and training are crucial but they must be adapted to the diffuse organizational context of peace operations.
- The key process is consensus building, and this requires different attributes both in the leadership and membership of the operation.

These themes are far enough from the conventional wisdom to be worthy of further exploration.

Notes

1. Chester Crocker, in his introduction to John L. Hirsch and Robert B. Oakley, *Somalia and Operation Restore Hope* (Washington, D.C.: United States Institute of Peace, 1995), p. xi.
2. Karen A. Mingst and Margaret P. Karns, *The United Nations in the Post–Cold War Era* (Boulder, Col.: Westview Press, 1995), p. 149.
3. Jonathan Moore, *The UN and Complex Emergencies: Rehabilitation in Third World Transitions* (Geneva: UNRISD, 1996), p. 24.
4. Fred Kaufman and Peter Senge, "Communities of Commitment: The Heart of Learning Organizations," in Sarita Chawla and John Renesch, eds., *Learning Organizations,* (Portland, OR: Productivity Press, Inc., 1995), p. 16.
5. Stanley B. Davis and Paul R. Lawrence, "Problems of Matrix Organizations," *Harvard Business Review,* May/June 1978, pp. 131–42; Richard E. Anderson, "Matrix Redux," *Business Horizons,* November 1994, pp. 6–10, 181–83.
6. Steven C. Wheelwright and Kim B. Clark, *Revolutionizing Produce Development: Quantum Leaps in Speed, Efficiency and Quality* (New York: The Free Press, 1992), pp. 151–60, 188–217.
7. Jay R. Galbraith, *Designing Organizations: An Executive Brief on Strategy, Structure, and Process* (San Francisco, Calif.: Jossey-Bass, 1995), p. 103.
8. Interview with Art Linden, Director of the Joint Program Office, Sikorsky Aircraft, May 30, 1996; See also Bruce F. Kay. "Comanche Airframe Design: PDT Approach," *Aerospace America,* April 1993, pp. 22–24.
9. Glenn M. Parker, *Cross-Functional Teams: Working with Allies, Enemies, and Other Strangers* (San Francisco, Calif.: Jossey-Bass, 1994), p. 10.
10. The Dallas-based DePalma Hotel Corporation has had success with self-directed teams in the operation of its 15 hotels. See Bradford McKee, "Turn Your Workers into a Team," *Nation's Business,* July 1992, p. 37.
11. Organizational learning is described as a "process whereby management teams change their shared mental models of their company, their markets, and their competitors." Peter Senge, *The Fifth Discipline: The Art and Practice of the Learning Organization* (New York: Doubleday, 1990), p. XXX.
12. David K. Banner and T. Elaine Gagné, *Designing Effective Organizations Traditional and Transformational Views* (Thousand Oaks, Calif.: SAGE Publications, 1995), p. 384.
13. Steven C. Wheelwright and Kim B. Clark, *Revolutionizing Produce Development: Quantum Leaps in Speed, Efficiency and Quality* (New York: The Free Press, 1992), pp. 153–54, 160–61.
14. For a more complete discussion, see Jerome H. Want, *Managing Radical Change* (Essex Junction, Vt.: OMNEO, 1995), pp. 139–60.
15. Stanley B. Davis and Paul R. Lawrence, "Problems of Matrix Organizations," *Harvard Business Review,* May/June 1978, pp. 131–42; Richard E. Anderson, "Matrix Redux," *Business Horizons,* November 1994, pp. 6–10; David K. Banner and T. Elaine Gagné, *Designing Effective Organizations Traditional and Transformational Views* (Thousand Oaks, Calif.: SAGE Publications, 1995), pp. 181–83.

16. Karl Albrecht, *The Northbound Train* (New York: AMACOM, 1994), p. 15.

17. Jon R. Katzenbach and Douglas K. Smith *The Wisdom of Teams* (Cambridge, Mass.: Harvard Business School Press, 1993), p. 49–50.

18. Ibid., pp. 50–52.

19. Wheelwright and Clark, p. 185.

20. Interview with Robert Rosati, Senior Vice President, International, Pratt & Whitney, May 30, 1996.

21. Jon R. Katzenbach and Douglas K. Smith, *The Wisdom of Teams* (Cambridge, Mass.: Harvard Business School Press, 1993), pp. 55, 98–104.

22. Glenn M. Parker, *Cross-Functional Teams: Working with Allies, Enemies, and Other Strangers* (San Francisco, Calif.: Jossey-Bass, Inc., 1994), p. 94.

23. See Russell A. Eisenstat, "Fairfield Systems Group," in J. Richard Hackman, ed., *Groups That Work (And Those That Don't): Creating Conditions for Effective Teamwork,* (San Francisco, Calif.: Jossey Bass, 1991), pp. 171–77.

24. David Chaudron, "Organizational Development: How to Improve Cross-Functional Teams," *Human Resources Focus,* Vol. 72, No. 8 (August 1995), p. 4; Wheelwright and Clark, pp. 175, 180.

25. Glenn M. Parker, *Cross-Functional Teams,* pp. 82–83. For the use of self-directed teams for medical treatment, see Jack D. Osburn, Linda Moran, Ed Musselwhite and John H. Zenger, *Self-Directed Work Teams: The New American Challenge* (Homewood, Il: Business OneIrwin, 1990), p. 96.

26. Jon R. Katzenbach and Douglas K. Smith, *The Wisdom of Teams* (Cambridge, Mass.: Harvard Business School Press, 1993), p. 56–59.

27. Interview with Robert Rosati, Pratt & Whitney, May 30, 1996.

28. See especially, David K. Banner and T. Elaine Gagné, *Designing Effective Organizations Traditional and Transformational Views* (Thousand Oaks, Calif.: SAGE Publications, 1995), p. 278; Glenn M. Parker, *Cross-Functional Teams: Working with Allies, Enemies, and Other Strangers* (San Francisco, Calif.: Jossey-Bass, 1994), pp. 164–65. See also Jay R. Galbraith, *Designing Organizations: An Executive Briefing on Strategy, Structure and Process,* (San Francisco, Calif.: Jossey-Bass, 1995).

29. Rosati interview.

30. Glenn M. Parker, *Cross-Functional Teams: Working with Allies, Enemies, and Other Strangers* (San Francisco, Calif.: Jossey-Bass, 1994), pp. 163–65.

31. Ibid., pp. 50–51; Jay R. Galbraith, *Designing Organizations: An Executive Briefing on Strategy, Structure and Process* (San Francisco, Calif.: Jossey-Bass, 1995), pp. 67–70; David K. Banner and T. Elaine Gagné, *Designing Effective Organizations Traditional and Transformational Views* (Thousand Oaks, Calif.: SAGE Publications, 1995), pp. 178–79.

32. This has been called *sapiential authority* by David K. Banner and T. Elaine Gagné, ibid., p. 30, 84, 178.

33. See Janet Webb and David Cleary, *Organizational Change and the Management of Expertise,* (London: Routledge, 1994).

34. For a more complete analysis of "the leaders' new work," see Peter Senge, *The Fifth Discipline: The Art and Practice of the Learning Organization* (New York: Doubleday, 1990).

35. Christopher A. Bartlett and Sumantra Goshal, "Matrix Management: Not a Frame of Mind," *Harvard Business Review,* July 1990, pp. 142–43.

36. For example, the OSCE instituted a training program for prospective mission members for their Missions of Long Duration for the first time in 1996, although such missions were first instituted ca. 1991, and even then, it was paid for by the Swiss government who served as chairman in office. See Note 81 in Chigas's chapter on the OSCE in Chayes and Chayes, eds.

37. Graham Allison, *The Essence of Decision: Explaining the Cuban Missile Crisis* (Boston: Little Brown and Co., 1971).

38. Christine Cervanak, "A Case Study of Organizational Interaction in El Salvador," 1991–1994 (Cambridge, Mass.: Conflict Management Group, unpublished paper, 1996), pp. 80–86.

39. Alvaro de Soto and Graciana del Castillo "Obstacles to Peacebuilding," *Foreign Policy,* No. 94 (Spring 1995), pp. 69–70.

40. Susan Woodward, *Implementing the Peace in Bosnia and Herzegovina: A Post-Dayton Primer and Memorandum of Warning* (Washington, D.C.: The Brookings Institution, 1996), p. 38.

41. See UN Charter, art. 57, 63, 64.

42. The IASC is chaired by DHA and composed of DHA, UNDP, UNICEF, WFP, DPA, International Organization for Migration, with ICRC and the International Federation of Red Cross/Red Crescent, and /International Committee for Volunteer Agencies participating as observers.

43. Ibid., Art. 71.

44. Although he must obtain the consent of the government, this is usually forthcoming without difficulty, since the government is loathe to offend the parent organization, the OSCE.

45. See Diana Chigas, with Elizabeth McClintock and Christophe Kamp, "Preventive Diplomacy and the Organization for Security and Cooperation in Europe: Creating Incentives for Dialogue and Cooperation," in Abram Chayes and Antonia Handler Chayes, eds., *Preventing Conflict in the Post Communist World: Mobilizing International and Regional Organizations* (Washington, D.C.: Brookings Institution, 1996), pp. 51–56.

46. John L. Hirsch and Robert B Oakley, *Somalia and Operation Restore Hope: Reflections on Peacemaking and Peacekeeping* (Washington, D.C.: U.S. Institute of Peace, 1995), pp. 67–69; Interviews with Ambassador Oakley, April 1996.

47. Abram Chayes, Thomas Erlich, and Andreas F. Lowenfeld, "Judicial Review by the International Court of Justice: Certain Expenses of the United Nations," in *International Legal Process: Materials for an Introductory Course* (Boston, Mass.: Little Brown and Company, 1968), pp. 176–89.

48. See Susan Woodward, *Implementing the Peace in Bosnia and Herzegovina: A Post-Dayton Primer and Memorandum of Warning* (Washington, D.C.: The Brookings Institution, 1996); Confidential interviews with American and European officials, March 1996.

49. In his article, Ambassador Yasushi Akashi adds economic reconstruction as one of the objectives recast in the field. See Akashi, "The Limits of UN Diplomacy and the Future of Conflict Mediation," *Survival*, Winter 1995–1996, pp. 83, 87–89.

50. DHA has a broad mandate to coordinate the activities of both UN and non-UN agencies responding to humanitarian disasters of all kinds. Despite significant potential, its efforts have often fallen short of the mark because of inadequate financial and staffing resources, bureaucratic infighting among UN offices, resistance from external agencies and organizations, and lack of meaningful support from the major powers. See Roger A. Coate, ed., *U.S. Policy and the Future of the United Nations* (New York: The Twentieth Century Fund Press, 1994), pp. 10, 232–34.

51. David Rieff, "Whose Internationalism, Whose Isolationism," *World Policy Journal*, Vol. 13, No. 2 (Spring 1996), pp. 1–11.

52. Susan Woodward, *Implementing the Peace in Bosnia and Herzegovina: A Post-Dayton Primer and Memorandum of Warning* (Washington, D.C.: The Brookings Institution, 1996), p. 15.

53. Ibid., pp. 14–15; confidential interviews by the authors at NATO Headquarters.

54. Confidential interview by the authors at the European Commission, March 1996.

55. Taylor Seybolt, *International Response to the War and Genocide in Rwanda* (Cambridge, Mass.: Conflict Management Group, unpublished paper, 1996), pp. 20–21, 37.

56. Confidential interview with OSCE official, March 1996.

57. Confidential interview with UN official, March 1996; Noah Rubins, "Organizational Interaction and Conflict in the Georgian Republic" (Cambridge, Mass.: Conflict Management Group, unpublished paper, 1996).

Informal Mediation by the Scholar/Practitioner[1]

HERBERT C. KELMAN

Introduction

For some years, I have been actively engaged in the development and application of an approach to the resolution of international conflicts for which I use the term "interactive problem solving." The fullest—indeed, the paradigmatic—application of the approach is represented by problem-solving workshops,[2] although it involves a variety of other activities as well. In fact, I have increasingly come to see interactive problem solving as an approach to the macroprocesses of international conflict resolution, in which problem-solving workshops and similar microlevel activities are integrally related to official diplomacy. The approach derives most directly from the work of John Burton.[3] While my work follows the general principles laid out by Burton, it has evolved in its own directions, in keeping with my own disciplinary background, my particular style, and the cases on which I have focused my attention. My work has concentrated since 1974 on the Arab-Israeli conflict, and particularly on the Israeli-Palestinian component of that conflict. I have also done some work, however, on the Cyprus conflict and have maintained an active interest in several other intense, protracted identity conflicts at the international or intercommunal level.

Interactive Problem Solving

Interactive problem solving—as manifested particularly in problem-solving workshops—is an academically based, unofficial third-party approach, bringing together representatives of parties in conflict for direct communication. The third party typically consists of a panel of social scientists who, among them, possess expertise in group process and international conflict, and at least some familiarity with the conflict region. The role of the third party in our model differs from that of the traditional mediator. Unlike many mediators, we do not propose (and certainly, unlike arbitrators, we do not impose) solutions. Rather, we try to facilitate a process whereby solutions will emerge out of the interaction between the parties themselves. The task of the third party is to provide the setting, create the atmosphere, establish the norms, and offer occasional interventions that make it possible for such a process to evolve.

Although the distinguishing feature of the approach (in contrast, for example, to traditional mediation) is direct communication between the parties, the objective is not to promote communication or dialogue as an end in itself. Problem-solving workshops are designed to promote a special type of communication—which I shall try to describe below—with a very specific political purpose. Problem-solving workshops are closely linked to the larger political process. Selection of participants and definition of the agenda, for example, are based on careful analysis of the current political situation within and between the conflicting parties. Moreover, the objective of workshops is to generate inputs into the political process, including the decision-making process itself and the political debate within each of the communities. Most broadly stated, workshops try to contribute to creating a political environment conducive to conflict resolution and to transformation of the relationship between the conflicting parties—both in the short term and in the long term.

Practically speaking, this emphasis usually means that problem-solving workshops are closely linked to negotiation in its various phases, although negotiation does not by any means fully encompass the process of changing international relationships.[4] In our work on the Israeli-Palestinian conflict over the years, problem-solving workshops have in essence been designed as contributions to a prenegotiation process: to creating the conditions that would enable the parties to move toward the negotiating table. Thus, in planning and following up on workshops, our focus has always been on the barriers that have stood in the way of opening negotiations and on ways of overcoming such barriers—for example, through mutual reassurance. Despite the close link between workshops and negotiations, we have been very clear in emphasizing that workshops are not to be confused with negotiations as such. They are not meant to be negotiations, or simulated negotiations, or rehearsals for negotiations, nor are they meant to serve as substitutes for negotiations. Rather, they are meant to be complementary to negotiations.

Binding agreements can only be achieved through official negotiations. The very binding character of official negotiations, however, makes it very difficult for certain other things to happen in that context—such as the exploration and discovery of the parties' basic concerns, their priorities, their limits. This is where problem-solving workshops—precisely because of their nonbinding character—can make a special contribution to the larger process of negotiation and conflict resolution. This special relationship to the negotiation process underlines one of the central difference between interactive problem solving and traditional mediation: unlike traditional mediation, problem-solving workshops are not designed to facilitate or influence the actual process of negotiation directly, although they do play a significant indirect role. Insofar as we mediate, it is not between the negotiators representing the two parties, but between their political communities. What we try to facilitate is not the process of negotiation itself, but communication that helps the parties overcome the political, emotional, and at times technical barriers that often prevent them from entering into negotiations, from reaching agreements in the course of negotiations, or from changing their relationship after a political agreement has been negotiated.

Central Features of Problem-Solving Workshops

To give the reader a more concrete image of problem-solving workshops, I shall begin by describing the format of a typical workshop. I want to stress, however, that most workshops are in fact "atypical" in one or more respects. Workshops conform to a set of fundamental principles, but they vary in some of their details, depending on the particular occasion, purpose, and set of participants. What I am presenting, then, is a composite picture, which most workshops approximate but do not necessarily correspond to in toto.

Most of our workshops have been held at Harvard University, under the auspices of the Center for International Affairs or in the context of my graduate seminar on international conflict. Workshop sessions usually take place in a seminar room, with participants seated at a round table, although in some cases, we have used a living-room setting or a private meeting room at a hotel. The typical workshop is a private, confidential event, without audience or observers. The discussions are not taped, but members of the third party take handwritten notes.

Participants in an Israeli-Palestinian workshop usually include three to six members of each party, as well as three to eight third-party members. The numbers have been smaller on some occasions. For example, I have arranged a number of one-on-one meetings, with the participation of one or two third-party members. These meetings have served important purposes and have retained many important features of problem-solving workshops, although one major feature—intraparty interaction—is obviously missing. In quite a few of our workshops, the size of the third party has been larger than eight. As an integral feature of my graduate seminar on international conflict, I have been organizing an annual workshop, in which the seminar participants—usually about twenty in number—serve as apprentice members of the third party. Only eight third-party members sit around the table at any one session, however: three "permanent" members (including myself and two colleagues with workshop experience) and five seminar participants on a rotating basis. When they are not around the table, the seminar participants are able to follow the proceedings (with the full knowledge of the parties, of course) from an adjoining room with a one-way mirror. Although they are not always around the table, the seminar participants are fully integrated into the third party; they take part in all of the workshop activities (preworkshop sessions, briefings, breaks, meals, a social gathering) and are always bound by the requirements and discipline of the third-party role. It should be noted that—apart from the large size of the third party—the workshops linked to my graduate seminar are similar to "regular" workshops in their purpose and format, and are widely seen as not just academic exercises, but serious political encounters.

The Israeli and Palestinian participants in workshops are all politically active and involved members of the mainstream of their respective communities. Many, by virtue of their positions or general standing, can be described as politically influential. Depending on the occasion and the political level of the participants, we may discuss our plans for a workshop with relevant elements of the political leadership on both sides, in order to keep them informed, gain their support, and solicit their advice on participants and agenda. For many potential workshop participants, approval and at times encouragement from the political leadership is a necessary condition for their agreement to take part. Recruitment, however, is generally done on an individual basis and participants are invited to come as individuals rather than as formal representatives. Invitees, of course, may consult with their leadership or with each other before agreeing to come. Whenever possible, we start the recruitment process with one key person on each side; we then consult with that person and with each successive invitee in selecting the rest of the team. At times, the composition of a team may be negotiated within the particular community (or subcommunity) that we approach, but the final invitation is always issued by the third party to each individual participant.

As an essential part of the recruitment process, I almost always discuss the purposes, procedures, and ground rules of the workshop personally with each participant before obtaining his or her final commitment. Whenever possible, this is done during a face-to-face meeting, although at times it is necessary to do it over the telephone. In addition to the individual briefings, we generally organize two preworkshop sessions, in which the members of each party meet separately with the third party. In these sessions, which generally last four to five hours, we first review the purposes, procedures, and ground rules of the workshop. We then ask the participants to talk about their side's perspective on the conflict, the range of views within their community, the current status of the conflict as they see it and the conditions and possibilities for resolving it, and their conceptions of the needs and positions of the other side. We encourage the participants to discuss these issues among themselves. We make it clear that the role of the third party—even in the preworkshop session—is to facilitate the exchange, in part through occasional questions and comments, but not to enter into the substantive discussion or to debate and evaluate what is being said.

The preworkshop sessions fulfill a number of important functions. They provide an opportunity for the participants to become acquainted with the setting, the third party, and those members of their own team whom they had not previously met, without having to confront the other party at the same time; to raise questions about the purposes, procedures, and ground rules of the workshop; to begin to practice the type of discourse that the workshop is trying to encourage; to gain a better understanding of the role of the third party; and to "do their duty" by telling the third party their side of the story and enumerating their grievances, thus reducing the pressure to adhere to the conflict norms in the course of the workshop itself. The preworkshop sessions also give the third party an opportunity to observe some of the internal differences within each team, and to compare the ways in which the parties treat the issues when they are alone and when they are together.

The workshops themselves generally last two-and-a-half days, often taking place over an extended weekend. The opening session, typically late Friday afternoon, begins with a round of introductions, in which the participants are encouraged to go beyond their professional credentials and say something about their reasons for coming. We then review, once again, the purposes, procedures, and ground rules of the workshop, stressing the principles of privacy and confidentiality, the nature of the discourse that we are trying to encourage, and the role of the third party. This review, in the presence of all of the participants, serves to emphasize the nature of the contract to which all three parties are committing themselves. After dinner, shared by the entire group, we reconvene for the first substantive session. On the second day, we have two sessions (each lasting one and a half hours) in the morning, with a half-hour coffee break in between. The same pattern is repeated after lunch. That evening, there is a dinner and social gathering for all participants, typically held at the home of the Kelmans. On the third day, there are again two sessions in the morning and two in the afternoon, and the workshop closes late that afternoon. Thus, in addition to the ten sessions around the table, the workshops provide ample opportunities for informal interaction during meals and coffee breaks. Sometimes participants create additional opportunities for themselves.

In opening the first substantive session, the third party—after describing the political context and the focus of the workshop—proposes a loose agenda. The specific agenda must depend, of course, on the stage of the conflict and the character of the group. The agenda followed in most of our workshops so far are appropriate for initial workshops (i.e., workshops whose participants are convening for the first time as a group) in a conflict that is still in a prenegotiation phase (like the Israeli–Palestinian conflict). The main task that we have set for our workshop participants in recent years has been to generate—through their interaction—ideas for bringing the parties to the negotiating table. To get the interaction started, we ask the participants to describe their view of the conflict and its current status, to define the spectrum of positions vis-à-vis the conflict in their own societies, and to place themselves along that spectrum. We try to move as rapidly as possible from this more conventional, descriptive discussion into the analytic, problem-solving mode of interaction that is at the heart of the agenda. First, we ask the participants on both sides to talk about their central concerns: the fundamental needs that an agreement would have to satisfy and the fundamental fears that it would have to allay in order to be acceptable to their communities. Only after both sets of concerns are on the table and each side's concerns have been understood by the other, are the participants asked to explore the overall shape of a solution that would meet the needs and calm the fears of both sides. Each is expected to think actively about solutions that would be satisfactory to the other, not only to themselves. Next, the participants are asked to discuss the political and psychological constraints that make it difficult to implement such solutions. Finally, the discussion turns to the question of how these constraints can best be overcome and how the two sides can support each other in such an effort. Depending on how much time is left and on the prevailing mood, the participants may try to come up with concrete ideas for unilateral, coordinated, or joint actions—by themselves or their communities—that might help overcome the barriers to negotiating a mutually satisfactory solution.

The agenda described here is not followed rigidly, but rather serves as a broad framework for the interaction. The discussions are relatively unstructured and, insofar as possible, are allowed to maintain their natural flow. We are careful not to intervene excessively or prematurely, and not to cut off potentially fruitful discussions because they appear to be deviating from the agenda. If the discussion goes too far afield, becomes repetitive, or systematically avoids the issues, the third party—usually with the help of at least some of the participants—will try to bring it back to the broad agenda. In general, the third party is prepared to intervene in order to help keep the discussion moving along productive, constructive channels. At times, particularly at the beginning or at the end of sessions, we also make substantive interventions, in order to help interpret, integrate, clarify, or sharpen what is being said or done in the group. On the whole, however, the emphasis in our model is on facilitating the emergence of ideas out of the interaction between the participants themselves. Consistent with that emphasis, we try to stay in the background as much as possible once we have set the stage.

Having drawn a general picture of the format and proceedings of a typical workshop, let me now highlight some of the special features of the approach.

Academic Context

In the work of my colleagues and myself, our academic base serves as the major venue of our activities and source of our authority and credibility. The academic context has several advantages for our enterprise. It allows the parties to interact with each other in a relatively noncommittal way, since the setting is not only unofficial, but also known as one in which people engage in free exchange of views, in playful consideration of new ideas, and in "purely academic" discussions. Thus, an academic setting is a good place to set into motion a process of successive approximations, in which parties that do not trust each other begin to communicate in a noncommittal framework, but gradually move to increasing levels of commitment as their level of working trust increases.[5] Another advantage of the academic context is that it allows us to call upon an alternative set of norms to counteract the norms that typically govern interactions between conflicting parties. Academic norms favor open discussion, attentive listening to opposing views, and an analytical approach, in contrast to the polemical, accusatory, and legalistic approach that conflict norms tend to promote.

Nature of Interaction

The setting, norms, ground rules, agenda, procedures, and third-party interventions in problem-solving workshops are all designed to facilitate a kind of interaction that differs from the way parties in conflict usually interact—if they interact at all. Within the workshop setting, participants are encouraged to talk to each other, rather than to their constituencies or to third parties, and to listen to each other—not in order to discover the weaknesses in the other's argument, but in order to penetrate the other's perspective. The principles of privacy and confidentiality—apart from protecting the interests of the participants—are designed to protect this process, by reducing the participants' concern about how each word they say during the workshop will be perceived on the outside. In order to counteract the tendency to speak to the record, we have avoided creating a record, in the form of audio or videotapes or formal minutes. The absence of an audience, and the third party's refusal to take sides, to evaluate what is said, to adjudicate differences, or to become involved in the debate of substantive issues, further encourage the parties to focus on each other, rather than attempt to influence external parties. These features of the workshop are in no way designed to help the participants forget about their constituencies or, for that matter, about relevant third parties; ideas generated in workshops must be acceptable to the two communities, as well as to outside actors, if they are to have the desired impact on the political process. Rather, these features are designed to prevent the intrusion of these actors into the workshop interaction itself, thus inhibiting and distorting the generation of new ideas.

A second central element in the nature of the interaction that workshops try to promote is an analytic focus. Workshop discussions are analytical in the sense that participants try to gain a better understanding of the other's—and indeed of their own—concerns, needs, fears, priorities, and constraints, and of the way in which the divergent perspectives of the parties help to feed and escalate their conflict. It is particularly important for each party to gain an understanding of the other's perspective (without accepting that perspective) and of the domestic dynamics that shape the policy debate in each community. To appreciate the constraints under which the other operates is especially difficult in a conflict relationship, since the parties' thinking tends to be dominated by their own constraints. But an analytic understanding of the constraints—along with the fundamental concerns—that inform the other's perspective is a sine qua non for inventing solutions that are feasible and satisfactory for both sides.

Analytical discussions proceed on the basis of a "no fault" principle. While there is no presumption that both sides are equally at fault, the discussions are not oriented toward assigning blame, but toward exploring the causes of the conflict and the obstacles to its resolution. This analytical approach is designed to lead to a problem-solving mode of interaction, based on the proposition that the conflict represents a joint problem for the two parties that requires joint efforts at solution.

Dual Purpose

Workshops have a dual purpose, which can be described as educational and political. They are designed to produce both changes in attitudes, perceptions, and ideas for resolving the conflict among the individual participants in the workshop, and transfer of these changes to the political arena—i.e., to the political debate and the decision-making process within each community. The political purpose is an integral part of the workshop approach, whatever the level of the participants involved. Workshops provide opportunities for the parties to interact, to become acquainted with each other, and to humanize their mutual images, not as ends in themselves, but as means to producing new learnings that can then be fed into the political process. Some of the specific learnings that participants have acquired in the course of workshops and then communicated to their own political leaderships or publics have included: information about the range of views on the other side, signs of readiness for negotiation, and the availability of potential negotiating partners; insights into the other side's priorities, rock-bottom requirements, and areas of flexibility; and ideas for confidence-building measures, mutually acceptable solutions to issues in conflict, and ways of moving to the negotiating table.

Because of their dual purpose, problem-solving workshops are marked by a dialectical character.[6] Some of the conditions favorable to change in the workshop setting may be antagonistic to the transfer of changes to the political arena, and vice versa. There is often a need, therefore, to find the proper balance between contradictory requirements if a workshop is to be effective in fulfilling both its educational and its political purpose. For example, it is important for the participants to develop a considerable degree of working trust in order to engage in joint problem solving, to devise direct or tacit collaborative efforts for overcoming constraints against negotiation, and to become convinced that there are potential negotiating partners on the other side. This trust, however, must not be allowed to turn into excessive camaraderie transcending the conflict, lest the participants lose their credibility and their potential political influence once they return to their home communities. Workshops can be seen as part of a process of building a coalition across the conflict line, but it must remain an uneasy coalition that does not threaten members' relationship to their own identity groups.[7]

The selection of participants provides another example of a central workshop feature for which the dialectics of the process have important implications. The closer the participants are to the centers of power in their own communities, the greater the likelihood that what they learn in the course of their workshop experience will be fed directly into the decision-making process. By the same token, however, the closer participants are to the centers of power, the more constrained they are likely to feel, and the greater their difficulty in entering into communication that is open, noncommittal, exploratory, and analytical. Thus, on the whole, as participants move closer to the level of top decision makers, they become less likely to show change as a result of their workshop experience, but whatever changes do occur are more likely to be transferred to the policy process. These contradictory effects have to be taken into account in selecting participants for a given occasion, *or* in defining the goals and agenda for a workshop with a given set of participants. In general, the best way to balance the requirements for change and for transfer is to select participants who are politically influential but not directly involved in the execution of foreign policy.

The workshops and related encounters that I have organized over the years have included participants at three different levels of relationship to the decision-making process: political actors, such as parliamentarians, party activists, or advisers to political leaders; political influentials, such as senior academics (who are leading analysts of the conflict in their own communities and occasional advisers to decision makers), community leaders, writers, or editors; and preinfluentials, such as younger academics and professionals or advanced graduate students, who are slated to move into influential positions in their respective fields. The lines between these three categories are not very precise; moreover, many participants who may have been "preinfluentials" at the time of their workshop have since become influential, and some of our "influentials" have since become political actors. Whatever the level of the participants, a central criterion for selection is that they be politically involved—at least as active participants in the political debate and perhaps in political movements. From our point of view, even this degree of involvement is of direct political relevance since it contributes to the shaping of the political environment for any peace effort. Another criterion for selection is that participants be part of the mainstream of their community and that they enjoy credibility within broad segments of that community. We look for participants who are as close as possible to the center of the political spectrum, while at the same time are interested in negotiations and open to the workshop process. As a result, workshop participants so far have tended to be on the dovish ("moderate" or pro-negotiation) side of the center.

Third-Party Contributions

Although workshops proceed on the principle that useful ideas for conflict resolution must emerge out of the interaction between the parties themselves, the third party plays an essential role (at certain stages of a conflict) in making that interaction possible and fruitful. The third party provides the context in which representatives of parties engaged in an intense conflict are able to come together. It selects, briefs, and convenes the participants. It serves as a repository of trust for both parties, enabling them to proceed with the assurance that their confidentiality will be respected and their interests protected even though—by definition—they cannot trust each other. It establishes and enforces the norms and ground rules that facilitate analytic discussion and a problem-solving orientation. It proposes a broad agenda that encourages the parties to move from exploration of each other's concerns and constraints to the generation of ideas for win/win solutions and for implementing such solutions. It tries to keep the discussion moving in constructive directions. And, finally, it makes occasional substantive interventions in the form of *content observations,* which suggest interpretations and implications of what is being said and point to convergences and divergences between the parties, to blind spots, to possible signals, and to issues for clarification; *process observations* at the intergroup level, which suggest possible ways in which interactions between the parties "here and now" may reflect the dynamics of the conflict between their communities; and *theoretical inputs,* which help participants distance themselves from their own conflict, provide them conceptual tools for analysis of their conflict, and offer them relevant illustrations from previous research.

Process observations are among the unique features of problem-solving workshops. They generally focus on incidents in which one party's words or actions clearly have a strong emotional impact on the other—leading to expressions of anger and dismay, of relief and reassurance, of understanding and acceptance, or of reciprocation. The third party can use such incidents, which are part of the participants' shared immediate experience, as a springboard for exploring some of the issues and concerns that define the conflict between their societies. Through such exploration, each side can gain some insight into the preoccupation of the other, and the way these are affected by its own actions. Process observations must be introduced sparingly and make special demands on the third party's skill and sense of timing. It is particularly important that such interventions be pitched at the intergroup, rather than the interpersonal level. Analysis of "here and now" interactions is not concerned with the personal characteristics of the participants or with their personal relations to each other, but only with what these interactions can tell us about the relationship between their national groups.

Social-Psychological Assumptions

The practice of interactive problem solving is informed by a set of assumptions about the nature of international/intercommunal conflict and conflict resolution. These assumptions are meant to be general in nature, although they may not be equally applicable in all cases. The problem-solving approach is likely to be most relevant in those conflicts to which these assumptions most clearly apply.

In my particular conception of the problem-solving approach, the guiding assumptions, derive from a social-psychological analysis, which provides a bridge between individual behavior and social interaction, on the one hand, and the functioning of social systems (organizations, institutions, societies) and collectivities, on the other. Social-psychological assumptions enter into our formulation of the structure, the process, and the content of problem-solving workshops.

Workshop Structure

By workshop structure I refer primarily to the role of workshops in the larger political context and their place within the social system in which the conflict is carried on. In effect, the focus here is on the relationship between the microprocess of the workshop and the macroprocess of conflict management or resolution.

Several assumptions underlie our view of this relationship and hence the way in which workshops are structured.

(1) I view international conflict as not merely an intergovernmental or interstate phenomenon, but also an intersocietal phenomenon. Thus, in addition to the strategic, military, and diplomatic dimensions, it is necessary to give central consideration to the economic, psychological, cultural, and social-structural dimensions in the analysis of the conflict. Interactions along these dimensions, both within and between the conflicting societies, form the essential political environment in which governments function. It is necessary to look at these intrasocietal and intersocietal processes in order to understand the political constraints under which governments operate and the resistance to change that these produce. By the same token, these societal factors, if properly understood and utilized, provide opportunities and levers for change.

This view has a direct implication for the selection of workshop participants. To be politically relevant, workshops do not require the participation of decision makers or their agents. In fact, as I argued in my earlier discussion of the dual purposes and dialectical character of workshops, the ideal participants may be individuals who are politically influential but not directly involved in the foreign-policy decision-making process. The important consideration is that they be active and credible contributors to the political debate within their own communities and thus can play a role in changing the political environment.

Another implication of the view of international conflict as an intersocietal phenomenon is that third-party efforts should ideally be directed not merely to a *settlement* of the conflict, but to its *resolution*. A political agreement may be adequate for terminating relatively specific, containable interstate disputes, but it is an inadequate response to conflicts that engage the collective identities and existential concerns of the societies involved.

(2) Following from the stress on the intersocietal nature of conflict is the assumption that conflict resolution represents an effort to transform the relationship between the conflicting parties. This assumption has direct implications for the type of solutions that third-party intervention tries to generate. First, solutions must emerge out of the interaction between the parties themselves: the process of interactive problem solving itself contributes to transformation of the relationship between the parties. Second, solutions must address the needs of both parties, thus providing the foundation of a new relationship between them. Finally, the nature of the solutions and the process by which they were achieved must be such that the parties will be committed to them: only thus can they establish a new relationship on a long-term basis.

(3) Another corollary of the stress on the intersocietal nature of conflict is the view of diplomacy as a broad and complex mix of official and unofficial processes. The peaceful termination or management of conflicts requires binding agreements

that can only be achieved at the official level. Unofficial interactions, however, can play a constructive complementary role, particularly by contributing to the development of a political environment conducive to negotiations and other diplomatic initiatives.[8] Problem-solving workshops and other informal efforts, as I pointed out earlier, can make such contributions precisely because of their nonbinding character. In such settings—in contrast to official fora—it is much easier for the parties to engage in noncommittal, exploratory interactions, which allow them, for example, to test each other's limits, to develop empathy, or to engage in creative problem solving. Accordingly, many of the features of problem-solving workshops are specifically geared to maximizing the noncommittal nature of the interaction: the academic context; the assurance of privacy and confidentiality; the eschewing of expectations of specific products; and the emphasis on interactions characterized by exploration, sharing of perspectives, playing with ideas, brainstorming, and creative problem solving—rather than negotiation.

(4) A further assumption relates to the interplay between intragroup and intergroup conflict. In many international and intercommunal conflicts, internal divisions within each party shape the course of the conflict between the parties. This phenomenon represents a special instance of the general observations of continuities between domestic and international politics. Understanding of the internal divisions within each party is essential to the selection of workshop participants, since the political significance of workshops depends on the potential impact these participants can have on the internal debate. The internal divisions in each society are also a major focus of concern within workshops, particularly when the discussion turns to the political and psychological constraints against compromise solutions and ways of overcoming these constraints.

More generally, I have already alluded to my conceptualization[9] of workshops and related activities as part of a process of forming a coalition across the conflict line—a coalition between those elements on each side that are interested in a negotiated solution. It is very important to keep in mind, however, that such a coalition must of necessity *remain* an uneasy coalition. If it became overly cohesive, it would undermine the whole purpose of the enterprise: to have an impact on the political decisions within the two communities. Workshop participants who become closely identified with their counterparts on the other side may become alienated from their own conationals, lose credibility, and hence forfeit their political effectiveness and their ability to promote a new consensus within their own communities. One of the challenges for problem-solving workshops, therefore, is to create an atmosphere in which participants can begin to humanize and trust each other and to develop an effective collaborative relationship, without losing sight of their separate group identities and the conflict between their communities.

(5) At the broadest level, my assumptions about international and intercommunal conflict rest on a view of the world system as a global society—a term that I use not only normatively, but also descriptively. To be sure, the global society is a weak

society, lacking many of the customary features of a society. Still, conceiving of the world as a society corrects for the untenable view of nation states as sole and unitary actors in the global arena. Clearly, nation–states remain the dominant actors within our current global society. The nation–state benefits from the principle of sovereignty and from its claim to represent its population's national identity—perhaps the most powerful variant of group identity in the modern world. (In intercommunal conflicts within established nation–states, the ethnic community is seen as representing the central element of identity and seeks to restructure, take over, or separate from the existing state in order to give political expression to that identity.) Despite the dominance of the nation–state, the world system has many of the characteristics of a society: it is formed by a multiplicity of actors, including—in addition to nation–states—individuals in their diverse roles, as well as a variety of subnational and supranational groups; it is marked by an ever-increasing degree of interdependence between its component parts; it is divided along many complex lines, with the nation–state representing perhaps the most powerful, but certainly not the only cutting line; and it contains numerous relationships that cut across nation–state lines, including relations based on ethnicity, religion, ideology, occupation, and economic interests. The embeddedness of the nation state in a global society, in which ethnic and other bonds cut across nation–state lines, accounts in large part for the continuity between the domestic and foreign policies of the modern state.

The view of the world system as a global society provides several angles for understanding the role of interactive problem solving within a larger context of conflict resolution. First, the concept of a global society with its emphasis on interdependence suggests the need for alternative conceptions of national and international security, which involve arrangements for common security and mechanisms for the nonviolent conduct, management, and resolution of conflicts. Such arrangements and mechanisms, in turn, call for the development of governmental, intergovernmental, and nongovernmental institutions to embody the emerging new conceptions of security. Interactive problem solving can be seen as the germ of an independent (nongovernmental) institutional mechanism, which can contribute to security through the nonviolent resolution of conflicts. Second, by focusing on multiple actors and crosscutting relationships, the concept of a global society encourages us to think of unofficial diplomacy in all of its varieties as an integral part of diplomacy and of a larger process of conflict resolution, and not just as a side show (as it tends to be viewed in a state-centered model). Finally, the multiple-actor framework central to the concept of a global society provides a place for the individual as a relevant actor in international relations. Interactive problem solving uses the individual as the unit of analysis in the effort to understand resistances to change in a conflict relationship despite changes in realities and interests, and in the search for solutions that would satisfy the human needs of the parties. Moreover, interactive problem solving is a systematic attempt to promote change at the level of individuals (in the form of new insights and ideas) as a vehicle for change at the system level.

Workshop Process

Several social-psychological assumptions underlie our view of the kind of interaction process that workshops are designed to promote.

(1) One assumption follows directly from the structural analysis that has just been presented—i.e., from the role of workshops in the larger political context. Somewhere within the larger framework of conflict resolution, there must be a place for direct, bilateral interaction between the parties centrally involved in a given conflict—such as the Israelis and the Palestinians, or the Greek and the Turkish Cypriots. Such direct, bilateral interactions are not a substitute for the multilateral efforts that are almost invariably required for the resolution of protracted conflicts. Greece and Turkey cannot be excluded from negotiations of the Cyprus conflict, nor can the Arab states and the superpowers be bypassed in efforts to resolve the Israeli-Palestinian dispute. Within this larger framework, however, there must be an opportunity for the parties immediately involved—the parties that ultimately have to live with each other—to penetrate each other's perspective and to engage in joint problem solving designed to produce ideas for a mutually satisfactory agreement between them.

Opportunities for interaction at the microlevel can also contribute some of the needed interactive elements at the macrolevel: a binocular orientation, such that each party can view the situation from the other's perspective as well as from its own; a recognition of the need for reciprocity in the process and outcome of negotiations; and a focus on building a new relationship between the parties.

(2) A second assumption underlying the workshop process is that products of social interaction have an emergent character. In the course of direct interaction, the parties are able to observe at first hand their differing reactions to the same events and the different perspectives these reflect; the differences between the way they perceive themselves and the way the other perceives them; and the impact that their statements and actions have on each other. Out of these observations, they can jointly shape new insights and ideas that could not have been predicted from what they brought to the interaction. Certain kinds of solutions to the conflict can emerge only from the confrontation of assumptions, concerns, and identities during face-to-face communication.

The emergence of ideas for solutions to the conflict out of the interaction between the parties (in contrast, for example, to ideas proposed by third parties) has several advantages. Such ideas are more likely to be responsive to the fundamental needs and fears of both parties; the parties are more likely to feel committed to the solutions they produce themselves; and the process of producing these ideas in itself contributes to building a new relationship between the parties.

In keeping with our assumption about the emergent character of interaction, we pay attention to the nature of the discourse during workshops.[10] How does the way parties talk to each other change over the course of the workshop? What are the critical moments in a workshop that have an impact on the continuing interaction? How do new joint ideas come to be formulated in the course of the interaction?

(3) Workshops are designed to promote a special kind of interaction or discourse that can contribute to the desired political outcome. As noted in the earlier discussion of the nature of the interaction, the setting, ground rules, and procedures of problem-solving workshops encourage (and permit) interaction marked by the following elements: an emphasis on addressing each other (rather than one's constituencies, or third parties, or the record) and on listening to each other; analytical discussion; adherence to a "no-fault" principle; and a problem-solving mode of interaction. This kind of interaction allows the parties to explore each other's concerns, penetrate each other's perspectives, and take cognizance of each other's constraints. As a result, they are able to offer each other the needed reassurances to engage in negotiation and to come up with solutions responsive to both sides' needs and fears.

The nature of the interaction fostered in problem-solving workshops has some continuities with a therapeutic model.[11] The influence of the therapeutic model can be seen particularly in the facilitative role of the third party, the analytical character of the discourse, and the use of "here and now" experiences as a basis for learning about the dynamics of the conflict (as mentioned in the earlier discussion of process observations). It is also important, however, to keep in mind the limited applicability of a therapeutic model to problem-solving workshops. For example, the focus of workshops is not on individuals and their interpersonal relations, but on what can be learned from their interaction about the dynamics of the conflict between their communities. Furthermore, there is no assumption that nations can be viewed as equivalent to individuals or that conflict resolution is a form of therapy for national groups.

(4) The workshop process is predicated on the assumption that the interaction between conflicting parties is governed by a set of "conflict norms" that contribute significantly to escalation and perpetuation of the conflict. There is a need, therefore, for interactions based on an alternative set of norms conducive to deescalation. Workshops are designed to provide an opportunity for this kind of interaction. As noted earlier, the academic context provides an alternative set of norms on which the interaction between the parties can proceed. The ground rules for interaction within the workshop make it both possible and necessary for participants to abide by these alternative norms. The safe environment of the workshop and the principle of privacy and confidentiality provide the participants with the protection they need to be able to deviate from the conflict norms.

(5) Finally, workshops operationalize a process that is social-psychological par excellence: a process designed to produce change in individuals as a vehicle for change in policies and actions of the political system. Thus, workshops have a dual purpose—educational and political, or change and transfer—as discussed above in

some detail. This dual purpose at times creates conflicting requirements that have to be balanced in order to fulfill both sets of purposes. I have already illustrated how such conflicts may affect the selection of workshop participants and the atmosphere of trust that workshops seek to engender. The relationship between change at the individual level and at the system level—which often lends a dialectical character to problem-solving workshops—is at the heart of the workshop process.

Workshop Content

A set of social-psychological assumptions also inform the substantive emphases of workshop discussions. These emphases include human needs, perceptual and cognitive constraints on information processing, and influence processes, as these enter into conflict relationships.

(1) I view the satisfaction of the needs of both parties—as articulated through their core identity groups—as the ultimate criterion in the search for a mutually satisfactory resolution of their conflict.[12] Unfulfilled needs, especially for identity and security, and existential fears typically drive the conflict and create barriers to its resolution. By pushing behind the parties' incompatible positions and exploring the identity and security needs that underlie them, it often becomes possible to develop mutually satisfactory solutions, since identity, security, and other psychological needs are not inherently zero-sum. Workshop interactions around needs and fears enable the parties to find a language and to identify gestures and actions that are conducive to mutual reassurance. Mutual reassurance is a central element of conflict resolution, particularly in existential conflicts where the parties see their group identity, their people's security, their very existence as a nation to be at stake.

(2) The needs and fears of parties involved in a conflict relationship impose perceptual and cognitive constraints on their processing of new information. One of the major effects of these constraints is that the parties systematically underestimate the occurrence and possibility of change and therefore avoid negotiations, even in the face of changing interests that would make negotiations desirable for both. Images of the enemy are particularly resistant to disconfirming information. The combination of demonic enemy images and virtuous self-images on both sides leads to the formation of mirror images, which contribute to the escalatory dynamic of conflict interaction and to resistance to change in a conflict relationship.[13]

By focusing on mutual perceptions, mirror images, and systematic differences in perspective, workshop participants can learn to differentiate the enemy image—a necessary condition for movement toward negotiation.[14] Workshops bring out the symmetries in the parties' images of each other and in their positions and requirements, which arise out of the dynamics of the conflict interaction itself. Such symmetries are often overlooked because of the understandable tendency of protagonists in a conflict relationship to dwell on the asymmetries between them.

Without denying these important asymmetries, both empirical and moral, we focus on symmetries because they tend to be a major source of escalation of conflict (as in the operation of conflict spirals) and reason for making the conflict intractable. By the same token, they can serve as a major vehicle for deescalation by helping the parties penetrate each other's perspective and identify mutually reassuring gestures and actions.[15]

(3) Finally, the content of workshop discussions reflects an assumption about the nature of influence processes in international relations. Workshops are predicated on the view that the range of influence processes employed in conflict relationships must be broadened. It is necessary to move beyond influence strategies based on threats and even to expand and refine strategies based on promises and positive incentives. By searching for solutions that satisfy the needs of both parties, workshops explore the possibility of mutual influence by way of responsiveness to each other's needs. A key element in this process, emphasized throughout this chapter, is mutual reassurance. In existential conflicts, in particular, parties can encourage each other to move to the negotiating table by reducing both sides' fear—not just, as more traditional strategic analysts maintain, by increasing their pain. At the macrolevel, the present approach calls for a shift in emphasis in international influence processes from deterrence and compellence to mutual reassurance. The use of this mode of influence has the added advantage of not only affecting specific behaviors by the other party, but contributing to a transformation of the relationship between the parties.

The expanded conception of influence processes that can be brought to bear in a conflict relationship is based on a view of international conflict as a dynamic phenomenon, emphasizing the occurrence and possibility of change. Conflict resolution efforts are geared, therefore, to discovering possibilities for change, identifying conditions for change, and overcoming resistances to change. such an approach favors "best-case" analyses and an attitude of "strategic optimism,"[16] or possible optimism—not because of an unrealistic denial of malignant trends, but as part of a deliberate strategy to promote change by actively searching for and accentuating whatever realistic possibilities for peaceful resolution of the conflict might be on the horizon. Optimism, in this sense, is part of a strategy designed to create self-fulfilling prophecies of a positive nature, balancing the self-fulfilling prophecies of escalation created by the pessimistic expectations and the worst-case scenarios often favored by more traditional analysts. Problem-solving workshops can be particularly useful in exploring ways in which change can be promoted through the parties' own actions and in discovering ways in which each can exert influence on the other.[17]

Relevance of Interactive Problem Solving

The principles of interactive problem solving have some applicability in a wide range of international conflict situations. Indeed, I would argue that problem-solving workshops and related activities—along with other forms of unofficial diplomacy—should be thought of as integral parts of a larger diplomatic process. This type of intervention can make certain unique contributions to the larger process that are not available through official channels—for example, by providing opportunities for noncommittal exploration of possible ways of getting to the table and of shaping mutually acceptable solutions. Moreover, the assumptions and principles of interactive problem solving can contribute to a reconceptualization of international relationships at the macrolevel by encouraging shifts in the nature of the discourse and the means of influence that characterize international relations today. Nevertheless, it must be said that problem-solving workshops, particularly in the format that has evolved in my style of practice, are more directly relevant in some types of conflict than in others and at certain phases of a given conflict than at others.

Since my primary case has been the Israeli-Palestinian conflict, it would not be surprising if my approach were most relevant to situations that share some of the characteristics of that conflict. I propose that the approach is most relevant to long-standing conflicts, in which the interests of the parties have gradually converged, and large segments of each community perceive this to be the case, but nevertheless they seem to be unable or unwilling to enter into negotiations or to achieve a negotiated agreement. The psychological obstacles to negotiation are not readily overcome despite the changes in realities and in perceived interests.

Interactive problem solving is not *feasible* if there is no interest among the parties—or significant elements within each party—in changing the status quo. It is not *necessary* if there are no profound barriers to negotiations; in that event, other forms of mediation—designed to enhance negotiating skills or to propose reasonable options—may be equally or more useful. However, when the recognition of common interests is insufficient to overcome the psychological barriers, interactive problem solving becomes particularly germane. These conditions are likely to prevail in intense, protracted identity conflicts at the international or intercommunal level, particularly conflicts in which the parties see their national existence to be at stake. The Israeli-Palestinian conflict, the Cyprus conflict, and the conflicts in Northern Ireland, Sri Lanka, and South Africa clearly share these characteristics. There are many other conflicts, however, that can benefit from a process designed to promote mutual reassurance and to help develop a new relationship between conflicting parties that must find a way of living together.

Since the goal of workshops is to help the parties translate their interest in changing the status quo into an effective negotiating process, by overcoming the barriers that stand in the way of such a process, it is necessary to select workshop participants from those segments of the two communities that are indeed interested in a negotiated agreement. They may be skeptical about the possibility of achieving such an agreement and suspicious about the intentions of the other side, but they must have some interest in finding a mutually acceptable way of ending the conflict. In addition, workshop participants must be prepared to meet and talk with members of the other community at a level of equality within the workshop setting, whatever asymmetries in power between the parties may prevail in the relationship between the two communities. Thus,

> participants from the stronger party must be *willing* to deal with the other on a basis of equality, which generally means that they have come to accept the illegitimacy of past patterns of discrimination and domination; participants from the weaker must be *able* to deal with the other on a basis of equality, which generally means that they have reached a stage of confrontation in the conflict.[18]

In their interactions within the workshop setting, it would be inappropriate for members of the stronger party to take advantage of their superior power, as they might in a negotiating situation. By the same token, it would be inappropriate for members of the weaker party to take advantage of their superior moral position in this setting, as they might in a political rally. Workshop interactions are most productive when they are based on the principle of reciprocity.

I emphasized earlier that workshops are not intended to substitute for official negotiations but they may be closely linked to the negotiating process. Our work on the Israeli-Palestinian conflict is primarily a contribution to the prenegotiation process. Thus, workshops have been designed to identify conditions required for negotiation and to help create a political environment conducive to movement toward the negotiating table. Workshops may also be useful, however, at a point in which negotiations are already in progress. For example, as in the Cyprus case, they may provide a noncommittal forum to explore ways of breaking a stalemate that has been reached in the negotiations. They may also allow the parties to work out solutions to specific technical, political, or emotional issues that require an analytical, problem-solving approach; such solutions can then be fed into the formal negotiating process. Finally, workshops may be useful in the postnegotiation phase, when they can help the parties address issues in the implementation of the agreement and explore a new relationship based on patterns of coexistence and cooperation.

The Israeli–Palestinian workshops that we have conducted over the years have suggested some of the ways in which workshops and related activities can contribute to the prenegotiation process, helping the parties to overcome the fears and suspicions that inhibit negotiations and to create the conditions that enable them to enter into negotiations. Workshops can help the participants develop more differentiated images of the enemy and discover potential negotiating partners on the other side, learning that there is someone to talk to on the other side and something to talk about. They can contribute to the development of cadres of individuals who have acquired experience in communicating with the other side and the conviction that such communication can be fruitful. They enable the parties to penetrate each other's perspective, gaining insight into the other's concerns, priorities, and constraints. They increase awareness of change and thus contribute to creating and maintaining a sense of possibility—a belief among the relevant parties that a peaceful solution is attainable and that negotiations toward such a solution are feasible.

Workshops also contribute to creating a political environment conducive to negotiations through the development of a deescalatory language, based on sensitivity to words that frighten and words that reassure the other party. They help in the identification of mutually reassuring actions and symbolic gestures, often in the form of acknowledgments—of the other's humanity, national identity, ties to the land, history of victimization, sense of injustice, genuine fears, and conciliatory moves. They contribute to the development of shared visions of a desirable future, which help reduce the parties' fear of negotiations as a step into an unknown, dangerous, realm. They may generate ideas about the shape of a positive-sum solution that meets the basic needs of both parties. They may also generate ideas about how to get from here to there—about a framework and set of principles for getting negotiations started. Ultimately, problem-solving workshops contribute to a process of transformation of the relationship between enemies.

Development of the Field

Our work in interactive problem solving has recently moved in a new direction, which promises to enhance its contribution to the resolution of the Israeli-Palestinian conflict. For the first time, with the help of several colleagues, I have convened a "continuing workshop."[19] Until now, the workshops and related opportunities for interaction that we organized were all self-contained events. To be sure, there has been continuity in our earlier efforts. A number of individuals have participated in two or more of our workshops. "Alumni" of the workshops also continue to be involved in a variety of other efforts at Israeli-Palestinian communication and collaboration, in which they draw on their earlier interactions. Moreover, our workshops have had a cumulative effect in helping to create a political environment conducive to negotiations, in the various ways described at the end of the last section. Because of logistical and financial constraints, however, I had never attempted to organize a workshop in which the same group of participants would meet regularly over an extended period of time. Such a workshop is now under way.

There are several unique contributions that a continuing workshop can make to the larger political process. It represents a sustained effort to address concrete issues, enabling us to push the process of conflict analysis and interactive problem solving farther and to apply it more systematically than we have been able to do in previous workshops. The longer time period and continuing nature of the enterprise make it possible to go beyond the sharing of perspectives to the joint production of creative ideas. Moreover, the periodic reconvening of a continuing workshop allows for an iterative and cumulative process, based on feedback and correction. The participants have an opportunity to take the ideas developed in the course of a workshop back to their own communities, to gather reactions, and to return to the next meeting with proposals for strengthening, expanding, or modifying the original ideas. It is also possible for participants, within or across parties, to meet or otherwise communicate with each other between workshop sessions in order to work out some of the ideas more fully and bring the results of their efforts back to the next session. Finally, a continuing workshop provides better opportunities to address the question of how to disseminate ideas and proposals developed at the workshop most effectively and appropriately.

The continuing workshop represents an important new phase in an effort that is still at an early stage of development. Only a small number of scholar/practitioners around the world are engaged in this kind of work and the experience they have accumulated is still quite limited.[20] However, the field is maturing. The number of centers devoted to this work is increasing. A new generation is emerging. My students, among others, are actively engaged in research and practice in the field and are taking increasing responsibility for organizing their own projects. By establishing their personal identities as scholar/practitioners in the field, they are giving the field itself an identity of its own. Both the older and the younger generations are building networks, whose members engage in collaborative work and are beginning to think systematically about the further development and institutionalization of problem-solving approaches to the resolution of international conflicts. Among the issues that need to be addressed and that are, indeed, receiving increasing attention are: the evaluation of this form of practice, the training of new scholar/practitioners, the requirements and pitfalls of professionalization, the formulation of principles and standards of ethical practice, and the development of institutional mechanisms that would strengthen the contribution of interactive problem solving to the resolution of intractable conflicts.

Notes

1. This chapter was written while the author was a Jennings Randolph Distinguished Fellow at the U.S. Institute of Peace. The views expressed in the chapter are the author's views alone; they do not necessarily reflect views of the U.S. Institute of Peace. The work on which this chapter is based has been supported by grants from the Ford Foundation, the Nathan Cummings Foundation, and the U.S. Institute of Peace to the Harvard University Center for International Affairs. I am greatly indebted, both to the granting agencies and to the Center, for their generous support of my action research program.
2. Herbert C. Kalman, "The Problem-Solving Workshop in Conflict Resolution," in R. L. Merritt (ed., *Communication in International Politics* (Urbana: University of Illinois Press, 1972) pp. 168–204; Herbert C. Kelman, "An Interactional Approach to Conflict Resolution and its Application to Israeli–Palestinian Relations," *International Interactions*, 6 (1979) pp. 99–122; Herbert C. Kelman, "Interactive Problem Solving: A Social-Psychological Approach to Conflict Resolution," in W. Klassen ed., *Dialogue toward Interfaith Understanding* (Tantur/Jerusalem: Ecumenical Institute for Theological Research, 1986) pp. 293–314; Herbert C. Kelman, "Interactive Problem Solving: The Uses and Limits of a Therapeutic Model for the Resolution of International Conflicts," in V. D. Volkan, J. V. Montville, and D. A. Julius, eds., *The Psychodynamics of International Relationships, Vol. II: Unofficial Diplomacy at Work* (Lexington, Mass.: Lexington Books, 1991) pp. 145–160; Herbert C. Kelman and Stephen P. Cohen, "Resolution of International Conflict: An Interactional Approach," in S. Worchel and W. G. Austin, eds., *Psychology of Intergroup Relations* (Chicago: Nelson-Hall, 1986) pp. 323–42.
3. John W. Burton, *Conflict and Communication: The Use of Controlled Communication in International Relations* (London: Macmillan, 1969); John W. Burton, *Deviance, Terrorism, and War: The Process of*

Solving Unsolved Social and Political Problems (New York: St. Martin's Press, 1979); John W. Burton, *Global Conflict: The Domestic Sources of International Crisis* (Brighton, Sussex: Wheatsheaf, 1984).

4. See Harold H. Saunders, "The Arab-Israeli Conflict in a Global Perspective," in J. D. Steinbruner (ed.), *Restructuring American Foreign Policy* (Washington, DC: Brookings Institution, 1988) pp. 221–51.

5. Herbert C. Kelman, "Creating the Conditions for Israeli-Palestinian Negotiations," *Journal of Conflict Resolution*, 26 (1982) pp. 39–75.

6. Kelman, "An Interactional Approach," Kelman and Cohen, "Resolution of International Conflict."

7. Herbert C. Kelman, "Forming Coalitions across International Conflict Lines: The Interplay of Conflicts within and between the Israeli and Palestinian Communities," paper presented at the 1990 Symposium on Group Dynamics, Texas A&M University.

8. Saunders, "The Arab-Israeli Conflict."

9. Kelman, "Forming Coalitions."

10. See Tamra Pearson, "The Role of 'Symbolic Gestures' in Intergroup Conflict Resolution: Addressing Group Identity," unpublished Ph.D. dissertation, Harvard University, 1990.

11. Kelman, "Interactive Problem Solving: The Uses and Limits of a Therapeutic Model."

12. Herbert C. Kelman, "Applying a Human Needs Perspective to the Practice of Conflict Resolution: The Israeli-Palestinian Case," in John W. Burton (ed.), *Conflict: Human Needs Theory* (New York: St. Martin's Press, 1990) pp. 283–97.

13. Urie Brofenbrenner, "The Mirror Image in Soviet-American Relations: A Social Psychologist's Report," *Journal of Social Issues,* 17 (3) (1961) pp. 45–56; Ralph K. White, "Images in the Context of International Conflict: Soviet Perceptions of the U.S. and the U.S.S.R.," in Herbert C. Kelman (ed.), *International Behavior: A Social-Psychological Analysis* (New York: Holt, Rinehart and Winston, 1965) pp. 238–76.

14. Herbert C. Kelman, "The Political Psychology of the Israeli-Palestinian Conflict: How Can We Overcome the Barriers to a Negotiated Solution," *Political Psychology,* 8 (1987), pp. 347–63.

15. Herbert C. Kelman, "Israelis and Palestinians: Psychological Prerequisites for Mutual Acceptance," *International Security* 3 (1978) pp. 162–86; Herbert C. Kelman, "A Behavioral Science Perspective on the Study of War and Peace," in R. Jessor (ed.), *Perspectives on Behavioral Science: The Colorado Lectures* (Boulder, Colorado: Westview, 1991) pp. 245–75.

16. Kelman, "Israelis and Palestinians": Kelman, "An International Approach to Conflict Resolution."

17. Kelman, "A Behavioral Science Perspective on the Study of War and Peace."

18. Kelman, "Applying a Human Needs Perspective," pp. 293–94.

19. The continuing workshop has been organized and conducted in close cooperation with Nadim Rouhana of Boston College. The third-party panel of facilitators includes, in addition, Harold Saunders of the Kettering Foundation and C. R. Mitchell of George Mason University.

20. For a recent review of the development and current status of the field, see Ronald J. Fisher, "Developing the Field of Interactive Conflict Resolution: Issues in Training, Funding, and Institutionalization," paper presented at the Fourteenth Annual Scientific Meeting of the International Society of Political Psychology, Helsinki 1991.

Intractable Conflicts

LOUIS KRIESBERG

Many conflicts, especially ethnic, religious, or other intercommunal conflicts (or interstate conflicts related to communal differences), often seem to be intractable. They are waged destructively and persist despite efforts to settle or to transform them, and some recur even after periods of dormancy. Such communal conflicts have become particularly salient with the end of the Cold War, as demonstrated in the former Yugoslavia and some parts of the former Soviet Union. However, not all communally associated struggles become intractable; many are conducted and settled through legitimate institutionalized means of handling conflicts. On the other hand, conflicts associated with differences in ideology, class position, or relative power sometimes also become protracted and appear intractable. For example, this was the case for the Cold War between the Soviet Union and the Western countries led by the United States.

This article is focused on the various kinds of large-scale conflicts that become intractable. First, we consider the concept and dimensions of intractable conflicts; then, the processes and policies by which conflicts become intractable are examined. Finally, the processes and policies that tend to transform a conflict so that it becomes tractable are also reviewed.

It is a premise of this article that conflicts are an inevitable aspect of social life. Conflicts include interpersonal disputes and long-lasting struggles between large-scale adversaries. Within societies utilizing institutionalized means of managing conflicts, the conflicts may be conducted so routinely that we hardly regard them as such. For example, the legal system and electoral politics are ways of settling disputes, even contests about who controls the government, in an agreed-upon manner. The focus of attention here, however, is on conflicts that are waged outside of such regulated and institutionalized forums.

Characteristics of Intractable Conflicts

The terms intractable, protracted, and deeply rooted are sometimes used interchangeably to characterize a class of large-scale conflicts. Each term has its own connotations and limitations. The term *deep-rooted* often refers to conflicts based on strife regarding the satisfaction of human needs by people sharing collective identities, often denoting a people.[1] The term *protracted* connotes simply long-lasting, but is often linked to ethnic and other identity-based conflict.[2] The term *intractable* suggests never-ending. The kind of conflicts considered here to be intractable are those that are resistant to settlement; they persist despite efforts to resolve them, although they do end or become transformed at some time.[3]

Intractable conflicts, as understood here, have interrelated characteristics. The characteristics should be regarded as continuous variables, not as qualities that are either present or absent. Consequently, we should recognize that conflicts are more or less intractable, varying in one regard more than another. The characteristics vary along four dimensions, each of which is discussed in terms of the relatively intractable end of the continuum.

First, large-scale intractable conflicts tend to be long-lasting, generally persisting for more than a generation. This means that young people are socialized to know who their enemies are and what terrible wrongs the enemies have inflicted on their people. Such socialization contributes greatly to sustaining the struggle. The persistent character of intractable conflicts is indicated by the failed efforts to resolve or to manage them acceptably. For example, in the struggle in Sri Lanka between the Sinhalese and the Tamils, the Indian government, using pressure, helped bring about an overall agreement in 1987.[4] An Indian peacekeeping force was sent to implement the arrangement, but violence erupted and the agreement failed.

Second, the leaders and most members of the adversary camps in an intractable conflict consider their goals regarding what they seek from the other to be irreconcilable. Furthermore, members of one or more of the opposing sides often believe that their very existence is threatened by their adversaries. Consequently they must fight on because if they cease, they will be destroyed.

Third, significant members of each side have vested interests in the conflict's continuation, at least at the level of the ongoing confrontation. The interests may be material or ideological ones. Many persons' identity or livelihood are invested in waging the struggle, as warriors, officials, or advocaters of ideology or religion. This too contributes to the self-perpetuation of the conflict. For example, the analyses of the role of the military industrial complex in the United States and in the Soviet Union during the Cold War indicated how the threat from the adversary was used to justify the need for increased military expenditures and how decisions to enhance military capabilities were perceived as threatening by the other side.[5]

Fourth, the conflict is conducted with recourse to destructive means. Violence is usually employed, including killing and otherwise physically damaging members of the other side. This violence may be targeted at noncombatants as well as combatants. Deep feelings of fear and hatred are generally aroused. Each side tends to view the other as the enemy, who also may be dehumanized.

Intractable conflicts, in spite of their persistence and viciousness, are nevertheless a kind of conflict and therefore share characteristics with other conflicts. As in all conflicts, two or more groups or their representatives manifest their belief that they have incompatible goals, but to some degree the adversaries are interdependent and the realization of each side's goals requires something from the opposing side. Furthermore, conflicts are conducted in more or less institutionalized fashion, using a variety of inducements including persuasion and positive sanctions, as well as violence and other forms of coercion. Finally, conflicts tend to move through a series of stages: emerging, escalating, deescalating, and settling.

Intractable conflicts, as the term is generally used, refers to large-scale conflicts that are waged between enduring antagonistic parties. But not all such conflicts are regarded as intractable. For example, class conflicts and labor management conflicts are endless, but they are not necessarily waged with deadly bitterness. What is peculiar to intractable conflicts is their persistence and the destructive means used to wage the conflict.

Becoming Intractable

Conflicts are not inherently intractable. Many conflicts emerge and are conducted through institutionalized means over a long time or they may erupt in a disorderly but relatively short-lived struggle. Only some conflicts persist and become intractable, and the explanations for such deterioration serve as the major subject matter of this contribution. The explanations are considered in three groupings: the relationship between the adversaries; internal characteristics of one or more of the antagonistic parties; and features of the external context. In conjunction with these explanations, we discuss policies pursued by the adversaries and by other actors that contribute to a conflict becoming intractable.

Relations between the Adversaries

Many explanations for a conflict's intractability emphasize the relations between the adversaries. A frequently noted factor is the relative power imbalance between different communities or countries. High levels of inequality between communal groups within a country or between countries make it possible for the stronger party to impose oppressive burdens on the weaker. Under propitious circumstances, the dominated group may challenge those who are dominant, seeking greater equality. The dominant group sometimes seeks to suppress such challenges, even if they were initially nonviolent. The consequent cycle of struggle then deteriorates into a mutually destructive intractable conflict, as happened in Sri Lanka.

The direction and degree of power asymmetry between groups, however, are matters of interpretation and are in flux. Frequently, adversaries on each side of a protracted struggle see themselves as beleaguered and threatened by the others, so they must fight hard to protect themselves. A few examples are worth noting: (1) during the years of apartheid, South African whites generally saw themselves as threatened by the much more numerous blacks in South Africa, while the South African blacks regarded themselves as militarily, economically, and politically dominated and exploited by the whites; (2) Israeli Jews generally see themselves as surrounded by a vast Arab world, while Arabs generally see themselves as threatened by the militarily mighty Israel, backed by Western imperialism; (3) Tamils in

Sri Lanka see themselves as a weak minority in a country dominated by the Sinhalese, while the Buddhist Sinhalese see themselves as threatened by the Hindu Tamils backed by the large Tamil population in southern India. Similar patterns can be noted for the Greeks and Turks in Cyprus, the Catholics and Protestants in Northern Ireland, and for the Serbs and Muslims in Bosnia.

Such different views of power and vulnerability help explain the protracted nature of many conflicts. They also suggest ways out of intractable conflicts, as the context and parties to a conflict can be modified. For example, in the 1980s, several Central American countries were racked by long-lasting and interlocked conflicts, making it difficult to settle any one of them in isolation. A large move toward resolution was made by the accord reached among the presidents of the five Central American countries, meeting in Esquipulas, Guatemala.[6] The accord is often called the "Arias Plan" to recognize the great mediating contributions of the President of Costa Rica, Oscar Arias. The accords included three components to be implemented simultaneously and according to a fixed time schedule; the components provided for ending the violent conflicts, promoting democracy, and fostering economic integration.

The view that adversaries have of their relationship and its bounded character may contribute to a conflict becoming intractable. Insofar as they view themselves as struggling within a clearly bounded system, they are likely to see themselves in a purely zero-sum conflict, in which whatever one side gains is at the expense of the other. This enhances the profoundly incompatible nature of their goals.

A very important aspect of the relations between the adversaries contributing to the intractability of their mutual struggle is the way they treat each other in waging the fight. Inhumane treatment deepens the antagonism and the desire to continue the struggle and even to seek revenge. The callous and indiscriminate use of violence, intended to intimidate and suppress the enemy is frequently counterproductive, prolonging a struggle and making an enduring peace more difficult to attain.

Another important policy affecting the increasing intractability of a conflict is the rejection by one or more sides of the other's claims regarding fundamental human rights, recognition, and minimal living conditions. Related to this, another fundamental policy affecting a conflict's intractability is the refusal by one side to recognize the other side as a legitimate collectivity and the consequent refusal by one side to communicate with the other.

Internal Developments

A variety of developments within one or more of the adversary parties can contribute to a conflict's becoming intractable. In the case of ethnic conflicts, widespread adoption of an ethnonationalist ideology by members of one or more adversaries is a likely source of intractability. Some political leaders, intellectuals, and mass media producers promote such ideologies, seeking to arouse emotions of fear and hatred toward ostensible enemies. They may not only extol particular qualities attributed to members of their own community, but condemn qualities attributed to an enemy.

For some members of a contending side, the sense of belonging to a larger entity engaged in a struggle provides meaning and significance for their lives; for others, it provides a livelihood as well as a sense of identity. For still others, it provides a vehicle for power and influence. Thus, the conflict itself creates a vested interest for some people to continue the struggle. Furthermore, the process of entrapment tends to lock some people to persisting in a course of action. Entrapment refers to a process whereby individuals increase their commitment in order to justify their previous investments or sacrifices.[7] Fighting on seems to justify what has already been expended in money, honor, or blood.

In addition, certain organizational developments contribute to a conflict's becoming intractable. For example, members of small groups, including elite decision-making groups, tend to pressure each other to conform to the prevailing views of the group. Dissenters within those groups are likely to withdraw or be excluded; consequently, dissenting voices are silenced and alternatives to continuing on the chosen path are not considered.

Social Context

Every conflict is embedded in a larger social system and interlocked with other conflicts. The nature of that larger social system and of the interlocking conflicts contributes greatly to a conflict's intractability. The larger social system may lack norms or institutions that would prevent a conflict from becoming intractable. They provide alternatives to a destructive escalation of a conflict.

A conflict also tends to become intractable as one conflict becomes superimposed by other conflicts. Thus, insofar as class, ethnic, religious, ideological, and other conflicts coincide rather than crosscut each other, the more intense and the more difficult it is to resolve any one of the conflicts.[8] Thus, the Cold War was superimposed on many conflicts in the Middle East, Central America, Africa, and Asia. The U.S. and the Soviet governments each justified its support of contending local parties as necessary to counter the actions of the other. Consequently, local adversaries were able to continue a struggle as each side gained support from opposing superpowers. The resulting local struggles were often intense and a final agreement difficult to reach and to sustain.

The Israeli-Egyptian relationship is illustrative. The Soviet assistance given Egypt, other Arab governments, and the Palestine Liberation Organization (PLO) seemed to promise ultimate victory and obviate the need to settle on terms acceptable to the Israelis. On the other hand, the American support of Israel offered assurances that allowed the Israelis to reject a settlement acceptable to the Arabs. In the 1970s, however, President Anwar Sadat led Egypt out of the Soviet camp and then the U.S. government undertook a strong mediating role and helped the Egyptian and Israeli governments conclude a peace treaty.

Tractable Conflicts

Intractable conflicts end with two kinds of outcomes. One way is the ending of the conflict itself; this may occur by the destruction or collapse of one of the antagonists as a viable contender or by the conversion or other transformation of one of the antagonistic sides. The more frequent outcome is that the conflict is transformed so that it is not conducted destructively. The adversaries may routinely negotiate their differences and use institutionalized means of struggle, and if they resort to coercion, rely largely on nonviolent forms. The conflict has become tractable.

Tractable conflicts are not entirely harmonious or exemplars of full justice. They may embody considerable inequality and domination of one party by another. They may be conducted by parties who have very little interaction or mutual dependency and result in separation. We are most interested, here, in tractable conflicts that entail ongoing interdependence, and ones that entail large components of mutual acceptance and mutual benefit. They are likely to be considered more just and to be more enduring.

The minimal benchmarks of tractable conflicts include the following three features. First, the adversary parties recognize considerable mutual interests and shared identity, and not only incompatible interests of distinct, exclusive identities. Second, significant members of each adversary side acknowledge minimal rights of the other and the propriety of the other's claims. Third, the adversaries agree to rely on nonviolent means of pursuing their conflict and procedures to settle specific issues in contention between them.

Becoming Tractable

Intractable conflicts move toward tractability as a result of several developments. Such movement arises from changes in the relationship between adversaries, from changes within one of the major adversaries, and from changes in the struggle's external context. Often elements from two or three of these sources converge and combine together to form ways out of the conflict. The process that brings about the transformation of an intractable conflict into a tractable one entails the interaction between a set of changing conditions and of new policies, both long-term and short.

Changes in adversarial relationships are important sources of paths out of intractable conflicts. One is the defeat of one side by the other, in which case the victorious party largely imposes its terms of settlement. Another way is for the weaker party to intensify the struggle, raising its cost to the dominant group until a settlement seems attractive. This is often the case in the resort to violence, even terrorism. Nonviolent coercive means may also be employed, including nonviolent protest, noncooperation, and the reduction of relations. Another important component may be the involvement of external supporters for one party to the conflict, shifting the balance of power and thus increasing coercive threats or experiences against the dominant party.

In addition to such coercive paths, or in conjunction with them, noncoercive means can also help terminate conflicts. They include new ways of thinking about the relationship, developed from gradual mutual interchange, dependency, and confidence-building measures, such as the end of the Cold War. They may also be the result of negotiated agreements. Changes within one party are also important. These include new political leaders, new thinking, and shifts in domestic forces, such as France's role in Algeria and the white role in South Africa. Changes in the social context of the focal conflict provide the bases for deescalation. Such changes include new common enemies—a shift in salience of fights—and external intervention, such as in Somalia.

In short, conflicts do not move out of intractability along a single path; there are many paths out. Which path is taken depends on many things. First, it depends on where the antagonists start from—whether from the defeat of one side, a protracted cold war, or a violent stalemate. Second, it depends on where the adversaries want to go. Thus, movement may be toward the utter defeat of one side or it may be toward mutual acceptance. The defeat of one side may sometimes result in reconciliation insofar as members of the defeated side can attribute the struggle to their rejected former leaders and join with their former enemies in significant ways, this, in significant degrees was the case in Franco–German relations after World War II.

Finally, an assessment of the path taken often depends on the time frame used. The same path, when viewed for a short distance, may appear quite different than when seen as a part of a much longer road. For example, even an intensification of a conflict may appear as a step toward reconciliation when considered over a fifty- or hundred-year span.

Many different parties within and outside an intractable conflict may pursue strategies to find a mutually acceptable outcome. Some of these efforts may be planned and others may be considered strategic only in hindsight, by outside analysts. Such strategies include selecting parties to the de-escalating efforts, issues to be emphasized, and the combination of inducements to be used. I will discuss a few cases to show how different parties can develop strategies that move adversaries toward settlements and peace.

Three relative successes in transforming apparently intractable conflicts are illustrative of various paths toward conflict tractability. The struggle in South Africa over apartheid had certainly been long and often violent. Yet in recent years it underwent a relatively peaceful transformation.[9] A gradual shift toward a more equal balance of resources between the dominant whites and the blacks in South Africa had been under way for years. This was made manifest not through violence, but by great external economic and moral opposition to white rule. Furthermore, the African National Congress and allied organizations stressed their desire for racial integration, not for an exclusively nonwhite society. Economic interdependency among all peoples in South Africa continued to grow. Ultimately, the leaders of the ANC and the South African National Party moved carefully to reassure each other and each other's constituency that a mutually beneficial outcome was possible and desirable.

Another example is the transformation of the Cold War. The long struggle between the United States and the Soviet Union did not end by a military defeat or militarily imposed settlement. Rather, the end resulted from a convergence of domestic Soviet developments and Cold War strains, but also from a series of conflict resolution efforts and achievements.[10]

A third example is Franco-German relations. For generations, French and German youth were raised knowing that they faced an implacable foe; wars were fought in 1870, 1914–18, and again in 1939–45. The humiliations suffered by the French in 1870 were to be redressed in 1914, and those the Germans suffered in 1918 were to be redressed in 1939.[11] Several new circumstances and strategies broke that cycle so that war between France and Germany is now unthinkable. The catastrophe of World War II was great, but so was that of World War I.

In the aftermath of World War II, however, the extremities of fascist nationalism were especially sobering. Moreover, a new common enemy quickly appeared for West Germany and the French. The integration of the two was put into a mutually beneficial context.

Like "successes," failed attempts at bringing about a resolution of intractable conflicts are also informative. These include the Indian-Pakistani antagonism relating to Kashmir, and struggles in Sri Lanka, Northern Ireland, and Israeli-Palestinian/Arab relations. What usually occurs in these conflicts is a reliance on violent coercion and a denial of legitimacy to the claims made by the adversary.

We can draw several inferences from this discussion: First, getting out of an intractable conflict is easy, if one side gives in to the adversary's terms. Getting out on terms that have mutual or joint benefits is much more difficult and often takes a very long time. Second, great inequalities in resources do not provide a sound basis for mutually acceptable, enduring relations. Ambiguities about power imbalances, however, may allow partisans to find equitable solutions: the parties to the dispute can be modified, as can the issues in contention, thus shifting the perception of power.

Third, for the subordinated party, strategies to create greater equality do not depend only on enhancing its ability to increase the violence it can inflict. Other means, often more effective in building an enduring, peaceful relationship, include (a) using nonviolent coercive means of protest and struggle; (b) drawing in outside allies, particularly by using moral claims; (c) offering some security to the basic interests of the dominant party; and (d) developing institutional arrangements for the peaceful settlement of disputes and for reconciliation.

Fourth, for the dominant party too, strategies that break through intractability usually must go beyond violent imposition if cycles of violence are to end. These strategies include (a) acknowledging the injuries suffered by the subordinated group, (b) developing institutionalized means to handle conflicts and allegations of injustice, and (c) exercising control over each side's hard-liners.

A frequent element in a deescalating process involves the growing sense by the adversaries that the old strategies are not working and will not succeed. The parties come to believe that changed conditions make it evident that they cannot succeed with their strategy, and it is costly. The parties find themselves in a hurting stalemate.[12]

New policies seem to promise an acceptable and mutually acceptable outcome. Failure of old policy may have made new ones seem more necessary. For example, the apartheid policy was not sustainable; instead, there was increasing integration and a growing black middle class. Black people had voted with their feet; they had migrated to the urban centers and integrated industry and residential areas, violating the official pass requirements.[13] Furthermore, it is important to recognize that although the ANC demanded the transfer of power to a government chosen by a majority of the people, it "recognized the equal right of whites to South Africa as their native land."[14] That reassurance was available to whites.

Internal Changes

In the course of a long struggle, changes inevitably occur within each party engaged in a struggle, and some of them foster deescalation and movement out of intractability. People become weary of the struggle and the burdens it imposes. The ending of the Cold War and of the struggle about the white's domination of South Africa are examples of remarkable transformations after decades of severe conflict, threatening even greater destructiveness. Changes within the Soviet Union and among the whites of South Africa certainly contributed significantly to the transformation of those intractable conflicts.

In the Soviet Union, beginning in the mid-1970s, the economy was clearly stagnating and living conditions were deteriorating. Life expectancy actually began to decline, unlike any other industrially developed country.[15] Improving relations with the West offered the prospect of limiting the immense military defense expenditures and gaining access to Western technological developments and more and better consumer products. In 1985, Mikhail Gorbachev was chosen by the Communist Party to lead it and the Soviet Union into a period of domestic reforms, and an accommodation with the West was regarded as a requisite for that. Furthermore, some members of the elite strata had begun to lose their convictions about Communist ideas and many had begun to admire the rule of law and the freedoms of the West.

In South Africa, many whites came to believe not only that apartheid was not working well, but that it was morally wrong. Religious support for segregation of the races was undercut, and in 1986, the general synod of the Dutch Reformed Church resolved that the forced separation of peoples cannot be considered a biblical imperative.

Social Context

Finally, external intermediaries can contribute to the management and resolution of intractable conflicts. Their contributions may include (a) arranging package deals to end the conflict, (b) expanding the pie to be divided by adding resources, (c) giving legitimacy to possible new options, and (d) helping implement and sustain the agreement that is reached. The availability of such intermediaries facilitates a conflict's transformation, when other conditions are propitious. The intermediaries can also help produce more propitious circumstances, for example, by lending support to one party or cutting off assistance to another or by helping to reframe the conflict and helping to provide the vision of possible mutually acceptable option for the adversaries.

Every conflict is interlocked with many others. A shift in the salience of one of those other conflicts can help move a conflict into greater or lesser intractability. The reduced salience of an old superimposed conflict is likely to allow others that had been superimposed to become tractable and even resolved. As previously noted, the U.S.-Soviet Cold War was superimposed on conflicts in the Middle East, Southern Africa, Central America, and Southeast Asia.

Changed conditions also affect one or more of the adversaries and the relations between them. This includes changes in economic, demographic, and social conditions. Normative and ideological changes affect the antagonists' sense of what alternatives are possible. More conciliatory elements of old strategies can become more likely to be recognized as such when conditions become more supportive of such interpretations. For example, the ANC goals had been nonracist, the whites being regarded as another African people in South Africa, and ANC leaders did not seek to expropriate and redistribute the wealth of the country so concentrated in the whites' hands. Such assurances became far more convincing after the disappearance of the Soviet Union and the accusation that the ANC was Communist lost credibility.

Intermediaries can contribute to the transformation of an intractable conflict in several ways. Intermediaries include officials from national governments and from international governmental organizations and also nonofficial persons based in nongovernmental organizations. They can foster new options by suggesting them and giving them support.

Short-term policies include gestures to the other side. What is also important is mobilizing support for conciliatory moves. Related to this is the development of strategies for dealing with constituency opposition, by suppression, cooptation, or persuasion. Finally, external intermediaries can also provide critical assistance in monitoring and implementing the provisions reached by the adversaries.

Conclusions

No particular kind of conflict is inherently intractable. Under certain combinations of conditions and with the application of particular policies, many can and do become intractable. The way the adversaries respond to each other's means of waging the struggle between them contributes greatly to the likelihood that a struggle will become protracted and destructive. If either side uses indiscriminate violence against an adversary or treats the members of the adversary group as subhuman, the chances of a conflict becoming intractable are immensely enhanced. The failure of external actors to condemn and to try to interrupt such conduct contributes to a conflict's persistence and escalation.

Intractable conflicts, however, eventually do come to an end and become tractable. They may even become transformed in such that the former adversaries are reconciled and develop relatively close and equitable relations. Such transformations require the convergence of many factors and well-considered strategies. Policies that acknowledge the humanity of the members of the other side and hold out the possibility of finding a mutually acceptable outcome inhibit a conflict from becoming intractable and raise the possibility of transforming the conflict into a tractable one.

Notes

1. John Burton, *Conflict Resolution and Prevention,* New York: St. Martin's Press, 1990
2. Edward A. Azar, Paul Jureidini, and Ronald McLaurin, "Protracted Social Conflict; Theory and Practice in the Middle East," *Journal of Palestine Studies,* 29 (Autumn, 1978): 41–60
3. Louis Kriesberg, Terrell A. Northup, and Stuart J. Thorson, eds. *Intractable Conflicts and their Transformation,* Syracuse: Syracuse University Press, 1989
4. David Little, *Sri Lanka: The Invention of Enmity.* Washington, D.C.: The United States Institute of Peace Press, 1994
5. C. Wright Mills, *The Power Elite* (New York: Oxford University Press, 1956); Arnold M. Rose, *The Power Structure* (New York: Oxford University Press, 1967); also see William Gamson and Andre Modigliani, *Untangling the Cold War,* Boston: Little, Brown, 1971, and Alan Wolfe, *The Rise and Fall of the "Soviet Threat": Domestic Sources of the Cold War Consensus,* Washington, D.C.: Institute For Policy Studies, 1979
6. See P. T. Hopmann, "Negotiating Peace in Central America," *Negotiation Journal,* 1988 4:361–80, and Paul Wehr and John Paul Lederach, "Mediating Conflict in Central America," *Journal of Peace Research* 1991 (28): 85–98
7. Joel Brockner and Jeffrey Z. Rubin, *Entrapment in Escalating Conflicts,* New York: Springer-Verlag, 1985
8. Ralf Dahrendorf, *Class and Class Conflict in Industrial Society,* Stanford, CA: Stanford University Press, 1959 and Louis Kriesberg, *Social Conflicts,* Second Edition, Englewood Cliffs, NJ: Prentice-Hall, 1982
9. Allister Sparks, *Tomorrow Is Another Country,* New York: Hill and Wang, 1995; also see Hendrik W. van der Merwe, *Pursuing Justice and Peace in South Africa.* London and New York: Routledge, 1989
10. Louis Kriesberg, *International Conflict Resolution,* New Haven and London: Yale University Press, 1992
11. Thomas J. Scheff, *Bloody Revenge: Emotions, Nationalism, and War.* Boulder/San Francisco/London: Westview Press, 1994
12. Saadia Touval and I. William Zartman, eds. *International Mediation in Theory and Practice.* Boulder, CO.: Westview, 1985
13. John Kane-Berman, *South Africa's Silent Revolution.* Johannesburg: South African Institute of Race Relations, 1990.
14. Benyamin Neuberger, "Nationalisms Compared: ANC, IRA, and PLO," pp. 54–77 in Hermann Giliome and Jannie Gagiano, eds. *The Elusive Search for Peace: South Africa and Northern Ireland.* Cape Town: Oxford University Press, 1990, p. 65
15. Christopher Davis and Murray Feshbaack, *Rising Infant Mortality in the USSR in the 1970's* U.S. Department of Commerce, Bureau of the Census (Washington, D.C.: U.S. Printing Office, 1980); and John Dutton, Jr., "Changes in Soviet Mortality Patterns, 1959–77," *Population and Development Review* 5 (June 1979): 267–91

The Tree Model:
Psychopolitical Dialogues and
the Promotion of Coexistence

VAMIK D. VOLKAN, M.D.

The work of most conflict resolution practitioners centers around opening and maintaining a dialogue between opposing ethnic or other large groups whether they are within one state or in neighboring states. The nature and content of such dialogues, as well as the related actions they attempt to facilitate, vary from one practitioner group to another. Similarly, participants in these dialogues range, according to the practitioner's philosophy and methodology, from grassroots types to influential members of a community or government. Yet practically every attempt to assist in the resolution of conflicts faces common problems: after a dialogue is initiated, how can a polarized and rigidified conflict be transformed into a *shared* one? How does one institutionalize the progress that has been made and prevent stagnation or slipping backward? How can one transfer the insights from the dialogues into concrete actions affecting the societies involved? What can be done to maintain peaceful coexistence and neighborliness among opposing groups after the facilitator leaves the region?

In this chapter I describe "The Tree Model," developed at the University of Virginia's Center for the Study of Mind and Human Interaction, a comprehensive approach to the reduction of tensions between large groups, institution building, and the promotion of democratization and coexistence. I will not attempt a comparative study between this model and other efforts of recognized conflict-resolution practitioners. The uniqueness of the Tree Model is its utilization of an interdisciplinary facilitating team that includes psychoanalysts, psychiatrists, (former) diplomats, historians, and other social and behavioral scientists. In utilizing such a diverse team, the complexities of real-world issues, such as political, economic, legal, and military friction, are studied in their own right, but also through a psychoanalytic lens. Thus attention is paid to unseen (unconscious) psychological factors that may blur realistic considerations, lead to irrational actions, and create resistances to change and progress toward adaptive negotiations.

The Tree Model describes a *process*—with time it grows and branches out like a tree. It begins with a diagnosis of the problems by the facilitating team, continues through the establishment of a "background of safety" (Sandler, 1960) for a series of psychopolitical dialogues between influential representatives of relevant groups (including decision makers who attend the meetings in an unofficial capacity), and then works toward a "vaccination" campaign to reduce poisonous emotions, first within the dialogue itself, and then in increasingly larger groups at the community, governmental, and societal levels. To achieve the latter, efforts are made to execute practical projects and build institutions to be left behind when the facilitators depart (new branches of the tree) so that the insights and new attitudes gained from the dialogues will continue to grow and develop.

Diagnosis

Large group (i.e., ethnic) problems have to be diagnosed on location. Before going on location, our interdisciplinary team studies the history and culture of the antagonist groups, collects information on the current situation, and identifies possible problems. Experts are consulted, as are the local newspapers when they are available, and other sources. At the end of this preparatory time, we draw up a list of problems and contact individuals on location who can receive us and provide further contacts and information if they are not available through the groups that have invited the facilitator's participation. Once on location, we conduct a series of in-depth interviews with a wide variety of people including government officials, parliamentarians, civic leaders, media people, scholars (historians, psychologists, and others), NGO representatives, and average citizens of all ages. We examine common themes, both overt and covert, to recognize anxiety-provoking issues as well as common fantasies and expectations from one's own group and from the enemy group.

Every ethnic conflict has its "hot" locations. These include national cemeteries, memorials to those who have died in conflicts, and other historically important symbolic locales. Visiting such locations with individuals in conflict allows the facilitating group to get quickly to the heart of what the locations represent and why they are perceived as hot in the context of the conflict. Examples of such places that I have visited include the National Cemetery in Latvia (from which Latvians wanted to remove Russian corpses after regaining independence), and the former Soviet military bases at Who and Pärnu, Estonia (which are now derelict and resemble huge waste dumps). Visiting such places is to large group psychology what recounting dreams is to an individual undergoing psychoanalysis, for both can provide a direct avenue to hidden and symbolic aspects of the psychological environment.

Another crucial factor in this diagnostic work is defining what I call the opposing groups' "chosen traumas" and "chosen glories" (Volkan, 1992), important markers of a group's ethnic identity. Chosen traumas refer to the shared mental representations of humiliating events where losses occurred. Chosen glories recount the shared mental representations of events of success or triumph. *The* "memories" of both kinds of events are often mythologized and passed from generation to generation although chosen traumas are typically stronger markers of a group's identity than the mental representations of past glories.

Losses associated with chosen traumas cannot be successfully mourned and humiliation and hurt cannot be resolved. Therefore, the "memories" of such traumas are handed down in the hope that they can be mourned, resolved, or avenged—when militarily or politically possible—in the future. Such handing down succeeds in perpetuating feelings of victimization, entitlement, and the desire for revenge rather than accomplishing acceptance of the change in the group's history. Traumas experienced many centuries in the past are still active in the identities of some groups. It is as if time collapses and feelings about ancient events are condensed and intertwined with current events. Elsewhere (Volkan, 1996) I describe how the mental representation of the Battle of Kosovo in 1389 was deliberately inflamed by the activities of Slobodan Milosevic, Radovan Karadzic, and other Serbian leaders, rekindling the trauma of Serbia's subjugation to the Ottoman Turks, and transferring these emotions to Bosnian Muslims.

After the collection and review of pertinent data, a diagnosis is formulated, and a list of the real world issues (economic, political, etc.) and the "hidden transcripts" (Scott, 1990) that lie beneath the surface is compiled. While the former may be difficult to resolve in practical terms, hidden transcripts that pertain to the group's identity and other collective motivations provide resistances and interfere with effective discussion of real world issues. For example, Estonians were obviously euphoric after regaining their independence from the Soviet Union in 1991. But an examination of their hidden transcripts reflected an underlying anxiety of "vanishing" as an ethnic group. The mental representation of living under foreign powers for centuries did not disappear even though Estonia was now independent, but paradoxically was reactivated to a heightened degree. Fear of foreign invasion and domination reemerged, for every third resident of Estonia was Russian. While this situation presented "real world" problems, the perception that Estonia would disappear provided resistance to consideration of policies of assimilation and integration. If Estonian and Russian "blood" were to "mix," the uniqueness of the Estonian people, whose sense of identity had managed to persist despite their small numbers and adverse conditions, might not survive. The diagnosis then indicated the necessity of helping Estonians differentiate real issues from fantasized fears so that they could deal with integration of Russians more adaptively.

In the schema of the Tree Model, the diagnosis of the conflict, and the contacts made with individuals, governmental, and nongovernmental organizations, civic and religious leaders and activists, form the roots of the tree. Funding, of course, is necessary to provide the "water" for the tree to grow through the initiation of a long-term dialogue that meets at least several times a year, or more frequently if possible.

Psychopolitical Dialogues

Conflict between nations, or between groups within multiethnic states, can make them more susceptible to political assaults that can destroy attempts at adaptive discussions and policies. Like a tree, healthy growth within a nation can be thwarted by pressures produced by inflamed ethnic or nationalistic animosities, or slowed by devoting undue energy to counterproductive issues, as a tree is weakened by "suckers," the detrimental shoots that form at the base of its trunk. To counter these hazards, it is crucial to engage conflicting groups in psychopolitical dialogues built upon participants who are selected during the diagnostic period. Individuals from opposing groups who are influential in their respective circles, and who come to the dialogue in an unofficial capacity, are therefore brought together for an extended series of meetings.

Psychopolitical dialogues are not academic conferences. They do not involve the presentation of academic papers. While we open and close each meeting with plenary sessions, the real work is done in small groups. The facilitators with expertise in the psychodynamics of small group discussions (typically those who are clinicians) are therefore crucial, for they can help establish functional "working groups" (Bion, 1961) upon a background of safety, and identify and deal with unconscious resistances. This enables opposing parties to find new ways of looking at the problems that they eventually acknowledge as shared. The dialogues thus become similar to the tape one wraps around the trunk of a young tree to protect it from damage so that new branches will grow and the tree will become strong. The following are some key steps and strategies that illuminate the process involved in such dialogues, gathered through my participation in three projects in "unofficial diplomacy": an Arab-Israeli dialogue conducted between 1979 and 1986 under the auspices of the American Psychiatric Association, and designed to generate new approaches to the lingering problems after the Camp David accords; the 1989 to 1991 Cypriot Turk and Cypriot Greek dialogues under the auspices of the Canadian Institute for International Peace and Security, and organized to address the continuing frictions that have plagued Cyprus since its independence in 1960; and an ongoing dialogue series (initiated in 1993) between Estonians, Russians, and Russians living in Estonia, conducted in cooperation between the Center for the Study of Mind and Human Interaction (CSMHI) and The Carter Center.

(1) Displacement onto a Mini-Conflict

A disruptive situation may evolve abruptly at the outset of any dialogue meeting. Such a situation is marked with a sense of urgency that absorbs the attention and energy of all participants, yet the content of this "crisis" is essentially insignificant in comparison to the salient aspects of the ethnic or national conflict for which the dialogue meeting has been organized. It is reminiscent of the extended debates on "who sits where" at a conference table that have occurred prior to important negotiations between nations. I call them *mini-conflicts,* and while seemingly inexplicable and incongruous, like the masques that preceded an Elizabethan tragedy, they provide condensed and symbolically suggestive treatments of what will be dramatically explored later in the play itself. Through the mini-conflict, many of the urgent concerns connected with large-group tensions are reduced to a more local and accessible realm.

For example, during a dialogue among Israeli, Egyptian, Palestinian, and facilitating American participants, a mini-conflict occurred to "protect" the participants from a heated discussion of a recent troublesome development in the ongoing Arab-Israeli conflict. The "problem" concerned the issue of spouses, for the spouses who had accompanied participants were restricted from participating in the dialogue itself. One Palestinian demanded that his wife be allowed to attend the meeting in an official capacity, and this unexpected development quickly took on critical importance. The larger issues were obscured and seemingly forgotten.

While this mini-conflict seemed to derail the dialogue, it was paradoxically in service of creating a leader. Such multiethnic or multinational gatherings are not "working groups" (Bion, 1961) at the outset, and a mini-conflict can initiate leadership within the facilitating group. The leader then "resolves" the mini-conflict, establishes his or her authority, and can redirect participants to work together, thus turning attention to the real issues at hand.

(2) The Echo Phenomenon

The "echo" of recent events involving the groups in conflict can often be heard when opposing groups open a discussion, further igniting emotions that exacerbate resistances to adaptive discussions. Therefore, the source of the echo must be addressed before effective discussion of pertinent issues and problems can take place. In one meeting in Estonia (between Russians, Estonians, and Russians living in Estonia) Vladimir Zhirinovsky's increasing popularity at that time was echoed in increased anxiety among Estonian participants. Zhirinovsky had recently been in Finland, where he made remarks skeptical of Estonian independence and promoted nationalistic policies for Russia's "near abroad" that Estonians considered threatening. Estonian fears of a surge in Russian aggressiveness and heated discussions pervaded the meeting until the facilitating team enabled Estonian participants to be reassured that Zhirinovsky's views were not held by Russians participating in the dialogue.

(3) Competition to Express Chosen Traumas and Chosen Glories

In a dialogue, members of opposing groups are frequently involved in a competition of historical grievances (chosen traumas) and a boosting of their self-esteem by references to their past glories. During the Estonian-Russian dialogue series, Estonians repeatedly brought up grievances with Russians that concerned the 1940 Soviet bombing of Tallinn (Estonia's capital); statistics of Estonians deported to Siberia, imprisoned, killed, or removed from their homes; and the humiliation of being forced to learn Russian and relinquish other ethnic traditions under Sovietization. Russians, on the other hand, recounted the many advances and advantages the Estonians gained under Soviet tutelage, such as industrialization or modernization, and the undeserved humiliation Russians now suffer from their former underling. Russians also directly and indirectly referred to their legacy as the sons and daughters of a powerful empire with many important achievements, thus boosting their shared self-esteem and holding onto the memories of chosen glories.

The same type of exchanges were seen in the series of meetings between Cypriot Greeks and Cypriot Turks (1988–89) over the future of the divided island. Although the intent of the dialogues was to determine what could be done now and in the future, exchanges dwelled on incidents of the past. The participants of Turkish descent continually referred to the 1963 events that drove them onto only 3 percent of Cyprus's land, when they had previously inhabited 35 percent. Those of Greek origin in turn repeatedly rehashed accounts of the Turkish military's intervention in Cyprus that resulted in the division of the island into northern Turkish and southern Greek sectors.

In such exchanges, there is little realistic integration of what "they" did to us, what "we" did to them, what "we" did for them, and vice versa. If left unchecked, both sides will continue to list their chosen traumas and glories, back and forth, in an endless and victoryless competition. However frustrating such exchanges may be, they are, nevertheless, necessary to the process itself. Through actively listening, the facilitating team absorbs the outpouring of the parties' emotions but avoids taking sides, and becomes a model of empathic listening. When the opposing groups begin to "hear" each other, more realistic discussions can ensue.

(4) The Accordion Phenomenon

After some airing of chosen traumas and chosen glories—when empathic communication starts—the opposing groups begin to become close. This closeness, however, is followed by a sudden withdrawal from one another and then again by closeness. The pattern repeats numerous times. I liken this to the playing of an accordion: squeezing together and then pulling apart.

For example, during the Arab-Israeli dialogue series, there would be sudden unity among the opposing participants during which the antagonists would enthusiastically note their mutual similarities. Statements such as "we are all brothers and sisters, descendants of a common grandfather, Abraham!" would be heard during these periods of unity. But before long, participants from opposing groups would reassert their difference and distance from one another, and the cycle of contradictory attitudes would continue.

Similarly, at a meeting in the Estonian-Russian dialogue series, the opposing representatives of both sides blamed the extremists in each camp for the problems between the two countries. Thus, the participants from each side squeezed together and appeared extremely friendly and agreeable. Such feelings of togetherness are illusory, however, for when two opposing groups become "friendly," the perception that they are far more similar than they previously thought causes anxiety. When a conflict is "hot," each group's identity depends on the belief that they are "good" and their enemy is "bad," but when these crucial distinctions blur, each group attempts to preserve its own identity and retreats from closeness.

More effective discussion of the real world issues cannot take place unless one allows the accordion playing to continue so that the pendulumlike swing in sentiments can be replaced by more realistic and stable conceptualizations. If an agreement is reached during a period of premature closeness, when the opposing groups are squeezed together, it will, most likely, be broken or renounced when the groups redistance themselves.

(5) Projections and Projective Identification

A group sometimes attempts to define its own identity through projection of their unwanted parts onto their enemy. For example, it is not *us* who are troublemakers, but *them.* Projections onto the opposing group reflect a clear "us" and "them" dichotomy of rigid positions—we are "good," they are "bad." However, projections can also involve a more complex relationship between two groups in a pattern that is similar to the mechanism of projective identification that psychoanalysts see with individual patients. At the group level, one group may project its own wish of how another group should think, feel, or behave onto that group. The first group then identifies with the group that houses their projections—the latter are perceived as actually acting in accordance with the expectations of the former, and the former responds accordingly. In effect, one group becomes the spokesperson for the other group, and since this process takes place unconsciously, the first group actually believes in its remarks about their enemy. However, the resulting "relationship" is not "real" but based on the processes of only one party. Some illustrations of these processes are helpful, for projection and projective identification can cause stubborn resistances to dialogue that must be addressed before progress can be made.

For example, Egyptian participants at one meeting began to make long statements on how Israelis feel, think, or react, what they believe in and what they do not, what they want and why, and so on, instead of talking about their *own* views. Israelis responded in turn with *their* summaries of what the Egyptians think, feel, and want. While appearing to address one another, the two sides were really talking to *themselves,* conducting a dialogue between their own position and what they believed (or expected or fantasized) was the position of the other. Facilitators then interceded and clarified for the group that what the Egyptians were saying about Israelis might be what they *wished* or *feared* the Israelis would think or do, and likewise for the Israelis in regard to the Egyptians. Both side's projective behavior may have had roots in reality, and may have been based on genuine concerns, yet also may have been inaccurate and exaggerated, or even wholly false. If both sides were allowed to speak for themselves, then they would be able to modify any faulty perceptions and tame their projections. We asked the Egyptians to allow the Israelis to report about their *own* feelings, thoughts and actions so that Egyptians could perceive a "reality" that had not been colored by fantasized and projected expectations, and the same was asked of the Israelis.

In another example, in the Canadian-sponsored dialogue concerning Cyprus, Cypriot Greeks would state that Cypriot Turks did not get along that well with mainland Turks, or that Cypriot Turks did not like the Turkish army's presence in Northern Cyprus. While this may actually be the case with some Cypriot Turks, this was primarily what the Greek Cypriots' *wished* the situation was, yet they believed it with no less certainty for that fact, and recommended policies based upon such "facts." It was therefore difficult for Cypriot Greeks truly to listen when the Cypriot Turks *did* express their own views, for the Cypriot Greeks already "knew" what Cypriot Turks thought, and discounted any information to the contrary.

(6) Personal Stories

Participants in dialogues invariably bring up personal stories pertaining to the large-group conflict at hand. Initially, personal stories often reflect an "us" and "them" (or "me" and "them") psychology in a black and white manner: the other is seen as all "bad" while one's own group is experienced as all "good." As empathy evolves, however, stories begin to include ambivalences. To have ambivalence means the beginning of acknowledgment of the other's identity as a total being who is both like and unlike oneself. In this way, the other becomes more human. One Estonian told the following story:

> Let me tell you what is "integration" [the integration of Estonians and Russian-speakers in Estonia after Estonia regained independence].
>
> When I was four years old, my family and some Soviet officers were "integrated." In our apartment we were forced to live in one room so that the Soviet officers could live in all of the other rooms. Furthermore, the new inhabitants of our home did not even bother to learn Estonian to communicate with us, but wanted us to learn Russian and adopt the Russian culture. They brought their wives and children also, but they would not learn Estonian either.

In this story, the "us" and "them," and "victim" and "victimizer," issues are clear. Yet, the next day, this same Estonian recalled a story his mother had told him. As a small girl, his mother would visit a Russian military hospital (during World War I) and make socks for the Russian soldiers. Ambivalence had (re)entered his perception of the other group. Alongside the enmity there had existed friendly relations between Russians and Estonians, but this Estonian was unsure when they would return. He further noted that in folklore it is Germans who are the historic enemy of Estonia and suggested that Estonians needed "self-analysis" in order to get rid of the feelings they projected onto the Russians.

During the dialogue between Cypriot Greeks and Cypriot Turks a genuine appreciation of the other's hurts was made possible when a Turk and a Greek told a similar story. Both described their ordeals of being separated from their families during outbreaks of fighting in Cyprus. Neither knew whether their loved ones were alive or dead, and both were emotionally distraught by the uncertainty of their respective family's condition for a time, but were finally reunited. Through their common experience, empathy was established between them, and instead of continuing to place blame on the other side, they acknowledged that the conflict caused innocent people to suffer on *both* sides.

Such exchanges allow the participants to see how their personal identities are intertwined with their large-group identities and what events have led them to hold onto their specific ideologies. Personal stories also allow the facilitating team to encourage discussion, and indirectly to ask members of the opposing group to come up with similar stories, and to underline empathic understanding. This leads to the development of empathy from members of the opposing group for both the person and his or her ethnic group.

(7) Hidden Transcripts

There are often practical and rational considerations that make it difficult for two opposing groups of participants to resolve an issue. However, beneath the surface of such pragmatic or logistical problems there are often hidden *resistances* that prevent parties from reaching agreement, even if practical obstacles can be overcome. Once a degree of empathy has been established, the "hidden transcript" (Scott, 1990; Harris, 1994) can be brought into the open.

After Estonia regained its independence, the issue of who could become an Estonian citizen developed into a critical issue. Estonians, among other things, required a non-Estonian to pass a language examination as a criterion for citizenship. Most Russians who found themselves in Estonia when it broke away from the Soviet Union did not speak or write Estonian, and it became evident that the language examination contained hidden transcripts. The examination was not standardized, and required a one-on-one interview between an Estonian examiner and the (Russian) applicant.

During the dialogue series there were many rational discussions pertaining to the language examinations. Russian-speaking people wanted Estonians to provide classes to prepare for this part of the citizenship requirement. Estonians countered that they lacked the resources to implement such a policy. Many on both sides agreed that the examination should be standardized; some suggested a review panel, others a multiethnic board to design and administer the program. Steps to overcome many obstacles were available, at least in theory, yet progress was elusive. Gradually we realized there were other reasons for the obsession with the language exam. Estonians did not want to standardize or systematize the exams because they wanted the Russian-speaking people to leave Estonia altogether. If the language examination were to be officially institutionalized, it meant, for the Estonians, that the presence of a substantial percentage of Russian-speakers in Estonia would also be institutionalized. At another level, in its unstandardized format, the language examination was a tool of revenge for the Estonians against the Russians.

On the other hand, Russians living in Estonia did not really want to learn Estonian, not simply because of practical problems, but because doing so would be a painful acknowledgment of their minority status in a country where they had recently been dominant. Russian-speakers were not ready to acknowledge this loss in status. We verbalized these hidden meanings, thereby allowing a deeper understanding of the issues, and a more realistic discussion—less colored by emotion—could proceed.

(8) Nonsameness and Minor Differences

As the meeting room evolves as a laboratory for large-group conflict, aspects of large-group rituals become prominent in small-group discussions. When parties become genuinely more empathic toward each other, they may become anxious if they begin to perceive themselves and their group as similar to their enemy. As each group's projection of unwanted aspects becomes unstable due to the perception that the other is similar to one's own group, they may exaggerate the importance of minor differences to maintain their separate identities. Minor differences thus function as a border separating the opposing parties so that their respective identities remain intact. A seemingly trivial disparity may then take on monumental importance and turn positive discussions sour.

For instance, in one meeting when the Estonian and Russian participants seemed to be expressing increasingly similar views, an Estonian abruptly got up and stated it was the birthday of a Russian-speaking participant. Everybody was asked to sing "Happy Birthday." While on the surface this seemed a gesture of camaraderie, it was in essence a defensive act. It seemed that coming close to an agreement made this participant anxious, but he was really responding to the anxiety of participants from *both* sides. By bringing up the birthday, the participants could be distracted from reaching an agreement and thereby remain at odds. In another illustration, as Cypriot Turks and Cypriot Greeks drew closer, discussion suddenly shifted to the preparation of baklava according to minor differences in Turkish or Greek recipes—one uses sugar and the other honey. In such situations the facilitating team interprets the meaning of the minor difference and its significance in the dialogue, and reassures participants from the opposing groups that to come to an agreement does not mean the loss of one's group identity.

(9) Symbolizing the Conflict and "Playing" with It

As a meeting series progresses, a symbol or metaphor may emerge that represents important aspects of the conflict. The participants begin to play with this metaphor, to kick it around like a ball. The metaphor, as a toy, captures the attention of the participants and transforms diffuse emotions and blurred reality into a more concrete understanding of the problem. The toy connects the participants, allowing them to share in the game while at the same time addressing a critical issue. As this play continues, poisonous emotions begin to disappear. Realistic discussion of issues can then ensue.

At one meeting in Estonia, one Russian introduced a metaphor equating Russia to an elephant, a friendly one. An Estonian participant added that if Russia was an elephant, then Estonia was a rabbit. It was difficult, the second participant noted, for the rabbit and elephant to have a relationship even if both are friendly, for the rabbit cannot help fearing that he will be stepped on by the elephant. A different participant then observed that if such was the case, then Russian-speakers in Estonia were like elephant eggs in the rabbit's nest—they could hatch and destroy the rabbit and his home, or the elephant could come to protect them if it thought they were threatened.

When anxiety-producing relationships are symbolized and played with, participants come to a better understanding of aspects of the relationship between them. Also, they begin to modify their perception of each other. For example, through the elephant-rabbit metaphor, the Russians elevated their image of Estonians from being ungrateful for past help from the Soviet Union, to being cautious. They sensed that the Estonians *had* to be careful and not easily friendly with the Russians.

(10) Initiation of Mourning

Mourning is a psychological response to loss and is exhibited by both individuals and groups (Volkan and Zintl, 1993). When we mourn adaptively, we accept the loss or change and come to terms with new situations. Under certain circumstances, however, the mourning process becomes complicated. Large groups' chosen traumas cannot be mourned adaptively because the loss is too big and/or anger, humiliation, the wish for revenge, and other related feelings are too great. As the feelings, memories, and perceptions related to the trauma are passed down from generation to generation, the inability to mourn the loss and the inability to work through the humiliation may lead to certain shared fantasies. These include the perpetuation of an entitlement for revenge or of a sense of victimization. Such attitudes, though they are primarily unconscious, are also shared by members of a group, and therefore may find their way into governmental policies.

In Estonia, for example, the mental representations of past hurts during the Soviet period, such as the deportation of Estonians to Siberia, have not been effectively mourned. As the mental representation of such destructive events was passed down from one generation to the next, it changed functions and became a shared anxiety that the Estonians are a vanishing ethnic group. Even after independence, this sense of endangerment remains and influences policy decisions. Such phenomena must be brought to the surface in order to initiate the mourning of past losses, thereby allowing acceptance of present reality and the taming of shared fantasy.

In another example, in a meeting with Egyptians and Israelis after Israel's withdrawal from the Sinai, Egyptians displayed irritation toward the Israelis for their reluctance to give up the Sinai. The Israelis continued to speak of having "given the Sinai back," to which the Egyptians would angrily retort, "It didn't belong to you in the first place, so why would you say you *gave it back?*" The facilitators helped the Egyptians to understand that the Israelis had a mental representation of the Sinai in which it appeared not only physically but, more importantly, mentally, as a buffer against the enemy. Thus, in withdrawing they had to mourn the loss of a psychological security blanket, and until the extended mourning process had been completed, the Israelis would continue to have a mental investment in that land. Change would certainly come, but not overnight.

(11) Initiation of Time Expansion and Dealing with Transgenerational Transmission

When a chosen trauma from the past is reactivated, the emotions and perceptions pertaining to it are felt as if the trauma occurred recently—those pertaining to the past collapse into emotions and perceptions pertaining to the present and are even projected to the future. What is remembered, felt, and expected come together. I call this a "time collapse" (Volkan, 1996). Allowing discussion about the mental representation of individual traumas or the chosen traumas of a group, with the guidance of the facilitating team, leads to a time expansion: feelings and issues about the past are distanced from present problems. When this happens, present problems can be more realistically discussed and future possibilities imagined.

In one meeting in Estonia, a leading Estonian politician shared an account of how he had been forced to wait alone for two hours past the scheduled time for a meeting with Mikhail Gorbachev to discuss Estonia's desire for independence from the Soviet Union. This humiliating incident at the hands of the Soviets (over five years earlier) seemed to color this participant's view of Russians at the dialogue, for he appeared to hold rigidly onto strong nationalistic views and to distance himself from Russian participants. Facilitators empathically acknowledged the humiliating nature of this previous experience with the Soviet system, and the Estonian politician later seemed to tame his anti-Russian rhetoric and interact in a less stiff and more congenial way with Russian participants. It seemed that the burden of combining his past and present feelings about Russians was eased, enabling him to deal better with the present relationship between the two countries now that time had "expanded."

Similarly, at the beginning of one series of dialogues, a young Estonian resolutely declared that her generation was very different from that of her grandfather's (who is very anti-Russian), and could better deal with the problems of integrating those of Russian origin into Estonia. In the course of the dialogue, however, as she was encouraged to examine her own perceptions of and feelings toward Russians living in Estonia, she came to recognize that she *was* expressing some of the chosen traumas of her grandfather's generation. Her recognition that she was unconsciously her grandfather's "spokesperson," and that traumas and corresponding attitudes had been passed on to her, despite some real differences in their generations, helped her find her own views about Russians.

Institution Building

Through the above process of the dialogue series, rigid and often hostile positions can be loosened, allowing the mode of discourse to shift from accusations and recriminations to explanations of each side's position, and then to a genuine negotiation. Because identity issues have caused participants to develop rigidified positions, they will not acknowledge the need or have the will to change unless they recognize that previous strategies have not worked. This situation must be addressed through the taming of projections, identification of hidden transcripts, modification of black-and-white thinking, the initiation of mourning, and the expansion of participant's psychological time frame. Although emotions will continue to flare up and resistances will again be encountered, the parties are then better equipped to talk and listen to each other, respond, and seek clarification of differing views. To return then to the concept of the tree, the process of psychopolitical dialogues allows a healthy trunk, insulated from dangerous environmental shocks, to develop. New branches can begin to grow.

At this point participants are asked to generate a list of real problems that need to be addressed so that relations can improve and crises be avoided. Then, using the new insights gained from earlier in the process, participants are asked to probe the dynamics of problematic aspects of their relations, including the specific elements of the problem, how each group has contributed to the problem, how each group's interests are affected, what direction constructive change might take, and where common ground might be reached.

While each psychopolitical meeting in a dialogue series has its own story that evolves over the four-day meeting period, the entire series goes through a progression from one gathering to the next (Julius, 1991). The series progression can be described phenomenologically. Harold Saunders (1995), for example, sees five stages for dialogues to change conflictual relationships. Briefly, they are (1) deciding to engage in dialogue; (2) mapping the relationships; (3) probing the dynamics of the relationships to generate the will to change; (4) designing scenarios to change relationships; (5) and putting scenarios into action. It is essential to underscore that these five stages are not rigid; one does not fully end before the next begins. Participants move back and forth across the stages as the larger political context changes or when they need to tackle new problems that cause new and old resistances to progress or appear. When stage 4 is reached, participants from opposing sides in collaboration with the facilitating team then can begin to design scenarios for actual projects to foster and maintain peaceful coexistence and cooperation, and extend the process of change into broader circles.

The creation of a *local contact group,* chosen in collaboration with the facilitating team and participants from each party to the conflict, then becomes necessary to coordinate the development of action scenarios into real projects. Facilitators then encourage the contact group to interact as a unit and form a new "working group" so that the participants involved will not fall back into projecting their fear and expectations onto contact group members from the other side. Thus they become extensions of the facilitating team as carriers of empathy and models for effective communication.

The ultimate aim is for the contact group to evolve into an NGO committed to a process of intergroup understanding and reducing and preventing ethnic tension by building community support. Through assimilating techniques from the facilitators, and with their deeper understanding of the roots, both conscious and unconscious, of the conflict their groups are party to, the contact group can continue to function and provide leadership and guidance, as well as work on their own sources of funding, after the facilitating team terminates its direct and regular involvement.

Timing is very important when building such institutions. Premature attempts to create institutions can be counterproductive in the long run, since members may succumb to malignant ethnic or nationalistic attitudes. In many newly independent states of the postcommunist world, concepts such as personal property, individual thinking and responsibility, community service, and civil law and regulation are evolving and need time to be experienced enough to be assimilated.

The next step for the contact group, once it is cohesive, is to identify possible new "branches" where practical projects can be studied, organized, and implemented—to replicate a part of the "trunk" in a different place (such as a different city, town, or community). This is the real test for the contact group, for it must be able to deal with the same problematic dynamics, as well as new challenges specific to the project environment, that the original facilitating team faced. The facilitators must therefore be prepared to provide continued guidance, encouragement, advice, and other periodic help along the way. Guidance is also provided by the continued support of the psychopolitical dialogues, and the growing networks of individuals and organizations that are connected through the dialogues.

Examples of Tree Branches

Some "branches" of a "tree" are currently growing in Estonia. In 1995, two years after the initiation of psychopolitical dialogues between Estonians, Russians, and Russians living in Estonia, three Estonian locales were selected as sites for specific projects to help build democratic institutions: Mustamäe (a suburb of Tallinn, the capital of Estonia), Klooga, a small village twenty-five miles from Tallinn, and Mustvee, a town on Lake Peipsi, which lies on the border of Estonia and Russia. In each location the population is roughly half Estonian and half Russian, although each has its unique problems that reflect the diversity of issues involved in the relations of Estonians and Russians living in Estonia.

Through the contact group in Estonia, ten Estonian citizens and ten Russian citizens were chosen in each location. They were given a simple instruction: "You will meet regularly once a month and discuss developing a project that will benefit both sides in your community. When a consensus is reached on what the project will be, it will be financed, up to a specified amount, by funds provided by the facilitators. You will continue to meet regularly until the project is completed. Your monthly meetings will continue for three years." The American team trained an Estonian and Russian-Estonian local contact group, mostly psychologists, in the methodology to provide leadership for these monthly meetings. The American group would visit each site three times a year to provide supervision. The main aim, of course, was to be a catalyst of the community's development of democratic and adaptive ways of dealing with problems as well as providing an antidote to possible tensions in multiethnic communities.

One site, Mustamäe, is a typical city suburb where a sophisticated dialogue regarding cultural diversity and democracy began to take place. The participant's focus already had been on "integration" and other issues of Estonian and Russian-Estonian kindergartens. The situation is very different in Klooga, a run-down area near a defunct Soviet military installation. Of the population, the Estonians are generally newcomers who moved into former military accommodations, while the Russians, mostly noncitizens, are primarily young women with children who were left behind after the base was shut down. The whereabouts of many of the husbands is unknown. No true sense of community exists here, ethnic divisions are severe, and other forms of infrastructure such as law enforcement, garbage collection, or a steady supply of heat from the dilapidated plant are lacking. The aim in Klooga is to develop a community without inflaming interethnic conflicts.

In Mustvee, a rural town dependent on fishing and farming, Estonians and Russians (mostly Old Believers, members of an Orthodox sect who settled in the area over 400 years ago) have coexisted peacefully for generations. Many residents can speak both Russian and Estonian. During the Soviet period, central control made life simple and predictable: a truck would arrive to collect the fish caught in Lake Peipsi and the onions and cucumbers grown on the nearby farms, and take them to St. Petersburg. With independence, Mustvee lost its primary market, and decisions were no longer provided by Soviet authorities, causing uncertainty and frustration that began to polarize the once-calm relationship of Estonian and Russian. Here, the aim is to help the villagers remain on peaceful terms.

At each of the three locations the psychological internalization of the Soviet system was evident, but it was most evident in Mustvee. When twenty Estonians and twenty Russians (mostly Old Believers) began to gather to discuss developing a community project, participants tended to give speeches instead of engaging in a genuine dialogue. While a man or woman gave a speech, standing up, other participants would talk among themselves and show no interest in the speaker's statements. They seemed only to be going through the motions of a "democratic" gathering, but expected someone in authority to make the decisions for them in the end. They needed help to "learn" how to make independent decisions, both as individuals and a community. In another example, when facilitators were investigating the area as a possible candidate for a community project, Mustvee's new Estonian mayor was very excited since he was being "forced" to decide on the purchase of new sewer pipes on his own instead of a Soviet official telling him what to do.

The initiatives in Mustamäe, Klooga, and Mustvee will continue through 1999. Meanwhile, efforts are also under way to develop leadership potential among young Estonians and young Russians living in Estonia who have participated in the psychopolitical dialogues.

Evaluation

A project based on the Tree Model takes time, like the growth of a tree itself, and also a good bit of funding. Sustained involvement and commitment, on both the part of the facilitators and funding organizations, are necessary, and genuine progress and growth are difficult if one component (roots, trunk, and branches/diagnosis, dialogue, action) is excluded. Given the investment of time and energy on the part of the facilitating team, and the financial investment of the funding agencies, evaluation of conflict resolution activities is both desirable and necessary. Yet it is also very difficult, since measuring changes in attitudes of the members of one group toward another is problematic, especially when complex emotional factors are involved. We are currently developing a psychometric test to scientifically demonstrate changes in one's own ethnic identity as well as that of the members of opposing ethnic groups.* The test is an adaptation of a scientific measurement of psychiatric patients' evaluation of their self-esteem and their perception of "others." Modifications have been made to apply the testing methodology to Russians and Estonians to enable them to report on changes in their own and the opposing party's mental representations as the project progresses. There is a control group that does not participate in the dialogues or projects. Two pilot studies initiating this scientific evaluation appear promising.

References

Bion, W. R. (1961). *Experiences in Groups.* London: Tavistock Publications.

Harris, M. (1994). "Reading the Mask: Hidden Transcripts and Human Interaction." *Mind and Human Interaction,* 5: 155–64.

Julius, D. A. (1991). "The Practice of Track Two Diplomacy in the Arab-Israeli Conferences." In *The Psychodynamics of International Relationships, Vol. 2: Unofficial Diplomacy at Work,* eds. V. D. Volkan, J. V. Montville, and D. A. Julius, pp. 193–205. Lexington, MA.: Lexington Books.

Sandler, J. (1960). "The Background of Society." *International Journal of Psycho-Analysis,* 41: 352–56.

Saunders, H. (1995) "Sustained Dialogue on Tajikistan." *Mind and Human Interaction,* 6: 123–35.

Scott, J. C. (1990). *Domination and the Art of Resistance.* New Haven, CT: Yale University Press.

Volkan, V. D. (1992). "Ethnonationalistic Rituals: An Introduction." *Mind and Human Interaction,* 4: 3–19.

———. (1996). "Bosnia-Herzegovina: Ancient Fuel of a Modern Inferno." *Mind and Human Interaction,* 7: 110–27.

———. and Zintl, E. (1993). *Life after Loss: Lessons of Grief.* New York, NY: Charles Scribner's Sons. (Paperback Edition, 1994).

---

*This test is being developed by Dr. Carrie Schaffer, a psychologist at the University of Virginia and faculty member of the Center for the Study of Mind and Human Interaction.

Conflict Resolution Moves East: How the Emerging Democracies of Central and Eastern Europe Are Facing Interethnic Conflict

RAYMOND SHONHOLTZ

This article focuses on some of the dilemmas presented to the new democracies of Central and Eastern Europe by the suppression, manipulation, and minimalization of the function of conflict under the Communist regimes. That legacy is presented as the background for a discussion of the importance of conflict for democratic institution building and the setting of new norms in the republics of Central and Eastern Europe and the Russian federation.

As mediating practice and theory in the West are understood from a democratic perspective, the evolution of democratic structures and mediating processes in the former Communist countries, and the limitations confronting them, are instructive to the American mediators working in these new international environments.

Since 1989, Partners for Democratic Change (hereafter, Partners) has established national centers on negotiation and conflict resolution at major universities in Moscow, Warsaw, Prague, Bratislava, Budapest, and Sofia. In addition to training national leaders in negotiation and conflict resolution skills and processes, each of these centers is actively engaged in two additional initiatives: introducing curricula on conflict prevention and resolution at the primary, secondary, and university levels and creating new institutions in civil society to engage conflict constructively.

I first proposed the concept of organizing local conciliation commissions to address border and ethnic conflict in July 1991 while serving as a member of the American delegation to the Conference on Security and Cooperation in Europe (CSCE). The commission concept became part of the official CSCE report. Beginning in September 1991, Partners and the national centers began to pursue the idea of local ethnic conciliation commissions. In March 1992, they published a model charter for such a commission, which became the frame of reference for the statute passed by the city of Plovdiv, Bulgaria, that created the first ethnic commission in Eastern Europe.

Ethnic conciliation commissions present several critical challenges to process designers. This paper focuses on one important dimension of the challenge: the intersection between the historical and cultural suppression of conflict and the democratic need for the expression and resolution of conflict.

Challenge to Conflict Resolution Theory and Practice

The emerging democracies of Central and Eastern Europe present dispute resolution professionals with a new field of work, inquiry, and development. Perhaps most pressing is the application of conflict prevention and early intervention mechanisms and structures to national minority, ethnic, and religious issues. Ethnic conflict poses three challenges for the new democracies. They must redefine *conflict*, develop a culture of democratic conflict resolution, and reassess the significance of minority groups as a motivating force for advancing and protecting the civil rights of all citizens.

Before we consider the values and functions of ethnic conflict, especially in terms of creating local capacity to address them peacefully, it is essential for us to appreciate that *conflict* and *conflict resolution* are culturally bound terms that can have contradictory meanings and significance in different societies (Rubenstein, 1992).

In the context of the democracies of North America or Western Europe, conflict is constitutionally protected (for example, First Amendment rights), channeled into prescribed institutional settings (courts, legislatures, private party bargaining sessions, and so on), and openly acknowledged by the citizenry and governmental authorities. To function, these democracies have developed a culture of conflict resolution that begins when citizens assert their rights in a conflictual setting and ends with the selection of a process for the expression and settlement of differences. The cultural foundation for the positive valuing and acceptance of conflict is rooted in the historical identity of American and Western European societies and in their struggle for individual rights and freedoms. In the West, conflict is inextricably linked to positive images of freedom, and it is perceived as a constructive engine for social change that warrants constitutional and institutional protection.

In the old Communist lexicon, conflict was defined in terms of class struggle, and a disputant was a person with a disputatious character. These simplistic definitions not only negated the existence of conflict between "comrades" but also defined conflict as being outside the harmonious values of "socialist society." Accordingly, Communist regimes equated conflict with deviant behavior that warranted professional attention in mental institutions or as the manifestation of political dissent requiring criminal punishment and isolation.

The old regimes created a set of norms that disavowed the value, utility, and healing power of conflict. These old norms included the notions that conflict was unacceptable, an opponent was an "enemy," and any conflict was necessarily win or lose. The new democracies of Central and Eastern Europe and the republics of the former Soviet Union lack the cultural, institutional, or psychological foundations needed to accept or engage conflict.

In seeking to promote and advance a culture of conflict resolution that can counter forty-five—in some cases seventy-five—years of Communist rule, we must address the concept and psychology of conflict and the absence of institutions in Central and Eastern Europe and the Russian federation that can engage conflict constructively.

Conflict Is Unacceptable. Under the old regimes, conflict was dangerous. Those promoting social unrest were viewed as working against the harmonious interests of the state and its security. Accordingly, persons espousing policies adverse to the state's were criminals. With dissent a criminal activity, there was no need to develop negotiation, mediation, or conflict management systems that could address opposing political perspectives peacefully. When political conflict is equated with state security, conflict suppression becomes a state initiative.

For minorities, the prohibition against expressing differences or promoting conflict resulted in the suppression of ethnic and national minority group positions and group identity. The inability to champion their opposition to state policies increased the subjugation of minorities to official assimilation programs. Efforts to advance minority concerns generated the type of conflict that the old regimes were systematically prepared to suppress. Accordingly, neither the state nor minority groups ever developed any methodology, psychology, or politically acceptable means for legitimating or mediating conflictual interests or concerns.

An Opponent Is an "Enemy." By depriving conflict of any interactive quality or value, the state could define opposing interests as the attitudes of persons or groups who were "enemies" of the state. As the state represented the best interests of society, the opposition could be characterized in depersonalized terms and linked to negative, individualistic aspirations.

The state's devaluation of conflict as confrontation with an enemy had the concomitant effect of making the state an enemy of all minority groups. Without a culture for engaging and legitimating conflict, Communist societies defined opposition as confrontational and inimical. Instead of becoming the arbiter of conflict and the creator of mediating mechanisms in society, the Communist state became the champion of one perspective to the detriment of all others. In short, the old regimes neither negotiated nor served to mediate differences.

Since the 1989 revolutions, the new democracies have officially disavowed suppression tactics and openly embraced the democratic principles set forth by the United Nations, the Conference on Security and Cooperation in Europe, and the European Community charters. The open expression of group identity has become possible, and it is officially supported by most of the new Central and Eastern European governments. For an example, we need only look to Hungary's new draft law on the rights of national and ethnic minorities.

The new democracies have disavowed the illegitimacy of conflict—a development paralleled by increasingly diverse newspapers and radio and television programs. However, this stance has not of itself created any new institutions, processes, or psychological frameworks that disputing parties or minority groups can rely on or trust. Few citizens or minority groups trust their governments to protect or advance their interests.

Shifting the Historical Paradigm of Conflict

As the preceding section underscores, the terrain in which the pioneers of dispute resolution are now working requires extensive cultivation. These laborers are not just Americans who come to share their training skills or conflict-resolution methodologies but also the citizens of the new republics who have cast their future in the direction of the values, if not the work, of the national centers on negotiation and conflict resolution.

One of the three main goals of Partners for Democratic Change and its centers is the establishment of mediating structures in civil society. In the latter part of 1991, Partners formally initiated an ethnic conciliation program following its groundbreaking work at the July 1991 meeting of the CSCE, which was devoted to national and ethnic minorities. The final document resulting from that meeting closely followed earlier Partners drafts that urged member states of the CSCE to establish local commissions for ethnic concerns, especially along border frontiers.

Prior to October 1992, when the first Bulgarian and Hungarian ethnic conciliation commissions were formed, Partners had initiated extensive discussions with minority leaders, local officials, and government ministries addressing the need to create new structures in civil society at the local level to address some dimensions of ethnic and national minority issues. This educational step sought to create an understanding that conflict can be used effectively to create new institutions and that such institutions can advance important democratic goals. In short, Partners and the centers have undertaken an educational initiative to counter the attitudes that prevailed in the old regimes.

Each center's ethnic conciliation program focuses on the creation of a physical place and visible process wherein disputing groups can express their needs. Of special import is the composition of the commission and the selection of commission members. In Bulgaria and Hungary, leaders from different ethnic and national groups met several times to discuss the development of commissions. These meetings focused on the role of the commissions in the community and on processes for selecting commission members.

The ethnic program seeks to develop new structures in civil society that can engage disputing parties; facilitate a dialogue focused on needs, interests, and possible options; and explore points of common or potential agreement. The commissions physically represent the transition point so difficult for the new democracies to move beyond, namely, the creation of a structure that is not a part of the formal governmental system but rather a new structure in civil society.

Minority Conflicts Can Strengthen Minority Interests and Democratic Society. Conflicts presented by minority groups in democratic society have the potential to create new norms, rules, and institutional structures that change consensual understandings concerning how the society functions.

In his famous work on the sociology of law, Max Weber asked what the new element that creates a new framework of norms and a new consensual understanding stems from. "In dismissing external conditions as insufficient, Weber states that 'the really decisive element has always been a new line of conduct which then results either in a change of the existing rules or in the creation of new ones. Several types of persons participate in these transformations. First . . . those individuals who are interested in some concrete communal action. Such an individual may change his behavior . . . either to protect his interests under new external conditions or simply to promote them more effectively under existing conditions.' As a result there arise new 'consensual understandings' and sometimes new forms of rational association with substantially new meanings; these in turn generate the rise of new customary behavior" (Rheinstein, 1954, p. 68).

In democratic society, ethnic conflict has the potential to bring the need to adopt new normative rules for addressing conflict into the consciousness of the disputing parties and the society as a whole. "Those who engage in antagonistic behavior bring into consciousness basic norms governing rights and duties of citizens. Conflict thus intensifies participation in social life" (Coser, 1956, p. 127).

In a democratic civil society, minority conflict becomes an indispensable vehicle for the clarification and adaptation of new social rules and the rationale for developing a physical venue for the interaction of these rules in society.

Conciliation Commissions Can Serve to Strengthen the New Democracies. Conflict has the ability to change the conditions that created it. "A flexible society benefits from conflict behavior inasmuch as this behavior, through the creation and modification of norms, assures its continuance under changed conditions. A rigid system, on the other hand, by not permitting conflict, will impede needed adjustments and so maximize the danger of catastrophic breakdown" (Coser, 1956, p. 128).

This observation succinctly states the condition of the Communist regimes before 1989. A case in point is the Polish social conciliatory commissions, which were created by Polish citizens but subsequently coopted by the Communist party. So rigid was the Communist system that, when confronted by a mild democratic initiative, the government was forced to suppress it completely (Shonholtz, 1986).

It is essential for the new democracies to understand the importance of creating a system that is flexible enough to modify its own normative conditions in the face of conflict. Only in this way can democracy survive under the ever-changing conditions of the democratic and free market world. Establishing commissions shows that the governing parties of the new democracies understand the importance of establishing mechanisms through which adjustment to new conditions can be brought about in civil society.

Within the civil societies of Western democracies, mediating structures engage conflict and reinforce the actual and perceived capacity of democracy to manage conflict. In the new democracies, the commissions are the first mediating structures in civil society. The creation of such commissions is axiomatic to the adaptability of the new democracies. If the commissions are successful in harnessing the social functions of conflict, then they will themselves promote democratic institution building and normative rule making.

The commissions can become synonymous with a societal form of consensual understanding concerning the way in which minority conflicts are to be addressed in civil society. From this perspective, minority conflict has an extremely important function in the evolving democracies.

Commissions Can Start a Dialogue That Presents Options. Minority groups are likely to support and participate in local conciliation commissions not only for the purpose of settling disputes but also for the opportunity to start and sustain a dialogue on the new rules of civic participation.

The psychological framework of enemies and winners that prevailed in the old regimes is dysfunctional in the context of a commission that focuses dialogue on needs, interests, and the exploration and analysis of options. Moreover, the state control factors that enabled this earlier form of "dispute settlement" to proceed no longer exist in an open commission setting.

Thus, the commissions enable disputing parties to engage in three necessary activities: expressing their needs and interests, examining their options, and exploring areas of mutual agreement. Moreover, commissions may offer another critically important function: the opportunity to evaluate the opposing party's strengths, weaknesses, and degree of investment in the conflict.

One motivating ingredient in any attempt to apply models of conciliation is the ability to evaluate the strength of the adversary in the conditions afforded by democratic society. Conflict has been transformed in the new democracies from something suppressed to something expected, anticipated, and encouraged. This open shift in the rules of the game has generated much confusion and uncertainty about appropriate attitudes and relative strengths of the actors in the conflict. By providing a container for the expression of conflict and the needs and interests of disputing parties, the commissions have become an agency for the clarification of values, affirmation of disagreements, and understanding of the consequences attached to the conflict.

It may well be that the conciliation commissions give the parties insight into the ramifications of unchecked conflict without having to resort to a test of the physical power of their opponent. "If the adversary's strength could be measured prior to engaging in conflict, antagonistic interests might be met without such conflict; but, where no means for prior measurement exists, only actual struggle may afford the knowledge of comparative strength" (Coser, 1956, p. 135). In such a context, "the mediator can achieve reconciliation only if each party believes that the situation justifies the reconciliation and makes peace advantageous" (Simmel, 1955, p. 147).

With assistance from a representative body, such as a commission that represents the community's diversity, disputants can reveal their relative strengths, commitments, opportunities, and limitations. In short, the commission can serve as an alternative means of appraising the relative strengths and weaknesses of disputing parties without their having to resort to a formal struggle.

Efforts to create a new mediating structure in society must employ the psychology and mechanisms of the old regime as background. The foreground is the new civil structure controlled and sustained by the power inherent in civil society and by the factors motivating the disputing parties to explore their respective needs and options with a view to settling their differences.

As mediating conciliators, commission members have a unique and important function to perform. It remains to be seen whether the commissioners can hold the antagonisms and feelings of people in the Central and Eastern European region in check as they perform their conflict resolution role. In societies that are highly fractured by histories of ethnic and national conflict and that lack any neutral or third group, it becomes essential to discover ways to create viable dispute settlement mechanisms.

Establishing a Local Conciliation Commission in Plovdiv, Bulgaria

In August 1992, the city of Plovdiv, Bulgaria, became the site of ethnic unrest as a result of the accidental shooting of a Gypsy man by the local police. Bulgaria's National Center on Conflict Resolution and Negotiation and I responded to the crisis by calling for a meeting of local authorities and Gypsy representatives.

Emotions ran high during the hot Saturday afternoon meeting that packed twenty-seven people into the cultural center. It was agreed that a forum was needed that could allow the different groups to talk with one another. The government was not fully trusted. The police and courts were controlled by the Bulgarian state. Churches were divided by national and ethnic loyalties. In short, there was no neutral space in which the community could come together to discuss the incident.

By bringing together representatives from city offices, the church, and the Gypsy, Bulgarian, and Turkish communities, the center demonstrated the ability to achieve a level of trust not given to any other group or organization in Plovdiv. The absence of an existing community capacity to meet and address ethnic tensions and the need for such a capacity became important themes of the center's organizing work in Plovdiv.

In bringing together the mayor's office, police officials, local administrators, educators, and representatives of the Bulgarian United Democratic Forces (UDF), the Turkish Movement for Rights and Freedoms (MRF), and several Roma (that is, Gypsy) organizations, the Bulgarian center and Partners achieved what many had considered to be impossible: a meeting of all the relevant parties at the same time in the same place. The August meeting brought the UDF and MRF together for the very first time, which underscored just how serious everyone considered the situation in the city to be.

The meeting not only laid the groundwork for the establishment of a local conciliation commission, it also resulted in the first set of agreements between the parties: They drafted a statute that would create a local conciliation commission; they asked the center and Partners to prepare the first draft; and they accepted a procedure for sharing the draft for comment between the parties.

On October 18, 1992, fourteen Turkish, Bulgarian, and Gypsy commissioners of the first ethnic conciliation commission in Eastern Europe completed their initial three-day training in the conciliation of local ethnic disputes. After further training, the Commission on Human Rights and Conflict Resolution will begin its work in January 1993.

The commission covers the ancient Roman district of Stolipinovo that is now crowded with Bulgarians, Turks, and Gypsies. The community commission joins three other educational commissions in Plovdiv established by Partners for Democratic Change and its national Center on Conflict Resolution at Sofia University. The Stolipinovo and educational commissions complete a nine-month effort by Partners to pursue with national and local political leaders the establishment of a conciliation commission in civil society that operates through the efforts of skilled citizens who have been selected and who are respected by their respective communities.

The October 15 training included a role play that was instrumental in highlighting the tensions currently felt between ethnic minorities in the regions and local and national officials. The fictional case involved a mayor from Plovdiv whose remarks about Turks and Gypsies had been misquoted by the international press while he was attending a conference in Vienna. Plovdiv television and newspapers picked up the disparaging comments and reinforced the mayor's statements with photos of the squalid conditions in which the Gypsies and Turks live. Neither Turkish nor Gypsy leaders were interviewed for the television or newspaper stories. The minority groups had called for the resignation of the mayor, the firing of the directors of the television station and newspaper, and the opportunity to present their opposing views to the public. Other actors in the dispute included the United Democratic Front (Bulgaria's ruling party; the mayor was their representative) and the Turks' Movement for Rights and Freedoms.

The role play was close to issues that concern Gypsies and Turks. One Turk who served in the role play as a commissioner had to remove himself from the process because he could not stay in the role. The exercise was too real. In fact, he viewed the mayor as the enemy of the Turks, and he wanted the mayor to resign. Similarly, the Gypsy and Turkish participants in the role play felt that the media were enemies and not entitled to having their positions heard.

As the role play unfolded, everyone learned that the mayor had not made the alleged comments and that he had been misquoted by the international press. The media apologized for the misquote and responded to the requests for outside control by noting that the media were a "public trust" and their actions could not be dictated by any one group. The UDF noted that the media were in fact subject to regulation and that, as a UDF mayor had been libeled, some action was necessary. The Turks and the Gypsies agreed that both the media and the mayor should increase their efforts to represent ethnic minorities more fairly.

To achieve their desired outcomes, the disputing parties were forced to evaluate their positions, objectives, and needs as well as their relative strengths and weaknesses. As a result, the disputants moved away from an inimical and confrontational stance toward open discussion of their problems with media (unfair coverage, unbalanced reporting, no minority representation in the media, and general powerlessness before the media).

The role play gave the participants an excellent opportunity to experience the real power of "enemy" thinking and enabled them to move through the process of developing options and discovering solutions. During the exercise, the future commissioners realized that such a process could help them to assess the relative strengths and investments of the disputing parties. They also realized that dialogues around options for change could shift the discussion away from historical conditions to present solutions.

Results of the training indicated that the conciliation model required further adaptation. Given the number of parties involved and the likely breadth of social issues presented, it needed to include the features of facilitated dialogue, negotiation, and cooperative planning and problem solving.

Conclusion

Those who take part in efforts to develop a culture of democratic conflict resolution in the new democracies of Central and Eastern Europe and the former Soviet republics will have to demonstrate the unifying aspects and positive functions of conflict. If the new democracies are to be flexible enough to adjust to the changing norms inherent in social conflict, they will have to create new structures and institutions that benefit from conflict. Ethnic conciliation commissions begin to provide the new democracies with the type of civil structure that engages conflict positively and that promotes its social functions and values.

Moreover, the new structures undermine the Communist legacy that views conflict as something that must be suppressed, that is fostered by enemies, and that has only one winner and many losers. Mediating structures expand the consensual understanding and tolerance that democratic society needs in order to function, and they serve to advance the values inherent in the peaceful expression and resolution of differences.

References

Coser, L. *The Functions of Social Conflict.* New York: Free Press, 1956.

Rheinstein, M. ed. *Max Weber on Law in Economy and Society.* Cambridge, Mass.: Harvard University Press, 1954.

Rubenstein, R. E. "Dispute Resolution on the Eastern Frontier: Some Questions for Modern Missionaries." *Negotiation Journal,* 1992, 8 (3), 205–13.

Shonholtz, R. "New Justice Theories and Practice." In H. Bianchi and R. Van Swaaringen eds., *Abolitionism: towards a Nonrepressive Approach to Crime.* Amsterdam: Free University Press, 1986.

Simmel, G. *The Sociology of George Simmel.* New York: Free Press, 1955.

·4·

TOOLS FOR
COEXISTENCE
WORK

The tools available for coexistence work are diverse. Most are borrowed from allied, more established fields like mediation, conflict management, peace research, international relations, antibias education, and others. A few of these tools are presented in this chapter. They stress primarily the recognition of a conflict's seemingly intractable nature and an awareness that the search for ideal solutions can get in the way of conflict avoidance. The coexistence worker is focused on the need for the parties to develop improved methods of living with each other, *in the meantime,* rather than on the need to solve those fundamental problems that form the basis of the conflict. Although the techniques of conflict resolution may be used, the aims are more limited. The focus is on getting through the day without having to kill or be killed. Coexistence work is about enhancing the living relationships between enemies, antagonists, and competitors, in as civilized a way as is feasible. Coexistence work thereby strengthens a de facto willingness to live together and to build community.

The tools of coexistence work outlined in this chapter address four major questions: (1) What methods are available to maintain the conversation between ethnic antagonists? (2) What methods are available to ethnic groups dominated by others who are stronger? (3) What methods are available to educators who wish to prevent intergroup antagonisms and enhance coexistence? (4) What are the advantages and disadvantages of mediation when dealing with ethnic conflict once it has crystallized into a set of grievances?

In the first article, Gene Sharp enumerates the nonviolent alternatives available to dominated-minority groups that enable them to coexist with and press their agendas upon dominating majorities.

Maria Volpe's article advocates the use of the "Town Meeting" to promote the goal of coexistence. While noting that there are many factors that contribute to the creation of peaceful coexistence, Volpe stresses that the themes of good communication and dialogue are generally central in these endeavors. Town meetings do not necessarily guarantee agreements or meaningful outcomes, but Volpe suggests that their potential for fostering coexistence between culturally and ethnically diverse groups on an ongoing basis is enormous and largely untapped.

Louise Derman-Spark's review of the literature on antibias educational programs gets to the heart of the attitudes and behaviors that prevent coexistence. She is a strong advocate of the series of methods and tools to be used in the educational context, particularly in the early grades, to enhance children's ability to appreciate diversity.

Antonia Handler Chayes and Abram Chayes address the following question: "What can international and regional organizations really do to manage ethnic conflicts, and where have they succeeded or fallen short—individually and collectively?" After illustrating the problems connected with specific attempts to manage conflict, they conclude their perceptive chapter by advocating a team-based approach of international organizations and NGOs, using different coalition and lead agencies in different situations.

In the section's concluding essay, Peter Coleman and Morton Deutsch summarize their position with regard to the tools of coexistence as follows: "A practical recommendation for dealing with these issues has also been outlined by Pruitt and Olczak . . . in a paper addressing intractable conflicts. After pointing to the impracticality of expecting to be able to confront and resolve every issue to a conflict through a win-win framework, these authors encourage a combination of problem solving and conflict avoidance. They note that parties to a conflict are frequently unable to distinguish between long-term idealistic objectives and those objectives that might be attainable within a realistic time frame. Thus the parties need to be helped to tone down their aspirations for agreement so as to address only what is currently possible, and to avoid or tolerate their remaining differences, as least temporarily." Coleman and Deutsch thus instruct us in the limitations of mediation as a tool to achieve coexistence between ethnic groups.

In addressing the questions presented with regard to the tools for coexistence work, the contributors insist that such work is focused neither on behavioral change nor on attitudinal change, but on both. Coexistence work is concerned with both short-term and long-range change as well as with macro-structural change concerning major societal arrangements as well as individual changes. In short, coexistence work, in their view, is an inclusive, total, multi-dimensional set of life-enhancing activities.

Nonviolent Action in
Acute Interethnic Conflicts

GENE SHARP

Persistent Acute Ethnic Conflicts

The tragic effects of interethnic violence are readily apparent in a number of devastating and bloody conflicts around the world. Northern Ireland, Israel/Palestine, India, Burma, and Nigeria are a few of such places. The recent killings in Rwanda and Bosnia reveal, sadly once again, the extremity such conflicts may reach. Clearly not all ethnic conflicts assume such genocidal proportions. However, some struggles between ethnic groups for greater autonomy, social equality, independence, cultural, and language rights, and responsive government lead to terrorism and guerrilla warfare. Such violence often has horrendous consequences for the populations involved.

A cursory glance at the daily news headlines is nearly all that is required to demonstrate that ethnic conflict remains a pervasive phenomenon in our world. Very few states are comprised of a single ethnic group. Also, groups within any given society will continue to contend with one another over issues of political power, self-determination, economic advantage, identity, cultural practices, religion, and the like. Therefore, it is safe to assume that there will be in the future many interethnic conflicts around the world.

The questions addressed in this chapter are these: What can be done to reduce the potential lethality of future interethnic conflicts? How can aggrieved ethnic groups pursue their objectives without adopting means that contribute to cycles of retributive violence? Can nonviolent action contribute to durable improvements in interethnic relations?

The focus here is on acute interethnic conflicts. These are defined as persistent conflicts between ethnic groups over perceived fundamental issues that have been, or are on the verge of being, carried out with mass direct action, either violent or nonviolent, or by harsh state action against an ethnic group. Many of today's acute interethnic conflicts involve demands for autonomy, independence, or power sharing by an ethnic group living within a state dominated by another ethnic group. This chapter posits two adversaries in conflict with one another, one often possessing the machinery of the state to enforce its will on the other. This is, of course, only one approximation of the many variants of ethnic conflict, but is not unrepresentative of the conflicts in today's world.

Cases of acute interethnic conflict should remind us that many such conflicts do not seem soluble by measures that attempt to achieve reconciliation or compromise. The protagonists are often unwilling or unable to abandon their feelings, beliefs, and goals or to compromise with their opponents. Submission to their opponents' claims is to them unthinkable. Compromise is viewed as a betrayal of one's principles and one's people. The prospect of defeat often seems preferable to a perceived betrayal of one's heritage, race, history, or religion.

These intransigent conflicts often persist for decades and even centuries, and commonly involve violence by one side or both. Clearly, conditions within the contested area and internationally may shift at any given time and create new opportunities for the redress of grievances. However, such changes in the "environment" of the conflict often cannot be anticipated or assumed. Ethnic groups are faced with the task of devising options for action in the present.

Other Dimensions of Some Interethnic Conflicts

It is commonly recognized that interethnic conflicts may involve relations between different religious groups, castes, racial groups, and peoples. Each group has its own views of the world and how its people should live. Commonly, members of one ethnic group have regarded themselves as superior to members of the other group by culture, religion, language, or race.

It is important also to remember that persistent interethnic conflicts frequently include other important elements in addition to ethnicity. When ethnic groups are in conflict, the dominant, stronger, group may have imposed conditions and practices that are to its own advantage, socially, economically, or politically, and to the disadvantage of the subordinate, weaker, ethnic group. Struggles to change those relations have often been identified as struggles for civil rights, human rights, self-determination, economic justice, and independence. In many such conflicts the resisting group has used forms of resistance that did not involve violence. These cases are significant in the search for means to defuse violent interethnic conflicts.

Additionally, it must be kept in mind that third parties for their own interests or governments that feel insecure may deliberately aggravate or even initiate interethnic conflict. The purpose may be to deflect pressure on themselves and turn sections of the potentially resistant population against each other. *Divide et impera.*

An Imperative to Struggle

As stated above, it is essential to recognize that emotions, convictions, prejudices, and issues are very real for the members of the contending ethnic groups. They are unable to remain passive observers, holding their beliefs quietly inside themselves. Members of each group will feel that they must act to try to apply their beliefs and to struggle to achieve their goals. Therefore, it is essential for them to have some strong means of expression. As long as the group retains its beliefs and goals, these means need to be seen by the aggrieved group as capable of achieving in the short run at least some minimal recognition of its rights, and in the long run to achieve the group's objectives.

Usually, almost by definition, these means must be noninstitutionalized means. Commonly, the dominant group has established institutions and procedures in society and government that favor its own status and interests to the disadvantage of the subordinate ethnic group. The subordinate group has in many cases been left without real access to these established legal and political procedures for correcting the power imbalance between it and the dominant group. With such limitations on effective access to established procedures and institutions, the subordinate ethnic group is left with the unacceptable alternative of doing nothing, and thus maintaining the existing power relationships, or, instead, it can use noninstitutionalized means which has often meant violence.

In these conflicts one side, or both, may claim that its resort to violence is not only justified but is required. When there seems little chance of success by other means, and when the dominant side is very powerful, the subordinate side may resort to extreme forms of violence, such as guerrilla warfare or terrorism. The dominant side is likely to use violent repression in the forms of states of emergency, suspension of civil liberties, police action, imprisonments, executions, assassinations, and military suppression.

To break this cycle, aggrieved ethnic groups need to adopt means that offer the prospect of altering the relative power relations between the conflicting groups. However, if their choice is to be rational, the means of action chosen must not lead to the group's own demise, to the permanent loss of its goals, or to wider catastrophe.

Problems of Terrorism and Guerrilla Warfare

Both terrorism and guerrilla warfare produce serious negative consequences for the group on whose behalf they are used. Terrorism can be used only by a small highly secretive group able to organize and conduct its acts of bombings, killings, hijackings, and the like that are intended to induce the atmosphere of terror. The general population on whose behalf such acts are supposedly conducted are excluded from participation. The terrorist acts provide the targeted group and government (which may itself have been the target) the grounds—or perceived justification—for harsh countermeasures and repression, while paying no attention to the grievances that motivate the terrorists. Similarly, public and international opinion hardens and is turned away from considering the grievances, which is now commonly accepted as "giving in to terrorism." Instead, the focus is placed almost entirely on the perceived outrageous and inhumane attacks that have commonly endangered and taken the lives of persons not responsible for the grievances. Previous sympathy and support from other groups may be damaged or lost. The needed change of the relative power relations between the conflicting ethnic groups does not occur. The weaker group usually remains weak and suffers greatly from the repression. Terrorism in many cases achieves little.

Guerrilla warfare also has negative consequences on the group on whose behalf it is waged. Almost universally, this technique results in massive repression and very high casualties among the civilian population and widespread destruction of social institutions. This occurs whether or not the population is supporting the guerrilla struggle. The opponents' machinery of repression, especially the military forces, is likely to increase greatly during such a struggle. If the guerrillas are defeated their opponents could therefore be significantly stronger and more repressive in the future than before the conflict.

On the other hand, if the guerrillas do win, the result is unlikely to be a democratic society respecting the rights of all. As Mao Zedong projected, successful guerrilla warfare is most likely to have developed sufficient manpower, military organization, equipment, and strategic development to have been transformed into conventional frontal military warfare. That produces a new very strong military establishment that will continue as a permanent institution after the defeat of the enemy forces. That military institution has a capacity that can easily be applied to impose or support a new dictatorship, as did the People's Liberation Army in China.

Both terrorism and guerrilla warfare have sufficient negative consequences that possible effective alternative ways to conduct an ethnic struggle should be carefully considered. Not the least of the potential consequences is that the dominant ethnic group may use the resisters' violence as a justification for mass slaughters and attempted genocide, cloaked in the guise of self-protection against the violent attacks.

A Shift in the Means of Conflict?

Whether chosen rationally or irrationally, violence is often the weapon of choice for many ethnic groups in sharp conflicts. It does little good for others who are offended by such violence to call for the abandonment of a group's long-held beliefs or goals. It is almost never realistic to expect that long and deeply held convictions and goals will be abandoned in order to limit or halt the resort to violence. As long as violent means of conflict are believed to be the most powerful and effective type of action available, they will not be abandoned and certainly not as a response to international pleas for peace and humanity.

However, violence can be abandoned without betrayal of one's people and one's cause if effective alternative types of action can be substituted. Such alternatives would need to have the following characteristics:

- enable the group to continue to struggle for their full claims, without feeling a personal betrayal or compromise on their beliefs and objectives
- provide participants in the new struggle with a sense of satisfaction and solidarity because of personal participation in an active struggle
- be capable of producing some positive gains and at least limited victories for their group

- provide the group with a technique of struggle able to wield power and to confront the power of the opposing ethnic group.

Does a realistic form of struggle exist that avoids the negative consequences of violence yet can powerfully and effectively address the convictions and interests of the aggrieved group?

Throughout history some groups facing acute conflict have adopted an alternative means of struggle. It is called nonviolent action or nonviolent struggle. The characteristics and requirements of this type of struggle potentially have significant advantages over violence for a dominated ethnic group.

Nonviolent Action as an Option

Nonviolent action is a way to conduct acute conflicts. It is a technique for mobilizing and applying the power potential of people, groups, and institutions for pursuing objectives and interests using nonmilitary "weapons": psychological, political, social, and economic ones. Overwhelmingly, the people using these nonviolent weapons might use violence under other circumstances, but for a given conflict use nonviolent methods of action because they have concluded that they offer better chances of success.

Nonviolent action involves a range of behavior. People using this technique either refuse to do things they are expected or required to do, or they insist on doing things they normally do not do or that are forbidden. The classes of specific methods, or forms, of action are: *nonviolent protest and persuasion* (symbolic acts, such as vigils, marches, and display of flags); *noncooperation* (including social boycotts, economic boycotts, labor strikes, and political noncooperation); and *nonviolent intervention* (such as sit-ins, hunger strikes, new institutions, and parallel governments).

Nonviolent struggle operates by mobilizing the power potential of people and institutions to enable them to wield power themselves and also to restrict or sever the sources of power of their opponents (sources such as authority or legitimacy, human resources, skills and knowledge, intangible factors contributing to support or obedience, material resources, and sanctions).

This capacity to wield power themselves and to undermine the power of opponents is important because the power of all oppressive groups, of all dictators and aggressors, depends upon the support they receive. This support refers to acceptance of their authority and the duty to obey, the operation of the economic system and the continued functioning of the civil service and the bureaucracy, the loyalty of the army and the reliability of the police, the blessing of the rulers by religious bodies, and the cooperation of workers and managers. Nonviolent struggle is a type of action uniquely suited to undermining and withdrawing these "pillars of support" that uphold an oppressive system.

The methods of nonviolent struggle attack the very sources of the opponents' power. Repression must therefore be expected. This repression, however, often fails to halt nonviolent struggle. Repression against nonviolent resisters can even drive more persons to join the resistance and also can alienate groups that usually have supported the opponents. The repression can at times even weaken the violent ethnic group and strengthen the nonviolent struggle group. That process is called "political jiujitsu": the violence of the opponents rebounds to undermine their own power position.

Of course, not all nonviolent struggles are successful. However, these struggles have a much higher success rate than is generally recognized. The identifiable conditions and capacities that lead to success must be present or created, and there is no substitute for wise strategy and courageous, persistent, disciplined action.

Nonviolent struggles may succeed in one of four ways, or in a combination of these. Rarely, though at times, the nonviolent action causes members of the opponent group to change their opinions or beliefs, so that they come to agree with the claims of the nonviolent group. This is called *conversion*. More commonly, through what is termed *accommodation*, the nonviolent group gains a part of its objectives, in recognition of changes produced by the struggle and in a compromise agreement with the opponent group. When noncooperation and defiance have been very powerful the opponent group may wish to continue the struggle but no longer has the ability to resist the demands that have been made on it. The opponents' effective power has been drastically reduced to the point that they have no alternative but to grant what has been asked. This is known as *nonviolent coercion*. Finally, in more extreme cases the noncooperation and defiance have so severed the opponent group's sources of power that the system or regime complete falls apart. No one has even enough power to surrender. This is called *disintegration*.*

Short-Term Advantages of Nonviolent Action

The choice of nonviolent struggle in an interethnic conflict has certain advantages for the group using it.

In those conflicts in which the dominant ethnic group controls the state apparatus, and thereby its police and military systems, and the subordinate ethnic group has insignificant or no such capacity, the subordinates have no real chance to defeat the regime by violence. Nonviolent struggle provides them with another, more advantageous, way to conduct the struggle.

Nonviolent struggle enables the subordinate, and previously weaker, group to mobilize the power potential of its people and institutions to make them stronger and more able to change the relationships between the ethnic groups in conflict. This provides the group using it with increased leverage for pressing its objectives or for resisting oppressive conditions or addressing grievances against the dominant group.

Members of the ethnic group that employs nonviolent struggle are likely to feel enhanced self-esteem and greater capacity to shape their own future. This is in part due to the sense of direct participation in the struggle that is increasing the

---

*For a fuller study of the nature of nonviolent struggle, see Gene Sharp, *The Politics of Nonviolent Action*. Boston: Porter Sargent, 1973.

group's power. This is especially likely to occur if the group achieves some specific objective for which it has struggled. This improvement in the participants' self-image may reduce the group's desperation in its relations with the other ethnic group.

The changes are, however, more than psychological. They can directly affect power relationships between the two groups. Nonviolent action in most cases has the potential to restrict or sever, directly or indirectly, the sources of power of the opponent group, as previously cited. Additionally, the adoption of nonviolent action—instead of violence—can reduce the solidarity of the dominant ethnic group, the members of which are not under violent attack. The nonviolent posture of the struggling ethnic group may persuade some members of the dominant group to support granting the resisters' claims. Such support would be far more difficult to obtain if the subordinate group instead had used violent resistance. Under those conditions the advocates of granting the claims of the resisting group would be more easily labeled as traitors and collaborators with murderers of their own people.

Nonviolent action has another advantage. It tends to bring a favorable public image to the ethnic group using it and can facilitate domestic and even international sympathy and assistance.

Subordinate ethnic groups often have limited economic resources. Here, too, the choice of nonviolent action has an advantage. Whereas the choice of violent struggle often requires major resources for guns, ammunition, and the like, nonviolent struggle places much more limited demands on economic resources.

The choice of nonviolent struggle instead of violence tends to limit casualties of wounded and dead among one's group. The reason for this is that violent repression against a nonviolent group will be more difficult for the dominant group to justify than will repression against violent resistance. When significant casualties do occur they are likely to stimulate condemnation of the perpetrators and increased support for the nonviolent group. Reduced suffering and a lower casualty rate are likely outcomes.

For such reasons as these, nonviolent struggle may provide a realistic and preferable alternative means of action for ethnic groups that would otherwise rely on forms of violence—such as terrorism and guerrilla warfare. Nonviolent action may provide ethnic minorities with an effective means of pressuring oppressive groups and unresponsive governments to address their grievances.

Especially for subordinate ethnic groups, the choice of using nonviolent action tends to increase their chance of gaining significant objectives. These include objectives that could not have been gained if the group had instead attempted to wage a violent struggle against the dominant ethnic group that usually has greater capacity to fight by violence.

Importance of Strategy

The development and application of wise strategy in nonviolent action are highly important. Yet only rarely do those seeking to use this type of struggle fully recognize the importance of preparing a comprehensive strategic plan before they act. For various reasons, resisters have often not attempted to think how best to apply their own resources towards the attainment of specific objectives. Often resisters even fail to articulate specific objectives for their actions (relying instead on such vagaries as "equality," "justice," or "freedom"). The failure to plan strategically dissipates one's strength. One's actions are less effective. Painful sacrifices may be wasted and one's cause is not well served.

On the contrary, the formulation and adoption of sound strategies increase the chances of success.* One's strength and actions are focused to serve the main strategic objectives. Casualties may be reduced. Action in accordance with a strategic plan enables the group to concentrate its strengths to move toward the desired goal.

Examples of Nonviolent Action in Ethnic Conflicts

There have been various acute interethnic conflicts in which the subordinate group has consciously used nonviolent struggle to advance its cause. At the time some of these conflicts were identified by other labels but had significant characteristics of interethnic conflict. A few of these cases are offered here merely to illustrate that ethnic groups can adopt nonviolent action to pursue their conflict with another ethnic group and thereby increase their ability to press their claims.

For centuries in Vykom in the princely state of Travancore, India, untouchables had been forbidden to use a particular road that went directly to their quarter but passed in front of an orthodox Brahman Hindu temple. In 1924–25 high caste Hindus and untouchables challenged that prohibition. Together, they walked down the road and stopped in front of the temple. Following some arrests and imprisonments, a police cordon was placed across the road. The volunteers waited there in shifts day and night, including during a flood. Sixteen months later the Hindu Brahmans said they were ready to receive the untouchables. The case had a major impact on improving the rights of untouchables elsewhere in India.

In the United States from the mid-1950s and throughout the 1960s African-Americans and other activists used nonviolent struggle extensively in the civil rights movement to end segregation and discrimination. Many of the methods are well known: bus boycotts, marches, sit-ins, picketing, economic boycotts, and the like. In hindsight, it is often assumed that the use of such methods was only to be expected. It is frequently forgotten that serious violence might well have been used, and that violence had its advocates. Indeed, following the assassination of Dr. Martin Luther King, Jr., there was widespread rioting in several cities. However, for the most part nonviolent action was used instead in the struggle, and it served well the cause of ending segregation and discrimination.

In the interethnic conflict in Northern Ireland violence has commonly been used by both the Protestant supporters of union with Britain and by Catholic supporters of union with the Irish Republic. It is less well remembered that nonvio-

---

*See Peter Ackerman and Christopher Kruegler, *Strategic Nonviolent Conflict: The Dynamics of People Power in the Twentieth Century*. Westport, Conn. and London: Praeger, 1994.

lent resistance has also on occasion been used by both sides. The 1974 Ulster unionist workers' strike was a dramatic departure from the violent activities of the Ulster Defense League. It was called to block perceived British attempts to be more conciliatory toward the Irish Catholic nationalists and supporters of legal equality for Catholics and Protestants. That strike brought down the Stormont government that the British had recently introduced as a moderating influence.

Hunger strikes were later used by Irish nationalists to advance their cause. In October 1980, Irish Republican Army (IRA) members imprisoned in Belfast, Northern Ireland, tried to achieve recognition of their political (or "special category") status in British jails. They sought very limited concessions, including the right to wear their own clothes. During this conflict, ten hunger strikers died in prison. The most famous of these was Bobby Sands, who had been elected to the British Parliament in a by-election while on hunger strike. The hunger strikes resulted in a massive outpouring of public sympathy for the hunger strikers, especially expressed in parades, revealing the greatest support for Irish unity in many years.

Prime Minister Margaret Thatcher, however, refused to budge even on the very limited demands. Unwilling to face further deaths, the hunger strikes were called off on October 3, 1981. The Irish Republicans returned to violent means and this was followed by a fall in their popular support as shown in elections, especially in the Irish Republic.

In South Africa nonviolent struggle was a principal technique in the struggle against *apartheid*. These struggles included the Defiance Campaign of 1952–53, involving civil disobedience against apartheid laws, and in later years, economic boycotts, rent strikes, school strikes, labor strikes, and stay-at-home demonstrations. These were collectively called "mass action." Violence was clearly also present, but these nonviolent forms of resistance combined with international economic boycotts and diplomatic isolation were major factors in ending apartheid and achieving nonracial elections.

Kosovo was previously an autonomous province within the Republic of Serbia in the former Yugoslavia, and has been the site of conflict between Slavs and Albanians for centuries. The population is 85 percent Albanian. In 1990, Serbia countered demands in Kosovo for greater autonomy with suspension of the region's autonomous status, declaration of martial law, and imposition of full Serbian rule. The population countered these measures with noncooperation with the Serbian institutions, holding their own multiparty elections and organizing their own independent parallel institutions including educational institutions. Despite repression and economic difficulties, the Kosovo struggle continues still in a changing situation in Serbia proper. Calls in Kosovo for violent resistance have not been widely supported.

A brief review of these illustrative cases suggests that if nonviolent action not been used to the extent that it was, the outcome in these conflicts might have been very different from what it was—perhaps tragically so. For example, the conflict in Kosovo has avoided the massive slaughters that have occurred in Croatia and Bosnia-Herzegovina.

In facing other interethnic conflicts in the future, the adoption of nonviolent action could be made more deliberately and with greater strategic sophistication than occurred in these past cases. That development could positively assist a wider shift away from the use of violence in interethnic conflicts.

Use of Nonviolent Action for "Wrong" Purposes?

Problems still remain when one ethnic group is using nonviolent struggle against another ethnic group. This is especially so when one side is (or both sides are) seeking to advance "unjust" or "wrong" objectives. For example, the goal may be to perpetuate racial segregation, a caste system, economic exploitation, or passive submission. No matter by what means those objectives are pursued, most thoughtful people maintain they are unacceptable. (Whether nonviolent means can in the long run really advance hierarchical domination is a separate question.)

When such goals, and the beliefs that underlie them, are firmly based and deeply rooted, there is almost *no* possibility that members of the group will abandon those beliefs and or compromise on those goals. Whether others want them to do so or not is irrelevant.

However, there often *is* a possibility that the same group might shift from violent to nonviolent means to conduct the conflict. The real question is therefore not whether one would prefer them to change their beliefs and goals (since that is almost certainly not going to happen); the real question is instead whether one prefers that group to struggle for its goals by violent or nonviolent means. That is often the realistic choice.

Given that choice, the adoption of nonviolent means minimally avoids the killings that continued mutual violence would bring and the escalation of that violence. For example, in the U.S. South in the 1950s and 1960s economic boycotts by segregationists against civil rights activists were preferable to the killings and bombings that also occurred.

In such cases when a hostile ethnic group adopts nonviolent means in place of violence, the targeted ethnic group is clearly not obligated passively to accept the changes demanded. The question becomes how the unacceptable objectives are to be opposed. The resort to violence by the targeted group will cause the situation to deteriorate to its predictable nadir. In some situations legal courses of counteraction are available, as by court action. In other situations the ethnic group that is the focus of harmful nonviolent pressures will have to pursue other responses. These may include tenacious persistence in refusing to capitulate, solicitation of external assistance, attempts to undermine support for the hostile policy among members of the opponent ethnic group, and the use of nonviolent counteraction.

Conclusion

An ethnic group in conflict may adopt nonviolent action while still adhering to its long-term objectives, fundamental convictions, and even its prejudices. However, the adoption of this technique introduces certain elements that may in time reduce the severity of the conflict and especially its lethality.

If the nonviolent group wants to succeed, it must adhere strictly to nonviolent discipline. The cessation of violent attacks on the other ethnic group means that the group that has adopted nonviolent action is no longer contributing to a reservoir of fear maintained within the opponent group that might fuel violent attacks on itself in the future. The pattern of reciprocal revenge may begin to weaken.

If the nonviolent resisters can maintain courage, persistence, and discipline, their behavior is likely in time to challenge negative ethnic stereotypes, which the other group may hold. In the long run that also may help to reduce the opponent group's hostility to the nonviolent group.

The newly nonviolent group may also realize that with this technique it need no longer be limited to making sweeping demands that cannot be realized. While not abandoning those goals, the group can potentially make concrete gains by conducting limited campaigns for achievable objectives. The attempt to win limited objectives can modify the extreme polarization in which each side demands nothing less than its total objectives—objectives that are in turn totally unacceptable to the other group.

In addition to building solid support for the nonviolent struggle from its own ethnic group, the nonviolent group may also make efforts to gain third-party and international sympathy and support. This may require presentation of more reasonable and justifiable objectives. At times the newly nonviolent group may even attempt to get sympathy and support from within the violent ethnic group that it opposes. In the long run, such efforts may help to soften the extreme hostility between the contending ethnic groups.

Similarly, the opponent ethnic group using violence will need to consider how to react to the newly developed nonviolent struggle, when it recognizes that its violent repression does not produce desired results and indeed may greatly undermine its position. This reconsideration, too, may have long-term consequences.

These efforts, stimulated by the shift by one side to the use of nonviolent action in place of violent struggle, may create sufficient pressure so that each group can begin to consider the claims and objectives of the other, and to view members of the opposing group as human beings, not simply as historical enemies, devils, or targets.

No one should expect a purely harmonious relationship to follow the use of nonviolent action in an acute interethnic conflict. Serious problems between the two ethnic groups will doubtless remain and conflict may well continue. The use of nonviolent action in an acute interethnic conflict will not produce a loving society, but it would result in a less violent one. Future forms of the conflict are likely to be different from those where previously both sides relied on violence. Less hostility and greater mutual understanding may have room to develop. Although not ideal, this situation would be a far cry from the results of interethnic conflict conducted by mutual violence.

Using Town Meetings to Foster Peaceful Coexistence

MARIA R. VOLPE

> In my mind [the town meeting forum] is the ultimate way to respect each other by listening to each other when we might not particularly want to, or we might realize that there is a very complicated answer we cannot get into in two minutes . . . but we have been able in this forum to grow, to listen, to laugh, to learn, to apologize, and to respect one another. . . . And while we have problems, we are facing them directly.
>
> President Gerald W. Lynch
> John Jay College of Criminal Justice—CUNY
> Closing remarks, Town Meeting,
> November 26, 1996

There is no magical formula or easy solution for fostering peaceful coexistence among ethnically diverse individuals and groups. Clearly, what works with some may be totally ineffective with others. Coexistence efforts are constructed and best understood within a context. While a host of factors contribute to successful peaceful coexistence, central to many endeavors are themes of good communication and dialogue. The cultivation and maintenance of constructive, comfortable, and civil dialogue sessions on an ongoing basis, however, can be particularly daunting.

This article will examine town meetings as a mechanism for creating and sustaining a culture and infrastructure for deliberate, facilitated public dialogue. More specifically, it will focus on the use and institutionalization of town meetings as a means of fostering ongoing peaceful coexistence.

Despite their potential for providing a means for conflict prevention, conflict management, or conflict resolution, town meetings have rarely been addressed by the growing body of literature in the rapidly emerging conflict resolution field [see Volpe and Witherspoon, 1992:346–49; Volpe, 1994:31–33]. I draw on eight years of experience convening town meetings in a culturally and ethnically diverse college environment, namely John Jay College of Criminal Justice,[1] a senior college of the City University of New York [CUNY].[2] The lessons drawn from this experience can be applied to other contexts where ongoing constructive dialogue between culturally and ethnically diverse individuals and groups is sought. Additionally, town meetings are explored as one more tool for the toolbox of those who strive to understand and foster peaceful coexistence initiatives.

This article departs from the traditional notion of town meetings occurring in small, relatively homogenous cultures or communities, particularly at the local level where individuals and groups share more in common than is possible in many contemporary, urban, highly diverse communities. This article also veers away from the more popular uses of town meetings as forums held during professional conferences or as sessions convened by elected officials to discuss particular concerns with their constituents or targeted groups. In such instances, town meetings are often convened as one-shot events when they are deemed necessary and targeted to meet specific needs. In this article, town meetings are discussed in the context of an organizational or community setting where they are used to serve as an ongoing proactive, preventative, and sometimes settlement mechanism for developing continuing dialogue between ethnically diverse individuals and groups.

Understanding Town Meetings

The town meeting concept is a simple one: bring people together and let them talk about concerns that are of relevance and interest to them. How, when, where, and why conflicts are managed in any organizational setting or community varies with practices, policies, procedures, philosophies, and human resources available. As used in this article, town meetings refer to the public convening of individuals or groups to discuss relevant and controversial issues with the assistance of a facilitator. The facilitated sessions can feature a specific theme or an open agenda. In an organizational setting, town meetings can be included as part of the organization's larger dispute system where they can play a role in helping to manage conflict situations and to encourage peaceful coexistence among culturally and ethnically diverse individuals and groups.

Town Meetings as a Conflict Resolution Concept

A significant challenge to interethnic coexistence are conflicts, often deep-rooted ones. Efforts to prevent, manage, and resolve these conflicts can take many forms. At the core of many endeavors is the difficulty of bringing people together to consider and talk about ways to handle their divergences. Sometimes the processes involve only the parties themselves, sometimes the use of third parties.

Regardless of the specific approach used, most conflict intervention processes confront similar challenges regarding the management of interactions. For example, who can or should convene the sessions? Who are or should be the participants at any session? Should sessions be open or restricted to nonstakeholders or observers? Who begins the sessions? What kind of discussion guidelines should be utilized? What other resolution processes can go on simultaneously? For instance, can litigation continue while another process is being used?

In some ways, town meetings may be easier to manage than other conflict resolution processes. For example, in face to face negotiations, the parties are usually trying to create doubt in each other's mind and striving for a suitable solution. In a mediation, the parties are working with a third party to work through their differences, and in many instances, hoping and trying to reach a mutually agreed upon settlement. In an arbitration, the parties present their concerns to a third party who is expected to make a decision for them. Town meetings, however, offer no expectations of agreements or meaningful outcomes, even though such may occur serendipitously as a result of the interactions engaged in by the participants.

From the perspective of implementing a process, a town meeting is quite easy. A meeting date is established, a site located, facilitators chosen, and ground rules developed. Depending on the context, town meetings are tailored to take into consideration a wide range of concerns by means of opening and closing statements, resource panels, and audience participation.

While town meetings may provide an opportunity to resolve conflicts between individuals and groups, that is not their manifest function. Town meetings are more likely to provide an occasion for individuals and groups to vent, express, and share their concerns and perspectives, acquire information, and obtain answers. The town meeting format enables individuals and groups to find ways to structure their interactions in such a way that they can coexist even if they do not see eye to eye or particularly like each other.

From Crisis Response to Institutionalization: One College's Experience with Town Meetings

Before proceeding with a more general discussion of town meetings, I will discuss how monthly town meetings became institutionalized at one college. During the spring 1989 semester, college students at John Jay College of Criminal Justice took over the college's buildings and locked everyone out for five days. Most of the students involved in the takeover were black or Latino, and with few exceptions, most key college administrators were white males. While the presenting problem and trigger for the takeover was the proposed tuition increase, the students used the takeover as an opportunity to address a variety of other concerns, better known as "local issues." Among the latter concerns was increased communication between the college's administration and students.

During the takeover, intensive negotiations between the administration and students focused not only on the release of the buildings, but on local issues as well. In response to the demand for increased communication, one of the agreements entered into by the parties was participation in a town meeting to be held at the conclusion of the takeover. This forum was envisioned as one where all members of the culturally diverse college community would have an opportunity to participate by asking questions or making comments.

The ensuing town meeting was extremely well attended by administration, faculty, and students, and as might be expected, was highly emotionally charged. Attendance mirrored the college community: predominantly white faculty and administrators, and a culturally diverse student population consisting of approximately one-third black, one-third Latino, and one-third white.

This town meeting could easily have been the college's first and last. The exchanges at the town meeting were not only impassioned about tactics used during the takeover, but reflected the interests of the black and Latino students to bring about changes in the college's organizational structure. Despite the town meeting's intensity (or "electricity" as the session's atmosphere was often referred to), respect for all in the huge room was maintained. So successful was this town meeting that during the subsequent academic year (1989–90), the students repeatedly asked for regularly scheduled town meetings. None were held. In one instance, the students even scheduled a town meeting, but college administrators did not attend and the meeting was not held.

Within a year of the first town meeting, in the spring of 1990, the College was again taken over for twenty-three days by many of the same students who had been involved in the previous takeover. The students had a long list of demands that included monthly town meetings.

Agreement between the college administration and the students to hold monthly town meetings was reached early during the 1990 takeover negotiations. A committee structure consisting of faculty, students, college administrators, and the director of the Dispute Resolution Program was created to plan future monthly town meetings. The monthly town meetings continue to the present time. They have been held under a wide range of conditions: in fact, one was held in the middle of the third student takeover in spring of 1991. Town meetings have focused on a wide range of intended and unintended topics, with none quashed or resisted even when sensitive or potentially volatile matters surfaced or the topics were unrelated to a town meeting's theme.

Isolated Event versus a Culture of Town Meetings

As one-shot events, town meetings meet a variety of needs for culturally diverse individuals and groups who attempt to or must coexist. When town meetings are institutionalized and incorporated into the culture of an organization or community, they provide a valuable opportunity for individuals and groups to structure communication for ongoing coexistence.

When convened as an isolated event, a town meeting is similar to many other forums. A format and agenda are developed and exchanges occur. Should a specific town meeting be perceived to have been a bad experience or unproductive event, it could be quickly forgotten by organizers and attendees since there are no expectations for any continuity. Similarly, if a town meeting is perceived to have been worthwhile or productive, particularly if the event was emotionally charged, the parties involved (including organizers) can move on to their other agendas. Such successful meetings, whether the result of deliberate design or serendipity, often end with a deep sigh of relief that they worked out. In short, regardless of perceived failure or success of one-shot town meetings, the prospects of continuing whatever transpired will, for the most part, soon fade away into memory.

The creation of a culture of institutionalized town meetings is markedly different from the orchestration of a town meeting as an isolated event. What this means is that there are shared meanings, norms, and knowledge transmitted over time by a group of people about a particular kind of communication forum. In a setting where town meetings are held on a regular basis, members of the community develop not only infrastructures to support the town meetings, but a mindset regarding dialogues among members of the community. This was evident at a recent John Jay College Faculty Senate meeting when faculty members, who were reflecting on the previous day's College Council meeting where some who wanted to speak were not recognized, "suggested that members of the College Council (and others wishing to speak) emulate the praiseworthy procedure of the College's Town Hall Meetings by lining up at the microphones and speaking when their turn at the microphone comes" (Faculty Senate Minutes No. 147, November 19, 1996, p. 2). The culture surrounding the town meeting also surfaces elsewhere in the college community. Consider the following reflections by an undergraduate student at John Jay College of Criminal Justice:

> After many decisions made by the 1996–1997 student government, the frustration that the student clubs felt was about to boil over. Each invitation that the Executive Officers of student clubs sent to the elected officers of Student Government was either ignored or dismissed since they felt they were right. The policies that this student government enforced were so unfavorable because they weren't enforced uniformly and the officers refused to sit down and explain why.
>
> The town meeting of October 24 [1996] was the last try for the Student Alliance, a democratic coalition of club officers, to be heard and have our concerns addressed. The town meeting relieved the tension students were feeling because it gave us a chance to address student government in an open forum where they couldn't run from answering our questions.
>
> The town meeting saved John Jay in a sense because the Student Alliance was ready to confront student government officers at their next meeting and demand to be heard. This would have probably led to a screaming match and nothing would have been accomplished. Through the town meeting, the student government realized the extent of our concerns and agreed to put our concerns on the agenda. . . . When people feel frustrated they want to riot and sit-in, but town meetings allowed us to be heard. Every university should have a town meeting. The town meeting saved us" (Singleton, 1996a, 1996b).

The Student Alliance Club is not unique in perceiving the town meeting as a mechanism to ask questions or make comments about matters of relevance to the college community. The monthly town meetings at John Jay College are widely viewed as opportunities for anyone to raise any issue in a structured, respectful, facilitated setting. When an issue surfaces, it is quite common to hear members of the community suggest that the concerns be brought up at the next town meeting or that a town meeting should be scheduled with a specific theme. This was reflected in a Faculty Senate resolution that stated "that the President immediately convene a town meeting to elicit the operational issues for the establishment of a branch campus" in Puerto Rico (Faculty Senate Minutes No. 102, 1994, p. 11). Furthermore, there have been instances on campus when other groups have held their own town meetings. For example, students have held their own town meetings with ground rules very similar to the collegewide meetings, and the Executive Director of the Ph.D. Program in Criminal Justice has held town meetings for doctoral students. The Executive Director has said that he got the idea for a town meeting after attending the college's town meetings (Levine, 1996). Moreover, the model is used to manage other forums: for example, recent candidates' forum for union elections mirrored the town meeting format very closely, including the use of the digital clock.

In a setting where town meetings are part of the members' worldview, individuals think of them much like the Student Alliance Club leaders did when they experienced communication roadblocks with elected leaders of student government. On a regular basis when concerns arise, it is very common for individuals to view the town meeting as a forum for communicating with others, raising relevant issues, and receiving information from others. On May 10, 1996, the President of John Jay College attended a Faculty Senate meeting and a faculty member asked about the college's retrenchment report proposals. According to the Faculty Senate minutes, the President remarked that "he would prefer not to take questions about the retrenchment plan until the May 13 Town Meeting at which time he will answer all questions, with the help of the Retrenchment Committee, whose members will be present as a resource panel: he said he has taken this position with every group that has asked to speak to him" (Faculty Senate Minutes No. 140, May 10, 1996, p. 7).

Institutionalizing Town Meetings as Part of the Local Culture

Although it is relatively easy to create town meetings as a communication forum, in order to maximize their potential for face-to-face dialogue on an ongoing basis, organizations and communities need to confront what commitment, personnel, resources, and time are necessary. Sustaining respectful town meetings where culturally diverse individuals and groups can participate over a long period of time requires careful attention regarding a wide range of details. Conveners need to understand and be sensitive to the context within which town meetings occur and find ways to ensure an impartial process. If a process is not perceived as a fair one, it will be limited in its potential to assist the participants in expressing concerns.

Over the years, the pilot efforts at John Jay College have provided significant insight into what ingredients contribute to success and what can derail attempts to achieve peaceful coexistence on a campus. What clearly emerges is the importance of paying attention to the preparation of each event. In the conflict resolution field, experts are increasingly addressing the significance of getting parties to the table, i.e., getting them ready to have those first difficult conversations. Preparing for a town meeting raises parallel concerns. Among the factors requiring attention are the following:

Location: Decisions need to be made regarding the physical setting where the town meeting will be held in terms of accessibility, image, and ability to accommodate the anticipated audience. What kind of seating arrangement is desired (formal or informal)? What proximity between participants is sought?

Dates and times: How frequently should town meetings be held? How long should they be? Whose schedules should be taken into consideration when planning town meetings? Clearly, if significant organizational or community decision makers are not present at town meetings, issues raised may or may not be able to be addressed, or might be addressed in less meaningful ways. Town meetings should also be convenient for constituencies for whom they are intended.

Agenda: Will town meetings focus on a specific topic or have an open agenda? If there is a specific agenda, is there a need for resource experts to be present? What will their role be? The agenda will help to anticipate the kinds of issues and questions that might be raised. Depending on the anticipated agenda, some provision for the media, security, or other resources may have to be made.

Ground rules: How will civility and respect be created? What will be the ground rules? How will they be shared with the audience? Will they be written? Will they be posted? Will they be announced? What happens if they are violated?

Timekeeping: Will time be kept? If so, how or by whom? How many minutes will be allocated per speaker? A timing device will have to be secured.

Audience participation: Under what conditions will the audience be permitted or encouraged to participate? Will there be any restrictions on how long and how often individuals can speak? Will follow-up questions or rebuttals be permitted? What if no one speaks? How will the lack of participation be handled?

Facilitators: What criteria and processes will be used to select facilitators? Will facilitators be drawn from the town-meeting community? Who will contact specific facilitators? What preparation do facilitators need? What guidance will facilitators be given to ensure the integrity of the process? Will facilitators have any facilitation assistance during the town meeting itself? If so, how will the assistance be provided?

Recording of sessions: Is there a desire to record sessions? How will they be recorded (audio, audiovisual, or in writing) and by whom? If taped, who will have access to the official tapes? Who will store them? Under what conditions will copies be made available? Will written records be distributed?

Amplification: Is amplification needed or desired? If so, how many microphones are needed? Where will they be positioned?

Publicity: What kind of publicity will be needed to attract an audience? Who will prepare it? How much lead time should be given? Is a specific audience desired? Should there be a targeted audience? How many participants are desired?

Planning committee: What kind of planning committee needs to be put in place to institutionalize town meetings? Who should be a member of the committee? Who will select the members of the committee? How often will the committee meet? What will the planning committee be responsible for?

Refreshments: Will any refreshments be made available at the town meetings? If so, how and when will they be distributed? Are some ground rules regarding cleaning up needed?

Special services: What provisions, if any, need to be made to address specific concerns regarding certain topics or an expected audience? Is a resource panel needed? If so, who will be recruited and by whom will they be recruited? Will audiovisual aids be needed (e.g., flip charts, VCRs, slide projectors, handouts, etc.)? Will special needs have to be met such as sign language for a hearing impaired, or translators for individuals speaking a different language?

The John Jay College Town Meeting: Lessons Learned

At John Jay College, the town meeting has evolved over the last eight years. With countless concerns raised by members of the culturally diverse community at each of the town meetings, there is evidence that town meetings have contributed to peaceful coexistence on campus, sometimes quite unintentionally. Individuals who speak have been provided with an opportunity to let others understand how they feel or what they know and, in turn, respondents have an opportunity to understand situations, to explain how they perceived them, and in many instances, to reach out and assist. There may or may not be any resolution.

Consider the following interaction: An African-American student shared a complaint she had regarding the use of the word "nigger" in the classroom by her professor (race or ethnicity was not specified). The student said that when she approached the professor about her concerns, the professor imposed a "gag order" on her in the classroom by not permitting her to discuss the matter. She said she went to the department chairperson who suggested that she drop the class. She then spoke to a counselor and dropped the class. The student wanted to know why professors are permitted to stay on the faculty if they use such terms in the classroom. As is often the case, when an emotionally charged topic is raised, audience participants share concerns, information, and in some instances, suggest remedies.

In the aforementioned situation, the College President responded by explaining that words in a classroom setting are sometimes used in a context—such as a play or the recounting of history—and that there is a need to hear the whole story since there are often two or more sides to every story. He recommended that the student see the provost to have him examine it, and if the facts are as the student reported, the use of this word would not be tolerated. The student then asked her counselor, an African-American professor who was in the room, to speak. Her counselor reported that he had spoken with the faculty member and that the word had been used in context. He then spoke to the issue of how important it is for faculty to explain to students how a specific word is being used in a context. The student who raised this concern proceeded to further explain what she heard when the word was used in class and disputed that it was used in a teaching context. The vice president of student government, a white male, remarked that students also have to watch the use of the word in the hallways. The student who initially raised the concern pointed out that faculty members are paid to be professionals. The college president reminded the student that she could see her counselor and the provost to feel satisfied or rectified, and that if the word was used without context, it would not be tolerated. After several speakers addressed different topics, an African-American student returned to this topic to express her views about the importance of teaching responsibilities around what is taught and the use of racially inflammatory language.

The town meetings have been held in large rooms where the audience could sit informally, in a circular arrangement. Several floor microphones are positioned close to the center of the circle, thereby minimizing the physical distance between speakers, college leaders and, when used, resource experts who give opening statements and field many of the ensuing questions and comments. Additionally, no tables are used in order to further reduce barriers in the room.

To ensure participation of key administrators, the president's schedule is confirmed before town meeting dates are set. Key college administrators, leaders of the faculty senate, and student government leaders always attend town meetings. Meetings are approximately two hours long and held once a month during the academic year. To meet the schedules of faculty and students, the meetings are held on different days of the week and rotated between the afternoon and evening hours.

Approximately one out of three town meetings is billed as an open town meeting. For the other town meetings during the year, the Town Meeting Planning Committee chooses a theme that is deemed to be of interest to the community. Over the years, themes have included: Civility and Mutual Respect on Campus: Profanity, Honoring Rules of the College, Student-Faculty-Administration Interactions; Does Race Play a Part in the Educational Process at John Jay College?; Preparing for a Smoke-Free Environment at John Jay College; Students and Faculty: Behavior and Obligations in the Classroom; The New CUNY Sexual Harassment Policy; Student-Faculty Evaluations; The CUNY Budget Crisis; Do You Feel Respected at John Jay? Quality of Life Issues Inside and Outside of the Classroom.

Even when there is a town meeting theme, nontheme issues can be addressed. At some town meetings, the theme has been completely ignored when members of the audience raised other concerns. The principle guiding the town meeting has always been that all participation is welcome, that speakers do not need to be constrained by a theme. For example, at one town meeting whose theme was "Evening Services for Students at John Jay," the interactions focused on the nonreappointment of an African American professor by the African American Studies Department. A large group of students and the nonreapppointed professor all made very passionate statements. The remarks ranged from personnel matters to strong feelings about race relations on campus. For instance, one African-American student commented "It is very important that we as a black community at John Jay College or a black community in New York City or a black community as a whole, even if we disagree with one another, we disagree in a way where we can still be respectful toward one another because in front of these white people we look like savages behaving in this fashion." He then urged everyone to be respectful in their exchanges.

When a theme town meeting is held, resource experts are often invited to be present. The resource experts could be members of the John Jay College community or individuals from most anywhere else who could contribute to a better understanding of the topic. The number of resource experts is usually quite small, no more than six, and when asked to make opening remarks, experts are allocated between three and five minutes to make opening statements. On some occasions, the resource experts are present only to answer questions or provide information during the audience participation component of the town meeting.

In addition to resource experts, theme meetings might mean managing other relevant details. For instance, when budget-related topics have been discussed, relevant financial data were disseminated. Another example of expertise included the availability of a voting machine for a town meeting focusing on the impact on the college of voting in the general elections.

Ground rules are central to maintaining civility at town meetings. Since the first town meeting at John Jay College, ground rules have been printed and conspicuously placed on every seat in the room.[3] Facilitators read the ground rules at the beginning of each town meeting and remind the audience whenever there seems to be a breach. On numerous occasions, members of the audience have also helped to encourage compliance with the ground rules by approaching the microphone and stating that everyone is expected to be respectful.

Over the years, the ground rules have evolved to address new or challenging conditions. Currently, if someone is speaking and another person is in line at one of the microphones, the former will have one minute to wrap up. If no one else is on line at a microphone, the speaker may continue speaking for an additional two minutes. Presumably, the speaker may continue to receive an additional two minutes until someone else approaches a microphone. The large digital clock with a buzzer that is used to keep track of time will be reset to buzz at each interval by a timekeeper. The clock is prominently positioned so that speakers can see how much time they have left.

There are three components of the college's town meeting: opening statements, audience participation, and closing statements. The opening statements are made by the president of the college and the president of student government, with each given up to five minutes. As mentioned earlier, if there is a resource panel, each panelist is given a few (usually three) minutes to address the audience. Audience members are given two minutes to ask a question or make a comment. Responses are given by those to whom the questions or comments are directed. To date, the town meeting sessions have not been designed to handle rebuttals since a debatelike atmosphere has not been permitted or encouraged.

Facilitators are key to managing successful town meetings. Careful attention must be paid to how facilitators can help or hinder peaceful coexistence by what they do or say during the town meeting. Every effort must be made to select individuals who are viewed as fairminded and nonjudgmental and who can behave nonjudgmentally throughout a town meeting. If "inappropriate" facilitators are chosen or if facilitators behave inappropriately, they will make it much more difficult for the forum to serve as one where parties can come to communicate their concerns and ideas. For example, if a facilitator thinks that all audience participants must stick to the theme of a town meeting and chooses to rebuff any participant who addresses a nontheme matter, there could be vociferous reaction from the audience directed at the facilitator.

Town meetings at John Jay College are managed by one facilitator who is briefed by the Director of the Dispute Resolution Program regarding the importance of subscribing to the ground rules constructed for the town meeting. During the town meeting, facilitators need to inform and remind the audience about the ground rules and to take care in not making any comments after any audience member speaks. Inevitably, there is someone in the audience who disagrees with something that is said. Any affirmation of a participant's comments can set the stage for a reaction by someone else in the audience. Facilitators at John Jay are encouraged to say thank you after individuals have spoken, rather than something like "That's a good or bad idea," "I like or don't like what you said," "That's what we need," etc. Additionally, facilitators are instructed to ask all speakers to identify themselves. This helps to increase the ownership of process by speakers.

John Jay College's town meetings are videotaped. The taping has been routinized and, while difficult to measure, does not seem to interfere with contributions that might otherwise be made. The video tapes are kept in the College's Instructional Services Department and are available for viewing upon request.

At the college, the town meeting is widely advertised through flyers and messages on voice mail. New techniques to make the community aware of the town meeting are always explored. For example, as a reminder, members of student government have distributed flyers on the day of the town meeting and large posters on easels have been placed at front doors.

To ensure ongoing town meetings, the college has relied on a Town Meeting Committee consisting of students (student government president and vice president), faculty (president of the faculty senate and a faculty senator), administration (vice president for administration and vice president for student development), and the director of the Dispute Resolution Program. The committee considers format, facilitators, themes, and any changes in ground rules.

At the conclusion of some of the early town meetings, the student government provided refreshments. Should funds become available, this component of the town meeting should be reconsidered. In terms of fostering an additional opportunity for coexistence, enabling individuals to spend time over food is a major contribution.

While there are many needs to be met in a culturally and ethnically diverse community, in general, the college's town meetings have a reputation for providing fair forums in which all members of the community can participate. The town meetings have attracted the attention of colleagues at other City University of New York campuses who are attempting to find ways to create safe, respectful forums to encourage individuals and groups to communicate. Based on anecdotal and impressionistic data we have collected, those who have attended John Jay's town meetings have been impressed by them. One observer noted in written correspondence that "it was a very valuable learning experience and as such very helpful. Hopefully we will be able to achieve the same positive outcome via such activities on our campus" (Carrasquillo, 1996). To date, that campus and one other CUNY campus have each held one successful town meeting. Additionally, the CUNY Dispute Resolution Consortium, which is housed at John Jay College, recently received a grant for a pilot project to explore the possibility of expanding and institutionalizing the concept of a town meeting to other CUNY campuses.[4]

Town Meetings: Promises and Challenges

The potential of town meetings as a mechanism for fostering coexistence between culturally and ethnically diverse individuals and groups on an ongoing basis is enormous and yet untapped. Town meetings can provide a low-cost opportunity for dialogue. Questions can be asked and ideas shared in a respectful, safe context, particularly if parties have limited occasions to interact.

The town meeting can also be used as a diagnostic tool to remedy problem situations. It gives individuals an opportunity to share concerns or raise questions that previously may not have been brought to anyone's attention. For instance, at one of the college's town meetings, a student questioned why a particular test was no longer being given on Fridays. In fact, it was being administered while the town meeting was in progress. Since the test had previously always been given on Fridays, everyone present assumed that that was the current practice. All administrators seemed to be hearing about the allegation for the first time. A representative from the Dean's Office who was certain that the tests were not being administered left the room. Shortly thereafter, he returned and announced to the audience at the town meeting, which was still in session, that indeed the tests were in progress and that they would henceforth be administered on Fridays.

Town meetings can empower members of a community. Problems and solutions can be delivered in the parties' own words. When town meetings are held on a regular basis, individuals and groups can plan to raise their concerns there. If they feel that their concerns have not been addressed elsewhere, the town meetings provide them with an opportunity to try to get assistance or responses.

When time limits are adhered to, town meetings compel parties to deliver their ideas in brief, precise terms. On a college campus, town meetings have a secondary effect of giving students an opportunity to develop their public-speaking skills.

While the purpose of the town meeting is not to resolve conflicts, in fact, differences between individuals might be worked out either at the town meeting or as a result of some proposed opportunity for interaction offered during or after the town meeting. In situations where the conflict has escalated, it might even be possible for someone to encourage "loop back" procedures that enable parties to return to lower cost approaches and perhaps help to deescalate the situation (Ury, Brett, and Goldberg, 1988:52–56). For instance, as a result of the sharing of information, individuals may then meet informally after the town meeting to work through their differences. It might even be possible for parties to come up with a working agreement that they can live with.

Holding town meetings on a regular basis can also pose a variety of challenges for those expecting to use them to foster ongoing peaceful coexistence. Given the unpredictability of town meeting sessions, organizing and convening town meetings on an ongoing basis can be immensely difficult. Therefore, preparation is imperative since challenges can surface from intentional and unintentional actions.

For town meetings to be successful, they often need to include influential leaders of the community or organization as planners and attenders. Unless they are committed to the concept of a town meeting, the initial challenge to many town meeting organizers is convincing such leaders that it is in their interest to participate. Town meetings could be seen as threatening by those who are in positions of authority for several reasons. First, embarrassing situations might be raised during the town meeting. There is little opportunity for preventing anyone's potential exposure while the issues are being addressed. Second, the town meeting offers a communication forum that suggests a set of values where participation by everyone is encouraged. This could be particularly unnerving for those working in contexts where decision-making is hierarchical.

While the purpose of the town meeting is not to eliminate powerbased relationships, its very format empowers individuals from diverse parts of a community or an organization to express their views. Questions can be posed either deliberately or unintentionally that could be disturbing and irritating. Individuals who are accustomed to being in charge may appear weak. Issues might be addressed for which one is unprepared or for which a public town-meeting forum is an inappropriate venue. At a college town meeting, for example, students may begin badgering the administration and other faculty decision makers about tenure and promotion decisions involving faculty.

Additionally, there is the prospect of being put on the spot, again and again, not only by one speaker but by successive speakers. Once a line of questioning or specific theme is raised, others may well follow up with related questions, comments, or points of information since contagious behavior is always a possibility.

Due to time constraints and the nature of the town-meeting structure, town meetings may not be the ideal or even appropriate forums to air issues thoroughly or to anticipate follow-up on concerns raised at previous sessions. This could be particularly frustrating for those who have looked forward to engaging in a meticulous information exchange or who might be seeking a follow-up report on what has happened regarding a particular matter, especially if there was significant interest or attention paid to it at an earlier meeting. Town meetings do not have representative constituencies who are required to attend, or recorders who could follow up on all concerns raised and report back. By their very nature, town meetings favor individuals who are able to think quickly on their feet. Questions often come in rapid succession. To encourage dialogue, particularly if one is interested in fostering peaceful coexistence, individuals must be careful about responses. Often, participants are functioning under a microscope, so if they say the "wrong thing" it could be quite disruptive.

Depending on the audience and the issues being discussed, town meeting sessions can be quite unpredictable. There can be some very long periods of silence, as well as highly repetitious and even boring interactions. Sessions can also be very emotionally charged and easily disrupted by participants who can become partisan, highly vocal, and even hurtful in their remarks. All of these situations emerge very quickly and publicly.

Facilitators who may be carefully chosen in advance may suddenly be seen as less than impartial by some members of the audience because of some recent issue that emerged after the facilitator was selected. In one instance, the faculty advisor to student government had been chosen as a facilitator of an open town meeting two months prior to the specific meeting date. At that town meeting, members of the aforementioned Student Alliance appeared in large numbers to raise concerns about the executive officers of student government. Subsequently, the Student Alliance members wondered if another facilitator unrelated to student government might have been better. Despite the facilitator's affiliation, there was agreement that he was scrupulous in carrying out his facilitation responsibilities. Prior to the meeting, like all facilitators, he had been carefully coached and cautioned to withhold comments after any of the participants' spoke.

The best of plans can also be challenged by circumstances unique to any town meeting. While ground rules are established to allow for respectful dialogue between individuals and groups with differing views, there may be occasions for departing from them, for example, when someone becomes extremely passionate and there is a strong interest in extending that participant's time limits. Questions for the facilitator include: Does one extend the time? What are the risks involved in doing so? What about everyone else, especially if there are others standing on line at the microphones? Facilitators have to think quickly about the implications of any actions taken since the ground rules are the objective criteria against which the meetings are run.

Town Meetings and Peaceful Coexistence: Some Observations

Around the world, countless diverse initiatives have proliferated to further ways of advancing positive, constructive, and creative orientations that hope to foster peaceful coexistence among culturally and ethnically diverse individuals and groups. Communities, institutions, and organizations are revisiting old efforts and striving to find new ones that work.

Clearly no one method will suffice to foster peaceful coexistence as the coexistence landscape emerges with a panoply of diverse processes. New approaches will become available for different situations and, when appropriate, combined with other systems, processes, and techniques. But when town meetings are held on an ongoing basis, they can play a role in helping to set the tone for culturally diverse parties to communicate with greater ease, a key ingredient for constructive ethnic coexistence.

References

Carrasquillo, E. (Counselor and Member, Network to Confront Racism at La Guardia Community College—CUNY), Letter to Dr. Maria Volpe, 4/26/96.

Faculty Senate Minutes, No. 147 (1996, November 19). City University of New York, John Jay College of Criminal Justice.

Faculty Senate Minutes, No. 140 (1996, May 10). City University of New York, John Jay College of Criminal Justice.

Faculty Senate Minutes, No. 102 (1994, February 23). City University of New York, John Jay College of Criminal Justice.

Gray, D. J. "John Jay College of Criminal Justice—Ethnic Survey Fall 1996," October 1966.

Levine, J. (Executive Director of the CUNY Ph.D. Program in Criminal Justice), interview, 11/21/96.

Singleton, T. 1996a (President of Political Awareness Club and Associate Judge of Judicial Committee at John Jay College of Criminal Justice—CUNY) Correspondence to Dr. Maria Volpe, 11/1/96.

Singleton, T. 1996b, interview, 11/5/96.

Ury, W. L., Brett, J. M., and Goldberg, S. B. *Getting Disputes Resolved: Designing Systems to Cut the Cost of Conflict*. San Francisco: Jossey-Bass, 1988.

Volpe, M. R. and Witherspoon, R. "Mediation and Diversity on College Campuses," *Mediation Quarterly*, Vol 9, No. 4, Summer, 1992, pp 341–51.

Volpe, M. R. "An Urban University-Based Conflict Resolution Program" *Education and Urban Society*, Vol. 27, No. 1, Nov 1994, pp 22–34.

Notes

1. According to a recent ethnic survey, John Jay College of Criminal Justice "is one of approximately 80 colleges out of over 3,300 nationally that is ethnically diverse—i.e., no one ethnic group constitutes

a majority" (Gray, 1996:1). More specifically, in 1996 the College's undergraduate population was reported as follows: whites constituted 22.6 percent, African Americans 31.9 percent, Hispanics 37.7 percent, American Indians .2 percent, Asians 3.7 percent (Gray, 1996:1).

2. The City University of New York (CUNY) is the largest urban university system and the third largest university in the United States. This urban, multicampus, publicly funded system is sprawled throughout the five boroughs of New York City. In the last twenty-five years, CUNY has undergone two major changes: in 1970, CUNY implemented a policy to provide open admissions to those holding high school diploma or its equivalent; in 1976, CUNY's historically tuition-free eduction ended.

3. Currently, ground rules at John Jay College of Criminal Justice consist of the following:

Part I: Opening Remarks—5 minutes each
            President of the College
            President of Student Government
            Resource Panel [when included]—3 minutes per person

Part II: Audience Participation
1.   Each audience participant will have *2 minutes* to make a statement or ask a question from the floor. When approaching the microphone, please identify yourself.
2.   Please direct questions to a specific person[s], if possible.
3.   *Two minutes* will be allowed for a response at which point the clock's buzzer will go off.
4a.   If no one is standing at any of the other floor microphones, you may speak for an *additional 2 minutes.*
4b.   If others are on line at any of the microphones, you may have *one minute* to conclude your statement.
5.   You may speak more than once *unless* there is someone else at a microphone has not yet had an opportunity to speak.

Part III: Closing Statements—2 minutes each
            President of Student Government
            President of the College

4. The Surdna Foundation awarded the CUNY Dispute Resolution Consortium a planning grant in September 1996 to research John Jay College's town meeting and explore ways of expanding the town meeting to other CUNY campuses.

Antibias Education:
Toward a World of Justice
and Peace

LOUISE DERMAN-SPARKS

Keep in mind always the present you are constructing. It should be the future you want.

(Walker, 1989, p. 238)

As the twentieth century comes to a close, tragic ethnic conflicts around the world are ripping apart the fabric of life for billions of people. The terrible consequences are nowhere felt more strongly than by the children who live in a state of chronic warfare, with its inhumane economic, cultural, family, and emotional toll. Some of these tragedies make world news—like the Israeli–Palestinian struggle or the erupting conflict among the various ethnic and national groups in the former Soviet Union or the conflict in Rwanda and Burundi. However, the psychological and physical toll of racism also happens in countries "at peace," like the United States.

Current statistics about the impact of racism in the lives of children document that American society is far from eliminating this scourge. The Los Angeles County Commission on Human Relations analysis of hate crimes in 1995 tells of an overall increase in reported hate crimes, with particular increases based on race, religion, and disability. Hate crime victims were more frequently targeted because of their race or sexual orientation, with these two categories accounting for over 86.3 percent of total crimes reported. More than 44 percent of all hate crimes, and 78 percent of attacks on gays were assaults with deadly weapons, assault and battery, attempted assault, murder, or attempted murder (Los Angeles County Commission on Human Relations, 1995). Moreover, although there is a relative lack of gender-based hate crimes in the report, this has more to do with how hate crimes are typically defined than with actual reality. For example, statistics about wife battering and rape do not usually come under the aegis of a report on hate crimes.

And, it is not only physical violence that destroys or damages children's hopes for a just and safe place to live, learn, and eventually work. For example, a 1995 survey of 248,000 students from all regions of the nation, grades six through twelve, carried out by the magazine *USA Weekend*, revealed 45 percent of the respondents said they had personally experienced racial prejudice in the past year (from name-calling to physical violence), and 84 percent answered "yes" to the question, "Do most people your age carry some form of racial prejudice?" (*USA Weekend*, Aug. 16–18, 1995, p.1). Significantly, the report also concluded that "Teens want to talk about issues of race. Not only did they flood us with essays, many told deeply personal stories. One Illinois teacher credited the discussion [following the students' filling out the survey] for helping students come to terms with a racially motivated shooting" (Pera, Aug. 16–18, 1995, p. 2).

To thrive, even to survive, in this more complicated world, children of the twenty-first century can no longer be psychologically bound by outdated and limiting assumptions about their fellow/sister citizens of this country and of the world. Rather, they need to learn how to function in many different contexts and to recognize and respect different histories and perspectives. To meet this complex challenge they must also know themselves and their cultural connections. Our country, and indeed the world, is at a crossroads: will we learn how to live productively and justly with the range of human diversity that exists on this planet, or will we destroy ourselves in the process of defending an ethnocentric, monocultural way of life?

Antibias Education, by definition, calls for an activist approach to challenging prejudice, stereotyping, and bias. In a society in which institutional structures create and maintain discrimination based on racial, ethnic, gender, class and other aspects of identity, one cannot do this work and remain nonbiased or choose only to be an observer. To embrace and participate in an antibias approach, each individual must actively intervene, challenge, and counter the personal and institutional behaviors that perpetuate oppression and violence (Derman-Sparks and the ABC Task Force, 1989). As Dr. Martin Luther King, Jr., made clear, "Peace is not simply the absence of conflict; it is the presence of justice."

The antibias educational approach emerged from work with children of preschool age. We believe it must begin very early, because the self-concept and attitudes toward others children construct in the period. During the years between two through five, children lay the foundations of self-concept and attitudes toward others in relation to racial and cultural identity upon which they will build throughout childhood and adolescence. Indeed, many researchers have come to believe that the developmental period from three through eight-years old is our best window of opportunity for fostering positive attitudes toward the range of human diversity.

Thus, this article focuses on the goals, implementation principles, strategies, and challenges of using an antibias educational approach with young children. In this sense, it is both a preventative and a long-term strategy for guiding growth toward a world of justice and peace.

Goals of the ABC Approach

The goals of antibias education are for all children and adults, though specific issues and tasks necessary for working toward each one vary depending on individual cultural backgrounds, ages, and life experiences. Building on each other, the combined intent of these goals is to empower individuals of all ages to resist the negative impact of racism, empowering children and adults to participate in the practice of freedom. Antibias educational work:

- Enables individuals to construct knowledgeable, confident self-concepts and group identities in a setting where each person can like her/himself without feeling superior to anyone else. Antibias work also guides individuals to develop biculturally—effectively interacting within their home culture and within the dominant culture.
- Promotes comfortable empathic interaction with people from diverse backgrounds. This goal involves guiding the development of cognitive awareness, emotional disposition, and behavioral skills needed to learn respectfully and effectively about differences, comfortably negotiate and adapt to differences, and cognitively understand and emotionally accept the common humanity that all people share.
- Fosters critical thinking about bias so that each individual is able to identify "unfair" and "untrue" images (stereotypes), comments (teasing, derogatory talk), and behaviors (discrimination) directed at oneself or others; and have the emotional empathy to know that bias hurts.
- Cultivates each individual's ability to stand up for her/himself and for others in the face of bias. This activism goal includes learning and practicing a variety of actions in response to bias acts directed toward oneself or others.

The underlying intent of these goals is not to end racism and other forms of prejudice in one generation, but to promote critical thinkers and activists who can work for social change and participate in creating a caring culture in a world of differences.

Children and Bias

The four antibias education goals are grounded in the research about children's development of identity and attitudes. A considerable body of research about children's development of identity and attitudes documents that the roots of bias begin early in life. Around three and four years of age, children become aware that differences in color, language, gender, and physical abilities are connected with levels of privilege and power. Spoken and unspoken messages about the differences and similarities in people have a profound influence on children's developing sense of self and of others. (Clark, 1963; Cross, 1991; Goodman, 1964; Derman-Sparks, Higa, & Sparks, 1980; Katz, 1989; Ramsey, 1991; Sheldon, 1990; Wong Fillmore, 1990).

Moreover, as Dr. Kenneth Clark (1963) pointed out many years ago, children form their ideas about diversity through their contact with the socially prevailing ideas about various groups even more than by actual contact with individual members of groups different from their own. Messages that communicate racial and other forms of prejudice gradually influence their developing perceptions, attitudes, and behaviors.

Consequently, the children we teach are not "blank slates" on the subject of diversity. From the preschool years onward, they bring along a personalized data bank that includes

- a developing sense of personal and group identity
- self-constructed "theories" about what causes diversity[1]
- learned positive or negative responses to various aspects of people's identities.

Absorption of the socially prevailing prejudices in their society is psychologically toxic to all children. The cumulative harmful impact of what Dr. Chester Pierce (1980) calls the daily "microcontaminants" of racism on young children of color's developing sense of personal and group identity has been long documented. (Clark, 1963; Dennis, 1981; Goodman, 1964; Ramsey, 1995; Wong Fillmore, 1990). Less well known (and less extensive) is the work about the impact of racial prejudice on the development of white children. For example, Kenneth Clark (1963) and Lillian Smith (1962) point to the ethical erosion created by the double messages of primary caregivers in home, place of worship, and school. These messages suggest first that people are all created equal, but then also that despite this equality, "we" don't live near, play with, learn with, worship with, or treat people different from ourselves by the same rules of respect. Moral hypocrisy and internal discord are the consequence. For example, Lillian Smith (1962) eloquently describes how being told to keep silent in the face of injustices she could clearly see forced her to deny what her heart knew from what she was being taught to do. Dennis (1980) argues that white children also learn early on to not speak out or act against perceived injustice for fear of rejection, punishment, or isolation from one's group. He further suggests that this internal discord either goes underground to emerge later at some critical encounter in adult life, or gets resolved by either buying into or completely rejecting the tenets of white superiority.

Children's absorption of prevailing gender stereotypes in their family and the society in which they live also limits full development. By the age of three and four children begin learning the rules about socially acceptable behavior for girls and boys, which deeply influence the kinds of activities in which they engage. A resultant pattern of uneven cognitive development, or what Serbin (1980) calls "practice deficits," begins to form from preschool age forward. These then influence later success or failure in subjects such as math or science or in human behaviors such as expressing feelings. Research also reveals that by two and three, children are curious about, and sometimes fearful of people with a disability and the equipment that they use (Froschl et al, 1984; Sapon-Shevin, 1983). Moreover, the impact of stereotypes and biases about people with disabilities affects primary-age children's treatment of any child who does not fit the physical "norms" of attractiveness, weight, height. By four and five years of age, children can also sort rich people from poor people based on clothing, residences, and possessions. Although they do not yet have an understanding of social class, they are beginning to grasp the advantages of wealth and the disadvantages of poverty. They are also beginning to develop a sense of fairness and to notice inequality, especially if they are at a disadvantage. (Ramsey, 1991, 1955)

Origins of the Antibias Curriculum

This research, plus the knowledge garnered by teachers and parents' experiences (Derman-Sparks, Higa, and Sparks, 1980) sparked the formation of the Antibias Curriculum Task Force—a multiracial/ethnic task force of early childhood educators at Pacific Oaks' Children's School in Pasadena, California, joined by a few additional educators from the Los Angeles Unified school district and the UCLA demonstration school. We came together in 1985, dissatisfied with the ways early childhood programs were addressing diversity. We began with the premise that the period between two and five years of age as a critical period when the construction of a strong foundation for the continued development of a healthy self-concept and attitudes toward human diversity is most possible and more easily achieved. We were also dissatisfied with the ways early childhood programs and teacher education courses were addressing diversity, particularly the prevailing simplistic, inadequate version of multicultural education we call to label "tourist" curriculum.

The "tourist" approach to diversity education "visits" cultures different from the dominant European-American culture and then "returns" to the regular curriculum, material and teaching methods that only reflect the latter culture. Signs of a tourist multicultural curriculum are:

- Multicultural activities are added on the curriculum as special times, rather than integrated into all aspects of the daily environment and life of the classroom. Add-ons might be a special bulletin board or an occasional parent visit to cook a special food or to show traditional clothing; but the family's current, daily life is not an integral part of the regular curriculum.
- Activities about "Other" cultures are also disconnected from the daily life of the ethnic groups whose culture is the subject of the lesson. One consequence is that cultures are treated as "quaint" or "exotic." Often, holiday activities are the *only* or *primary* vehicle for teaching about diversity. Since holidays are special days in any culture, children do not learn about how people live their daily lives, or how a particular holiday is part of a complex tapestry of life. Moreover, when a culture is experienced as exotic children do not learn about our human commonalities, and how these are expressed in different ways.
- Materials misrepresent ethnic groups. Too few images of a group oversimplify the variety within a group. Overuse of images and activities based on traditional or past life or on life in the group's country of origin rather than images of contemporary life in the U.S.A. confuse children. In addition, images and information may be inaccurate and stereotypic (e.g., all "Indians" do sand painting and eat fried bread).

The Antibias Curriculum Task Force set out to rectify this situation. We agreed to work together for a year observing the children in our early childhood programs, trying out new activities and materials, and reflecting on our experiences in monthly meetings. The outcome of this activity was the book *Anti-Bias Curriculum: Tools for Empowering Young Children* (Derman-Sparks & ABC Task Force, 1989).[2]

Children's Developmental Issues and Tasks

As teachers around the country began implementing an antibias educational approach with children three through eight-years-old, developmental tasks in relation to the four antibias goals began to emerge. The following charts, from an article entitled "Antibias, Multicultural Curriculum: What Is Developmentally appropriate?" (Derman-Sparks, 1992), provide general guidelines for determining educational content and activities.[3]

Goal One: To Foster Each Child's Construction of a Knowledgeable, Confident Self-Identity:

Threes:*

- are intrigued with their physical characteristics, including gender, anatomy, skin, eye, and hair color and texture, physical abilities, and differences.
- see themselves as single, unique individuals (for example, threes typically consider their name as a part of themselves and are therefore puzzled when another child has the same name as theirs). They also consider skin color, gender, anatomy, etc. as part of their individuality.
- begin naming their gender identity but are not yet clear which biological or social attributes determine it.
- do not yet have gender or "racial" constancy: they think their gender identification can change by dress or play preferences and that they can change their skin color or eye color.

Fours:

- continue strong interest in their physical characteristics, want names to describe them, and begin constructing gender, race, and ethnic identity constancy.
- while still focused on themselves as individuals, begin to see themselves (including their ethnic group name) as part of their immediate family, although not yet as members of larger groups.
- are rapidly absorbing the rules of behavior and the language of their home culture, not as formal lessons, but from their daily life experiences. In general,

---

*We start with *threes,* when the issues of identity become more focused.

their "egocentricism" involves them in thinking that their family's way of life is how everyone else lives.
- are vulnerable to the influence of societal norms and socially prevailing biases. Questions related to identity may reflect not only confusion about identity constancy, but also awareness of negative societal messages about themselves.

Fives:

- have established a rudimentary sense of gender and race identity that includes constancy.
- explore the meaning of each component of identity in relation to other children's ideas.
- are more likely to begin experiencing teasing/rejection based on an aspect of their identity.
- are more likely to absorb socially prevailing norms or negative stereotypes about oneself.

Sixes:

- have constructed a core sense of identity that includes their gender, race, and ethnicity, physical abledness, and beginning awareness of class.
- find it increasingly important to "hang out" with/identify with classmates who are like them: e.g., girls with girls, boys with boys.
- begin to identify themselves and their families as members of larger racial/ethnic groups.
- can be seriously damaged by societal biases both in terms of personal self-esteem, and a positive sense of racial/ethnic group identity.

Seven/eights:

- construct the understanding that an individual can have many different aspects of identity and still be one person, and that people who are not exactly the same can belong to the same ethnic group.
- begin to weave the various aspects of identity into a whole (I'm a boy, Mexican-American, speak English and Spanish, like rap, am Catholic, middle-class, etc.).
- demonstrate heightened interest in learning about their ethnic group in their community, city, and country, especially through oral histories and written autobiographies and biographies. Learning still needs to be concrete. They grapple with where they fit as an individual into their group identities: their gender, their ethnicity.

Goal Two: To Foster Each Child's Comfortable, Empathetic Interaction with Diversity among People:

Threes:

- Notice and ask about other children and adults' physical characteristics, although they are still more interested in their own.
- notice other children's specific cultural acts. (Elena speaks differently from me; Mei eats with chopsticks; Jamal's grandpa brings him to school, instead of his mother).
- may exhibit discomfort/fears with skin color differences and physical disabilities.

Fours:

- are increasingly interested in how they are alike and different from other children. Construct "theories" about what causes physical and apparent cultural differences among the children/adults they know that reflect "preoperational thinking, societal stereotypes, and discomforts."?
- while still focused on themselves and others as individuals, begin to classify people into groups by physical characteristics (same gender, same color, same eye shape) using their general classification rules (e.g., if your skin color is brown you can not be called "black")
- their ideas about who "goes together" and adult/society ideas do not always agree, and they are often confused about the meaning of adult categories. For example, how can a light-skinned child have a dark-skinned parent?; Why are children called black when their skin isn't black?; Mexican people speak Spanish so if I don't speak Spanish then I am not Mexican; Girls are supposed to have girl names, so how can "Sam" be a girl?; How can you be an "Indian" if you aren't wearing feathers?
- begin to become aware of and interested in cultural differences as they relate to the daily lives of children and adults they know (e.g., who makes up their family, what languages they speak, what jobs family members have, etc.)
- show influence of societal norms in their interactions with others ("girls can't do this, boys can") and learned discomforts with specific differences in their interactions with others ("You can't play; your skin is too dark").

Fives:

- show awareness of some aspects of socioeconomic class as well as age and aging.
- achieve new awareness of themselves and others as members of a family and demonstrate curiosity about how families of other children and staff live (e.g., "Can Sara have two mommies?").

- continue to construct theories to classify and explain differences among classmates.
- continue to absorb and use stereotypes to define others, and to tease/reject other children.

Sixes:

- have absorbed much of their family's classification systems for people, but still get confused about why specific people are put into one or another category by adults.
- use prevailing biases based on aspects of identity against other children.
- begin to understand through their own emerging group identity that others also have an ethnic identity, and various lifestyles.

Sevens/eights:

- are increasingly curious about other people's lifestyles (religion, traditions, etc.), including people with whom they do not have direct contact. Can begin to appreciate the deeper structural aspects of a culture (e.g., beliefs about humanity's relationship to the land, creation stories, impact of different environments on people's ways of life).
- their new cognitive tools enable them to understand there really are different ways to meet common human needs.
- can begin to appreciate the past if history is done concretely through storytelling about real people.
- in-group solidarity and tension/conflict between children based on gender, race/ethnic identity, social-economic class and exclusion of children with disabilities may increase.

Goal Three: To Foster Each Child's Critical Thinking about Bias

Threes:

- learning to be comfortable with various differences through repeated, supportive experience lays a foundation for later understanding of "fair"/"unfair" images and behaviors.

Fours:

- can begin to use concrete experiences and verbal feedback from adults to explore the reality of their "theories" or misconceptions about human differences.

- can begin to learn to distinguish between a person's action they don't like and a person's identity and accept limits of not teasing a person because of who they are.
- can develop emotional understanding (empathy) that teasing/rejection because of identity hurts too (just as hitting does).
- can begin underpinnings of critical thinking by comparing a fair and unfair image.

Fives:

- can begin engaging in critical thinking about individual stereotypic images: make comparisons, identify fair/unfair, real/not real.
- can begin engaging in critical thinking about unfair/hurtful behaviors (name calling, teasing) in specific, real situations
- can begin problem-solving appropriate ways to respond to differences.
- can begin engaging in critical thinking about specific societal norms, but only on an individual basis—"Some people say a person who uses a wheelchair can't be a teacher, but I know that Martha is a teacher."

Sixes:

- In addition to what fives can do, can also begin to engage in comparisons about correct/incorrect concrete beliefs about various groups (not just individuals), by gathering and using concrete data relevant to them (e.g., "Some people say men can't be nurses/take care of children, but we are learning they can"; "Girls can't do science, but we are learning"; "People who are visually impaired can't work, but we are learning").

Sevens and eights:

- although sevens and eights have absorbed and internalized many stereotypes and prejudice, they also have the cognitive tools to do critical thinking about their own ideas, and also about prevailing stereotypes around them: in books, TV, movies, greeting cards, etc.
- can use emerging reading and writing skills to help them gather data that challenges stereotypes and erroneous ideas about people as a result of their gender, race/ethnicity, disabilities, class, and sexual orientation.

Goal Four: To Foster Each Child's Ability to Stand up for Her/Himself and for Others in the Face of Bias

Threes:

- learning about acceptable ways to express their feelings when they want something, or when others hurt them.

Fours:

- engage in simple problemsolving and conflict-resolution techniques for dealing with incidents of teasing/rejection directed at their own and others' identity.

Fives:

- problem-solve and utilize ways to handle specific unfair comments and behaviors that arise in their school/home lives.
- gain emotional food-for-thought from stories about adults who have worked for social justice, especially adults they know.
- with adult help, create and engage in simple group actions, based on a concrete, meaningful experience in their daily life (e.g., making a handicapped parking space).

Sixes, sevens, and eights:

- develop fair rules for classroom behavior on identity issues with greater understanding, more autonomy, and depth.
- identify respectful ways to ask about cultural behaviors and ideas different from your own.
- learn about people who work for social justice in their communities.
- problem-solve conflict situations involving bias.
- problem-solve specific group actions related to a concrete discriminatory situation in their school or immediate community.

Implementation Principles and Strategies

Incorporating an antibias approach into daily programs for children requires that educators be "reflective practitioners" who adapt curriculum goals and general strategies to the needs of their setting and who understand that effective teaching is a continuous interaction between adults and children. On the one hand, teachers have the responsibility to do the brainstorming, planning, and initiating of antibias topics, based on their analyses of their children's needs. On the other hand, careful attention to children's thinking and behavior, and to "teachable moments" leads to modifications and additions to initial plans. To do this, teachers must:

Begin with themselves, gaining clarity about who they are and uncovering misinformation, stereotypes, discomforts, and prejudices toward people different from themselves.

Carefully evaluate all the materials and equipment in their classrooms or centers, for messages about diversity, determining which materials stay, which need modification, and which should be eliminated because of their stereotypical or inaccurate content.

Begin to incorporate antibias activities into daily curriculum planning. Antibias topics are integral to all the other subjects that comprise curricula. Most traditional preschool program units—e.g., "my body," "families," "work"—and the traditional content areas of the primary curriculum—science, math, language arts, physical and health curriculum—offer possibilities for incorporating diversity and antibias content. Be careful not to treat these activities as appendages or special events to regular curriculum.

Weigh the needs of their specific group of children and families and determine long-range overall goals, specific objectives and the starting point of their antibias work. Thoughtfully evaluate the program to see that it is culturally relevant—fostering children's development, as much as possible, in the context of their home culture. This happens automatically, for the most part, in all-white classrooms, since accepted early childhood education practices are grounded in Western European/American culture. However, always keep in mind that while cultural patterns/rules of behavior exist in every culture, each individual family carries out its own group's culture in their own ways. These are learned through ongoing interaction, observation, and conversation with each family. Appropriate antibias issues must be determined for each individual setting.

Use developmentally appropriate activities. Work is a journey that begins in early years and continues through secondary and postsecondary education. It means (a) starting with a child's experiences of self, (b) then moving outward in concentric circles to family, neighborhood, city, country, other countries, and (c) moving in a time continuum that begins with current experiences, to learning about the immediate past, and then to the more distant past and the future.

Plan how to intervene in all discriminatory interactions between children, on any kinds of bias, and teach children to care, think critically about and act against discriminatory behaviors. Discriminatory behaviors begin with four and five-year-olds, and exponentially increase in the primary and secondary years. Children at all ages can develop the critical thinking skills and the empathy to recognize and interpret discriminatory behaviors.

Plan how to engage children in planning and carrying out "activism" appropriate to their developmental level, cultural background, and interests. Activism activities should arise out of real-life situations that are of interest to the children with whom you are working. Their purpose is to provide opportunities for them to build their skills and confidence; consequently activities should reflect *their* ideas and issues, not the teacher's.

Plan how to involve parents and other adult family members in all aspects of antibias education. Education and collaboration with parents is ESSENTIAL. We have to be creative and ingenious in finding ways to make this happen. Parents can participate in the planning, implementing, and evaluating of environmental adaptations and curricular activities. They can serve on advisory/planning committees with staff, provide information about their family's lifestyles and beliefs, participate in classroom activities, and serve as community liaisons. Teachers can send home regular short newsletters to share ongoing plans and classroom activities, and elicit parent advice and resources. When a family member disagrees with an aspect of the curriculum, it is essential to listen carefully and sensitively to the issues underlying the disagreement. Find out all you can about the cultural and/or other issues that influence the family's concerns, and problem-solve with family members about ways to meet their needs while also maintaining the goals of antibias education.

Strategies for Working on Specific Goals

- Self-identity
  + visibility of the children's lives in all aspects of the educational environment and program
  + some staff reflective of the children's backgrounds
  + all staff knowledgeable about nurturing children's development in culturally sensitive and relevant ways
  + strong family-staff connections and partnerships
  + support for continued home language development while also gradually being introduced to English
  + ongoing dialogue with family members about nurturing their children's development of identity
  + staff work at becoming self-aware—conscious of their own culture and self-identity in a very practical sense: How are my child-caring and teaching beliefs, objectives, and behaviors influenced by my culture? How do I feel about who I am, and about other people from my own group?

- Respecting diversity
  + beginning with the children's own classroom/center, establish a culture of inclusion and fairness: how we are different and the same; fair ways to include everyone
  + bridge from children learning about themselves to people who are not part of the classroom; avoid overgeneralizations that stereotype groups, especially with preprimary children
  + keep developmentally appropriate guidelines in mind when designing activities
  + integrate learning about diversity into all aspects of daily life in the classroom, using accurate and authentic material/images

+ staff works at respectful learning about the cultural beliefs and practices of families and other staff, uncovering the misinformation, stereotypes, and prejudices toward others they have learned; and practices equitable negotiation and problem solving when cultural conflict arises.

- Critical thinking
  + uncover and identify the misrepresentations, stereotypes, and prejudices to which your children are exposed in their daily lives
  + find out how your children are thinking about people from various ethnic groups, gender roles, disabilities, family structures, etc.
  + help children learn to identify and resist stereotypes and prejudice directed at aspects of their own identity (e.g., culture, class, family structure, religion, weight, etc.)
  + never ignore biased interactions between children (e.g., teasing, rejection, name-calling based on an aspect of their identity)
  + develop critical thinking activities that challenge your children's misconceptions, using tried and true early childhood education methods to provide countering information and experiences and to explore feelings
  + staff works together at identifying and analyzing the underlying dynamics of both institutional and interpersonal prejudice and discrimination in their program, creates a social environment in which it is safe to give each other honest yet caring feedback about their work and do collaborative problem solving that improves the quality of their work.

- Taking action
  + follows from and extends children's critical thinking
  + issues come from children's lives at school and in their neighborhood
  + activities are developmentally and culturally appropriate to your group of children
  + highlight the contributions of the children's family and community as well as historic role models
  + staff model taking action in relation to issues that arise in the classroom/center and community.

The Teacher Is the Primary Tool for Success

Several years' experience working with early childhood educators wishing to implement an antibias educational approach throughout the country and internationally has led to deeper understanding of the teacher's vital role. First and foremost, antibias education is more a perspective and an approach than a specific curriculum. It cannot be done mechanically from a recipe. The teacher must be able to take the principles and basic strategies and figure out what they mean for the group of children and the community with whom they work. Consequently, antibias work has to be locally based, led by people who are part of and understand the conditions, needs, cultures, language, and learning styles of the people in their geographic area.

Furthermore, learning to implement an antibias educational approach is a developmental journey for adults as well as children. A growing literature about adult racial/cultural identity development provides a framework for guiding and supporting change in teachers (Cross, 1991; Darder, 1991; Helms, 1990; Tatum, 1992, 1995). It is also clear that time is an integral part in creating effective antibias education programs, including sufficient, on-the-job time for teachers to engage together in personal development and to reflect on and learn from their practice. It is one of the most difficult challenges to meet. Consequently, the majority of early childhood education teachers do not yet have either sufficient preservice preparation or continuing education to support and successfully incorporate antibias education into their programs.

What sustains those teachers who daily "walk the walk" rather than just talking about doing it? Themes that emerge from teachers' responses to this question include:

- their commitment to children and to the ethical mandates of their profession;
- their curiosity about others, enjoyment of diversity, and willingness to take risks and learn from mistakes;
- a sense of humor, creativity, flexibility, persistence;
- in-service training directly related to their particular teaching context;
- regular and frequent opportunities to do self-reflection, and to discuss, learn from, plan with, and support each other and parents/family members. Some directors have found ways to make this happen during work hours; in many cases teachers have had to look outside their work places to form support groups with other interested teachers in their city or geographic region;
- decent working conditions—fair wages, benefits, working hours.

Future Challenges

The need for education that teaches young people of all ages how to interact thoughtfully, respectfully, and fairly across different ethnic and cultural identities and boundaries has never been greater. Indeed, the Chronicle of Higher Education, recently reported that Nathan Glazer, a long-time critic of multicultural education, now argues that it is necessary—the price America must pay for its racism (Shea, 1997, p. A16).

However, as the antibias/multicultural/bilingual education movement gains momentum, critics accuse it of disuniting the nation, ignoring Western culture and thought, preaching censorship and mind control, and politicizing education. Christine Sleeter, a well-known and respected author on multicultural education points out—and I agree—that these critics are responding to "actual changes in curriculum required of white students as well as students of color, and particularly changes that challenge white supremacy" (Sleeter, 1995, p. 88).

We are at a crossroads. The debate about multicultural and antibias education reflects societal tensions between those who want to press forward toward creating a more open and equitable society and those who are desperate to maintain the status quo. Underlying this backlash are many fears and frustrations. People who have always been in control are frightened by the changing demographics in this country and are resistant to the idea that they might have to give up some of their economic and social power to groups that traditionally have been excluded. Others who may not be in positions of power are still afraid of the implications of social change and may not be able to see potential benefits to themselves. In the face of uncertainty, they yearn for the reassurance of familiarity and want to see that their children are going to the same schools and learning the same things that they did. Many people also resent the idea that they may have to change their ways of thinking and dismiss challenges to their long-held beliefs and assumptions as the narrow-minded preoccupations of the "politically correct" (Derman-Sparks & Ramsey, 1992).

The conservative backlash is evidence that the antibias/multicultural/bilingual movement now has a greater visibility to people outside the world of education, so in some ways, this reaction is encouraging. However, we must strive to persuade increasing numbers of people that as long as some groups are excluded and alienated from educational institutions and economic opportunities, our world is precarious. We also need to conduct research on classroom practices to keep improving the effectiveness of our work and to demonstrate the broad benefits of developing more open and just schools. New models of action research in which teachers are involved directly in defining questions and conducting studies would be a fruitful avenue to pursue.

Criticisms of antibias/multicultural education may help all educators define their mission and their goals more clearly and give them the determination to continue and expand their work. Alternatively, the harsh voice of the opposition may lead to retrenchment. Administrators and teachers may feel more apprehensive about embarking on curricular reforms that are potentially controversial. Nevertheless, "When it is clear that young people are learning racial hatred from a very early age, the imperative seems indisputable that the schools must formally teach young people the skills to counter the destructive messages reaching them" (Multicultural Collaborative, 1996).

I close with words from Carol Brunson Phillips, because she has already said it so well:

Antiracism and antibias curriculum won't be easy [to do], because racism and oppression are hard to talk about and no one has pat answers. People are afraid and uncertain about how to control them, and how to encourage honesty and create safety.

But because our dialogue is essential, these fears have to be put aside. We must create an atmosphere that allows us to take the risks required to begin the journey. A few agreed-upon ground rules will help:

We must share our uncertainty with each other and allow each other to make tentative statements.

We must acknowledge our misgivings and voice our ambivalence. As we expose our viewpoints to others, we must agree to listen to each other without judging.

We must, through our anger and hostilities, be open about our differing viewpoints and admit our hurts.

We must trust each other to find answers together and work toward change.

Nurturing diversity through our own variety of multicultural education will require some work—but to start involves only a simple commitment to self-enlightenment. For as we take on the challenge to redesign our institutions based on fuller understanding of the problems within society, we will do so with a stronger belief in our own power to resolve them. It is my wish that we take on this work and that our teaching will result in the liberation of the human spirit (Phillips, 1988, p. 47).

Notes

1. Young children use the same cognitive organizing "principles" for grappling with the realities of human diversity as they do for other aspects of their physical and social world. Consider, for example, the following conversation at my family's 1991 Passover Seder with my 4-year-old niece. After the telling of the story of the ancient Hebrews' liberation from slavery in ancient Egypt, she turned to me and said, "I'm half Jewish." "Uh Huh," I replied. My niece continued, "The Jewish people went through the water and they didn't get wet. They got to the other side. The people who weren't Jewish got drowned." "That is what the Passover story tells us," I affirmed, but her expression remained quizzical. "What do you think happened to the people who were half Jewish?" I then asked (recognizing that "half-Jewish" is not a category officially recognized in Judaism, but *is* how my young niece thinks about it at this stage in her life). "They got to the other side too," she replied—paused—and then concluded, "But they got a little bit wet." Her solution was cognitively clever and emotionally satisfying: she got to the other side safely, and she acknowledged her identity as she understands it at 4½ years old.
2. Published by the National Association for the Education of Young Children in 1989, the ABC book articulates an educational philosophy and set of values as well as offering teachers specific techniques for supporting all children's growth. To date, the book has sold more than 160,000 copies.
3. As with any developmental guidelines, however, the cultural, individual, and experiential context of a particular child must also be taken into account.

References

Clark, K. (1963). *Prejudice and your child.* (3rd ed.). Boston: Beacon.
Cross, W. E., Jr. (1991). *Shades of Black: Diversity in African-American Identity.* Philadelphia: Temple University Press.

Darder, A. (1991). *Culture and Power in the Classroom: A Critical Foundation for Bicultural Education*. New York: Bergin & Garvey.

Dennis, R. (1981). "Socialization and Racism: The White Experience." In B. Bowser & R. Hunt (Eds.), *Impacts of Racism on White Americans*. (pp. 71–86). Beverly Hills: Sage.

Derman-Sparks, L. (1992). "Anti-bias, Multicultural Curriculum: What is Developmentally Appropriate?" In S. Bredekamp & T. Rosegrant eds. *Reaching Potentials: Transforming Early Childhood Curriculum for Young Children*. Washington, DC: NAEYC

Derman-Sparks, L. & the ABC Task Force. (1989). *Anti-bias Curriculum: Tools for Empowering Young Children*. Washington, DC: NAEYC.

Derman-Sparks, L., Higa, C., & Sparks, B. (1980). "Children, Race and Racism: How Race Awareness Develops." *Bulletin of the Council on Interracial Books for Children, 11*, 3–9.

Derman-Sparks, L., & Ramsey, P. (1992). "Multicultural Education Reaffirmed." *Young Children, 47*, 10–11.

Froschl, M., Colon, L., Rubin, E., & Sprung, B. (1984). *Including All of Us: An Early Childhood Curriculum about Disability*. N.Y: Educational Equity Concepts, Inc.

Goodman, M. E. (1964). *Race Awareness in Young Children*. New York: Collier.

Helms, J. E. (1990). "Toward a Model of White Racial Identity Development." In J. E. Helms ed., *Black and White Racial Identity: Theory, Research and Practice*. Westport, CT: Greenwood Press.

Katz, P. (1982). "Development of Children's Racial Awareness and Intergroup Attitudes." In L. G. Katz ed., *Current Topics in Early Childhood Education*. (pp. 17–54). Norwood, N.J.: Ablex.

Los Angeles County Commission on Human Relations. (1995). *Hate Crime in Los Angeles County in 1995: A Report to the Los Angeles County Board of Supervisors*. Los Angeles.

MultiCultural Collaborative. (1996). *Race, Power and Promise in Los Angeles: An Assessment of Responses to Human Relations Conflict*.

Pera, G. (1995). "Teens and Race." *USA Weekend: Special Report*. August. (pp. 2–3).

Phillips, C. B. (1988). "Nurturing Diversity for Today's Children and Tomorrow's Leaders." *Young Children, 43*(2), 42–47.

Phinney, J., & Rotheram, M. J. eds., *Children's Ethnic Socialization: Pluralism and Development*. (pp. 10–28). Beverly Hills, CA: Sage Publications.

Pierce, C. M. (1980). "Social Trace Contaminants: Subtle Indicators of Racism." In S. Withey, R. Abeles, & L. Erlbaum eds., *Television and Social Behavior: Beyond Violence and Children*. (pp. 249–57). Hillsdale, NJ: Erlbaum.

Ramsey, P. G. (1991). "Young Children's Awareness and Understanding of Social Class Differences." *Journal of Genetic Psychology, 152*, 71–82.

Ramsey, P. (1995). "Growing up with the Contradictions of Race and Class." *Young Children*, 18–22.

Sapon-Shevin, M. (1983). "Teaching Young Children about Differences." *Young Children, 38*(2), 24–32.

Serbin, L. (1980). "Play Activities and the Development of Visual-Spatial Skills." *Equal Play, 1*(4), 5.

Sheldon, A. (1990). "Kings are Royaler than Queens: Language and Socialization." *Young Children, 45*(2), 4–9.

Shea, C. (1997, April 11). "Multiculturalism Gains an Unlikely Supporter." *The Chronicle of Higher Education*, April 11, 1997, A16, A18.

Smith, L. (1949, rev. 1962). *Killers of the Dream*. New York: Norton.

Sleeter, C. (1995). "An Analysis of the Critique of Multicultural Education." In J. Banks & C. M. Banks eds. *Handbook of Research on Multicultural Education* (pp. 81–94). New York: Macmillan.

Tatum, B. D. (1992). "Talking about Race, Learning about Racism: The Application of Racial Identity Development Theory in the Classroom." *Harvard Educational Review, 62*(1), 1–24.

Tatum, B. D. (1995, February). *Stages of Racial/Ethnic Identity Development in the United States*. Paper presented at the meeting of the National Association for Multicultural Education, Washington, D.C.

USA Weekend. (1995). *Special Report: Teens and Race*, August (pp. 1–8).

Walker, A. (1989). *The Temple of My Familiar*. New York: Pocket Books.

Wong Fillmore, L. (1991). "Language and Cultural Issues in Early Education." In S. L. Kagan ed., *The Care and Education of America's Young Children: Obstacles and Opportunities*. The 90th Yearbook of the National Society for the Study of Education.

Mobilizing International and Regional Organizations for Managing Ethnic Conflict*

ANTONIA HANDLER CHAYES

AND ABRAM CHAYES

Introduction

As we look ahead, the onus will clearly shift to the civilian agenda. There the signs are more troubling. The formal structures of civilian implementation—committees, commissions, and human rights chambers—are being set up according to Dayton. But we must look at the larger—and more disquieting—picture. By itself, the military can do little more than silence the guns and partition the country.

Thus wrote Carl Bildt,[1] former Prime Minister of Sweden and the High Representative of the international community—charged with the civilian task of social and economic reconstruction of Bosnia-Herzegovina—a little more than three months after Dayton. In fact, little tangible "peace-building" was started in the first ninety days. One official, working with OSCE on elections, returned from Sarajevo discouraged by the fact that although there were many international, regional, and nongovernmental organizations in evidence in Sarajevo, the only hammers and nails were supplied by the citizens themselves.[2] Responsibilities have been assigned to many organizations. However, although one-quarter of the critical year of NATO's commitment had passed, there was considerable creative improvisation, but little planning, cooperation, and flow of needed funds on the civilian side. The performance is depressingly familiar to those who have followed the efforts of international and regional organizations to deal with internal conflict in the post–Cold War world.

Although ethnic and tribal wars have raged throughout history, the efforts of international and regional organizations to deal with such conflicts is relatively recent. Historically, the UN, and before it the League of Nations (as well as regional political organizations such as the OSCE) focused on conflicts between states, the

*The authors wish to thank Chris Cervenak for her help in drafting this paper.

traditional domain of international law and politics. Although both states and individuals instinctively turned to international organizations in responding to the internal conflicts that have dominated the post–Cold War security agenda, the question remains: What can international and regional organizations really do to manage ethnic conflicts, and where have they succeeded or fallen short—individually and collectively?

Most of the analysis and criticism attempting to answer this question has focused on the United Nations, which has primary responsibility for the maintenance of international peace and security. But regional and other international organizations have been engaged in the enterprise to a greater or lesser extent. Nowhere is the concentration of such organizations richer or more sophisticated than in Europe. We focus on their experience in attempting to deal with ethnic conflict in Eastern and Central Europe (ECE) and in the former Soviet Union (FSU), in countries spawned in the collapse of Communism that are "fertile fields for spontaneous combustion." In societies experiencing transitional periods, "peoples struggling for the ethnic identity denied to them quickly become political groups demanding territory or social and linguistic concessions which they believe will enhance their security for all time."[3] There is no way of knowing which conflicts will be contained within accepted borders, threatening only the immediate participants, and which may spill over.

By "managing ethnic conflict" we mean to include more than preventive diplomacy in traditional terms, that is, activity that takes place before the outbreak of violent conflict. We include efforts in the course of violent confrontation to prevent escalation and provide the parties with breathing space to compose their differences. Also, we are concerned with preventing the recurrence of conflict after a settlement is reached. These phases cannot be kept entirely separate. A situation can move from one to another and back again. Often the same forces operate in each, and the same instruments must be used, although the different phases may call for different approaches or emphasis.

International and regional organizations are the formal vehicles through which consensus for action to deal with conflict is established by the relevant international community. They should have the capability of bringing greater resources, power, legitimacy, and expertise to bear on complex international problems than any one state or ad hoc grouping. Yet international organizations are made of states and concerted action even within a single organization requires building consensus. Typically, the necessary level of consensus is slow and cumbersome in coming. A single state or group can bring enormous pressure—positive or negative—on the organizations' decision-making process. Thus intervention is often too little, too late, or too tentative. Complicating the situation further, international organizations, like individual states, have multiple agendas, and as became clear in the EU recognition policy in the former Yugoslavia, these disparate agendas may play out in unexpected ways.[4]

Thus far the effectiveness of these organizations in coping with internal conflict in the ECE and FSU has been disappointing and their potential elusive. Not only is each organization struggling with internal impediments to action, but also a fully concerted strategy to mobilize the resources of this rich organizational structure is not yet available. Each organization has its own charter and its own mandate, priorities, bureaucracy, and budget. Memberships, though overlapping, are not identical. Within a single nation, organizational "stovepipes" lead to different domestic political actors. Although it is common and true to cite limitations of resources to explain deficiencies, it is also true that over $3 billion annually has been expended in the former Yugoslavia alone, with a deployment even before the Dayton Agreement of some 6,000 civilian personnel and 40,000 soldiers and police officers.[5]

Careful analysis of the record to date, however inadequate it has been, and the juxtaposition of the performance of relevant organizations suggest some ways in which their contribution could be improved over that of the first half-decade since the Cold War. Each organization operating in the ECE/FSU has a partial view of the problems and a different set of tools to apply. Some engage in intermediation, in traditional and newer guises. Other tools are the tangible inducements that regional and international financial institutions can offer, and the intangible inducements of belonging to the community of democratic nations that is the imprimatur of membership in the Council of Europe. Likewise, the powerful magnets of admission to the EU and NATO affect patterns of behavior among potentially conflictual communities. Still another tool, the threat and use of military force, has both potential and limits. Finally, further conflict may be prevented through the contribution organizations can make to reconstruction after conflict subsides.

For the purposes of discussion, we divide the organizations into three groups, excluding the UN. The first includes those that have an explicit focus on conflict prevention, but dispose of very limited resources. In this group are the trans-European regional organizations—the Organization for Security and Cooperation in Europe (OSCE) and the Council of Europe (COE)—which pursue the lowest-key and least coercive form of conflict prevention. The second group comprises organizations with political and economic resources, but with little or no focus on managing ethnic conflict. Here we find the international financial organizations—the International Monetary Fund (IMF), the World Bank and the European Bank for Reconstruction and Development (EBRD). They have power and influence to mount a conflict-prevention and management strategy, but have hardly begun to do so. Here too is the European Union and its offering of "conflict inhibitors," by the effect of its example and the aspiration for membership. In the third grouping are organizations with military power, but which, as products of the Cold War, have yet to address systematically the problem of ethnic conflict. These are the regional security organizations—the North Atlantic Treaty Organization (NATO) and the Western European Union (WEU).

1. Trans-European Political Organizations[6]

Membership in the OSCE and COE is confined to European countries (and by extension to the United States and Canada in the case of the OSCE) and is open to all of them, including the countries of Eastern Europe and the successor states of the Soviet Union. They are thus arguably the best suited for dealing with internal conflicts in these states, because they are the best informed and most closely concerned. Both organizations undertake low-key intervention in nascent conflicts, employing various forms of mediation, confidence building or norm development. Budgetary restrictions prevent more than very limited efforts at technical assistance or other kinds of material aid.

The OSCE's typical operation brings all stakeholders into dialogue in an attempt to prevent conflict from erupting. It requires detailed knowledge of the conditions in the area and more or less continuous mediatory activity. The work of the High Commissioner on National Minorities (HCNM) and various in-country missions illustrate this model. The COE develops human rights norms and standards of democratic governance, which it then imposes as conditions of membership for new applicants, thus placing pressure on them to improve their performance in these respects. The emergence of ethnic conflict in recent years has highlighted the tension between traditional individual rights and minority or group rights.

A. The Organization for Security and Cooperation in Europe

The most novel and potentially effective methods of preventing ethnic conflict have been developed by the OSCE.[7] The traditional "settlement-and-enforcement" model for international intervention in conflict begins with fact finding, the results of which are discussed by the organization's political decision-making body, typically resulting in directions to the parties to undertake certain actions (e.g., cease hostilities), as well as provisions for high-level intermediation. Coercive economic or military measures may be prescribed to help ensure cooperation by the parties. Whatever success this "settlement and enforcement" model has had in dealing with full-blown international conflict—and the record is at best doubtful—it is wholly unsuited to the earlier stages of a conflict:

> Traditional methods . . . [using] confrontation, pressure and advocacy will frequently only exacerbate conflict, while traditional strategies of mediation of conflict, with their emphasis on "carrots" and "sticks" to induce settlements, are inadequate to deal with long term psychological social, economic and political problems at the root of ethno-national conflict. . . . They implicate the most fundamental of human aspirations and needs (such as identity, recognition, security, meaningful participation in political processes) and cannot be "solved" through negotiation of legally binding and enforceable agreements.[8]

In the early stages of a conflict, neither the parties nor the issues are likely to be crystallized. The problem is to help set up processes that will get at underlying strivings and discontents before they harden into intractable and violent conflict.

The approach of the OSCE to conflict prevention is not limited to nor even primarily focused on settlement of the underlying dispute, but is based on cooperative management and dialogue. "[The OSCE's] strategy has been to build on its existing structures for multilateral discussion, and especially its inability to undertake any enforcement action. . . . It has proceeded by dialogue and 'jawboning' at early stages of conflict where large-scale intervention would be inappropriate."[9] Successful OSCE interventions are quiet and low key.

This approach to intervention fits the roles and structures of the OSCE. First, the OSCE has adopted a broad view of its security role to include ethnic conflict, economic cooperation, human rights within states, as well as the more traditional military and interstate relations.[10] Human rights and ethnic conflicts are not seen as matters of internal affairs out of bounds for the organization. This development dates back to Cold War days, when, in the Helsinki review conference of 1980, the Soviet Union attacked U.S. treatment of African-Americans and Native Americans, thus abandoning its traditional position that human rights was an internal affair and so exempt from OSCE jurisdiction.

Second, the OSCE is essentially a forum for multilateral discussion, operating on the basis of consensus, designed to promote security through dialogue, not coercion. Given the OSCE's inability to "enforce" commitments of participants, it has depended on and developed persuasive methods to gain adherence to its principles. At the OSCE summit in Budapest in 1994, this approach to conflicts was approved: the organization is to be a "primary instrument for early warning, conflict prevention and crisis prevention in the region," using a "flexible and dynamic" approach.[11]

Third, and ironically enough, the requirement for consensus[12] among the fifty-two nations that comprise the OSCE, so often cited as an impediment to action, may be its greatest strength. This principle is limiting to the extent that the OSCE is hampered in its ability to sanction violators of OSCE norms. Action requiring large resources, such as enforcement, is nearly impossible. But sanctions and enforcement action, in any case, do not have an enviable record in dealing with international conflict, and the consensus requirement has prompted the Organization to innovate and adopt creative approaches to conflict prevention. It has given the OSCE the flexibility to change its structures and procedures in response to changed circumstances after 1990.

The consensus requirement also enhances the legitimacy of OSCE norms, thereby generating pressure on governments to respect them. It becomes harder for a state to reject a normative command adopted by consensus after serious and lengthy debate within the organization in which all take part. The OSCE played a pioneering role in the effort to develop and promote international recognition of minority and group rights. In 1990, at its Copenhagen meeting, it adopted a trailblazing document containing an unprecedented enumeration of minority rights. This document served as the starting point for the Council of Europe's work in this field, discussed below.

The primary instruments for OSCE intervention in ethnic conflict are "the missions of short and long duration" and the High Commissioner on National

Minorities (HCNM).[13] The missions often cover a broader subject matter and are less localized geographically within a country than the activities of the HCNM. But they share the same goals. Both serve as early warning to the OSCE. They provide transparency within and outside the country and work with governments and the parties in conflicts to prevent escalation. The basis for successes achieved is not power but persuasive influence and the ability to offer alternatives to escalation.

The High Commissioner for National Minorities

The HCNM has been described as

> perhaps the most important and innovative of the OSCE's new preventive diplomacy instruments, and the core of the OSCE's preventive diplomacy approach. It was created explicitly as an "instrument of conflict prevention at the earliest possible stage," to provide early warning and early action on tensions involving national minorities that could escalate into conflict endangering peace and security. It is the first and only OSCE institution with authority to initiate preventive diplomacy activities on its own judgment and without a prior mandate.[14]

The formal mandate of the HCNM is a reflection of traditional conflict prevention practice. It provides for an information-gathering stage, followed by an "early warning" to political bodies of an impending dispute, then for authorization of "early action" in the form of mediation, and finally, the implementation of an action plan.[15] This procedure proved unworkable in practice, and has never been employed. In fact, the first HCNM, former Dutch foreign minister Max van der Stoel, said he would feel that his mission had failed if he had to issue a formal "early warning."

Instead, acting relatively independently of the OSCE bureaucracy, the HCNM enjoys independence of the governments and minority populations involved. He also has the authority to initiate country visits on his own responsibility, although he consults informally with the Chairman in Office (CIO) and interested OSCE states to assure political support.[16] But if he has a certain independence from the concerned government, neither is he a representative of minorities. As the HCNM explained his role:

> If the OSCE commitments such as contained in the Copenhagen Document are violated, the High Commissioner has, of course, to ask a government concerned to change its line, reminding it that stability and harmony are as a rule served best by ensuring full rights to persons belonging to a minority. However, he also has to remind the members of a minority that they have duties as well as rights.[17]

This independence allows the HCNM to act as a mediator, working to prevent conflict by promoting dialogue and cooperation among the parties. In contrast to the classical conception of the mediator, however, the HCNM acts as what has been characterized as an "insider third party."[18] "Insider" does not imply less neutrality but more continuous involvement closer to the ground than a typical international mediator might achieve. The HCNM operates within the state structure, putting pressures upon the government while attempting to win its confidence and that of the other parties. The objective is not a one-shot attempt at conflict resolution, but to start processes going, whether in politics, in the legislative forum or through intense round-table dialogues, in which the contending parties can begin to know and trust each other, thus creating the time and space for managing conflict.

The HCNM is working on issues relating to the minorities—Russian-speaking, Hungarian, Slovakian, Macedonian, Greek, or Albanian—in about ten countries. His activities have

> generally encompassed a process of visits and regular telephone communication for purposes of familiarizing himself with the situation, development of relationships with the parties, communication of recommendations to the governments concerned, and follow-up to address issues or tensions that arise during the course of his involvement or during the implementation phase of his recommendations.[19]

In-country missions

Unlike the HCNM's office, the in-country missions, otherwise known as "missions of long duration," are not mentioned in any of the OSCE constitutive documents. Rather, they were developed to respond to specific situations. There are now seven local missions, four of which are preventive diplomacy missions (Estonia, Latvia, Macedonia, and Ukraine), with the remaining three being crisis management missions (Georgia, Moldova, and Tajikistan).

Like the HCNM, the preventive diplomacy missions are aimed at deescalation and management of tensions in order to permit longer-term conflict resolution. However, the missions' structure and functions are somewhat different from those of the HCNM. The missions are resident in the country for at least six months and are visible and operational throughout the country. Their activities typically involve traveling from town to town to talk with officials, citizens, and NGOs and receiving individual complaints of mistreatment. The missions' mandate is often broader than that of the HCNM, including military, economic, social, and political issues as well as minority policy. In practice, they have also become involved in areas not originally envisioned.

In contrast to the relative independence of the HCNM, the missions may be described as "instruments of the political process" of the OSCE. They have no independent authority: the Senior or Permanent Council creates them, defines their mandate, and informally supervises them. The missions are dependent on the continuing consent of the host country. While the Permanent Council exerts pressure on the host governments not to withhold consent to the missions' activities, "the missions are forced to work cooperatively with the government and refrain from too much criticism of it, so as not to jeopardize their continued existence."[20]

As with the HCNM, the most effective missions have managed these pressures along with the need to gain the confidence of the minority populations by becoming "third-party insiders" to the conflict. They involve themselves with all the relevant parties, gaining knowledge and their confidence, and thereby building an effective third-party role. Successful preventive diplomacy missions, as in Estonia, Latvia, Macedonia, and even Serbia, also enjoy significant political support from countries such as the Scandinavians and the United States, which exert bilateral influence on the host governments. Such support is lacking for the crisis-management missions, presumably because at this stage it would require a greater investment of resources and political capital than the influential countries are prepared to make.[21] Without such backing and potential coercion, the crisis-management missions have not succeeded in compelling parties to negotiate. Nevertheless, they have sometimes played an important prenegotiation/mediation role, helping parties to set the groundwork that may lead to conflict resolution.

The in-country missions have enjoyed a number of successes in conflict prevention. For example, in Macedonia, the OSCE mission facilitated an agreement between the government and Albanian leadership to defuse a November 1992 riot. The OSCE mission in Latvia was instrumental in the negotiation and implementation of the agreement on the Russian withdrawal from the Skrunda military installation. The mission to Moldova helped to negotiate a release of hostages, engaged the breakaway "Trans-Dniester Republic" in dialogue in an effort to convey information about other parties and potential negotiation processes, provided support for delegations observing the parliamentary elections in 1994, organized a seminar for officials to discuss the principles of a democratic constitution, and advised the government on human rights issues. In Estonia, the mission is on the commission in charge of implementing a Russian-Estonian agreement on Russian military pensioners.

The OSCE processes are not necessarily an ideal or universal solution. They seem to have most success in relatively low-intensity situations. Homeopathic medicine does not cure pneumonia. The then-CSCE was ineffective in dealing with the raging conflict in the former Yugoslavia. The OSCE is pitifully underfunded, with a total budget of $27 million. Moreover, the processes established may not take permanent root by the time OSCE missions leave. And already there is some backlash, for example, in the Baltics, which express concern that they are being singled out, and in fact, the Baltic governments have pushed for the HCNM and missions to leave. A framework agreement for UN-OSCE cooperation exists. Although the OSCE consults regularly with the UN and the UN participates at OSCE meetings as an observer, much more is needed to ensure they work together effectively "in the field." All in all, however, the focus on conflict prevention, the willingness to become deeply involved as a quasi insider, the modest goals and the absence of bureaucratic sclerosis make the OSCE a very important model.

B. *The Council of Europe*

The focus of Council of Europe activities is only indirectly conflict prevention. Its mandate is to establish and to some degree enforce norms of civilized and democratic national behavior. The COE proceeds on the basic assumption that Western-type democracies operating under the rule of law and protecting fundamental human rights do not experience much violent internal conflict. Focusing on human rights issues in the context of its more general democracy mission, the COE works on elaborating norms of state conduct and increasing states' agreement to and compliance with them. Its potential conflict-prevention role flows from its powers to grant or withhold the imprimatur of COE membership on the basis of the applicant's compliance with norms of individual and minority rights.[22] The combination of recognized norms on these matters and more stringent application of admission requirements may have long term effects on the way the transitional states of the ECE and FSU address ethnonational conflict.

Norm Development and Promotion

In recent years, the Council has focused on completing a framework convention to the European Convention on Human Rights specifying the principles for the protection of national minorities.[23] In earlier times it had embraced the ideal of "republicanism," notably championed by France, which maintains that the state must strictly abjure formal nondiscrimination among citizens based on ethnic identity or other ascriptive characteristics. This conception sought to decouple the state and ethnic identity. But gradually, this traditional emphasis on individual human rights has come to be seen as not wholly adequate to societies racked by sharp ethnic division. A policy of formal nondiscrimination among individuals, it was argued, does not assure governmental neutrality or equality of status among groups. The shift to a minority rights emphasis, although resisted by some, was driven by the search for answers to secessionist impulses in the post–Cold War setting. The concept of minority rights concedes that ethnonationalism and public life cannot be delinked, and thus embodies a vision of the multicultural nation state. It requires that the state establish official mechanisms for the recognition and protection of minority ethnonational identities.

The COE has followed a convoluted path in developing norms of minority rights. As early as 1990, the Venice Commission, a COE organ, collaborated informally with the OSCE on the preparation of the Copenhagen Document noted above. In 1991, the Venice Commission presented a Draft European Convention for the Protection of Minorities, generally similar to the Copenhagen Document, but including provisions for enforcement through the European Court of Human Rights. Although this draft was not adopted, the COE created yet another commission of experts to draft a definitive instrument by 1993. But at the COE's Vienna summit in October 1993, the push for legal recognition of minority rights was aggressively challenged by defenders of the traditional view, including Václev Havel, in the wake of the dissolution of Czechoslovakia. Institutionalizing interethnic differences, it was argued, would impede efforts to forge a nation around other commonalities. The Vienna Summit contented itself with directing the preparation of an additional protocol to the European Convention on Human rights "in the cultural field" containing "provisions guaranteeing individual rights, in particular for persons belonging to national minorities."[24] In addition, the secretariat was instructed to draft a more general framework convention specifying the principles that governments must respect to assure the protection of national minorities living within their territory. The COE completed its work on its Convention on the Protection of National Minorities, which was signed by twenty-one states in early 1995.[25]

The Vienna Summit also charged the secretariat with following a minority conscious policy in helping member states and candidates for membership to consolidate their systems of democratic governance. Council outreach, however, is confined to modest confidence-building projects, workshops, and technical assistance designed to reinforce relevant norms. The activities include providing legal advice to East European states on the impact of legislation on minorities (e.g., of language and citizenship laws), support for bilingual radio stations in Croatia (Italian/Croat) and Estonia (Estonian/Russian), and conducting minorities/nationalities seminars. Like the OSCE, COE activities are low-key and cost little, since resources are extremely limited. They depend upon the power of persuasion, prestige, and the pressures of members to induce conformity with Council norms.[26]

The Allure of Membership

Norm elaboration and enforcement are inextricably linked to membership and the attraction of COE membership has been used by the Council to gain compliance with its norms. Membership is formally conditioned on a minimum respect for human rights, and the COE has tried, with varying degrees of success, to use the admissions process to pressure candidate states to improve their human-rights records. Generally, admission is coupled with the signature and ratification of COE human-rights instruments. All COE members are under the Council's human-rights supervisory mechanism. Under the European Convention on Human Rights, an offender state is subject to investigation by the European Commission on Human Rights and most have also accepted the jurisdiction of the European Court of Human Rights.

Since the end of the Cold War, the COE has had an onslaught of applications for membership from Eastern Europe. The motivations for seeking COE membership are varied: to show that the new governments are committed to human rights and democratic principles; for the accompanying boost membership gives to a government's legitimacy; to silence internal and external critics by arguing that the state's human-rights record meets COE standards; and to make explicit that the country has broken from past Soviet domination and is joining the circle of democracies. On this score, COE membership is an easier alternative to the NATO or EU clubs, where entry is more difficult.

Membership to the COE has not been granted as readily as in the OSCE. Approximately half of the applicants are not yet full members. The COE has tried expressly to use the application process as a tool for bringing about change in or testing the extent of democratic reforms by applicants.[27] During the admissions process, the COE reviews the applicant's human-rights record, makes recommendations, and may hold up admissions until the occurrence of some critical event, such as elections. Yet countries with mediocre human-rights records, such as Romania, have been admitted providing that they commit to certain reforms soon after admission and "appear to be making substantial progress toward democracy." In respect of minority rights norms, admission of new states will be conditioned on compliance with the new Convention,[28] and member states may be condemned if they violate it.

In order to maximize its leverage over nonmembers, the Parliamentary Assembly created "special guest status" for pending COE applicants. To be a "special guest," a country must ratify the UN Covenants on Civil and Political Rights and on Economic, Social, and Cultural Rights and accept the Helsinki Final Act and other CSCE declarations. Guest status establishes a framework for the COE to exert formal and informal pressures on the state through extended and intensive public discussion of the state's performance.

The need to be a member in good standing of the organized international community is a powerful motivator of state behavior, especially in countries emerging from long periods of totalitarian rule. Membership means access to economic resources and political status and legitimacy. But it would be a mistake to conceive the effect of norms of state conduct solely in terms of the "carrot" of membership or the "stick" of rejection or suspension (whether in the COE, or the other European organizations, all of which require adherence to democratic and human rights goals). A state accepting these norms also accepts an obligation to justify its conduct in the light of them, both within the bodies of the organization and in the larger community, and to submit to scrutiny when challenged. Grievances of minority groups are couched in terms of the norms, and negotiations and mediation are framed by them. The seemingly endless discussions of the meaning and application of the legal norms and standards in these forums not only strengthens their authority, but often elicits more detailed understanding of their content and commitments as to performance. For example, what starts out as the affirmation of a broad and generally accepted standard about respecting the rights of minorities to use their own language, may wind up in a detailed negotiation about street signs or the language in which official proceedings are to be conducted in a particular region. Agreements that emerge are very likely to be complied with, because they are tailored to this particular case and the state has participated in the process and explicitly committed itself to the outcome.[29] This leads to something of a dilemma in the use by the Council (and other organizations) of leverage based on admission to membership:

> [H]ow strict ought the Council be in interpreting and applying the requirements of democracy and respect for human rights as a prerequisite for admission? On the one hand the Council could take a relatively loose approach to these requirements, which would lead to the immediate admission of East European states. This, in turn, would consolidate these states' break from authoritarianism. With these states incorporated into the Council's human rights regime, the Council could

more effectively influence the conduct of those states. The loose approach has, however, a significant downside: since membership is the biggest incentive the Council has to offer, easy admission deprives the Council of its most important tool to effectuate changes in applicant countries.

On the other hand, the Council could take a stricter approach to the admission requirements. This stricter approach would ensure that the prize of membership would be granted only to the truly deserving. . . . Although this approach constitutes a good use of the membership tool, it risks depriving the Council of leverage over borderline states where the leadership is open to democratization and human rights, but is unwilling to move too rapidly in that direction.[30]

Trade and Development Institutions

The second group for discussion encompasses organizations with political and economic resources, but with at best a limited focus on conflict management. The international organizations represent an important pool of economic resources, far exceeding those available in bilateral assistance programs, that could be deployed to help resolve questions that might lead to conflict or to mitigate conflict once begun. The EU has economic power through its control of trade with the fifteen major European advanced industrial powers. Membership is thus one of the major boons available in the current international environment. If it is successful in its efforts to transform itself into a political power as well, the attraction will be correspondingly increased. Yet, for a variety of reasons rooted in the traditions of these institutions and, to some extent, in their constitutive documents, they have been hesitant to apply these powers in any very coherent or systematic way to the problems of internal conflict, even in cases that seem to threaten the overall goals of the institutions.

A. *International and Regional Financial Organizations*

Unlike the organizations discussed in Part 1, the IFIs—the International Bank for Reconstruction and Development (World Bank) and the International Monetary Fund (IMF)—and the European Bank for Reconstruction and Development (EBRD) have substantial funds to offer ECE and FSU nations. All three institutions are deeply involved in the economic transformation of the ECE and FSU. Thus far, however, they have not focused on the impact of their lending operations on ethnic conflict. Indeed, Susan Woodward argues that IMF policies in regard to the former Yugoslavia, which in the late 1980s was the sixth largest user of the Fund's resources, helped to dismantle the federal political structure and played into the hands of secessionist groups and nationalist leaders.[31]

The IFIs [32]

Traditionally, the World Bank and the Fund were supposed to be guided in their lending operations by purely economic considerations—in the case of the Bank, the ability of the project to repay the loan, and in the case of the Fund, the ability of the country to cure its balance of payments problems within a reasonable period. "Political" matters, particularly the internal social and governmental arrangements of the borrowing country, were supposed to be disregarded. It is apparent, however, that these business considerations alone dictate closer attention to the effect of ethnic conflict and conflict prevention on their investments. The IFIs are already deeply involved in system transformation, and are likely to be asked to pay the cost of reconstruction in the aftermath of conflict. Despite the reputation of institutional rigidity, the IFIs have begun to broaden their agenda to take account of the economic impact of such problems as environmental pollution, resource depletion, and population growth. However, it will require a considerable change in organizational culture, and in some cases, perhaps, changes in mandate and charter, to bring the IFIs to contemplate a conflict prevention and management strategy.

The World Bank was established in the aftermath of World War II to help rebuild the war-torn countries of Europe, as well as to "develop the resources and productive capacity of the world, with special reference to the less developed countries."[33] After the successful postwar recovery of Europe, the primary focus of the Bank's activities became the developing countries. With the end of the Cold War, ECE and the FSU became new areas of concentration. The Bank has traditionally insisted that under Article IV of its charter it can only consider the economic soundness of projects it funds, and cannot be diverted by political or social considerations. Indeed, it took the position that it could not respond to UN General Assembly resolutions calling for an embargo on economic relations with South Africa and Portugal because of their racial policies.

This purist perspective has already changed. Over the past decade, as the Bank has entered the field of structural adjustment lending, it has begun to pay attention to "enabling conditions" without which sound economic development is impossible. These conditions address matters such as environmental degradation, governance, poverty reduction and income distribution. The Bank has also begun to raise the issue of undue military expenditure. "What was once considered incidental to development has become instrumental for development."[34] The introduction of these heretofore extraneous criteria has led the World Bank into a far greater participatory process, involving publics and NGOs.

The International Monetary Fund (IMF) advances resources not for projects but to protect the currencies of its members in times of balance-of-payments difficulties. In order to ensure repayment of these advances, however, it conditions them on economic reform in the borrowing country. In general, these conditions have comprised standard monetarist prescriptions with little attention paid to social and political impacts of the policies. In recent years, however, along with the World Bank, the IMF has acknowledged the importance of these aspects to the problem of successful structural adjustment. The issues of poverty, good governance, and levels of military spending, though applied more narrowly than by the Bank, have become part of the Fund's policy-based criteria.

In wake of the recent changes in the ECE/FSU region, the IMF began to provide assistance there through the Systemic Transformation Facility (STF), founded in April 1993.[35] By January 1994, eleven countries including Russia had drawn on the STF for a total of SDR 1.5 billion. In order to access the funds of this facility, countries must adopt certain types of monetary policies and institutions. The IMF has set four reform goals for the ECE: *first*, replacing centralized planning and management with a market-oriented system; *second*, establishing a financial system with market-based interest rates; *third*, taking actions such as privatization to liberalize the operations of firms and markets; and *fourth*, creating a viable social safety net, with resources for unemployment insurance and job retraining.[36] While these four goals are primarily associated with economic system transformation, the IMF also has begun to include enabling conditions.

These enabling conditions and reform goals are justified as contributing to economic development and stability, and thus to the security of the organizations' advances and objectives. But if the conditions enumerated above are relevant to the soundness of World Bank funding, it seems hard to see why the issues of ethnic relations themselves should not be added to the list. Given that the IFIs are deeply involved in system transformation, including such transformation of multiethnic states, they cannot ignore the possibility that ethnic groups will compete, even violently, to redefine divisions of the economic, political, and cultural pie. Thus far, however, the IFIs have failed to employ seemingly obvious measures such as the requiring nondiscrimination among ethnic groups in Bank projects or ensuring that resources they provide do not go exclusively to the ruling majority or the regions where it is concentrated.

The IFIs also have a major role to play in providing economic backing for political/military solutions to ongoing ethnic conflicts. There was some such involvement in South Africa, where the Bank announced a major lending program to take effect immediately after successful elections. In the Middle East, a Bank study established overall assistance goals for the autonomous area. In Haiti too the Bank conducted studies of the requirements for economic rehabilitation. The reconstruction elements of the Bosnian peace settlements are also based on a major World Bank study. But the Bank needs to go further. As Wolfgang Reinicke explained:

> The resources of the IFIs, especially the Bank's, could help to make a financially and economically unattractive but otherwise acceptable settlement—including the division of a country—more attractive. For example, IFIs could promise the prospective new states not just membership in their organizations but a continuation of their support of system transformation. In fact, there are indications that the Washington Accords of April 1994 which led to the creation of the Muslim-Croat federation were backed by IFI commitments. Within a few months of the accord, the World Bank approved a $128 million loan to Croatia. A $250 million IMF loan is currently pending.[37]

A promising development is the Bank's planning effort for the reconstruction of Bosnia-Herzegovina which is being regarded as a framework for other donors. Financial support should be coordinated not only among IFIs, but also with other relevant international organizations.

The European Bank for Reconstruction and Development (EBRD)[38]

The EBRD was organized in the euphoria after the fall of the Berlin wall to be the premier financial instrument through which European resources would be channeled into ECE and the then transforming but still united Soviet Union. While the charters of the traditional IFIs call for neutrality as to the political and economic systems of borrowers, the EBRD charter (the Agreement Establishing the EBRD) contains an expressly political element. Article I enjoins the Bank

> to foster the transition towards open market–oriented economies and to promote private and entrepreneurial initiative in Central and Eastern European countries committed to and applying the principles of multiparty democracy, pluralism and market economics.

The EBRD is also different from other international financial institutions in that it focuses its funding on the private sector.[39] In fact, the EBRD finances infrastructure reconstruction or development only to the extent it is necessary for private-sector development and transition to a market economy. Unlike the World Bank, the EBRD need not obtain a sovereign guarantee in respect of its private and public sector activities.

The first president of the Bank, Jacques Attali, took the EBRD's political orientation seriously and implemented it aggressively. He established a Political Unit to monitor recipient state's compliance with Article I requirements. The EBRD became involved in the organization and sponsorship of activities on parliamentary processes, constitution drafting, and human rights protection. For example, the EBRD and the Council of Europe organized a closed conference on Baltic minorities and citizenship in October 1991.

Ethnonational conflicts were high on his agenda and he made a number of strong moves, not only in connection with the EBRD's investment activities, but as an independent political spokesman. For example, he protested, by letter, Estonia's threatened enactment of legislation that effectively prevented ethnic Russians from taking on Estonian citizenship. But Attali's commitment to Article I requirements as well as his flamboyant methods offended some of his European shareholders. The issue came to a head as Yugoslavia was disintegrating. Attali urged increased attention to minority-rights issues, pushed preparation of regional projects that would facilitate the economic integration of the countries in the region, and suggested that the Board, to demonstrate solidarity with those working for peace in the Balkans, convene its meeting scheduled for July 13, 1992, in Sarajevo, or, if this was impossible due to security considerations, in Split or some other location in the former Yugoslavia. Although the move for increased attention to multicountry projects was approved, the EBRD Board of Directors rejected the proposal to convene the July meeting in Sarajevo, arguing that it would improperly politicize the role of the Bank.[40]

After little more than two years in office, Attali departed in quasi disgrace. His replacement was Jacques de Larosière, a former Managing Director of the IMF, an impeccably conservative IFI bureaucrat. The new president disbanded the Political Unit and otherwise abandoned the "political mandate"; EBRD activities aimed at promoting democracy, human rights and the rule of law in ECE were ended. Since then, the EBRD's financing activities have gone forward with only the minimum legally required attention to the criteria specified in Article I. In February 1994, the Board of Directors adopted *Operation Policies: Guidelines for the Medium Term*, providing that the political aspects of the Bank's mandate should not be "a separate, 'proactive' task" for the EBRD, and so blessed Larosière's approach.[41]

Under the broad rubric of Article I, however, there certainly is room for the EBRD to be sensitive to considerations of democracy building and conflict prevention, without overt intervention in political affairs. As with the IFIs, the EBRD has a range of tools to assist in conflict prevention, from nonconfrontational confidential communiqués to suspension of loans. Indeed, existing EBRD projects are working in this direction by fostering interdependence (and so increasing the cost of conflict) in the ECE/FSU region. Examples include loans in April 1994 for Brest-Minsk-Russian border highway improvements and projects for promoting Czech-Slovak trade.

This discussion of the IFIs and the EBRD suggests that the enormous power of financial institutions can be harnessed to conflict prevention, even though that is not their primary purpose. It is not spurious to argue that "portfolio protection" alone should prompt these organizations to concern themselves with internal conflicts. Their prewar investment in the former Yugoslavia has been substantially lost.[42] If consciousness of their impact on potential conflict informed IFI and EBRD strategies more self-consciously, the leverage for conflict prevention might be increased significantly, especially in combination with the magnet of membership in the EU. Coordination with other international organizations would also increase the effectiveness of any IFI/EBRD conflict-management strategies.

B. *The European Union*

The European Union's potential for dealing with ethnic conflicts rests mainly on the attraction of membership, but also includes its own external economic and political policies towards states that are not members.[43] Given the EU's extraordinary economic power, history, and values, it has been argued that the aspiration to enter this community with little more will serve as a lever to prevent conflict in many of the former ECE nations and perhaps in those areas of western FSU where membership may be within reach. "The combination of prosperity, peace and freedom that Central and East Europeans saw embodied in the Community was attractive and encouraged them to throw off the Soviet system."[44] In fact, almost all the ECE countries and many in the CIS have expressed their desire to joint the EU, with Poland and Hungary making the first formal applications in 1994. Brussels has not yet decided who will be accepted and when.

It is widely accepted that EU membership itself will be a powerful guarantor of democracy and a market economy. Membership in the EU is premised upon liberal democracy, respect for human rights, the rule of law, and a market economy. Candidate countries must meet specified democratic and economic requirements, as well as accept the goals of political union.[45] Although EU states are not always models on the issue of ethnonational conflict—witness Greece and Turkey in Cyprus, Spain in the Basque region, France in Corsica, or Great Britain and Ireland in Ulster—the assumption is, as with the COE, that these elements will go a long way toward creating the climate in which internal peace can be maintained or restored.

But the very attraction of membership explains why it may be unlikely to happen in the near future. Agricultural and other forms of protectionism will not die easily. The effort to achieve democracy in transitional states will take some time, and membership deferred may make the transition harder. Nevertheless, the idea of early admission with the hope that membership criteria can be met once inside has not been viewed favorably. Each additional member complicates the EU's internal problems—its capacity to make decisions, take action, and develop its institutions.

Trade and economic assistance

The EU's budget is relatively small, its political powers are embryonic, and common currency remains a receding ideal, but it has substantially plenary power over internal and external trade. By far the most important assistance given to the ECE and FSU is in the form of trade.[46] Both exports and imports have grown rapidly, especially between the EU and the Visegrad countries, where economic reform was faster-paced than elsewhere in ECE.[47] A network of trade agreements has been concluded, the most important of which are the Europe Agreements, which are conceived as a critical first step toward ultimate membership.[48] These agreements contain provisions for regular political dialogue as well, thus introducing the other parties to the institutions and procedures of the Community. Nonetheless, protectionism in the EU remains serious, particularly in agriculture, steel, and other products of interest to ECE countries. It has embittered relations and hampered growth and transition to market economies.

There are a number of programs for direct assistance to democratization and marketization. The EU provided much of the impetus and funding for the EBRD. The Poland-Hungary Reconstruction Assistance program (PHARE) and Technical Assistance to the CIS (TACIS) contribute about ECU 1.5 billion a year each to the institution of market democracies and the building of infrastructure.[49] These EU democratization efforts include support for democratic infrastructure and interparliamentary cooperation, demarches in favor of democracy, assistance in creating a free media, and election monitoring. The proposed Trans-European Networks for transportation and communications infrastructure hold out particular promise for bringing the ECE countries into close and constructive relationship with the EU and with each other. All these programs have enjoyed varying degrees of success and have been criticized as being insufficiently aggressive in the face of countercurrents there.

The EU took a major political/economic initiative in committing $1.5 billion in support of the reconstruction aspects of the Dayton Agreements for peace in Bosnia. Of this about $150 million was earmarked for urgently needed assistance. But three months after the signature of the Accords, there was as yet little evidence of a prompt start for concrete activity on the ground in Bosnia.

Political action

The draw of membership and the value of trade and assistance has been supplemented by the EU's political initiatives to manage conflict in ECE and FSU. The EU is in the midst of its own transition from a mainly economic power to a political power, an actor and mediator on the global stage with capacity to further regional peace and stability. The Treaty on European Union (Maastricht Treaty), in force since 1993, created the Common Foreign and Security Policy (CFSP) as a framework to coordinate and ultimately unify EU foreign policy. "Theoretically, CFSP can draw on economic sticks and carrots of the Union, and on military support from WEU and NATO ... [In practical terms] this is the exception rather than the rule."[50] Thus far, it has resulted more in coordination than in unity, more in declarations than action. Nevertheless, a structure is in place for more ambitious concerted foreign and security policy undertakings in the future.

The first major venture in this domain, the EU policy toward recognition of the former Yugoslav republics, was launched while the ink was drying on the Maastricht Treaty. Far from generating a well-designed and deliberated common policy, the CFSP permitted Germany to hijack the EU and secure instant recognition of the breakaway republics. The Conference on Yugoslavia, in large part an EU instrument, laid down criteria that were to be met before the former Yugoslav and FSU republics would be granted recognition, including most particularly provisions for the protection of the rights of minorities. It also established an Arbitration Commission made up of the Chief Justices of the highest courts of five European countries to determine whether applications for recognition met these criteria. Before the Commission had even considered the issues, however, the EU, at Germany's insistence, announced on December 15, 1991, its intention to recognize Croatia and Slovenia a month later. On the appointed date, although the Commission advised that neither Croatia nor Bosnia fully complied with the criteria, the EU states went ahead with recognition on schedule. (At the same time, responding to a Greek veto, they refused to recognize Macedonia, although the Commission had ruled favorably on its compliance with the criteria.) Bosnia was recognized in April, after it declared its independence. Almost all observers of the Balkan crisis agree that recognition at this point was an egregious blunder. It made Bosnia's declaration of independence a certainty, and, by transmuting "republican" boundaries into "international borders" reduced the room to negotiate that might have truncated, if not averted the war. The CFSP, said the Italian Foreign Minister, was more important than Bosnia.

Two notable though lesser instances of CFSP action were the intermediation that helped lower tensions over the Gabcikovo-Nagymoros dam between Hungary and Slovakia, and funneled the dispute to the ICJ, and the assumption of responsibility for the administration of the town of Mostar in Croatia to stabilize an uneasy peace.

In the case of the Gabcikovo-Nagymoros dam, the disagreement between Hungary and Czechoslovakia over the future of this Communist-era project on the Danube was a flash point for nationalist passions. Hungary stopped working on the dam when the Communists lost power in 1989, but the separatist Slovak government viewed the dam as the symbol of its emerging national identity. The presence of 60,000 Hungarians in Slovakia exacerbated the tensions between the countries. The disagreement came to a head in October 1992, when Slovakia unilaterally started to divert water from the Danube. Hungarian appeals to the CSCE and UN Security Council were unavailing.[51] The EC had no formal standing in the dispute since neither party was an EC member, but it had a practical interest in the impact of the dam itself and in the consequences for relations between two potential EU members. Taking advantage of the political consultations prescribed in the Europe Agreements, it successfully mediated an agreement providing for eventual submission of the dispute to the International Court of Justice.

The EU also took action designed to prevent the resumption of fighting in Mostar, an ancient city in the south of Bosnia in an area dominated by Croats, which had been the site of widely publicized fighting among Muslims, Croats, and Serbs. In March 1994 the EU agreed to take over the administration of Mostar in order to end the fighting between Bosnian Croats and Muslims. The EU administrator's mandate was to make the city viable, repair local infrastructure, organize a unified police force of Croats and Muslims, and build up city administration. The ultimate objective was to turn over the administration to a freely elected municipal parliament. After an initial period of moderate success, the operation ran into trouble when, in the wake of the conclusion of the Dayton Accords, negotiations over the integrated police force broke down. The outcome of the effort remains in doubt.

On a broader scale, the Stability Pact for Europe initiated by French Prime Minister Baladur was a mechanism to get ECE and FSU countries to work on neighborly relations and address their own border and minorities problems in preparation for membership in the Union.[52] Although at first it was regarded as paternalistic, the initiative has been seriously engaged. Fifty nations attended the opening conference in May 1994. Two regional round tables, one in the Baltic and one for the Visegrad countries, held five meetings at which boundary problems and transborder issues were discussed. Settlements and agreements on these issues were reached on these issues and were consolidated in another stability pact, signed at the final meeting of the initiative in Paris in 1995. Further monitoring of the agreements was handed off to the OSCE.

Because of the EU's power and its draw for ECE and FSU nations, it should have a leading role in orchestrating the efforts and strategies of other European organizations.[53] This potential has yet to be realized. As noted above, there are difficulties in achieving consensus even within EU for CFSP action. It has not even begun to address the institutional rivalries between separate organizations with overlapping but not congruent membership and the difficulties of aligning complex international bureaucracies that wish to pursue their own policies in conflict prevention and otherwise.

Security Organizations

Before the Dayton Accords, traditional European security organizations had not played a significant part in the effort to manage ethnonational conflicts, although NATO was charged with some limited tasks in relation to the peacekeeping operations in Bosnia. These organizations are particularly the products of the bipolar Cold-War system and are shaped by that history. They are now seeking to adapt to the new realities of the post–Cold-War world, and a major test of their ability to do so looms in the deployment of a force in Bosnia to implement the peace agreement reached in Dayton. In this section, we look at the role and work of NATO and the WEU in this area, primarily for the period before the Bosnian peace agreements.[54]

A. *The North Atlantic Treaty Organization*

NATO efforts at policy reorientation in the post–Cold-War era show the organization's understanding of the critical importance of managing internal conflicts to security. In its final communiqué of June 10, 1993, NATO's North Atlantic Council (NAC)—its highest decision making body—declared:

> Conflict prevention, crisis management, and peacekeeping will be crucial to ensuring stability and security in the Euro-Atlantic area in the years ahead. . . . While reaffirming that the primary goal of Alliance military forces is to guarantee the security and territorial integrity of member states, we will contribute actively to these new tasks in order to enhance our security and European stability.

The contributions that NATO can make to conflict prevention and mitigation are varied. On one end of the spectrum has been the NATO role in large-scale peace operations. This role began with active, yet discrete participation in peace enforcement activities, such as its enforcement of the "no-fly" zone over Bosnia-Herzegovina and safe areas in the former Yugoslavia and of the embargo in the Adriatic Sea. It grew to the actual command of peace operations, through IFOR, the NATO-led multinational force in Bosnia in support of the Dayton agreements.

In the future, NATO may continue to carry out small military tasks of considerable, even crucial importance. Military forces may often serve as an adjunct to diplomacy, a form of "muscular diplomacy," in which military force is in the background and used in conjunction with diplomatic efforts and in coordination with a wide variety of civilian tasks. In a preconflict situation, security organizations may contribute a military presence that can play a part in coordination, communications, and logistics. They may prove particularly effective at the very early stages of a conflict when it has not hardened, and compromise and resolution may be possible. Even the show or shadow of military force can buy time and space for nurturing voluntary settlement options, as in the preemptive deployment of UN troops in Macedonia.[55]

Once hostilities have broken out, peace operations may require more military support or activity. The establishment and operation of headquarters for coordination and communication in a conflict zone, such as the one established by NATO in Zagreb for the United Nations Protection Force (UNPROFOR), requires considerable military skill and experience, particularly when it is multinational in character. Other military activities at this stage may include not only interposition of forces, but a demonstration of force to assure that innocent civilians are protected, that a full range of humanitarian missions can be accomplished, and that agreements will be respected.

NATO has for some time been preparing for this wide spectrum of potential conflict-management activities. To be sure, some of these activities may be performed by ad hoc UN forces with appropriate training and equipment. Nevertheless, there are clear advantages favoring NATO if the operation is complex, with diverse and perhaps changing components, requiring military sophistication and expertise. The Alliance currently possesses Europe's most effective multinational command, control, communications, intelligence, and logistical structures. Of course, NATO's advantages in military effectiveness are only the starting point for any discussion of its contribution to conflict prevention in specific contexts.

In terms of NATO's mandate and legal ability to engage in such activities in the post–Cold-War era, it should be first noted that NATO retains its Article V core function—deterrence against direct threats to its members. It probably also has existential credibility against any cross-border aggression that might spill over into its members' territory. The new question is: "On what basis does NATO perform any peace operation beyond the scope of its collective defense charter in the area of its member states—i.e., 'out of area'?"[56] Although NATO lawyers have not formally addressed the question of how NATO's legal mandate enables it to conduct peace support operations in ECE and FSU, it appears that such activities may be covered by Article II of the North Atlantic Treaty, which calls for cooperation "towards the further development of peaceful and friendly international relations by . . . promoting conditions of stability and well-being." The 1994 Brussels summit, without express reference to any authority in the treaty, decided to support, on a case-by-case basis, peacekeeping and other operations under the authority of the UN Security Council or the responsibility of the OSCE.

NATO's pre-Dayton participation as a partner of the UN in peace operations in the former Yugoslavia, which came early in its post–Cold War mission review, gave some sense of its capability in supporting peace operations. Although these early missions barely tested the coordinated military potential of NATO, the establishment of a headquarters unit in Zagreb and the participation in the Adriatic embargo suggests what it can contribute at this stage. The experience in enforcing the "no-fly" zones and safe havens in the former Yugoslavia illustrates both the potential and inherent difficulties of a UN-NATO partnership. These operations were conducted satisfactorily from a technical point of view, but they were not exacting operationally, and there were inherent limits to their practical effectiveness. Tensions arose from time to time over the objectives and implementation of policies announced by the UN Security Council.[57] Yet the limitations both of the UN Charter and the North Atlantic Treaty require that NATO perform its peace operations in ECE or FSU on the authority of the UN or OSCE, rather than on its own initiative, unless there were a direct threat to NATO territory.

With the establishment of IFOR to implement the military aspects of the Bosnian peace agreements, NATO finally had a peace operation that was commensurate with its resources and capabilities. The command and control problems that had plagued the earlier efforts at cooperation with UNPROFOR were obviated when the Security Council, in a very broad resolution, approved an arrangement whereby the force will be directly under NATO command and political guidance, without interposition by the UN. The deployment of almost 60,000 troops, including contingents from Russia and elsewhere in Eastern Europe, in the middle of winter over exacting terrain in a war-destroyed country was again carried out with admirable technical proficiency. The action underscored that NATO—and particularly U.S.—logistical, transport, and communications capability is indispensable for any large-scale deployment at a distance from home bases. Further, the initial military tasks of establishing a cease-fire line of almost 1,000 kilometers in length and supervising the withdrawal of the contending forces to a distance of two miles went off without serious incident.

Yet the fate of the total post-Dayton operation remains questionable. All the nonmilitary aspects, from return of refugees, to reconstruction, to war crimes, have been remitted to various independent civil entities, under the loose umbrella of the High Representative, Carl Bildt. Many of the organizations discussed above have been assigned roles: the EU, the World Bank, and the EBRD to fund and implement reconstruction; the OSCE to conduct elections; UNHCR to ensure the return and resettlement of refugees; the International War Crimes Tribunal to investigate war criminals and take them into custody. Resources in hand are limited. Coordination among these entities at the headquarters level is embryonic, although many are represented in a series of functional working groups that the Office of the High Representative has established in Sarajevo, dealing with subjects such as water supply, transport, communications, electricity, etc. Coordination with IFOR remained difficult after the first three months of 1996, since, from the beginning,

IFOR commanders tried to confine their mission narrowly to the military elements noted above. In the very first weeks, this effort at bifurcation came under pressure, when IFOR refused to accept responsibility for arresting war criminals and protecting mass grave sites and other evidence of war crimes. Although by mid-March there seemed to be growing awareness among some NATO officials that the success of the operation would depend importantly on the nonmilitary components, there was little in the way of practical action to deal with the diffusion of authority and responsibility. Most important, the whole mission operated in the shadow of the U.S. commitment to withdraw its forces—about a third of the total—at the end of a year. Almost nobody thought that either the military or civil aspects contemplated by the Dayton Accords could be completed by that time. There has been some relaxation of IFOR rigidity, as NATO leaders realize that certain tasks can be performed without the dreaded "mission creep" and without needless jeopardy of life. Thus, Joint Civilian Commission Subcommittees such as water and wastewater, electricity, and telecommunications are being staffed by "CIMIC" (Civilian-Military Committee) liaison, midlevel officers from the U.S. Army Reserves in their standard form of organization, and the American military sector has been paying local civilians to make necessary repairs. Constructive independent civil action is taking place—OSCE has plunged into its tasks of mounting elections in the autumn of 1996, and of preparing verification machinery for arms control. UNHCR continues its work with refugees. But the concerted effort needed to accomplish a peaceful society while IFOR is on the scene has not begun.

The largest political dilemma facing NATO is the issue of the enlargement of its membership. Like accession to the EU, membership in NATO is an important inducement for maintaining a democratic and market orientation in Eastern Europe. NATO has created a number of devices to begin to include ECE and FSU nations, starting with the North Atlantic Cooperation Council (NACC) in November 1992, which served as a useful first step towards the integration of the former communist bloc into NATO. Now, under the rubric of the Partnership for Peace (PfP), which was established in early 1994 and is open to any OSCE member, there is the possibility of more individualized contacts including joint training and exercises between the forces of NATO members and ECE and FSU states.[58] A number of the "partners" are participating in IFOR. Officials of NATO and of individual members have led some of the ECE states to believe that they are on a "fast track," and they have increased their pressures for membership.

However, the prospect of extending NATO eastward to the borders of Russia has stirred opposition especially from nationalist forces in Russia, contributing to the fragility of the present government. President Yeltsin's outburst at the December 1994 Budapest CSCE summit and later at the UN, and Russia's extended refusal to join PfP were not unpredictable manifestations of the problem. Again in March 1996, exchanges between Yeltsin and Russian Foreign Minister Primakov on the one hand, and U.S. Secretary of State Christopher and NATO Secretary General Javier Solana on the other, failed to reach any consensus on the issue. Thus enlargement presents a serious dilemma, and has been put off to a vaguer future consummation, while the relevance of NATO and its ability to participate in the actual conflicts of ECE and FSU continues to be in doubt.

B. *The Western European Union*

The nine-nation WEU has been denominated the "European pillar" of the North Atlantic Alliance, but the basic question is whether it will ever develop into an effective security force for Europe or will continue to be a shadow conception of the French, seeking an alternative to the U.S.-dominated NATO.[59] WEU member states have expanded its legal mandate to permit military operations outside of Western Europe and have pledged to undertake "the effective implementation of conflict-prevention and crisis management measures, including peacekeeping activities."[60] The WEU has played a small part, largely symbolic, in some military activities in relation to the Baltic conflict, such as naval operations in the Adriatic Sea and on the Danube River to enforce UN sanctions against the former Yugoslavia, and it has engaged in some peacekeeping activities under its own banner—minesweeping during the Iran-Iraq war and naval operations during the Gulf War. Yet, although the WEU would be free to act under circumstances when NATO may not, either because of legal restrictions or choice (presumably pressures from the United States), it has neither forces, command structure, nor capabilities of its own. It must rely entirely on contributions of its members—who are also the members of NATO and the EU—or of NATO itself.

The WEU in theory could provide a halfway house for ECE and FSU nations, through its "associate partner" status[61] or some other device, earlier than the current pace of integration in NATO or the EU will allow. But because the WEU has no military forces, it cannot now offer the security guarantees that these nations are seeking. Thus, such expedients are likely to be seen by the intended beneficiaries as yet another way of delaying entry into both the EU and NATO.

The root of the WEU's present ineffectiveness is the unwillingness of its members to commit the resources necessary to make it into an actual military force. Even if they were to do so, a significant part of the assets needed for any large operation, such as airlift and C4I, are U.S. forces, whether under its own or NATO command. And so, as the French have ruefully come to recognize, a WEU operation of any size would probably have to have NAC approval. The key relationship to watch is that of the WEU and the EU as the latter develops its CFSP. The gradual French rapprochement to NATO suggests that the umbrella may be NATO itself, but the idea of a European pillar is very much alive.

Thus, it remains unclear whether there is a capable and willing military force in Europe ready to shoulder the burdens of peacekeeping, should the situation require it. Recent developments show that the UN is now open to "subcontracting" peacekeeping functions to individual states or to other organizations, such as NATO. Under a "subcontract," the UN authorizes a single nation or group of states to implement UN decisions.[62] For example, the UN Security Council authorized Russia to deploy more troops in Georgia to end the three-year-old conflict there and by similar action approved the U.S. operation in Haiti. The latest example of this device—and its major test—is the NATO-led IFOR in Bosnia.

The Way Ahead: Are Effective Joint Strategies Available?

This chapter has described the strengths and weaknesses, activities and potential of a number of organizational players in preventing and managing ethnic conflict. Despite the rich array of regional organizations available in Europe, as well as the immense potential of the UN, the traditional pleas for "coordination" and "interlock" have achieved little in the way of concerted efforts. There has been some cooperation (and much tension) between the UN, EU, and NATO in the former Yugoslavia. But some highly relevant actors, such as the IFIs and even the EU, are only beginning to recognize the importance of the contribution they might make to conflict prevention and mitigation, and how important their capabilities could be if they were to exercise their potential leverage. As yet, these players do not avail themselves of potential synergies and possibilities for reinforcing action, nor do they find it easy to engage at the ground level where internal conflicts tend to have their origins and early growth.

A more multifaceted, concerted approach would necessarily include many of these organizations. But it will not be easy to achieve effective joint action on a sustained basis. The OSCE and COE, focused directly on preventing conflict, need more resources. The organizations with economic resources and political clout need to turn their attention more directly to conflict management. Security organizations need to adapt to the new challenges in the post–Cold War world of widespread ethnic conflict, including the challenge of working effectively with the other types of organization. If all the organizations worked together more effectively, the chances of successful intervention would be greater. For example, the modest successes of the OSCE in the Baltics might have been enhanced by greater availability of funds to develop language, job, and education programs and by closer synchronization with the process of integration of the European Union.

It will not be easy to achieve effective and sustained joint action, for both legal and institutional reasons. The organizations are highly centralized and slow-moving bureaucracies. They are all institutions in transition, trying to adapt to a radically changed environment. Many international organizations have yet to overcome the strictures against "intervention in matters within the domestic jurisdiction of states," which was a fundamental norm of the state system after World War II (the environment in which they were born and lived). Even though there is overlapping membership, the separate legal identities and bureaucratic hierarchies of the organizations operate to defeat effective and integrated deployment of available international resources. The states that comprise them have not provided clear direction, and it is problem enough for each organization to reach a consensus among its own members without trying also to reach agreement with other international organizations. The operational arms, with some exceptions like UNHCR, find it difficult to deal with unorganized and irregular groups of shifting composition and legitimacy that characterize internal conflict.

Joint action is not achievable with the existing ways of doing business. The usual prescription of consultants and study commissions is "better coordination." But there is no superordinate body to coordinate the activities of these organizations. In any case, "coordination" at the level of organizational headquarters will not produce a coherent basis for mobilizing the diverse resources of international organizations, both governmental and nongovernmental, to attack discrete and constantly shifting problem situations, each of which is to a considerable degree unique and thus inaccessible to bureaucratic routines.

If concerted strategy and effective joint action cannot be achieved by the methods of interagency coordination or "interlock," what are the alternatives? The experience of the past few years, while generally disappointing, holds some clues to a different approach. It seems relevant that such successes as we have been able to report, like the OSCE High Commissioner on National Minorities, are the result of flexible, nonhierarchical processes, working close to the ground in direct contact with the parties to the conflict. Useful "coordination" is more likely to emerge through ad hoc interaction among particular missions—and NGOs as well—working in particular situations. This more hopeful performance, we think, reflects a difference in strategy and organizational arrangements between the OSCE and traditional international organizations. The OSCE's lack of bureaucratic resources and its consensus decision process are sources of strength, or at least efficacy, rather than weakness.

This suggests that strategic mobilization and coordination may be more likely to emerge from ad hoc interaction among missions of international organizations and NGOs working in particular situations. The model would be a nonhierarchical, team-based approach, bringing together the capabilities and resources of the wide range of international organizations and NGOs in a particular conflict area. Although it is too early to specify the characteristics of such a model, it should be possible to conceptualize a way of catalyzing the early development of such a concerted strategy, tailored to the needs of particular situations, perhaps using different coalitions and lead agencies in different situations. Such a conception would have to address four main elements:

First, a method for activating problem solving groups that bypasses the elephantine decision-making processes of the standard bureaucratic organizations. It would be necessary to be able to form such groups quickly and in the early stages of a conflict. One of the main problems is that the political will for intervention does not emerge until the conflict has reached a relatively high level of intensity and violence, by which time the available resources may be inadequate to the task. The OSCE experience is important evidence that such an expedited decision process for early intervention is possible and can be combined with the necessary political accountability.

Second, it is important to find a formula for delegating broad operational control to the group in the field, as is the common doctrine of military organizations, reserving only broad policy guidance for headquarters. The UN experience has been that although the initial mandate passed by the Security Council is vague and general (due to the necessities of achieving political consensus), there are often subsequent efforts to micromanage both by the Council and the Secretariat. The initial mandate should concentrate on defining the overall mission and strategy of the operation in general terms and leave the task group with wide leeway in carrying it out.

Third, there must be a more realistic conception of the goals of intervention. Short of all-out enforcement action as in Kuwait, it cannot be to defeat one of the parties and impose a solution on the situation. The objective must be to initiate a process among the stakeholders that generates innovative possible solutions and broadly supported outcomes, a process by which the parties themselves can manage their continuing conflicts and disputes. This is the approach taken by the HCNM in creating ethnic round tables and other ongoing conciliation processes, and it might be equally effective even after the conflict intensifies.

Fourth, there must be a method for ensuring overall political accountability. Although operational control and responsibility should be lodged firmly in the field level problem-solving group, it cannot be permitted to proceed completely on its own without review or guidance from the ultimate political authorities of the parent organizations. The OSCE experience again shows that accountability can be achieved by informal consultative processes with key officials of the organization and its interested members, or by informal supervisory groups.

As this sketchy account suggests, much remains to be done in conceptualizing an effective mechanism for bringing organizations engaging in peace operations into an effective and synergistic relationship. A concerted effort of imagination to discover how to achieve joint action among the participants is now the top agenda item in efforts to mobilize international organizations for preventing ethno-national conflicts.

Notes

1. Carl Bildt "Keeping Bosnia in One Peace" *Washington Post,* March 31, 1996, c2.
2. Confidential interview, March 1996.
3. Keitha Saspin Fine, "NGOs on the Playing Fields of the Transitions in East Central Europe," in Antonia Handler Chayes and Abram Chayes, eds., *Preventing Conflict in the Post-Communist World: Mobilizing International and Regional Organizations,* (Washington, D.C.: The Brookings Institution, 1996) (hereinafter *"Preventing Conflict"*), p. 543.

4. EU recognition policy in the former Yugoslavia changed dramatically. Before the conflict erupted in mid-1991, the EC Commission's goal was to maintain a unified Yugoslav state. As the crisis progressed, countries backed off of this aim, with Germany in particular taking an inflexible position in support of recognition of separate states of Slovenia and Croatia and doing so in December of 1991. For a discussion of recognition policy and its consequences, see Mario Zucconi, "The European Union in the Former Yugoslavia: A Case Study" in *Preventing Conflict*, p. 237.

5. Jarat Chopra and Thomas G. Weiss, "The United Nations and the Former Second World: Coping with Conflict," in *Preventing Conflict*, p. 522. UNPROFOR's annual budget approaches $2 billion, UNHCR's is about $500,000, and another billion dollars are spent annually by other governmental, intergovernmental, and nongovernmental organizations.

6. Formerly the Conference on Security and Cooperation in Europe. The name was changed at Budapest in 1994.

7. This discussion is based on the chapter by Diana Chigas with Elizabeth McClintock and Christophe Kamp, "Preventive Diplomacy and the OSCE: Creating Incentives for Dialogue and Cooperation" in *Preventing Conflict* (hereinafter "Chigas). The primary author, Diana Chigas, is the Director of Conflict Management Group's Project on Preventive Diplomacy in the OSCE.

8. Chigas, pp. 28–29.

9. Chigas, p. 42.

10. The Helsinki Final Act defined the three "baskets" of basic principles governing relations between CSCE countries: (1) Questions relating to security in Europe; (2) Cooperation in the field of Economics, Science, Technology and the Environment; and (3) Cooperation in Humanitarian and Other Fields. .

11. Budapest Document, "Toward A Genuine Partnership in a New Era," Summit Declaration, para. 8 (December 1994).

12. "Consensus" is defined as the absence of any objection that would be an obstacle to the decision under consideration. Chigas p. 33.

13. In addition, there are other OSCE institutions involved in conflict prevention more generally. For example, there is the Conflict Prevention Centre in Vienna, which works primarily in the military realm, helping to implement Confidence-and-Security-Building Measures and to coordinate exchange of military information.

14. Chigas, p. 38, citing Helsinki Document, "The Challenges of Change," Summit Decisions, chapter I(15) (1992).

15. Helsinki Decisions, Chapter II (1 to 37) (1992).

16. For discussion of this point, see Chigas, p. 88, n. 66.

17. M. van der Stoel, "The Role of the CSCE high Commissioner on National Minorities in CSCE Preventive Diplomacy," in S. Carlsson, ed., *The Challenge of Preventive Diplomacy* (Ministry of Foreign Affairs, Sweden 1994), p. 44. An example of HCNM interventions in which he exercised this independence is in Estonia in mid-July 1993. At that time, he intervened to facilitate resolution of a dispute sparked by the call for refenda on "national-territorial autonomy" by two Russophone-dominated city councils and by the Estonian parliament's passage of a controversial law on aliens. Similar interventions were also undertaken in Macedonia, Ukraine and Albania. Chigas, p. 55.

18. See Chigas, pp. 49–50.

19. Chigas, p. 53.

20. Chigas, p. 57.

21. Chigas, p. 61.

22. Our discussion of this role draws upon many of the insights contained in Jean E. Manas, "The Council of Europe's Democracy Ideal and the Challenge of Ethno-National Strife," in *Preventing Conflict*, p. 99.

23. [Discuss status as of 1995].

24. Manas, p. 130–31, quoting the declaration of Vienna Summit, 1993. It is expected that this additional protocol would have an enforcement mechanism: violation by a signatory state would trigger the full European Convention on Human Rights system, including jurisdiction where applicable of the European Court on Human Rights. The new convention, however, is not expected to provide for an enforcement mechanism that is as strict as the European Convention on Human Rights system.

25. Twelve states must ratify this convention for it to enter into force; as of early 1996, only four states had done so. This problem also affects the European Charter for Regional or Minority Languages, which needs five ratifications for entry into force and has only three to date. British Broadcasting Corp., Jan. 24, 1996.

26. For example, the Demosthenes program, aimed at transmitting democratization expertise from Western officials to Central and Eastern Europe, had a budget of about 10 million U.S. dollars in 1994. This is modest, since much of the money is spent on transportation and lodging of government officials.

27. Unlike the CSCE, the COE did not immediately admit all applicants. See Manas, p. 140 note 22, for discussion of status of applicants since 1989.

28. See Order No. 484 (instructions to the Committee on Legal Affairs to examine applicant's respect for Protocol rights.) It should be noted that admission has not been denied for failure to comply with the Additional Protocol, although Romania and the Slovak Republic were admitted with the understanding that their legislation would be brought into compliance. Manas, p. 134.

29. For further discussion of the role of international organizations in generating compliance with norms, see Abram Chayes and Antonia Handler Chayes, *The New Sovereignty: Compliance with International Regulatory Agreements* (Cambridge, MA: Harvard University Press, 1995) (hereinafter *"The New Sovereignty"*).

30. Manas, p. 112.

31. Susan Woodward, *Balkan Tragedy*, (Washington, DC: Brookings Institution, 1995).

32. This portion of the chapter draws on the work of Wolfgang H. Reinicke, "Preventing Ethno-National Conflict: What Role for International Financial Institutions," in *Preventing Conflict*, p. 281.

33. World Bank Info Briefs, #A.02.4-94, quoting Lord Keynes.

34. Reinicke, p. 291.

35. Reinicke, p. 296, *citing Bretton Woods Commission*, 1994, p. C-266.

36. IMF Annual Report 1991.

37. Reinicke, p. 317 (footnotes omitted).

38. We draw on the work of Melanie H. Stein, EBRD Counsel, in her chapter "Conflict Prevention in Transition Economies: A Role for the EBRD?" in *Preventing Conflict*, p. 339.

39. As of the end of 1994, about 62 percent of EBRD funds were for private sector projects and 38 percent for state sector projects. Stein, p. 345.

40. Stein, pp. 350–51.

41. *Operational Polices* was based on the findings of the Task Force on Operational Priorities established by Jaques de Larosière in October 1993. The final report of the Task Force recommends that the Bank's political activities not be prominent and be confined to monitoring political conditions to the extent necessary for operational purposes.

42. Stein notes that to date, the EBRD has not sustained losses due to ethnonational conflict. Stein, *Preventing Conflict*, p. 354.

43. This discussion draws heavily on the work of three Europeans with close knowledge of the European Union, who authored the following chapters in *Preventing Conflict:* John Pinder, "Community against Conflict: The EC's Contribution to Ethno-National Peace in Europe;" Reinhardt Rummel, "The European Union's Politico-Diplomatic Contribution to the Prevention of Ethno-National Conflict;" and Mario Zucconi, "The European Union in the Former Yugoslavia."

44. Pinder, pp. 174–90.

45. The Maastricht Treaty provides that members' "systems of government are founded on the principles of democracy." Brussels is asking new applicants to meet the Copenhagen criteria—democratic requirements as well as preconditions for market economies and economic competition. For further discussion, see Pinder, pp. 185–90.

46. For example, for Bulgaria, the Czech Republic, Hungary, Poland, Romania, and Slovakia—the six countries with Europe Agreements—their total exports to the Community of transport equipment were 58 percent higher in the period January–August 1993 than a year earlier. Pinder, *Preventing Conflict*, p. 174. For more figures on trade, see Pinder, pp. 174–75.

47. The state parties to the Visegrad Agreement are the Czech Republic, Hungary, Poland, and Slovakia. They managed an export growth of at least 54 percent from 1990–92. Pinder, p. 174.

48. The Europe Agreements provide for establishing industrial free trade between the Community and partner states over a certain time. The Community has five years, while the partner has up to ten years, to remove all their tariffs and quotas. For further discussion, see Pinder, pp. 175–78.

49. The PHARE programme (Poland and Hungary aid for economic reconstruction) was launched by the EC and OECD to help economic reform and structural adjustment, with subsidiary goals such as the support of democratic institutions and the protection of minorities. TACIS (Technical Assistance for the CIS) is financed solely from the Community budget. Its purpose is similar to PHARE, and the mechanism is to pay for experts to CIS countries.

50. Rummel, *Preventing Conflict,* pp. 211–12.

51. Also, the Hungarian Prime Minister asked for help from the Danube Commission, made up of all Danube River riparian counties, with little response. Letters were sent to world leaders in an attempt to internationalize the dispute and ultimately bring it to the International Court of Justice were also unavailing. Rummel, pp. 219–20.

52. The goals and procedures of the plan were presented in a report annexed to the communiqué of the December 1993 European Council meeting in Brussels. The communiqué and the Annex I (Stability Pact: Summary Report) are reprinted in Agence Europe, no. 6127, December 12, 1993, pp. 1–12.

53. The CFSP tries to draw on other institutions or coordinate their work. The EU has interacted closely with the UN in conflict prevention in the former Yugoslavia. It has given major support to OSCE preventive diplomacy activities, and has participated in OSCE activities, such as fact-finding missions on human rights and compliance. Relations between the COE and EU have expanded recently. Finally, EU has worked with the WEU and NATO in developing dialogue with ECE/FSU countries and managing conflict together. See Rummel, pp. 223–27, for further discussion of EU relations with these organizations.

54. Two chapters in *Preventing Conflict* are the basis of this section: First, that authored by Antonia Handler Chayes and Richard Weitz, "The Military Perspective on Conflict Prevention: NATO," p. 381; and second, "A Peacekeeping Role for the Western European Union," by David S. Huntington, p. 429.

55. For a description of the composition and mission of this Macedonian requested deployment, which since January 1993 has involved about 1,200 military observers, infantry battalions, and civilian police from Canada, the United States, and various Nordic countries, see Julie Kim and Carol Migdalovitz, *Macedonia: Former Yugoslav Republic of Macedonia Situation Update* (Washington: Congressional Research Service, February 18, 1994), pp. 9–10.

56. For extensive discussion of this issue, see Chayes and Weitze, pp. 395–98.

57. For example, the "dual key" procedure, whereby NATO could propose military action but UN approval was required, has been frustrating to NATO. Response time has improved, but not without problems. For example, three hours elapsed before senior UN officials approved the request of the UN commander in Bosnia for NATO air strikes to defend French peacekeepers under attack by Serbs near Bihac. By the time NATO received the request, the Serb units had withdrawn. See Michael R. Gordon, "Serbian Gunners Slip Away as US Planes Await UN Approval," *New York Times,* March 14, 1994, p. 8.

58. The PfP Framework Document is reprinted in *RFE/RL Research Report,* vol. 3, no. 12 (March 25, 1994), pp. 22–23. Each participant agrees to a standard framework and to an individual "Partnership Program" specifying its military and political commitments and its level of anticipated collaboration with NATO. PfP participants must also agree to ensure the democratic control of their armed forces, promote the transparency of their defense planning, respect international law principles, the UN Charter, the OSCE, and be prepared to participate in certain operations under their auspices.

59. The WEU was formally linked to the Maastricht Treaty on European Union: under Article J4, the WEU is "an integral part of the development of the Union" and is to "elaborate and implement decisions and actions which have defense implications." This language represents a compromise between the French position that the WEU should be incorporated into the EU, and the British position, reluctant to refer to the WEU at all in Maastricht and resisting the concept of European defense integration.

60. Western European Union Council of Ministers, *Petersberg Declaration on WEU and European Security,* Bonn, June 19, 1992.

61. "Associate partner" status was offered first in May 1994 in response to NATO's PfP. This status, open to all of the Forum for Consultation countries, permits new associate partners to participate in WEU Council and working group meetings, establish links with the WEU planning cell, and join in certain operations carried out under WEU auspices. The status does not provide any security guarantees nor decision-making powers.
62. Chopra and Weiss, in *Preventing Conflict,* pp. 507, 525.

The Mediation of
Interethnic Conflict in Schools

PETER T. COLEMAN AND MORTON DEUTSCH

Introduction

In a recently published paper (Deutsch, 1993b), it was suggested that there are four key components to any comprehensive educational program intended to enable students to develop attitudes, knowledge, and skills for resolving their conflicts constructively rather than destructively. They are cooperative learning, conflict resolution training, the constructive use of controversy in teaching subject matters, and the creation of dispute resolution centers in the schools. A rationale for each of these components follows.

Cooperative Learning

Cooperative learning fosters a sense of positive interdependence ("we sink or swim together") and helps students to acquire the social skills involved in working together effectively. It also provides students with opportunities to interact cooperatively with other students who are different in ability, race, gender, ethnicity, religion, disability, and so on. Since Deutsch's early theoretical and experimental work on cooperation–competition (Deutsch 1949a, 1949b), there has been much research on cooperative learning. As Slaving (1983) and Johnson and Johnson (1989) have indicated in their extensive summaries of the research literature, cooperative learning has many positive effects on students, including a reduction in their prejudices toward students who are typically categorized as "different."

We want to emphasize that successful and effective cooperation with individuals and groups of different ethnic backgrounds is a necessary component of any comprehensive educational program to improve ethnic relations, whether among youths or adults. However, it is not sufficient, by itself, since cooperation tends to deteriorate and fail under conditions of destructive conflict.

Constructive Conflict Resolution

There is much to suggest that a two-way relaxation exists between effective cooperation and constructive conflict resolution. Good cooperative relations facilitate the constructive management of conflict; and the ability to handle constructively the inevitable conflicts that occur during cooperation facilitates the survival and deepening of cooperative relations.

In recent years, conflict resolution training programs have sprouted in a number of schools across the country. Although we believe these programs are very promising, little systematic research on their effectiveness has yet been done apart from "consumer satisfaction" studies (which generally indicate high levels of satisfaction). The International Center for Cooperation and Conflict Resolution at Teachers College, Columbia University, has recently completed a fairly extensive study in an inner-city alternative high school (Deutsch, 1993a), but its focus was not on ethnic relations. In brief, our data show that as students improved in managing their conflicts, they experienced increased social support and less victimization from others. This improvement in their relations with others led to increased self-esteem as well as to a decrease in feelings of anxiety and depression and more frequent feelings of positive well-being. The higher self-esteem, in turn, produced a greater sense of personal control over their own fates. Moreover, the increases in their sense of personal control and in their positive feelings of well-being led to higher academic performance.

Apart from the "victimization scale," which included items relating to whether the student was victimized in particular ways (robbed, assaulted, sexually harassed, insulted, etc.), we have no data specifically relevant to this conference. Nevertheless, we believe that a constructive conflict resolution training program in schools would be likely to have desirable effects in reducing destructive ethnic conflicts.

The Constructive Use of Controversy in Teaching Subject Matters

Our limited experience with training in constructive conflict resolution suggests that a single course or workshop is not usually sufficient, by itself, to produce lasting effects in most students; they must have repeated opportunities and encouragement to practice their skills of constructive conflict resolution in a supportive atmosphere. Constructive conflict resolution can be infused into "teachable moments" in various courses and student activities. In addition, the active use of constructive controversy in teaching different subject matters (Johnson and Johnson, 1992) can provide repeated and diverse opportunities for students to learn the skills of lively controversy rather than those of deadly quarrel.

There are difficult conflicts that the disputing parties, even when well trained, may not be able to resolve constructively without the help of third parties such as mediators. Informal mediation is one of the oldest forms of conflict resolution, and formal mediation has been practiced in behalf of international and labor-management conflicts for many years. More recently, formal mediation has been increasingly applied in such areas as divorce, small-claims cases, neighborhood feuds, landlord-tenant relations, environmental and public-resource controversies, industrial disputes, school conflicts, and civil cases. Following this explosion of the practice of mediation (coupled with the proliferation of textbooks and "how-to-do-it" books on mediation), there has been modest but important growth in research and theorizing on the topic. Kressel and Pruitt's book, *Mediation Research* (1989), provides a definitive review of the research being done in this area. They indicate that there is considerable evidence of user satisfaction with mediation and some evidence that the agreements reached through mediation are both less costly to the conflicting parties and more robust than traditional adjudication. However, there is also strong evidence to suggest that mediation has dim prospects of being successful under adverse circumstances. As Kressel and Pruitt (1989) have succinctly expressed it: "intensely conflicted disputes involving parties of widely disparate power, with low motivation to settle, fighting about matters of principle, suffering from discord or ambivalence within their own camps, and negotiating over scarce resources are likely to defeat even the most adroit mediators" (p. 405).

Third parties (mediators, conciliators, process consultants, therapists, counselors, etc.) who are called upon to provide assistance in a conflict require four kinds of skills if they are to have the flexibility required to deal with the diverse situations that mediators face.

In the *first* set of skills are those related to the third party's establishment of an effective working relationship with each of the conflicting parties so that they will trust the third party, communicate freely with the mediator, and be responsive to the mediator's suggestions regarding an orderly process for negotiations. In the *second* set are those skills related to establishing a cooperative problem-solving attitude among the conflicting parties toward their conflict. *Third* are the skills involved in developing a creative group decision-making process. This process clarifies the nature of the problems that the conflicting parties are confronting by reframing their conflicting positions into a joint problem to be solved. It also helps to expand the range of alternatives that are perceived to be available, facilitates realistic assessment of their feasibility as well as their desirability, and assists in the implementation of agreed-upon solutions. As for the *fourth* set of skills, it is often helpful for the third party to have considerable substantive knowledge about the issues around which the conflict is centered. Such knowledge can enable the mediator to see possible solutions that might not occur to the conflicting parties and thus permit the mediator to help them assess proposed solutions more realistically.

The mediation of interethnic conflict clearly calls for all four types of skills. In addition, it calls for an understanding of the specific social psychological processes involved in ethnic conflict. A mediator of such conflict should be tuned into (1) the misunderstandings and miscommunications that often arise from cultural differences; (2) the ethnocentrism characteristic of most groups; (3) the stereotypes of one group that are frequently held by the other; (4) the importance of an individual's ethnic membership in defining his or her self-identity; (5) the emblems, symbols, personages, and historic events that are central to the group's definition of itself; and (6) the prior relations between the conflicting ethnic groups—their rewarding experiences as well as those that have led to grievances.

Dispute Resolution Centers in Schools

We have searched the literature to see what research has been done on the mediation of interethnic conflict. And so far as we could determine, very little (if any) systematic research has been conducted. So we briefly discuss the existing research on school mediation instead. Only a few studies have assessed school-based dispute resolution or mediation programs in a systematic fashion (see Lam, 1989, for a review). Those studies that have explored their impact indicate that, in general, the participants are satisfied with the training and find it useful. Educators want conflict-resolution and/or mediation programs in the schools for several reasons. The reason most frequently given has to do with the increase in violence among students and between students and teachers. Such violence ultimately affects the quality of education in schools.

More than thirty-five college and university campuses now have mediation programs. Many more elementary, middle, and high schools offer training in conflict resolution and mediation, according to *The Fourth R,* the newsletter of the National Association for Mediation in Education (NAME). Rationales and evaluative summaries of some of these programs are given in Wilson-Brewer, Cohen, O'Donnell, and Goodman (1991) and in Lam (1989). Following the conflict resolution and mediation movement initiated in the United States, some schools in Canada have incorporated conflict resolution skills training into their curricula.

If popularity is an indicator of value, there is ample evidence to show that conflict resolution and mediation training are considered to be successful by many educators. Several feature articles have reported the beneficial aspects of these programs as ascertained by both subjective and objective measures. Evaluations of student mediation programs further show that the student disputants have been satisfied with the mediation outcomes (Lam, 1989). Additionally, studies of peer mediators show that their self-image is enhanced (Lam, 1989). A profile of one student mediator showed improvements not only in her feelings about her relationships but also in her grades.

Keeney (in Lam, 1989) reports that the principals and teachers of the schools involved in the New Mexico Mediation in the Schools program have reacted positively to the program. They feel that the school atmosphere and student interpersonal relations have improved now that there is a constructive and legitimate channel for dealing with conflicts. One good indicator of program acceptance in the school is that about 60 percent of the upper elementary students wanted to be trained to become mediators. No negative effects of the program have been noted.

Clark and Mann (in Lam, 1989) report that the mediation program at Poughkeepsie Middle School has been successful in improving attendance, building self-esteem, and creative a sense of responsibility within the student body. Positive effects of conflict resolution/mediation training have also been noted by parents. For example, the parents of student conflict managers in the New Mexico Mediation in the Schools program have reported being pleased with their children's involvement and have described a carry-over into the family of the skills that were learned in their school. In one district, parental training has actually been initiated at the request of parents. As Keeney (1989) indicates, it is often the changes that parents see at home that arouse their interest. These reports are encouraging because they point to the beneficial aspects of conflict resolution training in areas outside the school.

Parents have benefited from conflict resolution programs in other ways as well. In one study, the parents involved in disputes with the school were considerably more satisfied with conflict mediation after the school personnel had been trained in conflict resolution skills than they were prior to that training. The posttraining ratings made by independent observers of the performance of the participants were also higher (Maher, in Lam, 1989). In addition, the observers commented that such a program would be beneficial to themselves.

In short, many reports note that enthusiasm of the parties involved with school mediation/conflict resolution training programs. Several researchers and practitioners, however, point out the caveat involved in uncritically lauding these programs. Although the idea of mediation/conflict resolution is being sold to schools extensively, only very few intensive efforts have been made to evaluate what is working and what is not, thus possibly limiting the potential of such programs (Lam, 1989). Clearly there is a need for more systematic assessments of these programs following their implementation, using rigorous data collection and analysis procedures.

The Mediation of Interethnic Conflict

In light of the scarcity of research on the mediation of interethnic conflict, we decided to conduct an "experience survey" of a select group of expert mediators in the New York area who have served as mediators in interethnic conflicts. In the spring of 1992, coauthor Peter Coleman, who is a mediator and mediation trainer, interviewed eleven individuals who had mediated ethnic groups conflicts themselves. The interviews followed a semistructured format, using open-ended questions that focused on the conditions, processes, and effects of mediating ethnic group conflicts. A few follow-up interviews were also conducted with disputants who had been involved in the mediations and were willing to waive their right to confidentiality. A variety of ethnic groups were represented in the sample of disputants; among them were Hispanics, Asians, whites, African Americans, Africans, Hassidic Jews, Central Americans, American Indians, and Haitians. The disputants also ranged in years from high school age to adult, included both males and females, and came from a wide range of socioeconomic classes. The mediators represented a broad range of ethnic groups as well. The conflicts varied in level of severity from minor arguments and misunderstandings to organizational standstills, industrial sabotage, and acts of violence. Many of the conflicts had long histories. In a few of the cases, legal proceedings were pending over the issue of concern to the mediation. With one exception, all of the cases utilized a formal mediation process; however, many of the cases also utilized other conflict resolution strategies. The majority of the conflicts existed within some type of system, such as a school, government agency, or community.

What emerged from the interviews was a broad scope of information concerning ethnic group conflict mediation, which we have organized into five general categories of mediator activities. Kressel and Pruitt (1989), in describing what mediators do, have indicated that their diverse actions can be grouped under four major headings: (1) establishing a working alliance with the parties; (2) improving the climate between them; (3) addressing the issues; and (4) applying pressure for settlement. To these we have added a fifth: (5) ensuring implementation of the agreement.

In focusing our discussion on these five points we hope to articulate more specifically some of the "do's and don'ts" of effective ethnic group mediation, so as to broaden both our practical and our theoretical understanding of the processes involved.

Establishing a Working Alliance with the Parties

Initial Contact between the Disputing Parties and the Mediators. The mediator (or mediation center) may be approached by one or more of the disputing parties, or the mediation may occur as the result of third parties—for example, through the outreach of the mediator, through that of a school's mediation center, or at the insistence of teachers, administrators, parents, or the courts. Almost all mediators believe that mediation is more successful when the disputing parties participate in it on a voluntary basis. However, successes have been reported even when initial participation in mediation was not truly voluntary—particularly when the mediator is able to convince the conflicting parties that they *need* mediation. In any case, as a school's mediation center becomes well known and well respected, more and more students will bring their conflicts to it.

The mere existence of a conflict resolution curriculum in a school setting can provide a basic language for and familiarity with the process, thus facilitating the willingness of disputants to participate. Often the students involved in this curriculum become the "eyes and ears" of the mediation centers in the school, referring conflicts to mediation and encouraging their peers to use the service. Many of Coleman's interviews revealed that the involvement of these students, their own personal transformations, and the diffusion of their enthusiasm for mediation throughout the school were crucial to the success of the centers, forming the core of an actual culture change with regard to handling conflicts.

Some mediators believe that mediation should begin at an early phase of a dispute, before positions have hardened; others feel that the issues are clearer at a later stage, when polarization has occurred. We think the earlier, the better.

Establishing Trust. Of course, all mediators emphasize the importance of a trusting relationship between the mediator and the disputing parties. There are three interrelated bases of such trust: the personal credibility of the mediator, the credibility of the institution with which the mediator is affiliated, and the credibility of the procedures that the mediator employs. In interethnic conflict, the possible ethnic bias of the mediator or institution is sometimes an issue. To overcome such doubts, some mediators believe that the professional role of the mediator and its ethical code requiring impartiality should be stressed. Others emphasize that the mediator is only a facilitator, with all decisions being made by the disputing parties. Still others believe that it is helpful to have a team of mediators, so that each of the disputing ethnic groups is represented on the mediation team.

Personal credibility is often established through mediator contacts with each of the disputing parties prior to mediation. At such meetings, the mediator—in terms of appearance, manner, and behavior—must impress the party with whom he or she is meeting that he or she is impartial, fair, professional, and understanding of both the substance and the feeling of what is being said. The use of students who have been trained as mediators, rather than adults, has been recommended for student-student conflicts because of their greater ability to understand and speak the language of their fellow students.

Improving the Climate between the Parties

This initial aspect of the mediation process can be particularly difficult in interethnic conflicts, but successful mediation can provide an experience that will ultimately foster better relations between the ethnic groups. Improved climate between the parties can be approached in several ways.

Setting the Stage. One such way is illustrated in this quote from a mediator who was working on a conflict between faculty members at a school:

> So I did a lot of behind-the-scenes talking to everybody. I ran a multicultural sensitivity training for ½ day. Taught something about culture. Taught how culture could influence conflict. In the interim, The Black Teachers Caucus put on an evening [presentation] of a Black event which was spectacular! The Site Based Management negotiating team went. It was a first class event. Black spirituals and food and it was fabulous. This was the first time that the African American teachers had put on an evening. In this school people get status by putting on activities. So by the time mediation had evolved the multicultural thing had happened, and they had the Black cultural event [from Coleman's interviews].

Providing a Procedural Heuristic. Mediation can provide a cognitive framework that encourages the safe and constructive resolution of conflict. It provides disputants access to the other party, establishes ground rules to ensure civil discourse and safety, offers a forum on which to understand the other party's predicaments and concerns, and, most important, focuses the parties on future solutions rather than on past blame. This procedural heuristic is particularly important in cross-cultural mediation because it provides a common context within which differing cultures can communicate.

Allowing and Moving beyond Emotions. Allowing the appropriate ventilation of anger, frustration, and resentment of the parties enables disputants to "let out" and get beyond the intense feelings of hurt, loss, and fear that may be clouding their perceptions of the issues. Indeed, once such feelings have been expressed (within the limits of ground rules set by the mediator), the disputants may be better able to identify the real issues in the conflict.

Of course, there are considerable differences in cultural beliefs about what is an appropriate level of acknowledgment and expression of emotion. In interethnic conflicts, these differences should be identified by the mediator and openly stated.

Identifying and Clarifying Ethnic Assumptions. Culture can influence one's view of what conflict is, the appropriate way to respond to it, where responsibility lies in reaching an agreement, the role of the mediator, and what is possible under an agreement. Moreover, differing assumptions, beliefs, actions, and perceptions can polarize the groups, stirring ethnocentrism and stereotyping. Many of these assumptions are so subtle that they demand a considerable amount of patience from the mediator, who must listen carefully to the exchange, identify and confirm assumptions, and then share them with both sides. In short, mediators can facilitate the process by which different ethnic groups are made aware of how each group's background is affecting the conflict and its mediation.

Intervening in Ethnocentrism. In his book *Folkways*, Sumner (1906) defined *ethnocentrism* as "the technical name for the view of things in which one's own group is the center of everything. . . . Each group nourishes its own pride and vanity, boasts itself superior . . . and looks with contempt on the outsider" (pp. 12–13). This can be an issue even for conflicting groups that are not culturally different. Ethnic differences almost guarantee ethnocentrism.

The formula for intervening is as follows: (1) identify and clarify existing ethnic assumptions, misperceptions, and so on; (2) move on to the substantive issues (if they still exist); and (3) reframe the issues by focusing on the cooperative pursuit of resolving the reoccurrence of the problem in the future. This process is illustrated in the following example:

> What happened at the multicultural event was that I realized that many came from the "melting pot" approach. Whites came from old generation Italian, Jewish, and Irish, and had bought into the "melting pot" theory of race relations. Blacks were into the "salad bowl" theory. So in my head I thought how could this be solved. So I reframed it as a mediator that we need both soup and salad. I then asked them to brainstorm on the issue based on the reframing of how do you develop a governing structure that's fair and equitable and also includes representation of all the constituency groups. . . . The solution was that there would be a Multicultural Task Force made up of seven people appointed by the principal each year. The seven would be appointed based on the student demographics of the year, with proportional representation. So it seemed like a rational proposal that they all

contributed to and felt very happy that they agreed to it. There exists a better understanding between members of the team. It provided for the development of cohesion and team building. They are better friends. In this situation the main concern was a recognition of the fact that there were needs on both sides. The opposition dissolved after this was agreed. The results are very strong to date [from Coleman's interviews].

Avoiding Stereotypes. Stereotyping, as Walter Lippman once pointed out, is a natural process aimed at simplifying the complex set of data that impinge upon our perceptual and cognitive apparatuses. Negative stereotypes often develop to justify and explain hostilities that began with ethnocentrism and unresolved conflicts of interest. But once formed, they hamper the mediation process and constructive conflict resolution. Other issues involved in reducing prejudice and avoiding stereotypes must also be confronted by mediators. Indeed, they must, first of all, be aware of their own prejudices and curb them. Second, they must foster diverse, extended, informal interactions between members of different ethnic groups at meals, during coffee breaks, in recreational situations, in problem-solving subgroups, and so on. These informal interactions should be structured in such a way as to individuate the members of the different ethnic groups; to allow for the recognition of individual aspirations, hurts, and needs; and to enable the understanding of others' views in the context of the mediators' own life experiences.

Addressing the Issues

Before the issues can be addressed, they must be identified. But this task is often difficult in interethnic conflicts because the opposing groups may have been frozen into antagonistic positions that are not good representations of their underlying interests. In some conflicts, a group's interests may be hidden out of the group's fear of being exploited or because of a desire to exploit the other; but, in many instances, the members of a group do not have a clear picture of their own needs and interests. Often the emotional turmoil associated with interethnic conflict beclouds the true issues. In such cases, it is only after the emotional heat has been reduced and a working relationship has been established between the conflicting groups that these issues can be recognized and addressed.

There are several approaches that a mediator can take to help the conflicting groups identify and address the issues between them. When the hostility between the groups is so great that face-to-face discussions are unfeasible or unlikely to be productive, the mediator may work with each group separately to probe for the members' underlying interests and realistic aspirations, to identify a range of options for satisfying these interests, and to appraise the options in terms of their desirability, feasibility, and timeliness as well as in terms of objective criteria of fairness. The mediator may shuttle back and forth between the groups in an attempt to broaden the areas of agreement and narrow the differences between them. If this is successfully accomplished, the groups may be brought together to work out the details of a full agreement. If not, the mediator may draw up what he or she considers to be a fair agreement that addresses the interests of both. The mediator will then ask the two groups to use this text as the basis for negotiating a mutually acceptable agreement.

A second approach is to have the mediator facilitate a direct problem-solving interaction between the two parties. The basic steps involve identifying the problems between the two groups; analyzing their causes; developing suggestions for solving the problems; evaluating these suggestions in terms of their desirability, feasibility, and timeliness; selecting the preferred options and developing a plan for implementing them; and, finally, developing methods of checking how well they are being implemented and establishing a future time for assessing the progress in the two parties' relations. The typical rules of interaction during a mediation, to which the mediator continuously adheres, help to establish a civilized discourse during the process of cooperative problem solving.

A third approach to intergroup problem solving starts with ideals rather than problems. It involves several different steps. First, the mediator has the members of each group meet in separate parts of a room, where each group identifies what it thinks an ideal relationship between the two groups would be. Then, the two groups meet together to see if they can agree on the characteristics of such a relationship—and, with the help of the mediator, they often can. Next, the groups meet separately to discuss the nature of their present relationships. Again, they are brought together to see if, with the help of the mediator, they can agree on their present relationship. At this point, the mediator helps in identifying the various discrepancies between their ideal and the existing relationship. The two groups together or in mixed subgroups then develop specific suggestions for moving toward an improved relationship. Finally, these suggestions are evaluated in terms of their desirability, feasibility, timeliness, and fairness. And so on.

A practical recommendation for dealing with these issues has also been outlined by Pruitt and Olczak (in press) in a paper addressing intractable conflicts. After pointing to the impracticality of expecting to be able to confront and resolve every issue to a conflict through a win-win framework, these authors encourage a combination of problem solving and conflict avoidance. They note that parties to a conflict are frequently unable to distinguish between long-term idealistic objectives and those objectives that might be attainable within a realistic time frame. Thus the parties need to be helped to tone down their aspirations for the agreement so as to address only what is currently possible, and to avoid or tolerate their remaining differences, at least temporarily.

Applying Pressure for Settlement

Although mediators of interethnic conflicts cannot impose a settlement, they have an interest in obtaining an agreement that is responsive not only to the interests of the conflicting parties but also to those of the broader community of which they are a part: an agreement that is both fair and likely to endure. To obtain such an agreement, they may have to use pressure on one or both sides at various stages of the mediating process. There are various sorts of influence tactics that a mediator can employ, such as statements about the realistic consequences of no agreement or of the use of a given strategy or tactic; reliance on his or her own authority as an expert; expressions of approval or disapproval; the involvement of higher authorities than the local representatives of the conflicting ethnic groups (for example, the mediator can bring in national leaders of the conflicting ethnic groups); threats to withdraw as the mediator; provision of incentives for an agreement; and so on. It is evident that the use of pressure from the mediator can sometime help a stalled negotiating process to get moving. Yet such pressure may also backfire or fail to have a lasting desirable effect if it is not viewed as a legitimate influence attempt.

Ensuring Implementation of the Agreement

The mediator's role does not end with the achievement of an agreement between the conflicting parties. There are several other functions he or she can perform: providing advice and help in "selling" the agreement to the members of each ethnic group so that they will also support the agreement; identifying the steps involved in operationalizing the agreement, including, when necessary, access to the resources necessary to its implementation; establishing criteria and procedures for monitoring and evaluating compliance with the agreement; and creating procedures for appropriate responses to either intentional or unwitting noncompliance.

Another important function the mediator can perform to help ensure implementation of the agreement is to anticipate the conflicts and responses that may arise *within* each ethnic group as a result of the mediation process and agreement. Indeed, there may be extremists within a group who are committed to maintaining the struggle and who will intensify their opposition as progress is made toward an agreement. Consider, for example, the recent upsurge of militant violence in the West Bank of Israel that occurred just after the peace agreement between Israel and the PLO had been signed. This potentiality for increased resistance and/or violence needs to be identified and communicated to both parties in advance so that, in the event that the conflict does escalate, the parties responsible and not the peace process itself will be held accountable. Anticipation of these responses can inoculate the parties and act to partially nullify their effects.

Summary and Conclusions

We have tried to provide an overview both of the current state of research on mediation in the schools and of the procedures involved in the mediation of interethnic conflict. The research suggests that school mediation programs have such positive effects as reduction of violence and enhancement of the self-esteem and social skills of the mediator. Yet we must also note that this research is sparse, poorly funded, and of less than high quality.

The research on the mediation of interethnic conflict is almost nonexistent. It mainly consists of a few case descriptions written by mediators themselves. As noted, Peter Coleman supplemented these case studies by conducting interviews with eleven expert mediators who have worked on interethnic conflicts in schools and elsewhere. Combining our own knowledge and experience with insights garnered from these experts, we have discussed here some of the issues involved in mediating interethnic conflict. Many of these issues are the same as those involved in the mediation of any conflict. But the issues unique to interethnic conflict emerge from cultural misunderstandings, ethnocentrism, long-held stereotypes, and the importance of ethnic identity to self-identity. Although interethnic conflicts are not easy to mediate, our experts indicated many successful outcomes of such mediation.

In conclusion we now provide a brief outline of some suggestions for education and research in this area. Our model for the education of professionals in conflict resolution and mediation is based on a program of Graduate Studies in Conflict Resolution and Mediation that was recently instituted at Teachers College, Columbia University. And our suggestions for research are illustrated in relation to a systemwide conflict resolution intervention that was recently implemented by the New York City Board of Education.

Education

The recently established Teachers College program of Graduate Studies in Conflict Resolution and Mediation offers a set of core courses and practical as well as supplementary associated courses. The core courses provide students with knowledge of the theoretical and research basis for professional practice in the areas of cooperative learning, constructive conflict resolution, and mediation. They also provide students with supervised practice of the skills involved in these areas so that they can use these skills effectively in their personal lives as well as in their work. Advanced practical training enables them to train others in these skills. Additionally, as part of their education, students engage in continuous reflection on what they are learning; toward this end they are required to formulate significant researchable questions and to keep personal diaries related to their education and practice.

One set of associated, supplementary courses is directed toward providing students with the knowledge and skills to work effectively as facilitators, change agents, or administrators in an organization. Most conflict resolution specialists will work in organizational settings such as a school, industry, or community. To be influential and effective in such settings, students also need to be knowledgeable about consultation in organizations.

A second cluster of associated courses revolves around social and cultural diversity, dealing with the characteristics of different ethnic groups, cultural conflict, racism, sexism, ageism, and so on. In a multicultural society, conflict resolution specialists need to have knowledge of and skill in working with different cultural groups and in helping people from various backgrounds to work together cooperatively in resolving their mutual problems.

A third group of courses focuses on psychological development and personality and cultural differences. It is evident that conflict resolution and mediation must be taught in such a way as to remain responsive to the cognitive, emotional, moral, and social development of individual students. Being aware of the nature and stages of psychological development throughout the life span as it is influenced by the sociocultural context enables the mediator to formulate developmentally appropriate training. Similarly, recognition of the nature of individual differences in personality is helpful in individualizing training and in deciding whether or not a given person can benefit from it.

By itself, the Teachers College program of Graduate Studies in Conflict Resolution and Mediation does not yet lead to a degree. Its core courses can, however, be taken as components in any of several degree programs in various departments. Conflict resolution and mediation are inherently interdisciplinary and thus relevant to many different institutional contexts, whether interpersonal, family, intergroup, school, work, community, or international in orientation. In our own experience, it has been valuable to mix students from these different contexts in our program. They broaden their perspectives as they learn from one another in useful and unexpected ways.

To sum up, we favor the professional model of the "reflective practitioner." In this rapidly developing field, the cumulating experience of practitioners and, we hope, the increasing research will require professionals to be continuously reflective about their own work if they are to remain up to date.

Evaluation and Research

It is typical of practitioners in this field to support interventions around issues such as violence prevention and multicultural understanding, and yet not to support research and evaluation of the interventions that we implement. Due to the diverse nature of the types of interventions utilized, the differing levels of intensity with which they are introduced, the idiosyncratic differences among the trainers, and the vastly different environments into which they are introduced, research on the effects of the interventions is badly needed—indeed, essential to their refinement and level of efficacy. There is also a need for more general theoretical research on interethnic conflict mediation. Support from field studies and qualitative research such as the interview data presented earlier can begin to shed light on these issues, but such data have to be supplemented by more systematic, controlled studies of the phenomena. We now briefly describe an actual intervention in a school system and suggest some of the ingredients of a program of research to investigate it.

New York City Board of Education Conflict Resolution Project

Beginning in April 1992 and ending in June 1993, the International Center for Cooperation and Conflict Resolution (ICCCR) at Teachers College, Columbia University, undertook a project for the New York City Board of Education in conflict resolution in all of the city's high schools. The training project had two strands: one focused on starting a pilot program in conflict resolution in curricular areas; the other focused on establishing a peer mediation program within the schools. Two professionals from each school received ten days of training/support in one of the two strands over a period of several months. The aim of the program was for the two professionals to return to their schools and, with the support of their principal, a district conflict resolution specialist, and the ICCCR staff, to design a program of conflict resolution specifically tailored to the needs and limitations of their individual schools. Furthermore, these professionals received instruction enabling them to train both students and other school professionals in negotiation and mediation skills. Our overall objective was to begin to replicate and spread these skills and cooperative attitudes through the school system and, over time, to transform its predominantly competitive, violent culture into a safer, more cooperative one.

Unfortunately, we were unable to obtain funding for a research component to help monitor and evaluate the effectiveness of the interventions. We therefore outline a general program of research that we feel would be valuable in the way of assessing the effects of this intervention or any other systems-level intervention of conflict resolution.

We recommend that research in this area address the following three general questions:

(1) Was the initial training with the high school professionals successful?
(2) Were the high school professionals successful in getting a program started in their school?
(3) What were the short-term and long-term effects of the interventions on the students?

These general questions provide an overview of the most important issues at this stage in the development of and research on systems-level conflict resolution interventions. A more specific discussion of each of the areas follows.

Our first question concerns the effectiveness of the initial training and should address the issues of training integration and transfer of skills. Specifically, were the professionals actually able to integrate the attitudes and skills from the training and begin to use them in their own personal lives? The assumption here is that the trainers who are most effective with young people are those who use and can model the skills from the training, not only during the training but in other aspects of their personal and professional lives as well. In short, the repeated exposure of the students to the professional allows for the modeling and transfer of skills over time.

If the initial training was effective, we then ask whether the professionals can effectively train others. In other words, do they have the intelligence, energy, enthusiasm, creativity, and interpersonal style to help others learn, and can they effectively transfer their skills to other adults and young people? Again, our assumption is that young people will be most profoundly affected by trainers who both can train effectively and are seen to be living by their word. Although little research has been conducted on the integration of training or transfer of skills, both of these issues could be investigated through interviews with the professionals and students, through self-report questionnaires, and/or through behavioral-rating measurements of the work of the professionals.

Our second general question addresses issues of organizational change, support, and resource acquisition. As a corollary we must also ask, "What are the conditions necessary to enable the program to get started in a school and be most effective?" The answer requires that the following issues be addressed: Were the professionals successful as "change agents" in their system? Were they able to obtain "buy-in" early on from the sources of power (principal, deans, local youth officer, etc.) in their school and district? Were they able to obtain the necessary resources (time, space, students, etc.) to sustain the program? Did they network effectively through their peers and through the student body to promote the program and gain the needed support and "voice" for the program? Were they able to correctly identify and address areas of resistance to the project? Did they establish a mechanism to help monitor and fine-tune the interventions on an ongoing basis? And, finally, did the professionals receive the necessary training and/or assistance with these aspects of the intervention? There is a large body of research on organizational change and development that could be used to facilitate the investigation of these issues. It is usually best, however, to work with outside consultants for these types of inquiries because of the politically sensitive nature of the questions.

Our final question—concerning the effects of the interventions on students—is the most important and deserves the most thorough study. Deutsch (1992), with others, addressed this question by researching the effects of conflict resolution training and cooperative learning on students in an alternative high school in New York City. The study demonstrated that training in these areas led to an improvement in the students' social skills and ability to resolve conflict and work together constructively, which in turn led to more positive student relations (that is, to greater social support and less victimization), greater self-esteem, more frequent positive mental states, less frequent negative mental states, a greater sense of control, and greater achievement in terms of academic and vocational performance.

We strongly recommend the replication of this study, but we encourage the investigation of other issues as well. Particularly relevant to our discussion would be a more thorough exploration of the effects of these interventions on interethnic, intergroup categorizations and perceptions. It would be useful to obtain pre- and postintervention measures of individual-level cognitive categorization and recategorization of in-group/out-group distinctions for ethnic-group members to see if the interventions have short-term cognitive effects. It would similarly be useful to collect pre- and postintervention measures of perceptions of positive or negative interdependence between members of different ethnic groups to look for mediating effects here. Furthermore we might simply check for postintervention increases in cross-cultural awareness and acceptance. This type of research could build on past research dealing with Allport's contact theory (1954), Deutsch's theory of cooperation and conflict resolution (1949a), and Tajfel and Turner's social identity theory (Tajfel, 1982), as well as on recent advances in the area of social cognition.

We would also recommend an investigation into the specific conditions that enhance the effectiveness of the programs with young people. We might ask, for example, whether certain variables—such as the students' level of intelligence, communication skills, or ability to remain nonviolent—are necessary to ensure success in the program. And is the design of the program (in terms of teaching materials, examples, etc.) culturally sensitive enough to be effective with a multicultural population? Furthermore, it would be important to determine whether the effects of the training spread to the students' family, community, and work environments. And do the effects last? This question would entail a follow-up study of the young people past high school and into their college years or work life.

At a more general level, more valid and reliable instruments would have to be developed for the assessment of the individual, group, organizational, and larger system-level effects of mediation and other conflict-resolution interventions. As previously indicated, research in this area is sparse, and the instruments utilized are mostly ad hoc combinations of components of older instruments. It would also be useful to develop (through surveys, interviews, and observations) a typology of formal and informal conflict-resolution interventions that may exist at the disciplinary, curriculum, pedagogical, and cultural levels of schools, so as to begin to assess the relative effects of the mediation programs in these schools. Furthermore, some method of assessing the degree of exposure of each of the above conflict-resolution interventions at each of the school campuses should be developed so that the unique and/or combined contribution of each intervention could be weighed. The development of these instruments could better facilitate the measurement of the comparative effectiveness of the various different training approaches that exist for mediation and negotiation.

The current trend of research in this area appears to be oriented toward assessing the average effectiveness of these programs of intervention in general. What we encourage instead is specific research to identify the processes and conditions that determine whether or not a given type of intervention will be effective. It is through the answers to these questions that the field will truly move forward.

Clearly, then, there is a need to support both more education and more research in this area. It is our impression that only very few schools with educational programs would qualify their graduates to be experts in this field—experts with sufficient knowledge to be able to train other experts. Such educational programs are necessary if school mediation programs are to be developed in an effective and responsible manner. And given the insufficient research in this specialty of professional practice, there is an obvious need for the development of research institutes to develop the knowledge to guide professional practice and the procedures to evaluate and improve it.

References

Allport, G. W. (1954). *The Nature of Prejudice.* Cambridge, Mass.: Addison-Wesley.

Deutsch, M. (1949a). "Theory of Cooperation and Competition." *Human Relations, 2,* 129–51.

———. (1949b). "An Experimental Study of the Effects of Cooperation and Competition upon Group Processes." *Human Relations, 2,* 199–231.

———. (1992). *The effects of Training in Cooperative Learning and Conflict Resolution in an Alternative High School: A Summary Report.* New York: International Center for Cooperation and Conflict Resolution, Teachers College, Columbia University.

———. (1993a). "Cooperative Learning and Conflict Resolution in an Alternative High School." *Cooperative Learning, 13*(4), 2–5.

———. (1993b). "Educating for a Peaceful World." *American Psychologist, 48,* 1–8.

Johnson, D. W., and Johnson, R. T. (1989). *Cooperation and Competition. Theory and Research.* Edina, Minn.: Interaction Book Company

———, and Johnson, R. T. (1992). *Structuring Academic Controversies: Creating Conflict in the Classroom.* Edina, Minn.: Interaction Book Company.

Kressel, K., and Pruitt, D. G. (1989). *Mediation Research.* San Francisco: Jossey-Bass.

Lam, J. A. (1989). *The Impact of Conflict Resolution Programs on Schools: A Review and Synthesis of the Evidence.* Amherst, Mass.: NAME (National Association for Mediation in Education)

Pruitt, D. G., and Olczak, P. V. (in press). "A Multimodal Approach to Seemingly Intractable Conflict." In J. Z. Rubin and B. B. Bunker (eds.), *Cooperation, Conflict, and Justice: Essays Reflecting on the Work of Morton Deutsch.* New York: Sage.

Slaving, R. E. (1983). *Cooperative Learning.* New York: Longman.

Sumner, W. G. (1906). *Folkways.* New York: Ginn.

Tajfel, H. (ed.) (1982). *Social Identity and Intergroup Relations.* Cambridge, England: Cambridge University Press.

Wilson-Brewer, R., Cohen, S., O'Donnell, L., and Goodman, I. F. (1991). *Violence Prevention for Young Adolescents: A Survey of the State of the Art.* Revised version of working paper prepared for the conference "Violence Prevention for Young Teens," held in Washington, D. C., July 12–13, 1990.

°5°

Coexistence
in Israel

Each ethnic conflict has its own unique characteristics, and any attempt to engage in coexistence work must take into consideration the particular cultural, political, social, psychological, economic, and historical factors relevant to the conflict at hand. With this fact in mind, how then can one advocate a generic profession of coexistence work as we do in this *Handbook*? To address this challenging question, this section will take one particular intractable conflict and describe its distinctive factors as well as several of the existing programs currently in place that try to mitigate some of the negative aspects of that conflict. The authors in this chapter take the position that an intelligent application of existing coexistence programs to different aspects of individual cases of ethnic conflict can be accomplished, and that this constitutes the essence of the professional task.

The example we have chose to illustrate this professional task is the conflict between the Jewish and Arab citizens of the State of Israel who live within the pre-1967 borders of the State. Israeli Arabs are a minority ethnic group, many of whom see themselves and are regarded by others as Palestinians. They are part of the Arab people but their home is in the State of Israel. They are ethnically, nationally, and religiously distinct from the Jewish majority population, and most believe that the Palestinian nation has national rights in all areas of mandatory Palestine.

As citizens of the State of Israel they are entitled to vote, to be elected to Parliament, and to enjoy de jure the protection of their civil rights. However, although they benefit from other civil rights that are associated with a democratic system of government, they are regarded with distrust by Jewish citizens of the State of Israel who see them as potentially disloyal citizens. They have deep ethnic, cultural, political, and national ties to the Palestinian Diaspora around the world, and powerful memories of having been wronged by Zionist Jewish settlers when the State of Israel was established. While they support the efforts of the Palestinian people to establish an area in which there is Palestinian autonomy and to create the institutions of an emerging Palestinian State, most do not intend to leave their homes in Israel and settle in a Palestinian State should it come into being. Israeli Arabs are interested in strengthening their own national identity, while reducing the degree to which the State of Israel is defined legally and ideologically as a Jewish State.

By contrast, Israeli Jews are a majority ethnic group within the borders of the State of Israel. However, they feel themselves to be, and in fact are, a minority in the Middle East. Further, they feel themselves to be a beleaguered and isolated minority in a strategically uncertain situation, vulnerable to terrorist attack, fundamentalist acts of extremism, and destruction by unconventional weapons. Despite the strength of their army and the resourcefulness of their leaders, these feelings of vulnerability often prevent them from making the acts of compromise and concession needed to help create the conditions for peaceful coexistence. The haunting memory of a tragic history remains undiminished in the consciousness of Jews, both in Israel and elsewhere.

With all the challenges involved, surely if coexistence work is possible in Israel it should be possible in other situations as well. Making coexistence work in Israel relevant to ethnic conflicts around the world is the mission undertaken by the authors in this concluding section. Mitchell Bard leads the section with a comprehensive, descriptive study of coexistence work in Israel. Such a study provides the foundation from which professionally based coexistence programs can emerge elsewhere. Grace Feuerverger analyzes one particular experiment in integrated living and education, whereas Haviva Bar and Elias Eady challenge previous models of coexistence activity, and advocate their own. Helena Syna Desivilya considers the application of coexistence practices in professional services, and Rachel Hertz-Lazarowitz, Haggai Kupermintz, and Jennifer Lang evaluate an encounter between Jews and Arabs in particularly trying times. Eliezer Jaffe considers the professional challenges to traditional social work education with the resurgence of ethnic conflict. Finally, Nava Sonnenschein, Rabah Halabi, and Ariella Friedman present a unique program of coexistence intervention based on their own experiences.

While this section is culturally specific to Israel, within its complexity the way is pointed to effective models of coexistence work in other contexts. We have chosen Israel to exemplify not only the problems of coexistence work but also its promise. As Grace Feuerverger points out in her example of coexistence: Israel "is a flesh-and-blood place within a very difficult human circumstance where intergroup conflict in the wider society and the moral problems, and dilemmas that ensue, are constantly being played out and negotiated. Like the village of Neve Shalom/Wahat Al-Salam, Israel is a social-psychological experiment—a place where people of a certain level of education and personal conviction have chosen to come together to enact a collective vision of justice and care." The problem in the State of Israel, as in all other arenas of ethnic conflict, is that there is more than one vision of justice and care. These troubled places where ethnic conflicts flourish are dominated by conflicting visions that breed barbarism and inhumanity. These are precisely the places where the work of coexistence should take place and, as these articles show, it is where such work *is* taking place.

The Variety of Coexistence Efforts in Israel: Lessons for the United States

MITCHELL G. BARD

Once a fire breaks out—whether by accident or intention—the impact on life and property can be devastating. The best firefighting techniques and the most courageous firefighters can limit the damage, but the best defense against the destructiveness of a conflagration is prevention. The same is true for human conflict. It is possible to resolve disputes, sometimes before they escalate into violence, sometimes only after hostilities, but the ideal is to create a tolerant society where conflict does not exist, or at least does not intensify to the point of violence. This should remain our goal and our dream, but, realistically, the next best solution is a community where everyone coexists. As The Abraham Fund explained in its directory of Israeli coexistence projects:

> Coexistence is the minimal, least demanding way for people to relate to one another positively. It is not the same thing as love. It may not even be the same thing as friendship. To the contrary, it is an expression of distance, and an acknowledgment that boundaries will remain, that the possibilities of misunderstanding will never completely disappear. It is informed by an attitude of "live and let live" and that is precisely its message. Coexistence is an ideal without illusions. Its objective is not the seamless union of opposites, but a practical relationship of mutual respect among opposites. . . . In a pluralistic society, ethnic and cultural differences are not abolished. They are legitimated, and society strives to guarantee that the law will be blind to them.[1]

By promoting coexistence, we may not prevent human "fires," but we can reduce the risk of their occurrence, and minimize the intensity of those that do occur.

The recognition, implementation, and enforcement of the right to life, liberty, and the pursuit of happiness codified in the U.S. Constitution are necessary but not sufficient for coexistence. Despite all the work that has been done, and is being done to resolve conflicts in the United States, tensions, intolerance, and violence persist. Prejudice and intolerance are certainly not unique to American society; nevertheless, the intensity of hatred in the United States, and the violence it spawns, is deeply disturbing. According to the FBI, nearly 8,000 hate-crime incidents were reported in 1995. Sixty-one percent of the incidents were motivated by racial bias; 16 percent by religious bias; 13 percent by sexual-orientation bias and 10 percent by ethnicity/national origin bias. Some of the problems may be attributed to extremist groups. Ku Klux Klan, Neo-Nazi, and Skinhead organizations operate in every state of the union. More than 300 hate groups are scattered throughout the United States, according to the Klanwatch project of the Southern Poverty Law Center. Still, these relatively small organizations cannot be blamed for all the tensions that exist between Whites and non-Whites, Blacks and Koreans, Blacks and Hispanics, Jews and Blacks, gays and "straights," religious and secular and other identifiable groups in conflict.

The crimes are serious enough, but what is perhaps more alarming are the attitudes of others toward these acts. For example, a 1990 Harris survey asked high school students what they would do if confronted with a racial incident. Nearly half (47 percent) said they would either join in or feel the group being attacked deserved what it was getting. The results are particularly shocking given the fact that most people, even in anonymous surveys, are reluctant to give answers that might be construed as bigoted.

A neglected aspect of crime prevention is prejudice reduction. Though it is not hopeless at the adult level, the best chance for preempting conflict and fostering tolerance is among children. As schools around the United States become increasingly diverse, the challenge of promoting coexistence and training teachers to manage multicultural classrooms will continue to grow. Moreover, despite the increasingly hostile policies toward immigrants, this nation will remain a melting pot, and conflicts between adults of different religions, races, and ethnic groups will undoubtedly endure.

Israel has no magic solutions for eliminating conflict; however, Israelis have their own painful experience with similar problems and have developed innovative approaches to promote coexistence that offer lessons for Americans.

The Israeli Experience

The United States has not solved its problems in more than 200 years; therefore, it should not be surprising that Israel has not resolved its intergroup conflicts in its short forty-eight-year history. Moreover, unlike the United States, Israel has faced a daily fight for survival against neighbors seeking to destroy it. This reality has meant that the needs of minorities living within Israeli's borders were neglected and internal conflicts allowed to fester.

Israel is a small nation, about the size of New Jersey, with a population of fewer than six million people. More than 80 percent of Israelis are Jews, roughly 15 percent are Muslim, 3 percent Christian and 2 percent Druze and other groups. Israel has fought six wars and had numerous other military engagements with its neighbors and terrorist organizations, but relations between Jewish and non-Jewish citizens of the State have been remarkably free of violent confrontations. Israel has devoted an extraordinary amount of effort to prevent "fires" because everyone understands that a serious one could burn down the entire country.

When Americans think of Arab-Jewish relations, they usually have in mind Palestinians from the West Bank and Gaza Strip. Though many of the Arabs in Israel call themselves Palestinians and sympathize with the struggles of the Arabs outside the borders of the State, they have a distinct identity and have chosen to accept minority status as Israeli citizens. Israeli Arabs also have very different life experiences than Palestinians in the territories, who are locked in what has commonly been referred to as a conflict between two peoples over one land. Arab citizens of Israel have enjoyed the freedoms of a democratic society, such as the right to vote, freedom of expression and freedom of assembly, whereas the Arabs in the territories have lived under occupation, with all the hardships that entails. Other Palestinians have lived in Arab countries with few, if any, liberties.

The Arab citizens of Israel have been loyal, peaceful members of the society since the founding of the State. Thus, the level of hostility that exists between Jews and Palestinians from the territories does not pertain to relations with Arabs within the "Green Line" (i.e., those living inside the pre-1967 borders of the State). Nevertheless, mistrust and misunderstanding are characteristics of the relationship between Israeli Arabs and Jews. Though many Israeli projects seek to foster coexistence between the Palestinian and Jewish peoples, those described in this study focus primarily on building bridges between Jews and Arabs who share the common trait of citizenship in the State of Israel.

As in the United States, all Israeli citizens are assured equal protection under the law. Israel does not have a constitution, but is governed by a series of Basic Laws that encompass many of the principles in our Bill of Rights, which have been adopted by Israel's democratically elected legislature, the Knesset. Israel's Declaration of Independence is also considered a constitutional document. It clearly enunciates the principles of freedom and equality:

> The State of Israel . . . will promote the development of the country for the benefit of all its inhabitants; will be based on the precepts of liberty, justice and peace . . . will uphold the full social and political equality of all its citizens, without distinction of race, creed or sex; will guarantee full freedom of conscience, worship, education and culture. . . . We yet call upon the Arab inhabitants of the State of Israel to . . . play their part in the development of the State, with full and equal citizenship.

Many Israelis, like many Americans, find the promise of equality is not always matched by the reality. Arabs in Israel have suffered economic and social discrimination. By virtually any measure—health, education, welfare—Jews are better off. One reason is that government spending has historically been significantly higher in Jewish municipalities than Arab ones. In addition, Arabs have a far more difficult time getting university educations or jobs. Legally, Arabs are differentiated from Jews in one significant way: they are not required to serve in the military (Druze and Bedouin citizens do serve). The reason for this distinction was primarily to spare Israeli Arab the uncomfortable requirement of going to war against their fellow Arabs (who might even be relatives). Practically, this policy has limited employment possibilities for Arabs in Israel because military service plays a major role in the career opportunities of most Israelis.

Many inequalities between Jews or Arabs have been meaningfully reduced in the last few years. This has been a major objective of the Israeli government. Though noting a number of areas where more needs to be done, Sikkuy's 1994–95 Annual Progress Report "Equality and Integration," found "significant progress in the elimination of disparities" in Interior Ministry budget allocations to Jewish Arab municipal authorities; in resource allocation and employment in education; in National Insurance child allowances; in the level of service in Arab localities, and in the quality of health services.

The distinctions are not only economic. With the exception of a few cities, Jewish and Arab communities are largely segregated, with each group living in its own villages and attending its own schools. It is important to note that this is the preference of both communities. By maintaining a separate school system, the Arab students can study in Arabic (which, along with Hebrew, is a national language) and emphasize their culture whereas the Jewish students study in Hebrew and focus on Jewish culture.

This separation means the two groups have little interaction. For example, according to Neve Shalom/Wahat al-Salam, 83 percent of Israeli Jews have never visited an Arab home, even though they live no more than a fifteen-minute drive and often considerably, less—from each other. As a report by Givat Haviva notes, "This separation reinforces the barriers that obstruct good communication and understanding and fosters ignorance and suspicion between the two communities. In addition to this physical separation, there is a strong history of stereotyping and ethnic generalizations."

Coexistence Projects

According to the National Association for Mediation in Education (NAME), more than 5,000 dispute resolution programs are in schools across the United States, so the concept is widely accepted and hardly new. In Israel, the idea was not to discover *the* solution to conflict. The belief was that Israel had been forced to confront the issue of coexistence since before the state was established and that some of the lessons learned might be applicable in the United States and elsewhere.

In recent years, especially, a wide variety of programs have been created to promote coexistence in Israel and encourage professional work in the field. The methodologies employed in several projects have already been adapted to address conflicts in places such as Northern Ireland and the former Yugoslavia. Though some Americans in the field are familiar with techniques used in Israel, the programs are not widely known and some of the more innovative methodologies have not been tested here yet. Moreover, most of the coexistence projects in the United States are aimed at schools. This is true in Israel as well; however, many Israeli programs are designed for adults and could be adapted for use with older Americans.

Public Policy

It is possible for individuals and nongovernmental organizations to promote coexistence; however, to establish this goal as one of national importance, it is necessary to have the backing of the government. Symbolically, the government can demonstrate its commitment to the goal and, practically, it can contribute resources toward its achievement. The Israeli government has made the promotion of education for coexistence a priority. In 1986, the Ministry of Education established a Unit for Education for Democracy and Coexistence specifically to provide training for teachers and administrators; support educational programs; develop curricula and work with nongovernmental organizations to incorporate their programs in the schools. The idea for the department was predicated on the assumption that formal and informal educational activities have the power to combat existing stereotypes and preconceptions and to develop tolerant behavioral patterns, which center around accepting differences and acknowledging that all people are equally important.

The department focuses on subject matter taken from the principles of society and democratic rule. The department introduces curricula and instructional programs that encourage both teachers and students to debate and analyze highly controversial issues, while working to improve their skills in oral expression and stressing the importance of verbal civility. The department encourages students to take an active role in the community, the school, and the government, viewing this as a fundamental component of the democratic way of life. The department offers systemwide programs: preschool, elementary school, high school, and teacher seminars. The department also provides consultation and funding to voluntary institutions and organizations that are working to promote education for democracy.

The department's main areas of focus are:

(1) Education for life in a democratic society—education for tolerance, for accepting differences, for awareness that all people are equally important, and for sociopolitical involvement.

(2) Education for life in a multicultural society, with emphasis on promoting the relationship between Jews and Israel's Arab citizens.

(3) Education for democracy for students who immigrated from countries that have no democratic political culture.

(4) Educational involvement in current events, providing teachers with the tools to deal better with controversial political, cultural, and value-oriented issues.

(5) Familiarizing teachers and students with Israeli democracy.

(6) Instituting democratic processes in educational institutions and the educational system.

(7) Education toward peace.

The department provides in-service training for teachers in subjects such as education for life in a democratic society, ways to handle controversial value-oriented topics and methods to encourage involvement and participation in school. Joint study days and workshops are held for Jewish and Arab teachers who wish to explore Arab–Jewish relations and other current events. The department also cooperates with voluntary organizations and other institutions in arranging in-service training for teachers and principals and developing coexistence programs and materials for the state-approved curricula.

Competing Philosophies

Israeli programs reflect three different philosophies for promoting coexistence. One school of thought can be described as the "encounter approach." It holds that the key to understanding is bringing Arabs and Jews together for relatively short, intense encounters and forcing them to confront their prejudices and the issues at the root of the conflict.

A second school favors an "experiential approach," and believes that it is not sufficient to talk about coexistence and that it has to be practiced. Proponents argue that it is naive to believe that deep-rooted conflicts can be resolved by discussing them over a few days, or worse, that by beginning with dialogue, prior interethnic hatreds tend to be reinforced. This school's approach is to bring Jews and Arabs together over a long period of time and to concentrate on joint activities of mutual interest. The philosophy is that understanding is built by seeing the other group as composed of human beings with similar feelings and interests and that, over time, the contentious issues will arise and participants will know how to resolve them, or, at least, accept their differences.

The third philosophy approaches the problem more directly. This school emphasizes the importance of teaching the principles of democracy as a means of fostering tolerance. The programs described here are not mere civics lessons about the workings of government, but courses explaining the concepts and their implementation. "Teaching for democracy," Nivi Shinar of the Adam Institute says, "is education for recognition of the equal right of all people to freedom."

Americans can learn lessons from all three approaches. Much of what Israel has to offer is training for teachers who are interested in learning proven techniques and strategies for promoting coexistence. In fact, several organizations have already provided this assistance to other countries.

The Encounter Approach

The Israeli programs using the encounter approach typically bring participants together for relatively short-term, intense sessions in which they address their similarities and differences.

The School for Peace (SFP)

SFP is unique because it is located in Neve Shalom/Wahat al-Salam, a village where Jews and Arabs have chosen to build a community together. Beyond the day-to-day coexistence of the villagers, the school also offers several programs to promote familiarity between youths and adults who otherwise rarely mix.

The structure of the SFP, and of its workshops is guided by the principles of equality. The staff of facilitators is a permanent, professional team composed of Jews and Arabs. Decisions are made democratically. The workshops are conducted in Hebrew and Arabic. Each working group is headed by two facilitators, one Jewish and the other Palestinian. Part of the workshop is conducted in a "uninational" group setting (all Jewish/all Arab) to provide a secure, sheltered framework that can meet each group's separate learning needs. Numerical equality between Jews and Arabs is maintained throughout the workshop, and each people's needs are given equal priority.

SFP uses the encounter as the major experience of the project. The realities of Israel do not give the youth of the two peoples a chance to meet on equal terms. The encounters that take place are generally accompanied by feelings of fear, humiliation, disappointment, and distrust. The encounters provide an opportunity to process and understand these feelings, helping youth to cope better with the Jewish-Arab conflict. One key to the program is the use of both Arabic and Hebrew in the workshops. Language is at the base of one's national identity. Just as language creates bridges and ties between people, it can be an obstacle to contact.

Every workshop begins with separate all-Jewish and all-Arab groups, in which the participants get to know themselves, the other group members and their own people. The intensity of the encounter and the experience of meeting members of the other group creates tension and fear, in addition to curiosity and interest. NS/WAS has found that clear rules, within a framework known in advance, help the youngsters cope with these emotions.

Invitation to a Dialogue

Immigrants often have a particularly difficult time coexisting with "veterans." Like the United States, Israel is a melting pot with people from every corner of the globe. In recent years, a huge influx of immigrants has come from the former Soviet Union and faced difficulties overcoming cultural and emotional isolation. *Invitation to a Dialogue,* developed by the Joint Distribution Committee, uses a computer network, combined with face-to-face meetings, to reduce the isolation felt by teenagers.

The numerous stresses and difficulties of the immigration process are particularly problematic for the adolescent. All immigrants must confront the need for personal adjustment to their new environment. This includes the cognitive and emotional adjustments to learning to communicate in a new language and adapt to a new set of social norms, as well as a redefinition of their cultural identity. The adolescent, who is in any case undergoing the universal transition between childhood and adulthood leading to upheavals in their relationships with their families, their peers, and the outside world in general, is particularly vulnerable to the additional transition of immigration. The need to identify with a peer group is especially strong for this age cohort, so the language and cultural barriers compound their difficulties. The adolescent immigrant is also deeply affected by family crises often caused by the immigration process, such as material and financial hardship and a shift in social status. The growing numbers of young immigrants who are dropping out of school and, in some cases, drifting into delinquent behavior is an indication of the gravity of the situation in Israel.

Invitation to a Dialogue has set up groups of young immigrants, Na'aleh groups, and young Israelis at community centers, residential schools, and clubs for immigrant youth throughout Israel. The groups meet once or twice a week with a counselor who speaks their language and shares their cultural background. Group activities include discussion on issues of mutual interest, leadership courses, and journalism.

All the groups are linked by a computer network through which they can correspond both as individuals or as a group. The network offers them the opportunity to express themselves in their own language, Russian. The participants can also correspond with more veteran adult immigrants who serve as supportive role models for successful integration into the new environment and also lead specific activities. In addition to the electronic meetings, groups or group representatives meet periodically in person.

The computer network helps the young participants acquire skills in the use of advanced information technologies that will aid in their personal and professional development. This, together with the generally high-status aura of computers, helps initially to attract the youngsters to the project's activities. In addition, when communicating through a computer network rather than meeting face to face, most characteristics on which social groups build stereotypes of other groups (physical appearance, dress, mannerisms, accent) are hidden. This allows the youngsters to create relationships and "listen" to each other. After the relationships are formed, the participating groups have face-to-face meetings with people they already know and appreciate.

Education for Peace

Pelech Religious Experimental High School for Girls has created a program called *Education for Peace,* which uses techniques similar to many other programs to bring together Arabs and Jews. What makes this program unusual is that the Israeli school that started the encounters is a religious school. Generally, the "religious" schools in Israel have been reluctant to engage in dialogues with other groups.

The program, now in its third year, concentrates on the Middle East peace process and Palestinian autonomy. During the 1995–96 academic year, the project began to work with Abu Gosh High School. The program is divided into four units: 1. The study of democracy and human rights (Grade 10—two weekly hours); 2. Conflict and Conflict Resolution (Grade 11—two weekly hours); 3. Arab Culture and Customs (Grade 11—one weekly hour); and 4. Exchange visits with students of the Abu Gosh High School (Grade 12—two weekly hours).

This program is one of the few, if not the only, program that involves the *dati* (religious) community and therefore may serve as a good model for working with American religious and secular schools and resolving issues related to religious tolerance.

Children Teaching Children

In 1949, the founders of Givat Haviva recognized the need to build a place where Jews and Arabs could meet in safety to discuss their many problems. It was felt that with patience and understanding they could help plan a future of democratic coexistence among all the people of Israel.

Based on theories of humanistic education and conflict resolution, Givat Haviva's staff of Arab and Jewish educators believe that through dialogue and creative encounters children can overcome negative stereotypes they have about each other. The *Children Teaching Children* (CTC) program is, for most participants, their first opportunity for meaningful personal contact with members of the other community.

The class is divided into groups of 12–16 pupils, with one teacher and usually two assistants. Each class has a weekly two-hour lesson. After one to three months of preparation, the class begins a series of fortnightly encounters with its parallel group. In each encounter, mixed groups of 24–32 pupils are formed, so that two or three mixed classes work with two teachers each. The week when there is no mixed learning session is devoted both to the assimilation of the previous week's meeting through discussion, or activity focused on some of its specific aspects, as well as to preparation for the coming week.

Preparation Stage: This takes place in homeroom and is aimed at preparing for the mixed group. The participation of the children in planning and organizing is a precondition to success. Subjects such as conformism, stereotypes, and social pressure are discussed, as well as the legitimacy of expressing emotions, the creation of an atmosphere of acceptance in the group, and the ability to give attention and awareness to different points of view about any event or subjects.

Mixed Group Experience: The content is decided jointly by the pupils and the teachers during the preparatory period. This may include language studies; art projects; theater and dramatic expression; formal school subjects such as geography, agriculture, and computers; or social issues, such as the characteristics of adolescence in both groups, relations between adults and children and school culture. Students are encouraged to communicate with their counterparts through storytelling, drama, art, music, and other media, and to think about and openly discuss complex questions of identity. Through dialogue and shared activity, they confront and conquer their own stereotypes, prejudices, fears, and anxieties.

The learning process takes place on two levels—that of the teachers and that of the pupils. The program is perceived and accepted as an integral part of the school curriculum, and not as an external subject. Teachers' workshops and parents' meetings are an integral and dynamic part of the CTC program. Throughout the school year, the teaching and supervisory staff participates in twelve in-service training days, and meet once each week to plan activities and share ideas, experiences, and problems. Teachers attend summer workshops for ten days. The first is an encounter workshop. A second one is devoted to the role of the teacher in the program. During the academic year, teachers gather for day-long workshops. In additional, teachers participate in biweekly team meetings with teachers from the twin school and with their colleagues in the program. CTC thereby creates a growing core of teachers who have acquired new tools and gained significant experience in the sphere of the two major objectives of the program.

CTC is a two-year program with the potential of concluding it at the end of the first year or extending it beyond two years. While homeroom work concentrates on specific and largely different needs of the groups, the work in the mixed groups tries to answer common needs. The creation of a basis for mutual trust between teachers and teachers, between teachers and pupils, and between pupils and pupils is the primary objective and a necessary condition for continued operation of the program.

The Experiential Approach

Though many "experiential" programs involve encounters, the emphasis is less on dialogue than action, particularly joint activities that highlight the participants' similarity rather than their differences. By engaging in activities of mutual interest, coexistence is promoted without the concepts of difference and conflict.

Jewish–Arab Coexistence Project

Beit Shmuel is the Education–Cultural Center of the World Union for Progressive Judaism. It was established in 1987 as a community center designed to serve the primarily secular Israeli public. As a result of the growing Jewish-Arab conflict in Israel in general, and in Jerusalem in particular, increasing effort at Beit Shmuel has been devoted toward building mutual understanding and basic knowledge about the "other."

The *Jewish-Arab Coexistence Project* has two components. The first is the *Language Training Program,* which includes Hebrew and Arabic tracks. Courses meet two to three times a week for three hours in the evenings. Those studying Hebrew are mostly Palestinian business people who must command a sufficiently high level of Hebrew language skills to engage fully in their field within the larger Israeli context. Studying Arabic are Israelis whose professions fall primarily within the fields of civil service, social work, business, law and finance, and who require Arabic language skills.

The objectives of the classes are far broader than "mere" language acquisition. Also important—and meant to be transmitted through the language courses—is the understanding of another ethnic group's religious, historical, cultural, and social foundations. Language instructors are selected on the basis of their pedagogic skills and their ability to represent, in an engaging and interesting manner, the fundamental ethos of the ethnic group behind the language.

Beit Shmuel is especially well-suited to meet the needs of this project because it is situated at the meeting point of western and eastern Jerusalem (prior to the 1967 Six-Day War, it was considered no-man's-land between Israel and the Jordanian-controlled Old City). Arabs consider Beit Shmuel a "neutral" and "safe" environment because it is clearly a private, nongovernmental entity.

Two semesters of Hebrew courses were offered in 1995 as part of the Jewish-Arab Coexistence Project. The language acquisition stage is intended to prepare both Jews and Arabs for the personal encounters. This part of the program offers a number of joint field excursions and cultural activities. Participation is voluntary, though each encounter is generally attended by roughly the same number of Jews and Arabs. The nature of the field excursions is such that Jews and Arabs travel together to various parts of Israel to meet with a third ethnic group that is somewhat unfamiliar to both. These ethnic groups include Golan Druze and Negev Bedouin. The excursions include bus travel, outdoor activities, site tours, the ethnic meetings and presentations with question and answer periods. Most Arabs have never traveled around Israel or gone to places like the Israel Museum and get their first opportunity in outings with Jews in the program. In 1995, the groups began to travel to Jordan.

The Leo Baeck Education Center

The Leo Baeck Education Center is an organization dedicated to the advancement of progressive and humanist education in Israel. Connected with the World Union for Progressive Judaism (the Reform Movement), the center encompasses several institutions, including a junior and senior high school and a community center.

For eight years, the center has run a summer camp for Jewish and Arab children to initiate contact between the children based on attractive joint activities that can encourage formation of a group identity. The camp's activities include getting-to-know-you games, competition and contests between the groups, arts and crafts, computers, sports, and field trips. One innovative aspect of the camp is the approach to language. Since Arabs usually know Hebrew, but Jews do not know Arabic, Hebrew is the dominant language. To avoid confusion, all instructions for group activities were written in both languages so the Jewish and Arab counselors had to help one another to read and understand the instructions. The intermingling of the languages in the instructions was on the subsentence level, so neither counselor could understand the whole sentence without help from the other. In this way, mutual assistance between the counselors and an equalization between the Hebrew and Arabic languages was achieved. In the future, the plan is to continue some of the camp's activities during the school year to change the infrequent and superficial nature of contact between the two populations, and to dismantle any prejudices and mistrust between them by allowing a natural growth of friendship.

The Arab–Jewish photography class, "Film for Thought," is aimed at ninth graders. The project seeks to add social meaning to the production of photographs and to give an artistic component to the interaction between Jewish and Arab teens. The group will go on field trips to sites that reflect the diverseness of Israel's social fabric. Teamwork will be emphasized in professional training of photography skills.

As with other programs, the idea of working with young children, from kindergarten up, is to expose them at an early age to the "other" so they will grow up more tolerant. "Gan Yachad," Leo Baeck's day care center, aims to provide the special educational attention needed by children, ages four to nine, from extremely distressed emotional and economic backgrounds, to introduce Arab and Jewish children to one another at an impressionable age so they can learn to identify with one another and recognize their mutual humanity, and to serve as a model of coexistence with first-rate staff, equipment, and programming. The classes are separate, held in mirror-image wings, with a joint courtyard and play area. Daily interaction between the two groups of children facilitates their education in tolerance and coexistence. Joint programming is conducted in both Hebrew and Arabic, with the aim of providing both groups of children rudimentary knowledge of the other group's language. While many of the coexistence projects involve people who are predisposed toward tolerance, that is not the case in this program because of the population's poverty and emotional problems. Hungry, neglected children are not best suited for participating in any kind of coexistence activities; they are struggling hard enough merely to exist themselves. Therefore, the work done by the social worker and house mother to help these children is a crucial first step toward helping these children believe in themselves. Once this step has been taken, the next step, of helping the children to believe in one another, Arab and Jew alike, can be taken.

International YMCA

The Jerusalem International YMCA was formed in 1878 and is a branch of YMCA U.S.A. It is a voluntary association of members joined together for service, leadership, self-development, and fellowship. From the outset, the center has served as a meeting place for people of all races, faiths, and political persuasions and is run by a board comprising Jews, Christians, and Muslims. The YMCA's mission, inscribed at its entrance, is to be "a place whose atmosphere is peace, where political and religious jealousies can be forgotten and international unity fostered and developed."

The YMCA has many programs throughout the year designed to foster coexistence and tolerance. Two particular programs are pursued aggressively:

The Youth Leadership Club brings together thirty-two 15–17 year-olds, split evenly between Jews and Arabs, who are identified by Neve Shalom/Wahat al-Salam. The group meets for three hours every Thursday. For the first three months, they focus on activities like going to a movie and out for pizza. Later they use simulations to discuss issues and political problems (e.g., the future of Jerusalem). These young people get practical experience as assistant leaders in the spring, summer, and fall camps and graduate into leaders for the "Y" and other community centers. The program lasts two years and the third year the graduates can become teachers. One or two are assisted further if they choose to pursue a career in social group work on a higher education level.

The Integrated Nursery/Kindergarten Program has fifty Jewish and Arab boys and girls aged two to four. The integrated program comprises two separate classes of Jewish and Arab children, each of whom has two teachers—a Jew and an Arab. Each group learns about its own culture, language and folklore, in addition to learning about each other in joint activities. This group affects 500 persons—parents, grandparents, and other extended family members. Once a month an activity is organized for the parents, mostly lectures, picnics, and home visit. This is often the first exposure of parents to a different culture. Stereotypes are broken and barriers removed unconsciously.

Ein Dor Museum of Archaeology

Kibbutz Ein Dor is located in the eastern section of the Lower Galilee, a demographically diversified region. The staff of the Museum of Archaeology sees part of its function as affording a common meeting ground for the different communities and encouraging the undertaking of joint ventures between them. By familiarizing themselves with the region's ancient culture through investigation and the reenactment of ancient practices, museum visitors will hopefully learn to reexamine their own modern-day lifestyles and customs.

The emphasis in this project is on the ties made between Arab and Jewish children. The museum interests both Arab and Jewish children and thus provides an excellent setting for a meeting between the two communities. Through joint participation in an educational project it is hoped that Arab and Jewish children will get to know each other, and learn cooperation and mutual respect. The present-day realities of suspicion, animosity, fear, and estrangement are direct products of the distance and alienation that this project aims to combat. By affording the opportunity of a common positive experience through a systematic educational program where the other side's point of view is also examined, the museum staff hopes to bridge the gap between the two sides.

Students in grades five and six were chosen because the Arab children have mastered enough Hebrew to communicate with the Jews, and all the children are still young enough to be open to positive influences on the subject of coexistence.

The first steps in the project are to select schools interested in taking part in the project; to pair each Arab school with a Jewish school from the same area; to find teachers within the participating schools willing to work toward the project's success; and to conduct monthly meetings between the schools over a ten-month period. Preparation for the meetings is done by a committee comprising the museum staff and a special task force from each school that includes interested parents. The committee devises a creative, experiential, and educational enterprise for each meeting and works free time into the course of each meeting in which participants can meet in a more open environment.

The group is divided into subgroups of four pupils each (two Arabs, two Jews). An adult (teacher or parent) is then assigned to each subgroup. Parents are also invited to join the project as active participants. Meetings last three and a half to four hours and include study, hands-on experience, creative endeavors, free time, and a break for food and drink.

SHEMESH

In Israel today, approximately 80 percent of the population is Jewish and 20 percent Arab. In the lower Galilee however, the situation is the opposite: 80 percent Arabs and 20 percent Jews. As in the rest of the country, most Jews in the towns and rural settlements associated with the Misgav regional council have little or no contact with their Arab neighbors. There is little tension in the area, yet both Jews and Arabs are deeply influenced by the tension in the rest of the country. Children grow up with racist stereotypes, and the cycle of hatred and fear persists.

To break this cycle, residents from Moshav Shorashim and the village of Shaab created The Shaab-Shorashim Good Neighbors Program, which after six years culminated in the formation of SHEMESH (Shorashim-Misgav-Shaab). SHEMESH has grown beyond Shorashim, Misgav, and Shaab. Today it is a regional, nonprofit organization (Amuta), which includes members from many Jewish and Arab localities in the lower Galilee, and operates the following programs:

- *The Good Neighbors Summer Camps*—This summer camp is the mainstay of SHEMESH programming for Jewish and Arab children, six to thirteen years old. During the first session, a two-week long day camp for six to eleven year old Jewish and Arab children, the campers spend an intensive period together getting to know one another through arts and crafts, sports, music, day trips, community projects, and an overnight camping trip. Parents are encouraged to participate actively in the program, including a special evening of entertainment for all the families involved. In 1995, SHEMESH offered a second session of this camp for twelve to thirteen year olds, those who have outgrown the original camp.
- *Youth Leadership Training*—More than twenty Jewish and Arab teenagers from Misgav and Shaab meet together regularly in a program that includes leadership training, community and social action, and field trips and social activities together that stress group cohesiveness. This project has proven to be a success-

ful method for bringing together Jewish and Arab teenagers and for building a trained staff for SHEMESH activities.

- *Chugim*—Joint extracurricular activities *(chugim)* are a way to bring Jews and Arabs together through informal education in community schools. Jewish and Arab children, aged ten to twelve, meet weekly through the school year and participate in a wide range of activities, which have included computers, soccer, arts and crafts, and cooking. Each year new *chugim* are introduced. This combination of extracurricular activities, social events, and multicultural learning is a novel way in which to change the accepted norm of separate Jewish-Arab education.
- *NEIGHBORS*—A student newspaper in Hebrew, Arabic, and English is produced by Jewish and Arab eighth and ninth graders. The editorial staff meets regularly to decide on the content and layout of the newspaper. They learn together throughout the year how to publish a newspaper and what should be special about a joint newspaper. The process of working and learning together is just as important as the end product.
- *The Inbal Choir*—A joint choir of approximately thirty children, ages ten to fourteen, began working together in the middle of December 1993. The children in the choir come from the Misgav and Shaab community schools and from local schools in the village of Sakhnin. Music is an international language that should be used to build bridges between the two communities.

The Neighborhood Home

Friendship's Way: The Jewish-Arab Association for the Child and Family is a grassroots, multiservice organization that seeks to improve the conditions of socially, economically, and educationally deprived Jewish and Arab children and their families. It was created in 1983 by a handful of Jewish and Arab volunteers tutoring Arab youngsters in Hebrew and Arabic.

The Neighborhood Home is a daily, after-school enrichment program for fifty Jewish and Arab children of families at high risk. The majority of kids are referred to the home by school guidance counselors and social workers. Approximately 80 percent of the children are from welfare-supported families. Many children involved in the Neighborhood Home, who would otherwise be placed in a boarding school or foster home, receive an enriched education, social activities, and a hot, well-balanced lunch and dinner. The home allows children to maintain daily contact with their families and offers a haven from dangerous surroundings. The majority of children in the Home come from environments characterized by substance abuse, poverty, neglect, malnutrition, violence, and abuse.

The Friendship's Way minibus brings the children directly to the center at the end of their school day (2:00 P.M.). Upon arrival, the staff and children share a hot lunch together like a family. Throughout the day, the kids participate in a range of educational and social activities. At 5:45, the children take a break for an informal group discussion over sandwiches and tea. By 8:00 P.M., most of the children are returned home by the Friendship's Way van. The remaining sixteen kids consist of those from the most high-risk family situations. Spending an additional hour at Friendship's Way, they receive dinner and extra time for enrichment activities and personal attention.

It is Friendship's Way's philosophy that education is a path to equality. One of the main differences between the Neighborhood Home and other after-school centers is that children receive assistance with homework in addition to approximately fifteen hours a week of formal and informal lessons in Hebrew, Arabic, English, and math. Special interest clubs are also offered in sports, drama, chorus, music, science, dance, arts and crafts, and health education.

Periodic consultation meetings take place with school psychologists, guidance counselors, and teachers. In addition, Friendship's Way provides regular updates to Jaffa's Welfare services, reporting on the children's physical and emotional welfare and family situation. In cases of severe neglect and abuse, a Child Protection Official/Social Worker may remove children in danger from their homes as a result of Friendship's Way intervention.

To best meet the needs of the child, the Friendship's Way staff works in close coordination with their families. Parents are required to play an active role in their children's education They meet regularly with the Friendship's Way staff and pay a monthly symbolic fee. Fifteen mothers participate in a weekly discussion group on issues of child raising.

Special consideration has been placed on teaching the children tolerance and respect. Activities include group discussions that deal with stereotypes and prejudices, and celebrations of Jewish, Muslim, and Christian holidays and traditions. They learn about each other's folklore through songs, dance, and stories. All written material appears in both Hebrew and Arabic.

The cost for running these activities is minimal, since they are led by professional volunteers on the premises of Friendship's Way. Volunteers come from around the world and commit themselves to at least one year of service.

Traditional Creativity in the Schools Project

Since 1991, the Centre for Creativity in Education and Cultural Heritage has conducted a folklore and coexistence project called *Traditional Creativity in the Schools,* which focuses on three problem areas: cultural pluralism, social integration, and generation gaps within each community, and coexistence between neighboring Arab and Jewish communities.

The program is conducted with pairs of Jewish and Arab schools in Ramle and Jerusalem. These schools were chosen because the communities have mixed populations and the participants are more likely to encounter each other that in many other places in Israel. The program will soon be expanded to include schools with large populations of new immigrants.

Classes participate for a three-year cycle, meeting one another between ten to fifteen times over this period. Throughout the year, the children examine their own cultural environment and folklore, collecting information from parents and grandparents. The paired Jewish and Arab classes come together three to five times per school year to explore, for example, both communities' traditions in play, food, and oral history. So far, programs have been conducted in four schools involving 520 children, 120 active family members, and 35 teachers and principals.

The aim is for children to learn more about their own folklore and about the culture of the various other ethnic and religious groups and open a window into each other's daily life and traditions. With various family members helping to create a mosaic of family history and cultural heritage, the center expects to see a refreshed relationship between generations, with parents and grandparents acknowledged by the schools as having wisdom to impart. The two schools' staff work together on education whereas ordinarily they have no framework even to visit each other's schools. The children see their teachers, parents and grandparents working together, visible role models of coexistence and multiculturalism. The ultimate objective is that groups of people (children, parents, grandparents, teachers), having worked together for several years, help to develop a climate for coexistence, tolerance, and self-respect.

The programs run throughout the school year. They are ongoing from one school year to the next. The Project Team works with pupils and Form Teachers in weekly class meetings in each school. Joint activities between the paired Jewish and Arab classes take place every five to six weeks in alternate schools; separate or joint feedback classes are held every seventh week. Exhibitions and joint End of Year community events are also organized.

The themes for fifth and sixth grade, respectively, are *Traditional Play* and *Traditional Foodways*. Subjects of study are chosen in consultation with the school staff and pupils, based on folklore and traditions found in the students' homes. Pupils ask their parents and grandparents questions about these subjects and bring information and examples to class. Background lessons are given by project staff and teachers on, for example, outdoor games around the world, food acquisition, and preservation in hunter/gatherer societies, and the way information passes by word of mouth from one generation to another. The paired Jewish and Arab classes meet for joint activities. Members of students' families (as folk artists) teach, according to different traditions and practices of their childhood, activities such as jump rope and hopscotch, the making of rag dolls, hand puppets, kites, pickles, and clay pita ovens.

The third year theme (grade 7) is *Learning from Ourselves: Active Archives*. Students assemble and maintain bilingual Active Archives out of recipes, photographs, cassettes, and oral histories they collect over the three years. They record stories and songs from family members and work on family photograph albums and histories. In joint meetings, the pupils sing each other's songs and introduce their family stories. They annotate photographs of their joint past activities, reinforcing both their sense of having shared experiences and the knowledge they have acquired of each other's life. They design photographic exhibitions that are open to their communities.

Teaching Democracy

Israelis, like Americans, believe that democracy is the most tolerant form of government. By teaching the principles of democracy from an early age children learn that everyone has the right to live in freedom and that ethnic and cultural differences are legitimate components of a pluralistic society.

The Adam Institute for Democracy & Peace

The institute runs programs in approximately 100 schools (mostly junior and senior high schools, through a program for kindergarten and elementary schools is soon to begin). Programs are also run with youth movements, community centers and other groups outside the schools.

The democracy-education program for preschool and elementary school children was developed based on the assumption that children who encounter democratic options at an early stage are likely to choose it and adopt it as their worldview. The program helps children come to know their everyday reality and hones their ability to cope with the clash between the desires of different individuals in society.

This program begins with the recognition of the right to be different. The first section is devoted to recognizing the uniqueness of each individual, beginning with oneself, and acceptance of those who are different. The second part is devoted to clarifying the concept of equality. It is made up of the following subtopics:

(a) Understanding the distinction between mathematical equality and equality of worth.
(b) Examining the concept of equality in society.
(c) Recognizing the equal right to be different.

The education message is that "I am different from my friend, just as my friend is different from me, but that we are at the same time equal."

The program's second section deals with the principles of democracy. Democracy is defined as "a social covenant between people who agree to recognize the equal right of each person to live according to his or her beliefs and values, so long as he or she recognizes the corresponding right of others to the same."

The first two sections lay the foundations for internalizing the democratic concept. The last three sections look at the following topics:

• Rights—Clarification of the concept, clarification of the relationship between rights and obligations, conflicts between rights, rights of children and adults.

- Majority rule—Clarification of when the majority must decide, understanding the majority decision as a means and not as an end, recognition of the need for limits on majority decisions.
- The nature of law—Definition of the concept, clarification of the need for laws, equality under the law, limits to obedience.

The Rules of the Game: Understanding and Implementing Democratic Procedures

Jewish and Arab Israeli high school teachers jointly developed a curriculum and materials on democracy for use in their eleventh grade classes. The curriculum is aimed at acquainting students with the universal principles of democracy; the significance of human and minority rights within the principles of democracy; the historical and comparative background of democratic ideas and practices and the ways and means through which an informed and involved citizen is able to influence governments' decisions and actions. "Democracy" is examined from an interdisciplinary point of view—history, philosophy, psychology, sociology, logic, political science, communication, and legal studies. A cognitive approach is stressed, appealing to human reason rather than personal sentiments and feelings: distinguishing empirical findings from value judgments, evidence from hearsay and a logical argument from an emotional one.

The Rules of the Game allows Jewish and Arab Israelis, as well as secular and religious Jews, to find a common denominator. Stressing the themes of democracy, human rights, and coexistence, "The Rules" can be adapted to any context in which there is stress and conflict.

The program employs and teaches two kinds of strategies—knowledge-based and experiential-based. Knowledge-based strategies include an interdisciplinary curriculum, logical interconnections, rational orientation, and a multivocal text. Experiential-based strategies include simulations, role playing, encounter groups, and student self-government. The curriculum contains several volumes:

Volume 1

- the citizen and the democratic state: the individual's public involvement as sustaining democracy.
- Voluntary associations, interest groups, and political parties as the mediating bodies between the individual and the democratic state.
- The democratic civic culture: A necessary condition for a democratic government.
- Is there a democratic civil culture in Israel?

Volume 2

A. *Mass Media and Democracy*

- Mass media—between the citizens and the government.
- Mass media and civic liberties.

- Limitations on freedom of expression and the mass media.
- The media: A looking glass or a magnifying glass?
- Political propaganda: let us read between the lines.

B. *"Rule of Law" and the democratic state*

- The meaning of "Rule of Law." Is a constitution a "must" for a democratic state? An ongoing debate.
- The Rule of Law: Selected Issues.

(1) Law and national security
(2) The question of civil disobedience

- The rule of law in the Israeli context: some problems and dilemmas.
- Law and individual rights: civil liberties and legislation—the current situation in Israel.
- The Israeli High Court of Justice and civil liberties.

Conclusions

As noted at the outset, Israelis approach the same objective from three different approaches. All three have proponents who make a case for the value of their methodologies. No attempt has been made here to evaluate the individual programs; instead, descriptions have been offered to allow people from other countries to look more closely at those that are of interest and make their own determinations. Obviously, none of the programs would continue, or receive funding, if they were not believed to be accomplishing at least some of their goals. Nevertheless, perhaps the one major criticism of nearly all the Israeli projects, including those left out of this study, is that they fail to perform rigorous evaluations of their activities.

Along with the broad philosophical differences in approach, a few more specific differences also exist. For example, Israelis in the field do not agree on whether it is better to make programs voluntary or integrate them into the compulsory curriculum. The advocates of compulsory coexistence education maintain that students who are paired throughout the school year develop greater understanding and lasting friendships. By integrating the program into the school curriculum, the idea that coexistence is as important as any other subject is reinforced. In addition, working with schools legitimates the program. The proponents of voluntary programs believe it is better to distinguish the activities from their compulsory studies. The participants do not feel coerced and take part because they value the objective. The admitted downside of this is that the people who volunteer are those most inclined toward coexistence.

Israelis also disagree as to the proper age for beginning coexistence programs. Everyone agrees that it is better to grow up in an environment that promotes tolerance; however, the language difference is viewed by some as a barrier to younger children. Others insist that differences of culture and language can easily be overcome at a young age. The Adam Institute, for example, maintains that if the principles of democracy are conveyed to young children, they will become part of a child's worldview.

Other differences in theory and practice exist, but it is possible to identify several common elements that contribute to the success of the various programs.

- *Recognition of the importance of language.* Language is at the base of one's national identity. Just as language creates bridges and ties between people, it can be an obstacle to contact. Hebrew is the dominant language in Israel (although Arabic is also an official language). While most Palestinians are bilingual, most Jews do not have a command of Arabic. Such language differences must be taken into account. On the other hand, the study of language can be used as a bridge for coexistence.

- *Coexistence can be an unstated goal.* The premise behind most of the experiential programs is to engage parties in joint activities that everyone enjoys. The close proximity will, over time, promote coexistence.

- *Programs should be at neutral sites.* The site of meetings, particularly for "encounters," is significant, and effects the quality of the activity. Ideally, the site should not be identified exclusively with either side of the conflict. A neutral, safe environment will make participants feel more comfortable and encourage participation in coexistence projects.

- *Teachers and administrators must support projects run in their schools.* The principal must demonstrate a clear interest in the program to ensure that it is viewed as an important component of the curriculum. Similarly, teachers' support is vital to encouraging student participation and supporting the changes resulting from the program.

- *Parents should be involved.* The support and cooperation of parents are essential. Projects should be viewed as an opportunity to spread the message of coexistence beyond the classroom and into homes and communities. Joint activities that involve the communities and parents foster mutual tolerance.

- *Preparation is needed prior to interactions.* Before engaging in any joint activities, it is important to spend time preparing for the meetings. Students and teachers should be intimately involved in planning the interactions. Sessions to examine stereotyped thinking, generalizations and prejudice are important to prepare groups for encounters. The establishment in advance of clear rules also makes meetings work more harmoniously.

- *Promoting coexistence is facilitated by government support.* The Israeli Ministry of Education provides an example of how a governmental body can play an important role in introducing coexistence projects into the schools. The ministry also plays a role in developing curricula and training teachers. Ministry-sponsored study days and workshops for teachers from different schools and backgrounds offer opportunities for promoting coexistence on the professional level and reinforcing educational projects. The ministry provides a model for public, nonprofit and private sector cooperation in integrating coexistence and democracy curricula and projects in the schools.

- *Careful student selection enhances prospects for success.* Highly motivated students will influence their peers.

- *It is important for projects to be consistent and ongoing.* Ongoing multiyear programs reinforce a consistent commitment to improving cross-cultural relations.

- *Internships can contribute to individual and community coexistence.* By having interns commit themselves to long-term service to the community, the importance of the project is reinforced. Pairing of people from groups in conflict as interns creates bonds between the two individuals and sets an example for the community.

Applicability

People from other countries can learn lessons from all three Israeli approaches. The techniques developed in Israeli "encounters" could easily be adapted for use elsewhere. Similarly, the "experiential" programs could be applied in other contexts by either copying the Israeli models or using them as examples of creative ways to bring groups in conflict together for relatively long periods of joint activities. Even Americans, who often take democratic principles for granted, can learn from Israel's approach to teaching these principles, especially to immigrants who come from undemocratic nations.

Note

1. Excerpted from *Building Bridges: Lessons for America from Novel Israeli Approaches to Promote Coexistence,* by Mitchell G. Bard, sponsored by The Abraham Fund and The American–Israeli Cooperative Enterprise (DC: AICE, 1997), available from AICE, 2810 Blaine Dr., Chevy Chase, MD 20815, Tel. 301-565-3918, Fax 301-587-9056, E-mail mbard@capaccess.org

Oasis of Peace:
A Community of Moral
Education in Israel

GRACE FEUERVERGER

IN MEMORY OF FATHER BRUNO HUSSAR

Introduction

On a rocky hill some thirty kilometers west of Jerusalem rests the village of Neve Shalom/Wahat Al-Salam. It is a cooperative community where Jewish and Arab families live together in peace. Their goal is to create a social, cultural, and political framework of equality and mutual respect in which the residents maintain their own cultural heritage, language, and identity. The community was founded in 1972 as an intercultural experiment, and the first families took up residence there in 1978. Today it is a small but thriving village with a growing sheepfold and a large olive orchard planted on the slopes of its hillside.

A major focus of this study is on the bilingual/bicultural/binational elementary school that is coordinated by a teaching team of Jewish and Arab educators, some of whom are residents of the village and some of whom live in neighboring villages. My intention was to explore those interactions among the students and teachers, emanating from their sense of shared purpose that reflects their assumptions about the nature of education in their village and about the type of society they wish to promote through education. The Neve Shalom/Wahat Al-Salam School attempts to foster cooperation and mutual respect for its students of both Arab and Jewish backgrounds. It aspires to be a genuine bilingual, bicultural learning environment and could potentially provide a new and global dimension for exploring moral issues within the context of cultural and linguistic diversity and intergroup conflict. Although there has been substantial research on various aspects of language, identity, and intercultural relations in many parts of the world (see for example Cummins, 1989; Feuerverger, 1991; Lo Bianco, 1989; Ogbu, 1978; Samuda, 1986; Wong-Fillmore, 1989) there has been very little work on the specific consequences of bilingual/bicultural programs in which children from majority and minority groups learn together against a larger backdrop of intergroup conflict.

Moral Responsibility and a Theoretical
Framework: Objectives of the Study

There is very little qualitative research that focuses on a social grouping in which the residents are actively dedicated to issues of conflict resolution and peacemaking in their daily lives. This paper intends to explore the social and psychological complexities of moral development through this specific educational experience. "Moral experience" here will refer to the "lived experience" (see Dilthey, 1977 in Tappan and Brown, 1989) of my participants as they are confronted with everyday situations filled with moral conflicts, ambiguities, and dilemmas. I have focused on giving meaning to their "lived experiences" by presenting them in narrative form. There is a growing understanding in the research literature of narrative as a powerful way of giving meaning to human life experiences (see for example, Gilligan, 1982; Mishler, 1986; Polkinghorne, 1988; Sarbin, 1986; and so forth). This theoretical approach parallels Gilligan's focus on the analysis of moral voice and development by using narrative as a vehicle to examine conflicts and their possible resolution in interpersonal relationships (in Tappan and Brown, 1989, p. 199). Tappan and Brown (1989, p. 182) note that narrative is central to the study of, as well as to the teaching of morality, and that authorship of moral choices, actions, and feelings develops a sense of moral sensibility. Indeed, the deepening crisis in American schools and society (see Kozol, 1991) is obliging educators to explore educational programs that encourage moral development in its students through narrative. This study offers a narrative of what can be termed a peace education initiative and involves personal and professional accounts of teachers' and students' lives in terms of moral educational issues.

Some research questions that guided my inquiry were:

(1) What perceptions of the conflict and more generally of the world do these teacher/educators bring to the classroom and how do these perceptions interact with those of the students in the class?
(2) How do they envision themselves and their respective identities as Jews and Arabs caught in a very complex human struggle?
(3) How are these views enacted in their school curriculum choices and communication within the classroom?
(4) Does the school incorporate an egalitarian multicultural philosophy into its curriculum?

My observations in the school and my conversations with my participants affirm Giroux's claim that "[cultural] difference in this case . . . opens the possibilities for constructing pedagogical practices that deepen forms of cultural democracy that serve to enlarge one's moral vision" (1991, p. 509).

Moral Dilemmas and the Dialogic Relationship between Justice and Care

Kohlberg (1985) argued that the classroom atmosphere is crucial to moral development in the sense that students have the opportunity to make meaningful decisions in school as a means of self-empowerment. The "just community" school developed by Kohlberg emphasizes not only democratic principles but also the notion of gemeinschaft community with the ideals of group solidarity and a commitment to care and responsibility that promote a sense of integration and unity (Power,

Higgins, and Kohlberg, 1989). This approach to schooling was derived from the practice of a democratic communal education model that he witnesses on an Israeli kibbutz (see Kohlberg, 1971). What the kibbutz represented to Kohlberg, which was then incorporated into the "just community" model, was the emphasis on a collective or shared consciousness that would represent the norms and values of the group and thus create a strong basis for moral development and responsibility. The village of Neve Shalom/Wahat Al-Salam may reflect in some important respects a "just community" but there are also significant differences. The villagers do not share the same religious and cultural values and norms, nevertheless they do ascribe to similar underlying beliefs in equality and justice. In other words, there appears to be a collective consciousness about peaceful coexistence and respect for both the Arab and Jewish identity. Nevertheless, moral dilemmas arise frequently among individuals due to the intergroup conflict in the wider society that influences their daily lives.

It appears that these emotional issues cannot be explained solely through cognitive-development theory but rather through a new focus on a different methodology of interview and interpretation. Gilligan (1982) claims that a different development pattern could emerge when thinking is "contextual and inductive rather than formal and abstract." According to Gilligan (1982) and Gilligan et al. (1988) there are two different moral voices or ways in which to resolve moral issues: "justice" and "care" and there is a dialogic relationship between the two. Tappan (1991) elaborates on this notion by putting forth the Bakhtinian view of "an ongoing inner moral dialogue between justice and care. The dialogue between the voices goes back and forth—the justice voice speaks the language of fairness and equality and advocates one solution . . . while the care voice speaks the language of relationship and responsibility, and advocates another solution. . . . [People] frequently oscillate from one voice to another when responding to and resolving problems, conflicts, and dilemmas in their lives" (p. 248–49). In Neve Shalom/Wahat Al-Salam these moral voices are constantly being played out. In the school, the Jewish and Arab teachers are constantly negotiating the curriculum, especially in the case of history, social studies, and current events. I therefore see both theoretical approaches as significant in my paper on moral development at Neve Shalom/ Wahat Al-Salam. Firstly, there is Kohlberg's notion of the "just community" . . . with its emphasis on building a sense of gemeinschaft . . . Community here is a "normative concept that entails a valuing of the ideal of group solidarity and a commitment to norms of care and responsibility that promote this sense of unity" (in Power, 1988, p. 198–99). Secondly, there is Gilligan's research that uses a narrative approach in the study of moral development and moral education (see Gilligan, 1982; Gilligan, Brown, and Rogers, 1990; etc.)

An Interactive Methodology

My sojourn in the village took place in December–January of 1991/92. The study was based on a strong interactive relationship between myself and my participants through dialogue and conversation. The research approach for this study therefore involved a variety of qualitative methodologies. Case study and narrative methodologies were adopted in order to document the construction and reconstruction of the meaning of teaching and learning from a moral perspective for the individual teachers, students, and parents in the specific bilingual/bicultural school setting of the village of Neve Shalom/Wahat Al-Salam. (See Connelly and Clandinin, 1990; Eisner and Peshkin, 1990; Hopkins, 1987; Huberman and Miles, 1984; Yin, 1984.) I therefore chose a narrative approach in order to give voice to the moral/educational initiatives that these villagers are creating. Carol Witherell (1991) states that we "as educators are inescapably involved in the formation of moral communities as well as the shaping of persons" (p. 239) and I highlight the phrase Maxine Greene adapted from Toni Morrison's novel *Beloved* (1987) to say that "moral education requires becoming friends of one another's minds, even, perhaps especially, when the other is 'stranger'" (see Witherell, 1991, p. 238–39). In this process all participants were encouraged to reflect on their own personal philosophy on intergroup relations vis-à-vis the teaching and learning experience. Indeed, ethnographic and narrative research methodology was required here because of its emphasis on "thick" description, on process, and on the natural setting (i.e., the classroom, the home, the village) as the source of data (see for example Janesick, 1991).

Through the vehicle of narrative, I try to make sense of the personal as well as the professional experiences of my participants in their quest for intercultural harmony. Finally, within the theoretical framework of this study, the specific educational initiative of this school as a "moral community" provides a window through which the issues of schools' relationships to multicultural and multiracial communities can be observed and elucidated more generally in a global context. I documented the experiences of the children and teachers through in-depth interviews and participant observation in the school, and through a general "reflection-in-living" (see Schon, 1990) within the village. The interviews were unstructured and as open-ended as possible. The specific details of the project were worked out collaboratively with the school directors, teachers, parents, and the children in Neve Shalom/Wahat Al-Salam. Students and teachers shared with me their stories about why they decided to live in this village; about the dreams that they had for the children's future; about their great satisfaction with the school; and about the fragile sense of hope they nurtured for peace in their troubled land. The interviews were tape recorded and, in addition, field-note gathering and extensive journal writing took place. These data were transcribed after I returned to Canada and then were interpreted. In the telling of this research story, my intent is to contribute towards an understanding of the teaching-learning process taking place in an atmosphere of social-political conflict.

Moral Development through Narratives of Lived Experiences

The village of Neve Shalom/Wahat Al-Salam is a social-psychological experiment—a place where people of a certain level of educational and personal conviction have chosen to come together to enact a collective vision of justice and care. The villagers are on the whole well-educated, liberal-minded and interested in giving their children a chance at a more peaceful future. Their philosophy of a Jewish–Arab village in Israel living and teaching peace and equality is rooted in the democratic ideals of discussion and cooperative problem solving. But it is not as simple and idyllic as that. It is a "flesh-and-blood" place within a very difficult human circumstance where intergroup conflict in the wider society and the moral problems and dilemmas that ensue are constantly being played out and negotiated. It is probably safe to assume that most individuals from fundamentalist Islamic or Orthodox Jewish backgrounds would be opposed to this type of environment. Indeed, the impression I gained from informal discussions with people in various parts of Israel, both Arab and Jewish, was that this village is looked upon with uncertainty as experimental and is based on a self-selected group of committed people dedicated to an integrated school system and peaceful coexistence. The concern of many was whether such an endeavor could work in a larger context. To be fair, there are other areas in Israel where Jews and Arabs live together in relatively peaceful circumstances but in most cases the children are schooled separately. The Neve Shalom/Wahat Al-Salam school is open not only to the village children but now also serves children from various neighboring Jewish and Arab villages. It therefore finds itself within the wider arena of mutual fear and distrust and prejudice and stereotype. The village is not an island unto itself by any means. Many of the villagers work in nearby Jerusalem or Tel Aviv, and are subject to the social and political turmoil that envelops all of Israel.

The discussion that follows has two levels of discourse. Firstly it reflects my impressions of the village and the school, both the physical and psychological surroundings. Furthermore, it explores the process of narrating stories of moral development and thereby authoring one's moral lived experiences and ultimately taking responsibility for action. There are a number of metathemes that I will explore in the narrative structure of this study. They are:

- The commitment of the participants to confront the central question of Jewish-Arab coexistence on a grassroots level within the village and school;
- The school is a microsociety and a moral community that can be used as a role model for conflict resolution and peacemaking;
- The village as a symbol for creating a dialogue between Arabs and Jews in the larger Israeli society: negotiation and compromise in an atmosphere of moral dilemma and goodwill.

My imagination as an educator and researcher was captured by the stories that two of the educators, Salim and Joel. (see note 1, p. 512) began to tell about the history of the village and its people and about the bilingual/bicultural/binational school. I wanted to present a picture that conveys the tough moral struggles that confront these individuals on a daily basis. Their lives are, in fact, a microcosm of the Jewish–Palestinian dilemma.

Conversation/Dialogue as a Tool
in Data Gathering

Conversation became one of the most successful data-gathering tools during my stay. The following is a journal entry of mine in the first days of the sojourn:

I am so exhausted, it's hard to describe it. Everything is happening so fast and emotionally I feel as if I'm on a rollercoaster. I am stunned by how hard these people are trying to break through the Jewish-Arab impasse. There is an amazing sense of goodwill and sharing that permeates the whole village. Right now I want to mention how frustrated I've been—trying to interview some of the people. Every time I try to set up an appointment, I am faced with a very noncommittal attitude. And yet I feel that they are very pleased with my research project and with my being here. I've been invited to dinners and am having amazing discussions with many people. But the minute I try to formalize a time for an interview I'm staring at a blank wall. And yet I know they feel comfortable with me. Maybe I'm trying to go too fast! . . . Oh golly, I just realized what the problem is! I've been superimposing my own values onto their values. They perceive making "appointments" as distant and unfriendly. . . . I think. I've just worked out something important here. I will have to discard this North American urban approach and just go along with their rhythm. I will have to stop being in a hurry and just listen.

I began to realize that I had to slow down and allow the voices of the villagers to emerge at their own pace. I had to have faith in the participant-observation process. In order to optimize data collection, I have to let go of my own researcher needs and put the needs of my participants first. They needed to get to know me. I decided to cast a wide net and I began to simply enjoy being in this community. My most interesting data emerged out of very ad hoc situations. I would be walking along the road en route to someone's house or back to my room for some rest and I would bump into a villager and we would begin to talk. Spontaneously we would engage in conversation about the school and the raison d'être of the village in general. Conversations around dinner tables in people's homes and in the school staff room provided gold mines of information. These conversations were a collective, interactive process where we would learn how our individual life stories had been shaped by our specific family and social histories. It was often when the tape recorder was not running that I gained the most precious information. On these many occasions, I would reconstruct the conversations through notes that I wrote when I returned to my room.

The data were shaped by and evolved out of the relationships I formed through interaction with all sorts of people in the village. The conversations continually pointed to the underlying tension of differential cultural, linguistic, historical, and religious systems: many frameworks of meaning in competition with one another. What emerged, too, from my encounters was the significance placed by the villagers on interpersonal relationships as a means of conflict resolution. They reflected a sense of belonging to a community that articulated clearly the expectations for peace and equality between Israeli Jews and Arabs. My conversations revealed a group of people involved in the transformation of individual as well as collective consciousness; a society with a commonality of purpose towards mutual understanding. Power (1988) explains that "this shared consciousness represents the authority of the group and is the real agency of moralization" (p. 203). Through conversations with the participants, I gained a glimpse of how these people are constructing meaningful lives through their common goal of peacemaking.

The Village and School: A Brief Description

The Hebrew and Arabic words Neve Shalom/Wahat Al-Salaam mean "Oasis of Peace" in English. Indeed, the village is a small oasis within a deeply polarized country. It is nestled on a hilltop surrounded by green fields full of wild flowers and olive groves and other collective settlements in the area such as kibbutzim and moshavim. At the bottom of the hill several kilometers away is the Latrun Monastery and its vineyards run by French Trappist monks. There are two means of access to the village: an old dirt road that is very bumpy and muddy in bad weather, or the new blacktop road that circles around fields and orchards. In the fields not far from this road, but blocked from view by a small forest, are the tents and sheep of a Bedouin family who have lived there even before the existence of the village. As one enters the village, the first buildings are the youth hostel and dining hall. The view of the rolling and peaceful Avalon valley below is breathtaking. Looking westward on a very clear day at sunset one can catch a glimpse of the reflection of the Mediterranean sea in the far distance. There is a small main road with small white houses and red roofs on either side. They reflect the diversity of the population. Some have a traditional Arabic style; others are a mixture of European and Middle Eastern design. Each home has a pretty garden filled with all sorts of spices, vegetables, and fruits. Many plants grow wild all over the village.

The population of the village is approximately twenty-five families and three single members. There are fifty-four offspring from these families, ranging in age from eight months to twenty-two years. At this time (fall, 1994) there are three pregnant mothers. There is a waiting list of about fifty families who have applied to live in the village. The community is administered by a steering committee; the secretariat, which meets regularly once week and whenever necessary. All matters requiring a decision of principle are considered by the plenum. The plenum consists of all residents, but only full members are entitled to vote. The plenum may return matters to the secretariat with the authority to make a final decision. The secretariat may decide to put matters to a final vote in the plenum for a final decision. Once made, a final decision has to be adhered to by the community. The community is governed by a constitution that is reviewed from time to time. Several internal committees take care of various activities in the life of the community. All members of the secretariat and the committees are democratically elected each year. It is interesting to note that a balanced ratio of Jews and Arabs is observed throughout the community. The secretariat is always served by two Arabs and two

Jewish members, plus the secretary. The secretary is elected on merit and availability, but not strictly in rotation.

The school is at the northeast side of the village whereas the entrance to the village is at the southwest. The school consists of three small buildings: a kindergarten, the multigrade elementary schoolhouse with a kitchen/staff room in the middle, and a bomb shelter that is used as another classroom. It is an open plan designed allowing a lot of freedom of movement. It is a small, closely knit environment and most of the students have at least one sibling attending along with them. Some of the teachers have their own children in the school. There are approximately ninety-five children from kindergarten to Grade 8 with two kindergarten teachers and thirteen elementary teachers. Each class has one Jewish and one Arab teacher who work in a team-teaching mode. There is also a preschool class with nine toddlers. The children feel very comfortable in the school. It is definitely their school and one is immediately struck by their sense of ownership and the sense of empowerment that derives from it. Village dogs are always sniffing around the open porch of the school and in the yard, waiting for the children to come out and play with them at recess, lunch and at the end of the day. It is a noisy, gregarious, happy place.

The elementary school first opened its doors in September 1984; the preschool and kindergarten three years earlier. This school is innovative in its unabiding commitment to educate its students in a full Arabic-Hebrew bilingual, bicultural setting. Joel, my host and the English and history teacher in the school, took me to the preschool first, where the children were hopping around, amid toys and two very cheerful caregivers. Joel explained that one was Arab and one was Jewish, and this was the case for all levels of schooling. This way the children always had the opportunity to speak the language that they were most familiar with and to identify their teacher with their ethnic group. Joel and I then walked up a stony pathway to the kindergarten. Inside, a very busy scene greeted me. The children, about fifteen of them, were involved in making decorations for the Christmas tree, a pine tree standing bare at the back of the room. Scissors and colored paper and tinsel sparkled in the air.

Some of the children came up to me, curious to know who I was. In a small village, a stranger does not get lost. I spoke with the two teachers—Karima, the Arab teacher and Ronit, the Jewish teacher. The person in charge of the decorating lesson was a teacher's aide named Afwa and she was Arab too, but a Christian Arab. It should be noted that both Muslim and Christian Arabs live in Neve Shalom/Wahat Al-Salam as well as Jews. One part of the curriculum is devoted to the teaching of Jewish and Arab identity. Each child is taught to understand what their culture is all about and also learns about the other's culture. The goal is coexistence, tolerance, and friendship, but not assimilation. Maintaining personal, social, and national identity is of utmost importance. Religion is taught separately but there are joint discussions as well. The children learn about all the holidays of these three great religions within class time. They had just finished learning about Hannukah, the Jewish Festival of Lights, and Maouled, the birthday of the Muslim Prophet Mohammed before that. And now it was time to prepare for discussing Christmas. The children explained to me that it is important to respect each person's religion. All the children were sharing their decorations and helping each other with the cutting and pasting. Then Joel and I left the kindergarten and walked to the school not far away. It was a little stone building and there were a few dogs ambling about. I walked in and was swept away in a flurry of classroom activities. The first thing I noticed was how cheerful and busy the atmosphere was: easygoing and hard-working at the same time. The first drawing I noticed on the wall was a Santa Claus that had been painted by one of the students. It was a special picture and embodied, I think, the message of this village. There were gold Jewish stars on top of the Baba Noel and the Arabic for Baba Noel on the bottom. There was also a mural on the wall created by the children of drawings of Jerusalem from the different religious and cultural perspectives. For example there was the Al-Aqsa Mosque with the Arabic describing it; the Western Wall with a text in Hebrew explaining its significance; and the Church of the Holy Sepulchre with an Arabic explanation.

Stories of Moral Dilemmas

As participant–observer, I saw how the teachers were facilitators in the moral development of themselves and their students. The underlying message at the Neve Shalom/Wahat Al-Salam school in terms of teacher development was the constant need among the participants for negotiation, discussion, dialogue, and change in terms of what is "right or wrong" for curriculum development and classroom instructional practices. However, this need was often very difficult to put into practice. The discussions were frequently heated and problematic as a result of the moral dilemmas that shape the reality of the sociopolitical climate in which Neve Shalom/Wahat Al-Salam is located. I was witness to a great deal of "moral negotiation" among the teachers and students. On a cognitive level, what emerged as sacred was to present each side of the story, unresolved conflicts and all. On a deeper emotional level, the situation was much more complicated than that. The narratives that follow explore the complex nature of the participants' moral responses to one another and to themselves. I present excerpts of stories from various teachers and students in order to better understand their moral experiences and their moral development. The following section will examine more closely the difficult issues that were discussed through the telling of stories from the participants' life experiences.

Joel who teaches English and history at the school describes the delicate "pas de deux" that is necessary in order to sort out competing value systems and to bring equity into the history and social science curricula. He explains the risk taking that is involved in this endeavor and the benefits of shared decision-making that lead to shared ownership of the curriculum:

There's a lot of interaction between Ibrahim (a Palestinian teacher) and one regarding how we look at historical symbols. For example, the Israeli War of Independence is obviously not looked upon as independence for the Palestinians. Language is so powerful. We have to present both points of view and that's what we're grappling with. We've gotten onto some harsh disputes, sometimes noisily, sometimes in silence. It's such a delicate process. But we're moving forward and then you see the flash of a breakthrough and what a great feeling. It's all worth it because we're trying to give our children a better future. The children are being presented with both the Arab and Jewish perspective. Many times we can't resolve issues but at least we're facing the problem—which at least allows the children to reflect on these problems in a more balanced way.

One could argue that the village of Neve Shalom/Wahat Al-Salam offers an ideal of a small society in its attempts at respecting differences and inspiring a moral vision of dialogue and equality in the midst of a geopolitical framework of conflict. Nevertheless on the one hand there is a push for a sense of community and integration in the village; and on the other hand there is a need to maintain the Jewish and Arab identities as separate entities. The tension between these two goals is quite evident in the various moral dilemmas that constantly confront the villagers and also affect the objectives of the school. The following narratives are intended to provide a brief picture of various moral dilemmas that have no easy solutions and as such have significant implications for moral education in a larger perspective. These stories ask us to reconsider our "ways of knowing" (see Belenky et al., 1986) by illuminating very complex issues of human conflict.

Avi, a Jewish teacher who lives in the village, describes a moral conflict that enveloped the whole village during the Gulf War in January 1991.

The Gulf War affected the village in a very deep way. I think it was one of the very few times that you could feel a difference between the Jews and Arabs here. It polarized the community in a very unsettling way. Since I've been here (approximately ten years) I don't remember a more difficult separation emotionally. Of course it's never absolute and not everyone was polarized. But it did open up some deep splits. What surprised me most was that although we were all under the same threat (of being bombed by Iraq) and we were all anxious and frightened and living together and helping each other in the bomb shelter, I felt the Arabs were not as scared as the Jews. There was a difference in the feeling of threat. That's what I think—I mean we were all in this together—but it was different. Underneath it all, I think the Arabs still saw Iraq as an Arab country, and they reacted differently. We had discussions about this and they were very helpful and meaningful. We're still working through it.

Avi explained that, morally, the issue was difficult to resolve because a doubt was planted in the minds of many of the people in the village. An emotional rift had been created that needed repair.

We talked about the fact that naturally the Arabs will identify with their people in other countries in the Middle East but it left some of us feeling let down and worried. The Jews saw Saddam unequivocally as a mad dictator who was bent on destruction but many of the Arabs were ambivalent because after all Iraq was an Arab country and their identification is with the Arab world. In all fairness many Arabs in the village were just as against what Saddam Hussein was up to as the Jews were. Nevertheless, it brought up such complicated emotions that we are still working on and showed clearly that we are two different peoples with different histories and cultures. But that doesn't mean that we can't learn to live in peace. And the arguments didn't bring about clear divisions among Arab versus Jew: Many Jews disagreed with one another and same for many Arabs among themselves. It is important to mention that.

This kind of moral reasoning based on narrative provides Avi and the other participants the opportunity to "author" their own moral perspectives and in this way it encourages as Bakhtin (1986) claims the search for one's own (authorial) voice to be embodied, to become more clearly defined . . . to cast off reservations . . . not to remain tangential (but) to burst into the circle of life (and) become one among other people (p. 147).

Osamah who grew up in a small Arab village in the north of Israel and who lives in Neve Shalom/Wahat Al-Salam and works in Jerusalem explained the Gulf War conflict this way:

The Gulf War was unfortunate in one way, but clarifying in another. It pointed to the fact that Jews and Arabs in Israel do live separate lives culturally, religiously, politically. Our identities revolve around different symbols and different values and I think we have to be honest about that. As Arabs we have always felt isolated within the Israeli society, marginalized in many ways. So we certainly do not want to lose our ties with the rest of the Arab world. Our reaction to the Gulf War was more a question of retaining some thread to other Arabs. It doesn't mean that we necessarily agreed with Saddam Hussein's policies. But naturally we are emotionally involved with the people in Iraq as Arabs. Just as Jews would be involved with other Jews in different parts of the world. But living in this village teaches me daily that having different allegiances is not necessarily a bad thing as long as we have certain social and personal values that are based on sound moral principles. Maybe that's easier said than done. But we must teach our children to learn to respect each other's difference. It's an issue of trust that is most difficult.

Both Avi and Osamah reflect the psychological complexities inherent in the moral dilemma that emerged from the emotional "fallout" of the Gulf War. They both went on to describe that all the members of the village were encouraged to discuss these issues in ad hoc meetings. There were a great deal of ambivalent feelings that emerged and heavy arguments but the most significant outcome was that they were together thrashing out the issues. The teachers and directors of the school had to sit down and work out strategies in order to resolve these dilemmas with their students. These moral issues were not simply "add-ons" to the curriculum but inherent in and a part of the everyday classroom life in the school.

For example, the children were also greatly affected by the atmosphere created by the Gulf War and this issue became an explicit part of the class curriculum in all grades. Shuli, a third grader, and Yaakov, who is in Grade 6, were two young boys who discussed some moral conflicts in terms of the Gulf War from their point of view:

Shuli: You know in our school some of the Arab kids said things like: "Go Iraq, go Iraq!" And the Jewish kids said that Iraq was wrong.

Yaakov: We argued about it in class all the time all during the war. Even with my best friend. He's Arab and he kept saying that Saddam is right and is the son of all nations. And the Jewish kids felt that Saddam was crazy and bad. But we stayed friends because our teachers talked to us about what was going on and told us that we both have a right to our opinions but that when everything is all over we still will live together and it's better to live together as friends.

Mohammed, a child from a nearby Arab village, who is bussed to the Neve Shalom/Wahat Al-Salam school explained why he sang the pro-Saddam songs:

I sang the songs because the other kids in the village were singing them. They made me feel proud about being Palestinian and Arab. I didn't mean it to hurt my friends at the school who were Jewish. I don't think they understood how much better it made me feel about being Arab. I tried to explain it to them during our discussions with the teachers. It's hard because people were feeling angry and scared.

Zahar, a twelve-year-old girl who lives in another nearby Arab village and attends the Neve Shalom/Wahat Al-Salam school was torn between two allegiances. She described her moral dilemma:

In my village many of the kids got very excited about Saddam and shouted the slogans and sang the songs and I wanted to go along with them and be part of what my friends were doing. But at Neve Shalom/Wahat Al-Salam the teachers were telling us to see both sides of the problem. We have a class called actualia (current events) and both my Arab and Jewish teachers in the class talked with us for many days about trying to find peace and not war. They also explained how much better it would be if countries in the Middle East could be friends and not enemies. Not only are many Arabs enemies with Jews but many Arabs are enemies between themselves in different countries. But when I would go back home every day to my village some of my friends were mad at me because I was friendly with the Jewish kids. At least there were some of us from my village who go to the school so we stuck together. It made me very unhappy but I wasn't alone at least. And I decided not to shout those slogans or sing those songs. My parents wouldn't have wanted that.

Zahar's narrative and those of the other children tell an intricate tale of moral dilemma and development. They indicate the complex interrelationships in the lived experiences of the people involved with the Neve Shalom/Wahat Al-Salam school. As these participants explain, the issue of cultural identity and conflict of allegiance is an essential ingredient in the moral dilemma.

Another story of moral conflict in terms of identity formation and moral development was told by Ahmed who teaches in the school.

In the beginning I came here only to work. I was living in Jerusalem and was already married. I had been a student at the Hebrew University and became a journalist. I was getting tired of my journalist work and then I noticed an ad in the paper about the Neve Shalom/Wahat Al-Salam school needing teachers. It was 1988 and I worked there for two years and lived in Jerusalem. It was hard because I had to come by bus. It meant getting up very early and coming back very late every day. I was living in Arab Jerusalem (East Jerusalem) and there were events that forced me to decide where I belong. I knew these were my people, the Palestinians, but I didn't feel like I really belonged there. One morning when there was a general strike (as a result of the Intifada [see note 2, p. 512]) no one was working but I went to work at Neve Shalom/Wahat Al-Salam. It was very hard for me; I had to decide which side of the Green Line I belonged to. I had a little child by then and both my wife and I wanted to figure out a way to have our baby grow up in a good environment. So when they suggested to us to move to Neve Shalom/Wahat Al-Salam we decided to do it.

Ahmed's narrative was filled with moral ambiguities and challenges. Embedded within his story is the sense of guilt in having to choose "which side of the Green Line" he belongs. His narrative becomes a vehicle for exploring the cognitive and affective dimensions of his moral decision to leave his village in the West Bank and come to live in Neve Salom/Wahat Al-Salam. It reflects his intellectual and emotional struggle in attempting to solve a crucial moral dilemma. In "authoring" his own moral story, Ahmed offers insights into his personal development that bring a sense of meaning and moral value to the situation. As mentioned above, Bakhtin (1986) emphasizes the relationship between authoring one's own lived moral experiences and a sense of responsibility for action. This authorship allowed Ahmed to acknowledge his own moral perspective in the midst of conflict and tension and to emerge with a sense of his moral identity and authenticity (see Blasi, 1980).

It was such a difficult choice (to leave the West Bank village and move to Neve Shalom/Wahat Al-Salam) because I'm Palestinian but I have Israeli citizenship. That means—I don't know how to explain it—this feeling that you know they are my people, I belong to them, but because of the circumstances I have to move away from there and live in another place. I also realized that I was different from them because I was born and grew up in Israel and went to the Hebrew University. So that even though we (Ahmed's neighbors in the West Bank) speak the same language and have similar customs, we grew up in different places and have different mentalities. I had so many long discussions with my neighbors and friends. We spoke about the way we were feeling and it became clear that even though we had so much in common we did behave differently in terms of political choices. This was hard to admit. I had to recognize the fact that there was a split in my identity. For example, I made a pact with myself that I would not be involved in any stone throwing during demonstrations at the Israeli soldiers. I was in solidarity with my neighbors but I decided not to take part in violence. . . . This problem with identity for Israeli Arabs is very difficult. I think that Arabs even abroad now are beginning to understand this hard situation that we're in—that we don't feel like we totally belong in Israeli society but that we have different values from many in the West Bank.

It was through dialogue and reflection that Ahmed began to make sense of the moral dilemmas that had been thrust upon him. He began to shape his moral development by "authoring" his moral decisions on a gradual basis. The move to Neve Shalom/Wahat Al-Salam was a way of maintaining his Palestinian identity without having to reject his Israeli identification.

Abdul, a young Arab teacher who is new to the school and commutes from Jerusalem provides some insights into the special nature of the Neve Shalom/Wahat Al-Salam school in terms of Arab control over the curriculum and self-esteem:

What I like about this school is that the Arabs have more responsibility over their own education. This is not the case in most other schools in Israel. And this is one of the big problems for Israeli Arabs in terms of issues of identity and for a sense of self-esteem. At least in the West Bank, Arabs have their own school systems and universities. They have a clearer feeling of who they are, even with all the problems. Nobody is really looking at the problems that Arabs have in Israel proper. That's why Neve Shalom/Wahat Al-Salam is so special. It confronts that fact and tries to improve it and opens a line of communication. I get into a lot of arguments about it with the other teachers; we don't always know how to solve these problems but we're talking. That's so important. It means there's a chance for real change. It's also really good to see that the children are getting along well. They are given more opportunity to discuss their needs in terms of their language and cultural backgrounds.

Abdul explained that when there are disputes or arguments due to the political situation, the teachers don't "push it under the carpet." They discuss it with the children and listen to their voices.

Ariela, a Jewish teacher from a nearby village who is also new to the school expresses it this way:

I enjoy teaching here very much. It is good to have dialogue and to show us how things can work between Arabs and Jews. It is difficult but it works. There are so many emotions and years of hating and being afraid of each other. We have to learn not to blame each other. We have to try to live together side by side. If it's happening here, then it can happen elsewhere. The big thing is respect. That's what happens in this school and in this village. My ideas have become more open since I started to work here.

Ariela did have to interact with people in her village who were wary of the philosophical principles of the Neve Shalom/Wahat-Salam school; i.e., the idea that it is preferable for Jewish and Arab children to be schooled together on an everyday basis. She told me that some [of her villagers] were openly hostile to the idea. She was involved in a deep moral dialogue within herself and with these neighbors as far as arriving at the moral decision that her involvement in the Neve Shalom/Wahat Al-Salam school was the "right" thing to do.

It wasn't easy coming back home every day having to deal with some glowering faces. There are some in my village who feel that Arabs cannot be trusted and that they are all terrorists. So they see the school in Neve Shalom/Wahat Al-Salam as idealistically foolish at best and dangerous at worst. My feeling is that if they had had the opportunity of going to such a school maybe their attitudes would be more positive. I have been trying to discuss these issues with them and some are listening but others are too far away from the idea of the possibility of coexistence. What I find wonderful about the school is the hope that these attitudes can change with these Jewish and Arab children who are learning together side by side. They are being given the opportunity to see the situation in a different way on a more equal basis.

These teachers' comments support Giroux's (1991) notion of difference, equality, and social justice. The Neve Shalom/Wahat Al-Salam School explores ways to offer students curricula that will enable them to make judgments about how society is historically and socially constructed, and how existing social relationships structure inequalities around racism, sexism, and other forms of oppression (p. 508). Joel, for example, reflected on these issues as they relate to the current events classes:

> I originally taught that class with Salim (who is now one of the directors of the school) and we'd just both sit together and try to thrash it out. It doesn't mean that you don't get differences of opinion and that it's clear sailing. It's actually very hard but there's the significance of the fact that you have a Jewish and a Palestinian teacher trying to face the issues honestly and aboveboard. For example, after a terrorist attack that happened one morning in Jerusalem, Salim was directing the class and he brought out the issues of who profits from this type of activity. He said how it just increases the hatred and gives more power to the right-wing groups. The fact that an Arab teacher said that obviously meant something. It has an effect on both the Jewish and the Arab kids in the class. It opens up a line of communication, of real dialogue.

The daily events and interactions that take place at the school present a practical embodiment of Giroux's thesis that "educating for difference, democracy and ethical responsibility is not about enshrining reverence in the service of creating passive citizens. It is about providing students with knowledge, capacities, and opportunities to be noisy, irreverent and vibrant" (p. 509). Like Giroux, the teachers at Neve Shalom/Wahat Al-Salam speak to the necessity that students understand how cultural, ethnic, racial, and ideological differences enhance the possibility for dialogue, trust, and solidarity. They stress, as he does, the development of pedagogical contexts that promote compassion and tolerance rather than envy, hatred, and bigotry, and that provide opportunities for students to be border crossers (Giroux, p. 508). This idea of "border crossing" is a pedagogical approach that is being practiced on a daily basis in Neve Shalom/Wahat Al-Salam and it provides a new way of reading history as a way of reclaiming power and identity (see Aronowitz and Giroux, 1991). During my participant-observation at the school, I often witnessed the transformative power in the discourse of caring, equality, and justice in each classroom within the context of team teaching and cooperative learning.

There are two directors for the school; a Jewish woman and a Palestinian man. They both live in the village with their families. The team work that they display is enheartening. This school has been Chava's dream for many years and she was a key player in its development:

My husband and I met in Israel and then we spent some time in Sweden because he is Swedish. I then learnt about this village and we decided when we got back to Israel to move here. My dream was to open a school in the village and it is incredible that this dream has come true. And that it is not only growing but that children from Jewish and Palestinian villages outside of the village are now attending the school. Sometimes I can't believe that it is really happening! What is really exciting now is that the school is being formally recognized by the Ministry of Education, which means that we will be hopefully getting some funding and input from them. It gives a sense of normality and legitimization to the school that was missing up until now. Also we have hired some new teachers this year and they are excellent. There's a sense of "getting along" and things are going very smoothly because of that.

Salim explained the role that the school plays in enhancing a positive sense of identity for its students and commented on the moral development that is embedded within the daily educational discourse in the classes:

The Arab children who come to this school feel so much better about themselves. They feel a sense of equality here with the Jewish students. It really is a wonderful thing. There really are very few places where this happens on a formal and everyday level. In most cases Arabs feel very marginalized within Israeli society. In this school the children are able to share their stories and their experiences; their fears and their hopes. I think this school and this village is the hope for the next generation. There are all sorts of examples I can give you that would show how difficult moral issues are treated in the daily class lessons. The students and we the teachers live these problems all the time and they are there in every aspect of our teaching and learning.

The children had many opportunities for moral reflection and deliberation. They were encouraged to examine and communicate their view of a situation and to encounter those of their classmates. These classroom approaches reflect the words of Dewey (1909/1975) as quoted in Cuffaro (1995, p. 54): We need to see the moral principles are not arbitrary . . . that the term moral does not designate a special region or portion of life. We need to translate the moral into the conditions and forces of our community life, and into the impulses and habits of the individual.

I spent my first morning in the Grade 1 class with Arifa. Arifa lives in a nearby Arab village and commutes to the school every day. She is a natural teacher and all the children love her. She explained to me how important it is for a teacher to see the child first—not their cultural background:

You must see them with open eyes for the special qualities they have inside them. You must give them a chance to show you their unique self. And then I deal with whether they are Arab or Jewish. But only after we really get to know each other. I try so hard to keep an open mind. Nobody says it's easy. But it makes such a difference.

In her class, the children were collectively preparing their songs, poems, and stories for the Christmas party that was fast approaching. The atmosphere was festive and industrious. In this class Hebrew and Arabic were being used simultaneously. The children, guided by their teacher, were crafting themes revolving around war and loss and a hope for peace and normality. The class activities and discussions reflected the actual experiences that the children must deal with in their everyday lives. Their contributions to the curriculum were evident in this lesson. In fact, the teacher and her students shared in the development of the lesson and thus participated in the construction of knowledge and understanding of difficult moral issues within the social-political context in which they were situated. A few children recited this poem in Arabic, Hebrew, and English: I am a child with something to say/ Please listen to me/ I am a child who wants to play/ Why don't you let me?/ My toys are waiting for a chance/ Give us a chance/ Please, please give us a chance!/

What was remarkable about this presentation was that the children, Jewish, Moslem, and Christian, were singing in unison for peace and understanding: "We don't want guns, we want music and feasts and gifts from Baba Noel on this holiday." There was magic in this school. This little village school embodies a "moral community" where moral education focuses on the shaping of the self and the development of identity and equality. This philosophy concurs with Tappan and Brown's (1989) claim that such an educational endeavor can be called a "poststructuralist" or "postmodern" approach to moral development and moral education and provides a new vision of the relationship between developmental psychology and education. This vision—still in its nascent form—seeks to use education less to facilitate development along a hierarchical progression of structurally defined stages, and more to enable each student to resist and overcome social and cultural repression, and hence to authorize his or her own moral voice (p. 200). In Neve Shalom/Wahat Al-Salam School, a sense of moral responsibility towards constructing knowledge and relationships for coexistence and peacemaking informs all aspects of classroom activity.

Conversations with the School Children

All children in Israel possess a heightened awareness of cultural difference and intergroup conflict and violence, due to the ongoing struggle between Jews and Arabs. What sets the children who attend the Neve Shalom/Wahat Al-Salam School apart from most other children in Israel is the possibility for them as Jews and Arabs to learn together in bilingual/bicultural classrooms on a daily basis. The children who come from outside the village are encouraged to discuss their fears of each other in open dialogue. The teachers are constantly discussing issues of conflict and possible resolution in the staff room and in staff meetings. The two directors of the school play a large role in being available to their teachers to discuss problems. The children learn to work and play together and to examine their respective cultures, histories, religions, and languages within a context of safety, trust, and friendship. In my interviews with some of the children, they discussed their feelings about sharing and learning together in the school. They reflected on the Hebrew-Arabic bilingual program, on the specific social-political climate in their war-torn country and on their personal relationships with one another in and out of the village. They demonstrated a great sense of pride in their school. One Grade 6 boy said:

I think this school is a very good idea. Because it's where we learn to know each other and to learn Arabic as well as Hebrew. . . . We learn to live together and not be separated and have wars and stuff like that. . . . There is a desert of war in our country and here we have—how do you say it—an "oasis of peace." That's what "Neve Shalom/Wahat Al-Salam" means in English.

A boy in Grade 4 explained the ease with which he is learning both Arabic and Hebrew:

Many kids that I know who don't go to this school don't learn Arabic the way I do and they find it harder to read and write than Hebrew; it's more complicated for them. But because I'm learning it every day as much as I'm learning to read and write Hebrew it's much easier. Also there are Arab kids in my class who help me when I get stuck on something. And I can help them with Hebrew. Some of my friends who don't go to this school can't imagine that this works so well. They can't imagine speaking and reading Arabic so easily. Also we have Arab teachers here and they don't. . . .

A Grade 5 girl who lives in the village makes explicit the need for intergroup relations in order to dispel fear, hatred, and prejudice:

It's a terrible thing to say bad things about people especially when you don't know them. Like people say bad things about Arabs but that's because everybody is afraid. We have a lot of wars here and sometimes people get hurt or killed by terrorists. And that makes many people hate each other. I have so many friends who are Arabs and so we're not afraid of each other and we don't hate each other at all. But that's because we live here together and we know each other. I don't know what would happen if I lived in Jerusalem or Tel Aviv or something.

A little Grade 4 girl explores considerations of caring and concern for intergroup relationships. She discusses how daily "border crossing" from [an Arab village] to Neve Shalom/Wahat Al-Salam allows for the creation of new responses to cultural differences and conflicts. She also expresses her pleasure in the greater intimacy of the smaller school:

I come into this school every day by bus from [an Arab village]. I like the school here because there aren't so many kids in each class. The teacher has more time for us. I don't feel left out or ignored. I really know how to read and write Hebrew and when I go back to my village, I can't help but show off to my friends. I have Jewish friends because I go to school here and I like them the same way I like my

Arab friends. The kids in my village [an Arab village] who don't come to this school don't understand that. They think the Jews want to take away their homes. They don't realize that the Jews are just as afraid as they are. It's a real mess. When I'm in Neve Shalom/Wahat Al-Salam I feel different than when I'm in [my village]. I mean I feel special.

This Grade 2 boy illustrates the value of the bilingual/bicultural education that he is receiving. He explains how he is being taught an understanding and appreciation of his own Jewish heritage and a respect for the Moslem and Christian traditions. His words indicate an education towards a sense of community within a framework of diversity:

We learn about all the holidays of Christians, Jews, and Moslems. I like that because I get to understand other ways. But I celebrate my own holidays and learn to be Jewish but I know that you can't laugh on certain holidays, like when they celebrate Mohammed and you don't want to hurt them. You have to respect what they do. Like when they fast on Ramadan. You don't want to show them your food during the day or it will make them feel bad.

A Grade 5 girl who lives in a nearby Jewish village discussed her changing attitude towards Arabs now that she attends the school in Neve Shalom/Wahat Al Salam:

I find that since I'm at the school, I am less afraid of Arabs. Until now I used to be very afraid of them because of the war. . . . In our current events classes we have an Arab teacher and a Jewish teacher and so we have more of a chance to hear the Arab side. I'm still learning to speak Arabic and so the teacher translates what I don't understand. . . . My best friend in [a Jewish village] where I live doesn't know Arabs the way I do. She's a lot more afraid.

An atmosphere has been created in Neve Shalom/Wahat Al-Salam where differences can be appreciated and respected instead of feared. This girl continued:

In this village the children have respect for themselves and for one another, and for their different religions. That person is your enemy (referring to Arabs) not because you don't like him or her but because your people and her people are at war. But what I learn here is that we are all humans and we have to learn to get along. . . . This hatred is something to be ashamed of. Here we try to repair the hatred. Countries are always in competition with each other. They don't share anything. I think most people want peace in this world. If only Neve Shalom/Wahat Al-Salam could be the capital of the world!

One Grade 6 boy expressed it this way:

Many Arab families have more kids than Jewish families. But they love the same kinds of things we do. They love to play and watch television. We love to play and watch television. They're no different; they're people—like we are. We're alike. There's no such thing like I'm worth more than other people. If someone is better in mathematics, for instance, it's not because he's Jewish. Some Jews are good in mathematics and some Arabs are good in mathematics. I don't like people who think they are better and worth more than others.

These children are creating new realities, new expressions, and new images that give voice to a new collective consciousness of coexistence and hope for peace. By being given opportunities to reflect on their experiences in their classrooms with their teachers and with themselves, they have become aware of an educational discourse that is based on discussion and cooperative problem solving. Their teachers serve as role models in this respect.

Concluding Remarks

I returned to the village for a visit in the spring of 1993 and was impressed to see a larger number of children in attendance at the school. The atmosphere was robust and cautiously optimistic in view of the peace initiatives that were just beginning. In January 1994 I received some correspondence from a few of my participants on their first reactions to the signing of the Israeli–PLO peace agreement:

"It is difficult to describe my feelings in these days. I waited with my family and my friends and with thousands of Israelis and Palestinians who love peace (with compromise) for this historic moment when the two peoples would recognize the national rights of each other. For many years each side ignored and even denied the right of existence to the other, and now we are living the dream. . . . I expect many troubles and many difficulties on the way to achieving peace." (Arab male participant)

"When I first heard about the peace agreement, I couldn't believe it at first and thought it to be only rumor. Then I became hopeful and happy, and suddenly very afraid; as if this peace agreement is a small baby surrounded by so many dangers and people who will try to kill him." (Jewish female participant)

"The experience of seeing walls so heavily guarded suddenly collapsing in front of one's eyes is almost surrealistic. The rays of hope that come from plans for peace are dimmed by the extremists who cling to fanatical ideas that will only bring despair. Don't let [this ray of light] be only a dream." (Jewish male participant)

The village and its school as a "moral" endeavor appears to reflect the need for bringing about an understanding of the self in relation to the other in terms of Jewish and Palestinian conflict resolution. It is this quest for understanding between the two cultural/national groups and for awareness of the complexity of the Jewish–Arab issue that is at the heart of the peaceful coexistence between the villagers. In allowing my participants to share their multiple voices with me, I struggled to understand the moral dilemmas and complex interrelationships in their lived experiences. As a result of the constant social and political tensions that arise out of the Jewish–Palestinian conflict, moral negotiation in the village continues at all levels of discourse. I was struck by how the villagers were constantly negotiating the space between the tensions of competing national aspirations and their personal attempts at coexistence and goodwill. In spite of all the moral complexities and conflicts, my researcher self became more and more convinced that, at bottom, this was a caring educational community that was dedicated to peaceful coexistence. I include here excerpts of some of the correspondence from the two directors of the school:

"For the first time after nine years of working with the children of the two nations, I have the feeling that we are no longer alone in the battle. I can see this even in the eyes of the children in the school. Those who attend from outside the village no longer feel at odds with their friends at home. . . . There are many cities in Israel where Jews and Arabs live together. More than ever I believe [our school] can be a model to be emulated there . . . By playing together and exchanging knowledge . . . they can come to understand each other's traditions and culture. These children will grow into ambassadors and promoters of peace." (Jewish female director)

"The children who have been here longer better understand the meaning of the agreement and realize it is only a beginning and that many obstacles lie ahead. . . . We have a policy of equality in the management and teaching staff of the school and of numerical equality among the students. Outside the village it is very rare to find an Arab managing Jewish workers. In the school we always try to draw the connection between what happens here and what happens outside." (Arab male director)

In a short report written in August 1994, the directors discussed some of the problems that they are facing in terms of their educational objectives for Jewish-Arab coexistence. Briefly they identified three major points: (1) the need to address the issue of equality in the bilingual program; (2) the interest of the school to families outside the village and parental involvement; and (3) the need for more funding from public and private sources. First, in their attempt to give the two languages (Hebrew and Arabic) equal weight in the school curriculum, they constantly struggle against the asymmetry of the two languages in Israeli society. The common language between Jewish and Arab teachers is Hebrew, and the dominance of Hebrew in the wider society creates a situation in which the Arab children learn Hebrew far more quickly and easily than the Jewish children learn Arabic:

The Jewish children acquire a working level of Arabic, but in the playground the Jews and Arabs will almost always speak to each other in Hebrew. In the coming year we will address this problem by introducing more of a "corrective balance." The children will be expected to work with each other in more formalized language learning session (for example; language labs, computer language programs, etc.).

A second problem that they identified was the fact that outside of Neve Shalom/ Wahat Al-Salam the interest in the school remains higher for Arab families than for Jewish families. "The school will attract Jewish families with a strong ideological incentive, but ideology is not always enough. State-supported public schools require no tuition fees and present our school with serious competition." In some cases the small size of the school and its distance from certain villages become a major obstacle, especially for the older children who feel that their circle of friends become too limited. It turned out that the children of a certain village made a group decision to continue on to a larger and more established junior high school five minutes away from their homes. What the directors have suggested, in order to deal with these situations, is to encourage the parents from the other villages to become more involved in the school's educational content by setting up more social events for the families of the various villages. They did have a very successful picnic last spring and are planning more informal programs for this academic year. Also, at last count a number of new children from nearby Jewish villages have registered at the school, offsetting the departure of the junior high students from the above mentioned village.

Third, due to the fact that this is a private school very much "on the cutting edge" in terms of its bilingual/binational philosophy, it is looked upon with some uncertainty by the Ministry of Education. Nevertheless, the Ministry took a very important step in 1994 by declaring that it will fund 50 percent of the cost of each child up to fifth grade, not including transportation. Although this is a sign of real progress, it is still far from adequate. Therefore this school survives in part on the basis of private fund-raising, which is a collaborative effort of individual people from some European countries and North America who believe in this model of Jewish-Arab coexistence. Another interesting development is that the directors of the school have recently been invited by the Ministry of Education to attend monthly meetings of all directors of schools in the Jerusalem regional area. This is a very significant step forward in terms of providing the Neve Shalom/Wahat Al-Salam school a greater sense of legitimacy within mainstream Israeli society.

In this study I have tried to present some examples of a collective moral dialogue that has been weaving its way into the lives of each individual in the school and into the very fabric of this community. Directions for future research include an ongoing collection of data at the school in the wake of continued Middle East peace initiatives and subsequent increased extremist terrorist activity. It may very well be the case that this school has an important role to play in the moral education of culturally diverse communities not only in other parts of Israel but also in the international arena. Indeed, the ongoing quest for peace and equality, evidenced through their personal, social, and educational activities, provides the villagers with countless opportunities to interpret and contemplate their cultural and historical destinies. Their stories are simple and complex, ordinary and extraordinary, mundane and heroic, foreign and familiar, full of tension and of hope. I felt honored to be among them. When I asked some of the children what they would like me to tell others about their way of life, they responded with these words:

"It is very easy to call people names and to hate them. But when you begin to live with them and go to school with them and play with them, then you realize that, even though they may have different customs and beliefs, they are really very similar in many ways. You have to find a bridge and meet them halfway."

Acknowledgments

This project was funded by a grant from the Social Sciences and Humanities Research Council of Canada (SSHRC).

I wish to express my sincere gratitude to the people of Neve Shalom/Wahat Al-Salam and to those from the neighboring villages connected with the school who so generously shared their stories with me.

Very special thanks to the late Father Bruno Hussar, Anne Le Meignen, and Coral Aron who were a great inspiration to me throughout the project.

Notes

1. All names in this paper are pseudonyms.
2. The Intifada began in December 1988 as an uprising by the Palestinians in the Occupied Territories.

References

Aronowitz, S., and H. Giroux. (1991). *Postmodern Education: Politics, Culture and Social Criticism*. Minneapolis: University of Minnesota Press.

Bakhtin, M. (1986). *Speech Genres and Other Late Essays*. (V, McGee, Trans.). Austin: University of Texas Press.

Belenky, Mary Field, Blythe McVicker Clinchy, Nancy Rule Goldberger, and Jill Mattuck Tarule. (1986). *Women's Ways of Knowing: The Development of Self, Voice and Mind*. New York: Basic Books.

Blasi, Augusti. (1980). "Bridging Moral Cognition and Moral Action: A Critical Review of the Literature." *Psychological Bulletin 88*(1): 1–45.

Clandinin, D. J. (1988). *Metaphor and Folk Model as Dimensions of Teachers' Personal Practical Knowledge*. University of Calgary.

———, and F. M. Connelly. (1994). "Personal Experience Methods." I *Handbook of Qualitative Research*, eds. N. K. Denzin and Y. S. Lincoln. Thousand Oaks, CA: Sage Publications, (pp. 413–27, Chapter 26).

Connelly, F. M. and D. J. Clandinin. (1990). "Stories of Experience and Narrative Inquiry." *Educational Researcher, 19* (5 June/July): 2–14.

Cuffaro, H. (1995). *Experimenting with the World: John Dewey and the Early Childhood Classroom*. New York: Teachers College Press.

Cummins, J. (1989). *Empowering Minority Students*. Sacramento: California Association for Bilingual Education.

Denzin, N. (1988). *The Research Act*. (rev.ed.). New York: McGraw-Hill

Dewey, J. (1909/1975). *Moral Principles in Education*. Carbondale: Southern Illinois University Press, Arcturus Books.

Dilthey, W. (1977). "The Understanding of Other Persons and Their Expressions of Life." In W. Dilthey, *Descriptive Psychology and Historical Understanding* (trans., R. Zaner & K. Heiges,). The Hague: Martinus Nijhoff. [original work published 1894.].

Eisner, E. (1991). *The Enlightened Eye: Qualitative Inquiry and the Enhancement of Educational Practice*. New York: Maxwell MacMillan International Publ. Group.

Eisner, E. and Peshkin A. (1990). *Qualitative Inquiry in Education: The Continuing Debate*. New York: Teachers College, Columbia University.

Feuerverger, G. (1991). "University Students' Perceptions of Heritage Language Learning and Ethnic Identity Maintenance in Multicultural Toronto." *Canadian Modern Language Review, 47* (4 Spring Issue [Special Issue on Heritage Languages in Canada]); 660–77.

Geertz, C. (1988). *Works and Lives: The Anthropologist as Author*. Stanford CA: Stanford University Press.

Gilligan, C. (1982). *In a Different Voice: Psychological Theory and Women's Development*. Cambridge: Harvard University Press.

———, J. Ward, and J. Taylor, (eds.). (1988). *Mapping the Moral Domain: A Contribution of Women's Thinking to Psychological Theory and Education*. Cambridge MA: Harvard University Press.

————, L. Brown, and A. Rogers. (1990). "Psyche Embedded: A Place for Body, Relationships, and Culture in Personality Theory." In A. Rabin (ed.), *Studying Persons and Lives*. New York: Springer-Verlag.

Giroux, Henry A. (1988). *Schooling and the Struggle for Public Life*. Minneapolis: University of Minnesota Press.

————. (1991). "Democracy and the Discourse of Cultural Difference: Towards a Politics of Border Pedagogy." *British Journal of Sociology of Education*, 12 (4).

Glesne, C., and A. Peshkin. (1992). *Becoming Qualitative Researchers: An Introduction*. New York: Longman.

Greene, M. (1983). "The Humanities and Emancipatory Possibility." In Giroux, H. and Purpel, D., *The Hidden Curriculum and Moral Education: Deception or Discovery?* Berkeley, CA: McCutchan Publ., pp. 384–402.

Hopkins, D. (1987). *Enhancing Validity in Action Research*. (British Library Research Paper #16).

Huberman, A. M., and M. B. Miles. (1984). *Innovation up Close*. New York: Plenum.

Janesick, V. J. (1991). "Ethnographic Inquiry: Understanding Culture and Experience." In Short, E., *Forms of Curriculum Inquiry*. Albany: SUNY Press.

Kohlberg, L. (1971). "Cognitive-Developmental Theory and the Practice of Collective Moral Education." In Wolins and Gottesman, M. (eds.), *Group Care: An Israeli Approach*. New York: Gordon & Breach.

————. (1985). "The Just Community Approach to Moral Education in Theory and Practice." In *Moral Education: Theory and Application*. Edited by M. Berkowitz, and F. Oser. Hillsdale, NJ: Lawrence Erlbaum.

Kozol, J. (1991). *Savage Inequalities. Children in America's Schools*. New York: Crown Publ.

Lo Bianco, J. (1989). "Revitalizing Multicultural Education in Australia." *Multiculturalism*, 12:30–39.

Morrison, T. (1987). *Beloved*. New York: Alfred K. Knopf.

Mishler, E. G. (1986). *Research Interviewing: Context and Narrative*. Cambridge, Mass.: Harvard University Press.

Noddings, N. (1984). *Caring: A Feminine Approach to Ethics and Moral Education*. Berkeley, CA: University of California Press.

————. (1991). *Stories in Dialogue: Caring and Interpersonal Reasoning*." In *Stories Lives Tell: Narrative and Dialogue in Education*. Edited by C. Witherell and N. Noddings. New York: Teachers College Press.

Ogbu, J. (1978). *Minority Education and Caste*. New York: Academic Press.

Polkinghorne, D. E. (1988). *Narrative Knowing and the Human Sciences*. Albany: State University of New York Press.

Power, F. C., (1988). "The Just Community Approach to Moral Education." *Journal of Moral Education*, 17 (3): 195–208.

————, A. Higgins, and L. Kohlberg. (1989). *Lawrence Kohlberg's Approach to Moral Education*. New York: Columbia University Press.

Samuda, R. (1986). "The Canadian Brand of Multiculturalism: Social and Educational Implications." In *Multicultural Education*. Edited by S. Modgil, G. K. Verma, K. Mallick, and C. Modgil, London; Philadelphia: The Falmer Press.

Sarbin, T. R. (ed.) (1986). *Narrative Psychology: The Storied Nature of Human Conduct*. New York: Praeger.

Schon, D. (1991). *The Reflective Turn: Case Studies in and on Educational Practice*. New York: Teachers College Press, Columbia University.

Tappan, M. (1991). "Narrative, Language and Moral Experience." *Journal of Moral Education*, 20 (3).

————, and L. Brown. (1989). "Stories Told and Lessons Learned: Toward a Narrative Approach to Moral Development and Moral Education." *Harvard Educational Review*, 59:182–205.

Witherell, C. (1991). "Narrative and the Moral Realm: Tales of Caring and Justice." *Journal of Moral Education*, 20 (3).

Wong-Fillmore, L. (1989). "Language and Cultural Issues in the Early Education of Language Minority Children." In *The Care and Education of America's Young Children: Obstacles and Opportunities*. Edited by S. L. Kagan Chicago: NSSE, University of Chicago Press.

Yin, R. K. (1984). *Case Study Research*. London: Sage.

Education to Cope with Conflicts: Encounters between Jews and Palestinian Citizens of Israel

HAVIVA BAR AND

ELIAS EADY

Introduction

Israeli society has undergone a series of profound transformations in recent years. Apart from the peace process, these include: greater social consideration for individual status, together with a growing propensity for individuals to take part in public life, and consequently a demand for greater power and influence by minority groups; the growth of the media; and rapid, extensive developments in technology, communications, and information, with their implications at the individual level and for people's attitude toward society. Society's multiple classes are increasingly polarized socially, culturally, and economically, with tensions and conflicts characterizing the relations among them. We find, too, mutual dependence and interaction in the international arena, involving spheres such as economic well-being, quality of life, and political, ethnic, or religious conflicts.

We shall note several additional trends, mainly of a universal character, which impact on the individual's self-perception and ways of coping: in the ideational realm, pluralism and relativism of values (a gradual detachment from absolute values); in the social realm, the loss of the dichotomous, uniform definition of basic social roles ("children" vs. "adults," "men" vs. "women," "old" vs. "young") and of a dominant standard definition of the basic social cell ("the nuclear family"); in the psychological realm, greater individualism juxtaposed to socialization processes that emphasize the importance of group membership, with its inherent obligations and commitments. These trends, then, are marked by nonuniformity, nonlinearity, and instability; they display a multiplicity of contradictions and conflicts, and they necessitate the adaptation of ways of coping to the new reality that is emerging.

A key element in education to enable successful integration into a democratic society in general and into the Israeli society (as described above) in particular, is the progression of skills and capabilities to cope with conflicts.

This article, then, is geared to educators, interveners, funders, and researchers who are engaged in education for democracy and active citizenship, and who organize encounters between members of groups in conflict. More specifically, it is aimed at those who incorporate encounters between opposite groups in the educational process, seeking to guide them toward the questions they should ask before initiating encounters or before permitting schoolchildren to take part in encounters that are organized by experts.

Encounters are an educational channel that utilize intergroup processes to enhance personal growth and development by focusing on the idea of coping with a conflict—in this case, the Jewish–Arab, or Israeli–Palestinian, conflict (henceforth: the Conflict). Two peoples are involved in the Conflict (notwithstanding the notion that it is only a "Palestinian problem"), which is political and not interpersonal, and which assumes different forms in different periods. Encounters, according to this approach, are not meant to resolve concrete conflicts in the external world, but to help people understand them and to propose tools and a perspective to facilitate coping with them.

This is often defined as political education. It involves, in Lam's (1988) words, "preparing people to make optimal use of their intellectual abilities, their value judgment (distinguishing between what is possible and worthy, and what is not), their emotional attitude, and their will to rectify the political activity of the society and the individual based on a sense of personal responsibility." The point of departure of this definition is that attitudes and behavior are almost always learned.

The learning process in this case can extend over a lifetime. Education in this spirit emphasizes the need to engage aspects of socialization and learning that are acquired early in life and are characterized by automatism, simplism, and stereotypification (Bar-Tal, 1994). Among the abilities that should be encouraged are: a complex approach to events; a probing, unhindered view, accompanied by a critical view and conceptualization of a constantly shifting reality, which is heavily prone to ambivalence and polarization; wielding influence that derives from moral responsibility, involvement in the life of the community, and an active commitment to change; and the articulation of a worldview that upholds the values of equality, democracy, and humanism.

What Have Encounters Focused on in the Past?

The directory of the Abraham Fund (Weiner, Bar-On, and Weiner, 1992) lists 300 organizations that deal with "coexistence"—the most frequently used description of the contents and goals of the projects and programs implemented by those involved in this field—and most of them employ the technique of encounters to achieve their ends. The goal of the encounter is commonly described as addressing an intercultural and/or interethnic conflict in order to develop a pluralistic culture based on legitimization of the other and respect for other cultures (Circular of the Director-General [of the Education Ministry], March 1, 1984, quoted in Hareven,

1993). Such definitions are inadequate because they do not admit to the asymmetrical, conflictual essence of the relations between the two peoples: Jews and Arabs. In other words, the experience common to the two groups, and which holds out the promise of creating an equal opportunity for both, albeit only temporarily (while the encounter lasts), is that of the Conflict. Although no one doubts the great usefulness of the existing research in the field—which we will draw on—a number of pertinent concerns would seem to be in order:

(1) On the major questions raised by intergroup relations and encounters, researchers are divided about both the findings and their interpretation. The controversy stems from their perception of reality (Shamir, 1985).

(2) Adapting the underlying approach and conclusions of studies conducted elsewhere (especially in the United States) to Israel is fraught with drawbacks (Blalock, 1982; Leven and Campbell, 1972; Sharif, 1966; Tajfel, 1981). They deal with intercultural ethnic relations and with majority-minority relations. Such studies possess only partial relevance, and certainly no simple inferences can be drawn from them regarding the multidimensional Jewish–Arab conflict (Mikhlovitz, 1987; Bargal, 1990).

(3) It is insufficient to apply approaches and findings that derive from studies conducted in Israel to encounters between other groups of opposites, be they religious, communal, or cultural—i.e., having an ideological and/or ethnic source—or to majority-minority relations (Ben-Ari and Amir, 1988; Liebman, 1990; Peres, 1976). Jewish–Arab relations are shaped largely by a political conflict between two national groups (Smooha, 1993), with the Conflict defined by negative reciprocal dependence of two types: dominance, i.e., ruler–ruled; and competition, i.e., a struggle for scant resources, including water sources, realization of identity, and others (Campbell model, 1965). Nor should we overlook the part played by elements of Etzioni's spiral model (1970), in which the sides are dragged into a process of escalating hostility, at least until the last few years.

Common Models of Encounters

Educational activity involving encounters between two peoples has been based, whether consciously or not, on theoretical approaches that explain human aggressiveness, intergroup relations, and shifts of attitude in terms of interaction between groups. Two schools of thought on aggressive behavior are discernible among researchers. One school considers aggression to be an innate drive to ensure survival—for example, Freud's psychoanalytic conception holds that aggression is imprinted in the human psyche—while the other maintains that the roots of aggression lie in human experience and result from frustration and/or social learning (elaborated in Shavit-Ohion, 1994).

The theoretical explanations for the emergence of intergroup behavioral mechanisms that produce prejudice, negative stereotyping, discriminatory behavior, delegitimation, hatred, enmity, and conflict can be divided into two groups:

psychological (cognitive and personality-grounded) and societal-specific. The psychological-cognitive explanations refer to the overall mechanisms of information processing: categorization, ethnocentrism, the principle of diminished effort (Allport, 1954), and attributive processes. The psychological explanation focuses primarily on the crystallization of social identity and on social comparison. Society-specific explanations refer to modes of human socialization and its influencing factors, and to exploitation theory and the concrete Conflict (for further elaboration and a detailed survey of the literature, see Bar and Bargal, 1995).

One of the assumptions in theories about changing people's attitudes is that in order to alter attitudes and behavior it is necessary to create a meaningful reference group (Sherif, 1958) or to bring into being an alternative culture to enable the individual's "reeducation" (Lewin, 1945, 1958) (detailed theoretical survey in Bar and Bargal, 1995). Group membership is considered a mechanism for changing beliefs due to the following factors: group discussion; prior readiness to receive information and an active ability to process it; creation of an atmosphere of trust within the group; empathy by the agents of change toward the objects of change; the participants' receptiveness to their feelings and the feelings of others in the group; willingness to undergo exposure; group cohesion; self-insight; learning through identification with the Other; and airing one's feelings (Shulov-Barkan, 1993).

This complex of theories has given rise to various encounter models: the Contact Model; the Information Model; the Psychodynamic Model; and the Model of Conflict Resolution and Conducting of Negotiations (the last model is designed for policy makers and national leaders and is not germane to the educational system) (Kelman, 1979). These models—in their original form, later development, or in diverse combinations—have been applied to the Israeli reality (see elaboration in Mikhlovitz, 1987; Katz and Kahanov, 1990).

The *Contact Model* assumes that "intergroup contact will lead to a change in the mutual attitudes and relations. . . . Underlying this belief is the hypothesis that contact between people from different groups creates opportunities for mutual acquaintance, intensifies the understanding and mutual acceptance of the participants in reciprocal activities, and thereby reduces intergroup prejudices, confrontations, and tensions" (Ben-Ari and Amir, 1988). This model also stresses the bridging of gaps between individuals by creating common ground. In the reality of encounters in Israel, that common ground was coexistence and the fabric of shared civil life (Moaz, 1994). Allport (1954) maintains that when equal-status contact between groups that are united in the desire to achieve a common goal is supported by formal authorities, it has greater prospects to break down prejudices.

The *Information Model* takes as its starting point the assumption that insufficient information about the other group produces stereotypes, prejudices, and intergroup tensions. Therefore, anyone who is acquainted with the true facts and learns about the other group's cultural orientation will undergo a change of heart about them (Tabb and Mannheim, 1987).

A common model involving a combination of the Contact Model with the Information Model is *Task Groups,* i.e., groups that seek to achieve a joint professional goal (subject matter). The rationale here is that "acting together is important for developing reciprocal relations that go beyond mere discussions about Jewish–Arab relations, and it is common for additional initiatives to emerge afterward from this initial core in each pair (of schools)" (Hareven, 1993, p. 25). "At the same time, the model rejected direct engagement with the Jewish–Arab conflict and the attendant feelings, contending that this would underscore what is problematic, different, and conflictual in the situation, instead of emphasizing the common elements, [thus] generating feelings of hopelessness and helplessness" (Ottolenghi, 1990, in Moaz, 1994).

The *Psychodynamic Model* "presupposes that one's negative reactions toward members of the other group derive from problems in one's psychodynamic process, not necessarily from the target group itself" (Ben-Ari and Amir, 1988, p. 51). Katz and Kahanov (1990) note that the distinctive aspect of this model is its expanding of the individual's consciousness of his feelings and behavior toward the other group; the raw material is the "here and now," i.e., personal experiences, feelings, and thoughts that emanate from the participants. There is no deep probe of comprehensive, external data from a structural, social, or political-social perspective.

Main Limitations of the Models

Despite the extensive activity in recent years involving group encounters based on these models, experts are divided as to the optimal approach that should be adopted in such meetings; some question the quality, effectiveness, and results of the encounters. Hareven reports that "in some cases, the encounters actually caused a polarization and radicalization of attitudes among the participants" (1993).

Already a decade or more ago Stephan (1987) and Brown (1985) argued that "contact is not enough." They also explained why: (1) Hostility and racism toward the Other are not only the result of insufficient information and wrongheaded conceptions. They could be caused by a conflict of interests. (2) In some cases manifestations of similarity within the group do not occur; on the contrary, the differences turn out to be deeper than expected or than the stereotype had suggested. (3) Usually the contact between individuals does not produce the anticipated generalization toward everyone in the other group. (4) Stephan (1987) notes other variables to take into account in the form of historical and social background factors at the macro-level. Consideration must also be given to the participants' selection and prior preparation, the group's composition, the organizational conditions, and the techniques of influence. Moreover, the idea of encounters often rests on myths and fantasies holding that contact, information, and relations between opposites can affect reality.

A central assumption of those who organize encounters is that relations between Jews and Arabs can be transformed by breaking down prejudices and stereotypes and developing skills that are relevant to the intercultural dimension (Ben-Ari and

Amir, 1988). This assumption, apart from being one-sided and responding primarily to the interests and needs of the Jewish side, reinforces the depoliticization of reality and deliberately removes from the encounter agenda the conflictual issues that are central to the reality of the two peoples. The result is perpetuation of the status quo, including the relations of ruler and ruled.

Most of the models mainly underscore similarities and shared elements between the sides and are based on the equal status of the participants—a case in point is encounters of professionals from the same field (e.g., teachers or psychologists)—and ignore asymmetries and opposites. "The matter of equal status or symmetry between the sides is no simple question. Even if those involved are teachers from the two sides with a similar professional-educational or even socioeconomic status, and their aim is to discuss a common professional theme, the Jews' 'outside' dominance can, given various developments or issues that crop up in the encounter, be projected inward and bring about asymmetry even in this supposedly 'bubble-like' situation" (Moaz, 1994, p. 18).

The difficulties are even more pronounced if the encounter is not structured but is based instead on spontaneous (interpersonal and intergroup) processes of a "natural" and dynamic character, which rely predominantly on the participants' good intentions. Such encounters can cause psychological harm and frustration, mainly in the minority group (the Arabs), and a sense of missed opportunity and disappointment in the majority group (the Jews). This type of situation reconstructs and perpetuates the nature of encounters and the unequal relations that exist in the external world—in which the majority group is dominant and the minority group passive or uninvolved—and precludes the development of an educational-egalitarian process that is meaningful to both groups. In addition, an unstructured encounter heightens the uncertainty, hostility, and aggression that are present in large doses in every encounter between two asymmetrical groups living in a conflict situation.

A further limitation of the models described above is that often the differential needs of the two groups are not addressed equally; encounters, that is, are geared more toward one group and ignore the needs of the other group or even make use of them for a particular purpose. An example would be encounters which have set the goal of fomenting change in one group: usually of moderating attitudes of the Jewish majority through the agency of the Arab minority. This approach was especially pronounced in the mid-1980s and last year, when surveys showed that Jewish youngsters were adopting increasingly extreme antidemocratic attitudes, opposed the idea of equality with Arabs, and/or were advocating that Arab civil rights be clipped. It was also found that about a third of Jewish youngsters supported Kahanist ideologies (Hareven, 1993; Zemah, 1986, 1987). An example of such utilization of the other side is a "personal testimony" by an Arab to a group of Jewish pupils.

Jewish–Arab encounters have always been accompanied by various statements, some of them perhaps unrealistic (Bar and Bargal, 1986; Shavit-Ohion, 1994).

Examples are: "We are neither Jews nor Arabs, we are human beings," "We are both on the same side," "The extremists on both sides are the common enemy of us all," "If we can only meet, get to know one another, and become friends, everything will be different," and "Those who promote coexistence are 'world saviors,' and others are indifferent or bad." In many cases, even if such statements stem from positive motives and express good intentions, or are used to raise funds to underwrite encounters, they invariably preserve the status quo, perpetuate asymmetry, and even bolster the participants' illusion that believing in these slogans and behaving accordingly will resolve the Conflict.

Why Encounters?

As we saw, encounters can give rise to criticism, frustration, and disappointment. Moreover, the passage of time has brought fundamental disagreement over the rationale, goals, and methods of the implementation of encounters based on the models described above. The result was a growing tendency, particularly among Arab moderators, to address the issues separately, within uninational frameworks. It is certainly important that the Conflict be dealt with in the schools (in uninational groups, in current events lessons); encounters are not the only available channel. Still, planned encounters have several unique advantages:

(1) They are the major method for "experiencing" rather than "talking." In the encounter framework participants not only verbalize the issues, they live and undergo them directly and concretely. (For example, a sense of helplessness is important, since it is integral to the Conflict experience. Everyone is aware of its existence, but only rarely do we "permit" ourselves to experience the feeling of our own volition. The encounter process produces many situations of helplessness among the participants, and this clashes with their fervent desire to change the situation) (Shulov-Barkan, Bar, Oizerman, Vald, and Eady, 1992).

(2) The living encounter makes it possible to learn (i.e., to experience, to recognize, to acknowledge) "what we do not know about ourselves and about the other side," including feelings, attitudes, prejudices, and stereotypes (about ourselves and about the others) through a particularly meaningful method (Shulov-Barkan, et al., 1992).

(3) Encounters enable participants, through both structured and unstructured activity, to expose their inner being and to undergo a variety of experiences with concrete individuals from the other group in a situation of equals—a sharp contrast to the asymmetrical, charged, accidental meetings of everyday life. Such experiences can enrich and diversify one's images of the Other and of the other group (Mikhlovitz, 1987), and in particular they confront the Other with the ability to internalize complex reality.

(4) Similarly, encounters force individuals to face up to the disparity between the good intentions, declarations, and slogans in which they believe, and their ability to cope with the direct implications (on their feelings, behavior, and attitudes) of

complex realities and of the encounter between their own and the other group. The encounter participant thus experiences tension and contradictions—which are crucial to an ability to live with the conflict—in the following sequences: thoughts and attitudes/feelings and modes of behavior; insularity and en- trenchment/openness; similarity/difference; uniformity/diversity; simplistic, one- dimensional view/complex, multidimensional, multimeaningful approach; super- ficiality/depth; concrete and specific/universal and generalized; inner group real- ity/external reality; one-sidedness/mutuality; uninational/binational; harmony/ conflict; feeling and being: empathy/judgment; close/distant; victim/aggressor; tranquil/threatened; aggression and perhaps violence/dialogue; helplessness and despair/realistic hope. Tensions also arise between: individual and society; freedom and equality; law and religious law; actual and desired; stability and change; theory and practice; norm and reasoned discretion; freedom and security; personal free- dom and solidarity; equality and excellence; value education and neutrality; and autonomy and responsibility.

(5) The individual participant in the encounter can potentially gain personal, direct experience of real intergroup conflicts, with all that they entail.

Major Principles of the New Approach

The practical and research experience that was accumulated through the applica- tion of the models described above led to the emergence of an approach that is based on and specifically adapted to the developing experience of the two peoples in Israel. The foundations of the new approach are, on the one hand, theories from the realm of social psychology and intergroup relations, and on the other hand, constraints arising from the encounter process and its implementation in these two particular groups. The overriding goal of the approach is to construct encounters that will consolidate the concept of coexistence and enhance the indi- vidual's ability to live with the conflict. Understanding the complexity of the situ- ation and being aware that it is possible to improve one's ability to cope with it—therein lies the potential not to accept the situation but not to change it. This approach addresses what is realistically possible in encounters instead of purporting to attain an ideal that is beyond their power (Bar and Bargal, 1995; Shulov-Barkan, et al., 1992).

Prior Assumptions

(1) The encounter is not a goal in itself. It is insufficient (the process must begin beforehand and continue afterward), and it cannot encompass all the spheres that need to be engaged in terms of the relations between the two peoples. Similarly, there is an awareness that the conflict cannot be resolved either at the interpersonal or the intergroup level, nor is this the purpose of the encounter. On the other hand, encounters are troubling, complex experiences and therefore demand a serious, professional approach to the discrete parts that form them: the participants,

the attributes of the moderators (experience, training, ongoing in-service guidance), the scrupulous design of the encounter process and of several encounter models that are adaptable to different target audiences, and the content to be coped with (elaborated below).

(2) Encounters should be seen as the beginning of a meaningful process that extends beyond the duration of each particular encounter. The issues to be dealt with in the context of relations between the peoples and of the Conflict, and the psychological processes that are generated as a result are complex, powerful, and deep. They cannot be exhausted within the confines of an encounter, which is necessarily limited both in time and in the ability to foment change.

(3) This approach focuses on the individual's conception and abilities. All of us live in a reality context that comprises ourselves, our group, and other groups within a complex social-political situation. The attitude toward the individual is holistic, addressing three strata of the human psyche simultaneously: emotions, behavior, and conceptual insights. The encounter's spatial construction enables each individual to express a range of feelings and attitudes, including the most severe, such as hatred.

(4) An absolutely crucial element of encounters between the two peoples is a recognition of their asymmetry, which colors every aspect of their experience both in the real world and in the planned encounter. Asymmetry prevails in various areas: civil inequality and almost universal unequal opportunities; unequal legitimization to express personal and group identities; effects of majority-minority relations; directly vulnerability to the Conflict experience; disparities in awareness, in previous experience of encounters, and in opportunities of various kinds; "looking inward," expressing and sharing feelings with others by disclosing them in a group, crystallizing self-identities, and presenting arguments and standing firm in direct confrontations. Such difficulties, it bears noting, are not confined to only one group: individuals from both groups are found along the entire continuum represented by these abilities and opportunities. The entry into the less familiar situation of the encounter workshop heightens the disparities (see elaboration in Bar and Bargal, 1995; Shulov-Barkan, 1993).

(5) Encounters are based on needs, motivations, and expectations of the two groups, hence the goals must be common to both sides.

(6) The central theme is, as noted, the issue of the Conflict and the individual's ability to cope with it—something most people avoid in everyday life. Meaningful processing and airing of the issues are a sine qua non for learning how to cope with the Conflict. Moreover, dealing with the Conflict produces the most relevant content and is most promising in terms of furnishing an equal opportunity to both sides. This is also the conclusion reached by Moaz (1994) after a comparative evaluation of two projects conducted at the Van-Leer Institute.

(7) Acquiring the ability to cope with the Conflict is dependent on the social-political context. The findings of Bar and Bargal (1995) show clearly the differential effect of contrary political realities (wars and Intifada vs. the theme designated in

the Israeli school system for 1986–87: the Year of Coexistence and Democracy), and especially the contrary impact of the conflict on the two groups participating in the encounter. Even when encounters take place on what Lewin (1945) calls a "cultural island" (as they generally do: they are held at sites that remove the participants from their everyday lives), the reality they develop is nevertheless influenced by events in the outside world (on the significance of these findings, see Bar and Bargal, 1995).

(8) It is crucial to clarify the question of identities in encounters. In this connection, the following components should be addressed: (1) All individuals define their identities by themselves. Everyone possesses a range of social identities, which are interrelated in different ways (overlapping, complementary, conflicting, contradictory). (b) Every individual has a distinctive composition of identities (intensity, order of importance, and relations between them), and each group contains a broad range of identities. (c) The composition of individual/group identities is not static but dynamic, and it is influenced by external social-political events (Bar and Bargal, 1995). (d) Among both Jews and Arabs these different identities are perceived as distinct. At the same time, the Arabs consider Palestinian-ness and Israeli-ness to be antithetical (Bar and Asaqla, 1988; Smooha, 1989; for a detailed survey on the theme of identities, see Shulov-Barkan, 1993). (e) It is necessary to examine modes of coping in which claims by one side of the legitimization of its national identity and consequent aspirations will not automatically be construed by the other side as the delegitimation of its identity, and the reduction of the possibilities for the realization of their aspirations. (f) Participants in encounters, particularly Jews, tend to categorize those who define themselves as "Israeli Arabs" as good and loyal, whereas those who define themselves as "Palestinians" are perceived as threatening, disloyal to the state, and indeed as part of the enemy. (g) Any consideration of the question of identities as it relates to encounters raises the need to address the multitude of terms and names relating to them (Palestinian citizens of Israel, as many define themselves; others refer to Arabs, Israeli Arabs, Arabs of Israel, and more—this subject is discussed in Rabinowitz, 1993). The complex affiliations of the Palestinians who live in the territories must also be considered (Hertz-Leizerovich and Kupermintz, unpublished; Shavit-Ohion, 1990). (h) The processing of identities, like other aspects of content, necessitates dealing with the mechanisms of splitting and projection and with their political ramifications and attendant anxieties. (i) The new approach undercuts the common notion of "preaching to the converted," since the fact that one is "converted" signifies no more than possessing the motivation to take part in an encounter. The major thrust of encounters is less cognitive than experiential and emotional, and they evoke inner dimensions that are in part unconscious and unpredictable. No one in either nation is exempt from the important task of addressing and processing in depth—however painful the effort may be—the issues relating to the Conflict and the many themes that encounters address (e.g., anxieties, fears, stereotypes, prejudices, and the gap between beliefs and actions in everyday life and in shifting

external conditions): the whole occurring in a rare and distinctive situation with the other side also present. (j) An essential component if the participants are to make headway in the encounter process is the stage of loss and the incorporation of accompanying reactions. Both the previous world picture, which was based on prejudices, stereotypes, and fantasies, whether "rosy" or "dark," are discarded in this process. The resulting vacuum is a potential starting point for the stage of building a new world picture, which requires knowledge and acknowledgment of the presently existing reality, and prerequisites for altering it. For example, one of the universal fantasies in this realm claims that if (each participant) is well-intentioned and if the encounter is characterized by responsiveness, active participation, and empathy, then people will "really" be able to express everything they think and feel, they will find a common language, and the Conflict itself will be made less potent. A meaningful process makes it possible to understand that the Conflict is real, painful, and complex; that it involves more than one language; that we hurt others and are ourselves hurt even if this is not our intention; and that flights of fantasy about changing the world or changing others are of no use.

Conception and Skills

Underlying the new approach is the recognition that an Arab–Jewish Conflict exists, that it affects the life of everyone in the region, and that it is important to understand its political, social, and situational causes. Two peoples are involved in the Conflict, each playing a different role, but equal in many aspects. Each of the two peoples has a national identity and a legitimate leadership, each has its own history, each suffers from its own calamities and traumas, each is wracked by fears and has made mistakes that have produced the situation in which the two peoples find themselves today, and each has moderates and extremists among its members. Each side harbors its own yearnings, including national aspirations, which are perceived as legitimate, for full realization in the form of self-determination and an autonomous existence. Each side has preferred modes of reaching its goals and each employs aggression and violence against the other. Both peoples have their own—separate and distinct—perspective on reality. It is essential to know the viewpoint of the other side, even if one rejects it, and to discard the illusion that one side will be able to induce the other to understand its outlook absolutely. Each of these aspects is also fully represented in external reality, and equally in the encounter between individuals from each group. The development of tolerance, the recognition that every nation in the region has the right of existence, and the exercise of mutual trust between the two peoples can contribute much toward altering the Conflict situation. No solution can be what only one side considers desirable, ideal, or optimal; every solution will entail enormous difficulties and exact a high price. Still, the alternative—of not endeavoring to modify the situation—is liable to produce even greater difficulties and be even more costly to the two peoples, given the decades-long accumulation of enmity between them. In fact, the Conflict is not eternal: it exists within a reality that people have forged and that is, consequently, amenable to change, for the sake of a better future for both peoples.

Part of the composition is the development of abilities and skills to cope with the Conflict, and these can be summed up as follows: It is vital to know one's inner self—attitudes, values, emotions, reactions, behavior, and fantasies—and become confident of one's worth, as the way to bolster self-confidence and diminish the sense of threat. It is necessary to understand the situation as it truly is and possess the tools to examine it while not losing sight of its great complexity; to recognize the need for maintaining a delicate balance between a feeling of being in control and a sense of helplessness; to display responsibility and self-discipline, which become increasingly important as freedom expands; to be aware of the defense mechanisms of repression, denial, splitting, and projection, and to reduce their use; to develop a curiosity about the subject instead of turning away from it; to mobilize skills of empathizing, acceptance, and tolerance; to improve one's ability to listen and to incorporate unpleasant, frightening statements that contradict one's personal views; to take personal responsibility (in contrast to a pointless indulgence in guilt feelings) while also understanding collective responsibility; to activate a complex, critical consciousness that is driven by skepticism, sensitivity, and moral responsibility; to treat other human beings with humanity; to show responsibility and involvement in the life of the community; to seize the freedom to express directly, openly, and sincerely one's attitudes and to present substantive, complex, and convincing arguments in a debate; to recognize and acknowledge the richness that inheres in a pluralistic, multiethnic, and multicultural existence; and not to display passivity and accept the situation as ineluctable fate, but to demonstrate a desire to foment change in a broad range of spheres, from undergoing an inner transformation to engaging in overt activity.

The thrust toward change will be based on the awareness that there is no single right, good, and just way to achieve the desired transformation. Everyone has the right to choose their own way, and only the interfusion of the different approaches can improve the relations between the two peoples.

Conditions for a Successful Encounter

Irrespective of the approach that informs the encounter, it is important that conditions should enhance the prospects for its success and prevent possible adverse effects. Schools planning encounters will benefit from a knowledge of the preconditions for their success. Those responsible in the school should take into account the following points in planning, implementing, and evaluating encounters: constructing the entire process; selecting the participants; the group's composition; anticipatory socialization; ensuring an equal spatial presence for both sides; integration of a uninational forum; the program and the order of activities; and professional moderating.

Constructing the process: This is the most controversial subject among planners of encounters. Some take as their point of departure the idea that the group is a microcosm of reality and emphasize a constant linkage between the processes that take place during the encounter and events in external reality, and vice versa (Sonnenschein, Halabi, and Friedman [Cf. p. 600 ff.], 1992; Salter, 1966, in Katz and Kahanov, 1990). They also believe that it is crucial to foster natural and spontaneous interpersonal and intergroup processes during the encounter. A structured encounter, in this view, inhibits these processes and results in domination by the Jewish group. Others, however, including the present writers, maintain that the desired processes do not occur by chance and/or naturally, and that only a structured encounter will allow them to take place and give both sides an equal opportunity to express themselves—an opportunity that does not exist in the inegalitarian, asymmetrical world outside. Similarly, "in these groups elites are grown and when there is a combination between them and the myth of structurelessness there is no limit to their power" (Joreen, 1973). Structuring is also important so that individuals or a group (usually the weaker group) will not be able to "opt for" noninvolvement or escape; on the contrary, all participants will be able to choose confrontation on an equal footing and express their social and political awareness. In the specific situation of the Israeli Arabs, a minority group that is educated in an authoritarian atmosphere, the moderator and the structured framework represent an alternative authority, though in this case one that permits legitimate self-expression and provides space in which it can occur (Daviri and Oubeid, 1993). A structured encounter enables individual participants to observe and engage in confrontation in four spheres: with themselves, their conceptual approach, and their inner world; with other participants from the same group; with participants from the other group; and with the Conflict at the intergroup level.

Selecting the participants: Experience shows that despite the widespread custom of bringing together whole classes from two schools, it is crucial to select the participants (Stephan, 1987). An encounter cannot affect attitudes dramatically. Therefore, little purpose is served by the participation of youngsters who are deeply opposed to encounters or would rather not deal with the Conflict. The selection should focus on those who are most likely to be changed by the encounter: those who are sensitive to interpersonal relations, are endowed with cognitive openness and with the ability to perceive that they are like others, and especially if they are highly motivated to engage the subject and bring about change (Bar and Bargal, 1995). The psychological profile of adolescence means that young people are potentially good candidates to take part in encounters, though difficulties and dangers exist. The advantages of working with adolescents are: (1) Both their personality and their values are more susceptible to influence. (2) They show a readiness to internalize and identify with a worldview that emphasizes justice and equality. (3) As pupils, they are highly accessible and the most suitable are readily chosen. (4) Some youngsters, at least, are inclined to become involved in the life of the community and have the chance to realize their desire, which may be accompanied by a wish to reform the world. (5) Because of their place in the social scale, adolescents undergo personal experiences that can help them emphathize with the lot of a "deprived minority" and identify with its demand for freedom and self-determination. (6) Binyamini's (1983) findings show that grade level is importantly related to caring about social problems. Tenth grade was found to be particularly tolerant from the political point of view, and this was found to correlate with an index of social desirability. In other words, political tolerance at this age is a kind of social norm. But there are also disadvantages: strong vulnerability and sensitivity to personal and group image; intense dependence on primary groups, which do not always support the worldview implied in encounters; and a tendency to seek simple, one-sided answers that do not reflect an understanding of the complexities and difficulties involved in modifying the existing situation.

Composition of the group: Activity should be conducted in small groups made up of an identical number of participants from each nation who are highly matched. Correlation between the schools is required at various levels: involvement in and commitment to encounters; readiness for contact and also motivation to take part in an encounter; and educational and social projects. If this correlation is not possible, a decision should be made on whether to hold the encounter at all; if held, it is important that the members of the minority group possess a higher social status (Amir and Bizman, 1978).

Anticipatory socialization: Even in a direct encounter that enables personal, unmediated mutual acquaintance, the participants' predispositions will be apparent, and there is a risk of "self-fulfilling expectations." This stage, then, enables a certain defusing of the defensive and aggressive strategies toward the other side in both the verbal and the psychological sense (Shamir, 1992). The input that is processed at this stage is in part identical for both groups and in part distinct to meet each group's needs. The preferred forum in uninational, in the participants' school. It is important to implement this stage in both groups before every encounter, using the following guidelines: providing detailed, accurate information about what takes place in encounters (during both formal and leisure activity); raising the participants' consciousness as to the need to examine constantly each group's perceptions and images of the other, this through the personal and direct experience that encounters provide; inculcating an awareness of the need to develop empathy and tolerance for the Other; displaying sensitivity to cultural differences and to the centrality of group pressure and its preponderant use in group processes; allowing the participants to express openly feelings and fears about the encounter, legitimating such feelings and exposing the participants to new and diverse ways of coping with them; and toning down exaggerated and perhaps unrealistic expectations in order to reduce disappointment and enable the maximum to be gained from the opportunity. In the postencounter stage, a uninational format is again desirable.

Equal spatial presence: The encounter framework is supposed to provide place for each participant, and that place must be permanent, assured, and equal. The basic assumption is that people do not function equally or identically, especially not in groups or encounters, where a situation of equality in this regard is unattainable. Therefore, the plan of the encounter must assure each individual participant equal conditions throughout. This is accomplished in a number of ways: (1) Setting a structured time division for each activity limits the more garrulous speakers. (2) Each person must first be given the floor, the others listening without comment, before a general discussion is held. (3) Every feeling, attitude, and declared identity must be legitimated. (4) Another aspect of the assured, protected space involves a distinctive interfusion between direct confrontation and incorporation by the facilitators with respect to each individual and for the group as a single unit (Shulov-Barkan, et al., 1992).

Language: Generally the language of encounters is Hebrew, since few Jews speak Arabic. This situation entails a risk of dominance by the Jews due to their fluency in Hebrew. Even the Palestinian citizens of Israel who speak Hebrew are less fluent than Jews, for whom Hebrew is their mother-tongue. The Palestinian citizens of Israel do not know the latest slang and they lack the taken-for-granted Hebrew-language "codes"; more seriously, their inability to express themselves as accurately in Hebrew as they can in Arabic means that they cannot properly convey subtleties of thought, attitude, or emotion as called for by the charged and complex issues that are the themes of encounters. There is no total solution for this problem. However, the negative implications can be offset somewhat if the language issue is part of the processing of expectations that precedes the encounter and if Arabic is employed during the encounter, accompanied by authentic, consecutive translation. In situations where the Arab side is fluent in Hebrew and is ready to use it, the participants should be encouraged to communicate directly in that language, this being preferable to the limitations of translation by the facilitator.

Uninational forum: Activity in a uninational framework involves some of the participants from one of the nations and is led by a facilitator from the same nation. This forum affords a more equal opportunity and reduces the effects of asymmetry on the encounter. The advantages are: a more protected framework for disclosing personal doubts and difficulties (disappointment, anger, confusion, etc.) and for a sincere, deep sharing of feelings without having to confront members of the other group or to take their feelings and sensibilities into consideration; a warm, open, and supportive atmosphere based on years-long acquaintance and use of the mother tongue in conditions that can forge a cohesive, united membership group; capability to treat diverse needs in various ways, suited to the distinct character of each group; and finally, opportunity to deal with the effects of group pressure as well as the issue of tolerance for the Other. A uninational group helps strengthen national identity and individual pride. This framework also has the potential to provide support and reinforcement subsequent to the encounter.

The program and order of activities: The order of activities in encounters is of considerable importance. Activities that underscore similarities between the groups should be held before those that emphasize differences; feelings should precede attitudes; and activities that promotes skills and abilities for coping with the Conflict will take place before activities that require the implementation of those skills.

Facilitating the encounter: Facilitators convey a wide range of messages through their behavior. To generate a process that benefits all the participants, the encounter should be led by two facilitators, one from each group. They should function on as equal a footing as possible in order to ensure that individuals from both groups get equal space. This can be accomplished by ensuring a clear role division for every activity, as well as overall in the encounter (if the investment in training the facilitators to construct and plan the encounter has been insufficient and unequal, their presentation may reconstruct the external asymmetry). The facilitator's role is to permit individual participants to enhance their expertise by themselves. Since facilitators are not experts on the individuals, they should try to avoid absolute statements and psychological analyses. Facilitators can offer guidance, provide information, sum up participants' remarks, try to calm those who are agitated, express agreement and confirmation, and address participants' confrontations with their inner selves—but they should not challenge their attitudes. Their style should be warm, sincere, and empathetic. Empathy is not only a professional and mental attitude, it is also an important method of learning through which facilitators can obtain understanding and insight about themselves and others.

Harm and Risks

Encounters have the potential to induce change, but they can also be of no benefit and can even cause more damage than might result if individuals were to ignore the Conflict and not attend encounters. The following sections describe some of the more frequent types of harm and risks (the examples are based on complete records of encounters).

Hospitality encounters and personal relations: Encounters based on hospitality or that emphasize interpersonal relations may prove misleading (since the expectations of both sides are different and usually unrealistic). Such encounters almost always produce disappointment and frustration, particularly in the case of pupils (because the two groups have dissimilar perceptions of hospitality and consequently invest in it differently). The authors' experience shows that reactions to this situation tend to reinforce certain stereotypes: "Arabs are wonderful at hospitality," "Jews are stingy." In some cases the cultural sphere (which is expressed through the act of hospitality) acts as a touchstone for assessing the political attitudes of the other group, albeit without its knowledge. In this connection it is important to note that culture is not only reflected through home hospitality itself; it can be problematic if it becomes one of the themes of the encounter. For example, discussions of relations between the sexes or parent-children relations underscores and intensifies "stereotype-ridden differences and negative attributes."

Behavioral manifestations of inferiority: Such manifestations are the combined result of a pronounced dominance of one group and of a strong readiness by Palestinian citizens of Israel to form ties with Jews, though not always to confront them directly. This situation causes the Palestinian citizens of Israel difficulties that they refrain from expressing overtly. Moaz (1994) notes some of the behavioral manifestations that characterize this sense of inferiority: arriving late for activities, or not at all;

canceling activities without advance notice; fulfilling assignments incompletely or not at all; not controlling the subjects of a discussion; and giving passive responses to the other side's questions (instead of taking active initiatives).

Failure to process different expectations: Both groups have many different expectations. Palestinian citizens of Israel who attend encounters are expressing a desire to approach Jews and forge lasting relations with them, to gain recognition that they are deprived and active support for their claims to equality, and to create a comfortable, conflict-free atmosphere, while feeling strongly the need to present and justify their political stands. Jews, on the other hand, expect to discover together a shared set of apolitical, human values. Some are looking for the nonthreatening "Good Arab." Others expect to find the "Bad Arab" and thus justify their previous negative attitudes about Arabs. The level of expectations and their content should be adapted to what can realistically be achieved in an encounter (Shulov-Barkan, 1993).

Nontreatment of defense mechanisms: Repression, projection, splitting, and denial are some of the ways to cope with the assimilation of new information and with events in an intergroup process, and their use is heightened in situations of tension and conflict. If there is no awareness of these manifestations in encounters, if they are not addressed, the participants are deprived of a significant learning and action experience. In dealing with these phenomena it should be borne in mind that the greater the awareness of their existence, the greater the readiness to accept them and acknowledge their centrality, the less onerous will be their impact (Mikhlovich, 1987).

Guilt feelings: It is essential not to reinforce guilt feelings among participants as a method to cope with the difficult situation that is reflected by the other group in the encounter. Some Jews display a pronounced tendency to develop guilt feelings because they overidentify with the Palestinian side and lean to self-deprecation, or in the wake of the disparity that emerges in encounters between their self-perception, which rests on a collective history of victimization, and their image as aggressors in the eyes of the Arab participants. Undesirable guilt feelings are more likely to arise in encounters that seek to function as a microcosm of the external world, characterized by power struggles between the two groups.

Euphoric conclusion or despair and depression: Encounters that conclude with strong feelings of euphoria or despair reduce or nullify the participants' readiness to pursue the process of coping personally with the Conflict reality upon their return to everyday life. Such feelings can bring about a detachment from the issue either because of a sense of impotence in the face of all the problems that arose, or due to a feeling of "omnipotence" that holds that all the problems that came up in the encounter were "solved."

Unprofessional facilitation and its effects: Common examples of manifestations related to unprofessional facilitation include; judgmentalism; acceleration of the process without personal reference to participants (sometimes also at the group level); accusing participants of being incapable of expressing their views "creditably" in the confrontation with the other group; overidentifying with one of the groups instead of empathizing equally with both; exaggerated use of questions and failure to safeguard participants against deep exposure and against invasive questions put by other participants; and direct ideological brainwashing, perhaps in the guise of an objective, self-evident description of reality. All these phenomena affect the participants' feeling of their own worth and keep them from effectively engaging and coping with the issue at hand.

Greater change induced in one group: Studies conducted in recent years show clearly that Jewish groups are more influenced by encounters than Arab groups. This is the case at both the subjective level (including a sense of satisfaction) and the objective level of attitudinal change (Bar and Bargal, 1988; Masalha, 1987; Smith, 1982; Shulov-Barkan, 1993).

Conclusion and Recommendations

Encounters between Jews and Palestinian citizens of Israel are the beginning of a dialogue. Their importance lies in their potential to effect future change. If the underlying conception of encounters is to be internalized deeply, the skills they promote must be practiced diligently and honed constantly. They do not represent a sealed book and will require reprocessing, especially in cases of violent incidents between the two peoples.

Some of the encounters that were studied produced important achievements. The major change found in encounter participants (as compared with nonpartici-pants) is their acquisition of a more complex and realistic perception of the conflict. This is apparent in various areas: recognition that a conflict exists that is difficult and painful for both peoples; legitimization of the other nation's existence and recognition of its national affinity; awareness that both groups cause hurt and suffer hurt; recognition by Jews that they, too, have a concrete, active part in the conflict (Bar and Bargal, 1995; Shavit-Ohion, 1994; Shulov-Barkan, 1993). Another significant accomplishment of encounters is that they reduce the feeling of personal and group hatred that is attributed to the other nation (Bar and Asaqla, 1988).

The approaches we have presented can serve educators and interveners as guidelines to crystallize their viewpoint on the subject, examine the diverse activities involved, and compare the different organizations operating in this field.

As noted, many organizations deal with Jewish–Arab relations through the method of encounters (Hochman, 1986; Weiner, Bar-On, and Weiner, 1992), in addition to independent, local initiatives by schools. Every educator, intervener, and school should examine what is available to determine what best suits their needs. The plethora of organizations has not contributed much either to the deepening of knowledge in this sphere or to the raising of professional standards. All have good intentions and motivations, and funding is readily available from many sources. But these two elements in themselves—intentions and financing—can guarantee neither professionalism nor a positive experience for pupils. Before listing the questions that can help schools decide what is most suitable for their needs, we shall note that a study by Razael and Katz (1990) found that twice as many Arab schools (50 percent) reported the operation of some sort of coexistence program as compared with Jewish schools (24 percent). In the light of this finding, many approaches are likely to be made to Arab schools (either by organizations or independently by Jewish schools). The Arab educational institutions should take advantage of the situation and choose those proposals that most closely meet their needs and are in accord with their pedagogic orientation. It bears stressing that such caution should also be exercised in cases of local initiatives.

The following are relevant questions that can help schools (or any educational organization or institution that is planning an encounter between groups of opposites) choose the most suitable program. The fundamental question is whether the organization (or the school which initiates an approach independently) that is proposing an encounter has a comprehensive conception and the organizational ability to apply it in practice. That viewpoint should be uncovered through the following:

(1) What rationale and educational worldview underlie the encounter program?

(2) Do the goals of the encounter take into consideration the needs of both participating national groups?

(3) How are the participants selected (even in schools that bring whole classes to encounters there is a process of selection in terms of age group and sometimes even of classes and/or among the pupils in the chosen grade)?

(4) What experience do the facilitators have? Is this their principal occupation or a side job? What are their academic, organizational and professional qualifications in this field? Do they receive continuous in-service guidance and support (including emotional and political processing)?

(5) Does the encounter format take into account the prevailing asymmetry between the two groups, and how is this handled during the encounter?

(6) Is reference made to the shifting external political reality and in what way?

(7) Are the emphases of the encounter process correlated with the distinctive attributes of the pupils in this specific school?

(8) Does a process of anticipatory socialization occur before the encounter? Is there a subsequent processing of the experience? In what format (one-time or continuous, uninational or shared, etc.)?

(9) What are the central contents on which the encounter focuses?

(10) Does the organization carry out evaluations of its achievements? By what method (through an external body, systematically, openly and publicly, or otherwise)?

Encounters can make an important contribution to their participants if conditions exist to enhance the prospects for success and if the content is focused, shared, and relevant to both nations alike. In view of the crucial educational importance of encounters—never more than in the present—and the complexities involved, it is important to remember that encounters in themselves are insufficient. They should be held only when conditions can ensure success and prevent, or at least greatly reduce, the risks and possible harm liable to ensue from failure. We should always remember: "An encounter as such is not enough."

References

In Hebrew:

Amir, Y., and Bizman, A. (1978). *The Effect of Small-Framework Encounters between Jews and Arabs on Mutual Acceptance.* Ramat-Gan: Bar-Ilan University, Department of Psychology.

Bar, H., and Bargal, D. (1986). *School for Peace—Neve Shalom 1985: Description and Evaluation of Continuous Intervention among Pupils and Staff.* Jerusalem: Israel Institute of Applied Social Research.

—— and Bargal, D. (1988). *Encounter Workshops between Jewish and Palestinian-Arab Youth in the School for Peace: Evaluation of One-Time Intervention.* Jerusalem: Israel Institute of Applied Social Research.

—— and Bargal, D. (1995). *Living with Conflict: Encounters between Jewish and Palestinian Youth.* Jerusalem: Jerusalem Institute of Applied Social Research.

—— and Asaola, J. (1988). *Encounters of Jewish and Arab Youth at Givat Haviva: Evaluation of Attitudes "Before" and "After."* Jerusalem: Guttman Institute of Applied Social Research.

Ben-Ari, R., and Amir, Y. (1988). "Intergroup Confrontations in Israel: Situation Appraisal and Paths for Change." *Psychology, I,* 49–57.

Binyamini, K. (1983). "On Political Tolerance: Social-Political and Educational-Psychological Considerations." *Psychology and Counseling in Education* (1986 Yearbook), 31–45.

Daviri, M., and Oubeid, S. (1993). *Free vs. Guided Expressions of Feelings and Identification through Children's Literature.* Nazareth.

Director-General's Circular, Special Circular 14 (1994). *Central School-Year Subject for 1994–95: The Peace Process—Israel in the Middle East. General Guidelines.* Jerusalem: Ministry of Education and Culture.

Hareven, A. (1993). *Looking back; looking ahead: Personal Summation and Evaluation of Initiatives by the Van-Leer Institute in Jerusalem in the Area of Relations between Jewish and Arab Israeli Citizens, and between Israel and Its Neighbors, 1977–91.* Jerusalem: Van-Leer Institute.

Hertz-Leizerovich, R., and Kupermintz, H. (Unpublished). "Jewish–Arab Encounters in the Shadow of the Intifada."

Hochman, R. (1986). *Education for Coexistence between Jews and Arabs.* Jerusalem: Van-Leer Institute.

Katz, I., and Mannheim, B. (1987). Survey of Dilemmas in Moderating Encounter Groups between Jews and Arabs in Israel. *Megamot, 33* (1), 29–47.

Lam, Z. (1988). "Education for Political Involvement." *Psifas,* 5, 2–5. Jerusalem: Ministry of Education and Culture, Pedagogical Secretariat, Unit of Education for Democracy and Coexistence.

Lewin, K. (1945). "Behavior, Knowledge, and the Acceptance of New Values." In D. Bargal (Ed.) (1989). *Conflict Resolution* (pp. 111–222). Jerusalem: Keter.

Liebman, Y. (Ed.) (1990). *Living Together: Religious-Secular Relations in Israeli Society.* Jerusalem: Keter and Avi Hai Foundation.

Masalha, J. (1987). *Changing the Attitudes of Arab and Jewish High-School Pupils through Encounters.* Haifa: University of Haifa, Department of Political Science.

Mikhlovitz, Y. (1987). *Educational Encounters between Jewish and Arab Teachers.* Jerusalem: Van-Leer Institute.

Moaz, Y. 1994. *Encounters of Jewish and Arab teachers—Analysis and Comprehensive Evaluation.* Jerusalem: Van-Leer Institute.

Peres, Y. (1976). *Communal Relations in Israel.* Tel Aviv: Sifriat Hapoalim and Tel Aviv University.

Rabinovich, D. (1993). "Oriental Nostalgia: How the Palestinians Became "Israeli Arabs.'" *Theory and Criticism,* 4, 141–51.

Razael, K., and Katz, A. (1990). *Education for Coexistence between Jewish and Arab Citizens of Israel in Israeli Schools.* Jerusalem: Henrietta Szold Institute.

Shamir, S. (1985). "Teaching the Arabs and Teaching Ourselves, Getting to Know Nearby Peoples." In S. Hartman (1992). *Children Teaching Children* (collection of articles) (pp. 5–8), Givat Haviva Seminar.

Shavit-Ohion, V. (1990). "Living with the Conflict: Attitudes of Youth toward the Jewish–Arab Conflict in the Wake of Encounter Workshops at the School for Peace." Master's Thesis, Hebrew University of Jerusalem, Social Sciences Faculty, Department of Psychology.

Shulov-Barkan, S. (1993). *Coping with Intergroup Conflicts: The Jewish–Arab Conflict: Development of an Intervention Model for Activating Small Groups.* (Summation Report). Hebrew University of Jerusalem, School of Social Work.

———, Bar, H., Oizerman, D., Vald, A., and Eady, E. (1992). *Intervention Model for Activating Small Groups on the Subject of Intergroup Conflicts: The Jewish–Arab Conflict in Israel.* Hebrew University of Jerusalem, School of Social Work.

Smooha, S. (1993). "Class, Communal, and National Cleavages and Israeli Democracy." In U. Ram (Ed.), *Israeli Society: Critical Views* (pp. 172–202). Tel Aviv: Breirot Publishers.

Sonnenschein, N., Halabi, R., and Friedman, A. (1992). *Legitimation for National Identity and Examination of Change in Power Relations in a Workshop on Coping with the Israeli–Palestinian Conflict.* Neve Shalom: School for Peace. [Cf. the present volume, p. 600 ff.]

Tabb, G. I., and Mannheim, B. (1987). *The Human Factor in Work.* Tel Aviv: Dvir Publishers.

Tsemah, M. (1986). *Political and Social Attitudes among Youth.* Tel Aviv: Dahaf Research Institute.

——— (1987). *Political and Social Attitudes among Youth.* Tel Aviv: Dahaf Research Institute.

In English:

Allport, G. W. (1954). *The Nature of Prejudice.* Cambridge, Mass.: Addison-Wesley.

Bargal, D. (1990). "Contact Is Not Enough: The Contribution of Lewinian Theory to Intergroup Workshops Involving Palestinians Citizens of Arab Palestinians and Jewish Youth in Israel." *International Journal of Group Tensions, 20* (2), 179–92.

Bar-Tal, D. (1994, July). *Development of Stereotypes in Early Childhood: The Case of "Arab's" Concept Formation by Jewish Children in Israel.* Paper presented in the second international congress on prejudice, discrimination and conflict. Jerusalem.

Blalock, H. M. (1982). *Race and Ethnic Relations.* Englewood Cliffs: Prentice Hall.

Brown, R. (1985). *Contact Is Not Enough—Criticisms and Extensions of the Contact Hypothesis from an Intergroup Perspective.* Paper presented on Contact and the Reconciliation of Conflict.

Campbell, D. T. (1965). "Ethnocentric and other Altruistic Motives." In D. Levin (Ed.), *Nebraska Symposium on Riotivation.* Lincoln, Nebraska: University of Nebraska Press.

Etzioni, A. (1970). "The Kennedy Experiment." In E. I. Megaregee, & J. E. Hokanson, (Eds.) *The Dynamics of Aggression.* New York Harper & Row.

Joreen (1973). "The Tyranny of Structurelessness." In A. Koedt, E. Levine & A. Rapone (Eds.), *Radical Feminism.* New York: Quadrangle Books.

Kelman, H. C. (1979). "An Interactional Approach to Conflict Resolution and Its Application to Israeli–Palestinians Relations." *International Interactions, 6* (2), 99–122.

Leven, R. A., and Campbell, D. T. (1972). *Ethnocentrism: Theories of Conflict, Ethnic Attitudes and Group Behavior.* New York: Wiley.

Lewin, K. (1958). "Group Decision and Social Change." In E. Maccoby (Ed.), *Reading in Social Psychology* (pp. 197–211). New York: Holt-Rinehart.

Sharif, M. (1958). Superordinate Goals in the Reduction of Intergroup Conflicts. *American Journal of Society, 63,* 349–56.

——— (1966). *In Common Predicament: Social Psychology of Intergroup Conflict and Cooperation.* Boston: Houghton and Miflin.

Smith, M. W. (1982). *Improving Intergroup relations: The impact of Two Types of Small Group Encounters between Israeli Arab and Jewish Youth.* Ann Arbor, MI: University Microfilms International.

Smooha, S. (1989). *Palestinian Citizens of Israel and Jews in Israel* (Vol. 1). London: Westview press.

Stephan, W. G. (1987). "The Contact Hypothesis in Intergroup Relations." In C. Hendrick (Ed.), *Group Process and Intergroup Relations.* (pp. 7–40). Beverly Hills, CA: Sage.

Tajfel, H. (1981). *Human Groups and Social Categories: Studies in Social Psychology.* Cambridge: Cambridge University Press.

Weiner, A., Bar-On, A, and Weiner, E. (Eds.), (1992). *Directory of Institutions and Organizations Fostering Coexistence between Jews and Palestinian Citizens of Israel in Israel.* New York: The Abraham Fund.

Jewish–Arab Coexistence in Mixed Professional Teams: A Pilot Study

HELENA SYNA DESIVILYA

1. Introduction

A series of events in the course of the last two years, notably the signing of the "Declaration of Principles," the agreement on self-rule in Gaza and Jericho by Israel and the PLO, the peace treaty with Jordan, and establishing nearly diplomatic relationships with Morocco and the Persian Gulf states, have significantly promoted the odds for peace in the Middle East region. Kelman (1994) considers the agreements with the PLO a conceptual breakthrough, namely a transition from a zero-sum conflict to a mutual recognition of the other's national rights and existence in the region. Notwithstanding this positive trend, attaining comprehensive peace in the region will undoubtedly be a long process, paved with many obstacles. The difficulties stem to a large extent from the opposition of the extremists on both sides. Consequently, concerted efforts are needed to muster both the internal and external support to maintain the momentum, pushing forward the peace process. Successful coexistence between Jewish and Arab citizens in Israel undoubtedly constitutes a critical supporting factor.

The current study was designed to examine the success of professional coexistence between Jewish and Arab citizens, as reflected in mixed medical teams, and to evaluate its potential contribution to Jewish-Arab coexistence in general, i.e., beyond the specific professional arena. This research effort is a pilot study that can serve as a model for longitudinal, comprehensive investigations in the area of coexistence.

The medical profession appears compatible with coexistence due to its universal humanistic premise of providing health care and cure to any human being, regardless of his or her race, nationality, religion, or any other characteristics. However, both Jewish and Arab health-care providers belong to distinct national groups, whose relationship has evolved in the context of a prolonged escalated conflict. Thus, they have most likely been affected by stereotyped attitudes, animosity, mistrust, and pessimism with regard to the prospects of resolving the conflict (Carnevale and Pruitt, 1992; Ross and Stillinger, 1991). These adverse changes on the personal level along with structural changes at a group level (e.g., emergence of struggle oriented norms) are usually reflected in adoption of militant strategies to deal with the conflict, or at the very least in diminished motivation to cooperate with members of the adversary group (Lewicki and Litterer, 1985; Pruitt, Rubin, and Kim, 1994).

The positive force towards successful coexistence within medical teams encompasses two components: *superordinate goals* and *group incentives.* The medical profession, with its basis of rescuing human life, serves as a superordinate goal, transcendent various destructive influences thereby allowing successful collaboration between Jewish and Arab members within the mixed teams. Moreover, the medical team (as any other professional or work group) is certainly affected by *group incentives.* They encourage both sides (Jews and Arabs) to act so as to attain joint gains for the benefit of the team as a whole. Several studies have shown that group incentives facilitate information exchange, promote integrative agreements, and in general encourage cooperative tendencies along with positive attitudes towards the team members (Schulz and Pruitt, 1978; Kramer and Brewer, 1984; Johnson et al., 1981; 1984). In addition, there is a growing consensus among scholars in the organizational-behavior and ethnic relations areas, that heterogeneity in team membership and in certain levels of conflict, does not harm group performance. On the contrary, both elements can even improve the group outcomes, especially if the group norms and climate support expression of diverse opinions, which in turn allow optimal utilization of the members' competencies and skills (Worchel et al., 1993). In the specific context of Israeli medical teams, the binational team composition can enhance the quality of medical care provided to the mixed-patients population, due to improved understanding of the latter's needs and hence better matching of treatment.

In spite of the evidence in favor of nationally or ethnically mixed teams, other empirical data refute the "contact hypothesis" introduced by Allport (1954) and later implemented by Amir (1969; 1976): namely, joint activities within teams composed of members from opponent groups, notwithstanding the positive nature of these experiences, do not necessarily mitigate antagonistic attitudes towards the entire adversary group. Instead, these group members are viewed as "exceptional," nonrepresentative individuals of the resented category (Rothbart, 1993). Consequently, we can anticipate a positive effect within the small group—both at the behavioral and the cognitive level—but it is confined to the specific experiences with this group's members.

The contradictory evidence with regard to the "contact hypothesis" seems to indicate the importance of the cognitive mechanisms' limitations, namely, difficulties associated with the processing, storage, and retrieval of information, which contribute to the resistibility of stereotypes and prejudice.

Bearing in mind the above difficulties and limitations, we can argue then, that Jews and Arabs belonging to joint medical teams, with a salient superordinate goal and group incentives, are likely to derive positive social identities from such group membership (Taifel and Turner, 1986; Abrahms and Hogg, 1990). How solid is this professional identity? Can it indeed counteract the destructive forces stemming from social identity, most notably from the national identity?

Research Goals

This study examined the quality of coexistence within mixed medical teams (Jews and Arabs) and its effect on the team members' mutual national images. In addition, we explored the applicability of theoretical models in the areas of conflict management and intergroup dynamics.

At the micro level, members of mixed medical teams are simultaneously affected by two sets of forces: one stemming from their national identity, and the other derived from their professional identity—both on the personal level (internalization of medical professional goals) and on the group level (membership in a medical team). While the national identity may hamper cooperation due to the residues of protracted antagonism, professional identity does the opposite, pushing toward joint problem solving among the team members. This study examined the relative strength of the two forces, that is, assessed the extent of the negative impact of the psychological barriers and national identity in contrast with the benevolent influence of the superordinate goal and group incentives on the quality of professional interaction and the climate of relationship within the mixed medical teams. In addition, we examined the degree of transference of the quality of coexistence within the teams into mutual national images, namely, whether positive experiences within a work group can mitigate intergroup stereotypes and prejudice.

Our study was based on nationally mixed organic work teams, whose members maintain continuous professional relationships, in contrast with previous research in this area, which has been based on the *minimal contact paradigm*, that is, groups formed especially for research purposes or on ad hoc experiential groups (e.g., Benjamin and Levi, 1979; Blake, Mouton, and Sloma, 1965; Burton, 1969; Cohen, Kelman, and Miller, 1977). Our study examined the variables associated with work dynamics of organic and permanent medical teams we well as the team members' attitudes with respect to their mutual national images.

Beyond the theoretical aspects, this study also carries practical significance. Its results with regard to the effect of professional contact may contribute to intervention directed at improving the quality of coexistence between Jews and Arabs, far beyond the specific professional arena of medicine.

2. Method

This research project constituted a case study that applied the theoretical sampling technique (Eisenhardt, 1989) for selection of cases. This mode comprises inclusion of polar cases. In our study this referred to dissimilar sites: a large hospital versus small ambulatory clinics. In the former case we expected more effective professional coexistence, mainly due to the differences in working patterns (presence of team work) in comparison to the latter case (absence of team work).

Subjects. The study was conducted in the Haifa area and encompassed three hospital departments (forty-six subjects; twelve Arabs and thirty-four Jews) and two ambulatory clinics (fourteen subjects: four Arabs and ten Jews). The hospital is one of the largest medical centers in the northern region of Israel, and provides health care to a heterogenous patient population in terms of national and ethnic origin, socioeconomic status, and age. The ambulatory clinics are located in a small town near Haifa, and provided health care to a nationally mixed population, mainly from low socioeconomic strata. In addition to the sixty medical professionals, who served as our main subjects, five individuals at the management level in the hospital and in the clinics participated in informal interviews designed to explore their perspective on the issue of coexistence.

Instruments. A semi-structured interview, designed to map the work dynamics within the mixed medical teams, served as the major research instrument. In addition, a short self-report questionnaire was administered to assess the mutual national images of the Jewish and Arab team members. Most of the questionnaire items were identical to those used in the public opinion surveys on the Jewish-Arab relationships in Israel (Smooha, 1992).

The *semistructured interview* encompassed measures designed to map the patterns of professional interaction, the overall climate of relationships within the mixed medical teams, and the perceived effect of professional contact in binational teams on coexistence in the Israeli society. Specifically, it addressed the following issues: Subjects' perceptions regarding the team goals; the nature of incentives at work—individual vs. joint; members' evaluation of the team's professional competence; team cohesion and commitment; interaction patterns, notably communication flow, cooperation, scope, and intensity of conflicts and ways to manage them; the overall interpersonal climate within the team; the impact of terrorist acts on the team atmosphere and professional functioning; the members' perceptions about the effects of nationally mixed personnel on the quality of care of the nationally mixed patient population; and the subjects' appraisal concerning the impact of joint professional interaction of nationally mixed medical staff on coexistence between Jews and Arabs in Israel.

The *self-report questionnaire* focused on the mutual national images of the Arab and Jewish staff members. This instrument was based on a questionnaire developed by Smooha (1992) and used in two nationwide surveys on Jewish–Arab relationships in Israel. We utilized only a small subset of items, which comprised the following issues:

- the perceived legitimacy of coexistence, that is, to what extent each of the national groups recognize the other's right to exist;
- definitions of self-identity, i.e., whether it concentrates on the national origin, religion, profession, etc., and to what extent the definition of the Arabs' national identity by themselves matches the one adopted by the Jews;
- ethnocentrism, that is, a sense of low tolerance level and suspicion (a high tendency towards stereotyping, avoidance of contact, disinclination to be a

subordinate of the other groups' members etc.) of Jews toward Arabs and vice versa;

- perceptions with regard to equal opportunities vs. discrimination of the Arab Israeli citizens, particularly in terms of academic opportunities and public service jobs;
- political orientation (location on the doves–hawks continuum);
- institutional separation, i.e., to what extent Jewish and Arab citizens in Israel support or oppose institutional separation (this issue was examined with respect to a hypothetical option of military draft and civic service for Arab citizens);
- the perceived impact of professional contact on the mutual attitudes of Arabs toward Jews and vice versa.

Procedure. Data collection was managed by the principal investigator and a graduate student research assistant. The manager of the medical center and the regional management of the ambulatory clinics designated the specific departments and clinics to be included in the study. Their decisions were made on the basis of the national composition of the medical staff, namely, that the selected departments and clinics indeed comprised nationally mixed medical teams. Both investigators met initially with the designated department heads, their respective chief nurses, or clinic directors. The purpose of the study was explained along with the specific tasks requested from the subjects. Subsequently individual appointments were set with the members of the selected departments and clinics.

3. Results and Discussion

Since this investigation was a case study, most of our data were analyzed by means of a qualitative method. This approach provides several advantages, such as developing new theoretical models, high probability for derivation of measurable variables, and empirical validity due to the intertwined and concurrent processes of theory building and data collection in the field (Mintzberg, 1979). Nevertheless, the qualitative paradigm may also have some weaknesses, particularly the tendency for building excessively complicated models, which refer to unique, highly specific phenomena, thus having limited generalizability (Eisenhardt, 1989). Notwithstanding the potential flaws, we adopted a qualitative approach since the current research constituted an exploratory study designed to develop specific hypotheses for further investigations. Moreover, the latter paradigm is especially suitable for a case analysis through integration of different theoretical models, previously tested separately. Their conglomeration breeds a new perspective, which was indeed one of our aims in the current project.

The results are presented in accordance with the sequence of our research aims; Namely, the first section provides the findings with respect to coexistence within the mixed medical teams, emerging from the interview protocols. In the second section we present the questionnaire data on mutual national images. The third section addresses the issue of interrelationships between the work dynamics within the mixed teams and mutual national images. Finally, the fourth section provides theoretical explanations with regard to the association between coexistence within the teams and mutual perceptions of the Arab and Jewish members, followed by a presentation of an integrative model, which blends together the different theoretical explanations.

1. *The Nature of Coexistence within the Mixed Medical Teams*
a. *The Team Members' Background Characteristics*

All the teams that took part in this study provide health care to nationally mixed patient populations. The national composition of the investigated teams resembled the proportions of Jews and Arabs in the Israeli population—in each of the teams, Arab members constituted a minority.

In the ambulatory clinics, age differences between the Jewish and Arab members were quite evident. The former were usually older and had greater seniority in comparison to the latter, who were considerably younger and have had a rather short professional experience. In addition, the Jewish medical staff of the ambulatory clinics were, by and large, educated abroad, whereas the Arab members were educated in Israel. No Arab female physician was employed in either of the two ambulatory clinics that participated in the study.

All of the nursing staff in the ambulatory clinics who took part in the study, have had a long professional experience, and have been working in their particular clinic for an extensive period of time.

All of the Arab physicians in the hospital departments who participated in this project were educated in Israel. Among the Jewish physicians, the senior members were also educated in Israel, whereas among the residents there were a number of immigrants from the former Soviet Union who studied in medical school in their country of origin.

The chronological age of the hospital physicians was directly related to professional seniority, regardless of their national origin.

Among the Arab nursing staff in the hospital, all were educated in Israel, while some of the Jewish nursing staff were immigrants from the former Soviet Union, where they had acquired their professional education.

b. *The Working Patterns and Dynamics within the Medical Teams*

The major differences between our two research sites—the hospital departments and the ambulatory clinics—is that in the former work is clearly organized around professional teams: the physicians' group and the nursing staff, with reciprocal links between these two teams. By contrast, in the latter the family physicians are by and large autonomous, while the nursing staff constitutes a pool, supporting the entire clinic. Consequently, the working patterns in the ambulatory clinics do not necessarily conform to the typical team organization. The only teamlike feature retained within the ambulatory clinics is the pediatrician-nurse dyad. The ambulatory clinic staff meets once a week, primarily to discuss complicated cases, occasionally also to pass new regulations or hear a professional lecture by an outside speaker. Consequently, some of the interview questions, dealing directly with the teamwork processes, were irrelevant to the ambulatory clinic staff.

Perception of superordinate goal vs. divergence of interests. Overall, there was a wide consensus among most of the respondents: not surprisingly, in both research sites the dominant response was that the major aim is to provide high quality care to patients. Nevertheless, most subjects also stated having a parallel goal, notably individual interest in professional development as well as advancement in the organization. It should be mentioned that the two kinds of goals—group and individual—are inherently intertwined: individual development is by and large a function of the department/clinic professional level, reflected mainly in the quality of care. Thus; highly rated departments or clinics provide high-quality care and allow their staff most opportunities for professional growth.

In order to attain both goals, there is a need for cooperation and coordination of the staff members' efforts (especially in the hospital departments). In some cases, the respondents noted tensions, associated with the pursuit of the individual interest, or a perception of conflict between the two kinds of interests. In such situations, the subjects usually employed twofold coping modes: at the overt level they attempted to mobilize joint resources; however, at the hidden level they strove to advance individual interests. One manifestation of such coping efforts was the inclination of residents to refrain from taking responsibility for mistakes at night duties, which was reflected in frequent contacts or calls to superiors.

Notwithstanding the occasional tensions, the superordinate goal—providing quality care to patients—prevailed in both the hospital departments and in the ambulatory clinics.

The nature of incentives at work. Notable differences were found between the hospital teams and the ambulatory clinics. In the former the team incentive was integrated with the individual one. By contrast, in the ambulatory clinics, virtually lacking teamwork, the individual incentives prevail. Nevertheless, it should be noted that even in the hospital departments, individual incentives did play a role for some members, particularly for the Arab physicians, who tended to stress them somewhat more than their Jewish counterparts. This finding seems to hint at a sense of injustice in terms of unequal opportunities for Arabs in comparison with Jews. Consequently, the former appear especially committed to accomplishing their career goals.

Evaluation of the team professional level. The majority of respondents alleged that there is much variance in professional competence. Within the ambulatory clinics the sources of variance stem primarily from the place where the individual had acquired his or her professional education (in Israel or overseas, notably in the former Soviet Union), seniority, and age. The young Arab physicians claimed that their older and more senior counterparts suffer from burnout that adversely affects the quality of their professional performance. In addition, they were not very favorably impressed with regard to the Russian-Jewish immigrants' professional competence. In a similar vein, the evaluations of the hospital staff (both of the nursing staff and physicians') also reflected lower ratings with regard to immigrant physicians and nurses from the former Soviet Union in comparison to their counterparts who had been educated in Israel. Another relevant factor, associated with team professional levels was the employee's status in the professional hierarchy—senior physicians, not surprisingly, are perceived as more competent than residents, and similarly, certified nurses are viewed as more professional than noncertified nurses. Nevertheless, in the case of the nursing staff, seniority may compensate for low formal professional status.

One cannot conclude, then, that perceptions with respect to the Arab staff members' professional competence fall short of those of their Jewish counterparts. As long as members of the Arab minority were educated in Israel, their professional competence is viewed similarly to that of the Jewish majority. Nevertheless, it is not clear that patients share the same criteria for evaluation of the medical staff members' professional competence. The respondents in our study seemed to indicate that their Jewish patients hold stereotypic views with regard to the Arab physicians, i.e., evaluate them as inferior in terms of professional competence. Similar perceptions were demonstrated in several subjects' (both junior and senior staff members) statements, that Jewish patients refrain from coming to the Emergency Room on Saturday (Sabbath), since Arab staff members are in charge.

What about the Arab team members' self-evaluations? These also appear "infected" by the stereotypic views toward Arabs. When given a choice between two hypothetical alternatives—either work in a nationally homogeneous team or in a mixed team—the majority clearly opted for the latter. The prevailing argument for this preference was the superior professional level of mixed teams (or Jewish homogeneous teams) in comparison to the homogeneous Arab teams.

The above findings resemble the results from studies two decades ago on prejudice against women (Touhey, 1974a, 1974b). These studies had indicated that when women infiltrate traditional male jobs their prestige decreases, and vice versa: when men begin to occupy traditional female jobs their prestige increases. Akin to the sex prejudice, in our case, the entry of Arab physicians into hospital departments or ambulatory clinics adversely affects their perceived prestige.

Cohesion and commitment. Differences were found on both dimensions as a function of the type of facility—hospital departments vs. ambulatory clinic, and within each one especially between the physicians and nursing staff. Overall, the subjects' reports indicate higher cohesion within the nursing staff in comparison to the physicians' group. In the ambulatory clinics this distinction stems primarily from structural factors, i.e., the physicians hardly work as a team, whereas the nurses do. The differences among the hospital departments emerge primarily from their hierarchical structure. Consequently, the extent of cohesion among the various levels of the hierarchy is rather limited. Moreover, within each level of the hierarchy interpersonal tensions and competition interfere with cohesion. The major tensions between the nursing and physician staffs seem to be accentuated primarily due to increasing academization of the nursing profession. This in turn leads to role ambiguity, resulting on the one hand in overlap of responsibility but on the other hand in areas of neglect, where no one is in charge. Some of these incongruities are resolved by means of third-party intervention (e.g., department secretaries), and some via decisions of superiors (department heads, etc.).

One exceptional department was identified where the team cohesion crossed all the lines of the professional hierarchy as well as the professional identification (nurses vs. physicians). Members of this unique department tended to use the analogy of a "warm family" in depicting the atmosphere and the relationships within their professional team, including all levels and professions.

In spite of the difficulties and structural barriers that were identified in the cohesion domain, the superordinate goal promotes a sense of commitment, especially in the hospital departments, and within the nursing staff of the ambulatory clinics, and—to a somewhat lower degree—also among the physicians in the clinics. No relationship was found between national origin and perceptions with respect to cohesion and commitment, presumably due to the dominance of the professional identity in this area.

Characteristics of interpersonal interaction within the team. This section focuses on cooperation among the members' interpersonal communication, participation in decision-making processes, and the scope of conflicts as well as conflict-related coping modes.

In light of the paucity of teamwork in the ambulatory clinics, it is not surprising that the extent of cooperation in these facilities is rather limited, reflected primarily in the working relationship between the pool of nurses and each of the physicians, with the latter working as autonomous care providers, each responsible for a group of patients. Similarly, the communication among the clinic physicians is confined to the weekly staff meetings, where information is exchanged about complicated cases and possible courses of treatment are discussed. Most of the decisions are made by the clinic manager, occasionally after consultation with the head nurse.

Within the hospital departments, which certainly exemplify teamwork, the levels of cooperation varied. In two out of the three departments that participated in the study, there was quite successful cooperation within the physician as well as within the nursing staff, however it was less effective between the physicians and nurses. The third department evinced high levels of cooperation both within each subprofessional group and between the physicians and nurses.

Most of the subjects in the hospital departments reported high satisfaction levels regarding interpersonal communication. Even those indicating moderate cooperation levels claimed no barriers were posed on interpersonal communication, since this would be considered a violation of professional ethic standards.

The subjects' responses concerning decision-making processes by and large validate the hierarchical structure of medical teams: namely, most of the decisions are made by the department-head physician and the head nurse, although the other members remain involved, reflected in an exchange of opinions and suggestions among all levels of the professional ladder. More cohesive departments tend to encourage junior team members to voice their opinions and ideas in contrast with less cohesive departments.

No particular problems were found in the area of interpersonal conflicts, other than those related to role conflict of certified nurses with academic degrees and occasional clashes they experience with the physicians. Interpersonal conflicts are usually handled by means of direct communication and negotiation, with or without the presence of the supervisor (e.g., the head nurse of the department), decision by the supervisor, or as indicated in one of the departments, at the secretary's office, who serves as neutral third party. At any rate, no differences were found in interaction patterns at work as a function of national origin.

The findings presented so far concerning the working patterns within the mixed medical teams indicate a highly successfully professional coexistence between the Jewish and Arab members. In other words, national origin, by and large, is irrelevant to the quality of professional cooperation as well as the quality of interpersonal interaction within the mixed medical teams. Some of our study participants in senior positions support this contention, claiming that at the starting point, while appraising candidates for specific medical residencies, national origin does not carry any weight in the selection process, instead it is based on professional merits and interpersonal skills.

Notwithstanding the overall success of professional coexistence in mixed medical teams in the medical center, some residues of Jewish–Arab conflict have been traced. This has been reflected in indirect evaluation of the Arab members' professional competence, both as emerging from patients' perceptions as well as in their self-perceptions. In addition, Arab participants revealed a sense of discrimination regarding their advancement opportunities. This perception was expressed in a striving for excellence by Arab physicians so as to legitimize their claim for equal professional advancement opportunities.

c. *The Impact of Terrorist Assaults on Mixed Medical Teams*

Although the routine work dynamics within the mixed teams seem generally unaffected by their members' national origin, conceivably external events associated with the Jewish–Arab conflict might stir the system, thereby changing the daily patterns. Consequently, we opted to examine the perceived impact of terrorist assaults on the atmosphere and work dynamics in the mixed medical teams. It is important to note that the data-collection period for this study followed a period that was marked by a high incidence of terrorist assaults, such as the Hebron massacre, bus explosions in Afula and Hadera, as well as a major terrorist event in Jerusalem.

All the respondents reported that terrorist assaults have not directly affected their work, namely the quality of care, which allegedly is independent of the medical professional's and patient's national origin. However, several Jewish participants in one of the ambulatory clinics indicated that the Arab physician was usually absent in the clinic the day after a terrorist event, presumably due to uncomfortable feelings and perhaps apprehension that he would be tainted with blame and scorn. In addition, the respondents in ambulatory clinics reported that such events affect the overall climate, creating tension. They tended to cope with this adverse influence by separating the terrorist event and its meaning from work duties and workplace. Specifically, this meant that nobody raised the subject or even discussed related political issues at work. If these issues were discussed it occurred solely among the Jewish members of the staff.

Akin to their counterparts in ambulatory clinics, hospital respondents claimed that terrorist events have no impact on their work per se, notably on the qualify of care. Nevertheless, they also felt that influence penetrates into the overall atmosphere within the team, yet it is transient, that is, void of long-term impact. Similarly to the ambulatory clinics, some of the hospital participants also tended to choose avoidance as their dominant coping mode after a terrorist event. Several respondents noted that some whispering occasionally could be heard on the hospital corridors, albeit "slips of the tongue" with racist overtones were extremely rare. Respondents in the most cohesive departments out of those that participated in the study appeared especially cautious after terrorist event; they reported a sense of tension, and took special care not to hurt or offend the Arab team members. Consequently, they usually refrained from initiating discussions on the relevant issues, unless they were sure that those present and participating in the conversation shared political attitudes on the Jewish–Arab conflict. It should be indicated that most of the Arab respondents felt that terrorist events had no impact on their, or other team members' performance at work and opted to deal with tensions in the aftermath of such events through avoidance. The reports of the Jewish respondents revealed greater variety in their coping strategies with terrorist events. Some said they talked openly about the subject as they discussed other topics with their teammates. Several claimed that such events tended to enhance internal cohesion and solidarity within the mixed team—uniting all the staff members in their condemnation of brutality.

2. Mutual National Images

The data based on the self-report questionnaire, which examined the Jewish and Arab team members' perceptions and attitudes with regard to the other nation are provided in Table 1.

As can be seen in the table, the Arab participants' responses were presented in two separate categories—Muslim Arab and Christian Arabs—due to some differ-

TABLE 1

Mutual National Images of Joint Medical Teams Members

Note: the numbers in the table present the absolute frequencies.

	Jews (N=37)	Muslim Arabs (N=6)	Christian Arabs (N=4)
Legitimacy of Coexistence			
What proportion of the Israeli Arabs reconciled themselves to the existence of the State of Israel?	Most of them 2 Large number 20 Part of them 14 Few 1	Most of them 2 Large Number 2 Part of them 1	Most of them 4
What proportion of the Jews in Israel reconciled themselves to the existence of an Arab minority in Israel?	Most of them 11 Large number 15 Part of them 10	Large number 1 Part of them 3 Few 1	Most of them 1 Large number 3
Self-Identity			
What is your most important self-identity?	Israeli citizen 17 Profession 14 Jewish religion 2 Jewish nationality 1 Residence in the homeland 3	Israeli citizen 1 Muslim religion 1 Arab nationality 2 Palestinian nationality 1 Profession 3	Israeli citizen 1 Christian religion 1 Profession 2 1
In what terms would you define the Arabs in Israel?	Israeli Arabs 26 Arabs 5 Israelis 5 Palestinian Arabs 1	Palestinians 4	Israeli Arabs 3 Israelis 1
Ethnocentrism			
Do you have Jewish/Arab friends and have you visited them in the course of the last two years?	No, I do not have 10 I have, not visited 11 I have, visited 16	I have, not visited 2 I have, visited 4	I have, visited 4

TABLE 1: (cont'd) Mutual National Images of Joint Medical Teams Members

		Jews (N=37)		Muslim Arabs (N=6)		Christian Arabs (N=4)	
Ethnocentrism	Are you willing to have Jews/Arabs as friends?	I am certainly willing	28	I am certainly willing	5	I am certainly willing	4
		I am willing	6	I am willing	1		
		I am willing but prefer Arab/Jewish friends	2				
	Are you willing to let your son/daughter marry a Jew/Arab?	I am certainly willing	2	I am willing, but prefer an Arab	1	I am willing, but prefer an Arab	2
		I am willing	3	I am willing only an Arab	5	I am willing only an Arab	2
		I am willing but prefer a Jew	8				
		I am willing only a Jew	23				
	Are you willing to have a Jewish/Arab superior?	I am certainly willing	15	I am certainly willing	3	I am certainly willing	3
		I am willing	12	I am willing	2		
		I am willing but prefer a Jew	9				
Equality/Discrimination	Do you think that an Arab can live in Israel as an equal citizen?	Yes	19	Yes	1	Yes	2
		Perhaps	11	Perhaps	2	Perhaps	1
		Doubtfully	6	Doubtfully	3	Doubtfully	1
		No	1				
	Who should be admitted to the universities?	Those with greatest merit	35	Those with greatest merit	6	Those with greatest merit	4
		Mostly Jews	2				

ences found between these two groups. Since our sample was very small the data are presented as frequencies (number of respondents) rather than in percentages. In some sections our findings are compared to survey data obtained from a national and representative sample of Jewish and Arab citizens in 1988 (Smooha, 1992). It should be noted that such comparison is problematic for two major reasons: first, Smooha's survey was conducted during the Intifada (the uprisings in the occupied territories) whereas data collection for the current study took place after the "Declaration of Principles" accord in Oslo; second, the research populations were different. There was, however, an inherent problem in selecting an appropriate comparison or control group for this study. It is possible to find homogeneous (Jewish) medical teams, but they usually operate in a mixed environment; that is, in a hospital with many other mixed teams. Comparison to a different professional domain is also unfeasible due to the lack of another area with similar characteristics of professional coexistence of such a prolonged nature as is the case in the medical field. Consequently, we did involve comparisons to the 1988 survey as an anchor, notwithstanding the differences between the two studies, yet these comparisons should be regarded with great caution.

a. *Perceptions Concerning Legitimacy of Coexistence*

Questions in this area were designed to examine to what extent each of the national groups acknowledges the other's legitimacy to exist in the State of Israel. Our data indicate that both Jews and Arabs tended to view their own attitudes on this issue more positively than the other side evaluated these attitudes. Such discrepancies are especially pronounced among the Jewish respondents and the Muslim Arabs. Presumably Jewish participants made an attempt to "embellish" the views of their national group, namely they wished to present an impression that most Jewish citizens felt reconciled with the legitimacy of Jewish–Arab coexistence in Israel. Similarly, Muslim Arab respondents seemed to overestimate their compatriots' acceptance of the Israeli State legitimacy.

Overall, perceptions of our respondents regarding the legitimacy of coexistence were considerably more positive in comparison to the views of the participants in the 1988 survey. One possible explanation of this gap may be the inauguration of the peace process. However, due to the marked differences between these two projects this interpretation should certainly be taken cautiously.

b. *Definitions of Self-Identity*

The respondents were asked to characterize their sense of self-identity, that is, to what extent it is based on their nationality, religion, profession, etc. In addition, we examined the Jewish and Arab participants' definitions of the Israeli Arab citizens' national identity. As can be seen in the table, most of the Jewish respondents described their self-identity as rooted in Israeli citizenship or in their profession. The Arabs' responses revealed a wider range of definitions, with no single category emerging as the most dominant. Israeli citizenship was also the prevailing category selected by the Jewish subjects in the 1988 survey. By contrast, the dominant response among the Arabs was the Palestinian national identity.

Most of the Jewish respondents in our study used the term "Israeli Arabs" to define the Arab Israeli citizens' national identity. A similar trend was found in the reports of the Christian Arabs, whereas the Muslim participants opted for the term "Israeli Palestinians" or "Palestinian Arabs" to define the Arab citizens' national identity.

c. *Ethnocentrism*

This group of questions examined the subjects' levels of trust in members of the other nation and openness with regard to this "adversary" group. The specific questions centered around the amount of desired contact with members of the other nation and willingness to accept them in a supervisory role.

All the Arab respondents reported some form of contact with Jews, most of them reporting that they have visited Jewish homes. About 75 percent of the Jewish participants indicated that they have had social contact with the Arabs, over 40 percent also claimed that they have visited in Arab friends' homes in the course of the last two years. Our data seem to present a rather bright side of the Arab-Jewish relationships, not surprisingly far more positive than that which emerged in the 1988 survey. (Smooha's data indicated that 36 percent of the Arabs reported having Jewish friends whom they have visited, 30 percent reported having Jewish friends, but have not visited at their residence. Only 11 percent among the Jews reported social relationships with the Arabs, including visiting terms; 15 percent indicated having contact, but not including visits at their home). Our case, then, represents a small and unique group in terms of educational and professional characteristics, where social contact between Jews and Arabs emerge as a byproduct of their contacts at the workplace.

A similar trend to that indicated above was evinced when the respondents were asked about their willingness to establish friendships with members of the other nation. *All* the Arab participants expressed readiness for social contact with the Jews. The latter were also highly willing to have such relationships with the Arabs, only 5 percent appeared to have some reservations on this issues (they stated that they were ready to have Arab friends, but preferred Jewish friends). Here again our data are more favorable than Smooha's findings, where 63 percent of the Arabs and 38 percent of the Jews indicated readiness for social contact with members of the other nation. This discrepancy is not surprising in light of the unique nature of our sample, in which the subjects were members of mixed medical teams, experiencing daily professional contact at work.

To what extent can such high willingness for mutual contact be generalized to family relationships, particularly intermarriage? As can be seen in Table 1, this indeed seems to be the limit of the readiness for closeness. Most of our respondents (both Jews and Arabs) clearly preferred that marriages be confined to their own national category.

How much are the members of mixed medical teams open to having a supervisor from the other nation? It is important to note that the reality of Israeli hospitals hardly affords any opportunity for Arabs to be in supervisory positions over Jews. Consequently, the only question we could examine was the Jewish respondents readiness to work under an Arab supervisor. Our data indicate relatively high openness for such a relationship: about 75 percent claimed they were willing to have an Arab professional supervisor, with the rest expressing somewhat reserved acquiescence (namely, they are ready, but prefer a Jewish supervisor). These findings are clearly contradictory with the Smooha (1992) data, which reveal low tolerance levels and lack of openness to having an Arab supervisor (75 percent of the Jewish respondents reported opposition to working under an Arab supervisor).

Overall, our findings seem to suggest a positive effect of professional contact within the mixed medical teams, which appears to be reflected in a mitigation of ethnocentric perceptions and attitudes towards members of the other nation.

d. *Perceptions Regarding Equal Opportunities versus Discrimination against the Arab Minority in Israel*

We examined the respondents' views with regard to the issue of equal opportunities for the Arab minority in Israel, particularly in the academic education arena and public service jobs.

In general, the Jewish members of the mixed teams were more optimistic regarding equal opportunities for the Arab minority in Israel in comparison to their Arab counterparts. (With regard to the question "Is it possible for Arabs in Israel to be citizens with equal rights?" about half of the Jewish participants responded "definitely," another 32 percent responded "possibly," and less than 20 percent were doubtful. Among the Arab respondents 30 percent stated that it was definitely possible, 30 percent answered "possibly," and over a third of them expressed serious doubts). Nevertheless, perceptions of the members of the mixed medical teams were more favorable in contrast with the respondents in the 1988 survey.

As can be seen in Table 1, the majority of our Jewish subjects supported the need for providing equal opportunity for academic education to Israeli Arab citizens. However, there was much less enthusiasm with regard to advocating equal opportunities for the Arab minority within the domain of the public-service jobs.

Akin to previous issues, a significant discrepancy was shown between our findings and the 1988 survey. Our subjects, members of mixed medical teams, represent a rather tolerant and open-minded group, as far as coexistence is concerned, in comparison to the general Israel public, as emerged in the course of the second year of the Palestinian uprisings (the Intifada). This unique profile of our respondents gains additional support from data on their political proclivities, as presented in the following section.

e. *Political Attitudes*

One global question assessed the respondents' location on the political spectrum in Israel (hawk–dove continuum). The data clearly indicated that most of our participants espoused dovish attitudes (center and left on the "hawk–dove" continuum).

f. *Institutional Separation*

This study also investigated the preferences of members of mixed medical teams with regard to institutional separation versus integration. Examination of this issue was confined to the context of military and civic service. As can be seen in Table 1, the majority of our Jewish respondents were in favor of integrating the Arab citizens in the military service, albeit on a voluntary basis. They also tended to support compulsory or at least voluntary civic service for the Arab minority. By contrast, the Muslim participants opposed any form of military service for the Arab citizens. Their Christian counterparts, however, were in favor of voluntary military service for the Arab minority. Both Muslim and Christian Arabs supported integration of the Jewish and Arab sectors in Israel by means of civic service (preferably at first on a voluntary basis).

Again, our data reveals more openness for institutional integration in comparison to that indicated in the 1988 survey.

g. *Attribution of Change in the Mutual National Image to Joint Work Teams*

We examined the participants' perceptions regarding the impact of professional contact in mixed medical teams on their mutual national images, and particularly to what extent joint work teams have contributed to modifications in their views. Notwithstanding the overall positive flavor in the questionnaire responses, most of the subjects reported neither change in their attitudes toward the other national group nor modifications in their political attitudes as a result of the professional contact in joint work teams. This reluctance to attribute change in the mutual national image to joint work teams was especially pronounced among the Jewish respondents.

In summary, the questionnaire responses reveal rather positive mutual national images, with low levels of ethnocentrism, overall support for equal rights and opportunities for the Arab minority, considerable mutual reconciliation with regard to the legitimacy of coexistence and receptivity for institutional integration. However, this favorable trend was not viewed as a consequence of the joint professional contact.

3. *Relationships between Working Patterns within the Mixed Medical Teams and Mutual National Images*
a. *Ambulatory Clinics*

As stated earlier, the ambulatory clinics that participated in our study hardly applied the teamwork mode. The participants emphasized the separation between work-life and other domains. Consequently, judgment with regard to colleagues was confined solely to their professional and interpersonal capabilities at work, excluding their background characteristics, such as national or ethnic origin.

Notwithstanding this prevailing view, some individuals did state explicitly that nationally mixed medical teams had a positive impact on the quality of care for mixed patient populations. This positive effect was explained by the *capacity to practice ethnosensitive medicine and hence increase the fit between the patients' needs and the type of treatment.* A binational staff presumably promotes ethnosensitive medicine that attempts to reduce the incongruity between the patients' health-related beliefs and those of the health-care providers. Thus, having mixed medical teams of physicians and nurses who can communicate more effectively and understand their patients' health-related values and priorities can enhance the overall effectiveness of health services.

Some respondents in the ambulatory clinics contended that the degree of positive coexistence is contingent on the quality of interpersonal relationships within the team: The more cohesive the team, the higher the odds for transference of positive feelings with regard to members of the other national group beyond the work arena.

b. *Hospital Departments*

Four major views emerged from the interview responses with regard to the impact of mixed medical teams on mutual national images:

- *No impact.* This category represented the prevailing view of our study participants. They alleged that the quality of coexistence within the mixed team has not been transferred beyond the work arena. Accordingly, the members' background characteristics were irrelevant to the quality of professional performance, but rather professional competence and interpersonal skills were the key elements in successful team performance. Some respondents in this category, notably Jewish team members, also argued that their Arab counterparts hardly exhibited any distinctive features, especially if they had been educated in Israeli medical or nursing schools.

- *Unidirectional impact.* This group of respondents perceived the benevolent effect of mixed medical teams primarily in enhancement of professional development for the Arab employees (especially physicians). The Jewish majority has spurred a competitive atmosphere, invigorating the Arab physicians to exert special efforts so as to match the standards of their Jewish counterparts. It is interesting that both Arab and Jewish participants were included in this category. Another type of response, found in this category and provided by Jewish participants, focused on the negative impact of mixed medical teams. Thus, a number of Jewish nursing staff members stated that Arab members devoted greater effort in providing care to Arab patients than to Jewish ones. Some also claimed that senior Arab physicians abuse their authority with regard to junior Jewish physicians. Several Jewish nursing staff members felt they were constantly scrutinized by the Arab patients' relatives as if trying to ensure that they were not discriminated against in quality of care in comparison to the Jewish patients.

- *Bidirectional impact—promoting mutual understanding.* Responses in this category centered on the mutually positive effect of mixed medical teams on deepening of familiarity and understanding of the other nation's culture and customs due to the daily contact at work. This resulted both in improved interpersonal relationships within the team as well as higher quality of care provided to the mixed patient population. Like the ambulatory clinics' respondents, here again there was a sense that mixed medical teams promote ethnosensitive medicine. Not surprisingly, respondents in this category were by and large nurses. Presumably, nursing staff members tend to socialize more with their coworkers outside working hours in comparison to physicians, who have more limited leisure time. Consequently, the former were indeed more acquainted with the other nation's culture and customs. Notwithstanding the alleged positive impact of the professional contact, it has not affected the mutual national images, but was confined to deeper acquaintance with representatives of the other national group.

- *Bidirectional impact—promotion of mutual tolerance.* We identified several respondents in our study (Jews, both nurses and physicians) who viewed their work in mixed medical teams as an effective vehicle for promoting Jewish–Arab coexistence in Israel. They felt that professional contact between Jews and Arabs within work teams enhanced mutual tolerance that did generalize into interpersonal relationships outside the work arena. This positive effect was amplified in departments where new managerial practices were implemented, which were in principle patient-centered. Thus all team members collaborate to provide the best care. One participant in this category confirmed the "contact hypothesis": in his view, Jewish patients tended to change their attitudes towards Arabs following high quality care by an Arab physician.

c. *Relationships between Work Patterns and Mutual Attitudes*

An attempt was made to elucidate links between the work patterns within the mixed medical teams and their members' attitudes with regard to the other national group, based on our entire data set. It is important to note that these relationships were not derived from quantitative data but rather emerged from qualitative analyses.

As expected, an inverse relationship was found between team cohesion and ethnocentrism. In cohesive teams less evidence for ethnocentric behaviors or attitudes was found. These findings indicated a positive association between feeling at ease as a subordinate of a supervisor from the other national group, willingness to socialize with members of the other nation, optimism with regard to the potential of Arabs to materialize their professional aspirations, and endorsement of equal rights for the Arab minority. These results seem to suggest the positive influence of joint (universal) interests on the interpersonal relationships within the mixed medical team.

Beyond the associations presented above, no relationships were found between work-pattern variables within the mixed medical teams and the members' attitudes. Such was the case with regard to the specific issue of intermarriages, as well as the general feeling of no modification in either political or overall attitudes towards the other nation. One possible explanation for this paucity of evidence for the "contact hypothesis" might be the features of our sample: it was mainly composed of individuals characterized by relatively liberal, tolerant, and dovish attitudes. In other words, we might have encountered a "ceiling effect": since the respondents' attitudes were initially rather positive, no additional improvement could be expected as a consequence of daily professional interaction within the joint work teams. Our pilot study does not allow for drawing any firm conclusions with regard to the ceiling effect as a plausible explanation. However, there were some indications that other explanations may also be viable. Examination of the data obtained from the "deviant" respondents (primarily Jews) espousing "hawkish," unprogressive attitudes, claimed to have experienced no change in their views with regard to the Arab minority as a consequence of professional interaction within the mixed medical teams. They reported attempts to restrain themselves, withholding discriminatory or demeaning remarks with regard to Arab colleagues at work, particularly in highly cohesive teams, where the overall climate was characterized by mutual understanding and tolerance. Yet outside of the work domain their attitudes towards Arabs remained saturated with stereotypes and "hawkish" overtones. Such cognitive rigidity tended to be pronounced in the aftermath of a terrorist event. The "right wing" respondents experienced much greater difficulty interacting with Arab members within the teams in these unfortunate circumstances in comparison to their counterparts who embraced liberal and tolerant attitudes. In addition to these findings on the "deviant" subjects, we traced other indications of stereotypical perceptions of Arabs by Jews and vice versa, such as appraisal of professional inferiority with regard to the Arabs. Consequently, alternative or additional explanations need to be searched to account for the lack of transference of successful coexistence within the mixed medical teams to the mutual national images and coexistence of Jews and Arabs in general.

4. Theoretical Explanations

The following explanations of our data rest upon several theoretical approaches, such as theories on social identity, conflict resolution models, and cognitive-mechanism models, focusing on perceptual processes at the individual level.

a. Intragroup and Intergroup Processes

This explanation focuses on group-level phenomena or intergroup processes, addressing primarily *social identity,* including the *intergroup bias* phenomenon. According to social identity theory (Tajfel and Turner, 1986), individuals derive their self-identity primarily from membership in social categories. Each person belongs simultaneously to a number of social groups, but only the one with the highest contribution to positive self-image forms the core of his or her self-identity. For the member of a mixed medical team, self-identity can evolve around three components: personal identity, professional identity, and social identity, including the national identity.

Our quantitative data indicated that for the Jews, self-identity has been crystallized primarily from the professional component and membership in the Israeli State. For the Arabs, the elements of self-identity revealed greater variance, including Arabic or Palestinian nationality. Notwithstanding the contention of the motivational theory about the correlation of self-image and self-identity, conceivably the weight of the different components of self-identity can vary depending on the specific social context. Thus at work, the professional identity may gain the dominant position, but when the social milieu changes, e.g., at home with family and friends, it may lose its primacy and be succeeded by another component of the self-identity, such as the national identity. The dominance of professional identity was especially pronounced within the highly cohesive teams, where members were committed to pursuing both the joint objective of providing high-quality services as well as their individual interests of professional development and advancement. In the work arena, professional identity aids in blurring the differences, while emphasizing the similarities. Tangible discrepancies, such as language and culture, which remain salient notwithstanding the impact of professional identity, turn into real assets allowing effective fulfillment of the members' unique skills and proclivities. This in turn facilitates ethnosensitive medicine, thereby promoting the joint, superordinate goal.

In other words, our data appear to confirm conflict-resolution theory at the mixed team level: the members' interdependence on the one hand, and their aspiration to accomplish individual goals on the other hand, along with the superordinate joint goal all promote a problem-solving orientation, and in consequence contribute to the successful performance of the mixed medical teams.

The professional domain, then, serves as a refuge, especially for those who feel hostility towards the national out-group owing to the historical enmity between the two nations. The professional identity appears to free them from the bondage of divergence since it is based on universal values irrelevant to political inclinations or national membership. Moreover, the professional identity, especially medicine, contributes to the maintenance of a positive self-image due to its prestige as well as its importance to human society. It is not surprising, then, that in hospital departments with their prominent work-team structure, professional coexistence of the two national groups reaps significant achievements. However, outside the work domain, upon return to their family, neighborhoods, and social networks, the professional identity vanishes into the background, and the national identity becomes salient. In this nonwork realm, national identity has much greater appeal for the self-image than professional identity. Consequently intergroup bias is reinstated, amplifying the inclination to disparage the out-group. Preservation of the adverse stereotypical mutual national images is the obvious outcome of such a process.

According to the motivational explanation of the intergroup bias (Cialdini, 1976; Tajfel and Turner, 1986) the higher the identification with the in-group, the more intense is the intergroup bias. Hence, the mutual national image is affected by the intensity of national identity that undoubtedly becomes more potent outside the work arena. Similar predictions can be derived from the cognitive approach to social identity (cf. Rothbart and Lewis, 1988). According to this approach, perception of divergence of interests constitutes the key factor in aggravation of the intergroup bias.

Conceivably the perception of divergent interests becomes much more dominant outside the work domain where inequalities in standard of living and opportunities for political integration are salient, especially for the Arab minority. Consequently stereotypical perceptions with regard to the out-group members remain intact.

Interestingly enough, the professional identity was incapable of shielding the national vulnerabilities of the Arab team members. The perception of divergent interests managed to penetrate the work domain, reflected primarily in the Arabs' quest for excellence to justify equal opportunity for professional advancement, which may have to some extent interfered with the sense of cooperation among the mixed team members.

In summary, according to the aforementioned category of explanation, the odds for the success of professional coexistence among members of different national origin are rather high due to the dominance of their professional identity. Lack of transference of this success to the global level of coexistence between the two national groups stems from the potency of national identity outside the work domain.

b. *Coping Profiles with the Jewish–Arab Conflict*

This explanation discerns a variety of coping patterns with the Jewish–Arab conflict employed by Jews and Arabs. They are based on Smooha's (1992) typology of coping profiles, which was derived from the analysis of global views as well as specific attitudes of Jewish and Arab citizens with regard to the Middle East conflict. The emergent profiles reflect different trends within the Israeli political arena. Obviously, we cannot fully reconstruct Smooha's typology, but we have applied the key concepts, especially those associated with the Arab and Jewish citizens' views on the regional conflict and its possible solutions.

Smooha (1992) identified four distinct profiles among the *Arab* Israeli citizens:

- *Accommodationist,* prevalent among the Druze Israeli citizens, but also characterized by some of the Christian Arabs and Bedouins. Individuals who represent this profile believe that accommodation and integration within the Jewish-Zionist system constitutes the most effective means for advancing the status of minorities in Israel.

- *Reservationist,* representing primarily the Muslim Arabs, who are politically independent (do not vote for Zionist parties). They maneuver between some sort of adjustment within the Zionist establishment and opposition to the Zionist authorities. In their view the best way to improve the minority position is through autonomous organizing, albeit simultaneously negotiating with the Zionist establishment.

- *Oppositionist,* representing mainly members of the Communist parties, who acknowledge the Israeli State's right to exist, but oppose its Zionist essence. Consequently, individuals within this profile emphasize the necessity of independent organizing and launching a struggle against the Zionist establishment from outside.

- *Rejectionist,* comprising the supporters of the "village sons," who categorically oppose the Israeli State's right to exist and aspire to replace it by a Palestinian State.

The following profiles were identified among the *Jewish* Israeli citizens:

- *Conciliationist,* comprising Zionist Jews, notably supporting left-wing parties, who advocate equal rights and opportunities for the Arab minority, including their full integration within the Israeli society. They do not perceive any contradiction between a democratic Zionist state.

- *Pragmatist,* representing mainly supporters of the Labor party, who advocate selective and controlled integration of the Arab minority within governmental institutions. Advocacy of such policy toward Israeli Arab citizens stems from the view that their loyalty and contribution to the state is not conditioned on total identification with Israel. As long as the regional conflict is not entirely resolved, full equality and integration within the Jewish society are precluded, hence appropriate arrangements must be made to allow reasonable coexistence.

- *Hardliner,* comprising primarily the voters for the LIKUD right-wing party, who advocate granting Arab citizens partial rights as long as they comply with their status as a national minority within an essentially Jewish-Zionist state.

- *Exclusionist,* representing Jews who posit that Israeli Arab citizens should unequivocally submit themselves to Jewish rule or else leave the Israeli state. They believe that Jewish people can legitimately claim the entire territory of Israel.

If Smooha's typology of the coping profiles was applied as an explanation of our findings it would suggest that the likelihood of transference of successful coexistence within the mixed teams into overall mutual images is contingent on classification into one of these profiles. Consequently, the Arab accommodationist and the Jewish conciliationist would have much less need for transference from the team arena to overall image since they were from the outset more favorable and more optimistic with regard to coexistence. Conversely, the more extreme profiles, such as the "oppositionist," the "rejectionist," the "hardliner," and the "exclusionist," afford much lower odds for generalization of successful professional cooperation into domains beyond the work arena.

The latter interpretation of our findings reverts to the team composition in terms of general outlook on life as well as the specific political attitudes associated with the Middle East region. Yet, it still does not provide a full account of our pilot study. Let us then turn to the third interpretation.

c. *Cognitive Mechanisms*

This category pertains to the individual level interpretations, focusing on cognitive processes, presumably rational in nature. However, the emphasis in our interpretation rests on flaws and deviations from these rational processes, referred to as *cognitive biases.* Two phenomena are addressed: *subtyping* and *rebound effect.*

First we wish to refer again to the "contact hypothesis" (Allport, 1954; Amir, 1969; 1976), stating that positive interaction with members of an adversary group may mitigate mutual animosity and even improve mutual images, especially when these groups' representatives are of equal status. Such conditions have indeed been met in the investigated hospital departments, nevertheless no clear evidence was obtained as to modifications in the mutual national images. This may suggest that the contact hypothesis was in fact refuted. As Rothbart (1993) has suggested, contact among polarized groups often fails to produce the anticipated effect of prejudice reduction due to cognitive limitations. Positive experiences with the adversary do not modify overall attitudes. Instead of generalizing from these incidents to the entire category, the individual acts are interpreted as nonrepresentative, unique cases. Instead of changing perception with regard to the entire category (members belonging to the other national group) following positive experiences, there was a tendency to treat these individuals within the mixed teams as "exceptional" or nonrepresentative members. Consequently the category remains unchanged in the in-group's perceptions, yet its members may continue having positive experiences with the out-group's nonconforming members.

Kunda and Oleson (1995) proposed a mechanism whereby stereotypes with regard to social groups remain intact in spite of disconfirming evidence. Series of studies conducted by these researchers indicated that when individuals encounter deviant members of certain social categories, they seek for grounds to construct subtypes of this category in order to accommodate these exceptional individuals, while maintaining their perceptions with regard to the main category. Conceivably, Jewish and Arab members created subcategories of the other national group, namely treated Jewish or Arab health professionals as a subtype with distinct characteristics (presumably more positive), however their images of the entire national out-group have remained unchanged.

Indeed evidence for the subtyping phenomenon was reflected in frequent verbalizations of our Jewish subjects with regard to their Arab team members, such as:

They are just like us, they act as Jews do, not like Arabs.

Thus, it appears that global perceptions of social categories are highly resistant to change, especially after they have been solidified over extended periods of time.

Why are the stereotypical perceptions so resistant to change?

Attempts to suppress stereotypical thinking in the work arena, where a superordinate goal prevails, result in subsequent "rebound effect" (Macrae, et al., 1994), that is, the stereotypes reappear with even greater insistence in other arenas.

A study conducted by Macrae et al. (1994) revealed a *rebound effect* at the individual level, namely, a failure to suppress stereotypical thinking for the long run, particularly when deliberate emphasis is placed on refraining from such biased information processing. Mental control does succeed temporarily when pressure is exerted or clear instruction provided to abandon stereotypical perception, but such a tendency resumes with a mounting intensity when control is released. Within the mixed medical teams, especially the highly cohesive ones committed to a joint universal goal, undoubtedly the prevailing norm prescribes rational deliberation, based on professional competence, devoid of stereotypes and ethnocentric biases, and hence coexistence is quite successful. However, upon return to the nationally homogeneous home residence, the normative pressure towards universalistic, unbiased perception is lifted, perhaps even replaced by national demands. Consequently, the tendency for stereotypic thinking is reinstated and amplified. This "regressive" trend becomes even more prominent following terrorist events (for the Jews) and for the Arabs when they face their political reality in Israel.

Each of the preceding interpretations contributes some components to the understanding of the findings from our pilot study. They are not mutually exclusive, but rather complementary. To promote further insights on the issue of coexistence it seems important to develop an integrative model which encompasses a variety of interpretations and their interrelations. The following section constitutes a first step in this direction.

d. *The integrative model*

The proposed integrative model is schematically portrayed in Figure 1.

According to the proposed model, the odds for transference of successful coexistence at the professional level are not solely affected by the individual members and the team's characteristics but are also contingent on organizational features, including geographic location, as well as the stage of the peace process in the Middle East. Accordingly, our model is dynamic in nature, sensitive to the progressions in the peace process, which in turn influence the individual, team, and organizational

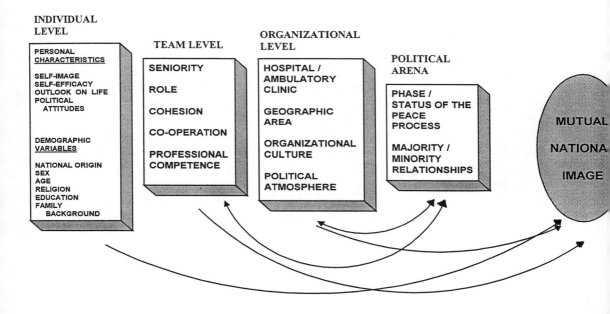

INDIVIDUAL LEVEL

PERSONAL
CHARACTERISTICS

SELF-IMAGE
SELF-EFFICACY
OUTLOOK ON LIFE
POLITICAL
  ATTITUDES

DEMOGRAPHIC
VARIABLES

NATIONAL ORIGIN
SEX
AGE
RELIGION
EDUCATION
FAMILY
  BACKGROUND

TEAM LEVEL

SENIORITY

ROLE

COHESION

CO-OPERATION

PROFESSIONAL
COMPETENCE

ORGANIZATIONAL LEVEL

HOSPITAL /
AMBULATORY
CLINIC

GEOGRAPHIC
AREA

ORGANIZATIONAL
CULTURE

POLITICAL
ATMOSPHERE

POLITICAL ARENA

PHASE /
STATUS OF THE
PEACE
PROCESS

MAJORITY /
MINORITY
RELATIONSHIPS

MUTUAL
NATIONA
IMAGE

Figure 1. Factors Affecting the Mutual National Image: *An Integrative Model*

level. The individual level is undoubtedly least amenable to change in comparison to the other levels.

Let us now demonstrate how the three interpretations provided in the previous section are integrated into a global model.

Changes at the political level, notably achievements in the peace process realm, may mitigate the perceived divergence of interests by both Jews and Arabs, diminishing in turn the magnitude of *inter group bias*. Conceivably, consistent progress in the direction of comprehensive peace in the region may also transform the coping profiles. For example, the "undecided" patterns may opt for the more moderate course, possibly even become advocates of equitable coexistence. At the *cognitive level*, the "contact hypothesis" may become a more viable means to rectify biased images and mitigate prejudice towards the out-groups. Moreover, if the peace process indeed involves transformation of the social reality it may dampen the "rebound effect," which again will minimize the use of stereotypes in processing information and reactions towards members of the out-group.

The organizational level was included in the proposed model on the assumption that the political atmosphere penetrates the organizational climate, thus affecting the interpersonal relationship at work, notably the characteristics of work teams (the importance of cooperation, joint goals, excellence, etc.).

The geographical location constitutes an additional important dimension due to its relevance to the political arena. Geographical regions where there are nationally mixed settlements and residences, and both groups are integrated in daily interaction, undoubtedly facilitate the transference of coexistence at the professional level into the more global level, in contrast with regions devoid of daily coexistence experiences.

Future research needs to further examine and validate the proposed integrative model, utilizing both quantitative and qualitative methods. The most suitable approach would be to launch a longitudinal investigation, initiated at the level of professional education and socialization, i.e., medical and nursing schools, followed up through the medical residency period, and later at the actual permanent placement. This would allow for carefully mapping of the process of transitions and elucidate the web of interrelations among the various dimensions in the proposed model.

4. Conclusions: Can Mixed Professional Teams Advance Coexistence between Polarized National Groups?

The results seem to suggest that the success of professional coexistence within the mixed medical teams is confined to the "local" boundaries. No evidence has been obtained that it generalizes into overall mutual national images and alleviates protracted antagonism, stereotypes, or prejudice. The forces associated with professional identity and the universal superordinate goal associated with the medical profession appear to have failed in counteracting the adverse impact of the national identity. The latter have encapsulated the structural changes, thus preserving the animosity between the two national groups.

The current pilot study does indicate the importance of professional coexistence as a necessary condition for establishment of an integrative problem-solving framework of relationships between the two nations in Israel. However, our study clearly points out that professional coexistence is insufficient. Notwithstanding its significant contribution to the reconciliation process, other influences—such as social reforms and transitions at the wider political level—undoubtedly constitute additional crucial components. This is merely the beginning of a dialogue. As Gurevitch (1994) stated, the handshake between Rabin and Arafat has symbolized a transition from communication by means of weapons to communication through words, nevertheless the process of gaining genuine mutual understanding would entail a prolonged progression of bilateral cognizance, including recognition and appreciation of differences. Denial of the sediments of the protracted conflict would only impede the constructive peace process. Instead, Jews and Arabs must engage in a search of novel alternatives, a new language that would allow for reconciliation of the interests and needs of both parties, thus creating a favorable framework of relationships.

Massive efforts of confidence building are necessary to advance the peace process and coexistence among adversaries who have experienced a protracted escalated conflict. Professional coexistence may be one necessary—albeit insufficient—component in this complex system of change, which should be supplemented by interventions in the educational arena, community work, and certainly further achievements in the political domain. As to internal policy, Rouhana (1992) emphasizes the importance of Israeli Arab citizens in shaping the future of the Israeli State.

In summary, notwithstanding the diversity in contentions and methodologies among scholars representing various disciplines and approaches who engage in analysis of the Jewish–Arab conflict, most share the idea that the integrative/problem solving orientation provides the best prospects for resolving the Middle Eastern conflict. Yet, one should be prepared for stumbling on barriers and obstacles, especially if the Israeli public has not reached a consensus, following a deep understanding of conflict dynamics, with regard for the need to implement this approach. Such widely adopted conviction can hardly be attained through professional contacts and the coexistence of members representing the two national groups; rather it requires a systematic and comprehensive intervention, focusing on education initiated in early childhood (Burton, 1990; Shamir, 1994), followed through the entire schooling years, and covering both students and educators.

References

Abrams, D., Hogg, M. A. (eds.) (1990). *Social Identity Theory: Constructive and Critical Advances*. New York: Springer-Verlag

Allport, G. W. (1954). *The Nature of Prejudice.* Reading, MA: Addison-Wesley

Amir, Y. (1969). "Contact Hypothesis in Ethnic Relations." *Psychological Bulletin,* 71, 319–42 [Cf. p. 162 ff.]

———. (1976). "The Role of Intergroup Contact in Change of Prejudice and Ethnic Relations." In P. A. Katz and B. A. Taylor (eds.), *Eliminating of Racism.* New York: Pergamon

Benjamin, A. J. and Levi, A. M. (1979). "Process Minefields in Intergroup Conflict Resolution: The Sdot Yam Workshop." *Journal of Applied Behavioral Science,* 40, 507–19, NTL Institute

Blake, R. R., Mouton, J. S., and Sloma, R. J. (1965). "The Union–Management Laboratory: Strategy for Resolving Intergroup Conflict." *Journal of Applied Behavioral Science,* 1, 25-57

Burton, J. W. (1969). *Conflict and Communication: The Use of Controlled Communication in International Relations.* London: Macmillan Publishers

Burton, J. (1990). "Unfinished Business in Conflict Resolution." In J. Burton and F. Dukes (eds.) *Conflict: Readings in Management and Resolution,* New York: St. Martins Press

Carnevale, P. J. and Pruitt, D. G. (1992). "Negotiation and Mediation." *Annual Review of Psychology,* 43, 531-82

Cialdini, R. B., Borden, R. J., Thorne, A., Walker, M. R., Freeman, S., and Sloan, L. R. (1976). "Basking in Reflected Glory: Three (Football) Field Studies." *Journal of Personality and Social Psychology,* 34, 366–75

Cohen, S. P., Kelman, H. C., Miller, F. D., and Smith, B. L. (1977). "Evolving Intergroup Techniques for Conflict Resolution: An Israeli–Palestinian Pilot Workshop." *Journal of Social Issues,* 33, 165–89

Eisenhardt, K. M. (1989). "Building Theories from Case Study Research." *Academy of Management Review,* 14, 532–50

Gurevitch, Z. (1994). "The Dialectics of a Handshake." *Palestine–Israel Journal,* 4, 38–44

Johnson, D. W., Maruyama, G. Johnson, R. T., Nelson, D., and Skon, S. (1981). "Effects of Cooperative, Competitive and Individualistic Goal Structure on Achievement: A Metaanalysis." *Psychological Bulletin,* 89, 47–62

———, Johnson, R., and Maruyama, G. (1984). "Goal Interdependence and Interpersonal Attraction in Heterogenous Classrooms: A Metaanalysis." In N. Miller and M. D. Brewer (eds.) *Groups in Contact: The Psychology of Desegregation.* New York: Academic Press

Kelman, H. C. (1994). Essay, *Psychology International,* 5, 5–6

Kramer, R. M., and Brewer, M. B. (1984). "Effects of Group Identity on Resource Use in a Simulated Commons Dilemma." *Journal of Personality and Social Psychology,* 46, 1044–57

Kunda, Z. and Oleson, K. C. (1995). "Maintaining Stereotypes in the Face of Disconfirmation: Constructing Grounds for Subtyping Deviants." *Journal of Personality and Social Psychology,* 68, 565–79

Lewicki, R. J. and Litterer, J. A. (1985). *Negotiation,* Homewood, Ill.: Richard Irwin, Inc.

Macrae, N. C., Brodenhausen, G. V., Milne, A. B., and Jetten, J. (1994). "Out of Mind but Back in Sight: Stereotypes on the Rebound." *Journal of Personality and Social Psychology,* 67, 808–17

Pruitt, D. G., Rubin, J. Z., and Kim, S. H. (1994). *Social Conflict: Escalation, Stalemate, and Settlement,* (second edition), New York: Random House

Ross, L. and Stillinger, C. (1991). "Barriers to Conflict Resolution." *Negotiation Journal,* 7, 389–404

——— and Lewis, S. (1988). "Inferring Category Attributes from Exemplar Attributes: Geometric Shapes and Social Categories." *Journal of Personality and Social Psychology,* 55, 861–72

Rothbart, M. (1993). "Intergroup Perception and Social Conflict." In S. Worchel and J. Simpson (eds.), *Conflict between People and Groups.* Chicago: Nelson-Hall Publishers

Rothman, J. (1993). "Bringing Conflict Resolution to Israel: Model Building, Training and Institutionalization." In: *Practicing Conflict Resolution in Divided Societies.* Selected and edited proceedings of a workshop held in 1992 at the Van Leer Institute, Jerusalem, Israel

Rouhana, N. (1992). "A Homeland for Us as Well." *Politics,* 45, 38–41. (In Hebrew)

Shamir, S. (1994). "There Is Something to Learn from Others." *Kol Adam,* 15, 2–3. (In Hebrew)

Smooha, S. (1992). *Arabs and Jews in Israel.* New York: Westview Press

Schulz, J. W. and Pruitt, D. G. (1978). "The Effects of Mutual Concern on Joint Welfare." *Journal of Experimental Social Psychology,* 14, 480–91

Tajfel, H. and Turner, J. C. (1986). "The Social Identity Theory of Intergroup Behavior." In S. Worchel and W. G. Austin (eds.), *Psychology of Intergroup Relations.* Chicago: Nelson-Hall

Touhey, J. C. (1974a). "Effects of Additional Women Professionals on Rating of Occupational Prestige and Desirability." *Journal of Personality and Social Psychology,* 29, 86–89

———. (1974b). "Effects of Additional Men on Prestige and Desirability of Occupation Typically Performed by Women." *Journal of Applied Social Psychology,* 4, 330–35

Worchel, S. Coutant-Sassic, D., and Wong, F. (1993). "Toward a More Balanced View of Conflict: There Is a Positive Side." In S. Worchel and J. A. Simpson (eds.), *Conflict between People and Groups: Causes Processes and Resolutions.* Chicago: Nelson-Hall Publishers

Arab–Jewish Student Encounter: Beit Hagefen Coexistence Programs*

RACHEL HERTZ-LAZAROWITZ,

HAGGAI KUPERMINTZ, AND JENNIFER LANG

Abstract

This study reports the results of an evaluation of a structured meetings program between Arab and Jewish youth in Israel. The meetings were held during the second year of the Intifada (Palestinian struggle for independence; see below, page 567). Two hundred ninety nine Jewish and 186 Arab high school students who participated in the meetings responded to an elaborate questionnaire, as well as 195 Jewish and 285 Arab control-group students. The questionnaire included measures of various aspects of intergroup relations, self-perceptions, stereotyping, and identity. A Pre-test–Post-test design was employed. Although program impact was not definite, some positive changes were detected—mainly for the Arab participants. The Arab youngsters showed a pattern of strong group identification and high self-esteem, as well as negative stereotyping of Jews. This marks a new psychosocial configuration for this group. The Israeli political context as well as subjects' political-orientation influences on the outcome measures are discussed. Recommendations for further research emphasize the need for a longitudinal-research plan.

Introduction

Over the past decade, despite the difficult and painful intergroup situation in Israel, the number of voluntary organizations that work on improving Jewish-Arab relations by educational programs for coexistence has increased significantly. A survey, conducted by the New Foundation for Israel, listed dozens of organizations, old and new, that work within the boundaries of the Green Line of the State of Israel (Rothman, Bray, and Neustadt, 1988). These programs range from privately initiated single meetings to intensive year-long programs (Peled and Bar-Gal, 1983). While organizations for adult coexistence have been operating within political and communal frameworks, the inclusion of school-age youth is a new development.

*We wish to thank Mr. Alfar H., project director of Beit Hagefen, and the trainers of the workshops. Mr. Ashkar T. assisted in the construction of the questionnaire. Special thanks to Mr. Israel Z, former head of Beit Hagefen, for his support and contributions.

As recently as 1986, the Ministry of Education and Culture formed a department to address the issues of democracy, coexistence, and tolerance within the curricula (Bein, 1990), and funded many programs in local settings. High status organizations, such as the Van-Leer Foundation and the majority of the Israeli universities, contributed to the theoretical and applied aspects of those programs. This new avenue was based on the belief that young people are less biased and have less prejudice toward the other nations, and are, therefore, more susceptible to change (Ben-Ari and Amir, 1988).

Historical Background of Coexistence Programs

Since the foundation of the State of Israel in 1948, four historical periods in the area of planned programs for coexistence can be delineated. The first period, from 1948 until the sixties, was characterized by ignoring the need for planned meetings, and by the lack of research on Arab–Jewish relations within Israel.

In the second period in the seventies, experimental semilaboratory research began. The framework for this research was sociopsychological in general, and group contact, conflict management, and conflict resolution in particular. Experimental meetings and/or workshops were held at Bar-Ilan University and University of Haifa. The Arab and Jewish students met, and the impact of these settings was researched. Those meetings were generally brief, in the tradition of "social laboratory experiments." During this time, the first large number of publications appeared (Levi and Binyamini, 1977; Hofman and Debbiny, 1970; Hofman, 1971; Amir, 1976; Smooha and Cibulski, 1978).

In the latter part of this period, Professor John Hofman did a significant amount of research on the effect of contact between Jews and Arabs. He carried out his research on readiness for social contact in two natural settings: one, the only pubic high school in Haifa where Jewish and Arab students learned in the same school but in separate home classrooms, and two, the newly born University of Haifa, which began absorbing many Arab students from Haifa and the Galilee (Hertz-Lazarowitz, 1988). In his pioneering research, Hofman examined a unique social reality, whose main component was equality between Arab and Jewish youth in the high school and university settings.

Hofman and his colleagues conducted this research using similar methodology and measurements, basically paper-pencil questionnaires. This enabled them to study readiness for relations over a period of two decades (Hofman, 1972, 1976, 1977; Hofman and Rouhana, 1976; Hofman and Beit-Hallahmi, 1977). Throughout the following years, Hofman and his colleagues at Haifa University (Hofman, 1982; Hertz-Lazarowitz, Hofman, Beit-Hallahmi, and Rouhana, 1978) and social psychologists at Bar-Ilan (Bizman and Amir, 1982; Ben-Ari and Amir, 1986; Ben-Ari and Amir, 1988) continued the research. Similar to research results during the seventies, the main finding was that while the two groups showed a high level of readiness for social contact, the Arabs' readiness and willingness to participate in such programs, and their desire for contact with Jews, was higher than that of the Jews.

The third period began in the late seventies and continued into the late eighties. It parallels the foundation of institutions and programs for Jewish–Arab coexistence. The focus of the research shifted from short experimental settings, or paper-pencil questionnaires, to action research in which lengthy programs of meetings were held.

Such action research were conducted in the School for Peace at Neve Shalom (Pelde and Bar Gal, 1983), the Arab Jewish Institute in Givat Haviva (Bar and Askalah, 1989), the Jewish–Arab Center, Beit Hagefen (Hofman, 1987a, Hertz-Lazarowitz and Kupermintz, 1989), the Van-Leer Foundation (Hareven, 1981), Tel Aviv University (Ben-Gal and Bar-Tal, 1989), Haifa University (Kalekin, 1987), and the Ministry of Education and Culture (Dolev-Gendelman, 1989; Bein, 1990). In these programs for coexistence, hundreds and thousands of Arab and Jewish youth were brought together in different coexistence workshops.

The fourth period began with the outbreak of the Intifada at the end of 1987. Since then, the level of conflict has risen, crystallized, and still prevails. Although this period cannot be detached from the dynamics of the previous decade, it no doubt started a new point in Jewish–Arab relations. At this point in time, which brought major political changes in Israel, as well as the West Bank and Gaza, and with the breakout of the Gulf crisis it is too difficult to predict the future. Surprisingly, all the organizations that work on Jewish–Arab coexistence are continuing the programs within and outside of the green lines, while adjusting the content and process to current events. Furthermore, the new reality makes such meetings in today's environment much more challenging (Bar and Ben-Gal 1995, Hertz-Lazarowitz 1993).

Coexistence Research in the Shadow of the Intifada

Just before the outbreak of the Intifada, from 1984 to 1987, Hofman observed the coexistence program that took place under the auspices of Beit Hagefen in Haifa (Hofman, 1987a). Variables related to intergroup and interpersonal domains were studied in a quasi-experimental control group pretest-posttest design.

Hofman's concluding findings indicated that Israeli–Arabs' readiness for social contact and relations with Jews was the highest during the seventies. Although a decline occurred in the eighties, Arabs living in Israel within the green lines, still scored higher than did Jews. A distancing trend is occurring among the Israeli-Arabs probably due to the Israeli army's occupation and control of the West Bank and of the Gaza Strip, and the emergence of the Palestinian-Arab identity (Abu-Bakr, 1990). Most of the Jews find it difficult to accept this emerging identity. They perceive it as a sign of disloyalty on behalf of the Israeli-Arabs, most of whom were born and raised in the State of Israel.

In measures of attitudes toward equality, democracy, and tolerance, Arab youths tend to score higher than the Jews. These findings are consistent with the minority groups' sensitivity as a result of their social vulnerability (Lewin, 1948). As for stereotyping, Hofman (1985, 1987b), like others (Binyamini, 1980), points out that stereotyping is extremely sensitive to outside events. Negative stereotyping of the Arabs by Jews primarily takes place on an intellectual level: i.e., they are considered less intelligent and less capable. Today, the issue of stereotyping is being studied in the context of delegitimation (Bar Tal, 1988). This research documents the extreme tendencies of stereotyping toward both Jews and Arabs in Israeli society. Ethnocentrism of Jews and Arabs is increasing as well (Smooha, 1988).

Findings concerning the Jews' and Arabs' self-perceptions consistently reported that Arab youths show less self-esteem and less self-worth (Hofman, Beit-Hallahmi and Hertz-Lazarowitz, 1982; Hertz-Lazarowitz, Hofman, Beit-Hallahmi, and Rouhana, 1978).

Since the beginning of the Intifada (December 1987), which can be characterized by increasing tension in the territories and in the Gaza Strip, as well as a high number of injuries among the Arab population in the territories, Palestinization of the Israeli-Arabs has increased dramatically. The Arab citizens of Israel are sympathetic to the Palestinian struggle for independence (Yogev, Ben Yehoushua, and Alper, 1989). The Intifada has polarized and intensified the political views among Arabs and Jews.

In spite of the deteriorating political situation and the Palestinization of the Israeli-Arabs, we should keep in mind that the shared life of Jews and Arabs in Israel has been taking place for over forty years. Up to now, the level of violence and tension within the Green Line has been relatively low as compared to other countries whose national groups are in conflict (e.g., Ireland, Turkey, Greece and Cyprus). In the Israeli context, work on coexistence, based on the principles of social psychology, is continuing, and even broadening its scope.

Beit Hagefen Jewish–Arab Center

Beit Hagefen is one of the oldest, most important organizations working on coexistence programs in Israel. Founded in Haifa in 1963, this Jewish–Arab Center is located in a city and neighborhood populated by both Arabs and Jews. The aim of the center was to create an atmosphere and the possibility for contact and cooperation between both ethnic groups—Jewish and Arab (Moslem, Christian, and Druze)—inhabitants of the State of Israel. It is a public organization that is supported by the Ministry of Education and Culture, the Haifa Municipality, and the Hillel Ziedel Foundation.

Over the years, Beit Hagefen's challenge has been to design different models in order to improve relations on the microlevel, set against a background of continuing conflict and lack of a political solution on the macrolevel. Beit Hagefen is aware of Hofman's reevaluation of the theoretical assumptions of underlying programs for improving intergroup relations as presented in a concluding chapter of his book (1988). He examined the obstacles for coexistence programs and highlighted the tension between intergroup (social) and interpersonal (human) models. The key question that he raised, as did others, was whether or not one can create positive contact working mainly on an interpersonal level in spite of the harsh problems that exist on the political level between Jews and Arabs. This is an open question, yet Beit Hagefen made a policy to continue basing their work primarily on interpersonal guidelines, with an emphasis on Arab–Jewish coexistence within the Green Line only.

Let us now turn to the description of the project as presented by Beit Hagefen (Alfar, 1988).

Youth Program Objectives

(1) To further cooperation on cultural, social, and interpersonal levels.
(2) To break the cycle of estrangement, prejudice, and stereotypes.
(3) To foster an atmosphere of tolerance, mutual understanding, trust, and cooperation.
(4) To lead youth toward an awareness of fruitful coexistence despite political conflict.
(5) To equip participants in the meetings with the interpersonal skills instrumental to better group relations.

Program Activities

In each of the coexistence meetings, two classes (about seventy to eighty students) participate. The students are matched according to their educational background and age. Each classroom works with two trainers from Beit Hagefen, one Arab and one Jew. The program follows the outline below.

(1) A meeting for trainers at Beit Hagefen.
(2) Twelve hours of uninational preparation, divided into three-to-four meetings, with Beit Hagefen trainers, held in the respective schools.
(3) First visit/meeting at the Jewish school. Arab class travels to Jewish school.
(4) Second visit/meeting at the Arab school. Jewish class travels to Arab school. The first two meetings focus on get-acquainted games, structured activities focusing on culture and social customs, food and holidays, stereotype reduction, and identity. The goal is to increase mutual liking, sensitivity, empathy, and understanding for one another.
(5) Second meeting of educators at Beit Hagefen—intermediary summary and evaluation of the process with regard to the specific youngsters at hand.
(6) Summary discussion related to the mutual visits in uninational groups with the Beit Hagefen trainers and classroom educators.

(7) Third meeting of students takes place at Beit Hagefen, during which they discuss topics related to political and civic issues.

(8) Fourth meeting involves a shared social activity, such as a picnic or an outing, depending on available funding and the youngsters' choice.

(9) Summary evaluation with Beit Hagefen trainers and classroom educators ends the year's activities for the two classrooms.

(10) Third meeting of trainers at Beit Hagefen to sum up activities.

All in all, the coexistence program is about forty hours, twenty-eight of which are Jewish–Arab meetings, and twelve are uninational meetings.

To give the reader a sense of the program, a participant observation of a second meeting and an agenda of a third meeting are presented in Appendix A.

Method

The research reported here, studied the effects of the coexistence program in 1988–89. The sample included 929 high school students from fifty-seven classes sampled randomly from schools in Northern Israel. The Jewish sample included 299 students who participated in the program (experimental group) and 159 who did not participate (control group). The Arab sample included 186 students who participated (the experimental group) and 285 who did not (control group).

The data was gathered twice, before (October 1988) and after the meetings (June 1989). The questionnaires were filled out with complete anonymity, due to the sensitivity of the questions asked, thus no identifying details were included with the completed forms. Students participating in the program came from comprehensive and noncomprehensive schools, mostly public with one or two private religious Arab schools. The students came from Jewish and Arab cities, small towns, and villages. Most of these settings are segregated in terms of Jewish and Arab inhabitants.

Instrumentation

The students responded to a 120-item questionnaire written in their mother tongue. After employing the back translation procedure, the questionnaires were administered in the classrooms by Jewish and Arab university students, and were identical for both populations. Most of the items were measured on a 1–4 Likert scale. In addition, stereotypes were measured by a seven point semantic differential (Osgood, Suci, and Tannenbaum, 1957), referring to self, their own nation, and the other nation. Identity measures were derived by directly asking the subjects (see details in measure 8).

The 120 items were subjected to a principal component analysis and a varimax rotation. Seven factors emerged by using this Factor analysis technique. They include the following:

(1) Readiness for relations with the other nation
(2) Democratic and political attitudes
(3) Social contact between Jews and Arabs
(4) Attitudes towards military and/or civil service
(5) Self-esteem
(6) Segregation between Jews and Arabs
(7) Perception of conflict

A reliability measure (Cronbach's alpha index of internal consistency) was computed for each scale (factor); for scales consisting of only two items the simple correlation was computed. Scores on each scale were the averages over items. The scales are introduced with representative items and the reliability measures.

(1) *Readiness for relations* (Alpha=.92)

This scale included fifteen items on readiness for relations with the other nation: "I am ready to be friends with Arabs/Jews," "I am ready to host an Arab/Jew in my house." Likewise, the items included: "The problems between Arabs and Jews living in Israel are solvable," and "Mixed marriage between Arabs and Jews harm the nation and the religion." The last items had a negative loading on the scale.

(2) *Democratic and political attitudes* (Alpha=.88)

This factor included ten items on equality between Jews and Arabs: "Give full equality to Jews and Arabs in Israel," and recognition of the P.L.O. and Palestinian independence: "The State of Israel needs to recognize the P.L.O." Likewise, it included civic satisfaction: "I am satisfied because I am a citizen of Israel," and trust: "Impossible to trust the majority of Arabs in the territories." Both of these had negative loadings.

Based on theoretical considerations, these items represent two different levels (ideological and practical), and could be considered separately. This factor was thus divided into two subscales: democratic ideology (Alpha=.83), which included six items representing a democratic view and favoring equality; and political solution (Alpha=.81), which included four items favoring the recognition of the P.L.O. and the foundation of an independent Palestinian state.

(3) *Social contact* (Alpha=.79)

This factor included four items on social contact with the other nation: "I am in contact with a Jew/Arab" or "I have Jewish/Arab friends."

(4) *Military/civil service* (r=.34)

This factor included two items: "Army service in the IDF (Israeli Defense Force) is required for all Israeli citizens, Jewish and Arab," and "National community service (substitution for the army) is required for all Israeli citizens, Jewish and Arab, who are exempt from the army."

(5) *Self-esteem* (r=.54)
This factor included two items on self-satisfaction and self-worth: "In general, I am satisfied with myself," and "I think that I am a worthwhile human being."

(6) *Segregation between Jews and Arabs* (r=.22)
This factor included two items: "I am ready to be in this country without having contact with Arabs/Jews," and "The way to reach peaceful coexistence is through maximum segregation between Jews and Arabs."

(7) *Perception of conflict* (r=.15)
This factor included two items: "There exists an unresolvable conflict between Jews and Arabs who live in the territories like Judea, Samaria, and Gaza," and "The conflict between Jews and Arabs in the territories destroys the relations between the Arab and Jewish citizens of Israel."

As for the last four factors, which were composed of two items each, there was a positive correlation (statistically significant P=.001) as well as content consistency.

Aside from these seven factors, additional measures were computed for identity and stereotyping.

(8). *Definition of an Arab identity*
The students were asked to relate to the definition of Arab identity in two ways. First, they were introduced to the following eight identity definitions, and asked to choose the most appropriate one for Israeli Arabs:

- Arabs
- Israeli-Arabs
- Israelis
- Palestinian-Arabs
- Israeli-Palestinians
- Palestinians in Israel
- Palestinian-Arabs in Israel
- Palestinians

In the second part, students were asked to rate the appropriateness of each definition on a 1-to-4 scale. A principal component analysis of the ratings revealed two main Arab identity definitions: Palestinian-Arab identity. This factor included the "Arabs," "Palestinian-Arabs," and "Palestinians" definitions. The second was Israeli-Arab identity, which included definitions of "Israeli-Arabs," "Israelis" and "Israeli-Palestinians." The Arab identity question was presented to Jews and Arabs regarding Arab identity only. Definitions of the Jewish identity were not investigated in this study, and emphasis was on Arab identity due to research reports of its changing nature (Smooha, 1987, 1988).

(9) *Stereotyping*

This scale was composed of distance scores between the stereotype perception of the other nation (Jewish/Arab Israeli) and self-perception (me as I am), measured by a nine items semantic differential (Osgood, Suci, and Tannenbaum, 1957) that included the following bipolar adjectives: Educated-Uneducated; Flexible-Stubborn; Stable-Unstable; Unselfish-Selfish; Cultured-Rude; Optimist-Pessimist; Honest-Devious; Strong-Weak; Sociable-Unsociable. For each trait, measured on a seven step scale, a distance score (between self and other nation) was computed and the final score on the scale was the square root of the sum of the squares of the distance scores (generalized distance score).

(10) *Feedback* (Alpha=.93)

At the end of the year, the students who participated in the meetings were asked to evaluate the program. The feedback questionnaire consisted of fifteen items (scaled 1–4). The evaluation included fifteen items relating to the content and process of the meetings. "The meetings demonstrated a chance for a peaceful coexistence between Jews and Arabs"; the role of leaders/trainers—"The activity with the trainers at school before the meetings was successful"; and the impact of the meeting on improving understanding between Jews and Arabs—"The meetings contributed to a better understanding of the other nation." Scores on this scale were computed as an average over items.

Results

A seria of two-way analyses of variance were performed. Time (pre vs. post) and group (experimental vs. control) were the independent variables. A between-group design was employed for the time effect since matching between pre and post measures was impossible, due to the lack of identifying information of the subjects. Table 1 presents the results for seven attitude factors for the Jews, while Table 2 shows the results for these same measures for the Arabs.

From Table 1, we learn that for the Jewish youth overall, the experimental group scored higher in the measures of Readiness, Social Contact, Democratic Ideology and Political Solution. This group scored lower on the measures of Self-Esteem and Segregation. Two measures showed significant time by group interaction; Democratic Ideology was lower for the experimental group after the program, and Self-Esteem was higher for that group after the program. Only Readiness was significant for the time factor.

Table 2 gives a different picture for the Arab youth. Arab youngsters in the experimental group maintained a stable level of Democratic Ideology over time, while there was a decrease in the control group. There was also a positive change in the amount of Social Contact reported by these students. However, there was a decrease over time in both groups in Readiness for social relations; the Perception of the conflict as well as the attitude toward Military/civil service became more negative.

TABLE 1
Means, SDs and F values by Group and Time—Jewish population

| | Control | | Experimental | | Time | F values Group | |
Variable	Pre	Post	Pre	Post	(A)	(B)	(AXB)
Readiness	2.23	2.21	2.80	2.57	*5.17	**71.09	3.44
	.69	.71	.69	.74			
Social Contact	1.43	1.33	1.84	1.88	0.41	**93.76	1.92
	.53	.44	.76	.71			
Democratic Ideology	2.00	2.06	2.50	2.28	2.56	**60.00	**7.42
	.59	.62	.64	.70			
Political Solution	1.75	1.72	2.00	1.87	3.19	**21.25	1.25
	.49	.52	.62	.58			
Army Service	3.13	3.01	3.06	2.97	2.46	0.73	0.07
	.91	.96	.88	.84			
Self-Esteem	3.50	3.39	3.28	3.36	0.15	**7.46	*4.40
	.50	.57	.65	.65			
Segregation	2.45	2.54	2.25	2.32	1.71	**12.31	0.02
	.82	.82	.79	.81			
Perception of	2.86	2.93	2.86	2.90	1.09	0.15	0.09
Conflict	.74	.69	.73	.70			

*P<.05   **P<.01

TABLE 2
Means, SDs and F values by Group and Time—Arab population

| | Control | | Experimental | | Time | F values Group | |
Variable	Pre	Post	Pre	Post	(A)	(B)	(AXB)
Readiness	3.05	2.93	3.10	2.94	**9.11	0.36	0.10
	.60	.64	.57	.68			
Social Contact	2.31	2.14	2.19	2.50	1.47	*4.26	**17.12
	.81	.77	.80	.82			
Democratic Ideology	3.44	3.26	3.45	3.45	**7.46	**8.95	**6.91
	.43	.52	.40	.42			
Political Solution	3.39	3.32	3.47	3.42	1.80	*4.69	0.00
	.52	.58	.53	.60			
Army Service	2.47	2.22	2.30	2.14	**10.46	*4.14	0.47
	.86	.86	.92	.80			
Self-Esteem	3.49	3.47	3.57	3.51	0.67	1.65	0.16
	.63	.69	.57	.59			
Segregation	2.24	2.13	2.03	2.02	0.94	*5.79	0.59
	.88	.87	.85	.89			
Perception of	2.59	2.77	2.65	2.77	*5.86	0.27	0.31
Conflict	.89	.86	.81	.78			

*P<.05   **P<.01

Overall, in comparing attitude factors for the Jews and Arabs, the latter scored significantly higher on the measures of Readiness (t=13.55; P<.001), Social Contact (t=16.41; P<.001), Democratic Ideology (t=20.32; P<.001), Political Solution (t= 25.61; P<.001) and Self-Esteem (t=4.86; P<.001). Jews scored higher on the measures of Military/Civil Service (t=17.63; P<.001), Segregation (t=18.97; P<.001), and Perception of Conflict (t=4.59; P<.001).

Table 3 presents the findings for the Stereotyping and Identity measures for the Jewish population. The experimental group had fewer stereotypes about the Arabs, and perceived their identity as more Israeli. An Interaction effect of time by group for the Arab/Israeli identity represents a decrease in that element in the experimental group after the program, compared to the controls.

Table 4 presents the findings for the same measures for the Arab population. The main finding here is that surprisingly all Arabs (experimental and control) showed a decrease over time in the measure of Arab/Palestinian element of their identity. This was accompanied by a similar non-significant trend of decrease in the measure of the Israeli's element of the Arab identity. the control group, however, perceived the Israeli element as more salient than the experimental group. The Stereotyping measure remained stable and similar for both groups.

The comparisons between Jews and Arabs showed that Arabs held significantly more stereotypes toward Jews (t=7.66; P<.001), and perceived the Palestinian element of Arab identity as much more salient (t=23.36; P<.001). Both groups evaluated the Israeli element of Arab identity similarly.

TABLE 3

Means, SDs and F values by Group and Time—Jewish population

Variable	Control		Experimental		Time (A)	F values Group (B)	(AXB)
	Pre	Post	Pre	Post			
Negative	7.86	7.56	6.55	7.08	0.23	**13.60	2.92
Stereotyping	2.69	2.84	2.77	3.33			
Arab/Palestinian	2.38	2.44	2.28	2.34	1.01	2.40	0.00
identity	.89	.91	.79	.80			
Arab/Israeli	2.04	2.14	2.36	2.21	0.24	**14.17	*5.26
identity	.66	.68	.64	.69			

*P<.05   **P<.01

Analyzing the distribution of the selection of the "most appropriate definition" for Arab identity revealed the following patterns: The Jewish youth defined the Arab identity as 26 percent Palestinian-Arabs, 62 percent Israeli-Arabs, and 12 percent as Arabs or Palestinians living in Israel. The Arab youth defined their identity in a mirror opposing way, as 52 percent Palestinian-Arabs, 17 percent as Israelis, and 31 percent as Arabs or Palestinians living in Israel. It is evident that

TABLE 4

Means, SDs and F values by Group and Time—Arab population

	Control		Experimental		Time	F values Group	
Variable	Pre	Post	Pre	Post	(A)	(B)	(AXB)
Negative	8.30	8.11	8.46	8.77	0.50	2.31	0.87
Stereotyping	3.57	3.68	3.01	3.40			
Arab/Palestinian	3.25	3.10	3.34	3.22	**32.70	0.06	3.72
identity	.58	.82	.70	.70			
Arab/Israeli	2.44	2.36	2.25	2.13	3.11	**14.13	0.14
identity	.80	.74	.73	.74			

*P<.05   **P<.01

the Jews perceive the Israeli component as more salient in the Arab identity than the Arabs themselves.

At the end of the meetings, the experimental groups were asked to evaluate the program. Overall, the Arab students gave more positive feedback of the meetings than the Jews. Mean score for the Arabs was 3.04 (sd=.64) and for the Jews 2.48 (sd=.74) (t=9.12; P<.001).

Discussion

The discussion will focus on several issues: whether or not it is possible to evaluate the direct impact of the coexistence programs on intergroup relations; if different configurations of Jews' and Arabs' perceptions exist, and if they can be conceptualized; and the practical lessons that can be learned from these results in order to structure effective programs. In addition, some methodological aspects of evaluating coexistence programs will be discussed.

The Impact of the Coexistence Program on Attitudes

We realize that the findings of this study are neither clear-cut nor definite. Rather, they create a puzzle that calls for various interpretations. In fact, no consistent patterns of change emerged as a result of the meetings. On a few measures, the programs have a positive impact, primarily for the Arabs, while on others, slightly negative impact can be detected. Still on others, no change is found at all.

Moreover, it is evident that the attitudes of Jews and Arabs are different from the start, with Arabs being overall more positive. And despite random assignment of groups, certain apparent differences exist between the control and experimental groups on pretext measures. This hinders chances for positive changes for the experimental group. Pretest differences and Jews-Arabs differences on attitude measures were documented often in other research in this field (Hofman, 1987a, Bar and Bar-Geal, 1995).

Despite these constraints, a few very important conclusions can be drawn. The findings indicate a positive effect among Arabs concerning social contact and democratic ideology, while Jewish youth's perception became more critical of the latter. This suggests that the discussions held during the meetings increase the Jews' awareness of and sensitivity toward the inequality of Arabs. For Arabs, it contributed to a more positive perception of Israeli democracy.

The effect of the political reality is one major reason for the result we obtained. The overall harsh and unstable political context of the Intifada has contributed to the minimization of the potential impact of the program. Daily violence occurs and shades each and every meeting. Most of the meetings can be metaphorically described as isolated islands surrounded by a stormy ocean. Such a reality affected the Arabs to a greater extent; their readiness for social relations with the Jews, as well as their willingness to serve in the army (civil), decreased. Moreover, their perception of the political conflict hardened.

The Impact of the Coexistence Program on Identity Definitions

Contrary to what one might expect, the Palestinian component of identity did not increase for the Arabs. Their Israeli part of identity remained strong and stable, but less as lenient than their Palestinian element. It seems that they are continually testing the different elements of their own identity, and the meetings served as a laboratory in which to do so. This search of identity is accompanied by high self-esteem and negative stereotyping of Jews. Thus, a twofold crystallization process can be conceptualized: on the one hand, self-identity as expressed through self-esteem is becoming stronger, while on the other hand, group identity as expressed through the Palestinian ethnic definitions is becoming more ethnocentric. Such a configuration marks for the Arabs a psychological departure from a self-perception as marginal and low status toward a more symmetric, and empowered self-and group identification (Hertz-Lazarowitz and Kupermintz, 1997; Hertz-Lazarowitz, Kupermintz, and Lang, 1991).

For the Jews, their perception of Arabs-identity definition and their attitudes remained the same throughout the course of the program with the experimental group being higher in the pretest and posttest than the control group. One reason may be due to the fact that Jews are removed from, and therefore less sensitive to, the political hardships of Intifada. Another reason may be related to the polarized political orientation of the Jewish youth, which may blur the picture. A few clarifications are due in order to elaborate on this important issue.

The Political Making of the Participants in the Coexistence Program

In the Beit Hagefen project (Hert-Lazarowitz and Kupermintz, 1989) we collected data on the political orientation of the participant students by asking the question:

"If you had to vote today in an election, for which party would you vote?" Arab youngsters had homogeneous political orientation: over 65 percent of them endorsed non-Zionist, left-wing parties. The Jews were polarized, and almost equally divided between right-wing (Hawks) and left-wing (Doves) parties. Thus, about half of the Jewish youth, the Hawks, entered the meetings with preconceived, antagonistic views, which might have put distance between them and the Arabs. Indeed the meetings, and especially the third one, were loaded with emotion. Discussions rallied around difficult issues, such as the daily terror, the Palestinians' right for self-determination, the meaning of the Intifada, Arabs' civil rights in Israel, and the occupation of the territories. In this meeting, the Hawks' views clashed with those of the Arabs and the Jewish Doves.

In spite of these confrontations, the meetings served as a legitimate scene for debate and discussion. Jews encountered, maybe for the first time, facts and perceptions with which they usually do not come into contact. Jews and Arabs had the chance to clarify and communicate painful issues like soldiers' actions in the territories during the Intifada on the one hand, and Arabs' personal accounts of discrimination on the other. Within the formal structure of the meetings, or even in informal settings, the roles of victim and victimizer were interchanged. It seems that the confrontations and self-revelations were meaningful, or at least not destructive, for both Jews and Arabs as proven by the fact that the dialogue continued and did not explode (Hertz-Lazarowitz, 1991).

Future Recommendations

The Israeli context of coexistence programs within a sociopolitical reality fosters many important research questions. One of which would be to consider political orientation as a significant variable and assess separately the impact of such programs on Jewish youth with left-wing political orientations compared to their right-wing counterparts. It seems that affective and cognitive distance from Arabs as well as attitudes on issues of identity, political solution and actualization of democracy and coexistence are different for these two Jewish groups. It might be that each group needs a different structures of meetings, or more uninational preliminary workshops (Bar Bar-Gel, 1995).

Another issue of importance is the age of the participants. This study reports on high school students. In Israel, Jewish youth ages sixteen to seventeen are preoccupied by their preparation for "becoming a soldier," which at the age of eighteen is compulsory. For these youngsters, it is a time of strong identification with the army, as well as the state (Gal and Mayseless, 1990), and they often find it difficult to cope with the dissonance between their civil duty and personal empathy (Liebes and Blum-Kulka, 1990).

Thus, the fact that most of the organizations to date work with adolescents makes the coexistence workshops a tough challenge. More systematic work with elementary school students has to take place. These age groups seems to be less politically and more willing to adopt the humanistic approach to coexistence meetings. Coexistence programs for young children (kindergarten to sixth grade) are less practiced. It seems that planning such programs for different age groups and collecting data on them would facilitate our understanding of the developmental processes related to group relations.

Finally, without a doubt, longitudinal research is needed. However, to date, due to a shortage of resources, most of the programs are only one year long, with limited meeting schedules, and are only evaluated once every few years. Thus, no consistent longitudinal body of data exists to assess the programs' impact on the development of attitudes towards Jewish–Arab coexistence. Personal observations and interviews reveal that young men and women, Jews and Arabs, who return to work in this field in their twenties to thirties report that they participated in coexistence programs at some point during their youth, and became committed to the field of coexistence (Raanan, Dora, and Hertz-Lazarowitz, 1991. Herz-Lazarowitz, 1993). This may partially explain the vitality of such programs in Israel and their impressive growth.

Appendix A

Below is a more detailed example of a day's activities at Beit Hagefen written by observer Jennifer Friedman-Lang.

A Participant's Observation of a Beit Hagefen Workshop

Two sixth-grade classes from two local elementary schools, one Arab and one Jewish, meet today for their second time in six weeks. These students are coming together to further get to know one another, to talk more about their backgrounds, to play sports, and to learn that perhaps they could be friends. This particular meeting is the second of a five-step process that is carried out over four months. The process first involves Beit Hagefen trainers, who total eight, half Arab and half Jewish, introducing their programs to the selected classes and preparing them for the four meetings to follow. The first meeting took place at the Jewish elementary school, the second at the Arab elementary school, the third at Beit Hagefen, where both classes come together outside of the school environment, and lastly, depending on funds and the children's decision, a field trip, i.e., hike or picnic.

It is a rainy day so the students are a bit rambunctious. Their excitement may be due to this second encounter, conjuring up memories of their first meeting one month prior. On an academic level, it can perhaps be attributed to their expectations of progressing towards a greater level of understanding of one another. In spite of the fact that they live side by side, they know very little about each other. The Arab class, this week's host, greets the Jewish class, including the teachers, at the door, and the day's activities begins.

One trainer makes an introduction in both Hebrew and Arabic. At this age, the students are not completely bilingual—the Jewish pupils only start learning Arabic in Sixth grade while the Arabs start learning Hebrew in fourth or fifth. Following the trainer's brief words, an Arab student, while carefully reading from his prepared speech, welcomes the visitors in both languages. A Jewish student then reciprocates, thanking their hosts in words, and presents a gift, a symbol of friendship, recommended although not required by Beit Hagefen trainers.

The activities begin. For the first introductory game, to help make the students feel more comfortable with one another, a trainer randomly picks a volunteer to stand in the middle of a big circle formed by the students' and trainers' chairs. The purpose of the game is to remove a chair and then the volunteer has to run and find another one to sit on before someone else takes it (otherwise known as musical chairs, without the music). The volunteer continues to run for the chair until he reaches an empty place and bumps someone else, at which point the bumped person stands in the middle and the game begins again.

Just as the students' level of energy and laughter are getting stronger, the trainer introduces a new game. Four students stand in the middle of the circle, two of whom are blindfolded and handed small ropes, and two of whom are given whistles. The unblindfolded blow their whistles at any time and the blindfolded swing their ropes towards the direction of the noise in order to find them while the unblindfolded try to dodge them. The purpose of this game is to loosen the children up and to involve them in physical play together. Spectators in the outside circle play a passive role simply watching and cheering on the "blind," and laughing when the "seeing" dodge them. An underlying twist in the game is that those with "sight" call and then dodge the "blind," thereby misleading them.

Following the two warm-up exercises, a trainer introduces a get-acquainted game or a mixer. It is a two-step group-forming process in which the trainer asks the children to stand up and change places in order to sit next to the person they remember best from the prior meeting. In other words, the students move and take a new seat next to their new friends from the other school. The next step is to form a larger group of seven–eight with other peripheral friends and then latch on to a trainer. They rearrange the chairs and sit next to their new friend. The goal of a two-step group formation is to make it a gradual process based on the first meetings' friendships and the students' choices. It really makes them refer back to the first meeting and build on that original contact.

Small group activities (my observations of one group's activities; there are several variations of the first and second mixers). The trainer introduces him/herself and then the students go around the circle and do the same. Then there is a verbal discussion on the following questions: What do you remember from the last meeting? Did you share it with your parents, brothers or sisters? Friends? What did you learn? What are your thoughts about this second meeting? This serves as a valuable recall for all the students to share their experiences following the last meeting that had a more serious and honest tone.

The next activity, a hand-name game, involved everyone's participation. The students say their name and then someone else's in the circle on the rhythmic beat of hand claps and snaps. The Arab names are difficult for the Jewish students to remember and to pronounce and vice versa, so it serves as a good review. This generally lasted until each student had the opportunity to be named and to name someone else a couple of times.

The following activity was a puzzle game. Placing a table in the middle of their circle of chairs, the trainer empties our puzzle pieces on it. The students were to take one piece each and put them together with or without talking, depending on the instructions.

Each of the seven–eight puzzle pieces had a word or a number on it written in Hebrew or Arabic. After fitting the pieces together, the students read what was written. The last one–two word(s) of each phrase or expression were missing and the goal of the exercise is for the students to find the missing word(s). Each phrase comes from within Jewish or Arab culture and is based on friendship, neighbors, family, and the like. If a Jewish student knows the expression in Hebrew he is to share and explain it until the others find what's missing and vice versa.

Then, a piece of paper with the other groups' expressions from their puzzles and the missing word(s) is handed out to the group to work on together. Again, for those who knew and understood the expression, they were to share and explain it with those who did not. The goal of the activity is for the students to cooperate, work together, and share the missing information, thereby explaining certain values and their sources inherent in their culture. Another aspect of this game involves values clarification in which the students themselves must understand the idea and its origin in order to explain it to others. This was followed by a thirty-minute break, giving the students the chance to let out some energy, have a snack and talk or play games among themselves.

Large group activity: Forming one large circle, the students and trainers stand up and take their neighbor's hand. One trainer breaks off and begins forming inner rings. Whether or not the circle breaks is secondary. What is important is the close physical contact between the students and the ability to cooperate and keep the circles going while still holding hands.

Teamwork: A trainer asks the students to break into the previous groups of seven–eight and form straight lines side by side each other in the room. The order of the line holds no importance. Those in the middle put their hands on the hips of the person ahead of them to form a chain. The first person in line holds up his hands and the last person receives a ribbon to tie to his pants. The object of the game is to keep the line linked, run together and have the first person in line capture the ribbon of the last person in another group, except for the one next to them. Again the emphasis is on physical contact and team work, to keep the group together and to work towards the same goal.

Group exploration: Two groups of seven–eight formed together so that in the end there were only four big groups. New introductions were made so that the two groups could get to know one another. In groups of two to three, with one from each school, the students were to draw what they thought about peace, the neighborhood, family, etc. This was a gradual winding down activity, quiet time, to see how the other views the world.

Personal feedback: Each student then received a sheet of paper to write his name, school and grade, and anything he/she thought about the last two meetings for the Beit Hagefen newspaper. They could write in either Hebrew or Arabic. This was good personal time for reflection and a lot of the students wrote some very personal thoughts.

Closing: Everyone came together slowly and formed a big circle with their chairs as they did at the beginning of the day. A trainer explained that there would be a third meeting at Beit Hagefen and everyone cheered. For those who wished, they were to stand up in front of the assembled two classes and share their feedback on the day's activities. The last thing I heard that day was an Arab boy who stood up and boldly said in Hebrew, "Before I came to this meeting, I didn't think Arabs and Jews could be friends. But after today, I don't think that anymore."

Agenda of a Third Meeting

8:30—9:00	Greetings and division into subgroups.
9:00—9:30	Get-acquainted games (mixers) in small groups. Summary of previous meeting.
9:30—10:30	Jewish–Arab areas of civic conflict—a role-playing activity. Processing the activity.
10:30—11:00	Break—light snack.
11:00—11:45	A film *Neighbors*—all groups in auditorium. The film presents an accelerated process of conflict over a flower that ends in the destruction of both neighbors (Canadian film). Small group discussion, reflection on the film and its meaning for Israeli Jews and Arabs.
12:00—13:00	Paired activities relating to different issues: identity, personal acquaintance, depending upon the age group. Feedback in small groups.
13:00—13:30	Break and home hospitality.
13:30—14:30	Summary of the workshop in small groups—what do we take home and how do we communicate it?
14:30—15:00	Sharing ideas for future interclass/personal meetings. Group cooperation game.
15:00—15:30	Closure and departure.

References

Abu-Bakr, M. (1990). "Arab–Jewish Reconciliation vis-à-vis an Irreconcilable Reality." In: Poggeler, F. and Yaron, K. (eds.), *Adult Education in Crisis Situations*. The Hebrew University: Magnes Press, Jerusalem

Alfar, H. (1988). *Beit Hagefen Encounters Program*. Beit Hagefen, Hafia (Hebrew)

Amir, Y. (1976). "The Role of Intergroup Contact in Change of Prejudice and Ethnic Relations." In P.A. Katz (ed.) *Towards the Elimination of Racism*

Bar, H. and G. Askalah (1989). *Arab–Jewish Youth Meetings: Evaluating Views Before and After*. Center for Arab Studies, Givat Haviva (Hebrew)

———— and Bar-Gel, D. (1995). *To Live with the Conflict*. Jerusalem Institute for the Research of Israel (Hebrew)

Bar Tal, D. (1988). *Group Beliefs*. New York: Springer

Bein, Y. (1990). *Education for Democracy and Coexistence in a Pluralistic Society: The Story of an Israeli Experiment*. Paper presented at the International Sociological Association (ISA) (World Congress. Madrid, Spain, July 9–13

Ben-Ari, R. and Y. Amir (1986). "Contact between Arab and Jews in Israel : Reality and Potential." In M. Hewystone and R. Brown (ed.) *Contact and Conflict in Intergroup Encounters*, pp. 45–58. New York: Basil Blackwell

————. (1988). "Promoting Relations between Arabs and Jewish Youth." In J. Hofman (ed.) *Arab–Jewish Relations in Israel*. Bristol, Indiana: Wyndham Hall Press

Ben-Gal, T. and D. Bar-Tal (1989). *Training Teachers for Jewish–Arab Coexistence in Israel*. Paper presented at the twelfth annual meeting of the International Society of Political Psychology, Tel Aviv

Binyamini, K. (1980). "The Image of the Arab in the Eyes of Israeli Youth—Changes over the Past 15 Years." *Studies in Education*, 27, 65–74

Bizman, A. and Y. Amir (1982). "Mutual Perceptions of Arabs and Jews in Israel." *Journal of Cross-Cultural Psychology*, 13, 461–59

Dolev-Gendelman, Z. (1989). *Intermediary Report: Population Project*. Hebrew University and Bureau of Education and Culture, Jerusalem (Hebrew)

Gal, R. and Mayseless, O. (1990). "Attitudes of Youngsters towards Military and Security Issues during the Intifade." in: Gal, R. (ed.). *The Seventh War: The Effects of the Intifada on the Israeli Society*. Hakibbutz Hameuchad Publishing House. Israel (Hebrew)

Hareven, A. (1981). "Israeli Arabs as a Jewish Problem." In A. Hareven (ed.) *Every Sixth Israeli*. Jerusalem: The Van Leer Institute

Hertz-Lazarowitz, R. (1988). "Conflict on Campus: A Social Drama Perspective." In: Hofman, J. (ed.) *Arab–Jewish Relations in Israel*. Bristol, Indiana: Wyndham Hall Press

————. (1991). *Dilemmas in Education toward Coexistence in the Political Reality of Israel*. Symposium presented in the Psychology of Nationalism. Third "Imut" conference, Jerusalem, Israel, June 2–3, 1991

————, Hofman, J., Beit-Hallahmi, B. and N. Rouhana (1978). *Identity and the Educational Environment*. University of Haifa: Center for Research and Development of Arab Education (Hebrew)

———— and Kupernintz, H. (1989). *Evaluation of Meetings Project—Beit Hagefen*. Research report, School of Education, University of Haifa (Hebrew)

————, Kupermintz, H. and Lang, J. (1991). *The Changing Nature of Prejudice: Jewish and Arab Youth in the Shadow of the Intifada*. Paper presented at the first International Congress on prejudice, discrimination, and conflict, Jerusalem, Israel, July 1–4, 1991

———— (1993). "Using Group-Investigation to Promote Arab–Jewish Relationship at Haifa University." *Cooperative Learning*, 13 (3), 26–28

———— and Kupermintz, H. (1997). "Arab and Jewish Youth Encounters in the Shadow of the Intifada." *Studies in Education: A Special Issue Dedicated to the Late Prof. J. Hofman*. Vol. 1, issue 2, pp. 35–70. (Hebrew)

Hofman, J. (1971). "Personal Contact as a Primary Factor in Attitude Change." *Hachinuch Hachevrati*, 28–31 (Hebrew)

———— (1972). "Readiness for Social Relations between Arabs and Jews in Israel." *Journal of Conflict Resolution*, 16, 211–52

———— (1976). *Identity and Intergroup Perception in Israel: Jews and Arabs*. Haifa: University of Haifa, Arab–Jewish Center. Occasional paper 7, 45 pp.

———— (1977). "Identity and Intergroup Perception in Israel." *International Journal of Intercultural Relations*, 1, 79–102.

———— (1982). "Social Identity and Readiness for Social Relations between Jews and Arabs in Israel." *Human Relations*, 35, 727–41

—— (1985). "Arabs and Jews, Blacks and Whites: Social Identity and Group Relations." *Journal of Multilingual and Multicultural Development*, 217–37

—— (1987a). *Projects of Meetings between Jewish and Arab High School Pupils: A Progress Report*, 1984–1987. Haifa: Beit Hagefen

—— (1987b). "Jewish–Arab Relations in Israel: Human Relations and Social Identity." *Patterns of Prejudice*, 21, 15–26

—— (ed.) (1988). *Arab–Jewish Relations in Israel*. Bristol IN. Wyndham Hall Press

—— and B. Beit-Hallahmi (1977). "The Palestinian Identity and Israeli Arabs." *Peace Research*, 9, 13–22

——, Beit-Hallahmi, B. and R. Hertz-Lazarowitz (1982). "Self-Concept of Jewish and Arab Adolescents in Israel." *Journal of Personality and Social Psychology*, 43, 786–92

—— and S. Debbiny (1970). "Religious Affiliation and Ethnic Identity." *Psychological Reports*, 26, 10–14

—— and N. Rouhana (1976). "Young Arabs in Israel: Some Aspects of a Conflicted Social Identity." *Journal of Social Psychology*, 99, 75–86

Icilov, O. (1990). *Political Socialization, Citizenship Education and Democracy*. Columbia University: Teachers College Press

Kalekin, D. (1987). *Coexistence Project Teachers*. School of Education, University of Haifa, Research grant from Ford Foundation

Levi, A. and A. Binyamini (1977). "Focus and Flexibility in a Model of Conflict Resolution." *Journal of Conflict Resolution*, 21, 405–25

Lewin, K. (1948). *Resolving Social Conflicts: Selected Papers on Group Dynamics*. New York: Harper. (1989) Hebrew translation. Gome Publishers

Liebes, T. and Blum-Kulka, S. (1990). "'Shoot and Cry?' On the Confrontation with Moral Dilemmas during Military Service in the 'Territories.'" in: Gal, R. (ed.). *The Seventh War: The Effects of the Intifada on the Israeli Society*. Hakibbutz Hameuchad publishing house, Israel (Hebrew)

Osgood, C. E. and Suci, C. J. and P. H. Tannenbaum (1957). *The Measurement of Meaning*. Urbana: University of Illinois Press

Pelde, T. and D. Bar Gal (1983). *Intervention Activities in Arab–Jewish Relations: Conceptualization, Classification and Evaluation*. Jerusalem: The Israeli Institute for Applied Social Research

Raanan, R., Dora, G., and Hertz-Lazarowitz, R. (1991). "In Front of the Class, behind the Encounter: On Jewish and Arab Trainers." Unpublished manuscript. Haifa University

Rothman, J. Bray, S. and M. Neustadt (1988). *A Guide to Arab Jewish Peacemaking Organization in Israel*. A publication of the New Israel Fund

Smooha, S. (1987). "Jewish and Arab Ethnocentrism." *Ethnic and Racial Studies*, 10, 1–26

—— (1988). "Jewish and Arab Ethnocentrism in Israel." In J. Hofman (ed.), *Arab–Jewish Relations in Israel*. Bristol, Indiana: Wyndham Hall Press

—— and O. Cibulski (1978). *Social Research on Arabs in Israel 1948–1976: Trends and an Annotated Bibliography*. Ramat Gan: Turtledove Publishers

Yogev, A., Ben-Yehoshua, N. S. and Y. Alper (1989) *Determinants of Readiness for Contact with Jewish Children among Arab Students in Israel*. Paper presented at International Society of Political Psychology, Tel Aviv

Ethnic and Minority Groups in Israel: Challenges for Social Work Theory, Values, and Practice

ELIEZER DAVID JAFFE

Ethnic and minority conflict seems to be an inherent part of social life. The study of specific ethnic and minority groups and their cultural backgrounds and coping mechanisms reflect the fact that people are very different as well as similar, that people live in very powerful competitive modern or traditional societies, and that group conflict and inequality is generally the social norm rather than the exception (Dahrendorf, 1969; Feagin and Feagin, 1979; Kitano, 1980; Weber, 1946; Peterson, et al., 1980; Myrdal, 1944).

Social workers deal primarily with inequities and personal problems of disadvantaged individuals and minority groups, often succeeding in removing or alleviating some of the pressures that clients face. Social work literature frequently describes interventions with populations negatively affected by such variables as race, ethnicity, minority status, sex group, marital status, color, physical disability, religion and nationality (Jacobs and Bowles, 1988; Schlesinger and Devore, 1991; Burgest, 1989; Norton, 1978; Chestang, 1976; Sottomayor, 1971; Glazer, 1975; Desai and Coelho, 1980). Social heterogeneity (in even seemingly homogeneous situations) and its effects on interacting diverse populations has taken a relatively prominent place in social work theory, practice, policy, and research. Special attention has been given to specific population groups such as Chicanos, Puerto Ricans, Blacks, and Indians, and specific categories of individuals such as immigrants, refugees, and people of color.

These activities reflect a greater contemporary sensitivity of social work to cultural diversity, and the introduction of sensitivity content into the social work education curriculum is a logical result, although based on earlier foundations (Cohen, 1958; Stein and Cloward, 1958; Pederson, 1976; Green, 1982; McGoldrich, et al., 1982; Lum, 1986).

Nevertheless, it is appropriate to ask about the purpose and outcome of this education, and the role of social work in affecting social change, diminishing ethnic conflict, and the alleviation of social forces that create social inequality for disadvantaged groups. Is there a relationship between sensitivity and social change? Does sensitivity change values and outcome? Does social work have a significant role for intervening in ethnic conflict and for social change? These are some of the questions discussed in this article.

The setting for this analysis is Israeli society, a Western, democratic, pluralistic enclave in the Middle East, where American, British, and indigenous Israeli social work practices and principles combine to form eclectic theoretical and practice norms. Multiple ethnic groups in Israel, mass immigration, religious diversity, a dynamic Western politico-socio-economic environment, and a cohesive, committed, and well-developed social work profession make Israel an ideal case in point for this analysis.

Ethnicity in Israel

Israel, the size of New Jersey, is a country of immigrants. Much has been written about the different "waves" of immigrants, their historical origins, the establishment of the social insurance and personal social services network, and clashes between various ethnic groups (Cohen, 1972; Inbar and Adler, 1977; Jaffe, 1975, 1977, 1982, 1988, 1992; Liebman and Don-Yehiya, 1984; Vital, 1978; Shumsky, 1955).

Ethnic relations in Israel can only be understood by a knowledge of the origins of the Jewish people, the history of Zionism and Palestine, the Ingathering of the Exiles, the Holocaust, the British Mandate period, and the creation of the State and its religious, social, and economic institutions. Also important is the role and ideology of the dominant Israeli Western culture that "absorbed" masses of successive Jewish immigrant groups, including Jewish refugees from Arab lands, from Russia, former Iron Curtain countries, and from Ethiopia. Although it is impossible to deal with all of these subjects in this article, we can discuss specific current ethnic dilemmas and background factors that influence them and provide the environment for social work practice.

The largest and most contentious ethnic division in Israel is of course that between Jews and Arabs. But even among Jews, the amount of ethnic diversity is striking. The two largest Jewish ethnic groups in Israel are the Ashkenazi (Western) and the Sepharadi (Middle-Eastern) populations. The latter group is referred to as the remnants of Jews dispersed in Exile throughout the Middle-Eastern, Arab lands as a result of the destruction of the First (Solomon's) Temple during the First Jewish Commonwealth Period by the Babylonians in 586 B.C.E. The Ashkenazi group stems from those Jews who eventually returned to Israel from Babylonia, where they had been taken as captive slaves, and who rebuilt the Second Temple during the time of Ezra and Nechemia (the Second Jewish Commonwealth Period). Jews again were subsequently exiled to southern Europe by the Romans who destroyed the Second Temple in 70 C.E. These Jews then migrated all over Europe and then to North and South America. Most contemporary American Jews are descendants of Ashkenazi Jews.

In the 1800s groups of pioneering European Jews came to Palestine to recreate a modern Jewish State and emancipate themselves from the anti-Semitism and racial and religious hatred of their inhospitable "host" countries. Sepharadi Jews had also immigrated and played a dominant role in the Jewish community, but the Western Jews set up predominantly Western social, democratic, economic, and educational institutions, and, together they established the State of Israel when the British left Palestine in 1948. The 600,000 predominantly Western (Ashkenazi) Jews then "absorbed" 750,000 Jewish refugees (Sepharadim) coming from the Moslem countries, between 1948 and 1956.

The Sepharadi population, with large extended families, deeply religious, patriarchal more fatalistic, and influenced by the preindustrial culture of the Middle East, faced the intensive competition of the veteran population, which was comprised mostly of secular, nuclear-family-oriented, protectionist Ashkenazi Establishment. The American melting-pot model (touted by Israeli sociologists at the time) was widely implemented and Sepharadi young people quickly adopted the Western secular model of the Ashkenazi Jews, and do so to this day (Glazer and Moynihan, 1965). Research conducted by this and other researchers shows clear preference among Sepharadim for Ashkenazi traits, often accompanied by feelings of inferiority and damaged self-image (Jaffe, 1988, 1990; Avineri, 1975; Patai, 1970; Cohen, 1972). Intermarriage between the two groups is high, amounting to nearly 20 percent of all marriages annually (Smooha, 1978). The preference pattern begins young: Sepharadi four-year-olds already show ambivalence about their ethnic identification. Children of Western origin preferred to identify with Western adults, and so, too, did a majority of children of Eastern background (Jaffe, 1988).

Today, most Israelis, including social workers, tend to play down, deny, or reject evidence of ethnic identification and a need for increasing their own ethnic sensitivity. They point to great strides in closing socioeconomic and educational gaps, political involvement of Sepharadim in mainstream political parties, intermarriage, and a pluralistic society. Nevertheless, the Likud party may have lost the elections in 1992 primarily because of internal Ashkenazi-Sepharadi fighting and posturing, which turned off many potential voters. Western paternalism still exists, with clear objective socioeconomic differences among different Jewish ethnic groups. One manifestation of ethnic conflict was the appearance in 1972 of the Israeli "Black Panthers," a social protest street-corner movement originating in the slums of Jerusalem, created by Sepharadi street-corner youths attempting to change their dead-end lives and enhance their life chances (Cohen, 1972; Jaffe, 1975; Iris and Shama, 1972). The movement was eventually neutralized by a combination of cooperation by government social and educational services, and by politicization and in-fighting among the Panther leadership.

The Ashkenazi-Sepharadi conflict described above has "cooled off" somewhat in recent years due to increased political participation of Sepharadi Jews, a slow but perceptive narrowing of objective socio-educational gaps, and increased second generation integration into the dominant Ashkenazi society.

The Russian Immigration

In late 1989, glasnost led to rapid disintegration and liberalization of the Soviet empire, and to a mass immigration to Israel of Jews from Russia and the Eastern

European former Iron-Curtain countries. Within two years, nearly 500,000 Soviet Jews immigrated to Israel. Over 60 percent of the adults are university graduates, and within a year they spoke Hebrew, entered government vocational retraining programs, organized their own immigrant associations, and vigorously began their own integration into Israeli society. Unlike those who arrived in 1948 as refugees from Iraq, Yemen, Morocco, and other Arab countries, the Russian immigrants were almost immediately attuned to the mixed-market economy and tempo of Israeli society. They began competing with veteran Ashkenazi and Sepharadi Jews alike. The citizen response to the Russians has generally been good, with many nonprofit organizations mobilized or formed especially to help them move into Israeli society. Russian immigrants have a strong ethnic affinity with many veteran Israelis, who themselves originated from Russia, Poland, and Eastern Europe before, during, and after World War II. The Israeli government has provided immeasurably better conditions and benefits to these latest immigrants than was economically possible during the Sepharadi mass immigration of 1948–56. This has led to some signs of resentment, especially among the veteran unemployed population. What took the Sepharadi Jews forty years to obtain (e.g., professional positions, status, university education, and housing) will happen for the Russians in less than one-third that time, and will probably surpass Sepharadi mobility even still. Moreover, the Russian immigration has now created a clear numerical majority for the Ashkenazi population, as opposed to the situation before the Russians arrived.

The Ethiopian Immigration

For many years, a population of Jews were believed to exist in Ethiopia (Kaplan, 1992). Theories about their origin suggest that they were one of the ten lost Israelite tribes, Jewish converts, descendants of King Solomon and the Queen of Sheba, or refugees from the destruction of the First Temple who fled south to Egypt and then up the Nile River into villages in the mountains of Ethiopia. Whatever the explanation, the Israel Chief Rabbinate recognized the Ethiopians as Jews because of many unmistakable ancient religious customs and rituals identical to Jewish ritual as mentioned in the Bible and existing at the time of the First Temple. Based on this recognition, the Israeli government made every effort to bring this group to Israel. In 1977, nearly 7,000 Ethiopians arrived in a clandestine American-assisted airlift from neighboring Sudan—for those Jews who survived the long and dangerous trek out of Ethiopia (Ben-Ezer, 1985; Rosen 1991).

Further Israeli efforts continued, despite the Marxist-Communist regime and civil war in Ethiopia, to rescue and bring out the rest of the Jewish community. Finally, in 1990, the cessation of Russian military and economic support and repeated losses inflicted by rebel forces resulted in the Ethiopian government allowing (for a steep head tax) the Israeli Air Force airlift to bring home 16,000 Ethiopian Jews within twenty-four hours. Today the Israeli Ethiopian community numbers over 40,000.

The integration of this community has been mixed thus far. There is general consensus that the younger Ethiopians are adjusting well in the educational system and in the army, and want very much to enter the dominant society. The 1977 group has generally been accepted by most Israelis, but also experienced cultural, religious, and economic problems that were still not settled when the 1990 immigrants arrived. Among these problems were the lack of rabbinical acceptance of Ethiopian Kessim (religious leaders), who were not deemed qualified to perform marriages and divorces in Israel because they had been totally cut off from Talmudic and Jewish Halachic (legal) developments and other Jewish communities after they fled Israel in 586 B.C.E. In 1977, the Israeli rabbinates under pressure of prolonged Ethiopian mass demonstrations, was forced to retreat from their demand that all Ethiopian immigrants undergo "symbolic conversion" to unequivocally clear up their status as Jews (Ashkenazi and Weingrod, 1985; Bard 1988; Abbink, 1984). Most Ethiopians adamantly refused and many are still in religious limbo as far as the State is concerned.

Other adjustment problems include the classic culture clash between children and their immigrant parents and elders, in-fighting among the new leadership, problems of personal adjustment to Western culture such as secularism, technology, relations between the sexes, family roles, political activity, and self-image (Munitz, et al., 1985; Suellen, 1989; Dothan, 1985; Schoenberger, 1975; Kaplan, 1988; Wolf, 1969; Well, 1988). Some of these problems are normative for all immigrant groups, but the Ethiopian situation is much more complicated because of the long historical, social, and religious separation from the rest of Jews in the world, and the intense desire to be accepted as modern Israeli Jews.

It is very important to note that the black skin color of Ethiopian Jews has apparently *not* greatly affected their acceptance into Israeli society and some intermarriage has taken place with Ashkenazim and Sepharadim. Unlike the situation of blacks in America, who were brought from Africa as slave labor by white importers, the black Jews of Ethiopia (as well as all other Jewish immigrants to Israel) are welcomed home along with the other dispersed exiled Jews from other countries. Since most of the Jews went into exile as prisoners or slaves, there is or was among most Israelis an immediate, nostalgic kinship affinity for the Ethiopians, regardless of color differences. The same is generally true regarding Sepharadi-Ashkenazi Jews, despite the fact that the Sepharadim generally are of darker skin color. The Israeli case, where religious kinship often, but not always, works to overcome conflict due to color differences, is outstanding on the international scene and a basic positive underlying feature of Israeli ethnic relations. It will be interesting to see how Israelis in general will relate to immigration of Falash-Mura Jews, who had converted to Christianity and returned to Judaism. This is currently a controversial issue even among parts of the Israeli-Ethiopian community.

The Arab Population

While Jews constitute 84 percent of the 5 million citizens of Israel, (excluding the Territories of Judea and Samaria), there are also 13 percent Moslem and Christian

Arabs and 3 percent Druze and other religious groups such as Bahai, Karaites, and Samarians (Central Board of Statistics, 1992). By the year 2005 the population forecast for Israel is 6.3 million.

Most Israeli (and West Bank) Arabs claim to be descendants of the ancient Philistines and Canaanites, but some American Jewish scholars believe they originate from Bosnia, which in ancient times was a Roman province called Illyricum, where Christianity was introduced in the Middle Ages. When Bosnia was invaded by Turkey in 1386, the entire population was forceably converted to Islam. When Turkey lost Bosnia to Germany at the Congress of Berlin in 1878, the Ottoman-Turkish Empire that same year granted lands in Palestine to Moslem refugees from Bosnia and Herzegovina for colonization, including a twelve-year tax exemption and exemption from military service in the Turkish army. Lands distributed were located in the Galilee, the Sharon Plain, and Caesaria. Other Moslem refugees from Russia (Georgia, Crimea, and the Caucasus) were resettled in Abu Ghosh near Jerusalem, and the Golan Heights, while Moslem refugees from Algeria and Egypt were later settled in Jaffa, Gaza, Jericho, and the Golan. Other Arab family clans migrated south to Palestine from Syria.

The different explanations of Arab origins clash with the Jewish historical accounts of an uninterrupted 3,350-year Jewish presence (despite the exile). These conflicting claims affect contemporary Jewish-Arab relationships where both peoples now live together in the same land. After the War of Liberation in 1948, military rule was imposed on Israeli Arabs and was subsequently abolished in 1966 when Israeli fears of Arab dual loyalty were less intense. Nevertheless, only in 1992 was the government "Office for Arab Communities" eliminated. As a democratic, pluralistic country, and as a result of Arab lobbying, all government Ministries now deal directly with Arab citizens as they do with everyone else. Also, the Labor government had committed itself to a further equalizing of the level of services to Arabs and other minorities to that existing for Jewish citizens.

The Israeli Ethnic Pyramid

In Israel there are innumerable cultural and ethnic subgroups within the Ashkenazi, Sepharadi, Ethiopian, Russian, and Arab groups, based on one or more of the common-denominator criteria noted above. For example, broad religious groupings include Orthodox, Conservative, and Reform. Each of these are subdivided, especially in the Orthodox camp, into hundreds of subgroups based on such variables as common country of origin and district of origin, identification with a rabbinical dynasty, degree of orthodoxy, historical and ideological affinity, language prior to migration, etc. (Jaffe, 1992).

It is important to clarify that this article refers to Jews as well as Arabs and all other Israeli groups as cultures, and not as a race. These groups have formed as an outcome of social, historical, and religious experience, rather than genetic and biological mutation transmitted through germ plasm.

All societies are socially stratified, and ethnic differentiation is an inherent reflection of the inequality in the distribution of power, privilege, and prestige in such societies. C. Wright Mills (1963) summarized typologies to describe features of stratification as follows:

(1) The economic order is of primary importance in determining social position, inequality, and the mechanisms of stratification.
(2) Group consciousness emerges among persons in a similar stratum, and may be an important dynamic for social change.
(3) Conflict and competition are inevitable between strata.
(4) Ideologies and beliefs of individuals are a reflection of the individual's position in the stratification system.
(5) Life histories and life chances from birth to death are shaped by position in the class structure.

In caste societies, unlike Israel, ethnic groups are locked into ascriptive forms of stratification and inequality, with no mobility allowed. Israel corresponds instead to a multiple hierarchy model of stratification in which class, ethnicity, sex, age, and other variables are considered separate but interrelated aspects of social inequality (Bengston, 1979). The "double jeopardy hypothesis" suggests that membership in more than one of these groups increases the degree and effects of inequality (Dowd and Bengston, 1978).

A stratified pyramid of ethnic groups based on status, income, and opportunity structure generally exists in Israel with the Ashkenazi veteran group on top, Sepharadi Jews next, followed by Russians, Arabs, and Ethiopians. Twenty years hence the Russians will most likely blend into the Ashkenazi group at the top with more Ethiopians moving ahead of the Arab population (Haidar, 1991), while the Sepharadi group remains second in the hierarchy. Perhaps all these groups, except the Russians, will maintain a clear ethnic identity.

This appraisal is based on objective and subjective criteria, the former indicated by income, political influence, education, ownership of goods and property, size of family, and personal well-being, and the latter by perceived ability or mobility to achieve expectations, and a sense of alienation and discrimination (Peres, 1977; Hassin, 1985, 1992; Amir and Shithot, 1975; Peres and Smooha, 1974; Zipperstein and Jaffe, 1981). Ethnic status, in Israel as in most countries, correlates highly with social advantage or disadvantage.

In addition to the stratification typology presented above, other theories have been applied to explain the status of Israeli ethnic groups, and especially the disproportionate distribution of minority ethnic youth as juvenile delinquents. Prominent theories are the "culture conflict theory" based on immigration maladjustment (Sellin, 1938), the "ecological influence and socialization theory" (Shaw and McKay, 1942; Cohen, 1955) based on the influence of reference groups and neighborhoods on behavior, and the "technology innovation versus retarded social change theory" (Ogburn, 1950), which ascribes social problems and inequality to the slow pace at which social programs are introduced to alleviate the detrimental societal effects of new technology.

All of these theories have differential relevance for explaining inequality in Israel and for describing ethnic groups and subcultures. For the most part, however, Jewish social cohesiveness is relatively prominent in Israel due to a strong basic common historical and cultural heritage, including the Holocaust experience, modern anti-Semitism, and physical danger from neighboring countries. Arabs, too, are generally united in a common culture and Pan-Arab identification based on strong religious and nationalist foundations.

Both the Arab and Ethiopian groups have a longer road to travel than other groups toward equality, the Ethiopians because of their late start in Western culture and the Israeli Arabs because of religious difference and the late opening to them of the opportunity structure. Both will continue to experience strong competition from the dominant and more powerful Ashkenazi and Sepharadi groups, but the basic democratic direction and nature of the society and its institutions will continue to enable more mobility for these groups.

Social Work Attitudes and Stereotypes

The social work profession is committed at individual, group, and societal levels to work for change in order to equalize power, close social gaps, preserve individual dignity, eliminate negative discrimination, and enable maximum participation of all individuals in the life of their society. The professional ethos suggests that social workers represent a humanistic force in society and are capable and willing to be agents for change in clinical practice and social policy.

Yet Israeli research has shown that these goals are not axiomatic or attainable for many social workers. In fact, despite years of experience in Israel with mass immigration, many social workers are still "culturally encapsulated," willing to engage clients only on their terms (Penderhughes, 1989), tending to adopt stereotypic explanations for behavior and prescriptions for treatment (Solomon, 1976). Keadar (1978) found that Israeli social workers, when presented with identical fabricated case material, responded with different diagnoses and intervention strategies when the material was attributed to an Ashkenazi or Sepharadi client respectively. They diagnosed the Sepharadi client's problems as environmental and deprivation-related, while the Ashkenazi client was thought to have serious interpersonal, psychological problems. Consequently, intervention recommendations for the Sepharadi client involved environmental manipulation and material assistance, while the Ashkenazi client needed long-term therapy and work on interpersonal relationships and personality problems. Keadar also found that these stereotypes were the same regardless of the ethnic background of the social worker. Almost identical findings were obtained twelve years later in a similar study of social work students at the Hebrew University (Wahab-Gilboa, et al., 1990). Programmatic research by Jaffe (1990, 1995) found that Sepharadi respondents from all ages and sectors of the Israeli population, including welfare clients, prefer Ashkenazi social workers to Sepharadi. Since his studies were based solely on the respondents' preferences for social workers pictured in random passport photos, Jaffe concluded that social workers (and all other respondents) rejected Sepharadi photos purely because of their ethnic stereotypes.

In brief, Israeli research shows strong ethnic stereotyping among clients and social workers alike, and these clearly influence differential diagnosis and intervention. These data become more urgent in view of the fact that Israelis, including social work practioners and students, tend to deny the existence of stereotypes. Even members of ethnic minorities are often reluctant to talk openly and frankly about this subject. Empirical data of behavior patterns show strong emphasis on the earlier assimilation-absorption-modernization model in Israel, in preference to the current official model of pluralism. Jaffe (1990) has suggested that this approach often leads to internalized feelings of negative self-concept and feelings of inferiority.

Very few social work research studies have documented the actual effects of ethnic insensitivity on Israeli social work practice (Greenwald, 1992). However, this has been studied by Israeli education researchers who documented negative effects of stereotype-based discrimination in public schools. Ironically, no serious institutional or personal changes have occurred in the educational system to remedy the situation. Teachers still relate to children with their own personal attitudes, stereotype, and values. Will this be the fate of social workers, even after "sensitization" from research findings and curriculum change? In the final analysis, when worker meets client, how much influence do personal values and stereotypes have over curriculum content? How can theory and information change values? These are vital questions for social work educators and practitioners in the post-melting-pot era.

Changes in Social Worker Attitudes and Values

Real change in practice requires changes in values. Many social workers in Israel still believe that ethnic conflict and inequality will go away over the years as a result of intermarriage, better education, and Westernization of the disadvantaged. But this will not take place unless there is a change in existing values. For example, in 1978, when only 10 percent of the students admitted to social work courses at Israeli universities were disadvantaged Sepharadim and Arabs, it was believed that they were simply not capable of studying and practicing social work. Subsequently, a seven-year research study on preferential admissions proved this hypothesis false, but there was still reluctance to liberalize admission procedures (Jaffe, 1989). In my view, social work today may have more theory and knowledge about ethnic and minority issues and social conflict than it is willing or able to act on.

Social workers do not come to the profession free of individual, family, and reference-group stereotypes and values. Research done by Bar-Gal (1978, 1981) found that most social work students already come to university schools of social work with humanist values and a desire to help people, rather than absorbing these from the curriculum. Bar-Gal found that social work study had only a slight impact on prior values. He also noted that these values stem from students' personal, economic, ethnic, and social background and from life experiences. The implication from Bar-Gal's research is that there is no homogeneous social ethic or consensus among social workers regarding major social, ethnic, and minority issues. This unclarity of attitudes and lack of consensus does not allow for social work to speak with one voice or to operationalize its desire for playing a significant role in social change.

From my experience of three decades as social work educator, researcher, and community organizer, I believe that social change occurs most decisively and rapidly when marginalized minorities who are hurting activate themselves and create coalitions that force majority interests to solve minority problems. Social workers, who choose to help people as a profession, can never attain the power of organized minority groups. They can be coalition partners, but they cannot walk around in clients' shoes. This is how change has occurred for the Sepharadi, Ethiopian, and Russian immigrants, Arabs, battered women, large families, the handicapped, and many other minority groups (Kahn, 1990; Jaffe, 1983). It is also true for the problems of African-Americans, Hispanics, and other groups in America.

The suggestion to be more realistic about social work's capacity to affect social change means, however, that social workers should excel at being "social warners," formulators of policy recommendations for the political echelon, engage in advocacy, and assist disadvantaged groups to mobilize their own resources and power (Korazin, 1989; Cox, et al., 1970; Grosser, 1976; Schneiderman, 1965). It also means that nonethnic-sensitive practice is inconceivable in contemporary social work. Shirley Jenkins made this abundantly clear in her pioneer research on ethnic factors and practices in American and other international social services (Jenkins, 1981).

Schools of social work can play a major role in attempting to inculcate values, empathy, and sensitivity to minority values (Schlesinger and Devore, 1991; Williams, 1988). Three specific vehicles are the following: careful selection and utilization of field-work settings and experiences, faculty and supervisors as role models, and provision of factual information and knowledge in the social work curriculum. Schools of social work in Israel have also become keenly aware of the impact of a heterogeneous student body on attitudinal changes, and as catalyst for generating serious dialogue among the students in and out of classes. Another important challenge for social work educators is to develop skills and knowledge that can be integrated into the curriculum specifically enabling some students to become professional change agents. These practioners should be educated to mobilize marginalized minorities to create coalitions that force majority interests to accommodate minority values.

Social Work Practice with Ethnic and Minority Groups

In recent years, the influx of over half a million Russian and Ethiopian immigrants has created a strong need and interest among Israeli social workers to understand the cultures and social backgrounds of these new clients. Hundreds of social work jobs were created by government and nonprofit agencies specifically to work with these communities and ease their integration into the country. The State of Israel several decades ago created a special Ministry of Absorption (a cabinet position) with funding for hundreds of programs and social workers devoted to providing social services to immigrant individuals, families, and groups. These include personal counseling, financial and concrete assistance, brokerage, therapeutic services, and networking with the Housing, Education, Welfare, and Health Ministries. Social workers are also employed in a wide range of nonprofit organizations such as youth villages of the Youth Aliyah organization, which care for over 8,000 children, the Tikva organization, which provides psychological counseling services, the Israel Interest-Free Loan Association, and hundreds of other organizations and programs.

Major professional national conferences have been convened on social work with minority communities yielding a fruitful exchange of information, research knowledge, and practice skills and approaches with different cultural groups. This has greatly influenced practice and sensitivity to methods and components of service delivery on a wide variety of specific topics such as marital therapy with Ethiopian immigrants (Ki-Tov and Ben-David, 1993), adjustment difficulties of adolescent immigrants from the former U.S.S.R. (Shraga and Slonim-Nevo, 1993), social work intervention with religious families (Schindler, 1987), affective responses to cultural changes (Banal, 1988), work with Holocaust survivors (Graaf, 1975) and others. Inventories of innovative services for children and other groups have been published (Tadmor, 1990) and prestigious prizes are offered annually to professionals and volunteers working with immigrants and other minority groups in distress.

A popular Israeli vehicle for working with families in extreme distress involves teams of social workers consisting of the family's social worker from the local welfare office (acting as case manager), a qualified family therapist, school psychologist, and other professionals. Interventions focus on child, couple, and parent systems, boundries, communication, and relationships with community institutions—all within a framework of focused short-term interventions (Sharlin and Shamai, 1991). Interdisciplinary cooperation and brokerage activity are seen as vital to successful work with families, which usually experience a multiplicity of problems. This is even mandatory regarding cases involving child placement in Israel. It has been found that interdisciplinary practice brings extensive knowledge regarding cultural practices and norms that may affect intervention planning and outcome.

Social Work in Fragmented Society

In the age of "the disuniting of America" (and Asia and Europe) where the mainstream, dominant society is giving ground to the celebration of ethnicity, the social work profession must find ways to help mediate cultural and interpersonal conflict (Schlesinger, 1992; Jacobs and Bowles, 1988; Burgest, 1983). In Israel, this means primarily cessation of denial of ethnic culture differences and gaps between ethnic groups. Ethnicity must stop being a nonsubject, ethnic pride should be revived as it was before immigration to Israel, and closer examination of social workers' practice performance, sensitivity and information about cultural groups must be undertaken. These goals are important for Israeli society, where the secular and religious, veterans and immigrants, Westerners and Easterners, Jews and Arabs need to improve communication and common effort to achieve their goals.

Both American and Israeli ethnic dynamics show that mobility among the disadvantaged is no longer homogeneous but rather heterogeneous, that poverty is multiethnic and thus lends itself to universal, government policy changes and that the dominant culture is more amenable to genuine ethnic pluralism and sharing than previously. These are positive indicators for social change that must be nurtured by everyone concerned (Kilson and Bond, 1992). Another positive factor, in my view, is the increasing role that nonprofit, third sector organizations can play in Israel, America, and other Western countries, in mediating social conflict and promoting dialogue and indigenous interventions to defuse social problems. Social work professionals may be able to learn from this model and play a larger role with nonprofit organizations (Wuthnow, 1991; Powell, 1986).

The discussion of ethnic and minority relations and treatment has moved far beyond issues of ethnic "sensitivity and information." As international and local communities undergo rapid and often violent change due to political, demographic, religious, and economic changes, the subject is now of crucial global importance for many nations and peoples. The migration of millions of displaced people to Western countries with high unemployment rates, following the breakup of the U.S.S.R., has led to rekindled ethnic, xenophobic nationalism rooted in unresolved historical conflicts. These present complicated problems for many groups and individuals and major challenges to the social work profession and the world community. Knowing how to understand and work with diverse populations and situations of ethnic and minority conflict may become one of the most important tasks of the twenty-first century.

References

Abbink, G. J. (1984). *The Falashas in Ethiopia and Israel—The Problem of Ethnic Assimilation.* Nijmegen, Holland.

Amir, M., and Shichor, D. (1973). "The Ethnic Aspect of Juvenile Delinquency in Israel," *Delinquency and Social Deviance,* 3:1–2, 1–18.

Ashkenazi, M., and Weingrod, A. (1985). "From Falasha to Ethiopian Jews," *Israel Social Science Research,* 3:1–2, 25–35.

Avineri, S. (1975). "Israel: Two Nations?" in E. Curtis and M. Chertoff, (eds.). *Israel: Social Structure and Change.* New Brunswick: Transaction Books.

Banal, Nurit (1988). *Ethiopian Absorption: The Hidden Challenge.* Jerusalem: Department of Immigration and Absorption of the Jewish Agency, pp. 105–23.

Bard, Mitchell (1988). "The Unfinished Exodus of Ethiopian Jews," *Midstream,* 34:2, 15–20.

Bar-Gal, David (1978). *Value Judgement and Development of Social Values Among Students of Social Work and Psychology.* Jerusalem: School of Social Work, The Hebrew University.

———. (1981). "Social Values of Social Work: A Developmental Model," *Journal of Sociology and Social Welfare*, 8:1, 45–61.

Ben-Ezer, Gadi (1985). "Cross-Cultural Misunderstanding: The Case of Ethiopian Immigrant Jews in Israeli Society," *Israel Social Science Research*, 3:12, 63–73.

Bengston, V. (1979). "Ethnicity and Aging: Problems and Issues in Current Social Science Inquiry," in D. Gelfand and A. Kutzik (eds.). *Ethnicity and Aging*. New York: Springer Publishing Co., pp. 9–31.

Burgest, David (ed.) (1989). *Social Work Practice With Minorities*. Metuchen, NJ: The Scarecrow Press.

———. (1983). "Principles of Social Casework and The Third World," *International Social Work*, 26:4, 7–23.

Central Bureau of Statistics (1992). *Statistical Abstracts of Israel, 1991*. Jerusalem: State of Israel.

Chestang, Leon (1976). "Environmental Influences on Social Functioning," in P. Cafferty and L. Chestang (eds.). *The Diverse Society: Implications for Social Policy*. New York: Association Press.

Cohen, A. (1955). *Delinquent Boys: The Culture of the Gang*. New York: The Free Press.

Cohen, Erik (1972). "The Black Panthers in Israeli Society," *Jewish Journal of Sociology*. 14:1, 93–109.

Cohen, Nathan (1958). *Social Work in the American Tradition*. New York: Dryden Press.

Cox, F. M., et al. (1970). *Strategies of Community Organization*. Hillsdale, NJ: Peacock Publishers.

Dahrendorf, Robert (1969). "On the Origin of Inequality among Men," in A. Beteille (ed.). *Social Inequality*. Baltimore, MD: Penguin Press.

Desai, P., and Coelho, G. (1980). "Indian Immigrants in America: Some Cultural Aspects of Psychological Adaptation," in P. Saran and E. Eames (eds.). *The New Ethnics*. New York: Praeger Publishers.

Dothan, Tamar (1985). "Jewish Children from Ethiopia in Israel: Some Observations on Their Adaptation Patterns," *Israel Social Research*, 3: 1–2, 97–103.

Dowd, J., and Bengston, V. (1978). "Aging in Minority Populations: An Examination of the Double Jeopardy Hypothesis," *Journal of Gerontology*, 33:3, 427–36.

Feagin, J., and Feagin, C. (1979). *Discrimination American Style: Institutional Racism and Sexism*. Englewood Cliffs, NJ: Prentice Hall.

Glazer, Nathan and Monihan, Patrick (1965). *Beyond the Melting Pot*. Cambridge: Harvard University Press.

Glazer, Nathan (1975). *Affirmative Discrimination: Ethnic Inequality and Public Policy*. New York: Basic Books.

Graaf, T. (1975). "Pathological Patterns of Identification in Families of Survivors of the Holocaust," *Israel Annals of Psychiatry and Related Disciplines*, 13:2, 335–73.

Green, J. W. (1982). *Cultural Awareness in the Human Services*. Englewood Cliffs, NJ: Prentice Hall.

Greenwald, Baruch (1992). "The Influence of Ethnic-Cultural Sensitivities of Rehabilitation Counselors on Treatment Process and Outcome." Jerusalem: The Hebrew University, (Masters Thesis in Progress).

Grosser, C. F. (1976). *New Directions in Community Organization: From Enabling to Advocacy*. New York: Praeger Publishers.

Haidar, Aziz (1991). *Social Welfare Services for Israel's Arab Population*. Boulder, CO: Westview Press.

Hassin, Yael (1985). "The Relationship between Country of Origin and Juvenile Delinquency in Israel; 1948–1977," *Delinquency and Social Deviance*, 79–99.

———. (1992). "Juvenile Delinquency in Israel: Objective and Subjective Disadvantagement among Immigrants from Islamic Countries to Israel," *Mifgash*, 2, 62–72.

Inbar, Michael, and Adler, Chaim (1977). *Ethnic Integration in Israel*. New Brunswick, NJ: Transaction Books.

Iris, Mark, and Shama, Abraham (1972). "Israel and Its Third World Jews: Black Panthers—The Ethnic Dilemma," *Society*, 9:7, 31–36.

Jacobs, Carolyn, and Bowles, Dorcas (eds.) (1988). *Ethnicity and Race: Critical Concepts in Social Work*. New York: National Association of Social Workers.

Jaffe, Eliezer David (1975). "Poverty in the Third Jewish Commonwealth: Sepharadi-Ashkenazi Divisions," *Journal of Jewish Communal Service*, 52:1, 91–99.

———. (1977). "Manpower Supply and Admissions Policy in Israel Social Work Education," ibid., 53:3, 242–49.

———. (1985). *Pleaders and Protesters: Citizen's Organizations in Israel*. New York: The American Jewish Committee.

———. (1988). "Ethnic Preferences of Israeli Pre-School Children," *Early Development and Care*, 39:1, 83–94.

———. (1989). "Disadvantaged Students in Israeli Social Work Education," *International Journal of Adolescence and Youth*, 1:2, 305–35

———. (1990). "The Effect of Age and Ethnic Background on Ethnic Stereotypes," *International Social Work,* 33:2, 325–38.

———. (1992). "The Role of Nonprofit Organizations within the Ultra-Orthodox Community in Israel," in K. McCarthy, et al., (eds). *The Nonprofit Sector in the Global Community.* San Francisco: Jossey-Bass.

———. (1995). "Ethnicity and Client's Social Worker Preference: The Israel Experience," *British Journal of Social Work,* 25:3, 615–33.

Jenkins, Shirley (1981). *The Ethnic Dilemma in Social Services.* New York: The Free Press.

Kahn, Arthur (1990). "Achieving Ethnic Equality in Israel," *Midstream,* 36:1, 13–18.

Kaplan, Steve (1988). "Falasha Religion: Ancient Judaism or Evolving Ethiopian Tradition?" *The Jewish Quarterly Review,* 79:1, 22–30.

———. (ed.) (1992). *Ethiopian Jews in Israel.* Detroit: Wayne State University Press.

Keadar, Shaul (1978). "The Influence of Client's Ethnic Origin on the Social Worker's Diagnosis Evaluation of the Client's Potential and Choice on Treatment." Ramat Gan: Bar Ilan University (M.S.W thesis).

Kilson, Martin, and Bond, George (1992). "Marginalized Blacks," *The New York Times,* May 7, 1992, p. 6.

Kitano, H. H. (1980). *Race Relations.* Englewood Cliffs, NJ: Prentice Hall.

Ki-Tov, Yael, and Ben-David, Amir (1993). "The Cultural Component in Marital Therapy with Immigrants from Ethiopia," *Society and Welfare,* 3:3, 287–99.

Korazim, Joseph (1989). "Deploying Social Workers for Advocacy and Social Warning Roles in a Period of Diminishing Public Resources," *Journal of Social Work and Policy in Israel,* 2:1, 45–56.

Liebman, C. S. and Don-Yehiya (1984). *Religion and Politics in Israel.* Bloomington: Indiana University Press.

Lum, D. (1986). *Social Work Practice and People of Color.* Monterey, CA: Brooks Cole Publishing.

McGoldrick, M. et al. (1982). *Ethnicity and Family Therapy.* New York: Guilford Press.

Mills, C. W. (1963). *Power, Politics and People.* New York: Ballantine Books.

Munitz, Sara, et al. (1985). "Color, Skin Color Preference and Self-Color Identification Among Ethiopian and Israeli-Born Children," *Israel Social Science Research,* 3:1–2, 74–84.

Myrdal, Gunnar (1944). *An American Dilemma: The Negro Problem and Modern Democracy.* New York: Harper and Row.

Norton: D. G. (1978). *The Dual Perspective: Inclusion of Ethnic Minority Content in the Social Work Curriculum.* New York: Council of Social Work Education.

Ogburn, W. F. (1950). *Social Change.* New York: Viking Press.

Patai, R. (1970). *Israel between East and West* (second edition). Westport, CT: Greenwood Publishers.

Pedersen, P. B. et al. (eds.) (1976). *Counseling across Cultures.* Honolulu: University of Hawaii Press.

Peres, Yochanan (1977). *Ethnic Relations in Israel.* Tel Aviv: Sifrat Hapoalim.

Petersen, William, et al. (1980). *Concepts of Ethnicity.* Cambridge: Harvard University Press.

Pinderhughes, E. (1989). *Understanding Race, Ethnicity, and Power.* New York: The Free Press.

Powell, Walter (ed.) (1986). *The Nonprofit Sector: A Research Handbook.* New Haven: Yale University Press.

Rosen, Chaim (1991). "Ethiopian Jews: An Historical Sketch," *Israel Journal of Medical Sciences,* 27:5, 242–50.

Schindler, Reuven (1987). "Intergenerational Theories in Social Work Practice with Religious Families," *Journal of Social Work and Policy in Israel,* 1:1, 99–113.

Schlesinger, Arthur Jr. (1992). *The Disuniting of America.* New York: Norton.

Schlesinger, Elfriede, and Devore, Wynetta (1991). *Ethnic Sensitive Social Work Practice.* St. Louis: C. V. Mosby Company.

Schneiderman, L. (1965). "A Social Action Model for the Social Work Practioner," *Social Casework,* 46:3, 490–93.

Schoenberger, Michelle (1975). "The Falashas of Ethiopia: An Ethnological Study." Cambridge: University of Cambridge (Ph.D. dissertation).

Sellin, T. (1938). *Culture Conflict and Crime.* New York: Social Science Research Council.

Sharlin, Shlomo and Shamai, Michal (1991). "Intervention with Families in Extreme Distress," *Society and Welfare,* 12:11, 91–112.

Shraga, Yona, and Slonim-Nevo, Vered (1993). "Adjustment Difficulties of Adolescent Immigrants From the Former U.S.S.R.," *Society and Welfare,* 13:3, 279–86.

Shaw, C., and McKay, H. (1942). *Juvenile Delinquency and Urban Areas.* Chicago: University of Chicago Press.

Shumsky, A. (1955). *The Clash of Cultures in Israel.* New York: Columbia Teacher's College.

Smooha, S. (1978). *Israel: Pluralism and Conflict.* Berkeley: University of California Press.

———— and Peres, Y. (1974). "Ethnic Gaps in Israel," *Megamot*, 20:1, 5–42.

Solomon, B. (1976). *Black Empowerment: Social Work in Oppressed Communities*. New York: Columbia University Press.

Sottomayor, M. (1971). "Mexican American Interaction with Social Systems," *Social Casework*, 5:3, 316–22.

Suelien, Zima (1989). "Forty-Two Ethiopian Boys: Observations of Their First Year in Israel," *Social Work*, (May, June).

Tadmot, Edna (ed.) (1990). *Innovative Services for Children in Israel, 1979–1989.* Jerusalem: Gefen Publishing House.

Vital, D. (1978). *The Origins of Zionism*. Tel Aviv: Tel Aviv University Press.

Israeli–Palestinian Workshops: Legitimation of National Identity and Change in Power Relationships

NAVA SONNENSCHEIN, RABAH HALABI,

AND ARIELLA FRIEDMAN

This chapter focuses on a description and analysis of a case study of an intergroup process for Jewish and Palestinian Arab adults in a model developed by the School for Peace of Neve Shalom/Wahat al Salam.* The analysis is based on courses for two adult groups.

The characteristic patterns of contact between Jews and Palestinian Arabs in Israeli society are faithfully played out at all stages of the group process in the room. The majority group (the Jews) shows a lack of recognition for the realities of oppression and discrimination felt by the minority group (the Arabs), as well as for the legitimacy of a Palestinian national identity. The minority group (the Arabs) is unwilling to sanction the legitimacy of the fears felt by the Jewish group. The majority group tries by various means to control or quash the expressions of nationalism from the Arab side. The minority group consolidates and, newly empowered, uses its assertiveness to bring about a change in the balance of power in the room. From a situation of majority control over a minority, there is a shift to a situation of equal dialogue.

Our premise, born out in the two groups under study, is that in order for an equal dialogue and fruitful negotiations to take place between participants of the two nations, two things must happen in the process:

(A) A change in the balance of power between the groups to one of equality. (B) Acceptance by the two groups of their independent national identities and the granting of legitimacy to the identity of the other group as it is, without feeling weakened by this granting of legitimacy.

---

*Neve Shalom/Wahat al Salam is the only village in Israel in which Jews and Palestinian Arabs of Israeli citizenship have chosen to live and work together in a cooperative village. The message for dialogue is imparted through the medium of the School for Peace, which is situated in the village. The school organizes Jewish–Palestinian encounter meetings for youth and adults as well as programs for the training of facilitators and teachers in this area.

The paper explores the working methods that enabled this process of transformation, identifying the various stages and kinds of intervention, and analyzing its important characteristics.

Introduction

This analysis focuses on the issue of the power struggle between Jews and Arabs in an extended group process, on the question of legitimation for Palestinian national identity, and on the fears of the Jewish group.

The working methods, the description of stages in the process, and the analysis are based on many years of work with Jewish–Arab youth encounters and specifically on the case study of two long-term-adult-group processes.

(1) A facilitators' course, April–June 1991: this group had ten participants; four Jews and six Arabs. The course included eighty-six hours of intergroup process, with six intensive workshops of ten hours each, and two of twenty-three hours. The second half of the course was dedicated to the training of the participants in facilitation.

(2) An experimental year-long course addressing the Jewish–Arab conflict, given as part of an M.A. degree program and conducted jointly with the psychology department of the Tel Aviv University: this group had fourteen participants; seven Jews and seven Arabs, all M.A. students of the University of Tel Aviv. The Jews were from the department of social psychology and the Arabs from various humanities and social studies departments. In the first semester of the course there was a series of fourteen weekly meetings each of three hours. The second semester was divided into (a) six meetings for the presentation of theories on conflicts, intergroup processes, stereotypes, and identity by the department of social psychology lecturers, and (b) seven additional meetings, each split into two sections of equal length. Here, the first section consisted of an open intergroup process, and the second section was given to analysis of the process in an open discussion directed by course lecturers and with the participation of students who had sat in to observe the process together with the lecturers.

Working Methods

The working method described here is based on intensive experience in intergroup process in Jewish–Palestinian encounters. The workshop format allows the participant to explore the Jewish–Palestinian conflict through the personal experience of conflict as it occurs in the microcosm of the group. The facilitators participate in the exploration of processes and contribute towards the attainment of the objective by:

(A) Positioning and keeping the conflict at the center of the group experience and focusing on intergroup aspects from the range of possible emphases. Working from a system approach, interactions between individuals are examined in their capacity to reflect relationships between the groups to which they belong rather than being explored for their significance on the personal level.

(B) Reflection of the conscious and unconscious group processes and enabling the participants to understand these processes and come to terms with them. Through the intergroup process the participants are made aware of the complexity of the conflict and their part in the creation of patterns characteristic to it (patterns of change and resistance to change).

(C) Constant linkage between events and group processes within the room and the reality outside of it, and vice versa, working from the premise that the group serves as a microcosm of the larger reality.

Example: When at the heat of the conflict in the group people experience discomfort and restlessness, some of them exit the room for the rest rooms—a situation that is interpreted as an expression of the desire to emigrate from the country/room when the conflict becomes unbearable.

The process of exploration is made in the binational forum (when the Jews and the Arabs are present in the room, most of the process is done in this forum) and the uninational forum (when each national group does its own process separately.*

The content of the discussion in the group is open to any subject that the participants raise. The work takes place in the format of third party consultation. In this context it is important that the two facilitators (one Jewish, one Arab) are intimately acquainted with the dynamics of the conflict explored.

Since at the heart of our working method is the linkage drawn between what happens outside and what happens in the group, the way in which reality is interpreted is of significance to this work. Conceptions about that reality will influence the choice of what is reflected in the group, how it is reflected, and what the foci will be. Thus it is important that the two facilitators share a common basis for interpretation.

Description of the Stages in the Intergroup Process

First Stage: Good Manners and, "We Are All Human Beings"

At this stage the group is busy with the building of a framework. There are attempts at the setting up of roles, rules, norms, and limits in the group. There is a checking of what is permissible and what is forbidden. Preconditions are established: "I will not sit with 'Moledet' party supporters and those who advocate 'transfer' (mass deportation) of the Palestinians." "Will you accept me if I am unwilling to feel guilty?" "Can I accept you if you support Saddam Hussein?" In this clarification of the preconditions and the limits of the group, attitudes of one group are checked against those of the other, concerning the meaning of the dialogue: "Is there room

---

*The group will meet only a few sessions in this forum, according to its needs.

for the expression of feelings in the room or must the focus be on the rational level?" "Are we representatives of a nation or individuals?"

The question of whether the focus will be on an interpersonal level is addressed, since the Jewish group favors this direction, or whether the focus will be more on a political level, since this is preferred by the Arabs. The Jewish group is interested in a blurring of the differences as a way of avoiding painful and threatening divisive factors.

(1) A Jewish participant: "It's better we get to know each other before we go to the controversial issues."

(2) An Arab participant: "It's scary to deal with the real issues but there is no other way."

The direction opted for by the Jews wins out and an unrealistic fantasy of "togetherness," holds sway in the room, with an emphasis on commonality and the blurring of differences. The watchword is "all of us are human beings." The Arab group, going along with this, talks about continual contacts with Jews. This situation causes the members of the minority group to feel they are losing a sense of their own identity. As one of the Arab participants said, "We tried to be like each other and I got lost. More and more I wanted to find my own voice. Always there was the attempt to return to commonality, that we are all human beings. Every time this inflamed a conflict and pain was the result."

The Jews do not expose the harsh images they have of the Arabs. The Jewish group pounces on individuals who attempt to lay bare such images. Exposing stereotypes of Arabs threatens the Jewish group, places them in a position of vulnerability. So in order not to lose control of the situation, the Jewish group will completely resist all such attempts. When at this stage a Jewish participant revealed the stereotypes he had of Arabs as "knife-wielding killers," everyone rushed to deal with him. He was called an imbecile. The group suppresses the individual who weakens it as a group, citing enlightened principles. The Jewish group will sometimes give itself credit for being just and fair. Stories will be told about instances where the participants came to the assistance of or defended Arabs. Every time a danger zone is entered, there is the inclination of the group to leave it. A Jewish participant expresses her feeling of carefulness and treading on ice: "We have many more meetings ahead of us so we'd better be careful." The group does not delve into any subject and jumps from one to the other. There are either silent pauses or too much chatter. There is an escape from dealing with the group's objective, which is the "exploration of the conflict."

Often the Arab group's internalization of oppression will be expressed at this stage as an exaggerated estimation of the Jewish majority group. H. Tajfel, S. Turner (1985) comment that a great deal of research shows that ethnocentricity between hierarchial groups is unidirectional. Groups discriminated against often are not ethnocentric but just the opposite. They will show deference for the discriminatory majority that oppresses them. An Arab participant spoke of his respect for the Israeli army and its power. Another participant expressed admiration for Western culture as against the "backwardness" of Oriental culture.

At this stage everyone still wants to protect the togetherness and not raise divisive factors. All the participants consolidate against everything that threatens and creates anxiety. This solidarity expresses itself in:

(1) Opposition to reflections given by the facilitators. There is opposition to reflections that disturb the group in its efforts to remain together and well-mannered, rather than raising separative factors so it will evolve into a work group as defined by Bion (1961).

(2) Solidarity against the difficult reality outside. The group emphasizes both in a general way and with personal stories the extent to which the participants in the room are good, enlightened, and reasonable, in contrast to the extremism and insanity of the "bad guys" in the world outside.

(3) The group will unite against individuals who bring out points of contention and conflict.

At this stage, the seating will be mixed in the room. During breaks there will be an inclination to go out together, to the cafeteria or other such places.

In accordance with the process in this stage, the role of the facilitators is to enable the group to build itself, mediate, and prevent the group from manipulating them into the direction it would like. They will reflect the processes occurring in the group, link between the realities inside the room and those outside, and focus on the dynamics of majority-minority relations.

Second Stage: The Consolidation into National Groups and the Struggle between Them

At this stage each national group begins to gel. Leaders emerge and representatives for negotiation are appointed by each group. Participants involuntarily assume the national roles parallel to the positions of the political world outside, according to their responses to the process. A Jewish participant: "Here I begin to feel like Geulah Cohen [a member of the right-wing "Tehia" party].

The seating arrangement in the room changes to unconsciously reflect the consolidation of participants into national groups. Without prior agreement, or even awareness that it is happening, Arabs occupy one half circle of the room, and the Jews the other, while the facilitators, who by convention sit opposite each other, find themselves defining the borders. Those who cross national borders in the intergroup process tend to cross them physically by the place they choose to sit. This subject of border crossers throws light on the process of consolidation of each national group in the process.

The desertion of the group by individuals according to H. Tajfel and J. Turner (1985) threatens the group's unanimity and it will therefore try its utmost to preserve unity and "keep order in its ranks."

Border crossers from the Jewish side are those who express understanding for the other side while the group is still at the stage of struggle between the two groups. The Jewish group describes them with words like: "fawning," "defeatist," even "treacherous." In the uninational forum the group expresses anger towards them. In one of the youth group sessions, in a simulation game on the peace talks, the Jewish group expelled the leftists among them from the room. If there is more than one border crosser in the group they will make a coalition between them. Sometimes the border crossing reaches the point of a fantasy where, "I don't actually belong to my nation at all, but my positions make me eligible to belong to the other side." The response of the Arab group in one of the groups was to present a clear line. An Arab participant: "It doesn't matter how leftist you are—you are still a Jew." In another group there was acceptance of Jewish border crossers by the Arab group on the basis of common opinions (it was expressed in the seating in the room until the end of the process) though with emphasis of the national differences in the realities of Jewish and Arab life. In this case, border crossers did not realign themselves until the end of the process. Despite the price that majority group participants must pay, border crossing and responding to it in front of the other national group is still more acceptable than for the minority.

Border crossers from the Arab side are those who express understanding of the other side. They tend to explain the motivations of the Jewish group in justifying the oppression of the minority. For example, an Arab participant tries to explain why Arabs must be searched at the airport for security reasons. Or he says he can understand why Jews shout "Death to the Arabs" after a murder committed in the name of nationalism. The Jewish group shows a high level of interest in border crossers of the Arab group. It will also compensate and strengthen them (cooptation). At this stage, the Arab group consolidates and returns the border crossers to the ranks of the national group. Sometimes it happens that these same individuals become the group's flag bearers of Palestinian Arab nationalism. In the Arab group, border crossing carries a much higher price, both for the individual and for the group. Thus the uninational forum is chosen by the Arab group as the more appropriate framework to deal with the subject.

This stage of a struggle, waged by the Arab group, begins over recognition of acts of injustice and oppression perpetrated against Arabs in the country, and over a shift from Jewish control in the room. The Jewish group will fight to maintain control of the situation in the room and try to win recognition of its fears. The Arab group will fight for recognition of its right for national identity.

When, at the peak of the battle, power relationships are measured against the issues of who is more a victim, who is more humane, and who is more guilty, there is a feeling of possible disintegration, of threat to the existence of the group. Sometimes there is an escalation so difficult that it is hard to remain in the room. The situation is felt to be unbearable. Anger is expressed towards the facilitators: "Why did you get us into this mess?"

There are expressions of desperation, stories of death and despair. An Arab participant told her nightmare of the "suicide of the Palestinian people." Arab participants express dejection and frustration over the intransigence in the room and the indifference of the Jewish side, and of their desire to leave the group. A Jewish participant expresses his frustration over the unwillingness of the Arab group to lay bare their points of weakness, over their refusal to recognize the fears of the Jews. There are more absences during this stage.

Sometimes during this stage very clear lines are drawn, up to the point of pinning stereotypes onto the other group. A statement made by a Jewish participant on his refusal to serve in the occupied territories was distorted by an Arab participant": "You, who serve in the territories." There is sometimes the attempt to exaggerate the description of the other group to the point of distortion and misrepresentation of what was said in the room, in order to preserve the stereotype given the group. The group no longer meets to have fun together in the cafeteria.

Another characteristic of this stage is the use of blows beneath the belt: "If you reveal your vulnerability, your weakness is taken advantage of, and there is a searching for additional places of weakness." A Jewish participant in the group told of a case in which she saved an Arab from a Jewish crowd that tried to beat him after the murder of a Jew, whose name was given. An Arab participant asked the Jewish participant and the other Jews why they never remember the names of Arabs slain by Jews, though they remember the name of every Jew killed by Arab aggression.

In the midst of this struggle, when a strong leadership in the Arab group evolves to press the demands of the group, the Jewish group will resist, but at the same time respect the strength embodied in the leadership. It will make this leadership the principal focus for the purpose of negotiation. At this point, a situation of equality is reached.

In accordance with the process described in this stage, the role of the facilitators is to reflect situations such as use of overpoliteness, and sidestepping the exploration of the conflict, in order that conflictive issues can be brought out and the process moved forward. Processes of control and oppression, the internalization of oppression, national consolidation, liberation, and power struggles are reflected, analyzed, and interpreted to the group, with constant linkage brought out between inside and outside. In segments where there is a return to a pattern that stalls the group's progress, it is important to point out the alternatives.

The Third Stage: Integration, Equal Dialogue, and a Working Group

At this stage, the group is more focused on its object of exploring the conflict. The participants are able to admit a greater complexity in their comprehension of identity; they are able to accept persons both as individuals and as part of the national group. There is a balance of power. A mutual acceptance emerges. The acceptance of the other side does not weaken me and I no longer see it as a "zero-sum game."

There is a reconciliation with the inability to actualize the imperfect fantasy; comfort with the fact that the conflict will not be solved here in the group, that when we part we will not have agreed on everything. The Jews will not all turn into leaders of protest demonstrations. It will not be possible to wrench all the answers from a process with a limited time frame. Even if we feel that some changes have begun in us, the reality of the conflict has a very different influence on the lives of members of each national group. In place of the fantasy there is a more sober and realistic vision. There is more willingness to take responsibility for the things said. There is less escapism and denial, and more awareness of the way every individual and national group helps to shape the dynamics of the conflict.

There is also the ability to joke in the group about subjects or words that formerly carried an explosive charge. There is a greater ability to listen to things that one does not agree with, and statements that formerly angered members of the group are now heard differently.

Sometimes towards the end of the process, there is a sensation of nearness, but there is difficulty in articulating this. The group possesses no suitable verbal repertoire (though nonverbal messages are present), and many issues remain unresolved.

The leader of the Arab group who represented Palestinian nationalism takes responsibility for pointing out even the smallest changes that have occurred and places them in the hard light of the conflict outside.

The two groups described here reached this stage. There are many groups that do not. They get stuck at the previous stage and are not able to move forward. One of the reasons for this is that outside the group there is still no solution. Even among the groups that reach this third stage there will be partial reversions though the quality of the discussion will be different.

To suit the needs of this stage, the facilitators intervene less since the group works by itself and takes more responsibility. The facilitators reflect constructive processes that enable the exploration of the conflict and recognition of processes of regression. Towards the end, the facilitators will help the group to remain on a realistic track, rather than allow them to drift into unrealistic fantasies.

Analysis of the Process

There are two foci that arise at each stage of the group process. These are:

(1) Failure to grant legitimacy.

The Jews are unwilling to give legitimacy to the feelings of oppression, dispossession, and discrimination felt by the Arabs. Moreover, they do all they can to control the situation and avoid the legitimation and realization of a Palestinian national identity. The Arabs are unwilling to grant legitimacy to the fears felt by the Jews.

(2) Power struggles—who controls the situation.

Giving legitimacy is taken as a zero-sum game. The recognition of fears is taken as a position of weakness, as is the recognition of acts of injustice, oppression or of Palestinian nationalism. According to this perspective, the recognition that the other side desires from me will be at my expense, will weaken me. For example, if I, as an Arab, agree to recognize the fears of the Jews, this will strengthen their inclination to continue to oppress me as a minority posing a threat to their security.

Or if I, as a Jew, recognize Palestinian Arabs as a strong and independent entity, they will use this to help them gain the upper hand, and then exact their revenge.

The power struggle is the central thread running through the dynamics of the conflict. During the group process, power will be continually measured and assessed by the groups, as they wrestle through various issues advanced by them. Three important issues in conflict are:

(1) Struggle over who is more humane.

(2) Struggle over who is more a victim.

(3) Struggle over Palestinian national identity as an entity of equal power in the room.

In many of these struggles, the same dynamics that characterize the conflictive situation outside the room will be found within it.

There are two stages to this struggle. Usually it is easier to attain recognition for acts of injustice and oppression than it is to attain recognition for Palestinian identity. One possible explanation may be that the recognition for acts of injustice, arising gradually in the room, may imply a degree of surrender and yielding of power to the Jewish group in the arena of who is the more humane and just, yet still the majority gives this recognition from its position of superiority and strength. When an atmosphere of change arises and there is recognition of injustice done to the Palestinian Arabs, the Arab group feels strong, unified, and begins to muster its forces. Now, even individuals toe the line behind a positive national group image. This strengthening is the beginning of a long struggle over recognition of Palestinian identity as an entity of equal power. Usually, such recognition of equal power begins much later in the process, and only when the Palestinians are able to state their case from a position of proven strength rather than from one of weakness. In such a position the making of demands takes the place of acquiescence.

The giving of legitimacy to the Palestinian identity as an identity of equal power in the room, and the giving of legitimacy to the fears of the Jews, are no longer conceived of in terms of a "zero-sum game." It can be seen as recognition given from a power position rather than from weakness.

It is important to note that this empowerment in the positive sense: it is liberating and assertive, exercised with responsibility for the welfare of the group, rather than in order to oppress. In the groups under study there was no exploitation of power for the purpose of controlling the Jewish group or "getting back at them."

A Description of Some Examples of the Power Struggle in the Process

The Struggle over Who Is More Humane

This struggle continues until very late in the process. Usually, after stories of acts of injustice and discrimination, the Arabs prevail and the balance of power in the room tilts in their favor, though at the cost of divulging painful stories from their everyday life as a minority. One of the options open to the Jews in order to maintain their position of power and control over the group is to question the humaneness of the Arab side. They ask about the murder of collaborators, about their position concerning terrorism: "If you don't condemn terrorism you are less humane than we are." They ask, "Why do you have no peace movements like us?" Images are raised of the cruelty of the Arab side; of sabotage, knives, and horrible murders. The question arises of Arab support for Saddam Hussein, who cruelly massacred the Kurds. The Arab gloating at the suffering of the Jews during the Gulf War is cited as inhumane. Images of the "primitivity" of the Levantine and tradition-bound Arab world, in contrast to the "enlightened" West are brought up. Jewish participants often raise the issue of the total oppression of women in Muslim Arab culture. A Jewish participant shares her conception of the Arabs as more cruel than the Jews, and how "One day, given the chance, they will do terrible things to the Jews, and that, although the Arabs in the room here seem pleasant and gentle, who knows? If the balance of power changes they may sit here like we do today, not lifting a finger, and only saying 'We are sorry.'"

The representation of the struggle over who is more humane is expressed in terms of the "zero-sum game." As one Jewish participant says: "Maybe it's true that we put you down and are still doing it. But if we stop, you will do the same to us, only more cruelly. It hurts me what happens but at least I am alive." Or in the words of another Jewish participant: "If power will be in your hands, when they come to slash me, or stab me—will you defend me?"

The Arab group in this struggle counters with examples of the cruelty of the Israeli army towards the Palestinians in the Occupied Territories, and towards Lebanese civilians. "You don't even think about the thousands of children murdered in Iraq under American bombings," an Arab participant says. Another asks "Why don't you refuse to serve in the Occupied Territories?" The indifference of the Jewish majority is portrayed as egoistic cruelty. An Arab participant asks "When they call 'Death to the Arabs'—will you protect me?"

The Jews know, at this point in the discussion, that by talking they only stand to lose more points, and so a group silence ensues that is interpreted by the Arab group as a wall of silence. The Jews are not only less informed, but in the dynamics of the discussion, in every argument on the facts of majority-minority relations, they emerge as less humane; and here it matters little whether they know the facts, deny them, or defend them and justify the establishment. The tactics of silence save them from this position of inferiority.

In the struggle over who is more humane, the groups articulate the images of cruelty they have of the other side. There is also the attempt to check their prospects for the future, in regard to what they can expect from the other group.

The Struggle over Who Is More a Victim

When the Arabs have won more points, having been able to demonstrate the acts of oppression and discrimination they suffer, and when there is recognition by the majority group of this discrimination, the struggle changes to one over the role of the victim in the group. The groups compete on who is more a victim. Even the majority group (the Jews) places itself in this role, chased and hounded into a corner by the cruel regimes of the Arab world, fearful of the cruelty of Saddam Hussein. The role of the victim carries moral capital. Every time stories of discrimination and acts of injustice towards the Arabs make their way into the discussion, immediately the Jewish group counters with stories of the Holocaust. When the Arabs speak of discrimination, Jewish women tell of how they feel as women discriminated against by men. Somehow it feels better to be on the side of the victimized. Naturally this macabre competition on suffering is linked to the competition on humaneness. The unwillingness of the Arab group to recognize the fears of the Jews only heightens the feeling of victimization for the Jews in the group. The Jewish group sometimes speaks of guilt feelings: "I don't want to sit here in the role of defendant." In fact, the Jews say, "We don't want to hear your tales." The rise of guilt feelings often seals channels of communication and prevents the Arab group from bringing more material to the discussion. Another way of dealing with the difficulty of guilt feelings is to detach oneself from the group: "I am not one of those who oppress you, and I am also a minority in my society."

The Struggle over Palestinian Identity as an Entity of Equal Power in the Room

When the Arabs in the room rally to the cause of establishing their Palestinian identity, when the leaders of the group stand and explain quietly, unemotionally, authoritatively, and assertively, the complexity of their identity, the Jews find it difficult to understand, and feel threatened. "How can you be Palestinians as well as Israeli Arabs? You have to choose one or the other!"

The Jews consolidate, as if to say: If we give legitimacy to your national identity, it will lead us to the point of throwing in the towel, abandoning our hard-won military achievements and our national pride. A Jewish participant says: "I am in a position of strength, and want to sustain this position." Individuals from the Jewish group who cross the border at this time are considered "Arab sympathizers," "quitters," and traitors who weaken the group.

In this struggle too, the Jewish group will attempt to use modes of dominance applied outside, such as "divide and rule" methods (splitting the Arabs into Christian, Moslem, Druze, and Bedouin factions). After the Arab participants of one group told of the expropriation of their families' lands, a Jewish participant asked, "What is your opinion of the murder of collaborators?" a subject over which there are internal differences of opinion on the Arab side.

The Jewish group raises its fears in a very obvious way in order to arrest the Arab group's consolidation behind a national identity with which they make demands. The fears are existential, however the particular circumstances under which they are raised in the room may suggest that they are being used as cards in the power play of the group and as justification for an unwillingness to relinquish control over the minority.

The Arab group unifies around the image that the fear of the Jews is like that of a thief, which an Arab participant brings in response to a disclosure by a Jewish participant that she fears the prospect of refugees' returning to claim a house inhabited now by one of her relatives. The Arab group brings personal stories to prove its claim of Jewish expropriation of lands and property. Jewish members tell why they will not relinquish control over the Arabs and the territories. The same Arab participant responds, "Your existence depends upon the legitimacy which I give to your power"—a power statement. The Jewish group will use all of its resources to try to win recognition of their fears from the Arab group, but without success. This puts them in a tight spot. The Arab group is unwilling to sanction their fears until the Jews stop using these as a means to oppress them, and as a pretext for dominance in the room. The Arab group struggles and consolidates, and a kind of "intifada" emerges on the Arab side.

It is not coincidental that at this stage a Jewish participant brings up the subject of the blocks thrown at a soldier before he pulls the trigger. The facilitators bring her statement back into the group and the same participant says that if there is a direction from which she fears the block being thrown, it is from that of certain Arab participants. The block epitomizes the danger that the Jews feel when confronted by the empowerment of the Arabs in the group.

A Jewish participant requests of an Arab participant that he will not take advantage of the situation when the balance of power tilts in his favor. And in fact, the balance of power in the room is changing already.

The Arabs in the room emerge as vindicated and strong in their position of power, and maneuver the Jews into a situation where they recognize this. The leader of the Arab group issues power statements: "I demand equal rights from the Israeli government. I demand that it leaves the Occupied Territories." The Jews ask, "How on earth can you demand anything?" But the Arabs have supplanted their image of oppressed and complaining victims with a new one of strength, of a power to be reckoned with. The same Arab participant said: "I was happy when the SCUD fell on Israel so the Israelis would know the Occupied Territories offer no security, so their pride would break and they would understand that power is not a solution—that they will need to find another way." The Arabs now control the situation and the Jews, confused and on the defensive, are much less clear in their responses. The Jews are startled by this meeting with Arab strength. It is the first time they have seen this degree of power in an Arab group. After this realization they give up the customary role of controlling the situation. From here on the dialogue is directed toward those Arab participants seen to command the greatest strength.

The Jews unite as one—consolidate their ranks—but the Arab group and its leader stand their ground. The atmosphere in the room is stormy and there is true dialogue with all its difficulty. There is a feeling of equal struggle between the groups, and less defensiveness.

When a shift begins in the balance of power in the room, the Arab group will express anger or depression over any retreat or attempts to erase changes that have been attained. Sometimes the struggle is extremely enervating. Every time there is a retreat from the position of equality back to Jewish control in the room, the Arabs experience desperation and frustration at the size of the task before them and express this as a desire to leave the group, emigrate from the room: "Why do I need to come here if it is just like everywhere else?" Usually when this happens, the group rallies to prevent the desertion.

Seeing the changes in the balance of power in these various rounds of the process, even when they are small encourages the participants to continue. Those who best express empowerment in the Arab group take a central place, become its leaders, and are sent to negotiate. If they are absent from a certain session, others take their place, as happens in the world outside.

From this point the Jews, startled to observe the new position of power occupied by the Arabs, speak directly to their best representatives. There is greater esteem for them.

This response contradicts the common premise that a powerful Palestinian leadership causes the Jewish side to dig in and harden its positions. In the groups with which we worked, though the Jewish participants state their objection to speaking with empowered Arabs—whom they call extremists—these become the focus of the principal communication, even when this fact is reflected to the group.

The truth is that the Jewish group begins to extend respect, legitimacy, and recognition for Palestinian nationalism only when there is a consolidation of the Palestinian group and when the identity is represented from a proud and assertive position of power by the leader of the group. From this point the dialogue becomes equal. There is also the ability to expose differences within the national group without any surrender of nationalism, even with differences of opinion in the Palestinian group. The Arab group and its leader are willing to recognize the fears of the Jews, and to express this.

When the balance of power changes in the room, the struggle over granting legitimacy to the feelings of oppression by the Arabs, to the fears of the Jews, and to a Palestinian national identity, are no longer taken as a "zero-sum game." The recognition of the other side can be made from a position of strength. This position of strength need not be oppressive. The Arab group, which is well versed in the role of the underdog beneath the heel of oppression, will show caution in using its newfound power, and rather than seek to reverse the roles, will tend to exercise its power with restraint, responsibility, and concern for the welfare of the group, rather than attempt to nullify the other side.

A new level of encounter is the result. The Arab group experiences empowerment; something quite new to it, and this in turn creates a new situation for the Jewish group. They are surprised when they must suddenly come to terms with Palestinian Arabs who show courage and equal power of speech, raising arguments in demand of their rights. Initially, the group will greet the phenomenon with resistance, but also with a degree of respect. In fact, the situation releases the majority group from the unwelcome cycle of oppression and control over the minority, to a place of equal dialogue, from where it is possible to advance. This process is similar to what Paulo Freire (1972) called liberation as a mutual process.

Summary

Since at the heart of the working method is the tracing of a linkage between Jewish–Palestinian conflict as it is waged inside the room and outside of it, the changes that got under way in the groups are encouraging from the point of view of the potential they demonstrate for the stalled negotiations between the two peoples.

The turning point in the process arrived when the Palestinian group emerged strong in its position of power. It was possible to advance in the dialogue when each national group gave up its customary role in the majority/minority relationship. The expression of power by the Palestinian group, and its acceptance by the Jewish group, changed the balance of power in the room. It enabled an equal dialogue, which opened the door to progress in negotiation. The change also expressed itself in the altered realization by the two national groups that recognition or giving of legitimacy to the needs of the other side does not necessarily weaken one's own side, but can issue from a position of power (ceasing to play the "zero-sum game"). The Arabs recognized the fears of the Jews after the Jews recognized the validity of a Palestinian national identity as an entity of equal power.

This change is encouraging, in that it may indicate the stages necessary before a breakthrough is possible in the stalled negotiations between the two peoples. Therefore it will be important to investigate more deeply the following questions.

(1) What are the conditions that permit change in the balance of power which, by turn, makes for a position of equality in negotiation?

(2) What are the processes that the Palestinian Arab group passes through in its progress toward liberation and empowerment?

(3) What are the characteristics of the powerful leadership that arises in the Palestinian Arab group and tilts the scales of power in the group, and yet does so with a sense of responsibility for the future of the dialogue, rather than with destructiveness?

(4) What are the processes sustained by the Jewish group that cause it to respond to the change in the balance of power as it does, rather than act with greater repression towards the minority group?

(5) Is there anything in the facilitation methods used in the intergroup process dealing with the Jewish–Arab conflict that might be advantageously applied to the Jewish–Palestinian peace process? Is there the same necessity in that context of changing the balance of powers to one of equality before effective negotiation can get under way?

Acknowledgments

We wish to express our gratitude to the following faculty members of the department of social psychology at Tel Aviv University who contributed analyses and many helpful comments derived from their observation of the group process:

Dr. Ariella Friedman, Prof. Nehamia Friedland, Prof. Arieh Nadler, Dr. Ya'acov Tropeh, and Dr. Yehiel Klar.

Naturally we thank the staff of the School for Peace; particularly Michal Zak for her feedback and Howard Shippin for translating this paper into English.

Lastly we must especially thank those who taught us more than anybody; the Palestinian and the Jewish participants of the courses.

We must specially thank the participants of the groups who taught us more than anyone else.

References

Bion, W. R. (1961). *Experiences in Groups.* Tavistock/Routledge

Freire, P. (1972, 1993). *Pedagogy of the Oppressed.* New York: Continuum

Tajfel, H. and Turner, J. C. (1985). "The Social Identity Theory of Intergroup Behavior." In S. Worchel, W. G. Austin (ed.), *Psychology of Intergroup Relations.* Chicago: Nelson-Hall

Appendix

COMPILED BY DEBORAH E. BING

Select Bibliography on Interethnic Coexistence

Philosophy of Coexistence

Arendt, Hannah. 1969. *On Violence.* New York, NY: Harcourt, Brace & World

Avruch, Kevin, and Peter Black. 1991. "The Cultural Question and Conflict Resolution." *Peace and Change* 16:22–45

Avruch, Kevin, and Peter W. Black, eds. 1991. *Conflict Resolution: Cross-Cultural Perspectives.* New York, NY: Greenwood Press

Axelrod, R. 1984. *The Evolution of Cooperation.* New York, NY: Basic Books.

Barth, Fresrik, ed. 1969. *Ethnic Groups and Boundaries.* Boston, MA: Little Brown.

Blackwell, James E. 1976. "The Power Basis of Ethnic Conflict in American Society." In *The Uses of Controversy in Sociology,* ed. Lewis A. Coser and Otto Larsen. New York, NY: The Free Press.

Bochner, Stephen, ed. 1981. *The Mediating Person; Bridges Between Cultures.* Cambridge, MA: Schenkman.

Breakwell, G., ed. 1992. *Social Psychology of Identity and the Self Concept.* London: Academic Press.

Brislin, Richard W., Kenneth Cushner, Craig Cherrie, and Mahleani Young. 1986. *Intercultural Interactions: A Practical Guide.* Cross Cultural Research Series, Vol. 9. Beverly Hills, CA: Sage.

Brislin, Richard W., Stephen Bochner, and Walter J. Lonner, eds. 1975. *Cross-Cultural Perspectrves on Learning.* New York, NY: Sage Publications.

Brock-Utne, Brigit. 1985. *Educating for Peace.* New York, NY: Pergamon Press.

Bunker, Barbara Benedict, Jeffery Z. Rubin, and Associates. 1995. *Conflict, Cooperation, and Justice: Essays Inspired by the Work of Morton Deutsch.* San Francisco, CA: Jossey Bass.

Burton, John, ed. 1990. *Conflict: Human Needs Theory.* New York, NY: St. Martin's Press.

Burton, John W. 1997. *Conflict Resolution: Its Language and Processes.* Lanham, MD: Scarecrow Press, Inc.

Burton, John. 1990. *Conflict: Resolution and Prevention.* New York, NY: St. Martin.

Bush, Robert A., Baruch and Joseph P. Folger. 1994. *The Promise of Mediation: Responding to Conflict through Empowerment and Recognition.* San Francisco, CA: Jossey-Bass.

Cohen, Stephen P., and Harriet Areone. 1988. "Conflict Resolution as the Alternative to Terrorism." *Journal of Social Issues* 44 (2): 175–90.

Connor, W. 1994. *Enthnonationalism: The Quest for Understanding.* Princeton, NJ: Princeton University Press.

De Reuck, Anthony, and Julie Knight, eds. 1966. *Conflict in Society.* London: J. and A. Churchill.

Dedring, Juergen. 1976. *Recent Advances in Peace and Conflict Research.* Newbury Park, CA: Sage Publications.

Deutsch, Morton. 1973. *The Resolution of Conflict: Constructive and Destructive Processes.* New Haven, CT: Yale University Press.

Doob, Leonard. 1981. *The Pursuit of Peace.* Westport, CT: Greenwood Press.

Fisher, Ronald J. 1990. *The Social Psychology of Intergroup and International Conflict Management.* New York, NY: Springer-Verlag.

Gulliver, P. H. 1979. *Disputes and Negotiations: A Cross-Cultural Perspective.* New York, NY: Academic Press.

Gurr, T. 1970. *Why Men Rebel.* Princeton, NJ: Princeton University Press.

Hermann, Margaret, ed. 1986. *Political Psychology.* San Francisco, CA: Jossey-Bass.

Hogg, M., and Abrams, D. 1988. *Social Identifications.* London and New York: Routledge and Keagan Paul.

Horowitz, Donald. 1985. *Ethnic Groups in Conflict.* Berkley and Los Angeles: University of California Press.

Kainz, Howard P., ed. 1987. *Philosophical Perspectives on Peace: An Anthology of Classical and Modern Sources.* London: Macmillan.

Kallen, H. 1956. *Cultural Pluralism and the American Idea: An Essay in Social Philosophy.* Philadelphia, PA: University of Pennsylvania Press.

Kelman, Herbert, ed. 1965. *International Behavior: A Social Psychological Analysis.* New York, NY: Holt, Rinehart and Wilson.

King, Jr., M. L. 1967. *Where Do We Go from Here: Chaos or Community?* New York, NY: Harper and Row.

Klassen, W., ed. 1986. *Dialogue toward Interfaith Understanding.* Tantur/Jerusalem: Ecumenical Institute for Theological Research.

Kreisberg, Louis. 1982. *Social Conflicts.* Englewood Cliffs, N J: Prentice-Hall.

Lederach, J. P. 1995. *Preparing for Peace: Conflict Transformation Across Cultures.* Syracuse, NY: Syracuse University Press.

Levine, Robert A., and Donald Campbell. 1972. *Ethnocentrism: Theories of Conflict, Ethnic Attitudes and Group Behavior.* New York, NY: John Wiley.

Lewin, Kurt. 1948. *Resolving Social Conflicts.* New York, NY: Harper.

Mandel, Robert. 1979. *Perception, Decision Making and Conflict.* Washington, DC: University Press of America.

Mehan H. and Wood, H. 1975. *The Reality of Ethnomethodology.* New York, NY: John Wiley and Sons.

Montville, Joe, ed. 1990. *Conflict and Peacemaking in Multi-Ethnic Societies.* Lexington, MA: Lexington.

Rubin, Jeffrey Z., Dean G. Pruitt, and Sung Hee Kim. 1986. *Social Conflict: Escalation, Stalemate and Settlement* (2nd Edition). New York, NY: Random House.

Schniedewind, and Ellen Davidson. *Open Minds to Equality.* Englewood Cliffs, NJ: Prentice-Hall.

Segall, Marshall H. 1979. *Cross-Cultural Psychology: Human Behavior in Global Perspective.* Monterey, CA: Brooks/Cole Publisher.

Slavin, Robert, et al., eds. 1985. *Learning to Cooperate, Cooperating to Learn.* New York, NY: Plenum Press.

Tajfel, Henri. 1981. *Human Groups and Social Categories: Studies in Social Psychology.* Cambridge: Cambridge University Press.

Tajfel, Henri, ed. 1982. *Social Identity and Intergroup Relations.* Cambridge: Cambridge University Press.

Worchel, Stephen, and J. Simpson, eds. 1993. *Conflict between People and Groups.* Chicago: Nelson-Hall.

Worchel, Stephen, and William G. Austin, eds, 1986. *Psychology of Intergroup Relations.* Chicago, IL: Nelson-Hall.

Volkan, Vamik D. 1988. *The Need to Have Enemies and Allies: From Clinical Practice to International Relationships.* New York, NY: Jason Aronson.

Yinger, J. Milton. 1976. "Ethnicity in Complex Societies: Structural, Cultural, and Characterological Factors." In *The Uses of Controversy in Sociology,* eds. Lewis A. Coser and Otto N. Larsen. New York, NY: The Free Press.

Applied Perspectives

Arrow, Kenneth, Robert H. Mnookin, Lee Ross, Amos Tversk, and Robert Wilson, eds. 1995. *Barriers to Conflict Resolution.* New York, NY: W.W. Norton & Company.

Azar, Edward. 1990. *The Management of Protracted Social Conflict.* Hampshire, UK: Dartmouth.

Azar, Edward E., and John Burton, eds. 1986. *International Conflict Resolution: Theory and Practice.* Boulder, CO: Lynne Rienner.

Bacow, Lawrence S., and Michael Wheeler. 1984. *Environmental Dispute Resolution.* New York, NY: Plenum.

Bazerman, M., and Lewicki, R. eds. 1983. *Negotiating in Organizations.* Newbury Park, Ca.: Sage.

Blake, R., Shepard. H., and Mouton, J. 1964. *Managing Intergroup Conflict in Industry.* Houston, TX: Gulf.

Becker, C., Chasin, L., Chasin, R., Herzig, M., and Roth, S. 1995. "From Stuck Debate to New Conversation on Controversial Issues: A Report from the Public Conversations Project." *Journal of Feminist Family Therapy: An International Forum.*

Bennet, Milton. 1986. "A Developmental Approach to Training for Intercultural Sensitivity." *International Journal of Intercultural Relations.* 10: 179–96.

Breslin, J. William, and Jeffrey Rubin, eds. 1991. *Negotiation Theory and Practice.* Cambridge, MA: PON Books.

Brown, L. 1983. *Managing Conflict at Organizational Interfaces.* Reading, Mass.: Addison-Wesley.

Burton, John, and Frank Dukes, eds. 1990. *Readings in Conflict Resolution and Management.* New York: St. Martin.

Deutsch, Morton. 1992. *The Effects of Training in Cooperative Learning and Conflict Resolution in an Alternative High School: A Summary Report.* New York, NY: International Center for Cooperation and Conflict Resolution, Columbia University.

Doyle, M., and D. Strauss. 1976. *How to Make Meetings Work.* New York, NY: The Berkley Publishing Group.

Faure, Guy Oliver, and Jeffrey Z. Rubin. 1993. *Culture and Negotiation.* Newbury Park, CA: Sage Publications.

Fisher, Ronald J. 1983. "Third Party Consultation as a Method of Intergroup Conflict Resolution." *Journal of Conflict Resolution.*

Goldberg, Stephen B., Nancy Rogers, and Frank E. A. Sander. 1992. *Dispute Resolution.* Boston, MA: Little Brown and Company, Inc.

Goldberg, Stephen B., Nancy Rogers, and Frank E. A. Sander. 1995. *Dispute Resolution: 1995 Supplement.* Boston, MA: Little Brown and Company, Inc.

Hewystone M., and R. Brown, eds. 1988. *Contact and Conflict in Intergroup Encounters.* New York, NY: Basil Blackwell.

Himes, Joseph S. 1980. *Conflict and Conflict Management.* Athens, Georgia: Georgia University Press.

Hocker, Joyce L., and William W. Wilmot. 1985. *Interpersonal Conflict.* Dubuque, Iowa: William C. Brown.

Isaacs, W. "Taking Flight: Dialogue, Collective Thinking, and Organizational Learning." *Organizational Dynamics.* #22, Vol 2. 24–39.

Kelman, Herbert, and Stephen P. Cohen. 1986. 'Resolution of International Conflict: An Interactional Approach," in S. Worchel and W. G. Austin, eds. *Psychology of Intergroup Relations.* Second Edition. Chicago, IL: Nelson Hall, pp 323–42

Kolb, Deborah M., and Associates. 1994. *When Talk Works: Profiles of Mediators.* San Francisco, CA: Jossey-Bass.

Kolb, Deborah M., and Jean M. Bartunek. 1992. *Hidden Conflict in Organizations: Uncovering Behind-the-Scenes Disputes.* Newbury Park, CA: Sage Publications.

Kreisberg, Louis, Terrel A. Northrup, and Smart J. Thorson. 1989. *Intractable Conflicts and Their Transformation.* Syracuse, New York: Syracuse University Press.

Lam, J. A. 1989. *The Impact of Conflict Resolution Programs on Schools: A Review and Synthesis of the Evidence.* Amherst: NAME.

Lewin, K. *Resolving Social Conflicts.* 1948. New York, NY: Harper.

Marcus, Leonard J., Barry C. Dom, Phyllis B. Kritek, Velvet G. Miller, and Janice B. Wyatt. *Renegotiating Health Care: Resolving Conflict to Build Collaboration.* San Francisco, CA: Jossey-Bass.

Matthews, Robert, Arthur Rubinoff, and Janice Gross Stein. 1984. *International Conflict and Conflict Management.* Scarborough, Ontario: Prentice-Hall of Canada.

Mitchell, C. R. 1981. *The Structure of International Conflict.* London: Macmillan.

Mitchell, C. R. 1981. *Peacemaking and the Consultant's Role.* New York, NY: Nichols.

National Institute for Dispute Resolution. 1991. *Forum: Special Issue on Dispute Resolution in Education.* Washington, DC: National Institute for Dispute Resolution.

Ross, Marc Howard. 1986. "A Cross-Cultural Theory of Political Conflict and Violence." *Political Psychology* 7:427–69.

Ross, Marc Howard. 1993. *The Culture of Conflict: Interpretations and Interests in Comparative Perspective.* New Haven, CT: Yale University.

Ross, Marc Howard. 1985. "Internal and External Violence: Cross-Cultural Evidence and a New Analysis." *Journal of Conflict Resolution* 29: 547–79.

Ross, Marc Howard. 1993. *The Management of Conflict: Interpretations and Interests in Comparative Perspective.* New Haven, CT: Yale University.

Rothman, Jay. 1997. *Resolving Identity Base Conflict: In Nations, Organizations and Communities.* San Francisco, CA: Jossey-Bass.

Sandole, Dennis J. D., and Ingrid Sandole-Staroste, eds. 1987. *Conflict Management and Problem Solving: Interpersonal to International Applications.* New York, NY: New York University Press.

Schon, Donald A. 1983. *The Reflective Practitioner: How Professionals Think in Action.* New York, NY: Basic Books.

Sherif, Muzafer, et al. 1988. *The Robbers Cave Experiment: Intergroup Conflict and Cooperation.* Middletown, CT: Wesleyan University Press.

Sherif Muzafer. 1966. *In Common Predicament: Social Psychology of Intergroup Conflict and Cooperation.* Boston, MA: Houghton Mifflin Co.

Smith, Kenwyn K., and David N. Berg. 1987. *Paradoxes of Group Life: Understanding Conflict, Paralysis, and Movement in Group Dynamics.* San Francisco, CA: Jossey-Bass.

Susskind, Lawrence. 1994. *Environmental Diplomacy.* New York, NY: Oxford University Press.

Susskind, Lawrence, and Jeffrey Cruishank. 1987. *Breaking the Impasse: Consensual Approaches to Resolving Public Disputes.* New York, NY: Basic Books.

Susskind, Lawrence, and Patrick Field. 1996. *Dealing with an Angry Public: A Mutual Gains Approach.* New York, NY: Free Press.

Umbreit, Mark. 1986. *Victim Offender Mediation in Urban/Multicultural Settings.* Valparaiso, Indiana: PACT Institute of Justice.

Walton, Richard E. 1969. *Interpersonal Peacemaking: Confrontations and Third Party Consultation.* Reading, MA: Addison-Wesley.

Walton, Richard E., and R. McKersie. 1965. *A Behavioral Theory of Labor Negotiations; An Analysis of a Social System.* New York, NY: McGraw Hill.

Walton, Richard E., and McKersie, R, 1966. "Behavioral Dilemmas in Mixed-Motive Decision Making." *Behavioral Science,* 11, 370–84.

Wichert, Susanne. 1989. *Keeping the Peace—Practicing Cooperation and Conflict Resolution with Preschoolers.* Philadelphia, PA: New Society Publishers.

The Role of Governments and NGOs in Coexistence

Agnew, John A. 1987. *Place and Politics: The Geographical Mediation of State and Society.* Boston and London: Allen & Unwin.

Ayres, Robert U. 1979. *Uncertain Futures: Challenges for Decision-Makers.* New York, NY: John Wiley.

Banks, Michael, ed. 1984. *Conflict in World Society: A New Perspective on International Relations.* New York, NY: St Martin's Press.

Bercovitch, Jacob, and Jeffrey Rubin. 1992. *Mediation in International Relations. Multiple Approaches to Conflict Management.* New York, NY: St. Martin's Press.

Burton, John W. 1969. *Conflict and Communication: The Use of Controlled Communication in International Relations.* New York, NY: Free Press.

Burton, J. 1979. *Deviance, Terrorism and War.* Suffolk: Martin Robertson.

Burton, John W. 1989. *Global Politics: The Domestic Sources of International Crisis.* Brighton, Sussex, England: Whetasheaf.

Carter, Jimmy. 1982. *Keeping Faith: Memoirs of a President.* New York, NY: Bantan.

Cohen, Raymond. 1991. *Negotiation across Cultures: Communication and Obstacles in International Diplomacy.* Washington, DC: United States Institute of Peace.

Cohen, S., and Arnone H. 1988. "Conflict Resolution as the Alternative to Terrorism." *Journal of Social Issues* 44 (2) pp. 175–90.

Chayes, Abram, and Antonia Handler Chayes. 1995. *The New Sovereignty: Compliance with International Regulatory Agreements.* Cambridge, MA: Harvard University Press.

Davidow, Jeffrey. 1990. *A Peace in Southern Africa: The Lancaster House Conference on Rhodesia, 1979.* Cambridge, MA: PON Books.

Enloe, Cynthia H. 1980. *Ethnic Soldiers: State Security in Divided Societies.* Athens, GA: University of Georgia Press.

Etzioni, A. 1968. "Social Psychological Aspects of International Relations." In Lindzey, G. and Aronson, E., eds. *Handbook Psychology.* Vol. 5. Reading, Mass.: Addison-Wesely.

Erdman, Sol, and Lawrence Susskind. 1995. *Reinventing Congress for the 21st Century: Beyond Local Representation and the Politics of Exclusion.* New York, NY: Fronteir Press.

Forsythe, David P. 1972. *United Nations Peacemaking.* Baltimore, MD: Johns Hopkins University Press.

Gosling, Jonathan. 1987. "The Anthropological Approach to Cross-Cultural Conflict Resolution: Another Perspective." *Conflict Resolution Notes.* 4(4): 38–39.

Haass, Richard N. 1990. *Conflicts Unending: The United States and Regional Conflict.* New Haven, CT: Yale University Press.

Habeeb, William M. 1988. *Power and Tactics in International Negotiation: How Weak Nations Bargain with Strong Nations.* Baltimore, MD: Johns Hopkins University Press.

Kahn, Robert L., and Mayer N. Zald, eds. 1990. *Organizations and Nation-States: New Perspectives on Conflict and Cooperation.* San Francisco: Jossey-Bass.

Kissinger, Henry. 1979. *The White House Years.* Boston, MA: Little Brown & Co.

Kissinger, Henry. 1982. *Years of Upheaval.* Boston, MA: Little Brown & Co.

Kriesberg, Louis, and S. Thorson. 1991. *Timing the Deescalation of International Conflicts.* Syracuse, N.Y.: Syracuse University Press.

Kremenyuk, Victor A., ed. 1991. *International Negotiation—Analysis, Approach, Issues.* San Francisco, CA: Jossey-Bass.

MacDonald, John Jr., and Diane Bendahmane, eds. 1987. *Conflict Resolution: Track-Two Diplomacy.* Washington, DC: U.S. Department of State, Foreign Service Institute, U.S. Government Printing Office.

MacDonald, John Jr., and Diane Bendahmane, eds. 1986. *Perspectives on Negotiation: Four Case Studies and Interpretations.* Washington, DC: U.S. Department of State, Foreign Service Institute.

Morgenthau, Hans J. 1949. *Politics among Nations: The Struggle for Power and Peace.* New York, NY: Knopf.

Osgood, C. 1962. *An Alternative to War or Surrender.* Urbana, Ill.: University of Illinois Press.

Park, Han S. 1984. *Human Needs and Political Development: A Dissent to Utopian Studies.* Cambridge, MA: Schenkman.

Rubenstein, Richard. 1987. *Alchemists of Revolution: Terrorism in the Modern World.* New York, NY: Basic Books.

Ruppesinghe, K. 1994. *Protracted Conflict.* London: McMillan.

Saunders, Harold. 1991. *Beyond Us and Them: Building Mature International Relationships.*

Shurke, Astri, and Leila G. Noble, eds. 1977. *Ethic Conflict in International Relations.* New York, NY: Praeger.

Smith, A. 1991. *National Identity.* Reno: University of Nevada Press.

Susskind, Lawrence, Esther Siskind, and William Breslin, eds. 1991. *Nine Case Studies in International Environmental Negotiation.* Cambridge, MA: PON Books.

Susskind, Lawrence, Eric J. Dolan, and J. William Breslin. 1992. *International Environmental Treaty Making.* Cambridge, MA: PON Books.

Steinbruner, J. D., ed. *Restructuring, American Foreign Policy.* Washington, DC: Brookings Institution.

Volkan, Vamik D., Demetriios A. Julius, and Joseph V. Montville, eds. 1990. *The Psychodynamics of International Relationships: Volume 1: Concepts and Theories.* Lexington, MA: Lexington Books.

Volkan, Vamik D., Demetriios A. Julius, and Joseph V. Montville, eds. 1991. *Psychodynamics of International Relationships: Volume II: Unofficial Diplomacy at Work.* Lexington, MA: Lexington Books.

Wein, Barbara J., ed. 1984. *Peace and World Order Studies.* New York, NY: World Policy Institute.

Young, Oran. 1967. *The Intermediaries: Third Parties in International Crises.* Princeton, NJ: Princeton University Press.

Tools for Coexistence Work

Argyris, Chris, Robert Puntnam, and Diana M. Smith. 1985. *Action Science: Concepts, Methods, and Skills for Research and Intervention.* San Francisco, CA: Jossey-Bass.

Argyris, C., and Schon, D. 1989. *Organizational Learning: A Theory of Action Perspective.* Reading, Mass.: Addison-Wesley.

Balakrishnan, P. V., Patton, C., and Lewis, P. "Toward a Theory of Agenda Setting in Negotiations." *Journal of Consumer Affairs,* Vol. 19, March 1993:637–54.

Bercovitch, Jacob. 1984. *Social Conflicts and Third Parties.* Boulder, Colorado: Westview Press.

Borisoff, D. and D. A. Victor. 1989. *Conflict Management; A Communication Skills Approach.* Engelwood Cliffs, NJ: Prentice-Hall.

Burton, John W. 1987. *Resolving Deep Rooted Conflict: A Hand-Book.* Lanham, MD: University Press of America.

Carbonneau, T. 1989. *Alternative Dispute Resolution: Melting the Lances and Dismounting the Steeds.* Chicago, IL: University of Chicago.

Casse, Pierre, and Surinder Deol. 1985. *Managing Intercultural Negotiations: Guidelines for Trainers and Negotiators.* Washington, DC: SIETAR International.

Chupp, Mark. 1991. "When Mediation Is Not Enough." *Conciliation Quarterly Newsletter* 10(3):2–12.

Coser, Lewis A. 1956. *The Functions of Social Conflict.* New York, NY: Free Press.

Costantino, Cathy A., and Christina Sickles Merchant. 1996. *Designing Conflict Management Systems.* San Francisco, CA: Jossey Bass.

Dodd, Carley H., and Frank F. Montalvo, eds. 1987. *Intercultural Skills for Multicultural Societies.* Washington, DC: SIETAR International.

The Encyclopedia of Peace. 1986. Oxford: Pergamon.

Fisher, Roger, and Scott Brown. 1989. *Getting Together: Building a Relationship That Gets to Yes.* New York, NY: Penguin Books.

Fisher, Roger, and Danny Ertel. 1995. *Getting Ready to Negotiate: The Getting to Yes Workbook.* New York, NY: Penguin Books.

Fisher, Roger, Elizabeth Kopelman, and Andrea Kupfer Schneider. 1996. *Beyond Machiavelli: Tools for Coping with Conflict.* New York, NY: Penguin Press.

Fisher, Roger, William Ury, and Bruce Patton. 1991. *Getting to Yes: Negotiating Agreement without Giving In* (2nd Edition). New York, NY: Penguin Books.

Folberg, Jay, and Alison Taylor. 1984. *Mediation: A Comprehensive Guide to Resolving Conflicts without Litigation.* San Francisco, CA: Jossey-Bass.

Folger, J. P., M. S. and R. K. Stutman. 1993. *Working through Conflict: Strategies for Relationships, Groups and Organizations.* New York, NY: HarperCollins.

Galtung, Johan. 1975–80. *Essays in Peace Research.* Copenhagen: Christian Ejlers.

Gurr, Ted Robert, ed. 1980. *Handbook of Political Conflict.* New York, NY: Free Press.

Hall, Lavina, ed. 1993. *Negotiation; Strategies for Mutual Gain.* Newbury Park, CA: Sage Publications.

Hoopes, Davis S., and Paul Ventura, eds. 1979. *Intercultural Sourcebook: Cross-Cultural Training Methodologies.* Chicago, IL: Intercultural Press.

Kottler, J. 1994. *Beyond Blame: A New Way of Resolving Conflicts in Relationships.* San Francisco, CA: Jossey-Bass.

Landis, Dan, and Richard W. Brislin, eds. 1983. *Issues in Theory and Design.* Vol. 1 of *Handbook of Intercultural Training.* New York, NY: Pergamon Press.

Lax, David A., and James Sebenius. 1986. *The Manager as Negotiator: Bargaining for Cooperation and Competitive Gain.* New York, NY: The Free Press.

Lederach, John Paul. 1990. "Training on Culture: Four Approaches." *Conciliation Quarterly.* 9(1): 6, 11–13.

LeResche, Diane Neumann, and Jennifer Spinill. 1990. "Training on Culture: A Survey of the Field." *Conciliation Quarterly.* 9(1): 2–25.

Madigan, Denise, Gerard McMahon, Lawrence Susskind, and Stephanie Rolley. 1990. *New Approaches to Resolving Public Disputes.* Washington, DC: National Institute for Dispute Resolution.

Mitchell, Christopher, and M. Banks. 1996. *Handbook of Conflict Resolution: The Analytical Problem Solving Approach.* London: Pinter.

Moore, Christopher W. 1987. *The Mediation Process: Practical Strategies for Resolving Conflict.* San Francisco, CA: Jossey-Bass.

Nader, Laura, and Harry F. Todd, eds. 1978. *The Disputing Process—Law in Ten Societies.* New York, NY: Columbia University Press.

Pneuman, Roy W., and Margaret E. Bruehl. 1982. *Managing Conflict: A Complete Process-Centered Handbook.* Engelwood Cliffs, N J: Prentice-Hall.

Princen, Thomas. 1992. *Intermediaries in International Conflict.* Princeton, NJ: Princeton University Press.

Raiffa, Howard. 1982. *The Art and Science of Negotiation.* Cambridge, MA: Harvard University Press.

Sherwood, J. and Glidewell, J. 1993. "A Planned Renegotiation: A Norm Setting OD Intervention." *Annual Handbook for Group Facilitators.* Iowa City: University Associates Press.

Stein, Janice G., ed. 1989. *Getting to the Table: The Process of International Prenegotiation.* Baltimore, MD: Johns Hopkins University Press.

Susskind, Lawrence, and Patrick Field. *Dealing with an Angry Public: A Mutual Gains Approach to Resolving Disputes.* New York, NY: Free Press.

Ury, William L., Jeanne Brett, and Stephen Goldberg. 1993. *Getting Disputes Resolved: Designing Systems to Cut the Costs of Conflicts.* Cambridge, MA: PON Books.

Ury, William L. 1991. *Getting Past No: Negotiating Your Way From Confrontation to Cooperation.* New York, NY: Bantam Books.

Watzlawicki, P., J. Wakland and R. Fisch. 1974. *Change: Principles of Problem Formulation and Problem Resolution.* New York, NY: Norton.

Wehr, Paul. 1979. *Conflict Regulation.* Boulder, CO: Westview Press.

Zartman, I. William, and Maureen Bennan. 1982. *The Practical Negotiator*. New Haven, CT: Yale University Press.

Coexistence in Israel

Alfar, H. 1988. *Beit Hagefen Encounters Program*. Beit Hagefen: University of Haifa.

Bar, H., and G. Askalah. 1989. *Arab–Jewish Youth Meetings: Evaluating Views Before and After*. Givat Haviva: Center for Arab Studies.

Bar-Tal, Daniel. "Israeli-Palestinian Conflict: A Cognitive Analysis." *International Journal of Intercultural Relations* 14: 7–29.

Benvenisti, Meron. "The Peace Process and Intercommunal Strife." *Journal of Palestine Studies* 17: 3–11.

Berger, Earl. 1965. *The Covenant and the Sword: Arab–Israeli Relations 1948–56*. London: Routledge & Kegan Paul.

Breslow, Mark. 1987. *Dialogue toward Israeli-Palestinian Peace*. Syracuse, NY: American Coalition for Middle East Dialogue.

Cohen, Raymond. 1990. *Culture and Conflict in Egyptian-Israeli Relations*. Bloomington: University of Indiana Press.

Esman, Milton J., and Itamar Rabinovitch. 1988. *Ethnicity, Pluralism, and the State in the Middle East*. Ithaca, NY: Cornell University Press.

Fuchs, Ina, Nancy Eisenberg, Rachel Hertz-Lazarowitz, and Ruth Sharanby. 1986. "Kibbutz, Israeli City, and American Children's Moral Reasoning about Prosocial Moral Conflicts." *Merrill Palmer Quarterly*. 32(1): 37–50.

Hareven, A. ed. 1981. *Every Sixth Israeli*. Jerusalem: The Van Leer Institute.

Hazan, Reuven. 1988 "Peaceful Conflict Resolution in the Middle East: The Taba Negotiations." *Journal of the Middle East Studies Society* 2 (1), 39–65.

Heller, Mark A. 1983. *A Palestinian State: The Implications for Israel*. Cambridge, MA: Harvard University Press.

Heller, Mark A., and Sair Nusseibeh. 1991. *No Trumpets, No Drums: A Two-State Settlement of the Israeli-Palestinian Conflict*. New York, NY: Hill and Wang.

Heradstveit, Daniel. 1981. *The Arab–Israeli Conflict: Psychological Obstacles to Peace*. Oslo: Universitestforlaget.

Hertz-Lazarowitz, R, J. Hofman, B. Beit-Hallahmi and N. Rouhana, 1978. *Identity and the Educational Environment*.

Herzl, Theodor. 1896. *The Jewish State: An Attempt at a Modern Solution of the Jewish Question*. New York, NY: American Zionist Emergency Council, 1946.

Hofman, J., ed. 1988. *Arab–Jewish Relations in Israel*. Bristol, Indiana: Wyndham Hall Press.

Hofman, J. 1976. *Identity and Intergroup Perceptions in Israel*. Haifa: University of Haifa.

Kellerman, Barbara, and Jeffrey Z. Rubin. 1988. *Leadership and Negotiation in the Middle East*. New York, NY: Praeger.

Kelman, Herbert. 1992. "Contributions of an Unofficial Conflict Resolution Effort to the Israeli-Palestinian Breakthrough." *Negotiation Journal* 11: 19–27.

Kelman, Herbert. 1978. "Israelis and Palestinians: Psychological Prerequisites for Mutual Acceptance." *International Security*, 3:162–86.

Kelman, Herbert. 1987. "The Political Psychology of the Israeli-Palestinian Conflict: How Can We Overcome the Barriers to a Negotiated Solution?" *Political Psychology* 8:347–63.

Khouri, Fres J. 1985. *The Arab–Israeli Dilemma* (3rd Edition). Syracuse, NY: Syracuse University Press.

Kollek, Teddy. 1988–89. "Sharing United Jerusalem." *Foreign Affairs* 67 (2): 156–68.

Kreisberg, Louis. 1992. *International Conflict Resolution: The U.S.-USSR and Middle East Cases*. New Haven, CT: Yale University.

Laquer, Walter, and Barry M. Rubin, eds. 1984. *The Arab–Israeli Reader: A Documentary History of the Middle East Conflict*. (4th edition). New York, NY: Penguin.

Lesch, Ann Mosley. 1980. *Political Perceptions of the Palestinians on the West Bank and Gaza Strip*. Washington, DC: The Middle East Institute.

Morris, Benny. 1988. *The Birth of the Palestinian Refugee Problem, 1947–1949*. New York, NY: Cambridge University Press.

Newman, D. 1985. *The Impact of Gush Emonim: Politics and Settlement in the West Bank.* London: Croom Helm.

Oz, Amos. 1983. *In the Land of Israel.* New York, NY: Harcourt Brace Jovanovich.

Peled, Tsionya, and David Bar-Gal. 1983. *Intervention Activities in Arab–Jewish Relations: Conceptualization, Classification and Evaluation.* Report. Jerusalem: Israel Institute of Applied Social Research.

Peters, Joan. 1984. *From Time Immemorial: The Origins of the Arab–Jewish Conflict over Palestine.* New York, NY: Harper & Row.

Quandt, William B. 1986. *Camp David: Peacemaking and Politics.* Washington, DC: Brookings.

Quandt, William B., Fuad Jabber, and Ann Mosley Lesch, eds. 1973. *The Politics of Palestinian Nationalism.* Berkley, CA: University of California Press.

Rosenbloom, David H. 1987. "Israel's Administrative Culture, Israeli Arabs, and Arab Subjects." *Syracuse Journal of International Law and Commerce* 13:435–73.

Rothman, Jay. 1992. *From Confrontation to Cooperation: Resolving Ethnic and Regional Conflict in the Middle East and Beyond.* California: Sage Publications.

Rothman, Jay. 1991. "Negotiation as Consolidation: Prenegotiations in the Israeli-Palestinian Conflict." *Jerusalem Journal of International Relations* 13: 22–44.

Rothman, Jay, with R. Land, and R. Twite. 1994. *The Jerusalem Peace Initiative: Project on Managing Political Disputes.* Jerusalem: The Leonard Davis Institute of International Relations.

Rothman, Jay, Sharon Bray, and Mark Neudstadt. 1987. *A Guide to Arab–Jewish Peacemaking Organizations in Israel* (3rd edition). New York, NY: New Israel Fund.

Rouhana, N., and Herbert C. Kelman. 1994. "Promoting Joint Thinking in International Conflicts: An Israeli-Palestinian Continuing Workshop." *Journal of Social Issues* 50 (1): 157–78.

Safran, Nadav. 1978. *Israel: The Embattled Ally.* Cambridge, MA: Harvard University Press.

Said, Edward. 1980. *The Question of Palestine.* New York, NY: Vintage.

Sanders, Ronald. 1964. *The View from Masada.* New York, NY: Harper & Row.

Saunders, Harold. 1991. *The Other Walls: The Politics of the Arab–Israeli Peace Process in a Global Perspective.* Washington, DC: American Enterprise Institute.

Sayigh, Rosemary. 1979. *Palestinians: From Peasants to Revolutionaries.* London, England: Zed.

Shipler, David. 1986. *Arab and Jew: Wounded Spirits in the Promised Land.* New York, NY: New York Times Books.

Shlaim, Avi. 1988. *Collusion across the Jordan.* New York, NY: Columbia University Press.

Smooha, S. 1989. *Palestinian Citizens of Israel and Jews in Israel* (Vol. 1). London: Westview Press.

Smooha, S., and O. Cibulski. 1978. *Social Research on Arabs in Israel 1948–76: Trends and an Annotated Bibliography.* Ramat Gan, Israel: Turtledove Publishers.

Stein, Janice G. 1985. "Calculation, Miscalculation and Conventional Deterrence I: The View from Cairo." In Robert Jervis, Richard Ned Lebow, and Janice G. Stein, eds, *Psychology and Deterrence,* pp. 34–59. Baltimore, MD: Johns Hopkins University Press.

Stein, Janice G. 1985. "Calculation, Miscalculation and Conventional Deterrence II: The View from Jerusalem," in Robert Jervis, Richard Ned Lebow, and Janice G. Stein, eds, *Psychology and Deterrence,* pp. 60–88. Baltimore, MD: Johns Hopkins University Press.

Stone, Russel A. 1982. *Social Change in Israel: Attitudes and Events, 1967–79.* New York, NY: Praeger Publishers.

Organizations Furthering Coexistence Work

As complex international conflicts continue to escalate around the world, both governmental and non-governmental organizations are increasingly looking to conflict resolution and interethnic initiatives as a way to foster positive coexistence between diverse ethnic groups. In recent years, there are numerous examples of this trend: The Oslo agreement in 1992 between Palestinian leader Yasar Arafat and the former Israeli Prime Minister was preceded by months of behind-the-scenes mediation facilitated by academics, practitioners, and diplomats. With the collapse of communism in Eastern Europe, academics and practitioners have developed and implemented coexistence workshops to address ethnic tensions between diverse identity groups in newly independent regions and to work toward future community development. With the decline of authoritarian regimes in Central America, many governmental and community-based organizations have called on the United States for conflict resolution and leadership training as they build future democracies based on interethnic coexistence.

As conflict resolution is increasingly being used as a means of working towards coexistence in divided nations and communities, a core of multidisciplinary conflict resolution professionals has emerged. Many organizations and institutes have developed programs that focus on coexistence initiatives, while others organizations, already dedicated solely to building positive coexistence, have extended their efforts to increasing numbers of communities, regions, and nations around the world.

The following list of organizations sponsoring coexistence work is broken down into two categories: organizations with diverse focus; and organizations with a focus on Israel. The list is certainly not exhaustive, since there are so many organizations undertaking this challenging work, but the list attempts to represent the spectrum of activities, visions, and goals of the coexistence/conflict resolution profession.

Organizations with Diverse Focus

African Center for the Constructive Resolution of Disputes (ACCORD)
University of Durban Westville
Private Bag X54001
Durban 4000
South Africa
Tel: 031-820-2812, 031-820-2894
Fax: 031-820-2815

ACCORD operates several training centers (with the national headquarters based at the University of Durban Westville) that offer skills building programs in conflict resolution, negotiation, mediation, and facilitation. They focus on identifying and training key individuals in organizations working toward peaceful conflict resolution.

Anti-Defamation League of B'nai B'rith
823 United Nations Plaza
New York, NY 10017
(212) 490-2525

The Anti-Defamation League combats anti-Semitism, all forms of bigotry and discrimination, and promotes harmonic relations among diverse religious and ethnic groups.

Carnegie Commission on Preventing Deadly Conflict
1779 Massachusetts Avenue, NW
Suite 715
Washington, DC 20036-2103
(202) 332-7900

The Carnegie Commission on Preventing Deadly Conflict addresses the looming dangers of intergroup violence, and advances new ideas for the prevention and resolution of deadly conflict.

The Carter Center
One Copenhill
Atlanta, GA 30307
Tel: (404) 420-5185
Fax: (404) 420-5196

Housed at Emory University, the Carter Center is led by former president Jimmy Carter, and aims to diminish imperative, intractable conflicts, using diverse resources and approaches. The Conflict Resolution Program of the Carter Center intervenes in international conflicts around the world, offering workshops, training, facilitation, and consultation.

CDR Associates
100 Arapahoe Avenue, Suite 12
Boulder, CO 80302
Tel: 1-800-MEDIATE or (303) 442-7367
Fax: (303) 442-7442

Founded in 1978 "to provide conflict management assistance to business, governmental agencies, and organizations in the public sector," CDR has trained and consulted in over twenty countries. Through mediation, facilitation, training, and consulting, CDR aims to encourage collaborative problem solving and to foster negotiations for mutually beneficial solutions in diverse countries and communities.

Center for Applied Studies in International Negotiations (CASIN)
11 la Avenue de la Paix
CH-1202 Geneva
Switzerland
Tel: 44-22-734-8950
Fax: 44-22-733-6440

Founded in 1979, CASIN is a trainer development program that operates under the supervision of the Swiss Federal Department of Domestic Affairs. CASIN works on domestic and international levels to offer peaceful alternatives to conflict through training and educational programs in conflict resolution.

Center for Peace and Reconciliation
Arias Foundation for Human Progress
Apartado 9-6410-1000
San Jose, Costa Rica
Tel: 506-255-2955
Fax: 506-255-2244

The Center for Peace and Reconciliation focuses their efforts in Guatemala by facilitating discussions between political, military, and social factions of the region. The discussions address methods of democratization in Guatemala and strategies to planning a stable future.

Center for Strategic and International Studies (CSIS)
1800 K Street, NW
Washington, DC 20006
Tel: (202) 887-0200
Fax: (202) 775-3199

Through its "Program on Preventive Diplomacy," CSIS analyzes ethnic and sectarian violence and develops coexistence strategies to reduce long-term violence and conflict. CSIS facilitates dialogue and collaborative solving workshops in diverse countries and communities, using psychological techniques and activities to encourage intergroup processes. Recent initiatives include the Program on Democratic Pluralism in Slovakia.

The Coexistence Project at the School of Public Affairs,
Baruch College, The City University of New York
17 Lexington Avenue
Box F1228
New York, NY 10010
(212) 802-5900

The Coexistence Project is a new academic, research, and service project focusing on intergroup coexistence as it relates to the formulation and implementation of public policy.

The Community Relations Service
National Office/Headquarters:
U.S. Department of Justice
55500 Friendship Blvd., Suite 330
Chevy Chase, MD 20815
(301) 492-5939

The Community Relations Service is an operation of the U.S. Department of Justice. In addition to their national headquarters, they have regional offices throughout the country that provide assistance to communities in resolving disputes, disagreements, or difficulties relating to race, color, or national origin. The regional offices also provide impartial conciliators and mediators to assess and reduce racial tension.

Conflict Resolution Network
P.O. Box 1016
Chatswood, NSW 2057
Australia
Tel: 02-419-8500
Fax: 02-413-1148

The Conflict Resolution Network was founded by the United Nations Association in Australia as an alliance of independent conflict-resolution programs throughout Australia. The main objective of the Network is to research and develop conflict resolution throughout the region and internationally. The Network's activities include training and public workshops, grants to community-based collaborative projects, educational resources, and program development.

Conflict Management Group (CMG)
20 University Road
Cambridge, MA 02138
Tel: (617) 354-5444
Fax: (617) 354-8467

CMG provides productive methods of negotiation and conflict resolution for individuals, organizations, and governments. CMG's initiatives aim to prevent and reduce ethnic, community, govemmental, and religious conflict CMG publishes the work of conflict resolution theorists and practitioners, and provides training and consulting services.

George Mason University, Institute for Conflict Analysis and Resolution (ICAR)
Fairfax, VA 22030-4444
Tel: (703) 993-1300
Fax: (703) 993-1302

ICAR houses scholars, practitioners, and graduate students, all working to advance the understanding of conflict analysis and resolution and of persistent conflicts among individuals, groups, communities, identity groups, and nations. ICAR offers degree programs in conflict analysis and resolution, and its activities include teaching, research, clinical work, and outreach.

Holywell Trust
10-12 Bishop Street
Derry BT48 6PW
IRELAND
Tel: (504) 261941/363729

The main concerns of the Holywell Trust have been in encouraging healthy relationships, both personal and cross-community; in campaigning, commenting on, and researching environmental issues; and in community arts and experiential group work.

Institute for Multi-Track Diplomacy
1819 H Street, NW, Suite 1200
Washington, DC 20006
Tel: (202) 466-4605
Fax: (202) 466-4607
E-mail: imtd@igc.apc.org

The Institute for Multi-Track Diplomacy promotes a systems approach to peace building and facilitates the transformation of deep-rooted social conflict through training, facilitation, publication, action research, and engagement.

Inter-Community Development Services (ICDS)
33 Norblen Road
Belfast, Northern Ireland
BT118EA
United Kingdom
Tel: 44-0232-62886

ICDS works with conflicts in Northern Ireland and the former Soviet Union through consulting and training services. The aim of ICDS is to provide comprehensive conflict-resolution education, by identifying regional problems and related needs, facilitating discussion and decision making through local and governmental agencies, and providing follow-up services with institutions they assist.

International Alert
1 Glyn Street
London SE11 5HT
United Kingdom
Tel: 44-171-793-8383
Fax: 44-171-793-7975

International Alert is a network of peace organizations working with conflict around the world. Local activists invite International Alert to train people in conflict resolution in an effort to provide people with the skills to reduce current conflict and prevent the escalation of future conflicts. Since 1993, International Alert has focused on Southern Russia, the Northern Caucus, and Georgia by analyzing the conflicts between the many ethnic groups in these regions and providing training to address interethnic tensions.

International Association for Conflict Management
252 Hubert Humphrey Center
301 19th Avenue South
Minneapolis, MN 55455
Tel: (612) 625-3046

The International Association for Conflict Management provides an interdisciplinary forum for scholars and practitioners interested in the study of social conflict and dispute resolution at all levels of society. Based at the University of Minnesota, it holds international conferences in a variety of venues.

National Association for Community Mediation
1726 M Street, NW, Suite 500
Washington, DC 20036-45092
Tel: (202) 467-6226

The National Association for Community Mediation is a membership organization for community mediation programs throughout the United States. The Association organizes conferences and training in the field of community mediation, publishes a newsletter, and provides other resources to its members.

National Coalition Building Institute
1835 K Street NW, Suite 715
Washington, DC 20006
(202) 785-9400

The National Coalition Building Institute works to eliminate prejudice and the intergroup conflicts in communities throughout the world. It begins with the training of community leaders who acquire the skills to deal effectively with intergroup conflicts.

National Conference on Peacemaking and Conflict Resolution (NCPCR)
George Mason University
400 University Drive
Fairfax, VA 22030-4444
Tel: (703) 934-5140

NCPCR organizes the largest annual national conference in dispute resolution and disseminates information about the field and other conferences.

National Institute for Dispute Resolution ("NIDR")
1726 M Street, NW, Suite 500
Washington, DC 20036-4502
Tel: (202) 466-4764
Fax: (212) 466-4769
E-mail: nidr@igc.apc.org

NIDR is a national dispute resolution think tank that organizes a wide range of nationwide conferences, publishes a newsletter and books on a variety of topics in the field. NIDR offers extensive training, written materials, and other resources covering the wide spectrum of dispute-resolution activities around the world.

National Peace Foundation (NPF)
1835 K Street NW, Suite 620
Washington, DC 20006
Tel: (202) 223-1770
Fax: (202) 223-1718

NPF is a private, nonpartisan membership organization that aims to promote peace building and conflict resolution at community, regional, national, and international levels. The Foundation facilitates dialogues, seminars, conflict-resolution training, and mediation programs in the United States and abroad.

Northern Ireland Community Relations Council
6 Murray Street
Belfast BT1 6DN
Northern Ireland
Tel: 011-44-1232-439953

The Northern Ireland Community Relations Council elicits and channels funding from larger institutional-type funding entities to a myriad of local grass-roots organizations that assist community projects.

Partners for Democratic Change
823 Uluo Street
San Francisco, CA 94127
Tel: (415) 665-0652
Fax: (415) 665-2732

Partners for Democratic Change was founded in 1990 to train local and national leaders from Poland and Russia in democratic principles. By 1993, the program also worked in Bulgaria, the Czech and Slovak Republics, Hungary, and Lithuania. The main focus of activities is to build a culture of conflict resolution in emerging democracies by providing training in conflict management skills, communication and negotiation strategies, and by developing curriculum for universities.

Project on Ethnic Relations (PER)
One Palmer Square, Suite 435
Princeton, NJ 08542-3718
Tel: (609) 683-5666
E-mail: ethnic@pucc.princeton.edu

Founded in 1991, PER aims to "encourage the peaceful resolution of ethnic conflicts in the new democracies of central and eastern Europe and the Russian Federation." They organize forums for ethnic group representatives and government officials to facilitate communication within and between countries, provide technical resources and support for grant writing, implement research projects and community development efforts, and bolster the international visibility of local scholars and research initiatives.

Program on International Conflict Analysis and Resolution (PICAR)
Harvard University
1737 Cambridge Street, Room 603
Cambridge, MA 02138
Tel: (617) 496-0680
Fax: (617) 496-7370

PICAR is part of the Center for International Affairs of Harvard University. The program develops and implements interactive problem-solving processes with diverse international conflicts, and provides academic training to scholars and practitioners in international-conflict resolution. Recent initiatives include the Balkans Peace Project, which facilitated conflict resolution workshops in the Balkans, Western Europe, and the United States.

Resolving Conflict Creatively Program National Center
163 3rd Avenue, Box 103
New York, NY 10003
Tel: (212) 387-0225

An initiative of Educators for Social Responsibility, Resolving Conflict Creatively Program National Center is a comprehensive, school-based program in conflict resolution and intergroup relations that provides a model for preventing violence, and creating caring and peaceable communities in learning. It serves 350 schools throughout the United States.

Search for Common Ground
1601 Connecticut Avenue NW, Suite 200
Washington, DC 20009
Tel: (202) 265-4300
Fax: (202) 232-6718
E-mail: searchcg@igc.apc.org

Search for Common Ground aims to use conflict resolution and collaborative problem-solving techniques to facilitate dialogue between adversaries in diverse international conflicts. Search has worked in the U.S., the former Soviet Union, the Russian Federation, the Middle East, South Africa, Macedonia, and Burundi, offering education, training, and counsel to institutions.

Seeds of Peace
370 Lexington Avenue
Suite 1409
New York, NY 10017
Tel: (212) 573-8040

Seeds of Peace works to secure peace in the Middle East by bringing together and training Arab and Israeli teenagers in conflict resolution through various activities, including a summer-camp program in the United States, an Arab–Israeli newspaper, and others.

Society of Professionals in Dispute Resolution ("SPIDR")
International Office:
815 15th Street, NW, Suite 530
Washington, DC 20005
Tel: (202) 783-7277
Fax: (202) 783-7281

SPIDR is an umbrella, membership organization for dispute-resolution professionals. SPIDR provides publications, conferences, and newsletters about developments throughout the field of dispute resolution. In addition to the national office, there are several regional chapters throughout the country.

Southern Poverty Law Center
400 Washington Avenue
Montgomery, AL 36104
Tel: (334) 264-0286

The Southern Poverty Law Center is dedicated to securing civil rights, eradicating intolerance and its attendant violence, and promoting justice for all people. It uses a threefold program of education (Teaching Tolerance), investigation (Klanwatch), and litigation (legal team).

UNESCO
2 United Nations Plaza
9th Floor
New York, NY 10017
Tel: (212) 963-5995

UNESCO, United Nations Educational, Scientific, and Cultural Organization, was established in order to contribute to peace and security by promoting peace among the nations through education, science, and culture. UNESCO works to advance mutual knowledge and understanding among peoples; to maintain, increase, and diffuse knowledge; and to encourage popular education and the spread of culture.

United States Institute of Peace
1550 M Street NW, Suite 700
Washington, DC 20005-1708

The U.S. Institute of Peace is mandated by Congress to strengthen the nation's capabilities to promote the peaceful resolution of international conflicts. The Institute works to expand basic and applied knowledge about international conflict and peace-building, to disseminate this knowledge, and to promote greater understanding among the U.S. public of the complex nature of international conflict.

World Learning
Kipling Road
P.O. Box 676
Brattleboro, VT 05302-0676
Tel: (802) 257-7551

Dedicated to enabling the participants to acquire the knowledge, skills, and attitudes needed to contribute effectively to international understanding and global development, the World Learning Project uses three operating divisions: its accredited college; the School for International Training; its International Education and Exchange Programs; and its private voluntary-organization activities.

Organizations with a Focus on Israel*

The Abraham Fund
477 Madison Avenue
New York, NY 10022-5802
Tel: (212) 303-9421
Fax: (212) 935-1834

The Abraham Fund was established in 1989 to enhance coexistence, specifically through funding and promoting Jewish–Arab coexistence programs in Israel. The Abraham Fund is nonpartisan, and strives to find common ground among all Israeli citizens. The Fund supports, publicizes, and rewards organizations and institutions that further Jewish–Arab coexistence through enhancing mutual understanding, fighting stereotyping, increasing tolerance and acceptance, and promoting national civility. In 1996, The Abraham Fund awarded sixty-eight grants totaling $826,000. The funded projects cover a wide array of fields including, but not limited to, the arts, community cooperation, curriculum development, early childhood education, economic development, the environment, interfaith dialogue, leadership development, medical care, and women's issues.

Adam Institute for Democracy and Peace
PO Box 3353
Jerusalem Forest, 91'033
Jerusalem
Israel

The goal of the Adam Institute is to explore the relationship between democracy and peace. The Institute organizes seminars and programs to introduce students to conflict resolution and the principles of democracy, and works with educators and educational administrators on ways to integrate democratic principles within schools. In 1993, the Adam Institute held the First International Conference on Education for Democracy in a Multicultural Society.

American Coalition for Middle East Dialogue (ACMED)
(East Coast)
Revrend Gordon Weber, Financial Coordinator for the East Coast
36 Crecent Drive
Brockport, NY 14420
Tel: (315) 445-9798

(West Coast)
Charles Davis, National Coordinator for the West Coast
1118 36th Avenue
Seattle, WA 98122
Tel: (206) 325-1776

---

*There are many organizations, both in Israel and abroad, working to foster positive coexistence between Arabs and Jews. They range from grassroots, community organizations that work within the structures of a civic society, to theory institutes that aim to create new methods of interaction and communication between the two communities. For a more comprehensive listing of coexistence efforts in Israel refer to Weiner, Anita, Arnon Bar-On, and Eugene Weiner. 1992. *The Abraham Fund Directory of Institutions and Organizations Fostering Coexistence between Jews and Arabs in Israel*. New York: The Abraham Fund.

ACMED was founded in Syracuse, New York, in 1986, as a national network of local American Middle East dialogue groups. The dialogue groups consist of Arabs and Jews, and they meet regularly to discuss current events and explore ways to promote coexistence between the two communities. ACMDE also publishes a newsletter, *Dialogue,* and sponsors collaborative study tours to Israel Gaza, the West Bank, and Jordan.

Beit Hagefen—Arab–Jewish Cultural Community and Youth Center
2 Hagefen Street
PO Box 9421
Haifa
Israel
Tel: 04-525251, 04-525252
Fax: 04-529166

Beit Hagefen was established in 1963 and today it is Israel's largest Arab–Jewish Community Center. Beit Hagefen's mixed Arab and Jewish staff run cultural, social, and educational activities for Jewish and Arab youth. They bring together Jewish and Arab high school classes to promote mutual understanding and foster positive interaction between the two groups, sponsor a joint folk dance troupe and an Arab theater company, offer classes in Arabic and tutoring for Arab children in Hebrew, and organize joint social and social-action activities.

The Dialogue Project
1225 15th Street NW
Washington, DC 20005
Tel: (202) 797-8961
Fax: (202) 462-2892

The Dialogue Project was initiated by American Jewish and Arab women after the start of the "Intifada" (uprising) in the West Bank and Gaza. The Project aims to build relationships between American Arab and Jewish women, explore areas of agreement and disagreement, and implement action projects to support peace by bringing together women from Jewish and Palestinian communities.

Givat Haviva
MP Menashe, 37850
Israel
Tel: 011-972-6-630-9249

Givat Haviva promotes mutual understanding, respect, and cooperation at the grass-roots level among Arabs and Jews by implementing dialogue projects, peace studies, education workshops for democracy, teacher training seminars, and other programs. It is well known for its "Children Teaching Children" program.

The Harry S Truman Research Institute for the Advancement of Peace
The Hebrew University of Jerusalem
Mt. Scopus, Jerusalem 91905
Israel
Tel: 02-882399, 02-882301
Fax: 02-322545

The Harry S Truman Research Institute for the Advancement of Peace was established in 1966 at the Hebrew University in Jerusalem to be an international center for the study of Third World and non-Western countries with a special emphasis on the Middle East. Today, the Institute is dedicated to fostering scholarly exchange between Jews and Arabs, sustained Palestinian-Israeli dialogue between professors and researchers, and advancement of the underrepresented Israeli Arab academics at Israeli universities. The Institute conducts research, sponsors conferences, gives grants and fellowships and implements projects aimed at enhancing communication between Arabs and Jews.

The House of Hope
PO Box 272
Shefar'am 20200
Tel: 04-868558

The House of Hope is a community center located in the lower Galilee Arab town of Shefar'am. The center is Arab initiated, and offers social and cultural programs to people of all nationalities and faiths. The center aims to provide a safe, open meeting place for Arabs, Jews, and others. The House of Hope activities include young leadership programs, "Children for Peace" summer day camp, and one-day meetings for Arabs and Jews to get to know each other and explore solutions to the challenges to coexistence in the Middle East.

The Institute for Coexistence, David Yellin Teachers College
(Israel)
Hamaagal Street
PO Box 3578
Jerusalem, 91035
Tel: 02-533111
Fax: 02-521548

(New York)
Friends of David Yellen Teachers College
1501 Broadway, Suite 1613
New York, NY 19936
Tel: (212) 391-8686
(212) 768-2012

Housed at the David Yellen Teachers College in Jerusalem, the Institute for Coexistence in Israel was founded in 1984 to help teachers create an atmosphere of tolerance and mutual respect between Jews and Arabs in the classroom. They train teachers to teach coexistence theory through a wide variety of subjects, to express all cultural communities in the classroom and to promote society and culture of Jews and Arabs at the theoretical and experiential level.

(Israel)
Interns for Peace
35 Ge'ula Street
PO Box 5796
Tel Aviv 61047
Israel
Tel: 03-656525
Fax: 03-657995

(New York)
Rabbi Bruce Cohen
270 West 89th Street
New York, NY 10024

Interns for Peace is a nonpartisan program aimed at fostering respect and understanding between Jewish and Arab citizens of Israel. The program sponsors recruits and trains interns to live in Jewish and Arab host communities in Israel and initiate and run joint social and community activities for Jewish and Arab youth.

The Interreligious Coordinating Council in Israel (ICCI)
P.O. Box 7805
Jerusalem 91078
Israel
Tel: 011-972-2-6726-430

ICCI is a council of over sixty Israeli religious and cultural organizations dedicated to enhancing interfaith dialogue.

The Israeli Center for Non-Violent Communication
c/o Yanoov, 6 Tor Hazahav Street
Herzlia 4652
Tel: 052-552485

(Sweden)
Tova Widstarnd, European Coordinator
Center for Non-Violent Communication
Prolavagen 13
Lindingo, Sweden 18160
Tel: (46-8) 766-3455

The Israeli Center for Non-Violent Communication was founded in 1990 to introduce to Israel a new communication model for resolving conflict. The model is based on a program developed by an American educator, Marshall Rosenberg, in the 1960s, and has been successfully used in many countries. The Center in Israel aims to reduce violence between Jews and Arabs by providing introductory meetings to the communication model and conducting intensive training sessions to joint groups of Jews and Arabs.

Neve Shalom/Wahat al-Salam
(Israel)
D.N. Shimshon 99761
Tel: 02-91222, 02-91628
Fax: 02-91208

(New York)
American Friends of Neve Shalom/Wahat al-Salam
Sharon Burde, Executive Director
121 6th Avenue, #502
New York, NY 10013
Tel: (212) 226-9246

Neve Shalom/Wahat al-Salam is a cooperative village of Arab and Jewish citizens of Israel. The community is dedicated to living by principles of coexistence and equality between the Arabs and Jews. The village also sponsors educational and conflict-resolution activities with Arabs and Jews, as well as discussion groups about Jewish–Arab relations, disputes between the communities, and personal identities. They operate a bilingual school system, a school for peace, and offer several types of intervention workshop models with visiting Jewish–Arab groups.

Open House
(Jerusalem)
Mr. Yehezkel Landau, Development Director
PO Box 26187
Jerusalem, 91261
Tel: 02-822-1874

(Ramle)
Michail Fanous
1 Klausnet Street
Ramle 72432
Tel: 9221874

Open House is located in the home of Dalia Landau in Ramle, Israel. In 1967, Dalia opened her door to three Palestinian men, the Alkhayfis, who had owned the house before Ramle's Arab population was expelled in 1948. In 1985, when Dalia inherited the house. she decided to use the house to help the Arab population in Ramle and to enhance coexistence between Arabs and Jews. Today, Open House runs a prekindergarten for Arab children, a weekend tutorial program, computer classes for Arab teenagers, parenting workshops for Jewish and Arab couples, adult classes in English and Arabic, and a summer peace camp for Arab and Jewish Children.

Peace Now ("Shalom Achshav")
(Israel)
6 Lloyd George Street
Jerusalem 93108
Tel: 02-660648
Fax: 02-690134

(New York)
Americans for Peace Now
27 West 20th Street
New York, NY 10011
Tel: (212) 645-6262
Fax: (212) 929-3459

Established in 1978 during the Israeli–Egyptian Camp David negotiations, today Peace Now is Israel's largest peace movement. The movement lobbies with the Israeli government and public to take action to enhance peaceful coexistence between Arabs and Jews. Peace Now officially calls for an answer to "the Palestinian Question" that is based on mutual, national recognition. Peace Now in Israel sponsors demonstrations, organized forums for discussion and special projects to promote their political stance, while American friends of Peace Now is a membership organization that lobbies with the U.S. government to take action that promotes peace in the Middle East and fund-raises for efforts in Israel.

Praxis Institute
1 Herzlia Street
Haifa 30095
Tel: 04-6693758

Praxis Institute is a collaboration of social science professionals dedicated to exploring moral issues in Israeli Society and developing an approach to conflict resolution in social education and social action. Through a specially designed process, Praxis teaches individuals and groups to identify social problems, explore the underlying interests of these issues, select intervention strategies based on democratic principles and implement interventions to have a positive impact on community coexistence. Praxis trains educators and other professionals to apply their design and conducts research projects on Israeli-Arab coexistence.

Shatil ("Support Project for Voluntary Action")
(Israel)
PO Box 7725
Jerusalem, 91077
Tel: 02-634079
Fax: 02-664503

(Washington)
1101 15th Street NW, Suite 304
Washington, DC 20005

Shatil was established by The New Israel Fund in 1982 to provide support and networking for Arab and Jewish volunteer organizations. Through consultation, interorganizational and management training, public relations and grant-writing assistance, lobbying and volunteer recruitment, Shatil aims to increase the cooperation between volunteer organizations and to help organizations be more effective in meeting their goals of productive citizen action. Shatil publishes a newsletter, *Shtion,* about its activities and the activities of diverse volunteer organizations.

SHEMESH: Organization for Jewish–Arab Friendship Coexistence in the Galilee
D.B. Misgav 20164
Israel
Tel: 972-4-902437

SHEMESH's mission is to demonstrate that Arab and Jewish students can peacefully study together and that integration of the two communities is essential to coexistence. Shemesh organizes educational, cultural, and social activites for Jewish and Arab students from the Misgav region of the Galilee, and aims to replace negative stereotypes between the communities with positive interactions. SHEMESH also hosts joint summer camps for Jews and Arabs, and organizes programs for adults and high school students.

Sikkuy—Association for the Advancement of Equal Opportunity
13 Ramban Street
Jerusalem, 92422
Israel
Tel: 011-972-2-566-5663

Sikkuy aims to induce government ministries and other public institutions to implement principles of equal opportunity and civic integration, and to enhance the development of civil society in Israel as a shared fabric between Jewish and Arab citizens. Activities include policy monitoring, dialogue with key government leaders and public figures, programs for municipal officials, civil education, and publication of newsletters and reports.

The Van-Leer Institute
43 Jabotinsky Street
PO Box 4070
Jerusalem, 91040
Tel: 02-667141
Fax: 02-666080

The Van-Leer Institute was established in 1965 to advance coexistence and reduce social tension in Israel and the Middle East. The Institute was officially named a national institute by special law of the Knesset in 1967, and it has been working to foster coexistence and advancement among socially disadvantaged groups through research, scholarship, and social intervention. The Institute publishes text books that promote coexistence between Jews and Arabs in Israel, sponsors a program of pairing Arab and Jewish teachers to meet and establish professional ties, organizes international conferences on Jewish–Arab relations, and has developed a model civic covenant between Arab and Jewish citizens of Israel.

Windows—Channels for Communication
P.O. Box 56096
Tel Aviv, 61560
Israel

Windows opens channels of communication between Jewish and Arab Israeli youth, primarily by publishing *Windows Magazine for All Children,* a bimonthly magazine researched, written, and edited by children from Israel, the West Bank, and Gaza.

A Select List of Graduate Programs in Dispute Resolution and Coexistence

The field of conflict resolution and coexistence is very multidisciplinary, reflecting the fact that conflict-resolution professionals come from a wide variety of backgrounds. As a result, there are many ways to study conflict resolution and coexistence formally: many undergraduate colleges and universities offer majors or concentrations in conflict and peace studies, global conflict resolution has become a main focus for many international relations programs, law schools offer courses and clinics in alternative dispute resolution and mediation, and schools of education incorporate special programs on teaching conflict resolution in the classroom.

While the field continues to draw together aspects of abundant disciplines, academic programs dedicated solely to the study of conflict resolution have also evolved over the last two decades, in effect producing a new academic discipline in and of itself.

The following is a list of select graduate programs which offer degrees in conflict resolution and coexistence.*

American University: School of Foreign Service
American University
Washington, DC 20016
Tel: (202) 855-1622
Degree: Master of International Peace and Conflict Resolution

Antioch University: The McGregor School:
The McGregor School of Antioch University
800 Livermire St.
Yellow Springs, Ohio 45387
Tel: (513)767-6325
Degree: Master of Arts in Conflict Resolution (2 years: 3 weeks of study in residence each year with work and study from student's own community for the remainder of the year)

California State University
Doinquez Hills Campus
1000 E. Victoria Street
Carson, CA 90731
(310) 516-3435
Degree: Masters of Negotiation and Conflict Resolution
Centre d'Etudes Pol. d'Afrique Centrale
University of Lubumbashi
PO Box 1825
Lubumbashi Zaire

Columbia University: International Center for Cooperation and Conflict Resolution
Columbia University, Teachers College
Box 171
New York, NY 10027
Tel: (212) 678-3402
Degree: Certificate Program in Conflict Resolution (also can be done in conjunction with any teacher's college degree program)

Eastern Mennonite University: Institute for Conflict Studies and Peacebuilding
Harrisonburg, VA 22801-2462
Tel: (703)432-4450
Degree: Master of Conflict Transformation

---

*George Mason University publishes a comprehensive list of academic programs in peace and conflicts-resolution studies. To order this list, contact: The Institute for Conflict Analysis and Resolution, 4400 University Drive, Fairfax, VA 22030-4444, (703) 993-1300.

European University of Peace Studies: European Peace University (3 campuses)
EPU Austria
A-7461
Stadtshlaining AUSTRIA (43) 3355 2498
EPU Ireland
Dromahair
CO. Leitrim
Ireland
Tel: (353) 71-64873

EPU Spain
Univesitat Jaume 1
Campus Borriol
12080 Castella
Spain
Tel: (34) 64-34-5700
Degree: Master of Arts in Peace and Conflict Studies

Fresno Pacific University: Center for Peacemaking and Conflict Studies
1717 S. Chestnut Avenue
Fresno, CA 93702
(209) 455-5840/(800) 909-8677
Degree: Master of Arts in Conflict Management and Peacemaking

George Mason University: Institute for Conflict Analysis and Resolution
4400 University Drive
Fairfax, VA 22030-4444
(703) 993-1300
Degree: Master of Science or Ph.D. of Conflict Analysis and Resolution

Harvard University: The Program on Negotiation at Harvard Law School
513 Pound Hall
Harvard Law School
Cambridge, MA 02138
(617)495-1684
Degree: Continuing, postgraduate, and executive education in conflict management and negotiation

Jawaharlal Nehru University: Center for International Politics, Organization, and Disarmament
School of International Studies
New Delhi 110067 INDIA
Tel: (11)667-676

Lesley College: Peaceable Schools Center
154 Auburn Street
Cambridge, MA 02139
(617)349-8405
Degree: Conflict Resolution Education

Nova Southeastern University: School of Social and Systemic Studies
Department of Dispute Resolution
3301 College Avenue
Fort Lauderdale, FL 33314
(305) 424-5700
(800) 262-7978
Degree: Certificate, Master, and Ph.D. in Dispute Resolution

Pepperdine University Law School: Institute for Dispute Resolution
Pepperdine University
Malibu, CA 90265
(310) 456-4655
Degree: Certificate and Master's in Dispute Resolution

Rutgers University: Negotiation and Conflict Resolution Center
Rutgers University
15 Washington Street
Newark, NJ 07102
(201)648-1534
Degree: Certificate in Conflict Management

Syracuse University: Program Analysis and Resolution of Conflicts
401 Maxwell Hall
Syracuse, NY 13244
(315) 433-2367
Degree: Certificate, Master, and Ph.D. in Analysis and Resolution of Conflicts

Trinity College and Seminary: Department of Conflict Management
4233 Medwell Drive
P.O. Box 717
Newburgh, IN 47629-0717
(800) 545-3306
Degree: Ph.D. and Master in Conflict Management

University of Copenhagen: Center of Peace and Conflict Research
Kobenhavns Universitet
Vandkunsten 5
1467 Copenhagen K
Denmark
Tel: (1)32 64 32

University of Hawaii: Program on Conflict Resolution
University of Hawaii
Department of Political Science
242 Maile Way, 717 Porteus
Honolulu, HI 96822
(808) 956-8984
Degree: Master in Conflict Resolution, Mediation, and Peacemaking

University of Massachusetts, Boston
100 Morrisey Blvd.
Boston, MA 02125-3393
(617) 287-7421
Degree: Certificate and Master

University of Peace
PO Box 199-1250
Escazu
Costa Rica
Tel: (49)10-72

The University of Phoenix: Center for Professional Education
Management Development Center
4615 East Elwood Street, 2nd Floor
Phoenix, AZ 85040
Degree: Master in Negotiation and Conflict Management

University of Ulster: Peace Studies Program
Magee College
Derry, BT48 7JL
Northern Ireland
Tel: (050)426-5621
Degree: Master of Arts in Peace Studies

University of Lund: Department of Peace and Conflict Studies
Dag Hammarskjölds Vag 2B
22364, Lund
Sweden
Tel: (46)145-460

University of Victoria: Institute for Dispute Resolution
Begbie Building
PO Box 2400
Victoria, British Columbia
Canada V8W 3H7
Tel: (604)721-8777

Uppsala University: Department of Peace and Conflict Research
Uppsala Universitat
Oestra Agatan 53
PO Box 278
75105, Uppsala
Sweden
Tel: (18)15 54 00

Wayne State University: College of Urban Labor and Metropolitan Affairs
Room 2320, Faculty Administration Building
Detriot, MI 48202
Tel: (303) 577-3453
Degree: Master of Arts in Dispute Resolution

The Contributors

YEHUDA AMIR was the Director of the Winston Institute for the Study of Prejudice at Bar Ilan University in Israel. He is deceased.

HAVIVA BAR was a senior researcher at the Guttman Institute of Applied Social Science in Jerusalem, and is currently a private consultant in the field of conflict relations between Arabs and Jews and other educational areas.

MITCHELL BARD is the Executive Director of the American-Israeli Cooperative Enterprise and a foreign-policy analyst, and a member of the board of directors of the U.S. Israel Biotechnology Council.

ABRAM CHAYES is Felix Frankfurter Professor of Law Emeritus at Harvard Law School and former Legal Adviser to the State Department.

ANTONIA HANDLER CHAYES is Senior Adviser at Conflict Management Group, Adjunct Professor at the Kennedy School of Government, Harvard University, and former Under Secretary of the U.S. Air Force.

PETER COLEMAN is co-director of the International Center for Cooperation and Conflict Resolution at Columbia University. He is also a mediator and a trainer in mediation and negotiation skills.

LOUISE DERMAN-SPARKS is on the faculty of Human Development at Pacific Oaks College in Pasedena, California, and Director of the Antibias Education Leadership Project.

HELENA SYNA DESIVILYA is Director of the Carmel Institute for Social Studies and Assistant Professor in Organizational Behavior at Emek Yezreel Academic College in Israel.

MORTON DEUTSCH is Professor Emeritus and Director of the International Center for Cooperation and Conflict Resolution at Teachers College, Columbia University.

ELIAS EADY is an educational consultant, the coordinator of the Karev Foundation educational program in the Arab sector, and a teacher at David Yellin College in Jerusalem.

WOLF B. EMMINGHAUS is an intercultural trainer, teacher, and researcher in Germany. He is a project manager for the German Red Cross in Saarland, and he serves on the international evaluation team of the Federation of the Red Cross and Red Crescent Societies.

AMITAI ETZIONI is University Professor at the George Washington University and founder and chairman of The Communitarian Network.

GRACE FEUERVERGER is Assistant Professor at the Joint Centre for Teacher Development at the Ontario Institute of Studies in Education.

ARIELLA FRIEDMAN is Professor in the Psychology department at Tel Aviv University.

RABAH HALIBI works at the School for Peace at Neve Shalom/Wahat al-Salam in Israel.

DAVID A. HAMBURG is President Emeritus of the Carnegie Corporation of New York. He is a member of the Defense Policy Board, the President's Committee of Advisers on Science and Technology, and Cochair of the Carnegie Corporation on Preventing Deadly Conflict.

RACHEL HERTZ-LAZAROWITZ is Professor of Educational Psychology at the School of Education of Haifa University in Israel.

ELIEZER DAVID JAFFE is Centraide–L. Jacques Menard Professor for the Study of Volunteering, Nonprofit Organizations, and Philanthropy at the Paul Baerwald School of Social Work of the Hebrew University of Jerusalem.

HERBERT KELMAN is Richard Clarke Cabot Professor of Social Ethics at Harvard University and Director of the Program on International Conflict Analysis and Resolution at Harvard's Center for International Affairs.

PAUL KIMMEL, Creative Conflict Management, is an Adjunct Professor at several major universities, an independent consultant in fields of cultural diversity and awareness and community-based public safety, and an actor.

LOUIS KREISBERG is Professor of Sociology, Maxwell Professor of Social Conflict Studies, and former Director of the Program on the Analysis and Resolution of Conflicts at Syracuse University.

HAGGI KUPERMINTZ is a Doctoral Candidate for Psychological Studies in Education at Stanford University School of Education.

JENNIFER LANG, received her M.A. from Haifa University and is currently writing a book on sibling relationships and religion.

JOHN PAUL LEDERACH is Professor of Conflict Studies as well as Founding Director of the Conflict Transformation Program and the Institute for Peacebuilding at Eastern Mennonite University.

SAUL H. MENDLOVITZ is Dag Hammarskjold Professor of Peace and World Order Studies at Rutgers University Law School and the Co-Director of the World Order Models Project.

JAY ROTHMAN is Executive Director of ARI Associates, a research and consulting firm focused on conflict resolution and "action evaluation," and Visiting Scholar and Associate Professor at the McGregor School of Antioch University in the Masters of Applied Conflict Resolution Program.

LESTER EDWIN J. RUIZ is Associate Professor of Political Science at the International Christian University in Tokyo, Japan.

AHMAD SADRI is Associate Professor of Sociology at Lake Forest College in Lake Forest, Illinois.

ELAINE SCARRY is the author of *The Body in Pain* and teaches at Harvard University.

GENE SHARP is Senior Scholar of the Albert Einstein Institution in Cambridge, Massachusetts. He has written several books on the nature and political potential of nonviolent struggle.

ALAN B. SLIFKA is co-founder and Chairman of the Board of The Abraham Fund. He is an investment banker in New York.

RAYMOND SHONHOLTZ, Jur. Dr., is President of Partners for Democratic Change.

NAVA SONNENSCHEIN is Director of The School for Peace at Neve Shalom/Wahat al-Salam in Israel.

EDWARD C. STEWART is Professor Emeritus of Psychology, having been an international teacher and trainer.

ROBERTO TOSCANO is the Deputy Permanent Representative at the Italian Embassy in Geneva.

VAMIK D. VOLKAN, M.D., is Professor of Psychiatry and Director of the Center for the Study of Mind and Human Interaction at the University School of Medicine in Charlottesville, Virginia.

MARIA VOLPE is Professor of Sociology and Director of the Dispute Resolution Program at John Jay College of Criminal Justice at The City University of New York.

EUGENE WEINER is co-founder of The Abraham Fund, as well as a professor, writer, rabbi, and social activist. He is currently the Head of Special Projects for the American–Jewish Joint Distribution Committee in Moscow.

MICHAEL WALZER is Professor of Social Science at the Institute for Advanced Study in Princeton, New Jersey.

JAMES WILL is Pfeiffer Professor of Systematic Theology at Garrett–Evangelical Theological Seminary in Evanston, Illinois.

Copyright Acknowledgments

Index